Canadian Fifth Edition

Volume II

Horngren | Harrison | Bamber | Lemon | Norwood

Accounting

Charles T. Horngren
Stanford University

Walter T. Harrison, Jr.
Baylor University

Linda Smith Bamber
University of Georgia

W. Morley Lemon
University of Waterloo

Peter R. Norwood
Langara College

Prentice
Hall

Toronto

Canadian Cataloguing in Publication Data

Main entry under title:

Accounting

Canadian 5th ed.
Canadian ed. published under title: Accounting/Charles T. Horngren,
Walter T. Harrison, W. Morley Lemon; with Carol E. Dilworth.
Contents: v. 1. Chapters 1–11—v. 2. Chapters 12–18—v. 3. Chapters 19–26.
ISBN 0-13-089693-4 (v. 1) ISBN 0-13-089694-2 (v. 2) ISBN 0-13-089695-0 (v. 3)

1. Accounting. 2. Managerial accounting. I. Horngren, Charles T., 1926-   .

HF5635.H8125 2002   657′.044   C00.933091-7

0-13-089694-2

Vice President, Editorial Director: Michael Young
Senior Acquisitions Editor: Samantha Scully
Executive Marketing Manager: Cas Shields
Developmental Editor/Copy Editor: Anita Smale, CA
Production Editor: Mary Ann McCutcheon
Production Coordinator: Deborah Starks
Page Layout: Bill Renaud
Permissions/Photo Research: Susan Wallace-Cox
Art Director: Mary Opper
Interior Design: Alex Li
Cover Design: Alex Li
Cover Image: Comstock, Inc.

1 2 3 4 5   06 05 04 03 02

Printed and bound in U.S.A.

B R I E F
Contents

Contents

---

*In each chapter, Assignment Material includes Questions, Exercises, Beyond the Numbers, an Ethical Issue, and
    Problems (Group A and B, and Challenge Problems).
**Extending Your Knowledge includes Decision Problems and a Financial Statement Problem.

Appendices

About the Authors

Charles T. Horngren is the Edmund W. Littlefield Professor of Accounting, Emeritus, at Stanford University. A graduate of Marquette University, he received his MBA from Harvard University and his Ph.D. from the University of Chicago. He is also the recipient of honourary doctorates from Marquette University and DePaul University.

A Certified Public Accountant, Horngren served on the Accounting Principles Board for six years, the Financial Accounting Standards Board Advisory Council for five years, and the Council of the American Institute of Certified Public Accountants for three years. For six years, he served as a trustee of the Financial Accounting Foundation, which oversees the Financial Accounting Standards Board and the Government Accounting Standards Board.

Horngren is a member of the Accounting Hall of Fame.

A member of the American Accounting Association, Horngren has been its President and its Director of Research. He received its first annual Outstanding Accounting Educator Award.

The California Certified Public Accountants Foundation gave Horngren its Faculty Excellence Award and its Distinguished Professor Award. He is the first person to have received both awards.

The American Institute of Certified Public Accountants presented its first Outstanding Educator Award to Horngren.

Horngren was named Accountant of the Year, Education, by the national professional accounting fraternity, Beta Alpha Psi.

Professor Horngren is also a member of the Institute of Management Accountants, where he has received its Distinguished Service Award. He was a member of the Institute's Board of Regents, which administers the Certified Management Accountant examinations.

Horngren is the author of other accounting books published by Prentice-Hall and Pearson Education: *Cost Accounting: A Managerial Emphasis*, Second Canadian Edition, 2000 (with George Foster, Srikant Datar and Howard D. Teall); *Introduction to Financial Accounting*, Third Canadian Edition, 2001 (with Gary L. Sundem, John A. Elliot, and Howard D. Teall); *Management Accounting*, Fourth Canadian Edition, 2002 (with Gary L. Sundem, William O. Stratton, and Howard D. Teall); and *Financial Accounting*, Fourth Edition, 2001 (with Walter T. Harrison, Jr.).

Horngren is the Consulting Editor for the Charles T. Horngren Series in Accounting.

Walter T. Harrison, Jr. is Professor of Accounting at the Hankamer School of Business, Baylor University. He received his B.B.A. degree from Baylor University, his M.S. from Oklahoma State University, and his Ph.D. from Michigan State University.

Professor Harrison, recipient of numerous teaching awards from student groups as well as from university administrators, has also taught at Cleveland State Community College, Michigan State University, the University of Texas, and Stanford University.

A member of the American Accounting Association and the American Institute of Certified Public Accountants, Professor Harrison has served as Chairman of the Financial Accounting Standards Committee of the American Accounting Association, on the Teaching/Curriculum Development Award Committee, on the Program Advisory Committee for Accounting Education and Teaching, and on the Notable Contributions to Accounting Literature Committee.

Professor Harrison has lectured in several foreign countries and published articles in numerous journals, including *The Accounting Review, Journal of Accounting*

Research, Journal of Accountancy, Journal of Accounting and Public Policy, Economic Consequences of Financial Accounting Standards, Accounting Horizons, Issues in Accounting Education, and *Journal of Law and Commerce*. He is coauthor of *Financial Accounting, Fourth Edition*, 2001 (with Charles T. Horngren) and *Accounting, Fifth Edition* (with Charles T. Horngren and Linda S. Bamber) published by Prentice Hall. Professor Harrison has received scholarships, fellowships, research grants, or awards from Price Waterhouse & Co., Deloitte & Touche, the Ernst & Young Foundation, and the KMPG Peat Marwick Foundation.

Linda Smith Bamber is Professor of Accounting at the J.M. Tull School of Accounting at the University of Georgia. She graduated summa cum laude from Wake Forest University, where she was a member of Phi Beta Kappa. She is a certified public accountant. For her performance on the CPA examination, Professor Bamber received the Elijah Watt Sells Award in addition to the North Carolina Bronze Medal. Before returning to graduate school, she worked in cost accounting at RJR Foods. She then earned an MBA from Arizona State University, and a Ph.D. from The Ohio State University.

Professor Bamber has received numerous teaching awards from The Ohio State University, the University of Florida, and the University of Georgia, including selection as Teacher of the Year at the University of Florida's Fisher School of Accounting.

She has lectured in Canada and Australia in addition to the U.S., and her research has appeared in numerous journals, including *The Accounting Review, Journal of Accounting Research, Journal of Accounting and Economics, Journal of Finance, Contemporary Accounting Research, Auditing: A Journal of Practice and Theory, Accounting Horizons, Issues in Accounting Education*, and *CPA Journal*. She provided the annotations for the *Annotated Instructor's Edition* of Horngren, Foster, and Datar's *Cost Accounting: A Managerial Emphasis*, Seventh, Eighth, and Ninth Editions.

A member of the Institute of Management Accounting, the American Accounting Association (AAA), and the AAA's Management Accounting Section and Financial Accounting and Reporting Section, Professor Bamber has chaired the AAA New Faculty Consortium Committee, served on the AAA Council, the AAA Research Advisory Committee, the AAA Corporate Accounting Policy Seminar Committee, the AAA Wildman Medal Award Committee, the AAA Nominations Committee, and has chaired the Management Accounting Section's Membership Outreach Committee. She served as Associate Editor of *Accounting Horizons*, and is serving as editor of *The Accounting Review* from 1999 to 2002.

W. Morley Lemon is the PricewaterhouseCoopers Professor of Auditing and the Director of the School of Accountancy at the University of Waterloo. He obtained his BA from the University of Western Ontario, his MBA from the University of Toronto, and his PhD from the University of Texas at Austin. Professor Lemon obtained his CA in Ontario. In 1985 he was honoured by that Institute, which elected him a Fellow. He received his CPA in Texas.

Professor Lemon was awarded the University of Waterloo Distinguished Teacher Award at the 1998 convocation at the University.

Professor Lemon is coauthor, with Arens, Loebbecke, and Splettstoesser, of *Auditing and Other Assurance Services*, Canadian Eighth Edition, published by Prentice Hall Canada, and coauthored four previous Canadian editions of that text. He is also coauthor, with Horngren, Harrison, Bamber, and Norwood, of *Accounting*, Canadian Fifth Edition, published by Pearson Education Canada. He coathored the four previous Canadian editions of that text.

He was a member of the Canadian Institute of Chartered Accountants' Assurance Standards Board. He has also served on the Institute of Chartered Accountants of Ontario Council, as well as a number of committees for both bodies. He has chaired and served on a number of committees of the Canadian Academic Accounting Association. Professor Lemon has served on Council and chaired and served on a number of committees of the American Accounting Association.

Professor Lemon has presented lectures and papers at a number of universities and academic and professional conferences and symposia in Canada and the United States. He has chaired and organized six audit symposia held at the University of Waterloo. He has served on the editorial board of and reviewed papers for a number of academic journals including *The Accounting Review, Contemporary Accounting Research, Issues in Accounting Education, Auditing: A Journal of Practice and Theory, Advances in Accounting, Journal of Accounting and Public Policy,* and *CA Magazine.* Professor Lemon has coauthored two monographs and has had papers published in *Contemporary Accounting Research, Research on Accounting Ethics, Journal of Accounting, Auditing and Finance, The Chartered Accountant in Australia, The Journal of Business Ethics,* and *CA Magazine.* He has had papers published in the following collections: *Educating the Profession of Accountancy in the Twenty-First Century, Comparative International Accounting Education Standards, Comparative International Auditing Standards,* and *The Impact of Inflation on Accounting: A Global View.* Professor Lemon served as a judge for *CA Magazine's* Walter J. Macdonald Award.

Professor Lemon has received a number of research grants and has served as the Director of the Centre for Accounting Ethics, School of Accountancy, University of Waterloo. He has written a number of ethics cases published by the Centre.

Peter R. Norwood is an instructor in accounting and the Chair of the Financial Management Department in the School of Business at Langara College. A graduate of the University of Alberta, he received his MBA from the University of Western Ontario. He is a Chartered Accountant and a Certified Management Accountant.

Before entering the academic community, Mr. Norwood worked in public practice and industry for over fifteen years. He is a member of the Board of Examiners of the Canadian Institute of Chartered Accountants and is the Chair of the Professional Development Management Committee of the Institute of Chartered Accountants of British Columbia. In addition, he has been involved in program development for the Certified Management Accountants of British Columbia and the Chartered Accountants' School of Business. Mr. Norwood has lectured at the University of British Columbia and is the Chair of the Langara Foundation.

Photo Credits

662 Peter R. Norwood; **708** The Canadian Press/Moe Doiron; **759** The Canadian Press/*Maclean's*/Todd Korol; **804** The Canadian Press/Kevin Frayer; **865** Marvin Moore Photography; **913** The Canadian Press/Canada News Wire Photo/EPIX; **980** Courtesy of Suncor Energy Inc.

To the Student

On behalf of the authors, we would like to welcome you to introductory accounting. Whether you plan to major in accounting or are taking this course for interest, rest assured that a basic understanding of accounting is fundamental to the world of business. Many of the principles you will learn in this course will be useful in whatever career you choose to pursue.

As you will discover in this course, accounting is more than bookkeeeeping. Accounting requires that you understand issues conceptually in addition to developing the technical ability to record, summarize, report, and interpret financial data. If you devote your efforts to understanding both of these aspects of accounting, you will be taking a large step towards developing a greater understanding of business fundamentals.

To maximize the benefit of this course and this text, there are certain responsibilities that you need to accept. As instructors, we know the volume of material covered in introductory accounting can be overwhelming. On a daily basis, you will learn new principles and techniques. In order to fully comprehend the new material, you should consider the following suggestions:

Read the textbook material in advance.   If you have had a chance to review the chapter before it is covered in class, you will find it much easier to grasp the material when it is presented in class.

Use the end-of-chapter material.   We have provided a multitude of exercises and problems at the end of each chapter. They range from single-objective, basic questions to comprehensive, multi-objective problems. These exercises and problems are designed to help provide a good understanding of the accounting issues you have covered in class. Check Figures have been provided at the end of the text to help you check your progress.

Use the resources available.   In addition to this text, there are several valuable resources available to help you understand accounting. The most important resource, of course, is your instructor. Other resources created to accompany this text are described below.

Accounting's **Companion Website**, with its on-line **Study Guide**, offers a number of opportunities to test your understanding of the material. Multiple-choice, true-and-false, fill-in-the-blanks, and short-answer questions are scored automatically by the computer, providing you with instant feedback. CBC videos and related cases are provided on-screen. Hot links are given for the companies mentioned in each chapter of the text allowing you instant access to these companies. Message board and chat areas let you contact other accounting students.

Study Guide with Demonstration Problems and Excel Templates provides you with a number of tools to master accounting. Each chapter provides a chapter review, Excel problems with templates on a disk, a Test Yourself section containing matching, multiple-choice, completion questions, exercises, and comprehensive demonstration problems. Solutions are provided for all *Study Guide* activities. A *Study Guide* to accompany Volume I and another to accompany Volume II are available from your bookstore.

Working Papers is a set of tear-out forms you can use to complete all the exercises and problems in Volume I and Volume II. Because the forms you need are already created, you avoid time-consuming set-up and focus on the accounting right away. The *Working Papers* are available from your bookstore.

Don't forget this text! Please look at the next few pages for all the features in the text that will help you succeed in accounting.

Features in *Accounting*

L<small>EARNING</small> accounting can be a bit overwhelming, especially if you have little business or accounting experience. But with a good text and instructor, you will succeed. To help you, we provide features in every chapter of this text to make accounting as easy to understand as possible. Please read through the next few pages to learn more about *Accounting* and the many ways it will help you understand, learn, and apply accounting concepts.

Chapter Objectives are listed on the first page of each chapter. This "roadmap" shows you what will be covered and what is especially important. Each objective is repeated in the margin where the material is first covered. The objectives are summarized at the end of the chapter.

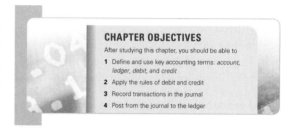

CHAPTER OBJECTIVES

After studying this chapter, you should be able to

1 Define and use key accounting terms: *account, ledger, debit,* and *credit*

2 Apply the rules of debit and credit

3 Record transactions in the journal

4 Post from the journal to the ledger

Chapter openers present a story about a real company or a real business situation, and show why the topics in the chapter are important to real companies. Some of the companies you'll read about include CanWest Global Communications Group, Sobeys Inc., Dofasco Inc., Suncor Energy Inc., and Intrawest. Students tell us that using real companies makes it easier for them to learn and remember accounting concepts.

"B<small>ecause</small> we are diversified across numerous locations in North America, we needed to put the right information systems in place. We've done that. We can now review on a moment's notice the status of any one of the dozens of real estate projects we are developing across the continent. Similar systems are now in place in our ski operations and this year we will have daily financial operating results for each resort available in Vancouver by 10 o'clock the following morning. This information intelligence has made our path of growth both clear and predictable." (Joe S. Houssian, Chairman, President and Chief Executive Officer of Intrawest Corporation.)

The 2000 Intrawest Annual Report describes Intrawest, headquartered in Vancouver, British Columbia, as "the leading developer and operator of mountain resorts across North America." The company owns year-round resorts at Whistler/Blackcomb and Panorama in British

Columbia, Tremb... Ste. Marie in C... Mountain in Onta... Colorado, Stratto... Snowshoe in W... Mammoth in C... Mountain Cre... Jersey. The com... an investment i... des Alpes, Franc... ski company in t... a golf resort, S... Florida.

Like all othe... Intrawest represents itself to outsiders... financial statements. But the accounting i... also used internally. Intrawest managers a... financial statement data for decision makin... track of the revenue and expenses at the cor... resort properties by using accounting reco... we illustrate in this chapter. Accounting help... profits and losses for each resort and for... as a whole.

Intrawest Corporation
www.intrawest.com

Vancouver Grizzlies
www.nba.com/grizzlies/index.html

Hudson's Bay Company
www.hbc.com/english.asp

Zellers
www.hbc.com/zellers/default.htm

C<small>HAPTER</small> 1 introduced transaction analysis and the fi... ments. But that chapter did not show how the financial statements a... Chapters 2, 3, and 4 cover the accounting process that results in the fin... ments.

Chapter 2 discusses the processing of accounting information as... done in practice. Throughout this chapter and the next two, we continu... accounting procedure with service businesses, such as Air & Sea Trav... design engineering company, or a sports franchise like the Vancouver... Chapter 5 we move into merchandising businesses such as The Bay... All these businesses use the basic accounting system that we illustrate...

By learning how accounting information is processed, you will unde... the facts and figures reported in the financial statements come from. Thi... will increase your confidence as you make decisions. It will also speed y... in your business career.

OBJECTIVE 1
Define and use key accounting terms: *account, ledger, debit,* and *credit*

The Account

The basic summary device of accounting is the **account**, the detailed... changes that have occurred in a particular asset, liability, or item of ow... during a period of time. For convenient access to the information...

Weblinks in the margin give you the internet address for the companies mentioned in the text. If you want to learn more about a company, use these handy references.

Objectives in the margin signal the beginning of the section that covers the objective topic. Look for this feature when you are studying and want to review a particular objective.

Student-to-Student boxes appear in every chapter. We asked real students to tell us which concepts or ideas they found particularly challenging and which feature or item in *Accounting* helped them overcome the challenge. One student said, "I think that the Student-to-Student boxes are great...they help students realize that other students have read and maybe even struggled with the same concepts that they are struggling with and they give them encouragement to continue."

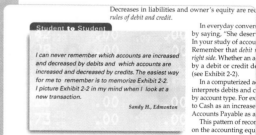

Decreases in liabilities and owner's equity are re... *rules of debit and credit.*

In everyday conver... by saying, "She deser... In your study of accou... Remember that *debit*... *right side.* Whether an a... by a debit or credit d... (see Exhibit 2-2).

In a computerized a... interprets debits and c... by account type. For ex... to Cash as an increase... Accounts Payable as a...

This pattern of recor... on the accounting equ...

ASSETS = LIABILITIES + OWN...

Student to Student

I can never remember which accounts are increased and decreased by debits and which accounts are increased and decreased by credits. The easiest way for me to remember is to memorize Exhibit 2-2. I picture Exhibit 2-2 in my mind when I look at a new transaction.

Sandy H., Edmonton

Learning Tips in the margin are suggestions for learning or remembering concepts that you might find difficult.

Debit
for
Increase,
50,000

Notice that Assets = Liabil

Exhibits are provided in full colour to make the concepts easier to understand and easier to remember.

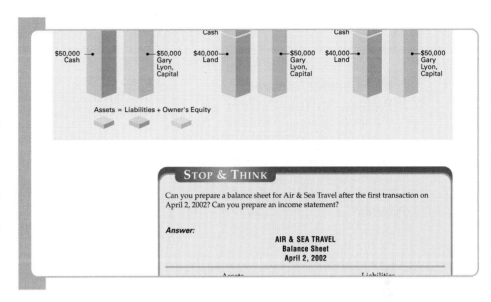

Assets = Liabilities + Owner's Equity

Stop and Think boxes are "speed bumps" that allow you to slow down for a moment, review and apply to a decision situation material just covered in the text. These serve as an excellent way to check your progress because the answers are provided in the same box.

STOP & THINK

Can you prepare a balance sheet for Air & Sea Travel after the first transaction on April 2, 2002? Can you prepare an income statement?

Answer:

AIR & SEA TRAVEL
Balance Sheet
April 2, 2002

DON'T FORGET the material in the margins! Some of these items allow you to pause and make sure you understand the material covered in the text. Others are excellent study aids because they help you find material you are looking for quickly. We already mentioned the Objectives, the Weblinks, and the Learning Tips in the margins. Here are some other margin items.

Working It Out are short calculation questions that appear throughout the chapter. Answers are provided to give you immediate feedback. You can use these questions to check your progress and to prepare for exams.

Thinking It Over are short questions about concepts just covered in the text. Answers are provided to give you immediate feedback. Like the Working It Out questions, you can use Thinking It Over questions to check your progress and to prepare for exams.

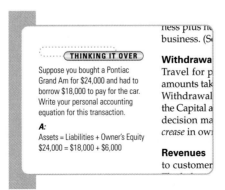

THINKING IT OVER

Suppose you bought a Pontiac Grand Am for $24,000 and had to borrow $18,000 to pay for the car. Write your personal accounting equation for this transaction.

A:
Assets = Liabilities + Owner's Equity
$24,000 = $18,000 + $6,000

ness plus n
business. (S

Withdrawa
Travel for p
amounts tak
Withdrawal
the Capital a
decision ma
crease in ow

Revenues
to customer

, Capital

(1)   10,000

3,000 cash.

e revenue ac-
Revenue.

,000

EVENUES
ice Revenue
3,000

evenue

(2)   3,000

e client for
ess $500

refore, debit
credit Service

500

WORKING IT OUT

Compute the missing amounts:

(1)   Cash

Bal.	10,000		
	20,000	13,000	
Bal.	X		

(2)   Accounts Payable

	X	Bal.	12,800
			45,600
		Bal.	23,500

(3)   S. Scully, Capital

		Bal.	X
	22,000		56,000
			15,000
		Bal.	73,000

A: (1) The ending balance (X) for Cash is
X = $10,000 + 20,000 − $13,000
X = $17,000
(2) We are given the beginning and ending balances. We can compute the debit entry as follows:
$12,800 + $45,600 − X
= $23,500
$12,800 + $45,600
− $23,500 = X
X = $34,900
(3) The Capital account has an ending credit balance of $73,000. We can calculate the beginning credit balance as follows:
X + $56,000 + $15,000
− $22,000 = $73,000
X = $73,000 − $56,000
− $15,000 + $22,000
X = $24,000

Key Points in the margin highlight important details from the text. These are good review tools for when you prepare for tests or exams.

Cash

| (Right side) |
| *Credit* |

e **debit** side, and the right side is called the
can be confusing because they are new. To
remember this:

left side
right side

Mid-Chapter Summary Problem for Your Review gives you another chance to review your understanding of the material covered in the first half of the chapter. A full solution is provided so you can judge whether you should look at the material again or proceed to the last half of the chapter.

Mid-Chapter Summary Problem
for Your Review

On August 1, 2003, Mary Woo opens Woo Computer Consulting. During the business's first ten days of operations, it completes the following transactions:

a. To begin operations, Mary Woo deposits $40,000 of personal funds in a bank account entitled Woo Computer Consulting. The business receives the cash and gives Woo capital (owner's equity).
b. Woo Computer Consulting pays $20,000 cash for a small house to be used as an office and $10,000 for the land on which the house is located.
c. The business purchases office supplies for $500 on account.
d. The business pays $6,000 cash for office furniture.
e. The business pays $150 on the account payable created in Transaction (c).
f. Woo withdraws $1,000 cash for personal use.

Required
1. Prepare the journal entries to record these transactions. Key the journal entries by letter.
2. Post the entries to T-accounts and calculate the ending balance.
3. Prepare the trial balance of Woo Computer Consulting at August 10, 2003.

Solution to Review Problem

Requirement 1

Accounts and Explanation	Ref.	Debit	Credit
a. Cash		40,000	
Mary Woo, Capital			40,000
Record initial investment from owner.			
b. Building		20,000	
Land		10,000	
Cash			30,000
Purchased building for an office and land.			
c. Office Supplies		500	
Accounts Payable			500
Purchased office supplies on account.			

Accounting and the E-World
or
Accounting Around the Globe
appears in each chapter. These boxes illustrate either how the world of e-commerce is influencing accounting or how accounting differs around the world. These boxes offer interesting views of accounting that might make you think about accounting in different ways.

Accounting and the *e*-World

Using Computers and the Internet to Be Successful

Computers and the internet are two reasons that companies have been able to grow to sizes unimaginable a decade ago and to spread throughout the world. Computers process vast amounts of data quickly and the internet allows companies to maintain constant contact with far-flung operations.

Bombardier Inc. **(http://www.bombardier.com)** has operations in twelve countries on three continents covering four major lines of business. Imagine the difficulty that Bombardier would have in gathering together all the company's financial data to prepare its 2000 financial statements if it did not have computers and world-wide data linkage through the internet.

Magna International **(http://www.magna.com)** employs 59,000 people at 174 manufacturing divisions and 33 product development and engineering centres in 19 countries—and Magna is able to produce its annual financial statements within five weeks of its December 31 year end. Magna can do this because of its extensive use of computers and because all its world-wide operations are connected by means of an electronic network.

Both of these companies are successful because they produce excellent products and are world leaders at what they do. Their success is based on their ability to make good decisions, and they are able to do this because they have excellent information technology working for them. Their accounting systems around the world are compatible with each other. Management is confident that the information they receive daily is both accurate and current. Computers and the internet provide this accurate information for decision making in real time.

Decision Guidelines show how the accounting concepts covered in the chapter are used by business people to make business decisions. This feature shows why accounting principles and concepts are important in a broader business context, not just to accountants. The Decision Guidelines also serve as an excellent summary of the chapter topics.

Intrawest management does not need to record in the journal all the transactions that would be affected by its decision. After all, the company has not completed a transaction yet. But management does need to know how Intrawest will be affected by the decision. If the decision makers know accounting, they can skip the journal and

Summary Problem for Your Review pulls together the chapter concepts with an extensive and challenging review problem. Full solutions are given so that you can check your progress.

Summary Problem
for Your Review

The trial balance of Tomassini Computer Service Centre on March 1, 2003, lists the company's assets, liabilities, and owner's equity on that date.

	Balance	
Account Titles	**Debit**	**Credit**
Cash	$26,000	
Accounts receivable	4,500	
Accounts payable		$ 2,000
John Tomassini, Capital		28,500
Total	$30,500	$30,500

During March the business engaged in the following transactions:

a. Borrowed $45,000 from the bank and signed a note payable in the name of the business.

b. Paid cash of $40,000 to a real estate company to acquire land.

c. Performed service for a customer and received cash of $5,000.

d. Purchased supplies on account, $300.

Cyber Coach appears after both the Mid-Chapter Summary Problem for Your Review and the Summary Problem for Your Review. It is a reminder to visit the *Accounting* Companion Website's Online Study Guide and other student resources for extra practice with the new material introduced in the chapter.

Salary expense	3,000	
Utilities expense	200	
Total expenses		5,100
Net income		$2,500

Cyber Coach Visit the Student Resource area of the *Accounting* Companion Website for extra practice with the new material in Chapter 2.
www.pearsoned.ca/horngren

Summary appears at the end of each chapter. It gives a concise description of the material covered in the chapter and is organized by objective. Use this summary as a starting point for organizing your review when studying for a test or exam.

Summary

1. **Define and use key accounting terms: *account, ledger, debit,* and *credit*.** Accounts can be viewed in the form of the letter "T." The left side of each T-account is its *debit* side. The right side is its *credit* side. The *ledger*, which contains a record for each account groups and numbers accounts by category in the following order: assets, liabilities, and owner's equity (and its subparts, revenues and expenses).

2. **Apply the rules of debit and credit.** *Assets* and *expenses* are increased by debits and decreased by credits. *Liabilities, owner's equity,* and *revenues* are increased by credits and decreased by debits. An account's *normal balance* is the side of the account—debit or credit—in which increases are recorded. Thus the normal balance

4. **Post from the journal to the ledger.** Posting means transferring to the *ledger* accounts. Posting references are used to trace amounts back and forth between the journal and the ledger.

5. **Prepare and use a trial balance.** The *trial balance* is a summary of all the account balances in the ledger. When *double-entry accounting* has been done correctly, the total debits and the total credits in the trial balance are equal.

6. **Set up a chart of accounts for a business.** A *chart of accounts* lists all the accounts in the ledger and their account numbers.

7. **Analyze transactions without a journal.** Decision makers must often make decisions without a complete

Self-Study Questions allow you to test your understanding of the chapter on your own. Page references are given for each of these multiple-choice questions so that you can review a section quickly if you miss an answer. The answers are provided after the Similar Accounting Terms (see below) so you can check your progress.

Accounting Vocabulary lists all the terms that were defined and appeared in bold type in the chapter. The page references are given so you can review the meanings of the terms. These terms are also collected and defined in the Glossary at the end of the text.

Similar Accounting Terms links the accounting terms used in the chapter to similar terms you might have heard outside your accounting class, in the media, in other courses, or in day-to-day business dealings. Knowing similar terms should make it easier to remember the accounting terms.

These are the Answers to the Self-Study Questions, mentioned above.

Self-Study Questions

Test your understanding of the chapter by marking the correct answer for each of the following questions:

1. An account has two sides called the (p. 55)
   a. Debit and credit   c. Revenue and expense
   b. Asset and liability   d. Journal and ledger
2. Increases in liabilities are recorded by (p. 56)
   a. Debits   b. Credits
3. Why do accountants record transactions in the journal? (p. 58)
   a. To ensure that all transactions are posted to the ledger
   b. To ensure that total debits equal total credits
   c. To have a chronological record of all transactions
   d. To help prepare the financial statements
4. Posting is the process of transferring information from the (p. 60)
   a. Journal to the trial balance
   b. Ledger to the trial balance
   c. Ledger to the financial statements
   d. Journal to the ledger
5. The purchase of land for cash is recorded by a (p. 61)
   a. Debit to Cash and a credit to Land
   b. Debit to Cash and a debit to Land
   c. Debit to Land and a credit to Cash
   d. Credit to Cash and a credit to Land
6. The purpose of the trial balance is to (p. 64)
   a. List all accounts with their balances
   b. Ensure that all transactions have been recorded

   c. Speed the collection of cash receipts fro[m] [cus]tomers
   d. Increase assets and owner's equity
7. What is the normal balance of the Acc[ounts] Receivable, Office Supplies, and Rent Expe[nse a]counts? (p. 71)
   a. Debit   b. Credit
8. A business has Cash of $3,000, Notes Paya[ble of] $2,500, Accounts Payable of $4,300, S[ervice] Revenue of $7,000 and Rent Expense of $[   ]. Based on these data, how much are its total [liabil]ities? (p. 74)
   a. $5,500   c. $9,800
   b. $6,800   d. $13,800
9. Smale Transport earned revenue on accoun[t. The] earning of revenue on account is recorde[d by] (pp. 74–78)
   a. Debit to Cash and a credit to Revenue
   b. Debit to Accounts Receivable and a cr[edit to] Revenue
   c. Debit to Accounts Payable and a cre[dit to] Revenue
   d. Debit to Revenue and a credit to Acc[ounts] Receivable
10. The account credited for a receipt of cash [on ac]count is (p. 77)
   a. Cash   c. Service Revenue
   b. Accounts Payable   d. Accounts Receiv[able]

   Answers to the Self-Study Questions follow the S[imilar] Accounting Terms.

Accounting Vocabulary

Account *(p. 52)*	Journal *(p. 58)*
Chart of accounts *(p. 70)*	Ledger *(p. 52)*
Credit *(p. 55)*	Posting *(p. 60)*
Debit *(p. 55)*	Trial balance *(p. 64)*

Similar Accounting Terms

Cr	Credit; right
Dr	Debit; left
The Ledger	The Books; the General Ledger
Entering the transaction in a journal	Making the journal entry; journalizing the transaction
Withdrawals by owner(s)	In a *proprietorship* or *partnership*, distributions from a company to its owner(s).

Answers to Self-Study Questions
1. a	3. c	5. c	7. a
2. b	4. d	6. a	8. b ($6,800 = $2,500 + $4,300)

9. b
10. d

THE END-OF-CHAPTER Assignment Material is

extensive because often the best way to make sure you grasp new accounting concepts is to practice, practice, practice! The number and variety of questions, exercises, and problems give you every opportunity to test your understanding of the chapter's concepts.

Questions require short, written answers or short calculations, often on a single topic.

Exercises on a single or a small number of topics require you to "do the accounting" and, often, to consider the implications of the result in the same way that real companies would. The objectives covered by each exercise are listed after the brief description of the concepts covered.

Serial Exercise in Chapters 2 to 5 follows one company and builds in complexity with each chapter, providing an excellent review of the accounting cycle.

Challenge Exercises provide a challenge for those students who have mastered the Exercises.

Beyond the Numbers exercises require analytical thinking and written responses about the topics presented in the chapter.

Ethical Issues are thought-provoking situations that help you recognize when ethics should affect an accounting decision.

Problems are presented in two groups that mirror each other, "A" and "B." Many instructors work through problems from Group A in class to demonstrate accounting concepts, then assign problems from Group B for homework or extra practice. The objectives covered by each problem are listed after the brief description of the concepts covered.

Challenge Problems encourage you to consider the effect of accounting information and apply it to decision situations.

THE EXTENDING Your Knowledge section contains
Decision Problems and a Financial Statement Problem.

Decision Problems allow you to prepare and interpret accounting information and then make recommendations to a business based on this information.

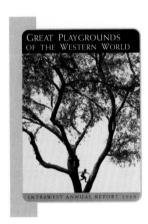

Financial Statement Problem allows you to use real financial information from Intrawest Corporation, the successful Canadian ski and resort company, to answer the problem. Selected information from Intrawest's 2000 Annual Report appears in Appendix A of Volume I and Volume II of *Accounting*.

A purple disk icon appears beside selected Exercises and Problems to remind you that Excel spreadsheets have been created to answer these questions. The spreadsheets are part of the *Study Guide with Excel Templates* that you can purchase from your bookstore. You don't have to use the spreadsheets to answer the questions but you may find they help to organize your answers.

In addition to the features above that appear in each chapter, two additional features appear at the end of each part of Volume I and Volume II.

Comprehensive Problem covers the content addressed in the book so far. This is a relatively long problem that provides an excellent review of all of the topics covered in the chapters in that part. See your instructor for the solution to this problem.

CBC **CBC Video Cases** appear at the end of each of the Parts in Volumes I and II. A CBC video of these interesting *Venture* segments is also available to your instructor to accompany these cases. The videos demonstrate the importance of accounting concepts to real businesses and real entrepreneurs in a truly interesting way.

To the Instructor

Welcome to *Accounting*! *Accounting*, Canadian Fifth Edition, provides full introductory coverage of financial and management accounting in a three-volume, full-colour format. Volumes I and II cover financial accounting topics, and Volume III covers management accounting topics. The three-volume format gives *Accounting* the flexibility to be used in a one-, two-, or three-semester introductory accounting course.

Instructors have told us their greatest challenges are effectively teaching students with very different business and accounting backgrounds, and motivating students to give accounting the study time and attention it deserves. *Accounting*'s approach and features were designed to help you address and overcome these challenges. The keys are a supportive text and supplements package, and motivated students.

Accounting continues its tradition of complete and comprehensive coverage of the most widely used accounting theory and practices. We have always believed that it is better to provide instructors with comprehensive coverage that could be trimmed if necessary rather than reduced coverage that might require instructor supplementation. This gives instructors the flexibility to tailor their presentations and coverage to their students' experience level.

Accounting continues to use the easy-to-understand writing style that sets it apart from other accounting texts. Instuctors have told us time and again that if students miss an accounting class, the instructor knows that students can keep up by reading the text. This should help students feel less overwhelmed by the thought of missing a class and having to catch up.

Accounting principles and procedures are illustrated using examples from real Canadian companies. This real-world business context runs throughout the chapters and assignment material, motivating students to think about companies and situations they know, which can help make difficult concepts easier to grasp. Familiar companies enliven the material and illustrate the role of accounting in business. In those situations where "live" data drawn from real companies would complicate the material for introductory students, we illustrate the accounting with realistic examples from generic companies to give students the clearest examples possible.

Changes in the Canadian Fifth Edition of *Accounting*

The most obvious change in this new edition is the attractive, inviting full-colour presentation of the material. Students have said they find concepts easier to understand when key material and exhibits are presented in colour. However, colour is only the beginning—colour cannot make weak features stronger. The features have to stand on their own.

A number of well-received features were introduced in the previous edition of *Accounting*, and most of these features remain in this edition, including Decision Guidelines, Similar Accounting Terms, Working It Out, and Thinking It Over items. A number of new features have been added to this edition—they are described below. For detailed descriptions of all of the features in this text, please refer to the To the Student section earlier in this Preface.

The most significant change in this edition of *Accounting* is the focus on proprietorships in Volume I, especially in Chapters 1 to 5. This change was made after considerable discussion with many instructors from across the country. While most instructors agreed that corporations, large and small, are increasing in number in Canada, the majority of instructors felt that students grasp owner's equity concepts more easily by learning about proprietorships before learning about corporations. However, for those instructors who prefer a corporate focus in Chapters 1 to 5, we will offer a website containing a parallel presentation of Chapters 1 to 5 with a corporate focus in the same full-colour layout as the text.

New **Student-to-Student** boxes appear in every chapter. We asked students to tell us which concepts or ideas they found particularly challenging and which feature or item in *Accounting* helped them overcome the challenge. One student said, "I think that the Student-to-Student boxes are great...they help students realize that other students have read and maybe even struggled with the same concepts that they are struggling with and they give them encouragement to continue."

A new **Accounting and the E-World** or **Accounting Around the Globe** box appears in each chapter. These boxes illustrate how the world of e-commerce is influencing accounting or how accounting differs around the world. These boxes offer interesting views of accounting that motivate students to think about accounting in different ways.

A new **Cyber Coach** box appears after both the Mid-Chapter Summary Problem for Your Review and the Summary Problem for Your Review. It is a reminder to students to visit the *Accounting* Companion Website's Online Study Guide and other student resources for extra practice with the new material introduced in the chapter.

A new **Management Accounting in the Real World** box appears in most chapters in Volume III. It shows how the management accounting concepts covered in the chapter, which are typically illustrated using large manufacturers, are used by real, small businesses.

Cash flow statements are introduced in Chapter 1 and covered fully in Chapter 17. To reduce possible student confusion, chapter-by-chapter introductions to portions of the cash flow statement have been eliminated in this edition.

The "generic" Financial Statement Problems in Chapters 1 to 18 have been moved from the text to the Companion Website and the *Instructor's Resource Manual and Video Guide*. However, the Intrawest Corporation Financial Statement Problems are still presented in the text.

What has *not* changed is the quantity, quality, and variety of exercises, questions, and problems presented in the text. All problems have been updated and revised, but the flexibility provided to instructors by the extensive assignment material remains.

Supplements

Accounting is supported by a variety of online course management solutions designed to meet the full range of instructor and student needs, including a Companion Website, a WebCT course, a BlackBoard course, and Pearson Education Canada's proprietary Course Compass course. For more information about any of these solutions, please contact your Pearson Education Canada Sales and Editorial Representative, or visit **www.pearsoned.com/dl**.

Also ask about the other supplements that accompany *Accounting*:

Instructor's Solutions Manual, Vol I: 013-093176-4; Vol II: 013-093177-2;
    Vol III: 013-093178-0
Instructor's Manual and Media Guide, Vol I: 013-093190-X; Vol II: 013-093201-9;
    Vol III: 013-093202-7
Test Item File, Vol I: 013-093193-4; Vol II: 013-093194-2;
    Vol III: 013-093195-0
Test Manager (Computerized Test Item File) for Volume I, II, III: 013-093276-0
CBC/Pearson Education Canada Video Library, 013-093270-1
Solutions Acetates, Vol I: 013-093275-2; Vol II: 013-093277-9;
    Vol III: 013-093279-5
Electronic Transparencies in PowerPoint, 013-093273-6
Adapting Your Lecture Notes if Using Larson et al., *Fundamental Accounting Principles*,
    9/C/E, 013-064588-5
Adapting Your Lecture Notes if Using Weygandt et al., *Accounting Principles*,
    Canadian Edition, 013-064589-3

Acknowledgements for the Canadian Fifth Edition

We would like to thank Chuck Horngren, Tom Harrison, and Linda Bamber for their encouragement and support.

Particular thanks are due to the following people for reviewing the manuscript for Volume I and/or Volume II of this new edition, writing the supplements, or performing technical checks, and for offering many useful suggestions:

Cécile Ashman, Algonquin College
Dave Bopara, Toronto School of Business
Nada Borden, College of the North Atlantic
Michael Bozzo, Mohawk College
Wayne Bridgeman, formerly with CGA-Canada
Chris Burnley, Malaspina University College
Maisie Caines, College of the North Atlantic
K. Suzanne Coombs, Kwantlen University College
Robert Dearden, Red River Community College
Vincent Durant, St. Lawrence College
David Ferries, Algonquin College
Dave Fleming, George Brown College
Augusta Ford, College of the North Atlantic
Donna Grace, Sheridan College
Laurence P. Hanchard, Edmonton
Elizabeth Hicks, Douglas College
Larry Howe, University College of the Fraser Valley
Stephanie Ibach, Northern Alberta Institute of Technology
Laurette Korman, Kwantlen University College
Rick Martin, College of the North Atlantic
Clifton Philpott, Kwantlen University College
Carson Rappell, Dawson College
David Sale, Kwantlen University College
Scott Sinclair, British Columbia Institute of Technology
Bob Sproule, University of Waterloo
Gregg Tranter, Southern Alberta Institute of Technology
H. Barrie Yackness, British Columbia Institute of Technology
Elizabeth Zaleschuk, Douglas College

We are also grateful to the instructors across the country who took the time to respond to surveys conducted during the planning stages of this edition. The thoughts and opinions of these instructors were a valuable guide as we mapped out a strategy for improving this new edition:

Cécile Ashman, Algonquin College
James E. Chambers, St. Clair College
K. Suzanne Coombs, Kwantlen University College
Richard Farrar, Conestoga College
Albert M. Ferris, University of Prince Edward Island
Reiner Frisch, Georgian College
Donna Grace, Sheridan College
Elizabeth Hicks, Douglas College
Wayne Irvine, Mount Royal College
Connie Johl, Douglas College
Allen McQueen, Grant MacEwan Community College
Ann MacGillivary, Mount Saint Vincent University
Tariq Nizami, Champlain Regional College CEGEP
Penny Parker, Fanshawe College

Gabriela Schneider, Grant MacEwan Community College
Scott Sinclair, British Columbia Institute of Technology
Bob Sproule, University of Waterloo
Elizabeth Zaleschuk, Douglas College

We especially want to thank those students who have generously and eloquently contributed Student to Student comments to the text and companion website. Our thanks go to those at the following schools who participated in this project. The students' and instructors' enthusiasm was greatly appreciated.

Assiniboine Community College
College of New Caledonia
College of the North Atlantic
Conestoga College
Douglas College
Humber College
Langara College
Malaspina University College
McGill University
St. Lawrence College
University College of the Fraser Valley
University of Waterloo

Thanks are extended to Intrawest Corporation for permission to use its annual report in Volumes I and II of the text. Thanks are extended to JVC Canada Inc. for permission to use its invoice in Chapter 5. Thanks are extended to the Canadian Institute of Chartered Accountants for permission to use materials published by the Institute. We acknowledge the support provided by *The Globe and Mail's Report on Business*, the *Financial Post*, and by the annual reports of a large number of public companies.

We would like to acknowledge the people of Pearson Education Canada, in particular Vice President, Editorial Director Michael Young and Senior Acquisitions Editor Samantha Scully. We would also like to acknowledge especially the editorial and technical support of Anita Smale, CA.

I would like to thank my wife Sandra for her support and encouragement.

W. Morley Lemon

I would like to thank my wife, Helen, and my family very much for their support, assistance, and encouragement.

Peter R. Norwood

Partnerships

CHAPTER OBJECTIVES

After studying this chapter, you should be able to

1 Identify the characteristics of a partnership

2 Account for partners' initial investments in a partnership

3 Allocate profits and losses to the partners by different methods

4 Account for the admission of a new partner to the business

5 Account for the withdrawal of a partner from the business

6 Account for the liquidation of a partnership

7 Prepare partnership financial statements

Bruce Dunn is a chartered accountant in Vancouver. He received his designation as a Chartered Accountant in 1982 after articling with one of the larger firms in Canada. Shortly after, he decided to open his own proprietorship. Initially, he specialized in accounting and tax services for small- and medium-sized businesses. His business grew quickly through the 1980s and 1990s. Bruce found that as his practice matured, he became much more of a tax specialist to his long-time clients.

"With the advent of computer accounting software packages, more of my clients were able to perform basic accounting duties and the skill they wanted me to provide the most was in the area of taxation," Bruce said. "The problem became that as my clients grew larger, they needed some other services, such as information systems consulting and treasury management consulting, that I could not provide. I was starting to lose clients to larger, full-service firms, and my practice was stagnant."

Bruce learned of another sole proprietorship, Wayne Grieve, a chartered accountant who specialized in information systems consulting and advisory services. After several meetings, the two CAs decided to merge their businesses and formed a partnership.

"The partnership has been in business for only eighteen months," Bruce said recently, "but we can already identify benefits. We are able to offer a full range of services to our clients, which allows us to compete for clients big and small. We have both noticed that our office operates more efficiently and we have seen some cost savings from that. An added benefit that I had not anticipated is that we can 'sound ideas off each other.' With the complexities that exist today in the business world, the ability to discuss alternatives with a partner is almost a necessity. Forming this partnership was the best thing that could have happened to my business."

THE PARTNERSHIP

form of business introduces some complexities that proprietorship avoids. How much cash should a new partner contribute to the business? How should the partners divide profits and losses? How should a partner who leaves the firm be compensated for her or his share of the business?

THINKING IT OVER

What are some reasons that Dunn and Grieve might form a partnership?

A: To raise more capital; to use the talents of both partners; to expand the business. Additional answers are possible.

A **partnership** is an association of two or more persons who co-own a business for profit. This definition is common to the various provincial partnership acts, which tend to prescribe similar rules with respect to the organization and operation of partnerships in their jurisdiction.

Forming a partnership is easy. It requires no permission from government authorities and involves no legal procedures, with the exception that most provinces require most partnerships to register information such as the name of the partners and the name under which the business will be carried on.[1] When two persons decide to go into business together, a partnership is automatically formed.

A partnership brings together the assets, talents, and experience of the partners. Business opportunities closed to an individual may open up to a partnership. Suppose neither Dunn nor Grieve has enough capital individually to buy a small building for an office. They may be able to afford it together in a partnership. They pool their talents and know-how. Their partnership thus offers clients a fuller range of services than either person can offer alone.

Partnerships come in all sizes. Many partnerships have fewer than ten partners. Some medical practices may have ten or more partners while some of the largest law firms in Canada have more than 130 partners. The largest accounting firms in

---

[1] Smyth, J.E., D.A. Soberman, and A.J. Easson, *The Law and Business Administration in Canada,* Ninth edition (Toronto: Pearson Education Canada Inc., 2001), pp. 580–585.

EXHIBIT 12-1

The Ten Largest Accounting Partnerships in Canada (data given are as of the date shown in brackets)

Rank 1999	Firm	Revenue (Millions)	Number of Partners/ Principals
1	PricewaterhouseCoopers LLP (June 1999)*	$845	534
2	Deloitte & Touche LLP (August 1999)	750	522
3	KPMG LLP (September 1999)	735	548
4	Ernst & Young LLP (September 1999)	616	412
5	Grant Thornton Canada (December 1999)	228	368
6	Arthur Andersen LLP (August 1999)	203	155
7	BDO Dunwoody LLP (December 1999)	172	287
8	Collins Barow/Mintz & Partners (January 2000)**	56	119
9	Richter Usher & Vineberg (February 2000)	54	55
10	HLB/Schwartz Levitsky Feldman (January 2000)	38	62

Source: "Canada Largest Corporations," *National Post Business,* June 2000, p. 164.

 * Formed by the combination of Price Waterhouse and Coopers & Lybrand in fiscal 1999.
** Mintz & Partners joined Collins Barrow in July 1999.

PricewaterhouseCoopers LLP
www.pwcglobal.com

Deloitte & Touche LLP
www.deloitte.ca

KPMG LLP
www.kpmg.ca

Ernst & Young LLP
www.eycan.com

Grant Thornton Canada
www.grantthornton.ca

Arthur Andersen LLP
www.arthurandersen.ca

BDO Dunwoody LLP
www.bdo.ca

Collins Barrow/Mintz & Partners
www.collinsbarrow.com

Richter, Usher & Vineberg LLP
www.richter.ca

HLB/Schwartz Levitsky Feldman LLP
www.slf.ca

Canada have from 150 to more than 500 partners.[2] Exhibit 12-1 lists the 10 largest public accounting firms in Canada.

Characteristics of a Partnership

Starting a partnership is voluntary. A person cannot be forced to join a partnership, and partners cannot be forced to accept another person as a partner. Although the partnership agreement may be oral, a written agreement between the partners reduces the chance of a misunderstanding. The following characteristics distinguish partnerships from sole proprietorships and from corporations.

The Written Partnership Agreement

A business partnership is like a marriage. To be successful, the partners must cooperate. However, business partners do not vow to remain together for life. To make certain that each partner fully understands how the partnership operates and to lower the chances that any partner might misunderstand how the business is run, partners should draw up a **partnership agreement**. This agreement is a contract between the partners, so transactions under the agreement are governed by contract law. The provincial legislatures in Canada have passed their respective versions of a partnership act, the terms of which apply in the absence of a partnership agreement or in the absence of particular matters in the partnership agreement.[3]

The partnership agreement should make the following points clear:

1. Name, location, and nature of the business
2. Name, capital investment, and duties of each partner
3. Method of sharing profits and losses among the partners
4. Withdrawals of assets allowed to the partners
5. Procedures for settling disputes among the partners
6. Procedures for admitting new partners
7. Procedures for settling with a partner who withdraws from the business
8. Procedures for removing a partner who will not withdraw or retire from the partnership voluntarily
9. Procedures for liquidating the partnership—selling the assets, paying the liabilities, and disbursing any remaining cash to the partners

OBJECTIVE 1
Identify the characteristics of a partnership

KEY POINT

A partnership is not required to have a formal written agreement. But a written agreement prevents confusion as to the sharing of profits and losses, partners' responsibilities, admission of new partners, how the partnership will be liquidated, and so on. A written agreement does not preclude discord, however.

[2] "Canada's Largest Corporations," *National Post Business,* June 2000, p. 164.
[3] Smyth, J.E., D.A. Soberman, and A.J. Easson, *The Law and Business Administration in Canada,* Ninth edition. (Toronto: Pearson Education Canada Inc., 2001), pp. 590–597.

LEARNING TIP

Note that when a partner leaves a partnership, it dissolves and its books are closed. If the remaining partners want to continue as partners, they form a new partnership with a new set of books. Dissolution does not require liquidation; that is, the assets need not be sold to outside parties.

As partners enter and leave the business, the old partnership is dissolved and a new partnership is formed. Drawing up a new agreement for each new partnership may be expensive and time-consuming.

Limited Life

A partnership has a life limited by the length of time that all partners continue to own the business. If Bruce Dunn of the chapter-opening story withdraws from the business, the partnership of Dunn & Grieve will cease to exist. A new partnership may emerge to continue the same business, but the old partnership will have been dissolved. **Dissolution** is the ending of a partnership. The addition of a new partner dissolves the old partnership and creates a new partnership. Large partnerships such as PricewaterhouseCoopers retain the firm name even after partners resign from the firm.

Mutual Agency

Mutual agency in a partnership means that every partner can bind the business to a contract within the scope of the partnership's regular business operations. If Bruce Dunn enters into a contract with a person or another business to provide a service, then the firm of Dunn & Grieve—not only Dunn—is bound to provide that service. If Dunn signs a contract to purchase lawn services for his home, however, the partnership would not be bound to pay because the lawn service is a personal matter for Dunn. It is not a regular business operation of the partnership.

Unlimited Liability

KEY POINT

Since all partners are personally liable for any debt of the business, it is extremely important to choose a partner carefully. This is one reason some investors/partners prefer the *limited partnership* form of business organization.

Each partner has an **unlimited personal liability** for the debts of the partnership. When a partnership cannot pay its debts with business assets, the partners must use their personal assets to meet the debt. Proprietors also have unlimited personal liability for the debts of their business.

Suppose the Dunn & Grieve firm had an unsuccessful year, and the partnership's liabilities exceed its assets by $20,000. Dunn and Grieve must pay this amount with their personal assets. Because each partner has *unlimited liability*, if a partner is unable to pay his or her part of the debt, the other partner (or partners) must make payment. If Grieve can pay only $5,000 of the liability, Dunn must pay $15,000.

Unlimited liability and mutual agency are closely related. A dishonest partner or a partner with poor judgment may commit the partnership to a contract under which the business loses money. In turn, creditors may force *all* the partners to pay the debt from their personal assets. Hence, a business partner should be chosen with great care.

Partners can avoid unlimited personal liability for partnership obligations by forming a *limited partnership*. In this form of business organization, one or more of the general partners assumes the unlimited liability for business debts. In addition, there is another class of owners, limited partners, who can lose only as much as their investment in the business. In this sense, limited partners have limited liability similar to the limited liability that shareholders in a corporation have.

Co-ownership of Property

KEY POINT

A personal investment of assets in a partnership becomes the joint property of all the partners.

Any asset—cash, inventory, machinery, and so on—that a partner invests into the partnership becomes the joint property of all the partners. Also, each partner has a claim to his or her share of the business's profits.

No Partnership Income Taxes

A partnership pays no income tax on its business income. Instead, the net income of the partnership is divided, and becomes the taxable income of the partners. Suppose Dunn & Grieve earned net income of $150,000, shared equally by partners

Dunn and Grieve. Dunn & Grieve would pay no income tax *as a business entity*. However, Dunn and Grieve would pay income tax as individuals on their $75,000 shares of partnership income.

Partners' Owner's Equity Accounts

Recall from Chapter 1, page 12, that owner's equity for a proprietorship has only one account, entitled "Capital." For example, when Bruce Dunn had his own accounting practice, owner's equity would have been the single account Bruce Dunn, Capital.

Accounting for a partnership is much like accounting for a proprietorship. We record buying and selling goods and services, collecting, and paying cash for a partnership just as we do for a proprietorship. But, because a partnership has more than one owner, the partnership must have more than one owner's equity account. Every partner in the business—whether the firm has two or two hundred partners—has an individual owner's equity account. Often these accounts carry the name of the particular partner and the word *capital*. For example, the owner's equity account for Bruce Dunn would read "Bruce Dunn, Capital." Just as a sole proprietor has a drawings or withdrawal account (a temporary account), each partner in a partnership has a withdrawal account. If the number of partners is large, the general ledger may contain the single account Partners' Capital or Owners' Equity. In this event, a subsidiary ledger is used for individual partner accounts.

Exhibit 12-2 lists the advantages and disadvantages of partnerships (compared to proprietorships and corporations).

LEARNING TIP

A partnership is really a "multiple proprietorship." Most features of a proprietorship also apply to a partnership—in particular, limited life and unlimited liability.

Types of Partnerships

There are two basic types of partnerships: general and limited.

General Partnerships

A **general partnership** is the basic form of partnership organization. Each partner is an owner of the business with all the privileges and risks of ownership. The general partners share the profits, losses, and the risks of the business. The partnership *reports* its income to governmental tax authorities (Canada Customs and Revenue Agency, or CCRA), but the partnership pays *no* income tax. The profits and losses of the partnership pass through the business to the partners, who then pay personal income tax on their income.

Partnership Advantages	Partnership Disadvantages
Versus Proprietorships:	1. Partnership agreement may be difficult to formulate. Each time a new partner is admitted or a partner leaves the partnership, the business needs a new partnership agreement.
1. Can raise more capital.	
2. Brings together the expertise of more than one person.	
3. 1+1>2 in a good partnership. If the partners work well together, they can achieve more than by working alone.	2. Relationships among partners may be fragile.
Versus Corporations:	3. Mutual agency and unlimited personal liability create personal obligations for each partner.
4. Less expensive to organize than a corporation, which requires articles of incorporation from a province or the federal government.	
5. Fewer governmental regulations and restrictions than a corporation.	

EXHIBIT 12-2

Advantages and Disadvantages of Partnerships

Limited Partnerships

A **limited partnership** has at least two classes of partners. There must be at least one *general partner*, who takes primary responsibility for the management of the business. The general partner also takes the bulk of the risk of failure in the event that the partnership goes bankrupt (liabilities exceed assets). In some limited partnerships, such as real-estate limited partnerships, the general partner often invests little cash in the business. Instead, the general partner's contribution is her or his skill in managing the organization. Usually, the general partner is the last owner to receive a share of partnership profits and losses. But the general partner may earn all excess profits after satisfying the limited partners' demands for income.

The *limited partners* are so named because their personal obligation for the partnership's liabilities is limited to the amount they have invested in the business. Usually, the limited partners have invested the bulk of the partnership's assets and capital. They therefore usually have the first claim to partnership profits and losses, but only up to a specified limit. In exchange for their limited liability, their potential for profits usually has a limit as well.

Most of the large public accounting firms in Canada are now organized as **limited liability partnerships** (LLPs), which means that each partner's personal liability for the business's debts is limited to a certain dollar amount. An example is PricewaterhouseCoopers LLP. The LLP must carry an adequate amount of malpractice insurance to protect the public.

OBJECTIVE 2
Account for partners' initial investment in a partnership

Initial Investments by Partners

Let's examine the start up of a partnership. We will see how to account for the multiple owner's equity accounts of the partners and learn how they appear on the balance sheet.

Partners in a new partnership may invest assets and their related liabilities in the business. These contributions are entered in the books by recording the assets and liabilities, in the same way as proprietorships record them, at their agreed-upon values. Each person's net contribution (assets minus liabilities) is credited to the owner's equity account for that person. Often the partners hire an independent firm to appraise their assets and liabilities at current market value at the time a partnership is formed. This outside evaluation assures an objective valuation for what each partner brings into the business.

Assume Karen Edwards and Linda McLean form a partnership to develop and sell computer software. The partners agree on the following values based on an independent appraisal:

Edwards' contributions

- Cash, $20,000; inventory, $140,000; and accounts payable, $170,000 (The appraiser believes that the current market values for these items equal Edwards' book values.)

- Accounts receivable, $60,000, less allowance for doubtful accounts of $10,000

- Computer equipment: cost, $800,000; accumulated amortization, $200,000; current market value, $450,000

McLean's contributions

- Cash, $10,000

- Computer software: cost, $36,000; current market value, $200,000

The partnership records receipts of the partners' initial investments at the current market values of the assets and liabilities because, in effect, the partnership is buying the assets and assuming the liabilities at their current market values. The partnership entries are as follows:

Edwards' investment

2003

June 1	Cash	20,000	
	Accounts Receivable	60,000	
	Inventory	140,000	
	Computer Equipment	450,000	
	Allowance for Doubtful Accounts		10,000
	Accounts Payable		170,000
	Karen Edwards, Capital		490,000
	To record Edwards' investment in the partnership ($670,000 – $180,000).		

McLean's investment

2003

June 1	Cash	10,000	
	Computer Software	200,000	
	Linda McLean, Capital		210,000
	To record McLean's investment in the partnership.		

The initial partnership balance sheet reports these amounts as shown in Exhibit 12-3. Note that the asset and liability sections on the balance sheet are the same for a proprietorship and a partnership.

KEY POINT

The major difference in accounting for a proprietorship versus a partnership is the number of capital and drawing accounts. The partnership balance sheet shows a separate capital account for each partner, and there is a separate drawing account for each partner. The asset and liability sections on the balance sheet and the income statement are the same for a proprietorship and a partnership.

EXHIBIT 12-3

Partnership Balance Sheet

EDWARDS AND McLEAN
Balance Sheet
June 1, 2003

Assets			Liabilities	
Cash		$ 30,000	Accounts payable	$170,000
Accounts receivable	$60,000			
Less: Allowance for doubtful accounts	10,000	50,000	**Capital**	
Inventory		140,000	Karen Edwards, capital	490,000
Computer equipment		450,000	Linda McLean, capital	210,000
Computer software		200,000	Total capital	700,000
			Total liabilities	
Total assets		$870,000	and capital	$870,000

STOP & THINK

How could a partner allow the partnership to use a personal asset, such as a car or money, without losing his or her claim to that asset?

Answer: The partner could lease the car to the partnership. If the partnership were liquidated, the car would have to be returned to its owner. The partner could also lend money to the partnership instead of investing it. Upon liquidation, the partnership would have to repay the loan to the lending partner before any distribution of capital to the partners.

OBJECTIVE 3
Allocate profits and losses to the partners by different methods

---

THINKING IT OVER

Notice the credits to Capital in the two journal entries on June 1 on page 667. Must the partners contribute equal amounts?

A: No, the partners can agree on the amounts invested. The amounts invested do not necessarily determine how profits and losses will be divided.

Sharing Partnership Profits and Losses

Allocating profits and losses among partners is one of the most challenging aspects of managing a partnership and can be a major source of disputes. Any division of profits and losses is allowed as long as the partners agree and it is in the partnership agreement. If the partners have not drawn up an agreement, or if the agreement does not state how the partners will divide profits and losses, then, by law, the partners must share profits and losses equally. If the agreement specifies a method for sharing profits but not losses, then losses are shared in the same proportion as profits. For example, a partner receiving 75 percent of the profits would likewise absorb 75 percent of any losses.

In some cases, an equal division is not fair. One partner may perform more work for the business than the other partner, or one partner may make a larger capital contribution. In the preceding example, Linda McLean might agree to work longer hours for the partnership than Karen Edwards in order to earn a greater share of profits. Edwards could argue that she should receive more of the profits because she contributed more net assets ($490,000) than McLean did ($210,000). McLean might contend that her computer software program is the partnership's most important asset, and that her share of the profits should be greater than Edwards' share. Arriving at fair sharing of profits and losses in a partnership may be difficult. We now discuss the options available in determining partners' shares of profits and losses.

Sharing Based on a Stated Fraction

Partners may state a particular fraction of the total profits and losses each individual partner will share. Suppose the partnership agreement of Sarah Cagle and Bill Elias allocates two-thirds of the business profits and losses to Cagle and one-third to Elias. If net income for the year is $270,000, and all revenue and expense accounts have been closed, the Income Summary account has a credit balance of $270,000:

Income Summary

	Bal.	270,000

The entry to close this account and allocate the profit to the partners' capital accounts is

Dec. 31	Income Summary	270,000	
	Sarah Cagle, Capital		180,000
	Bill Elias, Capital		90,000
	To allocate net income to partners.		
	(Cagle: $270,000 × ⅔; Elias: $270,000 × ⅓)		

Consider the effect of this entry. Does Cagle get cash of $180,000 and Elias cash of $90,000? No. The increase in the capital accounts of the partners cannot be linked to any particular asset, including cash. Instead, the entry indicates that Cagle's ownership in all the assets of the business increased by $180,000 and Elias's by $90,000.

If the year's operations resulted in a net loss of $132,000, the Income Summary account would have a debit balance of $132,000. In that case, the closing entry to allocate the loss to the partners' capital accounts would be

Dec. 31	Sarah Cagle, Capital	88,000	
	Bill Elias, Capital	44,000	
	Income Summary		132,000
	To allocate net loss to partners.		
	(Cagle: $132,000 × ⅔; Elias: $132,000 × ⅓)		

Just as profit of $270,000 did not mean that the partners received cash of $180,000 and $90,000, so the loss of $132,000 does not mean that the partners must contribute cash of $88,000 and $44,000. A profit or loss will increase or decrease each partner's capital account, but cash will not change hands.

Sharing Based on Capital Contributions

Profits and losses are often allocated in proportion to the partners' capital contributions in the business. Suppose Jim Antoine, Erica Barber, and Tony Culomovic are partners in ABC Company. Their capital accounts have the following balances at the end of the year, before the closing entries:

WORKING IT OUT

Ash, Black, and Cole share profits in a 30:40:30 ratio. Compute each partner's share of net income if the partnership income is $100,000.

A:
Ash:
($100,000 × 30%) = $30,000
Black:
($100,000 × 40%) = 40,000
Cole:
($100,000 × 30%) = 30,000
$100,000

WORKING IT OUT

Ash, Black, and Cole share profits on the basis of capital account balances of $20,000, $40,000, and $140,000, respectively. Compute each partner's share of net income if the partnership net income is $100,000.

A:
Ash:
($20,000/$200,000 × $100,000) = $ 10,000
Black:
($40,000/$200,000 × $100,000) = 20,000
Cole:
($140,000/$200,000 × $100,000) = 70,000
$100,000

Jim Antoine, Capital	$ 60,000
Erica Barber, Capital	90,000
Tony Culomovic, Capital	75,000
Total capital balances	$225,000

Assume that the partnership earned a profit of $180,000 for the year. To allocate this amount based on capital contributions, each partner's percentage share of the partnership's total capital balance must be computed. We simply divide each partner's contribution by the total capital amount. These figures, multiplied by the $180,000 profit amount, yield each partner's share of the year's profits:

Antoine:	($60,000/$225,000) × $180,000	=	$ 48,000
Barber:	($90,000/$225,000) × $180,000	=	72,000
Culomovic:	($75,000/$180,000) × $180,000	=	60,000
	Net income allocated to partners	=	$180,000

The closing entry to allocate the profit to the partners' capital accounts is

Dec.	31	Income Summary	180,000	
		Jim Antoine, Capital		48,000
		Erica Barber, Capital		72,000
		Tony Culomovic, Capital		60,000
		To allocate net income to partners.		

After this closing entry, the partners' capital balances are

Jim Antoine, Capital ($60,000 + $48,000)	$108,000
Erica Barber, Capital ($90,000 + $72,000)	162,000
Tony Culomovic, Capital ($75,000 + $60,000)	135,000
Total capital balances after allocation of net income	$405,000

Sharing Based on Capital Contributions and on Service

One partner, regardless of his or her capital contribution, may put more work into the business than the other partners. Even among partners who log equal service time, one person's superior experience and knowledge may command a greater share of income. To reward the harder-working or more valuable person, the profit-and-loss-sharing method may be based on a combination of contributed capital *and* service to the business. Most law firms take service into account in determining partner compensation.

Assume Sheila Randolph and Carolyn Scott formed a partnership in which Randolph invested $60,000 and Scott invested $40,000, a total of $100,000. Scott devotes more time to the partnership and earns the larger salary. Accordingly, the two partners have agreed to share profits as follows:

1. The first $50,000 of partnership profits is to be allocated based on partners' capital contributions to the business.

2. The next $60,000 of profits is to be allocated based on service, with Randolph receiving $24,000 and Scott receiving $36,000.

3. Any remaining amount is allocated equally.

If net income for the first year is $125,000, the partners' shares of this profit are computed as follows:

THINKING IT OVER

Under what circumstances would a partner make an initial contribution of a liability?

A: A partner could contribute an asset with a liability attached to it. For example, a partner could contribute a mortgaged building to the partnership. In transferring the building to the partnership, the partner would also be transferring the mortgage payable (a liability), as long as the original lender agrees to the transaction.

WORKING IT OUT

Ash, Black, and Cole have capital balances of $20,000, $40,000, and $140,000, respectively. The partners share profits and losses as follows:
(1) The first $50,000 is allocated on the basis of partners' capital balances.
(2) The next $38,000 is allocated on the basis of service, with Ash, Black, and Cole receiving $10,000, $12,000, and $16,000, respectively.
(3) The remainder is divided equally.
  Compute each partner's share of net income if the partnership earns $100,000.

A:
Ash:
($20,000/$200,000 × $50,000) + $10,000 + $4,000* = $19,000
Black:
($40,000/$200,000 × $50,000) + $12,000 + $4,000* = $26,000
Cole:
($140,000/$200,000 × $50,000) + $16,000 + $4,000* = $55,000

*Remainder shared equally:
$100,000 − $50,000 − $38,000 = $12,000
$12,000 / 3 = $4,000

	Randolph	Scott	Total
Total net income..			$125,000
Sharing of first $50,000 of net income, based on capital contributions:			
Randolph ($60,000/$100,000 × $50,000).....................	$30,000		
Scott ($40,000/$100,000 × $50,000).............................		$20,000	
Total			50,000
Net income remaining for allocation.............................			75,000
Sharing of next $60,000, based on service:			
Randolph..	24,000		
Scott...		36,000	
Total			60,000
Net income left for allocation...			15,000
Remainder shared equally:			
Randolph ($15,000 × ½)...	7,500		
Scott ($15,000 × ½)..		7,500	
Total			15,000
Net income left for allocation...			$ -0-
Net income allocated to the partners............................	$61,500	$63,500	$125,000

On the basis of this allocation, the closing entry is

Dec. 31	Income Summary..	125,000	
	Sheila Randolph, Capital.............................		61,500
	Carolyn Scott, Capital		63,500
	To allocate net income to partners.		

Sharing Based on "Salaries" and Interest

Partners may be rewarded for their service and their capital contributions to the business in other ways. In one sharing plan, the partners are allocated "salaries" (which are predetermined sums to be withdrawn, *not* employee salaries) plus interest on their capital balances. Assume Edward Massey and Pierre Vanier form an oil-exploration partnership. At the beginning of the year, their capital balances are $80,000 and $100,000 respectively. The partnership agreement allocates annual "salary" of $43,000 to Massey and $35,000 to Vanier. After these amounts are allocated, each partner earns 8 percent interest on his beginning capital balance. Any remaining net income is divided equally. Partnership profit of $96,000 for 2003 will be allocated as follows:

	Massey	Vanier	Total
Total net income..			$96,000
First, "salaries":			
Massey...	$43,000		
Vanier...		$35,000	
Total			78,000
Net income remaining for allocation			18,000
Second, interest on beginning capital balances:			
Massey ($80,000 × 0.08)...	6,400		
Vanier ($100,000 × 0.08)..		8,000	
Total			14,400
Net income remaining for allocation			3,600
Third, remainder shared equally:			
Massey ($3,600 × ½)..	1,800		
Vanier ($3,600 × ½)		1,800	
Total			3,600
Net income remaining for allocation			$ -0-
Net income allocated to the partners........................	$51,200	$44,800	$96,000

.... **THINKING IT OVER**

What factors influence the way profits and losses are shared?

A: Each partner's initial contribution of assets and liabilities; the fair market value of the assets contributed; the time each partner will devote to the business; the skills, abilities, reputation, clients, and such that each partner contributes.

In the preceding illustration, net income exceeded the sum of "salary" and interest. If the partnership profit is less than the allocated sum of "salary" and interest, a negative remainder will occur at some stage in the allocation process. Even so, the partners use the same method for allocation purposes. For example, assume that Massey and Vanier Partnership earned only $82,000 in 2003.

	Massey	Vanier	Total
Total net income...			$82,000
First, "salaries":			
Massey...	$43,000		
Vanier..		$35,000	
Total...			78,000
Net income remaining for allocation...........................			4,000
Second, interest on beginning capital balances:			
Massey ($80,000 × 0.08)...	6,400		
Vanier ($100,000 × 0.08)..		8,000	
Total...			14,400
Net income remaining for allocation...........................			(10,400)
Third, remainder shared equally:			
Massey ($10,400 × ½)...	(5,200)		
Vanier ($10,400 × ½)		(5,200)	
Total...			(10,400)
Net income remaining for allocation...........................			$ -0-
Net income allocated to the partners.........................	$44,200	$37,800	$82,000

A net loss would be allocated to Massey and Vanier in the same manner outlined for net income. The sharing procedure would begin with the net loss, and then allocate "salary," interest, and any other specified amounts to the partners.

For example, assume that Massey and Vanier Partnership had a loss of $12,000 in 2003.

	Massey	Vanier	Total
Total net income..			($12,000)
First, "salaries":			
Massey...	$43,000		
Vanier..		$35,000	
Total...			78,000
Net income (loss) remaining for allocation..............			(90,000)
Second, interest on beginning capital balances:			
Massey ($80,000 × 0.08)...	6,400		
Vanier ($100,000 × 0.08)..		8,000	
Total...			14,400
Net income (loss) remaining for allocation..............			(104,400)
Third, remainder shared equally:			
Massey ($104,400 × ½)...	(52,200)		
Vanier ($104,400 × ½)		(52,200)	
Total...			(104,400)
Net income remaining for allocation...........................			$ -0-
Net income (loss) allocated to the partners	($2,800)	($9,200)	($12,000)

We see that partners may allocate profits and losses based on a stated fraction, contributed capital, service, interest on capital, or any combination of these factors. Each partnership shapes its profit-and-loss-sharing ratio to fit its own needs.

Partner Withdrawals (Drawings) of Cash and Other Assets

Like anyone else, partners need cash for personal living expenses. Partnership agreements usually allow partners to withdraw cash or other assets from the business. These withdrawals are sometimes called *drawings,* and are recorded in a separate Withdrawals or Drawings account for each partner. (Drawings from a partnership are recorded exactly as for a proprietorship.) Assume that both Edward Massey and Pierre Vanier are allowed a monthly withdrawal of $5,000. The partnership records the March 2003 withdrawal with this entry:

Mar. 31	Edward Massey, Withdrawals	5,000	
	Pierre Vanier, Withdrawals...................................	5,000	
	Cash		10,000
	Monthly partner withdrawals of cash.		

During the year, each partner's withdrawal account accumulates 12 such amounts, a total of $60,000 ($5,000 × 12). At the end of the period, the general ledger shows the following account balances immediately after net income has been closed to the partners' capital accounts. Assume the January 1, 2003, balances for Massey and Vanier shown below, and that $82,000 of profit has been allocated on the basis of the illustration on page 672.

REAL WORLD EXAMPLE

According to the *Income Tax Act,* partners are taxed on their share of partnership income, not on the amount of their withdrawals.

Edward Massey, Capital

	Jan. 1, 2003 Bal.	80,000
	Dec. 31, 2003	
	Net income	44,200

Pierre Vanier, Capital

	Jan. 1, 2003 Bal.	100,000
	Dec. 31, 2003	
	Net income	37,800

Edward Massey, Withdrawals

Dec. 31, 2003 Bal. 60,000	

Pierre Vanier, Withdrawals

Dec. 31, 2003 Bal. 60,000	

The withdrawal accounts must be closed at the end of the period (as must be done for a proprietorship). The closing entry credits each partner's Withdrawals account and debits each partner's Capital account. The amount of the withdrawal does not depend on the partnership's income or loss for the year. In fact, it is possible for a partner to withdraw more than the balance in the capital account if, for example, profits were expected to be higher than they proved to be and withdrawals were made in anticipation of these high profits. This situation can only occur if the partnership has the cash required for the withdrawal and the other partners agree with the withdrawal and the ending capital balance.

OBJECTIVE 4
Account for the admission of a new partner to the business

Admission of a Partner

A partnership lasts only as long as its partners remain in the business. The addition of a new member or the withdrawal of an existing member dissolves the partnership. We turn now to a discussion of how partnerships dissolve—and how new partnerships arise.

Often a new partnership is formed to carry on the former partnership's business. In fact, the new partnership may choose to retain the dissolved partnership's name. PricewaterhouseCoopers LLP, for example, is an accounting and consulting firm that retires and admits partners during the year. Thus the former partnership dissolves and a new partnership begins many times. The business, however, retains the name and continues operations. Other partnerships may dissolve and then re-form under a new name. Let's look at the ways that a new member may gain admission into an existing partnership.

Admission by Purchasing a Partner's Interest

WORKING IT OUT

Ted and Fred are partners with capital balances of $32,000 and $48,000, respectively. Profits and losses are shared on the basis of capital balances. Ann offers Fred $120,000 for his interest in the business. What is the entry to record the transfer of capital?

A:

Fred, Capital 48,000
   Ann, Capital   48,000

A person may become a member of a partnership by gaining the approval of the other partner (or partners) for entrance into the firm, *and* by purchasing a present partner's interest in the business. Let's assume that Stephi Fisher and Carlo Levesque have a partnership that carries these figures:

Cash.....................................	$ 80,000	Total liabilities......................	$240,000
Other assets	720,000	Stephi Fisher, capital...........	220,000
		Carlo Levesque, capital	340,000
		Total liabilities	
Total assets...........................	$800,000	and capital......................	$800,000

Business is so successful that Fisher receives an offer from Linda Dynak, an outside party, to buy her $220,000 interest in the business for $300,000. Fisher agrees to sell out to Dynak, and Levesque approves Dynak as a new partner. The firm records the transfer of capital interest in the business with this entry:

Apr.	16	Stephi Fisher, Capital...	220,000	
		Linda Dynak, Capital		220,000
		To transfer Fisher's equity in the business to Dynak.		

The debit side of the entry closes Fisher's capital account because she is no longer a partner in the firm. The credit side opens Dynak's capital account because Fisher's equity has been transferred to Dynak. The entry amount is Fisher's capital balance ($220,000) and not the $300,000 price that Dynak paid Fisher to buy into the business. The full $300,000 goes to Fisher, including the $80,000 difference between her capital balance and the price received from Dynak. In this example, the partnership does not receive cash because the transaction was between Dynak and Fisher, not between Dynak and the partnership. Suppose Dynak pays Fisher less than Fisher's capital balance. The entry on the partnership books is not affected. Fisher's equity is transferred to Dynak at book value ($220,000).

The old partnership has dissolved. Levesque and Dynak draw up a new partnership agreement, with a new profit-and-loss-sharing ratio, and continue business

KEY POINT

The profit or loss on the sale of a partnership interest belongs personally to the partner selling the interest and will not appear on the partnership's books.

operations. If Levesque does not accept Dynak as a partner, the Fisher and Levesque partnership would be dissolved, and Dynak would be unable to buy Fisher's interest.

Admission by Investing in the Partnership

A person may be admitted as a partner by investing directly in the partnership rather than by purchasing an existing partner's interest. The new partner contributes assets— for example, cash, inventory, or equipment—to the business. Assume that the partnership of Robin Ingel and Michael Jay has the following assets, liabilities, and capital:

Cash	$ 30,000	Total liabilities	$ 90,000
Other assets	300,000	Robin Ingel, capital	105,000
		Michael Jay, capital	135,000
		Total liabilities	
Total assets	$330,000	and capital	$330,000

Laureen Kahn offers to invest equipment and land (Other assets) with a market value of $120,000 to persuade the existing partners to take her into the business. Ingel and Jay agree to dissolve the existing partnership and to start up a new business, giving Kahn one-third interest—[$120,000/($105,000 + $135,000 + $120,000) = ⅓]—in exchange for the contributed assets. Notice that Kahn is buying into the partnership at book value because her one-third investment ($120,000) equals one-third of the new partnership's total capital ($360,000). The entry to record Kahn's investment is

July	18	Other Assets	120,000	
		Laureen Kahn, Capital		120,000
		To admit L. Kahn as a partner with a		
		one-third interest in the business.		

After this entry, the partnership books show:

Cash	$ 30,000	Total liabilities	$ 90,000
Other assets		Robin Ingel, capital	105,000
($300,000 + $120,000)	420,000	Michael Jay, capital	135,000
		Laureen Kahn, capital	120,000
		Total liabilities	
Total assets	$450,000	and capital	$450,000

Kahn's one-third interest in the partnership does not necessarily entitle her to one-third of the profits. The sharing of profits and losses is a separate element in the partnership agreement.

Admission by Investing in the Partnership—Bonus to the Old Partners The more successful a partnership, the higher the payment the partners may demand from a person entering the business. Partners in a business that is doing quite well might require an incoming person to pay them a bonus. The bonus comes into the partnership, increasing the current partners' capital accounts.

Suppose that Hiro Nagasawa and Lisa Schwende's partnership has earned above-average profits for ten years. The two partners share profits and losses equally. The balance sheet carries these figures:

Cash	$ 80,000	Total liabilities	$200,000
Other assets	420,000	Hiro Nagasawa, capital	140,000
		Lisa Schwende, capital	160,000
		Total liabilities	
Total assets	$500,000	and capital	$500,000

WORKING IT OUT

Ted and Fred are partners with capital balances of $32,000 and $48,000, respectively. Profits and losses are shared on the basis of capital balances. Ted and Fred admit Jill to a 20% interest with a $24,000 investment. What is the entry to record Jill's admission to the partnership?

A:

Cash	24,000
Jill, Capital	20,800
Ted, Capital	1,280
Fred, Capital	1,920

Jill: $20,800 = ($32,000 + $48,000 + $24,000) × 0.2

Ted: $1,280 = $32,000/$80,000 × ($24,000 − $20,800)

Fred: $1,920 = $48,000/$80,000 × ($24,000 − $20,800)

The partners agree to admit Alana Parker to a one-fourth interest with her cash investment of $180,000. Parker's capital balance on the partnership books is $120,000, computed as follows:

Partnership capital before Parker is admitted ($140,000 + $160,000) ..	$300,000
Parker's investment in the partnership	180,000
Partnership capital after Parker is admitted	$480,000
Parker's capital in the partnership ($480,000 × ¼)	$120,000
Bonus to the old partners ($180,000 – $120,000)	$ 60,000

In effect, Parker had to buy into the partnership at a price ($180,000) above the book value of her one-fourth interest ($120,000). Parker's extra investment of $60,000 creates a *bonus* for the existing partners. The entry on the partnership books to record Parker's investment is

Mar.	1	Cash	180,000	
		Alana Parker, Capital..		120,000
		Hiro Nagasawa, Capital..................................		30,000
		Lisa Schwende, Capital		30,000
		To admit A. Parker as a partner with a one-fourth interest in the business. Nagasawa and Schwende each receive a bonus of $30,000 ($60,000 × ½).		

Parker's capital account is credited for her one-fourth interest in the partnership. The bonus is allocated to the original partners (Nagasawa and Schwende) based on their profit-and-loss ratio.

The new partnership's balance sheet reports these amounts:

Cash ($80,000 + $180,000)	$260,000	Total liabilities...................	$200,000
Other assets........................	420,000	Hiro Nagasawa, capital	
		($140,000 + $30,000).....	170,000
		Lisa Schwende, capital	
		($160,000 + $30,000).....	190,000
		Alana Parker, capital........	120,000
		Total liabilities	
Total assets	$680,000	and capital	$680,000

Admission by Investing in the Partnership—Bonus to the New Partner A potential new partner may be so important that the existing partners offer him or her a partnership share that includes a bonus. A law firm may strongly desire a former premier, cabinet minister, or other official as a partner because of the person's reputation. A restaurant owner may want to go into partnership with a famous sports personality like Wayne Gretzky or a singer like Shania Twain.

Suppose Jenny Page and Miko Osuka have a law partnership. The firm's balance sheet appears as follows:

Cash	$210,000	Total liabilities...................	$180,000
Other assets	540,000	Jenny Page, capital	345,000
		Miko Osuka, capital	225,000
		Total liabilities	
Total assets........................	$750,000	and capital	$750,000

The partners admit Martin Schiller, a former provincial Finance Minister, as a partner with a one-third interest in exchange for his cash investment of $150,000. At the time of Schiller's admission, the firm's capital is $570,000—Page, $345,000 plus Osuka, $225,000. Page and Osuka share profits and losses in the ratio of two-thirds to Page and one-third to Osuka. The computation of Schiller's equity in the partnership is

Partnership capital before Schiller is admitted ($345,000 + $225,000)	$570,000	
Schiller's investment in the partnership	150,000	
Partnership capital after Schiller is admitted	$720,000	
Schiller's capital in the partnership ($720,000 × ⅓)	$240,000	
Bonus to new partner ($240,000 – $150,000)	$ 90,000	

In this case, Schiller bought into the partnership at a price ($150,000) below the book value of his interest ($240,000). The bonus of $90,000 went to Schiller from the other partners. The capital accounts of Page and Osuka are debited for the $90,000 difference between the new partner's equity ($240,000) and his investment ($150,000). The existing partners share this decrease in capital, which is accounted for as though it were a loss, based on their profit-and-loss ratio. The entry to record Schiller's investment is

Aug. 24	Cash	150,000	
	Jenny Page, Capital ($90,000 × ⅔)	60,000	
	Miko Osuka, Capital ($90,000 × ⅓)	30,000	
	Martin Schiller, Capital		240,000
	To admit M. Schiller as a partner with a one-third interest in the business.		

The new partnership's balance sheet reports these amounts:

Cash		Total liabilities	$180,000
($210,000 + $150,000)	$360,000	Jenny Page, capital	
Other assets	540,000	($345,000 – $60,000)	285,000
		Miko Osuka, capital	
		($225,000 – $30,000)	195,000
		Martin Schiller, capital	240,000
		Total liabilities	
Total assets	$900,000	and capital	$900,000

Withdrawal of a Partner from the Business

A partner may withdraw from the business for many reasons, including retirement or a dispute with the other partners. The withdrawal of a partner dissolves the old partnership. The partnership agreement should contain a provision to govern how to settle with a withdrawing partner. In the simplest case, as illustrated on page 674, a partner may withdraw and sell his or her interest to another partner in a personal transaction. The only entry needed to record this transfer of equity debits the withdrawing partner's capital account and credits the purchaser's capital account. The dollar amount of the entry is the capital balance of the withdrawing partner, regardless of the price paid by the purchaser. The accounting when one current partner buys a second partner's interest is the same as when an outside party buys a current partner's interest.

If the partner withdraws in the middle of the accounting period, the partnership books should be updated to determine the withdrawing partner's capital balance. The business must measure net income or net loss for the fraction of the year up to the withdrawal date, and allocate profit or loss according to the existing ratio. An alternative is to set an amount in the partnership agreement to be allocated regardless of the final annual results. This could be appropriate in businesses that have seasonal fluctuations, where the selection of withdrawal date could lead to unfair allocations. After the books have been closed, the business then accounts for the change in partnership capital.

The withdrawing partner may receive his or her share of the business in partnership assets other than cash. The question then arises of what value to assign the partnership assets—book value or current market value? The settlement procedure may specify an independent appraisal of the assets to determine their current market value. If market

WORKING IT OUT

Jan and Ron are partners with capital balances of $45,000 and $60,000, respectively. They share profits and losses in a 25:75 ratio. Jan and Ron admit Lou to a 20% interest in a new partnership when Lou invests $15,000 in the business.
1. Journalize the partnership's receipt of cash from Lou.
2. What is each partner's capital in the new partnership?

A:

1. Cash	15,000	
Jan, Capital	2,250	
Ron, Capital	6,750	
Lou, Capital		24,000
To admit Lou with a 20% interest in the business.		

Partnership capital before Lou is admitted ($45,000 + $60,000)	$105,000
Lou's investment in the partnership	15,000
Partnership capital after Lou is admitted	120,000
Lou's capital in the partnership ($120,000 × 0.20)	$ 24,000
Bonus to the new partner ($24,000 – $15,000)	$ 9,000

Jan's decrease in capital is $2,250 ($9,000 × 0.25) and Ron's decrease is $6,750 ($9,000 × 0.75).

2. Partner's capital balances:	
Jan, capital ($45,000 – $2,250)	$ 42,750
Ron, capital ($60,000 – $6,750)	53,250
Lou, capital	24,000
Total partnership capital	$120,000

OBJECTIVE 5
Account for the withdrawal of a partner from the business

KEY POINT

When a partner leaves a partnership, she or he ceases to be an agent and no longer has the authority to bind the business to contracts. Third parties with whom the partnership has dealt should be notified that the exiting partner no longer can bind the partnership. For all other third parties, constructive notice, such as an advertisement in the newspaper, is sufficient.

WORKING IT OUT

Jane, Karol, and Leah are partners with capital account balances of $20,000, $30,000, and $50,000, respectively. They share profits in a 2:3:5 ratio. Karol is withdrawing from the business, so the partners have the assets appraised. The building's market value is $4,000 more than its book value. The inventory's market value is $6,000 less than cost. What are the journal entries to revalue these assets?

A:

Building	4,000	
Jane, Capital....		800
Karol, Capital...		1,200
Leah, Capital....		2,000
Jane, Capital......	1,200	
Karol, Capital	1,800	
Leah, Capital	3,000	
Inventory		6,000

values have changed, the appraisal will result in a revaluing of the partnership assets. Thus the partners share in any market value changes that their efforts caused.

Suppose Ben Isaac is retiring in midyear from the partnership of Green, Maslowski, and Isaac. After the books have been adjusted for partial-period income but before the asset appraisal, revaluation, and closing entries, the balance sheet reports the following:

Cash...		$ 52,000	Total liabilities.........................	$ 93,000
Inventory.................................		44,000	Joan Green, capital	54,000
Land		55,000	Ivan Maslowski, capital.........	43,000
Building.................	$95,000		Ben Isaac, capital	21,000
Less: Accumulated				
amortization	35,000	60,000	Total liabilities	
Total assets		$211,000	and capital.........................	$211,000

An independent appraiser revalues the inventory at $38,000 (down from $44,000), and the land at $101,000 (up from $55,000). The partners share the differences between these assets' market values and their prior book values based on their profit-and-loss ratio.

The partnership agreement has allocated one-fourth of the profits to Green, one-half to Maslowski, and one-fourth to Isaac. (This ratio may be written 1:2:1 for one part to Green, two parts to Maslowski, and one part to Isaac.) For each share that Green or Isaac has, Maslowski has two. The entries to record the revaluation of the inventory and land are

June	30	Joan Green, Capital ($6,000 × ¼)	1,500	
		Ivan Maslowski, Capital ($6,000 × ½)........................	3,000	
		Ben Isaac, Capital ($6,000 × ¼)	1,500	
		Inventory ($44,000 – $38,000)................................		6,000
		To revalue the inventory and allocate the loss in value to the partners.		
June	30	Land ($101,000 – $55,000)	46,000	
		Joan Green, Capital ($46,000 × ¼)		11,500
		Ivan Maslowski, Capital ($46,000 × ½)		23,000
		Ben Isaac, Capital ($46,000 × ¼)		11,500
		To revalue the land and allocate the gain in value to the partners.		

After the revaluations, the partnership balance sheet reports:

WORKING IT OUT

What are the partners' capital account balances after the revaluations in the previous Working It Out?

A:

Jane: ($20,000 + $800 – $1,200)
= $19,600
Karol: ($30,000 + $1,200 – $1,800)
= $29,400
Leah: ($50,000 + $2,000 – $3,000)
= $49,000

Cash		$ 52,000	Total liabilities.........................	$ 93,000
Inventory...............................		38,000	Joan Green, capital ($54,000 –	
Land		101,000	$1,500 + $11,500)	64,000
Building.................	$95,000		Ivan Maslowski, capital ($43,000 –	
Less: Accumulated			$3,000 + $23,000)	63,000
amortization ..	35,000	60,000	Ben Isaac, capital ($21,000 –	
			$1,500 + $11,500)	31,000
			Total liabilities	
Total assets		$251,000	and capital.........................	$251,000

The books now carry the assets at current market value, which becomes the new book value, and the capital accounts have been adjusted accordingly. As the balance sheet shows, Isaac has a claim to $31,000 in partnership assets. How is his withdrawal from the business accounted for?

Withdrawal at Book Value

If Ben Isaac withdraws by taking cash equal to the book value of his owner's equity, the entry would be

```
June    30    Ben Isaac, Capital........................................   31,000
                  Cash..........................................................               31,000
              To record withdrawal of B. Isaac from the part-
              nership.
```

This entry records the payment of partnership cash to Isaac and the closing of his capital account upon his withdrawal from the business.

Withdrawal at Less Than Book Value

The withdrawing partner may be so eager to leave the business that she or he is willing to take less than her or his equity. Assume Ben Isaac withdraws from the business, and agrees to take partnership cash of $10,000 and the new partnership's note for $15,000. This $25,000 settlement is $6,000 less than Isaac's $31,000 equity in the business. The remaining partners share this $6,000 difference—which is a bonus to them—according to their profit-and-loss ratio.

Because Isaac has withdrawn from the partnership, a new agreement—and a new profit-and-loss ratio—must be drawn up. Maslowski and Green, in forming a new partnership, may decide on any ratio that they see fit. Let's assume they agree that Maslowski will earn two-thirds of partnership profits and losses, and Green one-third. The entry to record Isaac's withdrawal at less than book value is

```
June    30    Ben Isaac, Capital .....................................   31,000
                  Cash ........................................................               10,000
                  Note Payable to Ben Isaac............................               15,000
                  Joan Green, Capital .......................................                2,000
                  Ivan Maslowski, Capital ..............................                4,000
              To record withdrawal of B. Isaac from the part-
              nership. Green's bonus is $2,000 ($6,000 × ⅓)
              and Maslowski's bonus is $4,000 ($6,000 × ⅔)
```

Isaac's account is closed, and Maslowski and Green may or may not continue the business as a new partnership.

Withdrawal at More Than Book Value

The settlement with a withdrawing partner may allow him or her to take assets of greater value than the book value of that partner's capital. Also, the remaining partners may be so eager for the withdrawing partner to leave the firm that they pay the partner a bonus to withdraw from the business. In either case, the partner's withdrawal causes a decrease in the book equity of the remaining partners. This decrease is allocated to the partners based on their profit-and-loss ratio.

The accounting for this situation follows the pattern illustrated for withdrawal at less than book value—with one exception. The remaining partners' capital accounts are debited because the withdrawing partner receives more than his or her book equity.

Suppose Linda is withdrawing from the partnership of Linda, Jacob, and Karla. The partners share profits and losses in a 1:2:3 ratio for Linda, Jacob, and Karla, respectively. After the revaluation of assets, Linda's capital balance is $100,000, and the other partners agree to pay her $120,000. The journal entry to record the payment to Linda and her withdrawal from the partnership is

```
              Linda, Capital...............................................  100,000
              Jacob, Capital...............................................    8,000
              Karla, Capital...............................................   12,000
                  Cash ......................................................              120,000
              To record withdrawal of Linda from
              the business. Jacob's capital is reduced
              by $8,000 [($120,000 – $100,000) × ⅖] and
              Karla's capital is reduced by $12,000
              [(120,000 – $100,000) × ⅗].
```

WORKING IT OUT

Refer to the Working It Outs on page 678. Assume that Karol is willing to accept $20,000 for his partnership interest. What is the journal entry to record his withdrawal from the business?

A:
```
Karol, Capital ....... 29,400
   Cash .................           20,000
   Jane, Capital......            2,686*
   Leah, Capital......           6,714†
```
*$9,400 × 2/7 = 2,686
†$9,400 × 5/7 = $6,714
Jane and Leah will now share profits in a 2:5 ratio.

WORKING IT OUT

Refer to the Working It Outs on page 678. Assume that Jane and Leah agree to pay Karol $40,000 for his partnership interest. What is the journal entry to record his withdrawal from the business?

A:
```
Jane, Capital......    3,029*
Karol, Capital .....  29,400
Leah, Capital......    7,571†
   Cash ................           40,000
```
*$10,600 × 2/7 = $3,029
†$10,600 × 5/7 = $7,571

Death of a Partner

Like any other form of partnership withdrawal, the death of a partner dissolves a partnership. The partnership accounts are adjusted to measure net income or loss for the fraction of the year up to the date of death, then closed to determine the partners' capital balances on that date. Settlement with the deceased partner's estate is based on the partnership agreement. The estate commonly receives partnership assets equal to the partner's capital balance. The partnership closes the deceased partner's capital account with a debit. This entry credits a payable to the estate.

Suppose Joan Green (of the partnership on page 678) dies after all accounts have been adjusted to current market value. Green's capital balance is $64,000. Green's estate may request cash for her final share of the partnership's assets. At this time the business has only $52,000 of cash, so it must borrow. Let's assume the partnership borrows $50,000 and then pays Green's estate for her capital balance. The partnership's journal entries are

July	1	Cash	50,000	
		Note payable		50,000
		To borrow money		
July	1	Joan Green, Capital..............................	64,000	
		Cash...		64,000
		To record withdrawal of Green from the business.		

Alternatively, a remaining partner may purchase the deceased partner's equity. The deceased partner's equity is debited and the purchaser's equity is credited. The amount of this entry is the ending credit balance in the deceased partner's capital account.

Liquidation of a Partnership

Admission of a new partner or withdrawal or death of an existing partner dissolves the partnership. However, the business may continue operating with no apparent change to outsiders such as customers and creditors. In contrast, business **liquidation** is the process of going out of business by selling the entity's assets and paying its liabilities. The final step in liquidation of a business is the *distribution of the remaining cash to the owners*. Before the business is liquidated, the books should be adjusted and closed. After closing, only asset, liability, and partners' capital accounts remain open.

Liquidation of a partnership includes three basic steps:

1. Sell the assets. Allocate the gain or loss to the partners' capital accounts based on the profit-and-loss ratio.
2. Pay the partnership liabilities.
3. Disburse the remaining cash to the partners in proportion to their capital balances.

In actual practice, the liquidation of a business can stretch over weeks or months. Selling every asset and paying every liability of the entity takes time. For example, the liquidation of a law firm of over 75 partners took almost a year.

To avoid excessive detail in our illustrations, we include only two asset categories—Cash and Noncash Assets—and a single liability category—Liabilities. Our examples also assume that the business sells the noncash assets in a single transaction and pays the liabilities in a single transaction. (In actual practice, each asset and its related amortization would be accounted for separately when it is sold, and each liability would be accounted for separately when it is paid.)

Assume that Jane Aviron, Elaine Bloch, and Kim Zhang have shared profits and losses in the ratio of 3:1:1. (This ratio is equal to ⅗, ⅕, ⅕, or a 60-percent, 20-percent, 20-percent sharing ratio.) They decide to liquidate their partnership. After the books are adjusted and closed, the general ledger contains the following balances:

Cash	$ 20,000	Liabilities	$ 60,000
Noncash assets	180,000	Jane Aviron, capital	80,000
		Elaine Bloch, capital	40,000
		Kim Zhang, capital	20,000
		Total liabilities	
Total assets	$200,000	and capital	$200,000

Sale of Noncash Assets at a Gain

Assume the Aviron, Bloch, and Zhang partnership sells its noncash assets (shown on the balance sheet at $180,000) for cash of $300,000. The partnership realizes a gain of $120,000, which is allocated to the partners based on their profit-and-loss-sharing ratio. The entry to record this sale and allocation of the gain is

Oct.	31	Cash	300,000	
		Noncash Assets		180,000
		Jane Aviron, Capital		72,000
		Elaine Bloch, Capital		24,000
		Kim Zhang, Capital		24,000

To sell noncash assets in liquidation and allocate gain to partners. Aviron's share of the gain is $72,000 ($120,000 × 0.60), Bloch's and Zhang's is $24,000 ($120,000 × 0.20).

The partnership must next pay off its liabilities:

Oct.	31	Liabilities	60,000	
		Cash		60,000

To pay liabilities in liquidation.

In the final liquidation transaction, the remaining cash is disbursed to the partners. *The partners share in the cash according to their capital balances.* (By contrast, *gains* and *losses* on the sale of assets are shared by the partners based on their profit-and-loss-sharing ratio.) The amount of cash left in the partnership is $260,000— the $20,000 beginning balance plus the $300,000 cash sale of assets minus the $60,000 cash payment of liabilities. The partners divide the remaining cash according to their capital balances:

Oct.	31	Jane Aviron, Capital ($80,000 + $72,000)	152,000	
		Elaine Bloch, Capital ($40,000 + $24,000)	64,000	
		Kim Zhang, Capital ($20,000 + $24,000)	44,000	
		Cash		260,000

To disburse cash to partners in liquidation.

A convenient way to summarize the transactions in a partnership liquidation is given in Exhibit 12-4.

After the disbursement of cash to the partners, the business has no assets, liabilities, or owners' equity. All the balances are zero. By the accounting equation, partnership assets *must* equal partnership liabilities plus partnership capital.

Sale of Noncash Assets at a Loss

Liquidation of a business often includes the sale of noncash assets at a loss. When this occurs, the partners' capital accounts are debited as they share the loss in their profit-and-loss-sharing ratio. Otherwise, the accounting follows the pattern illustrated for the sale of noncash assets at a gain.

EXHIBIT 12-4

Partnership Liquidation—Sale of Assets at a Gain

					Capital		
	Cash	+ Noncash Assets	= Liabilities	+	Aviron (60%)	+ Bloch (20%)	+ Zhang (20%)
Balances before sale of assets............................	$ 20,000	$180,000	$ 60,000		$ 80,000	$40,000	$ 20,000
Sale of assets and sharing of gain..............	300,000	(180,000)			72,000	24,000	24,000
Balances..............................	320,000	-0-	60,000		152,000	64,000	44,000
Payment of liabilities........	(60,000)		(60,000)				
Balances..............................	260,000	-0-	-0-		152,000	64,000	44,000
Disbursement of cash to partners....................	(260,000)				(152,000)	(64,000)	(44,000)
Balances..............................	$ -0-	$ -0-	$ -0-		$ -0-	$ -0-	$ -0-

EXHIBIT 12-5

Financial Statements of a Partnership and a Proprietorship

Panel A—Partnership

GRAY AND HUI CONSULTING
Income statement
For the Year Ended December 31, 2003

Revenues......................................		$460
Expenses.......................................		(270)
Net income..................................		$190
Allocation of net income:		
To Leslie Gray.........................	$114	
To Andrew Hui......................	76	$190

GRAY AND HUI CONSULTING
Statement of Owners' Equity
For the Year Ended December 31, 2003

	Gray	Hui
Capital, January 1, 2003	$50	$40
Additional investments	10	—
Net income...................................	114	76
Subtotal	174	116
Withdrawals	(72)	(48)
Capital, December 31, 2003	$102	$68

GRAY AND HUI CONSULTING
Balance Sheet
December 31, 2003

Assets	
Cash and other assets	$170
Partners' Equity	
Leslie Gray, capital	$102
Andrew Hui, capital	68
Total capital..	$170

Panel B—Proprietorship

GRAY CONSULTING
Income statement
For the Year Ended December 31, 2003

Revenues	$460
Expenses...	(270)
Net income..	$190

GRAY CONSULTING
Statement of Owner's Equity
For the Year Ended December 31, 2003

Capital, January 1, 2003.................................	$90
Additional investments.................................	10
Net income..	190
Subtotal...	290
Withdrawals	(120)
Capital, December 31, 2003	$170

GRAY CONSULTING
Balance Sheet
December 31, 2003

Assets	
Cash and other assets	$170
Owner's Equity	
Leslie Gray, capital..	$170

Partnership Financial Statements

OBJECTIVE 7
Prepare partnership financial statements

Partnership financial statements are much like those of a proprietorship. However, a partnership income statement includes a section showing the division of net income to the partners. For example, the partnership of Leslie Gray and Andrew Hui might report its income statement for the year ended December 31, 2003, as shown in Panel A of Exhibit 12-5 on page 682. A proprietorship's financial statements are presented for comparison.

Large partnerships may not find it feasible to report the net income of every partner. Instead, the firm may report the allocation of net income to active and retired partners and average earnings per partner. For example, Exhibit 12-6 shows how the accounting and consulting firm of Main, Price & Anders reported its earnings.

The Decision Guidelines feature on pages 684–685 summarizes the main points of accounting for partnerships.

EXHIBIT 12-6

Reporting Net Income for a Large Partnership

MAIN, PRICE & ANDERS
Combined Statement of Earnings
For the Year Ended August 31, 2002

Fees for Professional Services	$9,144,920
Earnings for the year	$2,978,800
Allocation of earnings	
To partners active during the year—	
Resigned, retired, and deceased partners	$ 199,010
Partners active at year end	2,620,291
To retired and deceased partners—	
Retirement and death benefits	83,100
Not allocated to partners—retained for specific partnership purposes	76,399
	$2,978,800
Average earnings per partner at year end (28 partners)	$ 106,400

STOP & THINK

Suppose the Aviron, Bloch, and Zhang partnership sold its noncash assets for $60,000 and all other details in Exhibit 12-4 remained the same. This creates a loss of $120,000 on the sale of the noncash assets. Allocate the loss to the partners. Identify ways that the partnership could deal with the negative balance (a capital deficiency) in Zhang's capital account.

Answer: Allocation of the $120,000 loss on the sale of assets is shown below.

	Cash	+	Noncash Assets	=	Liabilities	+	Aviron (60%)	+	Bloch (20%)	+	Zhang (20%)
									Capital		
Balances before sale of assets....................	$ 20,000		$180,000		$ 60,000		$ 80,000		$ 40,000		$ 20,000
Sale of assets and sharing of loss	60,000		(180,000)				(72,000)		(24,000)		(24,000)
Balances................................	80,000		-0-		60,000		8,000		16,000		(4,000)
Payment of liabilities...........	(60,000)				(60,000)						
Balances................................	20,000		-0-		-0-		8,000		16,000		(4,000)
Disbursement of cash to partners	(20,000)						(8,000)		(16,000)		4,000
Balances................................	$ -0-		$ -0-		$ -0-		$ -0-		$ -0-		$ -0-

To deal with the $4,000 capital deficiency in Zhang's Capital account, two possibilities are:

1. Zhang could contribute assets to the partnership in an amount equal to her capital deficiency. If Zhang contributed cash, the journal entry to record this is

Cash	4,000	
Kim Zhang, Capital		4,000

2. Kim Zhang's partners, Jane Aviron and Elaine Bloch, could agree to absorb Zhang's capital deficiency by decreasing their own capital balances in proportion to their remaining profit-sharing percentages: Aviron, 60/80; Bloch, 20/80. The journal entry to record this is

Jane Aviron, Capital.......................................	3,000	
Elaine Bloch, Capital	1,000	
Kim Zhang, Capital		4,000

DECISION GUIDELINES — Accounting for Partnerships

Decision	Guidelines
How to organize the business?	A partnership offers both advantages and disadvantages in comparison with proprietorships and corporations. (See Exhibit 12–2, page 665.)
On what matters should the partners agree?	See the list on page 663, under the heading "The Written Partnership Agreement."
At what value does the partnership record assets and liabilities?	Current market value on the date of acquisition, because, in effect, the partnership is buying its assets at their current market value.

How are partnership profits and losses shared among the partners?	• Equally if there is no profit-and-loss sharing agreement.
	 • As provided in the partnership agreement. Can be based on the partners'
	   a. Stated fractions
	   b. Capital contributions
	   c. Service to the partnership
	   d. "Salaries" and interest on their capital contributions.

What happens when a partner withdraws from the partnership?	The old partnership ceases to exist. The remaining partners may or may not form a new partnership.
How are new partners admitted to the partnership?	• *Purchase a partner's interest*. The old partnership is dissolved. The remaining partners may admit the new partner to the partnership. If not, the new partner gets no voice in the management of the firm but shares in the profits and losses of the partnership. Close the withdrawing partner's Capital account, and open a Capital account for the new partner. Carry over the old partner's Capital balance to the Capital account of the new partner. • *Invest in the partnership*. Buying in at book value creates no bonus to any partner. Buying in at a price above book value creates a bonus to the old partners. Buying in at a price below book value creates a bonus for the new partner.

How to account for the withdrawal of a partner from the business?	• First, adjust and close the books up to the date of the partner's withdrawal from the business.
	• Second, appraise the assets and the liabilities to determine their current market value.
	• Third, account for the partner's withdrawal
	  a. At book value (no change in remaining partners' Capital balances)
	  b. At less than book value (increase the remaining partners' Capital balances)
	  c. At more than book value (decrease the remaining partners' Capital balances)

What happens if the partnership goes out of business?	Liquidate the partnership, as follows:
	  a. Adjust and close the partnership books up to the date of liquidation.
	  b. Sell the partnership's assets. Allocate gain or loss to the partners' Capital accounts based on their profit-and-loss ratio.
	  c. Pay the partnership liabilities.
	  d. Pay any remaining cash to the partners based on their Capital balances.

How do partnership financial statements differ from those of a proprietorship?	• The partnership income statement reports the allocation of net income or net loss to the partners. • The partnership balance sheet (or a separate schedule) reports the Capital balance of each partner. • The cash flow statement is the same for a partnership as for a proprietorship.

Summary Problem
for Your Review

The partnership of Taylor and Uvalde is considering admitting Steven Vaughn as a partner on January 2, 2002. The partnership general ledger includes the following balances on that date:

Cash	$ 18,000	Total liabilities....................	$100,000
Other assets.........................	220,000	Debby Taylor, capital	90,000
		Thomas Uvalde, capital....	48,000
		Total liabilities	
Total assets.........................	$238,000	and capital....................	$238,000

Debby Taylor's share of profits and losses is 60 percent and Thomas Uvalde's share is 40 percent.

Required

(Items 1 and 2 are independent.)

1. Suppose Vaughn pays Uvalde $62,000 to acquire Uvalde's interest in the business after Taylor approves Vaughn as a partner.
   a. Record the transfer of owner's equity on the partnership books.
   b. Prepare the partnership balance sheet immediately after Vaughn is admitted as a partner.

2. Suppose that Vaughn becomes a partner by investing $62,000 cash to acquire a one-fourth interest in the business.
   a. Compute Vaughn's capital balance and record his investment in the business.
   b. Prepare the partnership balance sheet immediately after Vaughn is admitted as a partner. Include the appropriate heading.

3. Which way of admitting Vaughn to the partnership increases its total assets? Give your reason.

Solution to Review Problem

Requirement 1

a. 2002

Jan. 2	Thomas Uvalde, Capital..............................	48,000	
	Steven Vaughn, Capital...........................		48,000
	To transfer Uvalde's equity in the partnership to Vaughn.		

b. The balance sheet for the partnership of Taylor and Vaughn is identical to the balance sheet given for Taylor and Thomas Uvalde in the problem, except Steven Vaughn's name replaces Thomas Uvalde's name in the title and in the listing of Capital accounts.

Requirement 2

a. Computation of Vaughn's capital balance:

Partnership capital before Vaughn is admitted ($90,000 + $48,000)	$138,000
Vaughn's investment in the partnership	62,000
Partnership capital after Vaughn is admitted	$200,000
Vaughn's capital in the partnership ($200,000 × ¼)	$ 50,000

2002			
Jan. 2	Cash	62,000	
	Steven Vaughn, Capital..........................		50,000
	Debby Taylor, Capital.............................		7,200
	Thomas Uvalde, Capital		4,800
	To admit Vaughn as a partner with a one-fourth interest in the business. Taylor's bonus is $7,200 [($62,000 − $50,000) × 0.60] and Uvalde's bonus is $4,800 [($62,000 − $50,000) × 0.40].		

b.

TAYLOR, UVALDE, AND VAUGHN
Balance Sheet
January 2, 2002

Cash*	$ 80,000	Total liabilities	$100,000
Other assets	220,000	Debby Taylor, capital**..........	97,200
		Thomas Uvalde, capital*** ...	52,800
		Steven Vaughn, capital..........	50,000
		Total liabilities	
Total assets........................	$300,000	and capital	$300,000

*$18,000 + $62,000 = $80,000
**$90,000 + $ 7,200 = $97,200
*** $48,000 + $ 4,800 = $52,800

Requirement 3

Vaughn's investment in the partnership increases its total assets by the amount of his contribution. Total assets of the business are $300,000 after his investment, compared to $238,000 before. By contrast, Vaughn's purchase of Uvalde's interest in the business is a personal transaction between the two individuals. It does not affect the assets of the partnership regardless of the amount Vaughn pays Uvalde.

Cyber Coach

Visit the Student Resources area of the *Accounting* Companion Website for extra practice with the new material in Chapter 12.
www.pearsoned.ca/horngren

Summary

1. **Identify the characteristics of a partnership.** A *partnership* is a business co-owned by two or more persons for profit. The characteristics of this form of business organization are its *ease of formation, limited life, mutual agency, unlimited liability,* and *no partnership income taxes.* In a *limited partnership,* the limited partners have limited personal liability for the obligations of the business.

   A written *partnership agreement* establishes procedures for admission of a new partner, withdrawals of a partner, and the sharing of profits and losses among the partners. When a new partner is admitted to the firm or an existing partner withdraws, the old partnership is *dissolved,* or ceases to exist. A new partnership may or may not emerge to continue the business.

2. **Account for partners' initial investments in a partnership.** Accounting for a partnership is similar to accounting for a proprietorship. However, a partnership has more than one owner. Each partner has an individual capital account and a withdrawal account.

3. **Allocate profits and losses to the partners by different methods.** Partners share net income or loss in any manner they choose. Common sharing agreements base the *profit-and-loss ratio* on a stated fraction, partners' capital contributions, and/or their service to the partnership. Some partnerships call the cash withdrawals of partners *salaries* and *interest,* but these amounts are not expenses of the business. Instead, they are merely ways to describe the allocation of partnership net income to the partners.

4. **Account for the admission of a new partner to the business.** An outside person may become a partner by purchasing a current partner's interest or by investing in the partnership. In some cases the new partner must pay the current partners a bonus to join. In other situations the new partner may receive a bonus to join.

5. **Account for the withdrawal of a partner from the business.** When a partner withdraws, partnership assets may be reappraised. Partners share any gain or loss on the asset revaluation on the basis of their profit-and-loss ratio. The withdrawing partner may receive payment equal to,

greater than, or less than her or his capital book value, depending on the agreement with the other partners.

6. **Account for the liquidation of a partnership.** In *liquidation*, a partnership goes out of business by selling the assets, paying the liabilities, and disbursing any remaining cash to the partners.

7. **Prepare partnership financial statements.** Partnership *financial statements* are similar to those of a proprietorship. However, the partnership income statement commonly reports the allocation of net income to the partners, and the balance sheet has a Capital account for each partner.

Self-Study Questions

Test your understanding of the chapter by marking the correct answer for each of the following questions:

1. Which of these characteristics does not apply to a partnership? (*p. 664*)
   a. Unlimited life
   b. Mutual agency
   c. Unlimited liability
   d. No income tax paid by the business entity

2. A partnership records a partner's investment of assets in the business at (*p. 666*)
   a. The partner's book value of the assets invested
   b. The market value of the assets invested
   c. A special value set by the partners
   d. Any of the above, depending upon the partnership agreement

3. The partnership of Lane, Murdock, and Nu divides profits in the ratio of 4:5:3. During 2003, the business earned $40,000. Nu's share of this income is (*p. 669*)
   a. $10,000
   b. $13,333
   c. $16,000
   d. $16,667

4. Suppose the partnership of Lane, Murdock, and Nu in the preceding question lost $40,000 during 2003. Murdock's share of this loss is (*p. 670*)
   a. Not determinable because the ratio applies only to profits
   b. $13,333
   c. $16,000
   d. $16,667

5. The partners of Placido, Quinn, and Rolfe share profits and losses 1/5, 1/6, and 19/30. During 2004, the first year of their partnership, the business earned $120,000, and each partner withdrew $50,000 for personal use. What is the balance in Rolfe's capital account after all closing entries? (*pp. 673–674*)
   a. Not determinable because Rolfe's beginning capital balance is not given
   b. Minus $10,000
   c. $26,000
   d. $70,000

6. Barbara Fuller buys into the partnership of Graff and Harrell by purchasing a one-third interest for $55,000. Prior to Fuller's entry, Edward Graff's capital balance was $46,000, and Louisa Harrell's balance was $52,000; profits and losses were shared equally. The entry to record Fuller's buying into the business is (*pp. 675–676*)

a. Cash	55,000	
Barbara Fuller, Capital		55,000
b. Edward Graff, Capital...................	27,500	
Louisa Harrell, Capital..................	27,500	
Barbara Fuller, Capital		55,000
c. Cash	55,000	
Barbara Fuller, Capital		51,000
Edward Graff, Capital..............		2,000
Louisa Harrell, Capital		2,000
d. Cash	51,000	
Edward Graff, Capital...................	2,000	
Louisa Harrell, Capital.................	2,000	
Barbara Fuller, Capital		55,000

7. The partners of Tsui, Valik, and Wollenberg share profits and losses equally. Their capital balances are $40,000, $50,000, and $60,000 respectively, when Brenda Wollenberg sells her interest in the partnership to Brent Valik for $90,000. Raymond Tsui and Valik continue the business. Immediately after Wollenberg's retirement, the total assets of the partnership are (*pp. 674–675*)
   a. Increased by $30,000
   b. Increased by $90,000
   c. Decreased by $60,000
   d. The same as before Wollenberg sold her interest to Valik

8. Prior to Bill Hogg's withdrawal from the partnership of Hogg, Ho, and Lee, the partners' capital balances were $140,000, $110,000 and $250,000 respectively. The partners share profits and losses 1/3, 1/4, and 5/12. The appraisal indicates that assets should be written down by $36,000. Arthur Ho's share of the write-down is (*p. 679*)
   a. $7,920
   b. $9,000
   c. $12,000
   d. $18,000

9. The process of closing the business, selling the assets, paying the liabilities, and disbursing remaining cash to the owners is called (*pp. 680–681*)
   a. Dissolution
   b. Forming a new partnership
   c. Withdrawal
   d. Liquidation

10. Eric Hirst and Brenda Mallouk have shared profits and losses equally. Immediately prior to the final cash disbursement in a liquidation of their partnership, the books show:

Cash		Liabilities		Eric Hirst, Capital		Brenda Mallouk, Capital
$100,000	=	$-0-	+	$60,000	+	$40,000

How much cash should Hirst receive? *(p. 681)*

a. $40,000   c. $60,000

b. $50,000   d. None of the above

Answers to the Self-Study Questions follow the Similar Accounting Terms.

Accounting Vocabulary

Dissolution *(p. 664)*
General partnership *(p. 665)*
Limited partnership *(p. 666)*
Limited liability partnership *(p. 666)*
Liquidation *(p. 680)*

Mutual agency *(p. 664)*
Partnership *(p. 662)*
Partnership agreement *(p. 663)*
Unlimited personal liability *(p. 664)*

Similar Accounting Terms

Limited Liability Partnership LLP
Liquidation Winding up the business
Owner's equity Capital
Withdrawals Drawings

Assignment Material

Questions

1. List eight items that the partnership agreement should specify.

2. Ron Montgomery, who is a partner in M&N Associates, commits the firm to a contract for a job within the scope of its regular business operations. What term describes Montgomery's ability to obligate the partnership?

3. If a partnership cannot pay a debt, who must make payment? What term describes this obligation of the partners?

4. How is income of a partnership taxed?

5. Identify the advantages and disadvantages of the partnership form of business organization.

6. Robin Randall and Sylvia Smith's partnership agreement states that Randall gets 60 percent of profits and Smith gets 40 percent. If the agreement does not discuss the treatment of losses, how are losses shared? How do the partners share profits and losses if the agreement specifies no profit-and-loss-sharing ratio?

7. What determines the amount of the credit to a partner's Capital account when the partner contributes assets other than cash to the business?

8. Do partner withdrawals of cash for personal use affect the sharing of profits and losses by the partner? If so, explain how. If not, explain why not.

9. Name two events that can cause the dissolution of a partnership.

10. Briefly describe how to account for the purchase of an existing partner's interest in the business.

11. Jeff Malcolm purchases Sheila Wilson's interest in the Wilson & Kareem partnership. What right does Malcolm obtain from the purchase? What is required for Malcolm to become Paula Kareem's partner?

12. Sal Assissi and Barb Carter each have capital of $75,000 in their business. They share profits in the

ratio of 55:45. Kathy Denman acquires a one-fifth share in the partnership by investing cash of $50,000. What are the capital balances of the three partners immediately after Denman is admitted?

13. When a partner resigns from the partnership and receives assets greater than her or his capital balance, how is the difference shared by the other partners?

14. Distinguish between dissolution and liquidation of a partnership.

15. Name the three steps in liquidating a partnership.

16. The partnership of Ralls and Sauls is in the process of liquidation. How do the partners share (a) gains and losses on the sale of noncash assets, and (b) the final cash disbursement?

17. Compare and contrast the financial statements of a proprietorship and a partnership.

18. Summarize the situations in which partnership allocations are based on (a) the profit-and-loss ratio, and (b) the partners' capital balances.

Exercises

Exercise 12-1   *Partnership characteristics   (Obj. 1)*

Sandy Saxe and Ida Weiss are forming a business to imprint T-shirts. Saxe suggests that they organize as a partnership in order to avoid the unlimited liability of a proprietorship. According to Saxe, partnerships are not very risky.

Saxe explains to Weiss that if the business does not succeed, each partner can withdraw from the business, taking the same assets that she or he invested at its beginning. Saxe states that the main disadvantage of the partnership form of organization is double taxation: First, the partnership pays a business income tax; second, each partner also pays personal income tax on her or his share of the business's profits.

Correct the errors in Saxe's explanation.

Exercise 12-2   *Organizing a business as a partnership   (Obj. 1)*

Rhonda Hough, a friend from college, approaches you about forming a partnership to export software. Since graduation, Rhonda has worked for the World Bank, developing important contacts among government officials and business leaders in Poland and Hungary. Eager to upgrade their data-processing capabilities, Eastern Europeans are looking for ways to obtain computers. Rhonda believes she is in a unique position to capitalize on this opportunity. With your expertise in finance, you would have responsibility for accounting and finance in the partnership.

Required

Discuss the advantages and disadvantages of organizing the export business as a partnership rather than a proprietorship. Comment on the way partnership income is taxed.

Exercise 12-3   *A partner's investment in a partnership   (Obj. 2)*

Val Dierks invests a building in a partnership with Lena Marx. Dierks purchased the building for $600,000. Accumulated amortization on the date of forming the partnership is $160,000. A real estate appraiser states that the building is now worth $800,000. Dierks wants $800,000 capital in the new partnership, but Marx objects. Marx believes that Dierk's capital contribution into the partnership should be measured by the book value of her building.

Marx and Dierks seek your advice. Which value of the building is appropriate for measuring Dierks's capital—book value or current market value? State the reason for your answer. Give the partnership's journal entry to record Dierks's investment in the business.

Exercise 12-4   *Investments by partners   (Obj. 2)*

Duane Warner and Eli Broad are forming the partnership Sunshine Development to develop a theme park near Victoria. Warner contributes cash of $1 million and land valued at $15 million. When Warner purchased the land, its cost was $4 million. The partnership will assume Warner's $1.5 million note payable on the land. Broad invests cash of $5 million and construction equipment that he purchased for $3.5 million (accumulated amortization to date, $1.5 million). The equipment's market value is equal to its book value.

Required

1. Before recording any journal entries, compute the partnership's total assets, total liabilities, and total owners' equity immediately after organizing.
2. Journalize the partnership's receipt of assets and liabilities from Warner and from Broad. Record each asset at its current market value with no entry to accumulated amortization.
3. Use your journal entries to prove the correctness of total owners' equity from requirement 1.

Exercise 12-5 *Recording a partner's investment* *(Obj. 2)*

Ann Richards has operated an apartment-locater service as a proprietorship. She and Tara Holmes have decided to reorganize the business as a partnership, effective April 1. Richards' investment in the partnership consists of cash, $20,000; accounts receivable, $11,000 less allowance for uncollectibles, $1,000; office furniture, $3,000 less accumulated amortization, $1,000; a small building, $55,000 less accumulated amortization, $27,500; accounts payable, $4,000; and a note payable to the bank, $10,000.

To determine Richards' equity in the partnership, she and Holmes hire an independent appraiser. This outside party provides the following market values of the assets and liabilities that Richards is contributing to the business: cash, accounts receivable, office furniture, accounts payable, and note payable—the same as Richards' book value; allowance for uncollectible accounts, $3,000; building, $71,000; and accrued expenses payable (including interest on the note payable), $1,000.

Required

Make the entry on the partnership books to record Richards' investment.

Exercise 12-6 *Computing partners' shares of net income and net loss* *(Obj. 3)*

Matt Baines and Dave Bristow form a partnership, investing $80,000 and $140,000 respectively. Determine their shares of net income or net loss for each of the following situations:

a. Net loss is $104,000, and the partners have no written partnership agreement.

b. Net income is $88,000 and the partnership agreement states that the partners share profits and losses based on their capital contributions.

c. Net loss is $154,000, and the partnership agreement states that the partners share profits based on their capital contributions.

d. Net income is $220,000. The first $120,000 is shared based on the partner capital contributions. The next $90,000 is based on partner service, with Baines receiving 30 percent and Bristow receiving 70 percent. The remainder is shared equally.

Exercise 12-7 *Computing partners' capital balances* *(Obj. 3)*

Matt Baines withdrew cash of $124,000 for personal use, and Dave Bristow withdrew cash of $100,000 during the year. Using the data from situation (d) in Exercise 12-6, journalize the entries to close to each capital account the (a) income summary account, and (b) the partners' withdrawal accounts. Explanations are not required. Indicate the amount of increase or decrease in each partner's capital balance. What was the overall effect on partnership capital?

Exercise 12-8 *Admitting a new partner* *(Obj. 4)*

Gemma Mendez is admitted to a partnership. Prior to the admission of Mendez, the partnership books show Susan Hecker's capital balance at $150,000 and Louis Vitale's capital balance at $75,000. Hecker and Vitale share profits and losses equally. Compute the amount of each partner's equity on the books of the new partnership under each of the following plans:

a. Mendez purchases Vitale's interest in the business, paying $90,000. The $90,000 payment is not invested in the partnership but instead goes directly to Vitale.

b. Mendez invests $75,000 to acquire a one-fourth interest in the partnership.

c. Mendez invests $135,000 to acquire a one-fourth interest in the partnership.

Exercise 12-9 *Recording the admission of a new partner* *(Obj. 4)*

Make the partnership journal entry to record the admission of Mendez under plans a, b, and c in Exercise 12-8. Explanations are not required.

Exercise 12-10 *Withdrawal of a partner from a business* *(Obj. 5)*

After closing the books, Artemis & Chan's partnership balance sheet reports owner's equity of $36,000 for Artemis and $48,000 for Chan. Artemis is withdrawing from the firm. He and Chan agree to write down partnership assets by $18,000. They have shared profits and losses in the ratio of one-third to Artemis and two-thirds to Chan. If the partnership agreement states that a partner withdrawing from the firm will receive assets equal to the book value of his owner's equity, how much will Artemis receive?

Chan will continue to operate the business as a proprietorship. What is Chan's beginning capital on the proprietorship books?

Exercise 12-11 *Withdrawal of a partner* *(Obj. 5)*

Lana Brown is retiring from the partnership of Brown, Green, and White on May 31. The partner capital balances are Brown, $72,000; Green, $102,000; and White, $44,000. The partners agree to have the partnership assets revalued to current market values. The independent appraiser reports that the book value of the inventory should be decreased by $16,000, and the book value of the land should be increased by $64,000. The partners agree to these revaluations. The profit-and-loss ratio has been 5:3:2 for Brown, Green, and White, respectively. In retiring from the firm, Brown received $50,000 cash and a $50,000 note from the partnership.

Required

Journalize (a) the asset revaluations, and (b) Brown's withdrawal from the firm.

Exercise 12-12 *Liquidation of a partnership* *(Obj. 6)*

Marsh, Ng, and Orsulak are liquidating their partnership. Before selling the noncash assets and paying the liabilities, the capital balances are Marsh, $25,000; Ng, $15,000; and Orsulak, $10,000. The partnership agreement divides profits and losses equally.

Required

1. After selling the noncash assets and paying the liabilities, suppose the partnership has cash of $50,000. How much cash will each partner receive in final liquidation?
2. After selling the noncash assets and paying the liabilities, suppose the partnership has cash of $44,000. How much cash will each partner receive in final liquidation?

Exercise 12-13 *Liquidation of a partnership* *(Obj. 6)*

Prior to liquidation, the accounting records of Pratt, Qualls, and Ramirez included the following balances and profit-and-loss-sharing percentages:

					Capital		
		Noncash			Pratt	Qualls	Ramirez
	Cash +	Assets =	Liabilities +		(40%) +	(30%) +	(30%)
Balances before							
sale of assets	$10,000	$57,000	$21,000		$20,000	$15,000	$11,000

The partnership sold the noncash assets for $73,000, paid the liabilities, and disbursed the remaining cash to the partners. Complete the summary of transactions in the liquidation of the partnership. Use the format illustrated in Exhibit 12-4.

Exercise 12-14 *Liquidation of a partnership* *(Obj. 6)*

The partnership of Lee, Massé, and Nix is dissolving. Business assets, liabilities, and partners' capital balances prior to dissolution follow. The partners share profits and losses as follows: Cory Lee, 25 percent; Sandra Massé, 55 percent; and Clyde Nix, 20 percent.

Required

Create a spreadsheet or solve manually—as directed by your instructor—to show the ending balances in all accounts after the noncash assets are sold for $272,000 and for $180,000. Determine the unknown amounts, represented by (?):

	A	B	C	D	E	F
1			Lee, Massé, and Nix			
2			Sale of Noncash Assets			
3			(For $272,000)			
4				Cory	Sandra	Clyde
5		Noncash		Lee,	Massé,	Nix,
6	Cash	Assets	Liabilities	Capital	Capital	Capital
7						
8	$ 12,000	$252,000	$154,000	$24,000	$74,000	$12,000
9	272,000	(252,000)		? †	?	?
10						
11	$284,000	$ 0	$154,000	$?	$?	$?
12						
13						† ($A9 − $B8)*.25
14			(For $180,000)			
15						
16				Cory	Sandra	Clyde
17		Noncash		Lee,	Massé,	Nix,
18	Cash	Assets	Liabilities	Capital	Capital	Capital
19						
20	$ 12,000	$252,000	$154,000	$24,000	$74,000	$12,000
21	180,000	(252,000)		? **	?	?
22						
23	$192,000	$ 0	$154,000	$?	$?	$?
24						
						** ($A21 − $B20)*.25

Identify two ways the partners can deal with the negative ending balance in Nix's capital account.

Challenge Exercise

Exercise 12-15   *Preparing a partnership balance sheet*   *(Obj. 7)*

On October 31, 2003, Jill Mathers and Don Smith agree to combine their proprietorships as a partnership. Their balance sheets on October 31 are as follows:

	Mathers' Business		Smith's Business	
Assets	**Book Value**	**Current Market Value**	**Book Value**	**Current Market Value**
Cash..	$ 6,000	$ 6,000	$ 5,000	$ 5,000
Accounts receivable (net).......	22,000	20,000	8,000	7,000
Inventory	51,000	46,000	34,000	36,000
Capital assets (net)	122,000	105,000	54,000	60,000
Total assets..............................	$201,000	$177,000	$101,000	$108,000

	Mathers' Business		Smith's Business	
Liabilities and Capital				
Accounts payable	$ 24,000	$ 24,000	$ 10,000	$ 10,000
Accrued expenses payable.....	2,000	2,000	2,000	2,000
Notes payable	55,000	55,000		
Jill Mathers, capital	120,000	96,000		
Don Smith, capital...................			89,000	96,000
Total liabilities and capital	$201,000	$177,000	$101,000	$108,000

Required

Prepare the partnership balance sheet at October 31, 2003.

Beyond the Numbers

Beyond the Numbers 12–1   *Partnership issues*   *(Obj. 1, 5)*

The following questions relate to issues faced by partnerships.

1. The text suggests that a written partnership agreement may be drawn up between the partners in a partnership. One benefit of an agreement is that it provides a mechanism for resolving disputes between the partners. What are five areas of dispute that might be resolved by a partnership agreement?

2. The statement has been made that "If you must take on a partner, make sure the partner is richer than you are." Why is this statement valid?

3. Desaulles, Howard & James is a partnership of lawyers. Howard is planning to move to Australia. What are the options open to her to convert her share of the partnership assets to cash?

Ethical Issue

Gail LaRue and Cindy Ng operate The Party Centre, a party supply store in Burnaby, British Columbia. The partners split profits and losses equally, and each takes an annual withdrawal of $80,000. To even out the workload, Ng does the buying and LaRue serves as the accountant. From time to time, they use small amounts of store merchandise for personal use. In preparing for a large private party, LaRue took engraved invitations, napkins, place mats, and other goods that cost $2,000. She recorded the transaction as follows:

Cost of Goods Sold...	$2,000	
Inventory		$2,000

Required

1. How should LaRue have recorded this transaction?
2. Discuss the ethical dimension of LaRue's action.

Problems (Group A)

Problem 12-1A   *Writing a partnership agreement*   *(Obj. 1)*

Maria Rotor and Marie Deslauriers are discussing the formation of a partnership to import fabric. Rotor is especially artistic, so she will travel to Central America to buy merchandise. Deslauriers is an excellent salesperson, and has already lined up several large stores to sell the fabric.

Required

Write a partnership agreement to cover all elements essential for the business to operate smoothly. Make up names, amounts, profit-and-loss-sharing percentages, and so on as needed.

Problem 12-2A   *Investments by partners*   *(Obj. 2, 7)*

Jay Woeller and Claudette LeBlanc formed a partnership on March 15, 2003. The partners agreed to invest equal amounts of capital. Woeller invested his proprietorship's assets and liabilities (credit balances in parentheses):

	Woeller's Book Value	Current Market Value
Accounts receivable	$ 12,000	$12,000
Allowance for doubtful accounts	(1,000)	(1,500)
Inventory	44,000	31,000
Prepaid expenses	2,500	2,500
Store equipment	37,000	27,000
Accumulated amortization	(10,000)	(-0-)
Accounts payable	(22,000)	(22,000)

On March 15, LeBlanc invested cash in an amount equal to the current market value of Woeller's partnership capital. The partners decided that Woeller would earn 70 percent of partnership profits because he would manage the business. LeBlanc agreed to accept 30 percent of profits. During the period ended December 31, 2003, the partnership earned $90,000. LeBlanc's withdrawals were $32,000 and Woeller's withdrawals were $36,000.

Required

1. Journalize the partners' initial investments.
2. Prepare the partnership balance sheet immediately after its formation on March 15, 2003.
3. Journalize the December 31, 2003, entries to close the Income Summary account and the partner withdrawals accounts.

Problem 12-3A   *Admitting a new partner*   *(Obj. 4)*

Green Lake Resort is a partnership, and its owners are considering admitting Greg Rivers as a new partner. On July 31, 2003, the capital accounts of the three existing partners and their shares of profits and losses are as follows:

	Capital	Profit-and-Loss Ratio
Ellen Urlang	$ 72,000	1/6
Amy Sharp	96,000	1/3
Robert Hayes	132,000	1/2

Required

Journalize the admission of Rivers as a partner on July 31, 2003, for each of the following independent situations.

1. Rivers pays Hayes $75,000 cash to purchase one-half of Hayes' interest.
2. Rivers invests $75,000 in the partnership, acquiring a one-fifth interest in the business.
3. Rivers invests $60,000 in the partnership, acquiring a one-eighth interest in the business.
4. Rivers invests $45,000 in the partnership, acquiring a 15% interest in the business.

Problem 12-4A *Computing partners' shares of net income and net loss* *(Obj. 3, 7)*

Robin Kantor, Kami Karlin, and Joe Schipper have formed a partnership. Kantor invested $40,000, Karlin $80,000, and Schipper $120,000. Kantor will manage the store, Karlin will work in the store three-quarters of the time, and Schipper will not work in the business.

Required

1. Compute the partners' shares of profits and losses under each of the following plans:
   a. Net income is $174,000, and the partnership agreement does not specify how profits and losses are shared.
   b. Net loss is $94,000, and the partnership agreement allocates 45 percent of profits to Kantor, 35 percent to Karlin, and 20 percent to Schipper. The agreement does not discuss the sharing of losses.
   c. Net income is $208,000. The first $100,000 is allocated based on "salaries" of $68,000 for Kantor and $32,000 for Karlin. The remainder is allocated based on partners' capital contributions.
   d. Net income for the year is $182,000. The first $60,000 is allocated on the basis of partners' capital contributions. The next $60,000 is based on service, with $40,000 going to Kantor and $20,000 going to Karlin. Any remainder is shared equally.

2. Revenues for the year were $1,144,000 and expenses were $962,000. Under plan (d), prepare the partnership income statement for the year. Assume a year end of September 30, 2003.

3. How will what you have learned in this problem help you manage a partnership?

Problem 12-5A *Recording changes in partnership capital* *(Obj. 4, 5)*

Outdoor Equipment is a partnership owned by three individuals. The partners share profits and losses in the ratio of 30 percent to Jane Mutchler, 40 percent to John Voorhees, and 30 percent to Ivana Weill. At December 31, 2002, the firm has the following balance sheet:

Cash.............................		$ 35,000	Total liabilities................	$118,000
Accounts receivable...	$ 20,000			
Less: Allowance				
for uncollectibles..	1,000	19,000		
Inventory		98,000	Jane Mutchler, capital....	45,000
Equipment..................	150,000		John Voorhees, capital...	59,000
Less: Accumulated			Ivana Weill, capital........	50,000
amortization..........	30,000	120,000	Total liabilities	
Total assets..................		$272,000	and capital	$272,000

Jane Mutchler withdraws from the partnership on this date.

Required

Record Mutchler's withdrawal from the partnership under the following plans:

1. Mutchler gives her interest in the business to Lynn Arturo, her cousin, with the consent of Voorhees and Weill.

2. In personal transactions, Mutchler sells her equity in the partnership to Michel André and Steven Craig, who each pay Mutchler $20,000 for one-half of her interest. Voorhees and Weill agree to accept André and Craig as partners.

3. The partnership pays Mutchler cash of $5,000, and gives her a note payable for the remainder of her book equity in settlement of her partnership interest.

4. Mutchler receives cash of $20,000 and a note for $30,000 from the partnership.

5. The partners agree that the equipment is worth $200,000, and that accumulated amortization should remain at $30,000. After the revaluation, the partnership settles with Mutchler by giving her cash of $10,000 and inventory for the remainder of her book equity.

Problem 12-6A   *Liquidation of a partnership   (Obj. 6)*

The partnership of Cheung, Kosse & Lufkin has experienced operating losses for three consecutive years. The partners, who have shared profits and losses in the ratio of Fran Cheung, 15 percent, Walt Kosse, 60 percent, and Emil Lufkin, 25 percent, are considering the liquidation of the business. They ask you to analyze the effects of liquidation under various assumptions about the sale of the noncash assets. They present the following condensed partnership balance sheet at December 31, 2002:

Cash....................................	$ 34,000	Liabilities............................	$126,000
Noncash assets..................	306,000	Fran Cheung, capital.......	48,000
		Walt Kosse, capital...........	132,000
		Emil Lufkin, capital.........	34,000
		Total liabilities	
Total assets.........................	$340,000	and capital	$340,000

Required

1. Prepare a summary of liquidation transactions (as illustrated in the chapter) for each of the following situations:
   a. The noncash assets are sold for $350,000.
   b. The noncash assets are sold for $282,000.

2. Make the journal entries to record the liquidation transactions in requirement 1(b).

Problem 12-7A   *Liquidation of a partnership   (Obj. 6)*

Link Back to Chapter 4 (Closing Entries). RMG & Company is a partnership owned by S. Ryan, G. Morales, and D. Goldberg, who share profits and losses in the ratio of 1:3:4. The adjusted trial balance of the partnership (in condensed form) at June 30, 2003, follows:

Required

1. Prepare the June 30, 2003, entries to close the revenue, expense, income summary, and withdrawals accounts.

2. Using T-accounts, insert the opening capital balances in the partners' capital accounts, post the closing entries to the capital accounts, and determine each partner's ending capital balance.

3. The partnership liquidates on June 30, 2003, by selling the noncash assets for $150,000. Using the ending balances of the partners' capital accounts, prepare a summary of liquidation transactions (as illustrated in Exhibit 12–4).

RMG & COMPANY
Adjusted Trial Balance
June 30, 2003

Cash...	$ 36,000	
Noncash assets	174,000	
Liabilities...		$150,000
S. Ryan, capital		33,000
G. Morales, capital.....................................		61,500
D. Goldberg, capital....................................		93,000
S. Ryan, withdrawals..................................	21,000	
G. Morales, withdrawals...........................	52,500	
D. Goldberg, withdrawals	81,000	
Revenues..		162,000
Expenses..	135,000	
Totals	$499,500	$499,500

Problem 12-8A *Accounting for partners' investments; allocating profits and losses; accounting for the admission of a new partner; accounting for the withdrawal of a partner; preparing a partnership balance sheet (Obj. 2, 3, 4, 5, 7)*

2002
June 10   Amie Dhal and Marie Sung have agreed to pool their assets and form a partnership to be called D&S Consulting. They agree to share all profits equally and make the following initial investments:

	Dhal	Sung
Cash	$10,000	$20,000
Accounts receivable (net).............................	22,000	18,000
Office furniture..	24,000	16,000

2003
May 31   The partnership's reported net income was $130,000 for the year ended May 31, 2003.

June 1   Dhal and Sung agree to accept Mark Mason into the partnership with a $120,000 investment for 30% of the business. The partnership agreement is amended to provide for the following sharing of profits and losses:

	Dhal	Sung	Mason
Annual "salary".........................	$60,000	$80,000	$50,000
Interest on investment	10%	10%	10%
Balance in ratio of.....................	3 :	2 :	5

2004
May 31   The partnership's reported net income was $320,000.

Oct. 10   Dhal withdrew $56,000 cash from the partnership and Sung withdrew $38,000 (Mason did not make any withdrawals).

2005
May 31   The partnership's reported net income was $170,000.

June 2   After a disagreement as to the directions in which the partnership should be moving, Mason decided to withdraw from the partnership. The three partners agreed that Mason could take cash of $200,000 in exchange for his equity in the partnership.

Required

1. Journalize all of the transactions for the partnership.
2. Prepare the partners' equity section of the balance sheet as of June 2, 2005.

Problem 12-9A
Accounting for partners' investments; allocating profits and losses; accounting for the admission of a new partner; accounting for the liquidation of a partnership **(Obj. 2, 3, 4, 5, 6)**

Judy Chapin, Herb Nobes, and Jean Yee started a partnership to operate a management consulting business. The partnership (CNY Partners) had the following transactions:

2002

Jan. 2 Chapin, Nobes and Yee formed the partnership by signing an agreement that stated that all profits will be shared in a 3:2:5 ratio and by making the following investments:

	Chapin	Nobes	Yee
Cash	$ 2,000	$ 3,500	$11,500
Accounts receivable (net)	7,000	10,500	15,000
Office furniture	0	5,500	0
Computer equipment	13,000	0	4,500

Dec. 31 The partnership reported net income of $21,000 for the year.

2003

June 7 Chapin and Yee agreed that Nobes could sell his share of the partnership to Andre Dawson for $31,000. The new partners agreed to keep the same profit sharing arrangement (3:2:5 for Chapin:Dawson:Yee).

Dec. 31 The partnership reported a net loss of $25,000 for the year.

2004

Jan. 3 The partners agreed to liquidate the partnership. On this date the balance sheet showed the following items:

Cash	$ 6,500
Accounts receivable	123,000
Allowance for uncollectible accounts	6,000
Office furniture	30,000
Computer equipment	75,000
Accumulated amortization (total)	23,000
Accounts payable	137,000

The assets were sold for the following amounts:

Accounts receivable	$60,000
Office furniture	32,500
Computer equipment	45,000

Chapin and Dawson both have personal assets, but Yee does not.

Required

Journalize all of the transactions for the partnership.

Problems (Group B)

Problem 12-1B
Writing a partnership agreement **(Obj. 1)**

Mary Basdeo and Sue Keim are discussing the formation of a partnership to install payroll accounting systems. Basdeo is skilled in systems design, and she is convinced that her designs will draw large sales volumes. Keim is an excellent salesperson, and she has already lined up several clients.

Required

Write a partnership agreement to cover all elements essential for the business to operate smoothly. Make up names, amounts, profit-and-loss sharing percentages, and so on, as needed.

Problem 12-2B *Investments by partners* *(Obj. 2, 7)*

On June 30, 2003, Sean Russell and Chris Mak formed a partnership. The partners agreed to invest equal amounts of capital. Mak invested his proprietorship's assets and liabilities (credit balances in parentheses).

On June 30, 2003, Russell invested cash in an amount equal to the current market value of Mak's partnership capital. The partners decided that Mak would earn two-thirds of partnership profits because he would manage the business. Russell agreed to accept one-third of profits. During the remainder of the year, the partnership earned $105,000. Mak's withdrawals were $40,000, and Russell's withdrawals were $30,000.

	Mak's Book Value	Current Market Value
Accounts receivable	$ 8,000	$ 8,000
Allowance for doubtful accounts	(-0-)	(1,000)
Inventory	22,000	24,000
Prepaid expenses	2,000	2,000
Office equipment	46,000	28,000
Accumulated amortization—office equipment	(16,000)	(-0-)
Accounts payable	(20,000)	(20,000)

Required

1. Journalize the partners' initial investments.

2. Prepare the partnership balance sheet immediately after its formation on June 30, 2003.

3. Journalize the December 31, 2003, entries to close the Income Summary account and the partner withdrawals accounts.

Problem 12-3B *Admitting a new partner* *(Obj. 4)*

Hazelwood Consulting Associates is a partnership, and its owners are considering admitting Helen Oldham as a new partner. On March 31, 2003, the capital accounts of the three existing partners and their shares of profits and losses are as follows:

	Capital	Profit-and-Loss Ratio
Jim Zook	$ 80,000	15%
Richard Land	200,000	30%
Jennifer Lim	320,000	55%

Required

Journalize the admission of Oldham as a partner on March 31, 2003, for each of the following independent situations:

1. Oldham pays Lim $290,000 cash to purchase Lim's interest in the partnership.
2. Oldham invests $120,000 in the partnership, acquiring a one-sixth interest in the business.
3. Oldham invests $120,000 in the partnership, acquiring a one-fifth interest in the business.
4. Oldham invests $80,000 in the partnership, acquiring a 10% interest in the business.

Problem 12-4B *Computing partners' shares of net income and net loss* *(Obj. 3, 7)*

Larry Aplevich, Elinor Davis, and Paul Diehl have formed a partnership. Aplevich invested $30,000, Davis $36,000, and Diehl $54,000. Aplevich will manage the store, Davis will work in the store half time, and Diehl will not work in the business.

Required

1. Compute the partners' shares of profits and losses under each of the following plans:

   a. Net loss is $85,800, and the partnership agreement does not specify how profits and losses are shared.

   b. Net loss is $120,000, and the partnership agreement allocates 40 percent of profits to Aplevich, 25 percent to Davis, and 35 percent to Diehl. The agreement does not discuss the sharing of losses.

   c. Net income is $184,000. The first $80,000 is allocated based on "salaries," with Aplevich receiving $56,000 and Davis receiving $24,000. The remainder is allocated based on partner capital contributions.

   d. Net income for the year is $360,000. The first $160,000 is allocated based on partner capital contributions. The next $72,000 is based on service, with Aplevich receiving $56,000 and Davis receiving $16,000. Any remainder is shared equally.

2. Revenues for the year were $1,740,000 and expenses were $1,380,000. Under plan (d), prepare the partnership income statement for the year. Assume a January 31, 2003 year end.

3. How will what you learned in this problem help you manage a partnership?

Problem 12-5B *Recording changes in partnership capital* *(Obj. 4, 5)*

Personal Finance Services is a partnership owned by three individuals. The partners share profits and losses in the ratio of 28 percent to Katherine Smythe, 38 percent to Max Dune, and 34 percent to Emily Hahn. At December 31, 2003, the firm has the following balance sheet:

Cash..............................		$ 18,000	Total liabilities.................	$ 97,500
Accounts receivable ...	$33,000			
Less: Allowance				
for uncollectibles..	6,000	27,000	Katherine Smythe, capital	139,500
Building	$465,000		Max Dune, capital	75,000
Less: Accumulated			Emily Hahn, capital	93,000
amortization	105,000	360,000	Total liabilities	
Total assets..................		$405,000	and capital..................	$405,000

Dune withdraws from the partnership on December 31, 2003, to establish his own consulting practice.

Required

Record Dune's withdrawal from the partnership under the following plans:

1. Dune gives his interest in the business to Tony Dutoit, his nephew, with the consent of Smythe and Hahn.

2. In personal transactions, Dune sells his equity in the partnership to Bea Patell and Al Bruckner, who each pay Dune $75,000 for one-half of his interest. Smythe and Hahn agree to accept Patell and Bruckner as partners.

3. The partnership pays Dune cash of $22,500, and gives him a note payable for the remainder of his book equity in settlement of his partnership interest.

4. Dune receives cash of $15,000 and a note for $105,000 from the partnership.

5. The partners agree that the building is worth only $420,000, and that its accumulated amortization should remain at $105,000. After the revaluation, the partnership settles with Dune by giving him cash of $21,150 and a note payable for the remainder of his book equity.

Problem 12-6B *Liquidation of a partnership* *(Obj. 6)*

The partnership of Amping, Blair, and Trippi has experienced operating losses for three consecutive years. The partners, who have shared profits and losses in the ratio of Denise Amping, 10 percent, Bert Blair, 30 percent, and Toni Trippi, 60 percent, are considering the liquidation of the business. They ask you to analyze the effects of liquidation under various possibilities about the sale of the noncash assets. They present the following condensed partnership balance sheet at December 31, 2002:

Cash............................	$ 54,000	Liabilities.......................................	$242,000
Noncash assets............	404,000	Denise Amping, capital..............	62,000
		Bert Blair, capital........................	78,000
		Toni Trippi, capital......................	76,000
Total assets...................	$458,000	Total liabilities and capital.........	$458,000

Required

1. Prepare a summary of liquidation transactions (as illustrated in the chapter) for each of the following situations:
   a. The noncash assets are sold for $424,000.
   b. The noncash assets are sold for $344,000.
2. Make the journal entries to record the liquidation transactions in requirement 1(b).

Problem 12-7B *Liquidation of a partnership* *(Obj. 6)*

Link Back to Chapter 4 (Closing Entries). BP&O is a partnership owned by B. Bell, S. Pastena, and C. O'Donnell, who share profits and losses in the ratio of 5:3:2. The adjusted trial balance of the partnership (in condensed form) at September 30, 2003, follows:

BP&O
Adjusted Trial Balance
September 30, 2003

Cash	$ 50,000	
Noncash assets	177,000	
Liabilities..		$145,000
B. Bell, capital		57,000
S. Pastena, capital....................................		44,000
C. O'Donnell, capital		21,000
B. Bell, withdrawals.................................	45,000	
S. Pastena, withdrawals	37,000	
C. O'Donnell, withdrawals......................	18,000	
Revenues..		422,000
Expenses..	362,000	
Totals	$689,000	$689,000

Required

1. Prepare the September 30, 2003, entries to close the revenue, expense, income summary, and withdrawals accounts.
2. Using T-accounts, insert the opening capital balances in the partner capital accounts, post the closing entries to the capital accounts, and determine each partner's ending capital balance.
3. The partnership liquidates on September 30, 2003, by selling the noncash assets for $132,000. Using the ending balances of the partners' capital accounts, prepare a summary of liquidation transactions (as illustrated in Exhibit 12–4).

Problem 12-8B *Accounting for partners' investments; allocating profits and losses; accounting for the admission of a new partner; accounting for the withdrawal of a partner; preparing partnership balance sheet* **(Obj. 2, 3, 4, 5, 7)**

2002

June   10   Steven Dikolli and Sharon McCracken have agreed to pool their assets and form a partnership to be called D&M Logistics. They agree to share all profits equally and make the following initial investments:

	Dikolli	McCracken
Cash	$14,000	$24,000
Accounts receivable (net)..............................	28,000	14,000
Office furniture (net)	32,000	18,000

2003

May   31   The partnership's reported net income was $152,000 for the year ended May 31, 2003.

June   1   Dikolli and McCracken agree to accept Myra Pinos into the partnership with a $140,000 investment for 40% of the business. The partnership agreement is amended to provide for the following sharing of profits and losses:

	Dikolli	McCracken	Pinos
Annual "salary"	$80,000	$60,000	$40,000
Interest on investment	10%	10%	10%
Balance in ratio of	2 :	3 :	5

2004

May   31   The partnership's reported net income is $380,000.

Oct.   10   Dikolli withdrew $60,000 cash from the partnership and McCracken withdrew $40,000 (Pinos did not make any withdrawals).

2005

May   31   The partnership's reported net income is $150,000.

June   2   After a disagreement as to the directions in which the partnership should be moving, Pinos decided to withdraw from the partnership. The three partners agreed that Pinos could take cash of $340,000 in exchange for her equity in the partnership.

Required

1. Journalize all of the transactions for the partnership.
2. Prepare the partners' equity section of the balance sheet as of June 2, 2005.

Problem 12-9B *Accounting for partners' investments; allocating profits and losses; accounting for the admission of a new partner; accounting for the liquidation of a partnership* **(Obj. 2, 3, 4, 5, 6)**

William Press, Julie Harris, and Regina Visser started a partnership to operate a catering business. The partnership (PH&V Catering) had the following transactions:

2002

Jan.   2   Press, Harris, and Visser formed the partnership by signing an agreement that stated that all profits will be shared in a 2:3:5 ratio and by making the following investments:

	Press	Harris	Visser
Cash...	$18,000	$12,000	$22,000
Accounts receivable (net)	30,000	22,000	90,000
Office furniture (net)	0	0	22,000
Catering equipment (net).................	32,000	58,000	0

Dec.   31   The partnership reported net income of $80,000 for the year.

2003

June 7 Press and Visser agreed that Harris could sell her share of the partnership to Ray Ewing for $124,000. The new partners agreed to keep the same profit-sharing arrangement (2:3:5 for Press:Ewing:Visser).

Dec. 31 The partnership reported a net loss of $100,000 for the year.

2004

Jan. 3 The partners agreed to liquidate the partnership. On this date the balance sheet showed the following items:

Cash...	$ 26,000
Accounts receivable...	474,000
Allowance for uncollectible accounts	34,000
Office furniture...	112,000
Catering equipment...	360,000
Accumulated amortization (total)	74,000
Accounts payable...	578,000

The assets were sold for the following amounts:

Accounts receivable...	$286,000
Office furniture...	124,000
Catering equipment...	160,000

Press and Ewing both have personal assets, but Visser does not.

Required

Journalize all of the transactions for the partnership.

Challenge Problems

Problem 12-1C *Deciding on a capital structure* *(Obj. 1, 2)*

Rebecca Bernstein and Peter Tong have been in a partnership for five years. The principal business of the partnership is systems design for financial institutions. Gross revenues have increased from $82,000 in 1998 to $935,000 in 2003, the year just ended. The number of employees has increased from two in the first year to nine in the most recent year. Bernstein and Tong realized that they had to build up the partnership's capital and have withdrawn only part of the annual profits. As a result, their capital accounts have increased from $50,000 (Bernstein, $35,000; Tong, $15,000) in 1998 to $520,000 (Bernstein, $280,000; Tong, $240,000) in 2003.

The two partners realize that they must expand their capital base to expand their operations in order to meet the increasing demand for their systems designs. At the same time they wish to take personal advantage of the partnership's earnings. They have been trying to determine whether they should continue the partnership and borrow the necessary funds, take on one or more partners (several of their employees have expressed interest and have capital to invest), or incorporate and sell a portion of the business to outsiders. With respect to incorporation, Martin Askew, a former classmate of Bernstein's who works for a stockbroker, has indicated he knows of investors who would be interested in buying a share of the business.

Required

Bernstein and Tong have come to you to ask for advice. In response to your questions, they indicate they will need additional capital of $400,000 to $500,000.

Problem 12-2C *The effects of accounting decisions on profits* *(Obj. 3)*

Mary Antoine, Susan Chiu, and Alan May have been partners in a systems design business for the past eight years. Antoine and May work full-time in the business; Chiu has a public accounting practice and works about five to ten hours per week on the administrative side of the business. The business has been successful and the partners are considering expansion.

The partnership agreement states that profits will be distributed as follows:

1. Partners will get 6 percent on their average capital balances.

2. Antoine will get a "salary" of $50,000; Chiu will get a "salary" of $6,250; May will get a "salary" of $50,000.

3. The balance remaining will be distributed on the basis of Antoine, 40 percent; Chiu, 20 percent; and May, 40 percent.

The agreement also stipulates that the distributions outlined in parts 1 and 2 of the agreement will be made even if there are not sufficient profits and that any deficiency will be shared on the basis of part 3.

The capital structure was as follows at December 31, 2003:

Antoine	$ 112,500
Chiu	687,500
May	287,500
Total	$1,087,500

There has been some stress in the partnership of late because Antoine believes that she is contributing a major part of the effort but is earning much less than May; Chiu is upset because she believes that she is earning the least even though her capital is essentially funding the partnership.

Required

Mary Antoine, Susan Chiu, and Alan May have come to you to ask for advice as to how they might amicably settle the present dispute. Assume net income in 2003 was $262,500.

Extending Your Knowledge

Decision Problem

Settling disagreements among partners   (Obj. 3)

Barbara Jevons invested $40,000 and Tara Schlee invested $20,000 in a public relations firm that has operated for 10 years. Neither partner has made an additional investment. They have shared profits and losses in the ratio of 2:1, which is the ratio of their investments in the business. Jevons manages the office, supervises the 16 employees, and does the accounting. Schlee, the moderator of a television talk show, is responsible for marketing. Her high profile generates important revenue for the business. During the year ended December 2003, the partnership earned net income of $100,000, shared in the 2:1 ratio. On December 31, 2003, Jevons's capital balance was $210,000 and Schlee's capital balance was $140,000.

Required

Respond to each of the following situations:

1. What explains the difference between the ratio of partner capital balances at December 31, 2003, and the 2:1 ratio of partner investments and profit sharing?

2. Schlee believes the profit-and-loss-sharing ratio is unfair. She proposes a change, but Jevons insists on keeping the 2:1 ratio. What two factors may underlie Schlee's unhappiness?

3. During January 2004, Jevons learned that revenues of $15,000 were omitted from the reported 2003 income. She brings this to Schlee's attention, pointing out that her share of this added income is two-thirds, or $10,000 and Schlee's share is one-third, or $5,000. Schlee believes they should share this added income based on their capital balances: 60 percent (or $9,000) to Jevons, and 40 percent (or $6,000) to Schlee. Which partner is correct? Why?

4. Assume that an account payable of $12,000 for an operating expense in 2003 was omitted from 2003 reported income. On what basis would the partners share this amount?

Financial Statement Problem

Fortin, Lin & Royce (FLR) is a regional accounting firm with four offices. Summary data from the partnership's annual report follow:

(Dollars in thousands, except where indicated)	Years Ended June 30				
	2001	2000	1999	1998	1997
Revenues					
Assurance services	$1,234	$1,122	$1,064	$1,093	$1,070
Consulting services	1,007	775	658	473	349
Tax services	743	628	567	515	557
Total Revenues	$2,984	$2,525	$2,289	$2,081	$1,976
Operating Summary					
Revenues	$2,984	$2,525	$2,289	$2,081	$1,976
Personnel Costs	1,215	1,004	887	805	726
Other Costs	712	630	517	458	415
Income to Partners	$1,057	$ 891	$ 885	$ 818	$ 835
Statistical Data					
Average Number of Partners	9	9	9	8	8

Required

1. What percentages of total revenues did FLR earn by performing assurance services (similar to audit), consulting services, and tax services during 1997? What were the percentages in 2001? Which type of service grew the most from 1997 to 2001?

2. Compute the average revenue per partner in 2001. Assume each partner works 2,000 hours per year. On average, how much does each partner charge a client for one hour of time?

3. How much net income did each FLR partner earn, on average, in 2001?

13

Corporations: Capital Stock and the Balance Sheet

CHAPTER OBJECTIVES

After studying this chapter, you should be able to

1 Identify the characteristics of a corporation

2 Record the issuance of stock

3 Account for the incorporation of a going business

4 Prepare the shareholders' equity section of a corporation's balance sheet

5 Account for cash dividends

6 Use different stock values in decision making

7 Evaluate a company's return on assets and return on shareholders' equity

8 Account for a corporation's income tax

"MGI Software Corp. will not be making its debut on the U.S. Nasdaq exchange anytime soon," the company announced yesterday.

Toronto-based MGI Software Corp. has postponed the initial public offering of its shares of stock and its Nasdaq listing until market conditions improve.

"We strongly believe our stock is undervalued and this postponement will allow us to focus on our business," said Anthony DeChristofaro, chief executive officer.

"We considered our options and, given our strong cash position, did not feel the need to issue equity at the current share price," said Rodney Davis, chief financial officer.

Mr. DeChristofaro said the company will continue to monitor the markets, even though, these days, he said it is impossible to know when conditions will improve.*

Going public, through an initial public offering of stock, is often a good way for a company to raise the cash it needs. When a company is doing well, going public allows the company to raise money cheaply and easily. However, as the newspaper article above indicates, market conditions may affect a company's ability to raise funds through stock issues.

Typically, companies need cash to expand their operations and increase their profitability. While there are different sources available for raising cash, selling shares of stock is a common route for young, start-up companies. However, there are some hazards. If the value that the market is willing to pay for a share of stock is low, the company will need to issue more shares to raise the cash it requires. This can make it difficult to maintain control of the company.

Fortunately for MGI Software Corp., it has enough cash so that it can wait before issuing shares of stock. The hope is that the company's performance and the market conditions will improve so that the price that shareholders are willing to pay for the stock will increase.

*Source: David Steinhart, *The National Post*, November 15, 2000, p. C4.

KEY POINT

Corporations are owned by investors who usually are not involved in the daily operation. A corporation's financial statements should provide the information for investors and managers to make sound decisions.

MGI Software Corp.
www.mgisoft.com

Nortel Networks Corporation
www.nortelnetworks.com

Air Canada Corp.
www.aircanada.ca

BCE Inc.
www.bce.ca

OBJECTIVE 1
Identify the characteristics of a corporation

WHAT does it mean to "go public"? A corporation *goes public* when it issues its stock to the general public. However, the owners of the corporation—*shareholders*—can keep the stock *closely held*, that is, owned by a few shareholders. A common reason for going public is to raise money for expansion or to pay off debt. By offering its stock to the public, a company can hope to raise more money than if the shareholders are a limited group. MGI Software Corp. was probably planning to go public for that reason.

Corporations: An Overview

The corporation is the dominant form of business organization in Canada. MGI Software Corp. is an example. Although proprietorships and partnerships are more numerous, corporations transact more business and are larger in terms of total assets, sales revenue, and number of employees. Most well-known businesses, such as Nortel Networks Corporation, Air Canada Corp. and BCE Inc. are corporations. Their full names include *Limited, Incorporated*, or *Corporation* (abbreviated *Ltd., Inc.* or *Corp.*) to indicate they are corporations.

Characteristics of a Corporation

What makes the corporate form of organization so attractive? We now look at the features that distinguish corporations from proprietorships and partnerships, and some of the advantages and disadvantages of corporations.

Separate Legal Entity A corporation is a business entity formed under federal or provincial law. The federal or provincial government grants **articles of incorporation**, which consist of a document that gives the governing body's permission to form a corporation. Neither a proprietorship nor a partnership require federal or provincial approval to do business, because in the eyes of the law the business and the owner(s) are not separate entities.

From a legal perspective, a corporation is a distinct entity, an artificial person that exists apart from its owners, who are called **shareholders**. The corporation has many of the rights that a person has. For example, a corporation may buy, own, and sell property. Assets and liabilities in the business belong to the corporation rather than to the corporation's owners. The corporation may enter into contracts, sue, and be sued.

Continuous Life and Transferability of Ownership The owners' equity of a corporation is divided into shares of **stock**. The articles of incorporation specify how much stock the corporation can issue (sell) and lists the other details of its relationships with the federal or provincial government under whose laws it is incorporated. Most corporations have *continuous lives* regardless of changes in the ownership of their stock. The shareholders of Nortel or Air Canada or any corporation may sell or trade the stock to another person, give it away, bequeath it in a will, or dispose of it in any other way they desire. The transfer of the stock does not affect the continuity of the corporation. In contrast, proprietorships and partnerships terminate when their ownership changes.

No Mutual Agency *Mutual agency* means that all owners act as agents of the business. A contract signed by one owner is binding for the whole company. Mutual agency operates in partnerships but *not* in corporations. A shareholder of Loblaw Companies Limited cannot commit the corporation to a contract (unless he or she is also an officer in the business). For this reason, a shareholder does not need to exercise the care that partners must in selecting co-owners of the business.

Limited Liability of Shareholders Shareholders have **limited liability** for corporation debts. That means they have no personal obligation for corporation liabilities. The most that a shareholder can lose on an investment in a corporation's stock is the cost of the investment. In contrast, proprietors and partners are personally liable for all the debts of their businesses.

The combination of limited liability and no mutual agency means that persons can invest in a corporation without fear of losing all their personal wealth if the business fails. This feature enables a corporation to raise more money from a wider group of investors than proprietorships and partnerships can.

Separation of Ownership and Management Shareholders own the business, but a *board of directors*—elected by the shareholders—appoints corporate officers to manage the business. Thus shareholders may invest $100 or $1 million in the corporation without having to manage the business or disrupt their personal affairs.

Management's goal is to maximize the value of the firm for the benefit of the shareholders. However, the separation between owners—shareholders—and management can create problems. Corporate officers may decide to run the business for their own benefit and not for the shareholders. The distance between shareholders and management may make it difficult for shareholders to protest bad management. How else can shareholders protest? They can sell their shares of stock in that corporation.

Corporate Taxation Corporations are separate taxable entities. They pay a variety of taxes not borne by proprietorships or partnerships, such as federal and provincial income taxes. Corporate earnings are subject to **double taxation**. First, corporations pay their own income taxes on corporate income. Then, the shareholders pay personal income tax on the dividends (distributions) that they receive from corporations, although the tax rate is usually lower than for regular income to minimize double taxation. Proprietorships and partnerships pay no business income tax.

REAL WORLD EXAMPLE

Because of limited shareholder liability, many banks will lend money to a small corporation only if a third party (usually a corporate officer) guarantees payment of the loan personally in the event of default by the corporation.

THINKING IT OVER

Compare and contrast the characteristics of proprietorships and corporations.

A:
Proprietorship
1. Legally, the owner and the business are one entity
2. Limited to life of proprietor
3. Unlimited liability of the owner
4. Management by owner
5. Business income is included in calculating owner's taxable income

Corporation
1. Separate legal entity
2. Continuous life
3. Limited liability of shareholders
4. Often separation of ownership and management
5. Pays corporate income tax

····················
***** (THINKING IT OVER)

How does taxation of a
corporation differ from that of a
proprietorship?

A: (1) A corporation pays tax on its
income and is subject to some
different rules of taxation.
(2) Dividends distributed to the
shareholders are taxable to the
shareholders when received.
(3) Proprietorships are not tax-
paying entities: instead, the owner
pays tax on the business's income
regardless of how much is
withdrawn for personal use.

(KEY POINT)

Most corporations are authorized
to issue many more shares of
stock than they intend to issue
originally. The corporation can
raise additional capital by selling
stock in the future without having
to request government
authorization of more shares.

Instead, the tax falls solely on the owners who are taxed on their share of the proprietorship or partnership income.

Government Regulation   Because shareholders have only limited liability for corporation debts, outsiders doing business with the corporation can look no further than the corporation itself for any claims that may arise against the business. To protect persons who lend money to a corporation or who invest in its stock, the federal and provincial governments monitor the affairs of corporations. This government regulation consists mainly of ensuring that corporations disclose adequate business information for investors and creditors. For many corporations, government regulation is expensive.

Exhibit 13-1 summarizes the advantages and disadvantages of the corporation form of business organization.

Organization of a Corporation

The process of creating a corporation begins when its organizers, called the *incorporators*, submit articles of incorporation to the federal or provincial government for approval. The articles of incorporation include the **authorization** for the corporation to issue a certain number of shares of stock, which are shares of ownership in the corporation. The incorporators pay fees and file the required documents with the incorporating jurisdiction. Then the corporation comes into existence and becomes a legal entity. The incorporators agree to a set of **bylaws**, which act as the constitution for governing the corporation.

The ultimate control of the corporation rests with the shareholders, who usually receive one vote for each share of voting stock they own. The shareholders elect the members of the **board of directors**, which sets policy for the corporation and appoints the officers. The board elects a **chairperson**, who is the most powerful person in the corporation. The board also designates the **president**, who is the chief operating officer in charge of managing day-to-day operations. Most corporations also have vice-presidents in charge of sales, manufacturing, accounting and finance, and other key areas. Often the president and one or more vice-presidents are also elected to the board of directors. Exhibit 13-2 shows the authority structure in a corporation.

The structure of proprietorships, partnerships, and corporations is similar in that all three types of business have owners, managers, and employees. In proprietorships and partnerships, policy decisions are usually made by the owners—the proprietor or the partners. In a corporation, however, the managers who set policy are appointed by the board of directors, and may or may not be owners (shareholders).

All corporations have an annual meeting at which the shareholders elect directors and make other shareholder decisions such as appointing the external auditors. Shareholders unable to attend this annual meeting may vote on corporation matters by use of a *proxy*, which is a legal document that expresses the shareholder's preference and appoints another person to cast the vote.

A corporation keeps a record of its shareholders. The business must notify the shareholders of the annual shareholder meeting, send them financial statements,

EXHIBIT 13-1

**Advantages and
Disadvantages of a
Corporation**

Corporation Advantages	Corporation Disadvantages
1. Can raise more capital than a proprietorship or partnership	1. Separation of ownership and management
2. Continuous life	2. Corporate earnings subject to double taxation
3. Ease of transferring ownership	3. Government regulation
4. No mutual agency of shareholders	
5. Limited liability of shareholders	

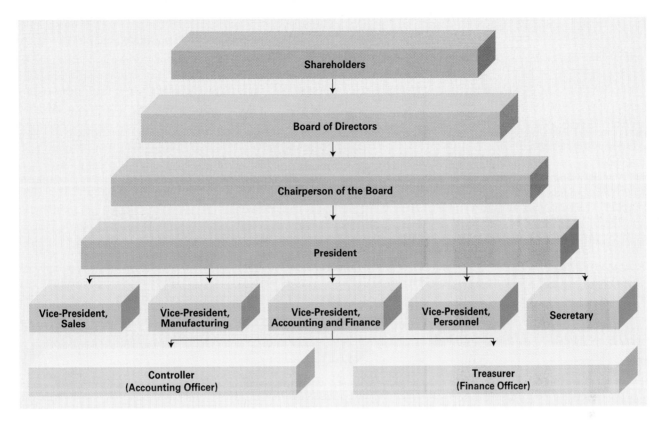

EXHIBIT 13-2

Authority Structure in a
Corporation

usually in the form of an annual report, and mail them dividend distributions (which we discuss later in this chapter). Large companies use a registrar to maintain the shareholder list and a transfer agent to issue stock certificates. Banks or trust companies provide these registration and transfer services. The transfer agent handles the change in stock ownership from one shareholder to another.

Capital Stock

A corporation issues *stock certificates* to its owners when they invest in the business. Because stock represents the corporation's capital, it is often called *capital stock*. The basic unit of capital stock is called a *share*. A corporation may issue a share certificate for any number of shares it wishes—one share, 100 shares, or any other number. Exhibit 13-3 depicts an actual share certificate for 200 shares of Intrawest Corporation stock. The certificate shows the company name, shareholder name, type of shares, and number of shares.

Stock that is held by a shareholder is said to be **outstanding**. The total number of shares of stock outstanding at any time represents 100 percent ownership of the corporation.

Shareholders' Equity: The Basics

The balance sheet of a corporation reports assets and liabilities in the same way as a proprietorship or a partnership. However, owners' equity of a corporation—called **shareholders' equity**—is reported differently. Incorporating acts require corporations to report the sources of their capital. The two most basic sources of capital are:

- **Contributed capital,** which represents investments in capital stock by shareholders in the corporation.

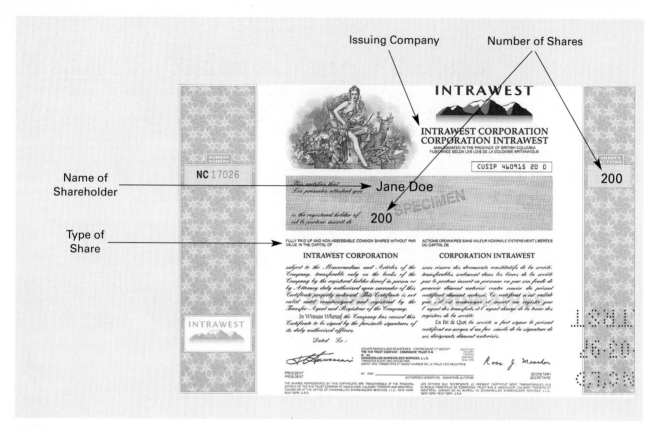

Issuing Company   Number of Shares

INTRAWEST

INTRAWEST CORPORATION
CORPORATION INTRAWEST
AMALGAMATED IN THE PROVINCE OF BRITISH COLUMBIA
FUSIONNÉE SELON LES LOIS DE LA COLOMBIE-BRITANNIQUE

CUSIP 460915 20 0

SHARES
ACTIONS
200

NUMBER
NUMÉRO
NC 17026

Name of
Shareholder

This certifies that
Les présentes attestent que   Jane Doe

is the registered holder of
est le porteur inscrit de   200

Type of
Share

FULLY PAID UP AND NON-ASSESSABLE COMMON SHARES WITHOUT PAR
VALUE IN THE CAPITAL OF

ACTIONS ORDINAIRES SANS VALEUR NOMINALE ENTIÈREMENT LIBÉRÉES
DU CAPITAL DE

INTRAWEST CORPORATION   CORPORATION INTRAWEST

EXHIBIT 13-3

Share Certificate

- **Retained earnings,** which is the capital the corporation has earned through profitable operations that has not been distributed to shareholders.

While the *Canada Business Corporations Act* and several of the provincial incorporating acts use the term *stated capital* to describe capital stock, this text will use the more common term, capital stock. Exhibit 13-4 outlines a summarized version of the balance sheet of The Forzani Group Ltd. to show how to report these categories of shareholders' equity.

The Forzani Group Ltd.
www.forzanigroup.com

Contributed Capital Is Received from the Shareholders

Common Stock is one type of capital stock. It is regarded as the permanent capital of the business because it is *not* subject to withdrawal by the shareholders. An investment of cash or any other asset in a corporation increases its assets and shareholders' equity. The Forzani Group Ltd.'s (FGL) entry to record the receipt of $2,000,000 cash and the issuance of its common stock to the shareholder is

Oct.	20	Cash..	2,000,000	
		Common Stock		2,000,000
		Issued stock to shareholder.		

EXHIBIT 13-4

Summarized Balance Sheet at January 30, 2000, of The Forzani Group Ltd. (Amounts in thousands)

Assets....................................	$208,316	Liabilities.............................	$125,627	
		Shareholders' equity		
		Contributed capital	82,681	
		Retained earnings.........	8	
		Total shareholders' equity	82,689	
		Total liabilities and		
Total assets..........................	$208,316	shareholders' equity......	$208,316	

Retained Earnings Are Earned from the Customers

Profitable operations produce income for the corporation and income increases shareholders' equity through a separate account called Retained Earnings. At year end, the net income (or net loss) balance of the Income Summary account is closed to Retained Earnings. For example, if FGL's net income is $14.3 million, Income Summary will have a $14.3 million credit balance. FGL's closing entry will debit Income Summary to transfer net income to Retained Earnings as follows:

2000				
Jan. 30	Income Summary...	14,300,000		
	Retained Earnings		14,300,000	
	To close Income Summary by transferring			
	net income to Retained Earnings.			

If operations of a corporation produce a net loss rather than net income, the Income Summary account will have a debit balance. Income Summary must be credited to close it. With a $100,000 loss, the closing entry is

June 30	Retained Earnings...	100,000		
	Income Summary...		100,000	
	To close Income Summary by transferring			
	net loss to Retained Earnings.			

Negative Retained Earnings is Called a Deficit   A large loss or an accumulation of several years of losses may cause a debit balance in the Retained Earnings account. This condition—called a Retained Earnings **deficit** or accumulated deficit—is reported on the balance sheet as a negative amount in shareholders' equity. Black Hawk Mining Inc. reported the following in a recent year:

Shareholders' Equity (in thousands)	
Contributed capital	$43,315
Deficit...	(9,474)
Total shareholders' equity..............................	$33,841

Corporations May Pay Dividends to Shareholders

If the corporation has been profitable and has sufficient cash, it may distribute cash to the shareholders. Such distributions—called **dividends**—decrease both the assets and the retained earnings of the business. Dividends are similar to a withdrawal of cash made by the owner of a proprietorship or by a partner of a partnership.

Some people think of Retained Earnings as a fund of cash. It is not, because Retained Earnings is an element of shareholders' equity; it is the balance of all of the company's income-earning activities. Remember that dividends are *paid out of assets*, not out of retained earnings. (Stock dividends are discussed in Chapter 14.)

Shareholders' Rights

The owner of a share of stock has certain rights that are set out in the corporation's articles of incorporation; these vary from company to company, and even between classes of stock within a company. In addition, the shareholder may have other rights granted by the legislation under which the corporation receives its articles. While those rights outlined in the articles of incorporation are specific to an individual company, those set forth by legislation are shared by shareholders of all companies incorporated under that legislation. The articles of incorporation, for example, may

specify that the shareholder of one class of common share is entitled to one vote per share at shareholders' meetings, while the shareholder of another class of common share is not entitled to vote. An example of a shared right is that, under the *Canada Business Corporations Act*, shareholders may require the directors of the company to call a meeting of the shareholders.

Some of the rights normally attached to common shares[1] are:

1. The right to sell the shares.
2. The right to vote at shareholders' meetings.
3. The right to a proportionate share of any dividends declared by the directors for that class of shares.
4. The right to receive a proportionate share of any assets, on the winding-up of the company, after the creditors and any classes of shares that rank above that class have been paid.
5. A preemptive right, the right to maintain one's proportionate ownership in the corporation. If a shareholder owns 5 percent of the outstanding common stock and the corporation decides to issue 100,000 new shares, the shareholder would be entitled to purchase 5,000 of the new shares. (This right, however, might not be given.)

Classes of Stock

Corporations issue different types of stock. The stock of a corporation may be either common or preferred.

Common and Preferred Shares

Every corporation issues shares of *common stock*, the most basic form of capital stock. Unless designated otherwise, the word *stock* or *shares* is understood to mean "common stock" or "common shares." Companies may issue different classes of common shares. For example, Rogers Communications Inc. has issued Class A common shares, which carry the right to vote, and Class B common shares, which are nonvoting. (Classes of common shares may also be designated Series A, Series B, and so on, with each series having certain unique features, such as a fixed, stated dividend or a redemption feature.) There is a separate general-ledger account for each class of common shares. In describing a corporation, we would say the common shareholders are the owners of the business.

Investors who buy shares of common stock take the ultimate risk with a corporation. The corporation makes no promises to pay them. If the corporation succeeds, it may distribute dividends to its shareholders, but if retained earnings and cash are too low, the shareholders may receive no dividends. The stock of successful corporations increases in value, and investors enjoy the benefit of selling the stock at a gain. But share prices can decrease, possibly leaving the investors holding worthless share certificates. Because common shareholders take a risky investment position, they demand increases in share prices, high dividends, or both. If the corporation does not accomplish these goals, the shareholders sell the shares, and the market price falls. Short of bankruptcy, this is one of the worst things that can happen to a corporation because it means that the corporation cannot easily raise capital as needed.

Preferred shares give their owners certain advantages over common shareholders. These benefits include the right to receive dividends before the common shareholders, and the right to receive assets before the common shareholders if the corporation liquidates. Corporations pay a fixed amount of dividends on preferred shares. Investors usually buy preferred shares to earn those fixed dividends. Often, preferred

KEY POINT

Most corporations are authorized to issue many more shares of stock than they intend to issue originally. If the corporation wants to issue more than the authorized shares, the articles of incorporation must be amended. Amendment of the articles of incorporation requires shareholder approval.

THINKING IT OVER

For the following list of characteristics of capital stock, indicate whether each characteristic would be likely to apply to preferred or common stock:

1. Stated dividend
2. Voting rights
3. Priority to receive assets in the event of liquidation
4. Cumulative

A:	Preferred	Common
1.	Yes	No
2.	Maybe	Yes
3.	Yes	No
4.	Maybe	No

---

[1]The rights enumerated are basic rights common to incorporating legislation generally. For a more complete listing, the interested reader is referred to the *Canada Business Corporations Act* in *The Revised Statutes of Canada*.

shares are cumulative, which means that if the preferred dividend is not paid in a year, the dividend from that year must be paid to the preferred shareholders before the common shareholders can receive a dividend in a later year. Because of the preferred shareholders' priorities, common shares represent the residual ownership in the corporation's assets after the liabilities and the claims of preferred shareholders have been subtracted. Often the right to vote is withheld from preferred shareholders. Westcoast Energy Inc., the energy transmission company, has several preferred shares issues. For example, Westcoast has $1.25 cumulative redeemable preferred shares and $1.40 cumulative preferred shares; $1.25 and $1.40 are the annual dividend rates. Companies may issue different classes of preferred shares (Class A and Class B or Series A and Series B, for example). Each class is recorded in a separate account.

Investors who buy preferred shares take less risk than do common shareholders. Why? Because corporations pay a specified amount of dividends on preferred shares. The preferred dividend may be a set amount, like that of Westcoast Energy Inc., or a fixed percentage of some number, such as the prime interest rate at the date of declaration of the dividend. For example, the 1999 annual report of The Thomson Corporation, the information and publishing company, reveals that the company has outstanding Series II preferred shares whose quarterly dividend is 70 percent of the Canada prime bank rate and Series V preferred shares whose quarterly dividend is $1.25. Investors usually buy preferred shares to earn those dividends. An increase in the market value of preferred shares is less important than an increase in the market value of common shares because preferred stocks' values do not fluctuate much.

The Thomson Corporation
www.thomcorp.com

Corporations issue preferred shares as opposed to common shares because preferred shares have no voting rights like common shares usually have, and equity (ownership) is not diluted when preferred shares are issued. Preferred shares may be preferred by corporations to debt because dividends are payable at the discretion of the corporation. As well, the corporation is not compelled to redeem the preferred shares at a certain date, whereas the corporation must repay the debt at a certain date.

Preferred shares operate as a hybrid somewhere between common shares and long-term debt. Like debt, preferred shares pay a specified dividend. But like shares, the dividend becomes a liability only after the board of directors has declared the dividend. Also, there is no obligation to redeem preferred stock in the manner required by debt. Preferred shares that must be redeemed (paid back) by the corporation are a liability masquerading as a stock. Experienced investors treat mandatorily redeemable preferred shares as part of total liabilities, not as part of shareholders' equity. In fact, types of preferred shares must be accounted for as debt for accounting purposes. Further discussion of this aspect of preferred shares is covered in advanced accounting texts. While issuing preferred shares is a common way for a corporation to raise funds, not all corporations issue preferred shares. All corporations must have at least one common share.

The method of financing affects net income and income taxes to be paid. Corporations may prefer debt to preferred shares because dividend payments are not tax deductible and interest payments are. Dividends are a distribution of assets

	Common Stock	Preferred Stock	Long-Term Debt
Investment risk	High	Medium	Low
Corporate obligation to repay principal	No	No	Yes
Dividends/Interest	Dividends	Dividends	Tax-deductible interest expense
Corporate obligation to pay dividends/interest	Only after declaration	Only after declaration*	At fixed dates
Fluctuations in market value under normal conditions	High	Medium	Low

*Some preferred stock is cumulative as to dividends.

EXHIBIT 13-5

Comparison of Common Stock, Preferred Stock, and Long-Term Debt

created by earnings. On the other hand, individuals might prefer to hold preferred shares because the income tax rate on dividends they receive is lower than the tax rate they pay on interest they receive. It's for that reason that the dividend rate on a company's preferred shares is usually lower than the interest rate on bonds the company issues. Exhibit 13–5, on page 715, summarizes the similarities and differences among common stock, preferred stock, and long-term debt.

No-Par-Value Stock

No-par-value shares are shares of stock that do not have a value assigned to them by the articles of incorporation. The board of directors assigns a value to the shares when they are issued; this value is known as the **stated value**. For example, Dajol Inc. has authorization to issue 100,000 shares of common stock, having no par value assigned to them by the articles of incorporation. Dajol Inc. needs $50,000 at incorporation, and might issue 10,000 shares for $5.00 per share, 2,000 shares at $25.00 per share, or 1,000 shares at $50.00 per share, and so on. The point is that Dajol Inc. can assign whatever value to the shares the board of directors wishes. Normally, the stated value would be credited to Common Stock when the shares are issued.

The recorded value of a corporation's capital stock or stated capital is the sum of the shares issued times the stated values of those shares at the time of issue. For example, if YDR Ltd. issued 1,000 common shares at a stated value of $8.00 per share, 2,000 shares at $12.00 per share, and 500 shares at $15.00 per share, its capital stock or stated capital would be $39,500 [(1,000 × $8) + (2,000 × $12) + (500 × $15)].

The *Canada Business Corporations Act* and most provincial incorporating acts now require common and preferred shares to be issued without nominal or par value. The full amount of the proceeds from the sale of shares by a company must be allocated to the capital account for those shares. For example, if Canadian Tire Corporation, Limited were to issue 100 shares of common stock for $2,500 (that is, the stock sold for $25.00 per share), $2,500 would be credited to Common Stock.

Issuing Stock

Large corporations such as Nortel Networks Corporation, McCain Foods Ltd., and Bombardier Inc. need huge quantities of money to operate. They cannot expect to finance all their operations through borrowing. They need capital that they can raise by issuing stock. The articles of incorporation that the incorporators receive from the federal or provincial government includes an *authorization of stock*—that is, a provision giving the government's permission for the business to issue (to sell) a certain number of shares of stock. Corporations may sell the shares directly to the shareholders, or they may use the services of an *underwriter*, such as the brokerage firm RBC Dominion Securities or Scotia Capital Markets. The agreement between a corporation and its underwriter will vary, but typically the underwriter will commit to placing all of the share issue it can with its customers, and to buying any unsold shares for its own account. In another form of contract, the underwriter agrees to do its best to sell all of the share issue but makes no guarantees. The underwriter makes its money by selling the shares for a higher price than it pays to the corporation issuing the shares.

The corporation need not issue all the stock that the articles of incorporation allow—authorized stock can, and often does, exceed issued stock. Management may hold some stock back and issue it later if the need for additional capital arises. The stock that the corporation does issue to shareholders is called *issued stock*. Only by issuing stock—not by receiving authorization—does the corporation increase the asset and shareholder's equity amounts on its balance sheet.

The price that the shareholder pays to acquire shares from the corporation is called the *issue price*. A combination of market factors—including the company's comparative earnings record, financial position, prospects for success, and general business conditions—determines issue price. Investors will not pay more than mar-

REAL WORLD EXAMPLE

If you looked at the balance sheet of a U.S. corporation, you might see that its common shares had been issued at *par value*. This means the Board of Directors assigned a value to the common shares. If the shares were sold for more than par value, the difference is credited to Contributed Surplus. Most Canadian corporations credit the capital account for those shares for the full amount of the net proceeds from the sale of the shares.

OBJECTIVE 2
Record the issuance of stock

KEY POINT

Owners invest in a corporation by buying stock. Issuance of stock increases the corporation's assets and shareholders' equity.

WORKING IT OUT

Answer the following question on the basis of this journal entry for stock issued at $25 per share:

Cash.................. 300,000
    Common
        Stock......... 300,000

How many shares of stock were issued?

A:
$300,000/$25 = 12,000 shares

ket value for the shares. The following sections show how to account for the issuance of stock.

Issuing Common Shares

Companies often advertise the issuance of their stock to attract investors. The Internet has now become the most popular medium for the advertisements. Exhibit 13-6 is a partial reproduction of Real Time Measurements Inc.'s initial public offering from the Website www.bay-street.com on January 10, 2001.

Altogether, Real Time Measurements Inc. hoped to raise approximately $750,000 of capital.

Issuing Common Shares at a Stated Value Suppose JDS Uniphase Corporation issues one million shares of its common stock for cash, and the directors determine that the shares will be issued with a stated value (selling price) of $100 per share. The stock issuance entry is

Jan.	8	Cash	100,000,000	
		Common Stock		100,000,000
		To issue common shares at $100.00 per share (1,000,000 × $100.00)		

We assume JDS Uniphase received $100,000,000. The amount invested in the corporation, $100,000,000 in this case, is called capital stock. The credit to Common Stock records an increase in the capital stock of the corporation.

The following example illustrates the shareholders' equity section of JDS Uniphase Corporation after it had issued the one million shares. Assume that the articles of incorporation granted to JDS Uniphase Corporation authorize it to issue an unlimited number of common shares, that 113,107,871 shares had been issued for an average value of $13.79 per share prior to January 8, and that the company had $648 million in retained earnings and a foreign currency translation adjustment of $20 million. The corporation would report shareholders' equity as follows:

Shareholders' Equity (in millions)	
Contributed capital	
Common stock, unlimited number of shares authorized, 113,107,871 shares issued	$1,560
Retained earnings	648
Foreign currency translation adjustment	20
Total shareholders' equity	$2,228

The authorized common stock reports the maximum number of shares the company may issue under its articles of incorporation.

Issuing Company	Number and type of shares	Issue price	Stated value of shares

This prospectus constitutes a public offering of these securities only in those jurisdictions where they may be lawfully offered for sale and therein only by persons permitted to sell such securities. No securities commission or similar authority in Canada has in any way passed upon the merits of the securities offered hereunder and any representation to the contrary is an offence.

INITIAL PUBLIC OFFERING   **January 10, 2001**

REAL TIME MEASUREMENTS INC.

3,000,000 Common Shares
$0.25 per share
($750,000)

Real Time Measurements Inc. (the "Corporation") hereby offers for sale 3,000,000 common shares ("Common Shares") of the Corporation at an issue price of $0.25 per Common Share (the "Offering"). The offering price of the Common Shares hereunder was determined by negotiation between the Corporation and Yorkton Securities Inc. (the "Agent").

REAL WORLD EXAMPLE

The financial section of a newspaper often gives the market price of a company's stock, its dividend per share, as well as the dividend yield (which is the dividend per share ÷ market price per share).

WORKING IT OUT

Prepare journal entries for each situation:
A company issues
1. 100,000 shares of common stock for $35 per share.

A:
Cash 3,500,000
  Common
    Stock 3,500,000

2. 160,000 shares of common stock in exchange for land valued at $55,000, a building valued at $125,000, and a computer valued at $5,000.

A:
Equipment 5,000
Building 125,000
Land 55,000
  Common
    Stock 185,000

EXHIBIT 13-6

Announcement of Initial Public Offering of Real Time Measurements Inc.

REAL WORLD EXAMPLE

Some corporations issue several classes of common stock—Class A shares and Class B shares. In a case like this, one class may have the rights of common shares and the other may have some restrictions or enhancements. For example, Magna International Inc.'s Class A shares have one vote each, while the Class B shares have 500 votes each.

STOP & THINK

Suppose JDS Uniphase Corporation actually had total liabilities of $2,184 million on the balance-sheet date just given. What was JDS Uniphase's debt ratio?

Answer: The debt ratio is 0.495, or 49.5%

$$\frac{\text{Total liabilities}}{\text{Total assets}} = \frac{\$2,184}{\$2,184 + \$2,228} = 0.495, \text{ or } 49.5\%$$

REAL WORLD EXAMPLE

Sometimes, with publicly traded corporations, it is most objective to use the market value of the shares given in exchange for an asset as a measure of the asset's value.

Issuing Common Shares for Assets Other Than Cash   When a corporation issues stock in exchange for assets other than cash, it debits the assets received for their current market value and credits the capital accounts accordingly. The assets' prior book value does not matter because the shareholder will demand stock equal to the market value of the asset given. Gillan Corporation issued 25,000 shares of its common stock for equipment worth $25,000 and a building worth $125,000. The entry is

Nov. 12	Equipment..	25,000	
	Building	125,000	
	Common stock...		150,000
	To issue 25,000 shares of common stock in exchange for equipment and a building.		

Common stock increases by the amount of the assets' *current market value*, $150,000 in this case; the stated value or value assigned to the shares would be $6.00 ($150,000/25,000) per share.

STOP & THINK

How did this transaction affect Gillan Corporation's contributed capital? Retained earnings? Total shareholders' equity?

Answer:

Contributed Capital	Effect on Retained Earnings	Total Shareholders' Equity
Increase $150,000	None	Increase $150,000

Issuing Preferred Shares

While not all corporations issue preferred stock, the recent edition of *Financial Reporting in Canada*[2] published by the Canadian Institute of Chartered Accountants reported that 77 of the 200 companies reporting, or 38.5 percent, mentioned preferred shares in the shareholders' equity section of their balance sheets. Accounting for preferred shares follows the pattern illustrated for common shares.

Assume the Arens Corporation articles of incorporation authorize issuance of 10,000 preferred shares with an annual dividend of $10.00 per share. On July 31, the company issues 1,000 shares at a stated price of $100.00 per share. The issuance entry is

[2]Byrd, C. and I. Chen, *Financial Reporting in Canada 2000,* Twenty-fifth edition. (Toronto: Canadian Institute of Chartered Accountants, 2000), p. 344.

July	31	Cash	100,000	
		Preferred Stock		100,000
		To issue 1,000 shares of preferred stock for		
		$100 per share (1,000 × $100).		

As was mentioned previously, sometimes preferred shares have characteristics that make them more like debt than equity. Such preferred shares are treated for accounting purposes as a liability rather than as part of equity. Investors also regard such preferred shares as debt rather than equity. Further discussion of the relevant issues is saved for a more advanced accounting course.

Ethical Considerations in Accounting for the Issuance of Stock

Issuance of stock for *cash* poses no serious ethical challenge. The company simply receives cash and issues the stock to the shareholders, giving them share certificates as evidence of their purchase.

Issuing stock for assets other than cash can pose an ethical challenge, however. The company issuing the stock often wishes to record a large amount for the noncash asset received (such as land or a building) and for the stock that it is issuing. Why? Because large asset and shareholders' equity amounts on the balance sheet make the business look prosperous and creditworthy. The motivation to look prosperous can inject a subtle bias into the amount recorded for the assets received and the stock issued.

As we discussed on page 718, a company is supposed to record an asset received at its current value. But one person's perception of a particular asset's market value can differ from another person's perception. One person may appraise land at a market value of $400,000. Another may honestly believe the land is worth only $300,000. A company receiving land in exchange for its stock must decide whether to record the land received and the stock issued at $300,000, at $400,000, or at some amount in between.

The ethical course of action is to record the asset at its current fair market value, as determined by a good-faith estimate of market value from independent appraisers. It is rare for a public corporation to be found guilty of *understating* the asset values on its balance sheet, but companies have been embarrassed by *overstating* their asset values. Investors who rely on the financial statements may be able to prove that an overstatement of asset values caused them to pay too much for the company's stock. In this case, a court of law may render a judgment against the company. For this reason, companies tend to value assets conservatively (that is, on the low side) to avoid an overstatement of their book value.

Donated Capital

Corporations occasionally receive gifts or *donations*. For example, a city council may offer a company free land to encourage it to locate in their city. The free land is called a donation. Also, a shareholder may make a donation to the corporation in the form of cash, land or other assets, or stock that the corporation can resell.

A donation is a gift that increases the assets of the corporation. However, the donor (giver) receives no ownership interest in the company in return. A transaction to receive a donation does not increase the corporation's revenue, and thus it does not affect income. Instead, the donation creates a special category of shareholders' equity called **donated capital**. The corporation records a donation by debiting the asset received at its current market value, and by crediting the Donated Capital account, which is a shareholders' equity account.

Suppose Burlington Ltd. receives 100 hectares of land as a donation from the city of Lethbridge, Alberta. The current market value of the land is $150,000. Burlington Ltd. records receipt of the donation as follows:

Apr. 18	Land		150,000	
	Donated capital			150,000
	To receive land as a donation from the city.			

Donated capital is reported in the Shareholders' Equity section of the balance sheet between Contributed Capital and Retained Earnings.

OBJECTIVE 3
Account for the incorporation of a going business

Incorporation of a Going Business

You may dream of having your own business someday, or you may currently be a business proprietor or partner. Businesses that begin as a proprietorship or a partnership often incorporate at a later date. By incorporating a going business, the proprietor or partners avoid the unlimited liability for business debts. Corporations often pay income tax at a lower rate than individuals. And as we discussed earlier, incorporating makes it easier to raise capital.

To account for the incorporation of a going business, we close the owner equity accounts of the prior entity and set up the shareholder equity accounts of the corporation. Suppose BC.com is a partnership owned by Joe Suzuki and Monica Lee. The partnership balance sheet, after all adjustments and closing entries, reports Joe Suzuki, Capital, of $100,000, and Monica Lee, Capital, of $140,000. They incorporate their business as BC.com Inc. with an authorization to issue 1,000,000 shares of common stock. Joe and Monica agree to receive common stock equal in stated value to their partnership equity balances. The equity balances represent the net assets of the partnership. The entry to record the incorporation of the business is

Feb.	1	Joe Suzuki, Capital...	100,000	
		Monica Lee, Capital...	140,000	
		Common Stock..		240,000
		To incorporate the business, close the capital accounts of the partnership, and issue common shares to the incorporators.		

Organization Cost

The costs of organizing a corporation include legal fees for preparing documents and advising on procedures, fees, and taxes paid to the incorporating jurisdiction, and charges by promoters for selling the company's stock. These costs are grouped in an account titled Organization Cost, which is an asset because these costs contribute to a business's start-up. Suppose BBV Holdings Inc. pays legal fees and incorporation fees of $5,000 to organize the corporation under the *Canada Business Corporations Act* in Newfoundland. In addition, an investment dealer charges a fee of $15,000 for selling 30,000 shares of BBV Holdings Inc. common stock for $225,000 and receives 2,000 common shares as payment. BBV Holdings Inc.'s journal entries to record these organization costs are

Mar.	31	Organization Cost...	5,000	
		Cash..		5,000
		Legal fees and incorporation fees to organize the corporation.		
Apr.	3	Cash..	225,000	
		Organization Cost	15,000	
		Common Stock..		240,000
		To record receipt of funds from sale of common shares and issue of shares to investment dealer for selling stock in organization.		

Organization cost is an *intangible asset*, reported on the balance sheet along with patents, trademarks, goodwill, and any other intangibles. We know that an intangible asset should be amortized over its useful life, and organization costs will benefit the corporation for as long as the corporation operates. But how long will that be? We cannot know in advance. The *Income Tax Act* allows corporations to expense a portion of organization costs against taxable income. While the *CICA Handbook* does not require organization costs to be amortized, most companies amortize organization costs over a short time period because of their relatively small size. As is true with other intangibles, amortization expense for the year should be disclosed in the financial statements.

Summary Review of Accounting for Stock

OBJECTIVE 4
Prepare the shareholders' equity section of a corporation's balance sheet

Let's review the first half of this chapter by showing the shareholders' equity section of Envoy Corporation's balance sheet at December 31, 2002, in Exhibit 13-7. (Assume that all figures, which are arbitrary, are correct.) Note the two sections of shareholders' equity: capital stock and retained earnings. Also observe the order of the capital stock accounts: preferred stock, common stock, and contributed surplus.

EXHIBIT 13-7

Part of Medina Corporation's Balance Sheet

ENVOY CORPORATION
Partial Balance Sheet
December 31, 2002

Shareholders' Equity

Contributed capital	
Preferred stock, $5.00, 10,000 shares authorized,	
1,000 shares issued	$ 50,000
Common stock, 10,000 shares authorized,	
4,000 shares issued	80,000
Total contributed capital	130,000
Contributed surplus—Donated capital	40,000
Retained earnings	15,000
Total shareholders' equity	$185,000

STOP & THINK

Examine Envoy Corporation's shareholders' equity in Exhibit 13-7, and answer these questions.

1. How much did Envoy Corporation's preferred shareholders invest in the corporation?
2. How much did the common shareholders invest in Envoy Corporation?
3. What did the shareholders get for their investments in the company?
4. How does the donated capital differ from the other capital accounts?

Answers:

1. $50,000
2. $80,000
3. The shareholders received stock, which represents their ownership in the net assets of the corporation.
4. Donated capital represents a donation to the company for which the donor received no ownership interest in the assets of the company. The contributed capital accounts represent what the shareholders paid for their ownership in the company's assets.

Now review the Decision Guidelines feature to solidify your understanding of shareholders' equity as it is reported on the balance sheet.

DECISION GUIDELINES Reporting Shareholders' Equity on the Balance Sheet

Decision	Guidelines
What are the two main segments of shareholders' equity?	• Contributed capital • Retained earnings
Which is more permanent, contributed capital or retained earnings?	Capital stock is more permanent because corporations may use their retained earnings for distributing dividends to the shareholders.

How are contributed capital and retained earnings
• Similar?
• Different?
	• Both represent the shareholders' equity (ownership) in the net assets of the corporation.
	• Contributed capital and retained earnings come from different sources:
	  a. Contributed capital comes from the corporation's shareholders, who invested in the company.
	  b. Retained earnings comes from the corporation's customers. It was earned by the company's profitable operations.

What categories of contributed capital appear most often on corporation financial statements?	• Preferred stock • Common stock

Mid-Chapter Summary Problems

for Your Review

1. Test your understanding of the first half of this chapter by answering whether each of the following statements is true or false:

   a. A shareholder may bind the corporation to a contract.

   b. The policy-making body in a corporation is called the board of directors.

   c. The owner of 100 shares of preferred stock has greater voting rights than the owner of 100 shares of common stock.

   d. A company incorporated under the *Canada Business Corporations Act* must assign the proceeds of a stock issue to the capital account for that stock.

   e. All shares of common stock issued and outstanding have voting rights.

   f. Issuance of 1,000 common shares at $12 per share increases shareholders' equity by $12,000.

   g. The stated value of a stock is the value assigned to the stock by the company issuing it at the date issued.

   h. A corporation issues its preferred shares in exchange for land and a building with a combined market value of $200,000. This transaction increases the corporation's shareholders' equity by $200,000 regardless of the assets' prior book value.

   i. Preferred shares are a riskier investment than common shares.

2. Leith Technologies Inc., incorporated under the *Canada Business Corporations Act*, had three transactions during the year involving its common shares. On January 15, 2002, 50,000 Class A voting shares were issued with a stated value of $8.00 per share. On February 28, 2002, 10,000 Class B non-voting shares with a stated value of $10.00 per share were issued. On August 8, 2002, 15,000 Class B shares were issued in exchange for land with a market value of $165,000. Leith's articles of incorporation state that 100,000 Class A voting and 200,000 Class B non-voting common shares are authorized.

Required

a. Prepare the journal entry to record the transaction of January 15, 2002.

b. Prepare the journal entry to record the transaction of February 28, 2002.

c. Prepare the journal entry to record the transaction of August 8, 2002.

d. Create the shareholders' equity section for Leith Technologies Inc. after the three transactions have taken place.

e. What is the total capital stock of the company?

f. How did Leith Technologies Inc. withhold the voting privilege from its Class B common shareholders?

Solutions to Review Problems

1. Answers to true-false statements:

a. False	b. True	c. False	d. True	e. False
f. True	g. True	h. True	i. False	

2. a. Jan. 15 Cash.. 400,000
                        Common Stock—Class A 400,000
                        To issue Class A common shares at $8.00
                        per share (50,000 × $8.00).

  b. Feb. 28 Cash.. 100,000
                        Common Stock—Class B.................... 100,000
                        To issue Class B common shares at
                        $10.00 per share (10,000 × $10.00).

  c. Aug. 8 Land 165,000
                        Common Stock—Class B....................... 165,000
                        To issue 15,000 shares of common stock at
                        $11.00 per share in exchange for land.

  d. Shareholders' Equity
      Capital stock
          Common stock, Class A voting,
             100,000 shares authorized,
             50,000 shares issued...................... $400,000
          Common stock, Class B
             non-voting, 200,000 shares
             authorized, 25,000 shares issued.. 265,000
          Total capital stock $665,000

  e. Capital stock is $665,000.

  f. The voting privilege was withheld by specific agreement; the articles of incorporation specified the Class B common shares were non-voting.

Cyber Coach

Visit the Student Resources area of the *Accounting* Companion Website for extra practice with the new material in Chapter 13.
www.pearsoned.ca/horngren

Accounting for Cash Dividends

Corporations share the company's wealth with their owners, the shareholders, through dividends. Corporations declare dividends from *retained earnings* and may pay the dividends with *cash*. The corporation must have enough retained earnings to declare the dividend and enough cash to pay the dividend.

Dividend Dates

A corporation must declare a dividend before paying it. The board of directors alone has the authority to declare a dividend. The corporation has no obligation to pay a dividend until the board declares one, but once declared, the dividend becomes a legal liability of the corporation. Three relevant dates for dividends are

1. *Declaration date*   On the declaration date, the board of directors announces the intention to pay the dividend. The declaration creates a liability for the

corporation. Declaration is recorded by debiting Retained Earnings and crediting Dividends Payable.

2. **Date of record** At declaration, the corporation announces the record date, which follows the declaration date by a few weeks. The shareholders who own the shares on the date of record receive the dividend when it is paid. The corporation makes no journal entry on the date of record because no transaction occurs. Nevertheless, much work takes place behind the scenes to identify the shareholders of record on this date, because the stock is being traded continuously.

3. **Payment date** Payment of the dividend usually follows the record date by two to four weeks. Payment is recorded by debiting Dividends Payable and crediting Cash.

Dividends on Preferred and Common Stock

OBJECTIVE 5
Account for cash dividends

Declaration of a cash dividend is recorded by debiting Retained Earnings and crediting Dividends Payable as follows:

Oct.	3	Retained Earnings...	XXX	
		Dividends Payable		XXX
		To declare a cash dividend.		

Payment of the dividend occurs, as was noted above, on the payment date, and is recorded as follows:

Nov.	15	Dividends Payable..	XXX	
		Cash..		XXX
		To pay a cash dividend.		

Dividends Payable is a current liability. When a company has issued both preferred and common stock, the preferred shareholders receive their dividends first. The common shareholders receive dividends only if the total declared dividend is large enough to pay the preferred shareholders first.

Cascade Industries Inc., in addition to its common stock, has 15,000 shares of cumulative preferred shares outstanding. Preferred dividends are paid at the annual rate of $2.00 per share. Assume that Cascade Industries Inc. declares an annual dividend of $200,000 for the 2002 fiscal year. The allocation to preferred and common shareholders is

	Total Dividend of $200,000
Preferred dividend (15,000 shares × $2.00 per share)......................	$ 30,000
Common dividend (remainder: $200,000 – $30,000)........................	170,000
Total dividend...	$200,000

If Cascade Industries Inc. declares only a $50,000 dividend, preferred shareholders receive $30,000 and the common shareholders receive $20,000 ($50,000 – $30,000).

This example illustrates an important relationship between preferred stock and common stock. To an investor, the preferred stock is safer because it receives dividends first (as well as ranking ahead of common shares on dissolution). For example, if Cascade Industries Inc. earns only enough net income to pay the preferred shareholders' dividends, the owners of common shares receive no dividends at all. However, the earnings potential from an investment in common shares is much greater than from an investment in preferred shares. Preferred dividends are usually limited to the specified amount, but there is no upper limit on the amount of common dividends.

We noted that preferred shareholders enjoy the advantage of priority over com-

WORKING IT OUT

CRS Robotics Inc. was organized on Jan. 1, 2003, with 500,000 shares of stock authorized; 200,000 shares were issued on Jan. 5, 2003. CRS Robotics Inc. earned $250,000 during 2003 and declared a dividend of $0.25 per share on Nov. 30, 2003, payable to shareholders on Jan. 5, 2004.
(1) Journalize the declaration and payment of the dividend.
(2) Compute the balance of retained earnings on Dec. 31, 2003

A:
(1) Nov. 30, 2003, declaration
Retained
  Earnings.............. 50,000
    Div. Payable.... 50,000
    (200,000 shares × $0.25)

Jan. 5, 2004, payment
Div. Payable 50,000
  Cash................. 50,000
(2) The balance in retained earnings is $200,000 ($250,000 – $50,000). The declaration on Nov. 30, 2003—not the payment on Jan. 5, 2004—reduced retained earnings.

mon shareholders in receiving dividends. The various features or sweeteners for preferred shares are explained on page 714. The dividend preference is normally stated as a dollar amount. For example, the preferred shares may be "$3 preferred," meaning that the shareholders are entitled to an annual dividend of $3 per share. (In those rare cases where the preferred shares have a par value, the dividend preference may be stated as a percentage of the par value rate.)

Dividends on Cumulative and Noncumulative Preferred Stock

The allocation of dividends may be complex if the preferred stock is *cumulative*. Corporations sometimes fail to pay a dividend to their preferred shareholders. The missed dividends are said to be *in arrears*. The owners of **cumulative preferred stock** must receive all dividends in arrears plus the current year's dividend before the corporation pays dividends to the common shareholders. The cumulative feature is not automatic to preferred shares but must be assigned to the preferred shares in the articles of incorporation.

As noted above, the preferred shares of Cascade Industries Inc. are cumulative. Suppose the company did not distribute the 2001 preferred dividend of $30,000. Before paying dividends to its common shareholders in 2002, the company must first pay preferred dividends of $30,000 for both 2001 and 2002, a total of $60,000.

When a company has more than one class of preferred shares or common shares, the division of dividends among the various classes of stock follows this same pattern: the most senior preferred stock gets the first dividends, and so on.

Assume that Cascade Industries Inc. did not distribute its 2001 preferred dividend. In 2002, the company declares a $200,000 dividend. The entry to record the declaration is

2002					
Sept.	6	Retained Earnings	200,000	
		Dividends Payable, Preferred........................		60,000
		Dividends Payable, Common		140,000
		To declare a cash dividend. Preferred		
		dividends are $60,000 ($30,000 × 2); common		
		dividends are $140,000 ($200,000 – $60,000).		

If the preferred shares are not designated as cumulative, the corporation is not obligated to pay dividends in arrears. Suppose that the Cascade Industries Inc. preferred stock was not cumulative, and the company did not distribute the 2001 preferred dividend of $30,000. The preferred shareholders would lose the 2001 dividend forever. Of course, the common shareholders would not receive a 2001 dividend either. Before paying any common dividends in 2002, the company would have to pay the 2002 preferred dividend of $30,000.

Having dividends in arrears on cumulative preferred shares is *not* a liability to the corporation. (A liability for dividends arises only after the board of directors declares the dividend.) Nevertheless, a corporation must report cumulative preferred dividends in arrears in the notes to the financial statements. This information alerts common shareholders to how much in cumulative preferred dividends must be paid before the common shareholders will receive any dividends. This gives the common shareholders an idea about the likelihood of receiving dividends and satisfies the disclosure principle. Most preferred shares are cumulative.

Student to Student

I think the most difficult part of allocating dividends between preferred and common shares happens when the preferred dividends are cumulative. I found the Learning Tip on this page and the Working It Out on page 727 helped me understand dividend allocation, especially when the preferred-share dividends are in arrears.

Harjit S., Prince George

KEY POINT

Dividends are *not* an expense, but a distribution of earnings to owners. Cash dividends, like withdrawals, reduce assets and shareholders' equity.

KEY POINT

To declare cash dividends, a corporation must have (1) a credit balance in Retained Earnings, (2) adequate cash, and (3) approval by the Board of Directors.

LEARNING TIP

"Cumulative" means that any dividends not declared in a given year will accumulate, or carry over, to the future. Dividends cannot accumulate on common stock.

Note disclosure of cumulative preferred dividends might take the following form. Observe the two references to note 3 in this section of the balance sheet. The "$3.00" after "Preferred stock" is the dividend rate.

Preferred stock, $3.00, 10,000 shares authorized, 2,000 shares issued (Note 3)	$100,000
Common stock, 100,000 shares authorized, 40,000 shares issued	200,000
Retained earnings (Note 3)..	414,000

Note 3: Cumulative preferred dividends in arrears. At December 31, 2002, dividends on the company's $3.00 preferred stock were in arrears for 2001 and 2002, in the amount of $12,000 ($3.00 × 2,000 × 2 years).

Convertible Preferred Stock

Convertible preferred stock may be exchanged by the preferred shareholders, if they choose, for another specified class of stock in the corporation. For example, the preferred stock of Renewal Resources Inc. is convertible into the company's common stock. A note to Renewal's balance sheet describes the conversion terms as follows:

> The . . . preferred stock is convertible at the rate of 7.00 shares of common stock for each share of preferred stock outstanding.

If you owned 100 shares of Renewal's convertible preferred stock, you could convert it into 700 (100 × 7.00) shares of Renewal Resources Inc. common stock. Under what condition would you exercise the conversion privilege? You would do so if the market value of the common stock that you could receive from conversion exceeded the market value of the preferred stock that you presently held. This way, you as an investor could increase your personal wealth.

Renewal Resources Inc. convertible preferred stock was issued at $100 per share, and the common stock at $1. The company would record the conversion at the value of the 100 preferred shares on the Renewal Resources Inc. books, or $10,000 (100 × $100). The conversion of the 100 shares of preferred stock into 700 shares of common stock would be recorded as follows:

Mar.	7	Preferred stock..	10,000	
		Common stock		10,000
		Conversion of preferred stock into common. (100 shares of preferred stock converted into 700 shares of common stock).		

At this point, the new common shares cannot be converted back to preferred shares.

Summary

Preferred stock, as we see, offers alternative features not available to common stock. Preferred stock may be cumulative or not cumulative, and convertible or not convertible. In addition, preferred stock is usually preferred when dividends are distributed, and when the assets are distributed to shareholders upon liquidation of the company.

Different Values of Stock

The business community refers to several different *stock values*. Market value, liquidation value, and book value are used for various investor decisions.

WORKING IT OUT

Trivision Corp. has outstanding 20,000 shares of common stock and 10,000 shares of $2.00 cumulative preferred stock. The company has declared no dividends for the past two years but plans to pay $90,000 this year. Compute the dividends for the preferred and common stock.

A:
Preferred Stock:
Dividends in arrears
  ($2.00 × 10,000 × 2)

.... $40,000
Current dividend........... 20,000
Total to Preferred $60,000

Common Stock:
Remainder of dividend
  ($90,000 − $60,000)

.... 30,000
Total dividend.............. $90,000

KEY POINT

Convertible preferred stock may be exchanged for common stock at the shareholder's option.

WORKING IT OUT

Record the conversion of 100 shares of $10.00 convertible preferred stock that was originally issued at $150 per share. Each preferred stock is convertible into 4 shares of common stock.

A:
Preferred Stock
(100 × $150) 15,000
  Common Stock* 15,000

*4 × 100 = 400 common shares would be issued.

OBJECTIVE 6
Use different stock values in decision making

Market Value

A stock's **market value**, or *market price*, is the price for which a person could buy or sell a share of the stock. The issuing corporation's net income, financial position, its future prospects, and the general economic conditions determine market value. The Internet and most newspapers report the market price of many stocks. Most companies' Websites track their stock prices. Corporate annual reports generally provide quarterly market price data for the past five or ten years. *In almost all cases, shareholders are more concerned about the market value of a stock than any of the other values discussed below.* Recently, BCE Inc. common shares were *listed at* (an alternative term is *quoted at*) 37.00 which meant they sold for, or could be bought for, $37.00 per share. The purchase of 100 common shares of BCE Inc. would cost $3,700 ($37.00 × 100), plus a commission. If you were selling 100 shares of this stock, you would receive cash of $3,700 less a commission. The commission is the fee an investor pays to a stockbroker for buying or selling the stock. If you buy shares in BCE Inc. from another investor, BCE Inc. gets no cash. The transaction is a sale between investors. BCE Inc. records only the change in shareholder name.

Liquidation Value

The *liquidation value* of a share of company stock is equal to the net realizable value of the assets less the cash required to pay the liabilities divided by the number of shares outstanding. Liquidation value is rarely equal to either market value or book value.

For example, Douglas Ltd. has 10,000 common shares outstanding. The shares are trading on the stock market at $29.50; that is, they have a market value of $29.50 per share. The company's assets have a net realizable value of $336,000, while liabilities amount to $62,000; the liquidation value per share is $27.40 ($336,000 − $62,000 divided by 10,000 shares).

Occasionally, you will read in a business newspaper like *The Financial Post* that a company's break-up value (liquidation value) per share is greater than its market value per share. That means that the total market value of the company's individual assets, minus its liabilities, exceeds the total market value of the company's shares.

Book Value

The **book value** of a stock is the amount of shareholders' equity on the company's books for each share of its stock. Corporations often report this amount in their annual reports. If the company has only common stock outstanding, its book value is computed by dividing total shareholders' equity by the number of shares outstanding. A company with shareholders' equity of $180,000 and 5,000 shares of common stock outstanding has book value of $36 per share ($180,000/5,000 shares).

If the company has both preferred and common stock outstanding, the preferred shareholders have the first claim to shareholders' equity. Ordinarily, preferred stock has a specified liquidation value. The book value of preferred stock is usually its liquidation value plus any cumulative dividends in arrears on the stock. Its book value *per share* equals the sum of the liquidation value and any cumulative dividends in arrears divided by the number of preferred shares outstanding. After the corporation computes the preferred shares' book value, it computes the book value per common share. The corporation divides the common equity (total shareholders' equity minus preferred equity) by the number of common shares outstanding.

Assume that a company's balance sheet reports the amounts shown on the next page.

Suppose that four years (including the current year) of cumulative preferred dividends are in arrears and preferred stock has a liquidation value of $120 per share.

REAL WORLD EXAMPLE

A change in the market price of a company's stock does not affect the corporation unless the corporation decides to issue additional stock or repurchase its own stock. Most stock transactions are between shareholders.

LEARNING TIP

Book value per share uses the number of shares outstanding, not the number of shares authorized.

Shareholders' Equity

Contributed capital	
Preferred stock, $7.00, 5,000 shares authorized,	
1,000 shares issued...	$100,000
Common stock, 20,000 shares authorized,	
5,000 shares issued...	150,000
Total contributed capital	250,000
Retained earnings..	90,000
Total shareholders' equity..	$340,000

The book value per share computations for this corporation follow:

Preferred	
Liquidation value (1,000 shares × $120)...	$120,000
Cumulative dividends (1,000 × $7.00 × 4)	28,000
Shareholders' equity allocated to preferred...	$148,000
Book value per share ($148,000/1,000 shares)...	$148.00

Common	
Total shareholders' equity	$340,000
Less: Shareholders' equity allocated to preferred	148,000
Shareholders' equity available	
for common shareholders...	$192,000
Book value per share ($192,000/5,000 shares)..	$38.40

Book Value and Decision Making   How is book value used in decision making? Companies negotiating the purchase of a corporation may wish to know the book value of its stock, especially if the stock is not publicly traded. The book value may affect the negotiation of the purchase price. Corporations—especially those whose shares are not publicly traded—may purchase the shares of a retiring executive, agreeing to pay the book value of this person's stock in the company.

Some investors have traditionally compared the book value of a share of a company's stock with the stock's market value. The idea was that a stock selling below its book value was underpriced and thus was a good buy. The relationship between book value and market value is far from clear, however. Some investors believe that a company whose stock sells at a price below book value must be experiencing financial difficulty. Exhibit 13-8 contrasts the book values and ranges of market values for the common stocks of three well-known companies.

Evaluating Operations

OBJECTIVE 7
Evaluate a company's return on assets and return on shareholders' equity

Investors and creditors are constantly evaluating the ability of managers to earn profits. Investors search for companies whose stocks are likely to incease in value. Creditors are interested in profitable companies that can pay their debts. Investment and credit decisions often include a comparison of companies. But a comparison of Nortel Network Corporation's net income to the net income of a new company in

EXHIBIT 13-8

Book Value and Market Value

	Year-End Book Value	Fourth-Quarter Market-Value Range
Shaw Communications Inc.		
Class B (August 31, 2000)	$ 7.37	$29.75 – 36.30
The Molson Companies Limited,		
Class B (March 31, 2000)	17.32	23.00 – 25.00
Telus Corporation (December 31, 1999)	17.91	28.50 – 37.00

Chapter Thirteen Corporations: Capital Stock and the Balance Sheet   **729**

the electronics industry simply is not meaningful. Nortel's profits run into hundreds of millions of dollars, which likely exceed the new company's total sales. Does that automatically make Nortel a better investment? Not necessarily. To make relevant comparisons between companies different in size, scope of operations, or any other measure, investors, creditors, and managers use some standard profitability measures. Two of the most widely used are the rate of return on total assets and rate of return on shareholders' equity.

Rate of Return on Total Assets

The **rate of return on total assets**, or simply **return on assets**, measures a company's success in using its assets to earn income for those who are financing the business. Creditors have lent money to the corporation to earn interest. Shareholders have invested in the corporation's stock and expect the company to earn net income.

The sum of interest expense and net income is the return to the two groups that have financed the corporation's assets, and this is the numerator of the return on assets ratio. The denominator is average total assets. Return on assets is computed as follows, using the actual data from the 1999 annual report of Alberta Energy Company Ltd. (amounts in millions of dollars):

Alberta Energy Company Ltd.
www.aec.ca

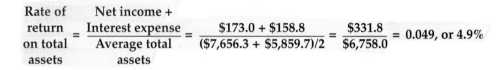

$$\frac{\text{Rate of return on total assets}} = \frac{\text{Net income + Interest expense}}{\text{Average total assets}} = \frac{\$173.0 + \$158.8}{(\$7,656.3 + \$5,859.7)/2} = \frac{\$331.8}{\$6,758.0} = 0.049, \text{ or } 4.9\%$$

WORKING IT OUT

The financial statements of Chain Energy Corp. reported:

	2003	2002
Net income	$80,000	$90,000
Interest expense	20,000	24,000
$6.00 Pfd. stock	100,000	100,000
(1,000 shares)		
Common stock	200,000	200,000
Retained earnings	180,000	160,000
Total assets	840,000	760,000

Dividends were paid to preferred shareholders in 2002 and 2003. Dividends of $54,000 were declared and paid to common shareholders in 2003. Compute for 2003 (1) the return on assets and (2) the return on common shareholders' equity.

A:

(1) 12.5%:

$$\frac{\$80,000 + \$20,000}{(\$840,000 + \$760,000)/2}$$

$$= 0.125$$

(2) 20%:

$$\frac{\$80,000 - (\$6.00 \times 1,000)}{(\$380,000 + \$360,000)/2}$$

$$= 0.20$$

Net income and interest expense are taken from the income statement and the notes. Average total assets are computed from the beginning and ending balance sheets. How is this profitability measure used in decision making? It is to compare companies. By relating the sum of net income and interest expense to average total assets, we have a standard measure that describes the profitability of all types of companies.

What is a good rate of return on total assets? There is no single answer to this question because rates of return vary widely by industry. For example, consumer products companies earn much higher returns than do utilities or grocery store chains. In most industries, a return on assets of 10 percent is considered good.

Rate of Return on Common Shareholders' Equity

Rate of return on common shareholders' equity, often called **return on equity**, shows the relationship between net income and average common shareholders' equity. The numerator is net income minus preferred dividends. This information is taken from the income statement and statement of retained earnings. Preferred dividends are subtracted because the preferred shareholders have the first claim to dividends from the company's net income. The denominator is average *common shareholders' equity*—total shareholders' equity minus preferred equity. Alberta Energy Company Ltd.'s rate of return on common shareholders' equity for 1999 is computed as follows (amounts in millions):

$$\frac{\text{Rate of return on common shareholders' equity}} = \frac{\text{Net income - Preferred dividends}}{\text{Average common shareholders' equity}} = \frac{\$173.0 - \$6.7}{(\$3,792 + \$2,578)/2} = \frac{\$166.3}{\$3,186} = 0.052 \text{ or } 5.2\%$$

Observe that the return on equity (5.2 percent) is higher than the return on assets (4.9 percent). This difference results from the interest expense component of return on assets. Companies such as Alberta Energy Company Ltd. borrow at one rate, say, 7.3 percent, and invest the funds to earn a higher rate, say, 9.3 percent. Borrowing at a lower rate than the return on investments is called *using leverage*. During good times, leverage produces high returns for shareholders. However, too much can make it difficult to pay the interest on the debt. The company's creditors are guaranteed a fixed rate of return on their loans. The shareholders, conversely, have no guarantee that the corporation will earn net income, so their investments are riskier. Consequently, shareholders demand a higher rate of return than do creditors, and this explains why return on equity should exceed return on assets. If return on assets is higher than return on equity, the company is in trouble.

Investors and creditors use return on common shareholders' equity in much the same way as they use return on total assets—to compare companies. The higher the rate of return, the more successful the company. A 12 percent return on common shareholders' equity is considered quite good in most industries. Investors also compare a company's return on shareholders' equity to interest rates available in the market. If interest rates are almost as high as return on equity, many investors will lend their money to earn interest rather than invest in common shares. They choose to forego the extra risk of investing in stock when the rate of return on equity is too low.

Accounting for Income Taxes by Corporations

Corporations pay taxes on their income in the same way that individuals do. Corporate and personal tax rates differ, however. The federal tax rate for manufacturing corporations with income in excess of $200,000 was 21% in 2000. Canadian-controlled private corporations with income of less than $200,000 and meeting certain other conditions pay taxes at a lower rate. In addition, all the provinces and the Yukon, Nunavit, and Northwest Territories levy taxes on corporations at rates ranging from 2.5 percent to 17.0 percent.

For each period, the corporation measures income tax expense and the related income tax payable. Corporate strategy is almost always directed at minimizing the income tax payable because that is the amount of cash the company must pay the government. But the main accounting issue centres on the measurement of net income. Therefore accountants strive for a reasonable measure of income tax expense. Total revenues minus total expenses, including income tax expense, produces net income.

Income Tax Expense, an expense on the income statement, is based on **pretax accounting income**, or income before income tax, from the income statement. Income Tax Payable, a liability on the balance sheet, is based on **taxable income** from the income tax return filed with Canada Customs and Revenue Agency and the provincial government. Taxable income is the basis for computing the amount of tax to *pay* the governments. Pretax accounting income and taxable income are rarely the same amount.

$$\begin{array}{c} \text{Income} \\ \text{tax} \\ \text{expense} \end{array} = \begin{array}{c} \text{Pretax} \\ \text{accounting} \\ \text{income} \\ \text{(from income} \\ \text{statement)} \end{array} \times \begin{array}{c} \text{Income} \\ \text{tax} \\ \text{rate} \end{array} \qquad \begin{array}{c} \text{Income} \\ \text{tax} \\ \text{payable} \end{array} = \begin{array}{c} \text{Taxable} \\ \text{income} \\ \text{(from tax} \\ \text{return)} \end{array} \times \begin{array}{c} \text{Income} \\ \text{tax} \\ \text{rate} \end{array}$$

The authors thank Jean Marie Hudson for suggesting this presentation.

Some revenues and expenses enter the determination of accounting income in periods different from the periods in which they enter the determination of taxable income. Over a period of many years, total pretax accounting income may equal total taxable income, but for any one year the two income amounts are likely to differ.

There are a number of reasons why pretax income might not equal taxable income. We will discuss the most common reason, which is a **temporary difference,** or **timing difference.**[3]

A temporary difference can arise when an expense is deducted on the financial statements in one year but is not deductible for tax purposes until the expense is paid. Warranty expense is an example. The matching principle requires that warranty expense be deducted from income in the same period the product or service is sold. However, Canada Customs and Revenue Agency does not allow warranty expense to be deducted from income for tax purposes until the expense is incurred and paid. For example, suppose SR Electric Products Ltd. sells a toaster oven in 2002 for $80 and the product is warrantied for one year. SR Electric Products Ltd. estimates a warranty cost of $20 and deducts that amount as an expense on its income statement when calculating *pretax accounting income* for the year ended December 31, 2002. This $20 must be added back to pretax accounting income to calculate SR Electric Products Ltd.'s *taxable income* for 2002. If we assume the company has a pretax accounting income of $100 (which reflects the $20 warranty expense) and an income tax rate of 40%:

Income tax expense	=	pretax accounting income × tax rate
	=	$100 × 0.40 = $40
Income tax payable	=	taxable income × income tax rate
	=	($100 + $20) × 0.40 = $48
Difference	=	$48 − $40 = $8

When income tax expense and income tax payable amounts are not the same in a given period, the difference is known as a future income tax asset or a future income tax liability, depending on the effect of the timing difference. Section 3465 of the *CICA Handbook* calls the $8 difference in the example above a **future income tax asset** because it represents a future benefit to SR Electric Products Ltd. The $8 difference will reverse in a future year when cash is actually paid for a repair under warranty and this warranty payment then becomes deductible for income tax purposes.

The journal entry to record SR Electric Products Ltd.'s income tax expense and income tax payable is:

2002			
Dec. 31	Future income tax asset	8	
	Income tax expense	40	
	Income tax payable		48
	To record income tax expense for 2002.		

Another common temporary difference occurs when a company uses amortization rates for accounting purposes that are different from the Canada Customs and Revenue Agency capital cost allowance rates used for income tax purposes. In this situation, the temporary difference will lead to *either* a future income tax asset or a future income tax liability. Often, the amortization expenses deducted for accounting purposes are less than the capital cost allowances allowed for income tax purposes, which leads to a **future income tax liability.** You would follow the same method as above to calculate the future income tax liability.

---

[3]*CICA Handbook,* Section 3465.

Decision	Guidelines
Dividends	
Whether to declare a cash dividend?	• Must have enough retained earnings to declare the dividend.
	• Must have enough cash to pay the dividend.
What happens with a dividend?	• The corporation's board of directors declares the dividend. The dividend then becomes a liability of the corporation.
	• The date of record fixes who will receive the dividend.
	• Payment of the dividend occurs later.
Who receives the dividend?	• Preferred shareholders first receive their dividends at a specified rate.
	• Common shareholders receive the remainder.
Stock Values	
How much to pay for a stock?	Its market value.
What value is used if the company is going out of business?	Liquidation value—the market value of net assets after liabilities and preferred shareholders are paid, divided by the number of common shares outstanding.
What is book value's role in decision making?	Sometimes used to help determine the market value of a stock that is not traded on a stock exchange.
Evaluating Operations	
How to evaluate the operations of a corporation?	Two measures that relate earnings to the amount that shareholders have invested include
	• Rate of return on assets
	• Rate of return on common shareholders' equity
	For a healthy company, return on common shareholders' equity should exceed return on assets.
Accounting for Income Tax	
What are the three main accounts?	• Income tax expense
	• Income tax payable, a current liability
	• Future income tax asset or liability, a current or long-term asset or liability
How to measure	
• Income tax expense?	Income before income tax (from the income statement) $\times$ Income tax rate
• Income tax payable?	Taxable income (from the income tax return filed with Canada Customs and Revenue Agency) $\times$ Income tax rate
• Future income tax asset or liability?	Difference between income tax expense and income tax payable for any one year

Summary Problems
for Your Review

1. Use the following accounts and related balances to prepare the classified balance sheet of Whitehall, Inc. at September 30, 2003. Use the account format of the balance sheet.

Common stock,		Inventory	$ 85,000
50,000 shares authorized,		Property, plant, and	
20,000 shares issued	$125,000	equipment, net	225,000
Dividends payable	4,000	Donated capital	18,000
Cash	9,000	Accounts receivable, net	25,000
Accounts payable	28,000	Preferred stock, $0.75,	
Retained earnings	69,000	10,000 shares authorized,	
Organization cost, net	1,000	2,000 shares issued	24,000
Long-term note payable	74,000	Accrued liabilities	3,000

2. The balance sheet of First Line Corporation reported the following at March 31, 2003, the end of its fiscal year.

Shareholders' Equity

Contributed capital:	
Preferred stock, $4.00, cumulative, 4,000 shares authorized	
and issued	$ 220,000
Common stock, 100,000 shares authorized, 50,000 shares issued	963,000
Total contributed capital	1,183,000
Contributed surplus—Donated capital	110,000
Retained earnings	660,000
Total shareholders' equity	$1,953,000

Required

a. Are the preferred shares cumulative or noncumulative? How can you tell?

b. What is the total amount of the annual preferred dividend?

c. Assume the common shares were all issued at the same time. What was the selling price per share?

d. What was the market value of the assets donated to the corporation?

e. Compute the book value per share of the preferred stock and the common stock. No prior year preferred dividends are in arrears, but First Line Corporation has not declared the current-year dividend.

Solutions to Review Problems

1.

WHITEHALL, INC.
Balance Sheet
September 30, 2003

Assets		Liabilities	
Current:		**Current:**	
Cash	$ 9,000	Accounts payable	$ 28,000
Accounts receivable, net.....................	25,000	Dividends payable	4,000
Inventory	85,000	Accrued liabilities..................................	3,000
Total current assets.........................	119,000	Total current liabilities	35,000
Capital assets, net......................................	225,000	Long-term note payable	74,000
Intangible assets:		Total liabilities...	109,000
Organization cost, net.........................	1,000	**Shareholders' Equity**	
		Contributed capital:	
		Preferred stock, $0.75,	
		10,000 shares authorized,	
		2,000 shares issued.............	$ 24,000
		Common stock,	
		50,000 shares authorized,	
		20,000 shares issued...........	125,000
		Donated capital.....................	18,000
		Total contributed capital	167,000
		Retained earnings	69,000
		Total shareholders' equity	236,000
		Total liabilities and	
Total assets..	$345,000	shareholders' equity..............	$345,000

2. Answers to First Line Corporation questions:

a. The preferred shares are cumulative as is noted in its description.
b. Total annual preferred dividend: $16,000 (4,000 × $4.00)
c. Price per share: $19.26 ($963,000/50,000 shares issued)
d. Market value of donated assets: $110,000
e. Book values per share of preferred and common stock:

Preferred

Book value..	$220,000
Cumulative dividend for current year (4,000 × $4.00).....	16,000
Shareholders' equity allocated to preferred	$236,000
Book value per share ($236,000/4,000 shares)	$ 59.00

Common

Total shareholders' equity..	$1,953,000
Less: Shareholders' equity allocated to preferred	236,000
Shareholders' equity available for common shareholders...	$1,717,000
Book value per share ($1,717,000/50,000 shares)	$ 34.34

Cyber Coach

Visit the Student Resources area of the *Accounting* Companion Website for extra practice with the new material in Chapter 13.

www.pearsoned.ca/horngren

Summary

1. **Identify the characteristics of a corporation.** A corporation is a separate legal and business entity. Continuous life, the ease of raising large amounts of capital and transferring ownership, and limited liability are among the advantages of the corporate form of organization. An important disadvantage is a degree of double taxation. Corporations pay income taxes, and shareholders pay tax on dividends. Shareholders are the owners of the corporations. They elect a board of directors, which elects a chairperson and appoints the officers to manage the business.

2. **Record the issuance of stock.** Corporations may issue different classes of stock: common and preferred.

3. **Account for the incorporation of a going business.** Close the owner's equity accounts of a proprietorship or partnership, and open the shareholders' equity accounts of the corporation.

4. **Prepare the shareholders' equity section of a corporation's balance sheet.** The balance sheet carries the capital raised through stock issuance under the heading Contributed Capital in the shareholders' equity section. Donated assets, such as land, are reported under the heading Contributed Surplus—Donated Capital. Retained Earnings are listed last.

5. **Account for cash dividends.** Only when the board of directors declares a dividend does the corporation incur the liability to pay dividends. Preferred stock has priority over common stock as to dividends, which are stated as a dollar amount per share. In addition, preferred stock has a claim to dividends in arrears if it is cumulative. Convertible preferred stock may be exchanged for the corporation's common stock.

6. **Use different stock values in decision making.** A stock's *market value* is the price for which a share may be bought or sold. *Liquidation value* and *book value*—the amount of shareholders' equity per share of company stock—are other values that may apply to stock.

7. **Evaluate a company's return on assets and return on shareholders' equity.** *Return on assets* and *return on shareholders' equity* are two standard measures of profitability. A healthy company's return on equity will exceed its return on assets.

8. **Account for a corporation's income tax.** Corporations pay income tax and must account for the income tax expense and income tax payable. A difference between the expense and the payable creates other accounts, Future Income Tax Assets or Future Income Tax Liabilities.

Self-Study Questions

Test your understanding of the chapter by marking the best answer for each of the following questions:

1. Which of the following is a *disadvantage* of the corporate form of business organization? (*pp. 709–710*)
   a. Limited liability of shareholders
   b. Double taxation
   c. No mutual agency
   d. Transferability of ownership

2. The person with the most power in a corporation is the (*p. 710*)
   a. Accountant   c. President
   b. Chairperson of   d. Vice-president
      the board

3. The dollar amount of the shareholder investments in a corporation is called (*p. 711*)
   a. Outstanding stock   c. Contributed capital
   b. Total shareholders' d. Retained earnings
      equity

4. The arbitrary value assigned to a share of stock by the board of directors is called (*p. 716*)
   a. Market value   c. Book value
   b. Liquidation value   d. Stated value

5. Stock issued by a corporation incorporated under the Canada Business Corporations Act normally has (*p. 716*)
   a. No par value
   b. A par value set by management

   c. A par value set by the government
   d. A par value of $10.00

6. Mangum Corporation receives a building for 1,000 shares of common stock. The building's book value is $385,000 and its current market value is $640,000. This transaction increases Mangum's capital stock by (*p. 718*)
   a. $0 because the corporation received no cash
   b. $100,000
   c. $385,000
   d. $640,000

7. Organization cost is classified as a (an) (*p. 721*)
   a. Operating expense
   b. Current asset
   c. Contra item in shareholders' equity
   d. None of the above

8. Trade Days, Inc. has 10,000 shares of $3.50 cumulative preferred stock, and 100,000 of common stock issued and outstanding. Two years' preferred dividends are in arrears. Trade Days, Inc. declares a cash dividend large enough to pay the preferred dividends in arrears, the preferred dividend for the current period, and a $1.50 dividend per common share. What is the total amount of the dividend? (*p. 726*)
   a. $255,000   c. $150,000
   b. $220,000   d. $105,000

9. The preferred stock of Trade Days, Inc. in the

preceding question was issued at $55 per share. Each preferred share can be converted into 10 common shares. The entry to record the conversion of this preferred stock into common is (*p. 727*)

a. Cash   550,000

       Preferred Stock   500,000

       Common Stock   50,000

b. Preferred Stock   500,000

   Cash   50,000

       Common Stock   550,000

c. Preferred Stock   550,000

       Common Stock   550,000

d. Common Stock   550,000

       Preferred Stock   550,000

10. When an investor is buying stock as an investment, the value of most direct concern is (*p. 728*)

a. Par value   c. Liquidation value

b. Market value   d. Book value

Answers to the Self-Study Questions follow the Similar Accounting Terms.

Accounting Vocabulary

Articles of incorporation (*p. 709*)
Authorization of stock (*p. 710*)
Board of directors (*p. 710*)
Book value (*p. 728*)
Bylaws (*p. 710*)
Chairperson (of board) (*p. 710*)
Common stock (*p. 712*)
Contributed capital (*p. 711*)
Convertible preferred stock (*p. 727*)
Cumulative preferred stock (*p. 726*)
Deficit (*p. 713*)
Dividends (*p. 713*)
Donated capital (*p. 719*)
Double taxation (*p. 709*)
Future income tax asset (*p. 732*)
Future income tax liability (*p. 732*)
Limited liability (*p. 709*)
Market value (*p. 728*)

No-par-value shares (*p. 716*)
Organization cost (*p. 721*)
Outstanding stock (*p. 711*)
Preferred shares (*p. 714*)
President (*p. 710*)
Pretax accounting income (*p. 731*)
Rate of return on common shareholders' equity (*p. 730*)
Rate of return on total assets (*p. 730*)
Retained earnings (*p. 712*)
Return on assets (*p. 730*)
Return on equity (*p. 730*)
Shareholder (*p. 709*)
Shareholders' equity (*p. 711*)
Stated value (*p. 716*)
Stock (*p. 709*)
Taxable income (*p. 731*)
Temporary difference (*p. 732*)
Timing difference (*p. 732*)

Similar Accounting Terms

Capital stock   Share capital
Donated capital   Contributed surplus
Shareholder   Stockholder
Stated capital   Capital stock
Temporary difference   Timing difference

Answers to Self-Study Questions
1. b
2. b
3. c
4. d
5. a
6. d
7. d   Intangible asset
8. a   [(10,000 × $3.50 × 3 = $105,000) + (100,000 × $1.50 = $150,000) = $255,000]
9. c
10. b

Assignment Material

Questions

1. Identify the characteristics of a corporation.

2. Explain why owners of shares in corporations face a tax disadvantage.

3. Briefly outline the steps in the organization of a corporation.

4. How are the structures of a partnership and a corporation similar and how are they different?

5. Name the four rights of a shareholder. Are preferred shares automatically nonvoting? Explain how a right may be withheld from a shareholder.

6. Which event increases the assets of the corporation: authorization of shares or issuance of shares? Explain.

7. Suppose Watgold Ltd. issued 1,000 shares of its $6.65 preferred shares for $120 per share. How much would this transaction increase the company's capital stock? How much would it increase retained earnings? How much would it increase annual cash dividend payments?

8. Woodstock Ltd. issued 100 shares of common stock for $15.00 per share and 200 shares for $16.00 per share. What would be the journal entry to record the combined issue?

9. How does issuance of 1,000 shares of common stock for land and a building, together worth $150,000, affect capital stock?

10. Give an example of a transaction that creates donated capital for a corporation.

11. Journalize the incorporation of the Barnes & Connally partnership.

12. Rank the following accounts in the order they would appear on the balance sheet: Common Stock, Organization Cost, Contributed Surplus—Donated Capital, Preferred Stock, Retained Earnings, Dividends Payable. Also, give each account's balance sheet classification.

13. What type of account is Organization Cost? Briefly describe how to account for organization cost.

14. Briefly discuss the three important dates for a dividend.

15. Mancini Inc. has 3,000 shares of its $2.50 preferred stock outstanding. Dividends for 2002 and 2003 are in arrears, and the company has declared no dividends on preferred stock for the current year, 2004. Assume that Mancini Inc. declares total dividends of $35,000 at the end of 2004. Show how to allocate the dividends to preferred and common (a) if preferred is cumulative, and (b) if preferred is noncumulative.

16. As a preferred shareholder, would you rather own cumulative or noncumulative preferred? If all other factors are the same, would the corporation rather the preferred stock be cumulative or noncumulative? Give your reason.

17. How are cumulative preferred dividends in arrears reported in the financial statements? When do dividends become a liability of the corporation?

18. Distinguish between the market value of stock and the book value of stock. Which is more important to investors?

19. How is book value per share of common stock computed when the company has both preferred stock and common stock outstanding?

20. Why should a healthy company's rate of return on shareholders' equity exceed its rate of return on total assets?

21. Explain the difference between the income tax expense and income tax payable of a corporation.

Exercises

Exercise 13-1 *Characteristics of a corporation* *(Obj. 1)*

Suppose you are forming a business and you need some outside money from other investors. Assume you have decided to organize the business as a corporation that will issue stock to raise the needed funds. Briefly discuss your most important reason for organizing as a corporation rather than as a partnership. If you had decided to organize as a partnership, what would be your most important reason for not organizing as a corporation?

Exercise 13-2 *Organizing a corporation* *(Obj. 1)*

Kristen Smith and Anita Samuels are opening a limousine service to be named S&S Limo Ltd. They need outside capital, so they plan to organize the business as a corporation. Because your office is in the same building, they come to you for advice. Write a memorandum informing them of the steps in forming a corporation. Identify specific documents used in this process, and name the different parties involved in the ownership and management of a corporation.

Exercise 13-3 *Issuing stock* *(Obj. 2)*

Centurion Technologies Inc. made the following stock issuance transactions:

June	19	Issued 2,000 shares of common stock for cash of $12.00 per share.
July	3	Sold 500 shares of $2.00 Class A preferred stock for $10,000 cash.
	11	Received inventory valued at $46,000 and equipment with market value of $20,000 for 3,300 shares of common stock.
	15	Issued 1,000 shares of $3.00 Class B preferred stock with a stated value of $30 per share.

Required

1. Journalize the transactions. Explanations are not required.
2. How much contributed capital did these transactions generate for Centurion Technologies Inc.?

Exercise 13-4 *Issuing stock and preparing the shareholders' equity section of the balance sheet* *(Obj. 2, 4)*

The articles of incorporation for IMI International Inc. authorizes the company to issue 500,000 shares of $3 preferred stock and 1,000,000 shares of common stock. During its start-up phase, IMI International Inc. completed the following transactions:

2003
July	3	Issued 1,000 shares of common stock to the promoters who organized the corporation, receiving cash of $20,000.
	12	Issued 300 shares of preferred stock for cash of $15,000.
	14	Issued 2,000 shares of common stock in exchange for land valued at $42,000.
	31	Earned a small profit for the fiscal year and closed the $8,000 net income into Retained Earnings.

Required

1. Record the transactions in the general journal.
2. Prepare the shareholders' equity section of the IMI International Inc. balance sheet at July 31, 2003.

Exercise 13-5 *Recording issuance of stock* *(Obj. 2)*

The balance sheet of BCE Inc. at December 31, 1999, reported the adapted shareholders' equity section shown below. BCE Inc. has six classes of preferred stock labelled as First Preferred Series P, Q, S, U, W, and Y.

Shareholders' Equity	
First preferred share, authorized an unlimited number of shares	
Outstanding	
Series P shares	$400,000,000
Series Q shares	200,000,000
Series S shares	200,000,000
Series U shares	350,000,000
Series W shares	300,000,000
Series Y shares	250,000,000
Common shares, authorized an unlimited number of shares	
Outstanding	
640,804,984 shares	$6,559,000,000

The preferred shares were issued for $25.00 per share. Series U, W, and Y were issued in 1997.

Required

1. What was the average price at which the common shares were issued?
2. Make a summary journal entry to record the issue of the preferred shares in 1997. Explanations are not required.

Exercise 13-6 *Recording issuance of common stock* *(Obj. 2)*

Creo Products Inc., located in Burnaby, B.C., imports sports equipment. The corporation issues 10,000 shares of common stock for $10 per share. Record issuance of the stock.

Exercise 13-7 *Issuing stock to finance the purchase of assets* *(Obj. 2)*

This exercise shows the similarity and the difference between two ways to acquire capital assets.

Case A—Issue stock and buy the assets in separate transactions:

High River Technologies Inc. issued 10,000 shares of its common stock for cash of $1,000,000. In a separate transaction, High River then used the cash to purchase an office building for $700,000 and equipment for $300,000. Journalize the two transactions.

Case B—Issue stock to acquire the assets:

High River Technologies Inc. issued 10,000 shares of its common stock to acquire an office building valued at $700,000 and equipment worth $300,000. Journalize this transaction.

Compare the balances in all accounts after making both sets of entries. Are the account balances similar or different?

Exercise 13-8 *Capital stock for a corporation* *(Obj. 2)*

FPI Corp. has recently organized. The company issued common shares to a lawyer who provided legal services of $10,000 to help organize the corporation. It issued common shares to another person in exchange for his patent with a market value of $50,000. In addition, FPI Corp. received cash both for 3,000 shares of its $2.00 preferred stock at $30 per share and for 26,000 shares of its common stock at $20 per share. The city of Oshawa donated 50 hectares of land to the company as a plant site. The market value of the land was $500,000. Without making journal entries, determine the total contributed capital created by these transactions.

Exercise 13-9 *Incorporating a partnership* *(Obj. 3)*

The Moose Jaw Warriors are a semiprofessional baseball team that has been operated as a partnership by Linda Arnold and Martin Gerson. In addition to their management responsibilities, Gerson also plays third base and Arnold operates the concession. Journalize the following transactions in the first month of operation as a corporation:

April 14 The incorporators paid legal fees of $1,000 and other fees of $500 to obtain articles of incorporation.

14 Issued 2,500 shares of common stock to Arnold and 1,500 shares to Gerson. Arnold's capital balance on the partnership books was $25,000, and Gerson's capital balance was $15,000.

18 The city of Moose Jaw donated 20 hectares of land to the corporation for a stadium site. The land's market value was $80,000.

Exercise 13-10 *Shareholders' equity section of a balance sheet* **(Obj. 4)**

The articles of incorporation for ACD Systems Inc. authorizes the issuance of 100,000 shares of Class A preferred stock, 50,000 shares of Class B preferred stock, and 100,000 shares of common stock. During a two-month period, ACD Systems Inc. completed these stock-issuance transactions:

Jan. 23 Issued 10,000 shares of common stock for cash of $15.00 per share.
Feb.   2 Sold 1,000 shares of $2.00 Class A preferred stock for $20,000 cash.
      12 Received inventory valued at $50,000 and equipment with market value of $27,000 for 3,500 shares of common stock.
      17 Issued 1,000 shares of $2.50 Class B preferred stock. The issue price was cash of $40 per share.

Required

1. Journalize the transactions, with explanations.
2. Prepare the shareholders' equity section of the ACD Systems Inc. balance sheet for the transactions given in this exercise. Retained Earnings has a balance of $50,000.

Exercise 13-11 *Shareholders' equity section of a balance sheet* **(Obj. 4)**

Comstate Corporation has the following selected account balances at June 30, 2003. Prepare the shareholders' equity section of the company's balance sheet.

Common stock,		Inventory	$125,000
500,000 shares authorized,		Machinery and equipment........	130,000
150,000 shares issued......................	$150,000	Preferred stock, $1.00,	
Donated capital....................................	100,000	100,000 shares authorized,	
Accumulated amortization—		10,000 shares issued	120,000
machinery and equipment............	65,000	Organization cost, net................	3,000
Retained earnings................................	130,000	Cost of goods sold..................	81,000

Exercise 13-12 *Dividing cash dividends between preferred and common stock* **(Obj. 5)**

Refer to the shareholders' equity of Envoy Corporation in Exhibit 13–7, page 722. Answer these questions about Envoy 's dividends.

1. How much in dividends must Envoy Corporation declare each year before the common shareholders receive cash dividends for the year?
2. Suppose Envoy Corporation declares cash dividends of $10,000 for 2003. How much of the dividends go to preferred shareholders? How much goes to common shareholders?
3. Is Envoy Corporation's preferred stock cumulative or noncumulative? How can you tell?
4. Suppose Envoy Corporation did not pay the preferred dividend in 2003 and 2004. In 2005, Envoy declares cash dividends of $10,000. How much of the dividends go to preferred? How much goes to common?

Exercise 13-13 *Computing dividends on preferred and common stock* **(Obj. 5)**

The following elements of shareholders' equity are adapted from the balance sheet of Glentel Communications Inc. All dollar amounts, except the dividends per share, are given in thousands.

Shareholders' Equity

Preferred stock, cumulative (note 7)
Series A, 100,000 shares authorized, 60,000 shares issued	$ 30
Series B, 750,000 shares authorized, 400,000 shares issued	400
Common stock, 2,000,000 shares authorized, 200,000 shares issued.......	2,000

Note 7: Preferred stock:

**Designated Annual
Cash Dividend Per Share**

Series A	$0.08
Series B	0.10

The Series A preferred has preference over Series B preferred, and the company has paid all dividends through 2001.

Required

Compute the dividends to both series of preferred and to common shareholders for 2002 and 2003 if total dividends are $15,000 in 2002 and $200,000 in 2003. Round to the nearest dollar.

Exercise 13-14   *Book value per share of preferred and common stock*   *(Obj. 6)*

The balance sheet of UTS Energy Ltd. reported the following:

Cumulative preferred stock; 100 shares issued, liquidation value $7,200	$ 6,000
Common stock; 10,000 shares issued	200,000

Assume that UTS has paid preferred dividends for the current year and all prior years (no dividends in arrears). Retained earnings was $150,000. Compute the book value per share of the preferred stock and the common stock.

Exercise 13-15   *Book value per share of preferred and common stock; preferred dividends in arrears*   *(Obj. 5, 6)*

Refer to Exercise 13-14. Compute the book value per share of the preferred stock and the common stock, assuming that three years' preferred dividends (including dividends for the current year) are in arrears. Assume the preferred stock is cumulative and its dividend rate is $3.00 per share.

Exercise 13-16   *Evaluating profitability*   *(Obj. 7)*

Tempo Services, Inc. reported these figures for 2003 and 2002:

	2003	2002
Income statement:		
Interest expense..	$ 34,800,000	$ 24,200,000
Net income...	24,000,000	37,400,000
Balance sheet:		
Total assets	702,000,000	634,000,000
Preferred stock, $1.30, 200,000		
shares issued and outstanding..............................	5,000,000	5,000,000
Common shareholders' equity...................................	328,000,000	302,000,000
Total shareholders' equity..	333,000,000	307,000,000

Compute rate of return on total assets and rate of return on common shareholders' equity for 2003. Do these rates of return suggest strength or weakness? Give your reason.

Exercise 13-17 *Accounting for income tax by a corporation* *(Obj. 8)*

DSI Datatech Inc. is taxed at the rate of 30 percent. Income before taxes was $200,000 for 2002. The company had neither future income tax assets nor liabilities at January 1, 2002. The following two situations are independent:

A. DSI Datatech Inc. claimed $20,000 for warranty expense in 2002 in arriving at $200,000 income before taxes. The $20,000 was actually incurred in 2003.

B. DSI Datatech Inc. purchased capital assets for $60,000 in 2002. The company claimed amortization of $6,000 in arriving at $200,000 income in 2002. Maximum capital cost allowance was $10,000 in 2002.

Required

For each of the two situations:

1. Decide if DSI Datatech Inc. has a future income tax asset or a future income tax liability.
2. Calculate the future income tax asset or liability at December 31, 2002.
3. Show the journal entries DSI Datatech Inc. would make with respect to income taxes for 2002.

Challenge Exercise

Exercise 13-18 *Accounting for shareholders' equity transactions* *(Obj. 2, 5)*

Fairfax Stores Inc. reported these comparative shareholders' equity data:

	December 31,	
	2003	2002
Common stock	$ 430,000	$168,000
Retained earnings	1,250,000	967,000

During 2003, Fairfax Stores Inc. completed these transactions and events:

a. Net income, $683,000.

b. Cash dividends, $400,000.

c. Issuance of common shares for cash, 1,000 shares at $22 per share.

d. Issuance of common shares to purchase other companies (Fairfax debited the Investments account), 10,000 shares at $24 per share.

Required

Without making journal entries, show how Fairfax Stores Inc.'s 2003 transactions and events accounted for the changes in the shareholders' equity accounts. For each shareholders' equity account, start with the December 31, 2002, balance and work toward the balance at December 31, 2003.

Beyond the Numbers

Beyond the Numbers 13-1 *Characteristics of corporations' capital stock* *(Obj. 2, 6)*

Answering the following questions will enhance your understanding of the capital stock of corporations.

1. Why do you think contributed capital and retained earnings are shown separately in the shareholders' equity section?
2. Lynn Liu, major shareholder of L-S, Inc., proposes to sell some land she owns to the company for common shares in L-S, Inc. What problem does L-S, Inc. face in recording the transaction?
3. Preferred shares generally are preferred with respect to dividends and on liquidation. Why would investors buy common shares when preferred shares are available?

4. What does it mean if the liquidation value of a company's preferred shares are greater than their market value?

5. If you owned 100 shares of stock in Cara Corporation and someone offered to buy the stock for its book value, would you accept the offer? Why or why not?

Ethical Issue

Note: This case is based on a real situation.

George Campbell paid $50,000 for a franchise that entitled him to market Success Associates software programs in the countries of the European Union. Campbell intended to sell individual franchises for the major language groups of western Europe—German, French, English, Spanish, and Italian. Naturally, investors considering buying a franchise from Campbell asked to see the financial statements of his business.

Believing the value of the franchise to be greater than $50,000, Campbell sought to capitalize his own franchise at $500,000. The law firm of McDonald and LaDue helped Campbell form a corporation authorized to issue 500,000 common shares. Lawyers suggested the following chain of transactions:

1. A third party borrows $500,000 and purchases the franchise from Campbell.

2. Campbell pays the corporation $500,000 to acquire all its stock.

3. The corporation buys the franchise from the third party, who repays the loan.

In the final analysis, the third party is debt-free and out of the picture. Campbell owns all the corporation's stock, and the corporation owns the franchise. The corporation balance sheet lists a franchise acquired at a cost of $500,000. This balance sheet is Campbell's most valuable marketing tool.

Required

1. What is unethical about this situation?

2. Who can be harmed? How can they be harmed? What role does accounting play?

Problems (Group A)

Problem 13-1A *Organizing a corporation* *(Obj. 1)*

Al Raffan and Elaine Morishita are opening a restaurant in a growing section of Vernon, B.C. There are no competing family restaurants in the immediate vicinity. Their most fundamental decision is how to organize the business. Raffan thinks the partnership form is best. Morishita favours the corporate form of organization. They seek your advice.

Required

Write a memo to Raffan and Morishita to make them aware of the advantages and the disadvantages of organizing the business as a corporation. Use the following format for your memo:

Date:	_____
To:	Al Raffan and Elaine Morishita
From:	Student Name
Subject:	Advantages and disadvantages of the corporate form of business organization

Problem 13-2A *Journalizing corporation transactions and preparing the shareholders' equity section of the balance sheet*   **(Obj. 2, 3, 4)**

The partnership of Ed Lee and Sarah Starr needed additional capital to expand into new markets, so the business incorporated as Winpak Technologies Inc. The articles of incorporation under the *Canada Business Corporations Act* authorize Winpak Technologies Inc. to issue 200,000 shares of $3.00 preferred stock and 1,000,000 shares of common stock. In its first month, Winpak Technologies Inc. completed the following transactions:

2002

July   2   Paid incorporation fees of $1,000 and paid legal fees of $6,000 to orga-
              nize as a corporation.
       2   Issued 10,000 shares of common stock to Lee and 15,000 shares to Starr
              in return for the net assets of the partnership. Lee's capital balance on
              the partnership books was $60,000, and Starr's capital balance was
              $80,000.
       8   Received a small parcel of land valued at $100,000 as a donation from
              the municipality in which the company is located.
      10   Issued 500 shares of preferred stock to acquire a computer system with
              a market value of $25,000.
      16   Issued 12,000 shares of common stock for cash of $72,000.

Required

1. Record the transactions in the general journal.
2. Prepare the shareholders' equity section of the Winpak Technologies Inc. balance sheet at December 31, 2002. The ending balance in Retained Earnings is $40,000.

Problem 13-3A *Issuing stock and preparing the shareholders' equity section of the balance sheet*   **(Obj. 2, 4)**

Patheon Inc. was organized in 2003. At December 31, 2003, Patheon Inc.'s balance sheet reported the following shareholders' equity:

Preferred stock, $4.50, 100,000 shares authorized, none issued	$ —
Common stock, 1,000,000 shares authorized, 100,000 shares issued	200,000
Retained earnings (Deficit)	(50,000)
Total shareholders' equity	$150,000

Required

Answer the following questions, making journal entries as needed.

1. What does the $4.50 mean for the preferred shares? After Patheon Inc. issues preferred shares, how much in cash dividends will Patheon Inc. expect to pay on 1,000 shares?
2. At what price per share did Patheon Inc. issue the common shares during 2003?
3. Were first-year operations profitable? Give your reason.
4. During 2004, the company completed the following selected transactions:
   a. Issued for cash 1,000 shares of preferred stock at $50 per share.
   b. Issued for cash 2,000 shares of common stock at a price of $2.50 per share.
   c. Issued 50,000 shares of common stock to acquire a building valued at $150,000.
   d. Net income for the year was $100,000, and the company declared no divi-
       dends. Make the closing entry for net income.
   Journalize each transaction. Explanations are not required.
5. Prepare the shareholders' equity section of the Patheon Inc. balance sheet at December 31, 2004.

Problem 13-4A *Shareholders' equity section of the balance sheet* *(Obj. 4)*

The following summaries for Magellan Fotographic Inc. and Teksystems Inc. provide the information needed to prepare the shareholders' equity section of the company balance sheet. The two companies are independent.

Magellan Fotographic Inc. Magellan Fotographic Inc. is authorized to issue 100,000 shares of common stock. All the shares were issued at $10 per share. The company incurred net losses of $100,000 in 2000 (its first year of operations) and $25,000 in 2001. It earned net incomes of $70,000 in 2002 and $75,000 in 2003. The company declared no dividends during the four-year period.

Teksystems Inc. Teksystems Inc.'s articles of incorporation authorize the company to issue 100,000 shares of cumulative preferred stock and 1,000,000 shares of common stock. Teksystems Inc. issued 1,000 shares of the preferred stock at $20 per share. It issued 100,000 shares of the common stock for $500,000. The company's retained earnings balance at the beginning of 2003 was $100,000. Net income for 2003 was $60,000, and the company declared the specified preferred share dividend for 2003. Preferred share dividends for 2002 were in arrears. The preferred dividend was $3.00 per share per year.

Required

For each company, prepare the shareholders' equity section of its balance sheet at December 31, 2003. Show the computation of all amounts. Entries are not required.

Problem 13-5A *Analyzing the shareholders' equity of an actual corporation* *(Obj. 4, 5)*

The purpose of this problem is to familiarize you with financial statement information. Inco Limited is one of the world's leading producers of nickel and an important producer of copper, precious metals, and cobalt. Inco Limited reported the following information in its December 31, 1999 annual report:

Shareholders' Equity (adapted) (amounts in millions)	
Preferred shares, $2.75 cumulative, convertible, redeemable Preferred Series E	
Issued 9,427,261 shares..	$ 471
Class VBN shares	
Issued 25,892,469 shares (Note)..	753
Common shares	
Issued 181,569,141 shares	2,747
Retained earnings	637
	$4,608

(Note: The company issued a special class of [common] shares in connection with its purchase of Voisey's Bay Nickel Company Limited.)

Required

1. Identify the different issues of stock Inco Limited has outstanding.

2. Are the VBN shares redeemable? How can you tell?

3. Suppose Inco Limited did not pay its preferred dividends for one year. Would the company have to pay these dividends in arrears before paying dividends to the common shareholders? Give your reason.

4. What amount of preferred dividends must Inco Limited declare and pay each year to avoid having preferred dividends in arrears?

5. Assume preferred dividends are in arrears for 1999.
   a. Write note 6 of the December 31, 1999, financial statements to disclose the dividends in arrears.

b. Journalize the declaration of a $250 million dividend for 2000. An explanation is not required.

Problem 13-6A *Preparing a corporation balance sheet; measuring profitability (Obj. 4, 7)*

Link Back to Chapter 1 (Accounting Equation). The following accounts and related balances of Viking Supplies Inc. are arranged in no particular order.

Accounts payable	$ 62,000	Accrued liabilities	$ 34,000
Retained earnings	?	Long-term note payable	208,000
Common stock,		Accounts receivable, net	204,000
100,000 shares		Preferred stock, $0.40	
authorized, 22,000		25,000 shares authorized,	
shares issued	220,000	7,400 shares issued	74,000
Dividends payable	6,000	Cash	64,000
Total assets, Nov. 30, 2002	1,162,000	Inventory	362,000
Net income	72,400	Property, plant, and	
Common shareholders'		equipment, net	556,000
equity, Nov. 30, 2002	1,046,000	Prepaid expenses	26,000
Interest expense	25,600	Patent, net	74,000

Required

1. Prepare the company's classified balance sheet in the report format at November 30, 2003.
2. Compute rate of return on total assets and rate of return on common shareholders' equity for the year ended November 30, 2003.
3. Do these rates of return suggest strength or weakness? Give your reason.

Problem 13-7A *Computing dividends on preferred and common stock (Obj. 5)*

Highpoint Corporation has 10,000 shares of $1.00 preferred stock and 200,000 shares of common stock outstanding. During a three-year period, Highpoint Corporation declared and paid cash dividends as follows: 2001, $2,000; 2002, $19,000; and 2003, $40,000.

Required

1. Compute the total dividends to preferred stock and common stock for each of the three years if
   a. Preferred is noncumulative.
   b. Preferred is cumulative.
2. For requirement 1b, record the declaration of the 2003 dividends on December 22, 2003 and the payment of the dividends on January 14, 2004.

Problem 13-8A *Analyzing the shareholders' equity of a corporation (Obj. 5, 6)*

The balance sheet of Silverstone Manufacturing Inc. reported the following:

Shareholders' Equity	($ thousands)
Cumulative convertible preferred stock; authorized 20,000 shares	$ 50
Common stock, authorized 40,000 shares; issued 20,000 shares	240
Deficit	(90)
Total shareholders' equity	$200

Notes to the financial statements indicate that 10,000 shares of $0.25 preferred stock were issued and outstanding. The preferred stock has a liquidation value of $8.00 per share, and preferred dividends are in arrears for two years, including the current year. On the balance sheet date, the market value of the Silverstone Manufacturing Inc. common stock was $7.90 per share.

Required

1. Are the preferred shares cumulative or noncumulative? How can you tell?
2. What is the amount of the annual preferred dividend?
3. What is the total contributed capital of the company?
4. What is the total market value of the common shares?
5. Compute the book value per share of the preferred stock and the common stock.

Problem 13-9A   *Computing and recording a corporation's income tax   (Obj. 8)*

The accounting (not the income tax) records of GSO Solutions Inc. provide the income statement for 2003:

	2003
Total revenue	$1,000,000
Expenses:	
Cost of goods sold	$ 470,000
Operating expenses	330,000
Total expenses before tax	800,000
Pretax accounting income	$ 200,000

The company has unearned revenue of $25,000 at the end of 2003. For tax purposes, revenue that is collected in advance is included in the taxable income of the year when the cash is received. In calculating taxable income on the tax return, this revenue belongs in 2003.

GSO Solutions Inc. calculates amortization of capital assets for accounting purposes at the maximum rate allowed by the Income Tax Act. Therefore, amortization and capital cost allowance for 2003 was $80,000.

Required

(Assume a corporate income tax rate of 40 percent.)

1. Compute taxable income for 2003.
2. Journalize the corporation's income taxes for 2003.
3. Prepare the corporation's single-step income statement for 2003.

Problem 13-10A   *Accounting for the incorporation of an ongoing business; recording the issuance of stock; allocating cash dividends; preparing the shareholders' equity section of the balance sheet   (Obj. 2, 3, 4, 5)*

Craig Jones and Tom Suto are partners in a small tools business with capital account balances of $100,000 and $160,000 respectively. They are considering incorporating and taking advantage of an offer from the Region of Waterloo to establish a new manufacturing plant. The following transactions then took place:

2002

Jan. 2 Jones and Suto incorporated their partnership into JS Technologies Inc. with an authorization to issue 100,000, $1 convertible preferred shares and 500,000 common shares. Jones received 100,000 common shares and Suto received 160,000 common shares.

9 The Region of Waterloo donated land to the new corporation in exchange for establishing the business in that area. The land had cost the Region $60,000 when purchased 10 years ago, but has a market value today of $160,000.

15 Paid $6,000 and gave 2,000 common shares to the corporation's legal firm for incorporating the business. The total legal fee was $10,000.

Mar. 7 Sold 12,000 preferred shares for $48,000. The preferred shares are convertible on the basis of 4 common shares for each preferred share.

Dec. 31 The company reported net income after taxes of $110,000 for the year, and then closed the income summary account.

2003

Feb. 14   Declared cash dividends of $24,000, payable on April 10, 2003, to the shareholders of record on March 1, 2003. Indicate the amount that would be payable to the preferred and to the common shareholders.

Apr. 10   Paid the cash dividend declared on February 14, 2003.

Sept. 7   The preferred shareholders converted 2,000 preferred shares into common.

Dec. 31   The company reported net income after taxes of $142,000 for the year, and then closed the income summary account.

2004

Feb. 16   Declared cash dividends of $48,000, payable on April 10, 2004, to the shareholders of record on March 13, 2004. Indicate the amount that would be payable to the preferred and to the common shareholders.

Required

1. Record the transactions in the general journal.
2. Prepare the shareholders' equity section of the balance sheet as of the close of business on February 16, 2004.

Problem 13-11A   *Recording the issuance of stock; allocating cash dividends; accounting for corporate income taxes; preparing the liability and shareholders' equity sections of the balance sheet*   **(Obj. 2, 4, 5, 8)**

At January 1, 2002, Crispin Manufacturing Ltd.'s balance sheet reported the following shareholders' equity:

Shareholders' Equity	
Contributed capital:	
Preferred stock, $3, cumulative (2 years in arrears),	
liquidation price of $52.50, 100,000 shares authorized,	
10,000 shares issued..	$ 500,000
Common stock:	
Class A, 50,000 shares authorized and issued	500,000
Class B, unlimited number of shares authorized,	
100,000 shares issued..	2,400,000
Total contributed capital	3,400,000
Contributed surplus—Donated capital	100,000
Retained earnings...	500,000
Total shareholders' equity..	$4,000,000

The company had the following transactions on the dates indicated:

2002

Dec. 1   The company declared dividends of $165,000, payable on January 15, 2003, to the shareholders of record on December 31, 2002. Indicate the amount that would be payable to the preferred shareholders and to the common shareholders. Class A and Class B shares receive the same per-share dividend.

     31   The company reported pretax accounting income of $150,000 and taxable income of $100,000 (income tax rate = 40%). Record the income taxes and close the income summary account.

2003

Jan. 7   The company sold 5,000 shares of preferred stock at $45 per share.

     15   Paid the dividend declared on December 1, 2002.

Feb. 14   The company sold 10,000 shares of Class B common stock at $20 per share.

Apr. 17   The company paid the income taxes payable from 2002.

Dec. 2   The company declared dividends of $160,000, payable on January 15, 2004, to the shareholders of record on December 31, 2003. Indicate the amount that would be payable to the preferred shareholders and to the common shareholders.

     31   The company reported pretax accounting income of $320,000 and taxable income of $280,000 (income tax rate = 40%). Record the income taxes and close the income summary account.

2004

Jan. 15 Paid the dividend declared on December 2, 2003.

Required

1. Record the transactions in the general journal.

2. Prepare the liability and shareholders' equity sections of the balance sheet as of the close of business on December 31, 2003.

3. Calculate the book value per share of the preferred stock and of the common stock (Class A and Class B combined) on December 31, 2003.

4. What was the average price at which the Class A common shares were sold?

Problems (Group B)

Problem 13-1B *Organizing a corporation*   *(Obj. 1)*

Jim Kirkham and Jane Gustafson are opening an office supply store in a shopping centre in Moncton. The area is growing, and no competitors are located in the immediate vicinity. Their most fundamental decision is how to organize the business. Kirkham thinks the partnership form is best. Gustafson favours the corporate form of organization. They seek your advice.

Required

Write a memo to Kirkham and Gustafson to make them aware of the advantages and disadvantages of organizing the business as a corporation. Use the following format for your memo:

Date:	_____
To:	Jim Kirkham and Jane Gustafson
From:	Student Name
Subject:	Advantages and disadvantages of the corporate form of business organization

Problem 13-2B *Journalizing corporation transactions and preparing the shareholders' equity section of the balance sheet*   *(Obj. 2, 3, 4)*

The partners who own Mason & Reeves wished to avoid the unlimited personal liability of the partnership form of business, so they incorporated the partnership as Computer Solutions Ltd. The articles of incorporation from the federal government authorizes the corporation to issue 100,000 shares of $6.00 preferred stock and 250,000 shares of common stock. In its first month, Computer Solutions Ltd. completed the following transactions:

2003

Jan. 2 Paid incorporation costs of $3,000 and legal fees of $4,000 to organize as a corporation.

3 Issued 10,200 shares of common stock to M. Mason and 7,600 shares to R. Reeves in return for the net assets of the partnership. Mason's capital balance on the partnership books was $102,000, and Reeves' capital balance was $76,000.

12 Issued 100 shares of preferred stock to acquire software with a market value of $12,000.

22 Issued 3,000 shares of common stock for $12 cash per share.

Required

1. Record the transactions in the general journal.

2. Prepare the shareholders' equity section of the Computer Solutions Ltd. balance sheet at December 31, 2003. The ending Retained Earnings balance is $50,000.

Problem 13-3B *Issuing stock and preparing the shareholders' equity section of the balance sheet* **(Obj. 2, 4)**

Mill City Corporation was organized in 2002. At December 31, 2002, Mill City Corporation's balance sheet reported the following shareholders' equity:

Preferred stock, $0.40, 50,000 shares authorized, none issued	$ —
Common stock, 100,000 shares authorized, 10,000 shares issued	100,000
Retained earnings (Deficit)	(10,000)
Total shareholders' equity..	$ 90,000

Required

1. What does the $0.40 mean for the preferred shares? After Mill City Corporation issues preferred shares, how much in cash dividends will Mill City Corporation expect to pay on 1,000 shares?

2. At what price per share did Mill City Corporation issue the common shares during 2002?

3. Were first-year operations profitable? Give your reason.

4. During 2003, the company completed the following selected transactions. Journalize each transaction. Explanations are not required.

   a. Issued for cash 10,000 shares of preferred stock at $5 per share.

   b. Issued for cash 1,000 shares of common stock at a price of $12 per share.

   c. Issued 20,000 shares of common stock to acquire a building valued at $240,000.

   d. Net income for the year was $50,000, and the company declared no dividends. Make the closing entry for net income.

5. Prepare the shareholders' equity section of the Mill City Corporation balance sheet at December 31, 2003.

Problem 13-4B *Shareholders' equity section of the balance sheet* **(Obj. 4)**

Shareholders' equity information is given for Atrium Inc. and Carnival Corp. The two companies are independent.

Atrium Inc.   Atrium Inc. is authorized to issue 100,000 shares of common stock. All the shares were issued at $12 per share. The company incurred a net loss of $50,000 in 2001, its first year of business. It earned net income of $75,000 in 2002 and $100,000 in 2003. The company declared no dividends during the three-year period.

Carnival Corp.   Carnival Corp.'s articles of incorporation authorize the company to issue 20,000 shares of $2.50 cumulative preferred stock and 250,000 shares of common stock. Carnival Corp. issued 2,000 shares of the preferred stock at $50 per share. It issued 60,000 shares of the common stock for a total of $360,000. The company's retained earnings balance at the beginning of 2003 was $100,000 and net income for the year was $150,000. During 2003, the company declared the specified dividend on preferred and a $0.50 per share dividend on common. Preferred dividends for 2002 were in arrears.

Required

For each company, prepare the shareholders' equity section of its balance sheet at December 31, 2003. Show the computation of all amounts. Journal entries are not required.

Problem 13-5B *Analyzing the shareholders' equity of an actual corporation* **(Obj. 4, 5)**

The purpose of this problem is to familiarize you with the financial statement information of a real company, Domtar Inc. Domtar Inc. included the following shareholders' equity on its year-end balance sheet at December 31, 1999:

Shareholders' Equity	($ millions)
Preferred shares, unlimited authorization, authorized 100,000 shares in each class:	
Series A—issued 69,576 shares..	$ 2
Series B—issued 2,070,000 shares	52
Common shares, unlimited authorization, issued 184,139,827 shares.........	1,234
Retained earnings	503
	$1,791

Note: Series A preferred shares are non-voting and carry a cumulative cash dividend per share of $2.25 per annum.
　　　Series B preferred shares are non-voting and redeemable, and carry a cumulative cash dividend equivalent to 72% of the bank prime rate.

Required

1. Identify the different issues of stock Domtar Inc. has outstanding.

2. Give the summary entries to record issuance of all the Domtar Inc. shares. Assume that all the shares were issued for cash. Explanations are not required.

3. What amount of preferred dividends must Domtar Inc. declare and pay each year to avoid having preferred dividends in arrears on the Series A shares?

4. Assume that Series A preferred dividends are in arrears for 1999.
   a. Write note 5 of the December 31, 1999, financial statements to disclose the dividends in arrears.
   b. Record the declaration of a dividend for Series A preferred shares in the year ended December 31, 2000 to pay the amount in arrears and the current-year dividend.

Problem 13-6B　*Preparing a corporation balance sheet measuring profitability*　**(Obj. 4, 7)**

Link Back to Chapter 1 (Accounting Equation) The following accounts and related balances of Red Star Supply Ltd. are arranged in no particular order.

Trademark, net..........................	$ 18,000	Common shareholders'		
Preferred stock, $0.50,		equity, June 30, 2002...........	$444,000
10,000 shares		Net income	62,000
authorized and issued	54,000	Total assets, June 30,	
Cash	26,000	2002......................................	808,000
Accounts receivable, net..........	92,000	Interest expense	12,200
Accrued liabilities....................	52,000	Property, plant, and	
Long-term note payable...........	84,000	equipment, net....................	522,000
Inventory..................................	162,000	Common stock, 500,000	
Dividends payable....................	18,000	shares authorized;	
Retained earnings	?	236,000 shares issued	510,000
Accounts payable	62,000	Prepaid expenses....................	20,000

Required

1. Prepare the company's classified balance sheet in the report format at June 30, 2003.
2. Compute rate of return on total assets and rate of return on common shareholders' equity for the year ended June 30, 2003.
3. Do these rates of return suggest strength or weakness? Give your reason.

 Problem 13-7B　*Computing dividends on preferred and common stock*　**(Obj. 5)**

CHK Wireless Inc. has 10,000 shares of $4.00 preferred stock and 50,000 shares of common stock outstanding. CHK Wireless Inc. declared and paid the following dividends during a three-year period: 2001, $30,000; 2002, $100,000; and 2003, $225,000.

Required

1. Compute the total dividends on preferred shares and common shares for each of the three years if
   a. Preferred is noncumulative.
   b. Preferred is cumulative.
2. For requirement 1b, record the declaration of the 2003 dividends on December 28, 2003, and the payment of the dividends on January 17, 2004.

Problem 13-8B *Analyzing the shareholders' equity of a corporation* **(Obj. 5, 6)**

The balance sheet of Williams Creek Company Limited reported the following at December 31, 2002:

Shareholders' Equity	
Redeemable non-voting cumulative preferred stock,	
authorized 10,000 shares (liquidation value $716,000)	$ 640,000
Common stock, authorized 200,000 shares; issued 72,000 shares	570,000
Retained earnings	238,000
Total shareholders' equity...	$1,448,000

Notes to the financial statements indicate that 16,000 shares of $2.60 preferred stock were issued for $40 per share. Preferred dividends have not been paid for three years, including the current year. On the balance sheet date, the market value of the Williams Creek Company Limited common shares was $7.50 per share.

Required

1. Are the preferred shares cumulative or noncumulative? How can you tell?
2. What is the amount of the annual preferred dividend?
3. Which class of shareholders controls the company? Give your reason.
4. What is the total contributed capital of the company?
5. What was the total market value of the common shares?
6. Compute the book value per share of the preferred shares and the common shares.

Problem 13-9B *Computing and recording a corporation's income tax* **(Obj. 8)**

The accounting (not for income tax) records of Virtual Technology Inc. provide the income statement for 2003:

	2003
Total revenue..	$1,400,000
Expenses:	
Cost of goods sold	$ 600,000
Operating expenses...	370,000
Total expenses (before tax)	970,000
Pretax accounting income...	$ 430,000

Revenue for 2004 will include rent of $50,000 that was received late in 2003. This rent will be included in 2004 total revenue because the rent will be earned in 2004. However, rent revenue that is collected in advance is included in taxable income when the cash is received. In calculating taxable income on the tax return, this rent revenue belongs in 2003.

Virtual Technology Inc. calculates amortization of capital assets for accounting purposes at the maximum rate allowed by Canada Customs and Revenue Agency. Therefore, amortization and capital cost allowance for 2003 was $60,000.

Required

(Assume a corporate income tax rate of 30 percent.)

1. Compute taxable income for 2003.
2. Journalize the corporation's income taxes for 2003.
3. Prepare the corporation's single-step income statement for 2003.

Problem 13-10B *Accounting for the incorporation of an ongoing business; recording the issuance of stock; allocating cash dividends; preparing the shareholders' equity section of the balance sheet   (Obj. 2, 3, 4, 5)*

Pardeep Gillan and Tara Ralston are partners in a glass recycling business with capital account balances of $90,000 and $120,000 respectively. They are considering incorporating and taking advantage of an offer from the City of Victoria to establish a new recycling plant. The following transactions then took place:

2002

Jan.   2   Gillan and Ralston incorporated their partnership into URGreen Corporation, with an authorization to issue 100,000 of $1.00 convertible preferred shares and 500,000 common shares. Gillan received 60,000 common shares and Ralston received 80,000 common shares.

         9   The City of Victoria donated land to the new corporation in exchange for establishing the business in that area. The land had cost the city $120,000 when purchased 10 years ago, but had a market value today of $180,000.

        15   Paid $5,000 and gave 5,000 common shares to the corporation's legal firm for incorporating the business. The total legal fee was $12,500.

Mar.   7   Sold 5,000 preferred shares for $40,000. The preferred shares are convertible on the basis of 4 common shares for each preferred share.

Dec.   31   The company reported net income after taxes of $100,000 for the year, and then closed the income summary account.

2003

Feb.   14   Declared cash dividends of $40,000, payable on April 8, 2003, to the shareholders of record on March 1, 2003. Indicate the amount that would be payable to the preferred and to the common shareholders.

Apr.   8   Paid the cash dividend declared on February 14, 2003.

July   7   The preferred shareholders converted 2,000 preferred shares into common shares.

Dec.   31   The company reported net income after taxes of $70,000 for the year, and then closed the income summary account.

2004

Feb.   16   Declared cash dividends of $50,000, payable on April 10, 2004, to the shareholders of record on March 13, 2004. Indicate the amount that would be payable to the preferred and to the common shareholders.

Required

1. Record the transactions in the general journal.
2. Prepare the shareholders' equity section of the balance sheet as of the close of business on February 16, 2004.

Problem 13-11B *Recording the issuance of stock; allocating cash dividends; accounting for corporate income taxes; preparing the liability and shareholders' equity sections of the balance sheet   (Obj. 2, 4, 5, 8)*

At January 1, 2002, Rival Technology Inc.'s balance sheet reported the following shareholders' equity:

Shareholders' Equity

Contributed capital:	
Preferred stock, $2.50, cumulative (3 years in arrears), liquidation price of $60, 100,000 shares authorized, 25,000 shares issued	$1,000,000
Common stock,	
Class A, 10,000 shares authorized and issued	100,000
Class B, unlimited number of shares authorized, 50,000 shares issued	900,000
Total contributed capital..	2,000,000
Contributed surplus—Donated capital	100,000
Retained earnings	400,000
Total shareholders' equity	$2,500,000

The company had the following transactions on the dates indicated:

2002

Dec. 1 The company declared dividends of $300,000, payable on January 15, 2003, to the shareholders of record on December 31, 2002. Indicate the amount that would be payable to the preferred shareholders and to the common shareholders. The dividend rate for Class A and Class B shares is the same.

31 The company reported pretax accounting income of $120,000 and taxable income of $100,000 (income tax rate = 30 percent). Record the income taxes and close the income summary account.

2003

Jan. 7 The company sold 5,000 shares of preferred stock at $40 per share.

15 The company paid the dividend declared on December 1, 2002.

Feb. 14 The company sold 20,000 shares of Class B common stock at $20 per share.

Apr. 17 The company paid the income taxes payable from 2002.

Dec. 2 The company declared dividends of $80,000, payable on January 15, 2004, to the shareholders of record on December 31, 2003. Indicate the amount that would be payable to the preferred shareholders and to the common shareholders.

31 The company reported pretax accounting income of $100,000 and taxable income of $80,000 (income tax rate = 30 percent). Record the income taxes and close the income summary account.

2004

Jan. 15 Paid the dividend declared on December 2, 2003.

Required

1. Record the transactions in the general journal.

2. Prepare the liability and shareholders' equity sections of the balance sheet as of the close of business on March 31, 2004. Assume no other transactions occurred after January 15, 2004.

3. Calculate the book value per share of the preferred shares and of the common shares on March 31, 2004.

4. What was the average price at which the Class A common shares were sold?

Challenge Problems

Problem 13-1C *The pros and cons of incorporation* *(Obj. 1)*

Your friend Mary Lam has come to you for advice. She has a very successful antique store that had sales of more than $400,000 in the year just ended. She would like to expand and will need to borrow $300,000 to finance an enlarged inventory. She has learned that she can buy the store adjoining hers for $200,000 and estimates that $40,000 of renovations would be needed to make the store compatible with her present store. Expansion would mean adding three or four employees to the two employees Mary already has.

Mary's accountant has suggested that she incorporate her business and that Mary hold all the shares. She cited several reasons to Mary including the benefits of limited liability. Mary has talked to her banker about the possibility of incorporating; he pointed out that if she did incorporate, the bank would need personal guarantees for any loans Mary arranged with the bank.

Required

Consider Mary's situation and discuss the pros and cons of incorporation for Mary. What would you suggest?

Problem 13-2C *Deciding on an investment in shares* **(Obj. 6, 7)**

You have just received a bequest from an aunt of $1,000 and you have decided to invest the money in shares of Super Sounds Television (SSTV), a cable television channel that shows music videos. The company that owns SSTV has: common shares; cumulative preferred shares; noncumulative, convertible preferred shares; and noncumulative preferred shares. The common shares are trading at $20.00 and currently have been paying a dividend of $1.00 per share. The cumulative preferred shares are selling at $30.00 and have a stated dividend of $1.80. The convertible preferred shares are selling for $86.35 and are convertible at the rate of 4 common for 1 preferred; the dividend rate is $4.75. The noncumulative preferred shares are trading at $40.00 and have a dividend rate of $2.10.

Required

Evaluate each of the four different shares as an investment opportunity. After performing your analysis, select which shares you will buy and explain your choice.

Extending Your Knowledge

Decision Problem

Evaluating alternative ways of raising capital **(Obj. 2, 4)**

Alan Adams and Judy Hoy have written a computer program for a video game system that they believe will rival Nintendo. They need additional capital to market the product, and they plan to incorporate their partnership. They are considering alternative capital structures for the corporation. Their primary goal is to raise as much capital as possible without giving up control of the business. The partners plan to receive 110,000 shares of the corporation's common stock in return for the net assets of the partnership. After the partnership books are closed and the assets adjusted to current market value, Adams' capital balance is $60,000 and Hoy's balance is $50,000.

The corporation's plans for the articles of incorporation include an authorization to issue 5,000 shares of preferred stock and 500,000 shares of common stock. Adams and Hoy are uncertain about the most desirable features for the preferred shares. Prior to incorporating, the partners have discussed their plans with two investment groups. The corporation can obtain capital from outside investors under either of the following plans:

Plan 1 Group 1 will invest $105,000 to acquire 1,000 shares of $5.00, cumulative preferred stock and $70,000 to acquire 70,000 shares of common stock. Each preferred share will receive 50 votes if preferred dividends are more than two years in arrears.

Plan 2 Group 2 will invest $160,000 to acquire 1,400 shares of $6.00 nonvoting, noncumulative preferred stock.

Required

Assume the corporation receives its articles of incorporation.

1. Journalize the issuance of common shares to Adams and Hoy.

2. Journalize the issuance of shares to the outsiders under both plans.

3. Assume net income for the first year is $160,000 and total dividends of $19,100 are properly subtracted from retained earnings. Prepare the shareholders' equity section of the corporation balance sheet under both plans.

4. Recommend one of the plans to Adams and Hoy. Give your reasons.

Financial Statement Problem

Shareholders' equity   (Obj. 2)

The Intrawest Corporation financial statements appear in Appendix A. Answer the following questions about the company's common stock.

1. Where can you find information about Intrawest's capital stock? What classes of capital stock has Intrawest issued and are outstanding? How many shares are authorized and how many are issued?

2. Was any common stock issued during the year? If yes, at what price were the shares issued?

3. Intrawest has a plan whereby the company finances share purchases by employees. What is the name of the plan? How many common shares is the company holding as security for loans made under the plan at June 30, 2000?

4. What is the book value per share at June 30, 2000? The market price of the shares ranged between $12.50 and $21.50 at that time. Why is the market price different from the book price?

5. What did Intrawest earn per common share in 2000? Where did you find that information?

14

Retained Earnings, Stock Repurchases, and the Income Statement

CHAPTER OBJECTIVES

After studying this chapter, you should be able to

1 Account for stock dividends

2 Distinguish stock splits from stock dividends

3 Account for repurchased capital stock

4 Report restrictions on retained earnings

5 Identify the elements of a corporation's income statement

6 Prepare a statement of retained earnings

"Our investors are interested in the level of income a company can expect to earn in the future. Therefore, we are most likely to base our recommendations on our review of a company's income from continuing operations rather than its net income." (Peter J. Miller, Investment Executive, ScotiaMcLeod Inc.)

Investment advisors, like Peter J. Miller, receive information about potential investments for their clients from investment analysts employed by their firm. Suppose a ScotiaMcLeod Inc. analyst is evaluating Shaw Communications Inc.'s operations. Which 2000 income figure—net income of $118.3 million (line 11 in Exhibit 14-1) or net income from continuing operations of $118.5 million (line 8)—should the analyst use to evaluate Shaw Communications Inc.'s operations during 2000?

The answer depends on the decision analysts will make. If they want to measure how well the company has performed in light of all its activities, then they should look at net income (line 11). But if they want to predict the level of income the company can expect to earn in the future, they should consider only those aspects of its operations that Shaw Communications Inc. can repeat from year to year. Peter J. Miller and his staff are probably more interested in net income from continuing operations than in net income. Most sophisticated investors and lenders concentrate their analysis on income from continuing operations, which can be expected to generate income for the company in the future.

EXHIBIT 14-1

Shaw Communications Inc. Consolidated Statement of Income (partial, adapted)

SHAW COMMUNICATIONS INC.
Consolidated Statement of Income (partial, adapted)
For the Years Ended August 31, 2000 and 1999

(Dollars in thousands)	2000	1999
1. Revenue	$971,000	$709,412
2. Operating, general and administrative expenses	573,337	399,539
3. Amortization	222,653	155,515
4. Interest expense	120,991	99,934
5. Other items (other revenue and gains in excess of other expenses)	(135,907)	(73,609)
6. Income from continuing operations before income taxes	189,926	128,033
7. Income taxes	71,427	81,483
8. Net income from continuing operations	118,499	46,550
9. Net loss from media business, including separation costs	—	(301)
10. Net loss from discontinued paging operations	(239)	(456)
11. Net income	$118,260	$ 45,793

IN this chapter, we discuss continuing operations, discontinued operations, and other operating activities reported on the corporate income statement. We explain special gains and losses that affect net income but differ from basic revenues and operating expenses on corporate income statements. First, however, we continue the discussion of shareholders' equity that we began in Chapter 13. Here we go more deeply into retained earnings, dividends, and stock repurchase transactions, which are important to corporations.

> **LEARNING TIP**
>
> Recall that in a proprietorship, investments, net income, and withdrawals are all recorded in the Capital account. In a corporation, shareholders' equity is split into Capital Stock and Retained Earnings. The Capital Stock section holds investments of capital. Retained Earnings is used to record net income, net loss, and dividends. Retained Earnings are calculated as:
>
> Beginning Retained Earnings
> +Net Income
> −Net Loss
> −Dividends
> =Ending Retained Earnings

Retained Earnings and Dividends

We have seen that the equity section on the corporation balance sheet is called *shareholders' equity*. The capital stock accounts and retained earnings make up the shareholders' equity section.

Retained Earnings is a corporate account that carries the balance of the business's net income less all net losses from operations and less any declared dividends accumulated over the corporation's lifetime. *Retained* means "held" or "kept." Retained earnings is the shareholders' claim against total assets arising from accumulated income. Successful companies grow by reinvesting the assets they generate from profitable operations. A survey of 200 Canadian corporations in 1999 indicates that the term "Retained Earnings" is used by 75.5 percent of those reporting. Of the 20.5 percent of companies reporting negative retained earnings, most used the term "Deficit".[1]

A debit balance in Retained Earnings, which arises when a corporation's accumulated net losses exceed its accumulated net income, is called a *deficit*. This amount is subtracted from the sum of the credit balances in the other shareholders' equity accounts on the balance sheet to determine total shareholders' equity. As was noted above, in 1999, 15.5 percent of 200 companies surveyed had a retained earnings deficit (Exhibit 14-2).

At the end of each accounting period, the Income Summary account—which carries the balance of net income for the period—is closed to the Retained Earnings account. Assume the following amounts are drawn from a corporation's temporary accounts:

Income Summary

Dec. 31, 2002	Expenses	750,000	Dec. 31, 2002	Revenues	850,000
			Dec. 31, 2002	Bal.	100,000

This final closing entry transfers net income from Income Summary to Retained Earnings:

2002				
Dec.	31	Income Summary	100,000	
		Retained Earnings		100,000
		To close net income to Retained Earnings.		

EXHIBIT 14-2

Retained Earnings of the *Financial Reporting in Canada* 200 Companies

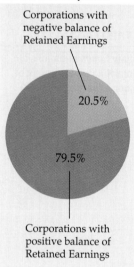

Corporations with negative balance of Retained Earnings

20.5%

79.5%

Corporations with positive balance of Retained Earnings

STOP & THINK

Assume that the beginning balance of Retained Earnings was $720,000. The net loss for the year was $810,000. What will the Retained Earnings balance be after this net loss?

Answer:

Retained Earnings

Dec. 31, 2002	Net loss	810,000	Jan. 1, 2002	Bal.	720,000
Dec. 31, 2002	Bal.	90,000			

---

[1] Byrd, C., I. Chen and H. Chapman, *Financial Reporting in Canada* 2000, Twenty-fifth edition (Toronto: Canadian Institute of Chartered Accountants, 2000), p. 342.

When you see a balance sheet, remember these facts about Retained Earnings:

1. *Credits to the Retained Earnings account arise only from net income.* To learn how much net income a corporation has earned and retained in the business, look at Retained Earnings. Its balance is the cumulative, lifetime earnings of the company less all net losses and all dividends.

2. *The Retained Earnings account is not a reservoir of cash waiting for the board of directors to pay dividends to the shareholders.* Instead, Retained Earnings is an owners' equity account representing a claim on all assets in general and not on any asset in particular. In fact, the corporation may have a large balance in Retained Earnings but not have the cash to pay a dividend. Why? The company may have used its cash to purchase a building or other asset or to pay off liabilities.

- To *declare* a dividend, the company must have a credit balance in Retained Earnings both before and after the declaration of dividends.

- To *pay* the dividend, it must have the cash.

Cash and Retained Earnings are two entirely separate accounts with no particular relationship.

KEY POINT

Retained Earnings is *not* a bank account. A $500,000 balance in Retained Earnings means that $500,000 of capital has been created by profits reinvested in the business.

Stock Dividends

OBJECTIVE 1
Account for stock dividends

A **stock dividend** is a proportional distribution by a corporation of its own stock to its shareholders. Stock dividends are fundamentally different from cash dividends because stock dividends do not transfer the assets of the corporation to the shareholders. Cash dividends are distributions of the asset cash, but stock dividends

- Affect *only* the accounts within shareholders' equity (Retained Earnings and Common Stock)

- Have *no* effect on total shareholders' equity

A stock dividend increases Common Stock and decreases Retained Earnings. Because both of these accounts are elements of shareholders' equity, total shareholders' equity is unchanged. There is merely a transfer from one shareholders' equity account to another, and no asset or liability is affected by a stock dividend.

The corporation distributes stock dividends to shareholders in proportion to the number of shares they already own. For example, suppose you owned 300 shares of The Bank of Montreal common stock. If The Bank of Montreal distributed a 10 percent common stock dividend, you would receive 30 (300 × 0.10) additional shares. You would now own 330 shares of the stock. All other Bank of Montreal shareholders would receive additional shares equal to 10 percent of their prior holdings. You would all be in the same relative ownership position after the dividend as you were before.

The Bank of Montreal
www.bmo.com

Stock dividends, like cash dividends, are taxable in the hands of the recipient. The value of the stock dividend is equal to the amount of the increase in the capital of the company paying the dividend. The increase is usually the fair market value of the shares issued.

Reasons for Stock Dividends

In distributing a stock dividend, the corporation gives up no assets. Why, then, do companies issue stock dividends? A corporation may choose to distribute stock dividends for these reasons:

1. *To continue dividends but conserve cash.* A company may want to keep cash in the business in order to expand, buy inventory, pay debts, and so on. Yet the company may wish to continue dividends in some form. To do so, the corporation may distribute a stock dividend.

2. *To reduce the market price per share of its stock.* Distribution of a stock dividend may cause the market price of a share of the company's stock to decrease because of the increased supply of the stock. Suppose the market price of a share of Quebecor World Inc. is $34. Doubling the number of shares of its stock outstanding by issuing a stock dividend is likely to drop the market price of the stock by approximately half, to $17 per share. The objective of such a large stock dividend is to make the stock less expensive and thus more attractive to a wider range of investors.

Recording Stock Dividends

The board of directors announces stock dividends on the declaration date. The date of record and the distribution date follow. (This is the same sequence of dates used for a cash dividend.) The declaration of a stock dividend does *not* create a liability because the corporation is not obligated to pay assets. (Recall that a liability is a claim on *assets*.) Instead, the corporation has declared its intention to distribute its stock. Assume General Communications Corporation has the following shareholders' equity prior to a stock dividend:

Shareholders' Equity	
Contributed capital	
Common stock, 100,000 shares authorized, 40,000 shares issued.........	$400,000
Retained earnings...	100,000
Total shareholders' equity...	$500,000

Of concern about stock dividends is how to determine the amount to transfer from retained earnings to the capital stock account. The *Canada Business Corporations Act* suggests that the market value of the shares issued is the appropriate amount to transfer, while other incorporating acts allow the directors to set a value on the shares. If market value were to be used, it would be the market value on the date the dividend is declared. If any other value were to be used, it would be determined by the directors at the time of declaration. This issue is not dealt with in the *CICA Handbook*. The market value of the shares issued, on the declaration date, would seem to be an appropriate valuation in any event and will be used in this text.

Assume General Communications Corporation declares a 10 percent common stock dividend on November 17. The company will distribute 4,000 (40,000 × 0.10) shares in the dividend. On November 17 the market value of its common stock is $16 per share. Using the market value approach, Retained Earnings is debited for the market value of the 4,000 dividend shares and Common Stock Dividend Distributable is credited. General Communications Corporation makes the following entry on the declaration date.

Nov. 17	Retained Earnings	64,000	
	Common Stock Dividend Distributable		64,000
	To declare a 10 percent common stock dividend. (40,000 × 0.10 × $16)		

The accounting equation for this transaction shows that a stock dividend affects neither assets, liabilities, nor total shareholders' equity.

Assets	=	Liabilities	+	Shareholders' Equity
				−64,000
0	=	0		+64,000

On the distribution date, the company records issuance of the dividend shares as follows:

Dec.	12	Common Stock Dividend Distributable	64,000	
		Common Stock		64,000
		To issue common stock in a stock dividend.		

Common Stock Dividend Distributable is a shareholders' equity account. (It is *not* a liability because the corporation has no obligation to pay assets.) If the company prepares financial statements after the declaration of the stock dividend but before issuing it, Common Stock Dividend Distributable is reported in the shareholders' equity section of the balance sheet immediately after Common Stock. However, this account holds the value of the dividend shares only from the declaration date to the date of distribution.

The following tabulation shows the changes in shareholders' equity caused by the stock dividend:

Shareholders' Equity	Before the Dividend	After the Dividend	Change
Contributed capital			
Common stock, 100,000 shares			
authorized, 40,000 shares issued......	$400,000		
44,000 shares issued		$464,000	Up by $64,000
Total contributed capital......................	400,000	464,000	Up by $64,000
Retained earnings	100,000	36,000	Down by $64,000
Total shareholders' equity	$500,000	$500,000	Unchanged

Compare shareholders' equity before and after the stock dividend. Observe the increase in the balance of Common Stock and the decrease in Retained Earnings. Also observe that total shareholders' equity is unchanged from $500,000.

Amount of Retained Earnings Transferred in a Stock Dividend   Stock dividends are said to be *capitalized retained earnings* because they transfer an amount from retained earnings to capital stock. The capital stock accounts are more permanent than retained earnings because they are not subject to dividends. As we saw in the preceding illustration, the amount transferred from Retained Earnings in a stock dividend is the market value of the dividended shares. Therefore, many shareholders view stock dividends as distributions little different from cash dividends.

Stock Splits

A stock dividend may decrease the market price of the stock. A stock *split* also decreases the market price of stock—with the intention of making the stock more attractive. A **stock split** is an increase in the number of authorized and outstanding shares of stock coupled with a proportionate reduction in the book value per share of the stock. For example, if the company splits its stock 2 for 1, the number of outstanding shares is doubled and each share's book value is halved. Many large companies in Canada—Dofasco, The Toronto-Dominion Bank, St. Lawrence Cement, and others—have split their stock.

Assume that the market price of a share of Ballard Power Systems Inc. Class A common stock is $150 and that the company wishes to decrease the market price to approximately $75. Ballard decides to split the common stock 2 for 1 in the expectation that the stock's market price would fall from $150 to $75. A 2-for-1 stock split means that the company would have two times as many shares of stock outstanding after the split as it had before and that each share's book value would be halved. Assume Ballard had 70,000,000 shares of common stock issued and outstanding before the split.

Shareholders' Equity (before stock split; adapted)	($ millions)
Contributed capital	
Class A Common stock, unlimited number of shares authorized,	
70,000,000 shares issued	$1,568
Retained earnings	1,302
Total shareholders' equity	$2,870

After the 2-for-1 split, Ballard would have 140,000,000 shares (70,000,000 × 2) of Class A common shares outstanding. Total shareholders' equity would be exactly as before the stock split. Indeed, the balance in the Common Stock account does not even change. Only the number of shares authorized and issued, and the book value per share change. Compare the highlighted figures in the two shareholders' equity presentations.

Shareholders' Equity (after stock split; adapted)	($ millions)
Contributed capital	
Class A Common stock, unlimited number of shares authorized,	
140,000,000 shares issued	$1,568
Retained earnings	1,302
Total shareholders' equity	$2,870

Because the stock split affects no account balances, no formal journal entry is necessary. Instead, the split is often recorded in a *memorandum entry* such as the following:

Aug. 19   Distributed one new Class A common share for each old share previously outstanding. This increased the number of Class A shares issued from 70,000,000 to 140,000,000.

A company may engage in a reverse split to decrease the number of shares of stock outstanding. If the number of shares outstanding is decreased, then existing shareholders may have a better chance of maintaining control over a corporation's shares of stock. There are fewer shares available to be traded and purchased by new shareholders. For example, Ballard could split its stock 1 for 4 which would reduce the number of shares issued from 70,000,000 to 17,500,000. Reverse splits are rare.

Similarities and Differences between Stock Dividends and Stock Splits

OBJECTIVE 2
Distinguish stock splits from stock dividends

Stock dividends and stock splits both increase the number of shares of stock owned per shareholder. Neither a stock dividend nor a stock split changes the investor's total cost of the stock owned. For example, assume you paid $32,000 to acquire 1,000 shares of Power Corporation common stock. If Power Corporation distributes a 100 percent stock dividend, your 1,000 shares increase to 2,000, but your total cost is still $32,000. Likewise, if Power Corporation distributes a 2-for-1 stock split, your shares increase in number to 2,000, but your total cost is unchanged.

Where stock dividends and stock splits differ, however, is in the way they are treated for tax purposes. A stock split does not create taxable income to the investor, but a stock dividend does because stock dividends are taxed in the same way as cash dividends. The stock dividend is valued at the market value of the shares on the date the stock dividend is declared, and this amount is included as taxable income. This is one reason why stock dividends are less popular than stock splits: investors must pay income tax on a stock dividend even though no cash is received.

Both a stock dividend and a stock split increase the corporation's number of shares issued. For example, a 100 percent stock dividend and a 2-for-1 stock split both double the outstanding shares and are likely to cut the stock's market price per share in half. They differ in that a stock *dividend* shifts an amount from retained earnings to capital stock, leaving total book value unchanged. However, the book value per share will decrease because of the increased number of shares outstanding. A stock *split* affects no account balances whatsoever but instead changes the book value of each share of stock.

Exhibit 14-3 summarizes the effects of dividends and stock splits on total shareholders' equity.

Repurchase of Its Stock by a Corporation

OBJECTIVE 3
Account for repurchased capital stock

Corporations may **repurchase stock** from their shareholders for several reasons: (1) the company may have issued all its authorized stock and needs the stock for distributions to officers and employees under bonus plans or stock purchase plans; (2) the purchase may help support the stock's current market price by decreasing the supply of stock available to the public; and (3) management may gather in the stock to avoid a takeover by an outside party.

The *Canada Business Corporations Act* requires a corporation that purchases its own stock to cancel the shares bought; it may do so by treating the purchased shares as authorized but unissued, and issue them in the normal way at a later date or it may cancel them outright. Several of the provincial incorporating acts also require that the shares be treated this way, while other incorporating acts permit the corporation to hold the shares as treasury stock (in effect, the corporation holds the stock in its treasury) and resell them.

Shares that are canceled outright may not be re-issued. The effect of purchasing an outstanding share is to reduce the number of shares issued; the effect of canceling a share outright is to reduce the number of shares authorized.

For practical purposes, treasury stock is like unissued stock: neither category of stock is in the hands of shareholders. The company does not receive cash dividends on its treasury stock, and treasury stock does not entitle the company to vote or to receive assets in liquidation. The difference between unissued stock and treasury stock is that treasury stock has been issued and bought back.

The repurchase of its own stock by a company decreases the company's assets and its shareholders' equity. The size of the company literally decreases, as shown on the balance sheet. The *Canada Business Corporations Act* and most of the provincial incorporating acts do not permit a corporation to acquire its own shares if such reacquisition would result in the corporation putting itself into financial jeopardy and being unable to pay its liabilities as they become due.

For companies incorporated under the *Canada Business Corporations Act* and in jurisdictions where repurchased stock must be canceled or treated as unissued, the

> ## Student to Student
>
> *For me, the hardest part of shareholders' equity was the journal entries required when companies buy back their own shares. I thought the Primex Forest Products example on pages 767–769 was great. Also, the Working It Out on page 768 was a really good reminder of the process involved. The Decision Guidelines on page 769 were really helpful too.*
>
> *Jennifer B., Richmond*

EXHIBIT 14-3

Effects of Dividends and Stock Splits on Total Shareholders' Equity

	Effect on Total Shareholders' Equity	
	Declaration	Payment of Cash or Distribution of Stock
Cash dividend	Decrease	None
Stock dividend	None	None
Stock split	None	None

Source: Adapted from Beverly Terry.

Common Stock account is debited. In those jurisdictions in Canada where treasury stock is permitted, the entry to record a purchase of treasury stock would include a debit to Treasury Stock and a credit to Cash. The Treasury Stock account has a debit balance, which is the opposite of the other shareholders' equity accounts. Therefore, Treasury Stock is a contra shareholders' equity account; it is deducted from the total of capital stock and Retained Earnings to compute total shareholders' equity. Treasury stock is permitted in the U.S. but is rare in Canada. For this reason, the remainder of this text will *not* deal with treasury stock.

Repurchase of Capital Stock

The *CICA Handbook* requires a company that purchases its own shares at a price less than the *average issue price* to debit Common Stock (or Preferred Stock, as the case may be) for the average issue price; the excess of the average issue price over the purchase price should be credited to Contributed Surplus—Stock Repurchase. When a company purchases its own shares at a price equal to or greater than the average issue price, the excess should first be debited to Contributed Surplus—Stock Repurchase to reduce the balance in this account to $0 and any remaining excess should then be debited to Retained Earnings. Under the *Canada Business Corporations Act*, any subsequent issues of repurchased shares are treated as new share issues, with the proceeds credited to the Common Stock account. The Contributed Surplus—Stock Repurchase account is not adjusted.

Accounting Around the Globe

Aktienrueckkauf, Rachat des actions, Recompra de acciones: Stock Buybacks Catch On in Europe

Stock repurchase plans—often called stock buybacks—are most common in the United States, but are new to Europe. Until a few years ago, European companies were either prohibited from repurchasing their own stock or charged harsh tax penalties for doing so. These companies normally invested their spare cash conservatively or used it to acquire other companies. The Europeans may turn out to be smarter than their American counterparts, who have rushed to buy back company stock. In Europe, 1999 saw only an estimated $50 billion in buybacks, whereas American companies bought back that much in the first two months of 2000.

Do buybacks really support or "prop up" the price of a stock? In one view, a buyback sends a message that a company's top managers think its stock is undervalued. After all, who knows the most about the company's backlog of sales and future prospects? But the stock prices of Anheuser Busch, Carnival Corp., and Germany's Siemens—all of which announced buybacks in 2000—barely budged. It may show that a company lacks imagination, that it has no interesting new investment projects on the horizon. "…I'm skeptical you can make a profit buying the 'buyback' story," said Rory Powe, head of European equities at London's Invesco. "I'd rather invest in growth companies that can find better uses for their cash by investing in new business."

Based on: Robert O'Brien, "Deals & Dealmakers: Stock Buybacks Gain Popularity, But Price Pops Aren't Guaranteed," *Wall Street Journal*, March 6, 2000, C17. David Nicklaus, "Stock Buybacks Have Lost Their Magic for the Area's 'Old Economy' Companies," *St. Louis Post-Dispatch*, March 18, 2000, p. Biz 1. Joan Warner, "Buyback Fever Hits Europe," *Business Week*, May 11, 1998, p. 46. Suzanne McGee, "Buybacks Catch On in Europe With Mixed Results," *Wall Street Journal*, January 25, 1999, p. C14. Caspar Busse and Angela Cullen, "Germany's Siemens Posts Surge in Profit; Stock Buyback, U.S. Spinoff Are Planned," *Wall Street Journal*, April 28, 2000, p. A17.

Suppose Primex Forest Products Inc. had the following shareholders' equity before repurchasing 10,000 of its own shares. Its 80,000 shares were issued at the same price, as follows:

Shareholders' Equity	
Contributed capital	
Common stock, 100,000 shares authorized, 80,000 shares issued................	$200,000
Retained earnings..	150,000
Total shareholders' equity	$350,000

On November 22, Primex Forest Products Inc. purchases 10,000 of its common shares, paying cash of $7.50 per share; the shares had been issued at $2.50 ($200,000/80,000). The shares are to be canceled. Primex records the purchase as follows:

Nov. 22	Common Stock...	25,000	
	Retained Earnings...	50,000	
	Cash..		75,000
	Purchased 10,000 shares of stock at $7.50 per share.		

The shareholders' equity section of Primex Forest Products Inc. balance sheet would appear as follows after the transaction:

Shareholders' Equity	
Contributed capital	
Common stock, 90,000 shares authorized, 70,000 shares issued	$175,000
Retained earnings	100,000
Total shareholders' equity	$275,000

Observe that the purchase of the shares decreased the number of shares authorized and decreased the number of shares issued and outstanding. Only outstanding shares have a vote, receive cash dividends, and share in assets if the corporation liquidates. Notice that the dollar amount shown for Common Stock and Retained Earnings decreased by $25,000 and $50,000 respectively.

Assume the articles of incorporation for Atlantic Exploration Ltd., issued under the *Canada Business Corporations Act*, authorized it to issue 100,000 common shares. By February 28 of this year, Atlantic Exploration Ltd. had issued 40,000 shares at an average price of $20.00 per share. Common Stock on the balance sheet amounted to $800,000. Retained Earnings was $187,396.

On March 20, Atlantic Exploration Ltd. repurchases 2,000 shares at $15.00 per share with the intention of reissuing the shares to employees in the future. The company records the transaction as follows:

March 20	Common Stock...	40,000	
	Contributed Surplus —Stock Repurchase		10,000
	Cash..		30,000
	Purchased 2,000 shares at $15 per share.		
	Since the common shares repurchased had		
	an issue value of $40,000 (2,000 × $20),		
	the contributed surplus was		
	$10,000 [2,000 × ($20 – $15)].		

The shareholders' equity section of Atlantic Exploration Ltd.'s balance sheet would appear as follows after the transaction:

Anderson Products Inc. issued 100,000 shares of common stock at $10. Later, when the market price was $15 per share, the company distributed a 10% stock dividend. Then Anderson Products Inc. repurchased 500 shares at $20 per share. What is the Common Stock balance?

A: $1,144,773:
100,000 shares × $10

$$= \$1,000,000$$
$$+ \ 10\% × 100,000 × \$15$$
$$= \ \ \ \underline{150,000}$$
$$\ \ \ \ 1,150,000$$
$$- \ 500 \text{ shares} × 10.45*$$
$$= \ \ \ \ \ \ \underline{5,227}$$
$$\ \ \ \ \underline{\$1,144,773}$$

*$10.45 = $1,150,000 ÷ 110,000 shares

Shareholders' Equity

Contributed capital	
Common stock, 100,000 shares authorized, 38,000 shares issued	$760,000
Contributed surplus—Stock Repurchase (note 6)	10,000
Total capital stock	$770,000
Retained earnings	187,396
Total shareholders' equity	$957,396

Note 6: During the year, the company acquired 2,000 common shares at a price of $15.00 per share; the shares had been issued at $20.00 per share. The company intends to re-issue these shares in the future.

Sale of Repurchased Capital Stock

A company incorporated under the *Canada Business Corporations Act* may re-issue the shares that it previously had repurchased. The sale would be treated like a normal sale of authorized but unissued stock.

STOP & THINK

Stock repurchase transactions have a serious ethical and legal dimension. A company buying its own shares must be extremely careful that its disclosures of information are complete and accurate. Otherwise, a shareholder who sold shares back to the company may claim that he or she was deceived into selling the stock at too low a price. What would happen if a company repurchased its own stock at $17 per share and one day later announced a technological breakthrough that would generate millions of dollars in new business?

Answer: The stock would likely increase in response to the new information. If it could be proved that management withheld the information, a shareholder selling stock back to the company may file a lawsuit to gain the difference per share. The shareholder would claim that, with the knowledge of the technological advance, he or she would have held the stock until after the price increase and been able to sell the stock at a higher price.

No Gain or Loss from Repurchased Capital Stock Transactions

The repurchase and sale of its own stock do not affect a corporation's net income. Stock repurchase affects *balance sheet accounts*, not income statement accounts. Under the *Canada Business Corporations Act*, any sale of repurchased shares is treated like a new share issue, and no gain or loss is recognized. The fact that a company may have repurchased shares at a price different from their average issue price and then reissued shares later is not relevant. If the repurchased shares are canceled outright, the number of shares authorized and issued is reduced. These shares, therefore, cannot be reissued. If the repurchased shares are not cancelled, the number of shares authorized remains the same but the number of shares issued is reduced. These shares may be reissued at some point in the future. At that point, the issue of shares is treated in the normal way, as a credit to Common Stock.

Suppose Primex Forest Products Inc. sold 500 common shares at $10.00 per share shortly after the repurchase of 10,000 shares at $7.50 per share described previously. Primex records the sale as follows:

Primex Forest Products Inc.
www.primex.com

Dec.	5	Cash	5,000	
		Common Stock...		5,000
		To sell 500 common shares at $10.00 per share.		

If Primex had sold the 500 shares for $2.00 per share, the sale would be recorded as follows:

Dec.	5	Cash...	1,000	
		Common Stock..		1,000
		To sell 500 shares of stock at $2.00 per share.		

Does this mean that a company cannot increase its net assets by repurchasing stock low and selling it high? Not at all. Management may repurchase stock because it believes the market price of its stock is too low. For example, a company may buy 500 shares of its stock at $10 per share. Suppose it holds the stock as the market price rises and resells the stock at $14 per share. The net assets of the company increase by $2,000 [500 shares × ($14 − $10 = $4 difference per share)]. This increase is reported as contributed capital and not as income.

DECISION GUIDELINES — *Accounting for Retained Earnings, Stock Dividends and Stock Splits, and Stock Repurchases*

Decision	Guidelines

How to record:
• Declaration of a stock dividend?
	Retained Earnings...................... Market value
	  Common Stock Dividend
	  Distributable.......................... Market value

• Stock split?	Memorandum only: Split the common stock 2 for 1. Distributed one new common share for each old share outstanding.

What are the effects of stock dividends and stock splits on each of the following?	Effects of	
	Stock Dividend	**Stock Split (for example, a 2-for-1 split)**
• Number of shares authorized	No effect	Increase
• Shares issued	Increase	Increase
• Shares outstanding	Increase	Increase
• Total assets and total liabilities	No effect	No effect
• Total shareholders' equity	No effect	No effect
• Common Stock account	Increase	No effect
• Retained Earnings account	Decrease	No effect

Decision	Guidelines
How to record repurchase of shares: • At issue price?	Common stock.......................... Issue price Cash....................................... Issue price
• Above issue price (with no relevant Contributed Surplus)?	Common stock.......................... Issue price Retained earnings...................... Excess* Cash....................................... Amount paid *Excess of amount paid over issue price

• Below issue price?	Common stock.......................... Issue price
	  Contributed surplus—stock repurchase Gain**
	  Cash....................................... Amount paid
	**Gain is equal to issue price minus amount paid.

What are the effects of the repurchase and subsequent sale of the repurchased shares on:	Effects of	
	Repurchase of Stock	**Sale of Repurchased Stock**
• Total assets?	Decrease by full amount of cash disbursement	Increase by full amount of cash receipt
• Total shareholders' equity?	Decrease by full amount of cash disbursement	Increase by full amount of cash receipt

Restrictions on Retained Earnings

Dividends and repurchases of capital stock require payments by the corporation to its shareholders. In fact, repurchases of capital stock are returns of their investment to the shareholders. These outlays decrease the corporation's assets, so fewer assets are available to pay liabilities. Therefore, its creditors may seek to restrict a corporation's dividend payments and capital stock repurchases. For example, a bank may agree to loan $500,000 only if the borrowing corporation limits dividend payments and repurchases of its stock.

To ensure that corporations maintain a minimum level of shareholders' equity for the protection of creditors, as was noted above, incorporating acts restrict the amount of its own stock that a corporation may repurchase. The maximum amount a corporation can pay its shareholders without decreasing capital stock is its balance of retained earnings. Therefore, restrictions on dividends and stock repurchases focus on the balance of retained earnings.

Companies usually report their retained earnings restrictions in notes to the financial statements. The following disclosure in the 1999 financial statements by TransCanada PipeLines Limited is typical:

TransCanada PipeLines Limited
www.transcanada.com/

> **Note 11—Restriction on Dividends**
>
> Certain terms of the Company's preferred shares, preferred securities, junior subordinated debentures, and debt instruments could restrict the Company's ability to declare dividends on preferred and common shares. At December 31, 1999, such terms did not restrict or alter the company's ability to declare dividends.

STOP & THINK

Why would a borrower such as TransCanada PipeLines Limited agree to restrict dividends as a condition for receiving a loan?

Answer: To get a lower interest rate. Other things being equal, the greater the borrower's concessions, the more favourable the terms offered by the lender.

Appropriations of Retained Earnings

Appropriations are restrictions of Retained Earnings that are recorded by formal journal entries. A corporation may appropriate (segregate in a separate account) a portion of Retained Earnings for a specific use. For example, the board of directors may appropriate part of Retained Earnings for building a new manufacturing plant, for meeting possible future liabilities, or other reasons. A debit to Retained Earnings and a credit to a separate account—Retained Earnings Restricted for Plant Expansion—records the appropriation. The appropriated retained earnings account appears directly above the regular Retained Earnings account on the balance sheet.

Retained earnings appropriations are rare. Corporations generally disclose any retained earnings restrictions in the notes to the financial statements, as shown in "Note 11" above. The notes give the corporation more room to describe the nature and amounts of any restrictions. Thus corporations satisfy the requirement for adequate disclosure.

Variations in Reporting Shareholders' Equity

Real-world accounting and business practices may use terminology and formats in reporting shareholders' equity that differ from our general examples. We use a more detailed format in this book to help you learn the components of the shareholders' equity section. Companies assume that readers of their statements already understand the details they omit.

One of the most important skills you will learn in this course is the ability to understand the financial statements of actual companies. Thus we present in Exhibit 14-4 a side-by-side comparison of our general teaching format and the format of the Bank of Nova Scotia taken from its 2000 annual report. Note the following points with respect to the real-world format illustrated in Exhibit 14-4 and also with regard to actual financial statements:

1. The Bank of Nova Scotia uses the heading Capital Stock. Companies may use Share Capital or other headings instead of Contributed Capital.

2. Some companies combine all classes of capital stock into a single line item and provide specifics in the notes. The Bank of Nova Scotia has combined eight series of preferred shares in a single line item but does show preferred and common separately.

3. The preferred and common shares are described fully in the notes with respect to shares authorized and issued; the information in the balance sheet is limited to a description of the class and total amount for which the two classes of shares were issued.

4. Often total shareholders' equity is not specifically labeled.

EXHIBIT 14-4

Formats for Reporting Shareholders' Equity*

General Teaching Format		Real-World Format	
Shareholders' Equity **($ amounts in millions)**		**Shareholders' Equity** **($ amounts in millions)**	
Contributed capital		Capital stock (note 12)**	
Unlimited number of preferred shares authorized (Proceeds not to exceed $4 billion), 61,250,000 issued	$ 1,775	Preferred shares	$1,775
		Common shares	2,765
Unlimited number of common shares authorized (Proceeds not to exceed $5 billion), 497,964,733 issued	2,765		
Retained earnings	8,435	Retained earnings..............................	8,435
Total shareholders' equity	$12,975		$12,975

**Note 12: Capital Stock
Authorized
An unlimited number of Preferred Shares without nominal or par value. The aggregate consideration shall not exceed $4 billion.

Unlimited number of Common Shares without nominal or par value. The aggregate consideration shall not exceed $5 billion.

* GAAP suggests the presentation of comparative data; in order to simplify the illustration, data are presented for 2000 only.

Mid-Chapter Summary Problem
for Your Review

Pierre Caron Inc. reported the following shareholders' equity:

Shareholders' Equity

Preferred stock, $1.00	
Authorized: 10,000 shares	
Issued: None..	$ —
Common stock	
Authorized: 100,000 shares	
Issued: 13,733 shares	98,532
Retained earnings	178,640
	$277,172

Required

1. What was the average issue price per share of the common stock?
2. How many Pierre Caron Inc. common shares are outstanding?
3. Journalize the issuance of 1,200 shares of common stock at $8.00 per share. Use Pierre Caron Inc.'s account titles.
4. How many common shares would be outstanding after Pierre Caron Inc. splits its common stock (computed in requirement 3) 3 for 1?
5. Using Pierre Caron Inc. account titles, journalize the declaration of a stock dividend when the market price of Pierre Caron Inc. common stock is $6.00 per share. Consider each of the following stock dividends independently:
   a. Pierre Caron Inc. declares a 10 percent common stock dividend on the shares outstanding, after the entry in requirement 3.
   b. Pierre Caron Inc. declares a 50 percent common stock dividend on the shares outstanding, after the entry in requirement 3.
6. Journalize the following repurchase and sale of its stock transactions by Pierre Caron Inc., assuming they occur in the order given (Requirement 6 is independent of Requirement 5.)
   a. Pierre Caron Inc. purchases 500 shares at $16.00 per share.
   b. Pierre Caron Inc. purchases 500 shares at $6.00 per share.
   c. Pierre Caron Inc. sells 100 shares for $18.00 per share.
7. How many Pierre Caron Inc. common shares would be outstanding after the transactions in requirement 6 take place? Ignore the transactions in requirements 4 and 5.

Solution to Review Problem

1. Average issue price of the common stock was $7.17 per share ($98,532/13,733 shares = $7.17).
2. Shares outstanding = 13,733.
3. Cash 9,600
      Common Stock... 9,600
   To issue common shares for cash of $9,600 (1,200 × $8).
4. Shares outstanding after a 3-for-1 stock split = 44,799 (13,733 + 1,200 = 14,933 shares outstanding × 3).

5. a. Retained Earnings 8,960
        Common Stock Dividend Distributable...............   8,960
        To declare a 10 percent common stock dividend
        valued at $8,960 (14,933 × 0.10 × $6).

    b. Retained Earnings... 44,799
        Common Stock Dividend Distributable   44,799
        To declare a 50 percent common stock dividend
        valued at $44,799 (14,933 × 0.50 × $6).

6. a. Common Stock (500 × $7.24)*..................................... 3,620
        Retained Earnings [500 × ($16.00 – $7.24)*]............. 4,380
        Cash   8,000
        To purchase 500 shares at $16.00 per share.

    b. Common Stock (500 × $7.24)*..................................... 3,620
        Contributed Surplus—Stock Repurchase
        [500 × ($7.24* – $6.00)]   620
        Cash   3,000
        To purchase 500 shares at $6.00 per share.

    c. Cash 1,800
        Common Stock   1,800
        To sell 100 shares at $18.00 per share.

7. Shares outstanding = 14,033 (13,733 + 1,200 – 500 – 500 + 100)

_____
*[($98,532 + $9,600)/(13,733 + 1,200)] = $7.24

Cyber Coach   Visit the Student Resources area of the *Accounting* Companion
Website for extra practice with the new material in Chapter 14.
www.pearsoned.ca/horngren

The Corporate Income Statement— Analyzing the Quality of Earnings

OBJECTIVE 5
Identify the elements of a corporation's income statment

Now that we have covered shareholders' equity in detail, we turn to the corporate income statement. A corporation's net income (revenues plus gains minus expenses and losses) receives more attention than any other item in the financial statements. In fact, net income is probably the most important piece of information about a company. Net income measures the business's ability to earn a profit and indicates how successfully the company has managed its operations. To shareholders, the larger the corporation's profit, the greater the likelihood of dividends. To creditors, the larger the corporation's profit, the better able it is to pay its debts. Net income builds up a company's assets and shareholders' equity. It also helps to attract capital from new investors who hope to receive dividends from future successful operations.

Suppose you are considering investing in the stock of Shaw Communications Inc. You would examine Shaw's income statement in Exhibit 14-1 (page 759). Shaw's income (the sum of lines 1–5) is up 48.3 percent to $189.9 million. To understand the composition of net income, let's examine the various types of income in detail. Exhibit 14-5 provides a comprehensive example that we will use in the following discussions. It is the multi-step income statement of Allied Electronics Corporation, a small manufacturer of precision instruments. (Refer to Chapter 5, page 238, for single-step and multi-step income statements.)

KEY POINT

Businesses operate to generate profits; without profits a business will not exist for long. The main source of income for an ongoing business must be from regular, continuing operations, not from sources such as selling off a business segment.

The first income tax expense listed on the income statement relates solely to income from continuing operations. Therefore, the tax effect of the discontinued segment's operating income (or loss) is not included in income tax expense; rather, it is added or deducted in the discontinued operations part of the income statement.

Continuing Operations

Income from a business's continuing operations helps financial statement users make predictions about the business's future earnings. In the income statement of Exhibit 14-5, the topmost section reports income from continuing operations. This part of the business is expected to continue from period to period. In the absence of other information, we may use this information to predict that Allied Electronics Corporation will earn income of approximately $54,000 next year.

The continuing operations of Allied Electronics Corporation include three items deserving explanation. First, during 2003, the company had a $10,000 loss on restructuring operations. Restructuring costs include severance pay to laid-off workers, moving expenses for employees transferred to other locations, and environmental cleanup expenses. The restructuring loss is part of continuing operations because Allied Electronics Corporation is remaining in the same line of business. But the restructuring loss is highlighted as an "other" item (unusual item) on the income statement because its cause—restructuring—falls outside Allied's main business endeavor, which is selling electronics products.

Second, Allied Electronics Corporation had a gain on the sale of machinery, which is also outside the company's core business activity. This explains why the gain is reported separately from Allied's sales revenue, cost of goods sold, and gross margin. (For a review of sales, cost of goods sold, and gross margin, see Chapter 5.)

EXHIBIT 14-5

Corporation Income Statement

ALLIED ELECTRONICS CORPORATION
Income Statement
For the Year Ended December 31, 2003

Sales revenue		$500,000	
Cost of goods sold		240,000	
Gross margin		260,000	
Operating expenses (listed individually)		181,000	
Operating income		79,000	
Other gains (losses)			Continuing operations
Loss on restructuring operations	($10,000)		
Gain on sale of machinery	21,000	11,000	
Income from continuing operations before income tax		90,000	
Income tax expense		36,000	
Income before discontinued operations			
and extraordinary items		54,000	
Discontinued operations			
Operating income, $30,000, less			
income tax of $12,000	$18,000		
Gain on disposal, $5,000, less			
income tax of $2,000	3,000	21,000	Special items
Income before extraordinary items		75,000	
Extraordinary flood loss	(20,000)		
Less income tax saving	8,000	(12,000)	
Net income		$ 63,000	
Earnings per common share			
(30,000 shares outstanding)			
Income before discontinued operations and			
extraordinary items		$ 1.80	
Income from discontinued operations		0.70	Earnings per share
Income before extraordinary items		2.50	
Extraordinary loss		(0.40)	
Net income		$ 2.10	

Third, income tax expense has been deducted in arriving at income from continuing operations. The tax corporations pay on their income is a significant expense. The combined federal and provincial income tax rates for corporations varies from time to time, for type and size of company, and from province to province; the current rates range from 14.5 percent to a maximum rate of 46.25 percent. We will use an income tax rate of 40 percent in our illustrations. This is a reasonable estimate of combined federal and provincial income taxes. The $36,000 income tax expense in Exhibit 14-5 equals the pretax income from continuing operations multiplied by the tax rate ($90,000 × 0.40 = $36,000).

Discontinued Operations

Most large corporations engage in several lines of business. For example, Canadian Pacific Ltd. is best known for transportation, but it also has subsidiaries in mining, forestry products, real estate, hotels, and other activities. Bombardier Inc., best known for its Skidoos and Seadoos, also owns aerospace companies in Canada, the U.S., and Ireland for a world market, and manufactures subway cars for a world market. We call each significant part of a company a **segment of the business**.

A company may sell a segment of its business. Such a sale is not a regular source of income because a company cannot keep on selling its segments indefinitely. The sale of a business segment is viewed as a one-time transaction. Financial analysts typically do not include income or loss on discontinued operations to predict a company's future income. The discontinued segments will generate no income in the future.

The *CICA Handbook*, in Section 3475, "Discontinued Operations," requires that the income statement carry information on the segment that has been disposed of under the heading *Discontinued Operations*. This section of the income statement is divided into two components: (1) operating income or (loss) from the segment that is disposed of and (2) gain (or loss) on the disposal. Assume income and gain are taxed at the 40 percent rate. They would be reported as follows:

Discontinued operations
Operating income, $30,000, less income tax, $12,000 .... $18,000
Gain on disposal, $5,000, less income tax, $2,000.. 3,000
$21,000

Trace this presentation to Exhibit 14-5.

It is necessary to separate discontinued operations into these two components because the company may operate the discontinued segment for part of the year. This is the operating income (or loss) component; it should include the results of operations of the segment from the beginning of the period to the disposal date. There is usually also a gain (or loss) on disposal. The transaction may not have been completed at the company's year end and so the gain (or loss) may have to be estimated. Following the conservatism concept, the estimated net loss should be recorded in the accounts at year end while an estimated net gain would not be recognized until it was realized.

It is important that the assets, liabilities, and operations of the segment can be clearly identified as separate from those of other operations of the company. The notes to the financial statements should disclose fully the nature of the discontinued operations and other relevant information about the discontinued operations, such as revenue to the date of discontinuance.

Discontinued operations are common in business. Recent examples include the sale by Molson Inc. of its 25 percent interest in The Home Depot Canada and its sale of Beaver Lumber to Home Hardware Stores Limited.

Extraordinary Gains and Losses (Extraordinary Items)

Extraordinary gains and losses, also called **extraordinary items,** must meet three criteria to be classed as extraordinary. They must have all of these characteristics (*CICA Handbook*, Section 3480):

KEY POINT

Income from continuing operations includes income from only those operations expected to remain in existence the following year. In Exhibit 14-5, if Allied Electronics Corporation had no discontinued operations and no extraordinary loss, then the $54,000 income from continuing operations would be the net income.

REAL WORLD EXAMPLE

Segments represent major lines of business or geographic areas. TransCanada Pipelines Limited lists its segments as transmission, power, gas marketing, and corporate.

WORKING IT OUT

On Sept. 1, 2002, Acme Equipment Corp. sells its division that manufactures mobile homes. The assets are sold at a gain of $1,700,000. The loss from operations for the year up to the date of sale was $960,000. Tax rate is 30%. How would you present the loss for the year and the sale of the division on the 2002 income statement?
A: In the Discontinued Operations section you would list two items:
Operating loss,
  $960,000, less income tax savings,
  $288,000........... $(672,000)
Gain on disposal,
  $1,700,000, less income tax,
  $510,000........... 1,190,000

Molson Inc.
www.molson.com

The Home Depot Canada
www.homedepot.ca

1. An item is extraordinary only if it is not expected to occur frequently. For example, a company that had property on a flood plain that was covered with water every four or five years could not treat losses from flood waters as extraordinary.

2. An item is extraordinary only if it is not typical of the normal business activities of the company. For example, inventory losses or gains, or losses from the sale of property would not be considered extraordinary, since a company that owned either one might normally expect to suffer a loss as a result of that ownership.

3. A gain or loss is extraordinary only if it does not depend on decisions or determinations made by management or owners. For example, the gain on the sale of property held for expansion would not be an extraordinary gain, whereas the gain on the expropriation of land by a municipality would normally be considered extraordinary because management cannot choose to refuse the transaction.

WORKING IT OUT

How would you report on an income statement:
(1) $100,000 extraordinary gain, 30% tax rate, and
(2) $150,000 extraordinary loss, 35% tax rate?

A:

(1) Extraordinary gain..... $100,000
Less income taxes 30,000
Extraordinary
gain, net of tax.....$ 70,000

(2) Extraordinary loss $150,000
Less tax savings........ 52,500
Extraordinary
loss, net of tax......$ 97,500

In short, to be classed as extraordinary, a transaction must be infrequent, unusual, and its result determined externally.

Extraordinary items are reported along with their income tax effect. Assume Allied Electronics Corporation lost $20,000 of inventory in a flood. This loss, which reduces income, also reduces the company's income tax. The tax effect of the loss is computed by multiplying the amount of the loss by the tax rate. The tax effect decreases the net amount of the loss in the same way that the tax effect on income reduces the amount of net income. An extraordinary loss is reported along with its tax effect as follows:

Extraordinary flood loss..	$(20,000)
Less income tax saving...	8,000
	$(12,000)

Trace this item to the income statement in Exhibit 14-5. An extraordinary gain is reported the same way, net of the income tax on the gain.

Gains and losses from unusual or infrequent transactions that are not extraordinary, such as gains or losses from capital asset disposals or losses resulting from employee strikes, could be classified as *unusual* and would be separately disclosed on the income statement as part of income before discontinued operations and extraordinary items. An example is the gain on the sale of machinery in Exhibit 14-5. These items are *not* shown net of tax effects.

Earnings Per Share (EPS)

The final segment of a corporation income statement presents the company's earnings per share, abbreviated as EPS. In fact, GAAP requires that corporations disclose EPS figures on the income statement or in a note to the financial statements.

Earnings per share is the amount of a company's net income per share of its outstanding common stock. EPS is a key measure of a business's success. Consider Plaza Corporation with net income of $200,000, no preferred dividends, and 100,000 shares of common stock outstanding. Its EPS is $2 ($200,000/100,000). Quaid Corporation may also have net income of $200,000, and no preferred dividends but only 50,000 shares of common stock outstanding. Its EPS is $4 ($200,000/50,000).

$$\text{Earnings per share} = \frac{\text{Net income} - \text{preferred dividends}}{\text{Weighted average number of shares of common stock outstanding}}$$

$$\text{EPS} = \frac{\$200,000}{100,000} = \$2$$

Plaza Corporation
Net income: $200,000
Shares of common stock outstanding: 100,000

$$\text{EPS} = \frac{\$200,000}{50,000} = \$4$$

Quaid Corporation
Net income: $200,000
Shares of common stock outstanding: 50,000

Just as the corporation lists separately its different sources of income from continuing operations, discontinued operations, and so on, it must list separately the EPS figure for income before discontinued operations and extraordinary items and net income for the period. The *CICA Handbook*, in Paragraph 3500.11, suggests that this be done to emphasize the significance of discontinued operations and extraordinary items to a company's overall results.

Consider the income statement of Allied Electronics Corporation shown in Exhibit 14-5; in 2003, it had 30,000 common shares outstanding. Income before discontinued operations and extraordinary items was $54,000, income from discontinued operations net of tax was $21,000, and there was an extraordinary loss, net of tax saving, of $12,000. Adhering to the *CICA Handbook*, it presents the following disclosures:

Disclosure required
 Income per share before discontinued operations and
  extraordinary items ($54,000/30,000) $1.80
 Net income per share [($54,000 + $21,000 − $12,000)/30,000] 2.10
Disclosure not required, but suggested for clarity
 Income per share from discontinued operations ($21,000/30,000) 0.70
 Loss per share from extraordinary items ($12,000/30,000) .... (0.40)

Note that the details of calculations shown above are for illustrative purposes only. They would not appear in formal financial statements.

Remember that the disclosure required by the *CICA Handbook* is a minimum. It is often in the user's interest to exceed that minimum as was done in Exhibit 14-5. The income statement user can better understand the sources of the business's EPS amounts when presented in this detail.

Weighted Average Number of Shares of Common Stock Outstanding

Computing EPS is straightforward if the number of common shares outstanding does not change over the entire accounting period. For many corporations, however, this figure varies as the company issues new stock and repurchases its own stock over the course of the year. Consider a corporation that had 100,000 shares outstanding from January through November, then purchased 60,000 of its own shares for cancellation. This company's EPS would be misleadingly high if computed using 40,000 (100,000 − 60,000) shares. To make EPS as meaningful as possible, corporations use the weighted average number of common shares outstanding during the period.

Let's assume the following figures for IMC Global Communications Corporation. From January through May, the company had 240,000 shares of common stock outstanding; from June through August, 200,000 shares; and from September through December, 210,000 shares. We compute the weighted average by considering the outstanding shares per month as a fraction of the year:

Number of Common Shares Outstanding		Fraction of Year			Weighted Average Number of Common Shares Outstanding
240,000	×	$\frac{5}{12}$	(January through May)	=	100,000
200,000	×	$\frac{3}{12}$	(June through August)	=	50,000
210,000	×	$\frac{4}{12}$	(September through December)	=	70,000
			Weighted average number of common shares outstanding during the year	=	220,000

The 220,000 weighted average would be divided into net income to compute the corporation's EPS.

The calculation of weighted average number of common shares outstanding becomes complicated when there have been stock dividends or stock splits during the year. These issues are studied more fully in intermediate and advanced accounting courses.

WORKING IT OUT

The net income of Hart Corp. amounted to $3,750,000. Hart Corp. had 200,000 shares of $9.00 preferred stock and 310,000 shares of common stock at the end of the year. At the beginning of the year, Hart had 270,000 shares outstanding and issued 40,000 shares on April 1. Calculate Hart's EPS.

A:

Weighted average:
270,000 × 3/12 = 67,500
310,000 × 9/12 = 232,500
= 300,000 shares

$$EPS = \frac{\$3,750,000 - (200,000 \times \$9)}{300,000 \text{ shares}}$$

$$= \frac{\$3,750,000 - \$1,800,000}{300,000}$$

$$= \$6.50$$

Preferred Dividends   Throughout the EPS discussion we have used only the number of shares of common stock outstanding. Holders of preferred stock have no claim to the business's income beyond the stated preferred dividend. Even though preferred stock has no claims, preferred dividends do affect the EPS figure. Recall, the EPS is earnings per share of common stock. Also recall that dividends on preferred stock are paid first. Therefore, preferred dividends must be subtracted from income subtotals (income before discontinued operations and extraordinary items and net income) in the computation of EPS.

If Allied Electronics Corporation had 10,000 shares of preferred stock outstanding, each with a $1.50 dividend, the annual preferred dividend would be $15,000 (10,000 × $1.50). The $15,000 would be subtracted from the two income subtotals resulting in the following EPS computations:

Income before discontinued operations and extraordinary items [($54,000 − $15,000)/30,000]	$1.30
Net income [($63,000 − $15,000)/30,000]	1.60

Dilution   Some corporations make their bonds or preferred stock more attractive to investors by offering conversion privileges, which permit the holder to convert the bond or preferred stock into some specified number of shares of common stock. Holders of convertible bonds or convertible preferred stock may exchange their securities for common shares. If in fact the bonds or preferred shares are converted into common stock, then the EPS will be diluted (reduced) because more common shares are divided into net income. Because convertible bonds or convertible preferred shares can be traded in for common stock, the common shareholders want to know the amount of the decrease in EPS that would occur if conversion took place. To provide this information, corporations with convertible bonds or preferred shares outstanding present two sets of EPS amounts: EPS based on outstanding common shares (*basic EPS*), and EPS based on outstanding common shares plus the number of additional common shares that would arise from conversion of the convertible bonds and convertible preferred shares into common (*fully diluted EPS*). The topic of dilution can be very complex and is covered more fully in intermediate accounting texts.

EPS is the most widely used accounting figure. Many income statement users place top priority on EPS. Also, a stock's market price is related to a company's EPS. By dividing the market price of a company's stock by its EPS, we compute a statistic called the *price-to-earnings* or *price-earnings ratio*. *The National Post* reports the price-earnings ratios (listed as P/E) daily for hundreds of companies listed on the Toronto, Montreal, Canadian Venture, New York, and other stock exchanges.

STOP & THINK

What makes earnings per share so useful as a business statistic?

Answer: Earnings per share is useful because it relates a company's income to one share of its stock. Stock prices are quoted at an amount per share, and investors usually consider how much they must pay for a certain number of shares. Earnings per share is used to help determine the value of a share of stock.

OBJECTIVE 6
Prepare a statement of retained earnings

Statement of Retained Earnings

Retained earnings may be a significant portion of a corporation's shareholders' equity. The year's income increases the retained earnings balance, and dividends decrease it. Retained earnings are so important that some corporations prepare a financial statement outlining the major changes in this equity account, much as the

EXHIBIT 14-6

Statement of Retained
Earnings

ALLIED ELECTRONICS CORPORATION
Statement of Retained Earnings
For the Year Ended December 31, 2003

Retained earnings, January 1, 2003	$ 130,000
Net income for 2003	63,000
	193,000
Dividends for 2003	(21,000)
Retained earnings, December 31, 2003	$172,000

statement of owner's equity presents information on changes in the equity of a proprietorship. The statement of retained earnings for Allied Electronics Corporation appears in Exhibit 14-6.

Some companies report income and retained earnings on a single statement. Exhibit 14-7 illustrates how Allied Electronics Corporation would combine its income statement and its statement of retained earnings.

Accounting for Errors and Changes in Accounting Policy

What happens when a company makes an error in recording revenues or expenses? Detecting the error in the period in which it occurs allows the company to make a correction before preparing that period's financial statements. But failure to detect the error until a later period means that the business will have reported an incorrect amount of income on its income statement. After closing the revenue and expense accounts, the Retained Earnings account will absorb the effect of the error, and its balance will be wrong until the error is corrected.

Corrections to the beginning balance of Retained Earnings for errors of an earlier

EXHIBIT 14-7

Statement of Income and
Retained Earnings

ALLIED ELECTRONICS CORPORATION
Statement of Income and Retained Earnings
For the Year Ended December 31, 2003

Income statement	Sales revenue	$500,000
	Cost of goods sold	240,000
	Gross margin	260,000
	Operating expenses (listed individually)	181,000
Statement of Retained Earnings	Net income for 2003	63,000
	Retained earnings, January 1, 2003	130,000
		193,000
	Dividends for 2003	(21,000)
	Retained earnings, December 31, 2003	$172,000

Earnings per share of common stock (30,000 shares outstanding)	
Income before discontinued operations and extraordinary items	$1.80
Income from discontinued operations	0.70
Income before extraordinary items	2.50
Extraordinary loss	(0.40)
Net income	$2.10

period or to reflect retroactive application of a change in accounting policy are called **prior-period adjustments.** To correct an error, the correcting entry includes a debit or credit to Retained Earnings for the error amount and a debit or credit to the asset or liability account that was misstated. The prior-period adjustment appears on the corporation's statement of retained earnings to indicate to readers the amount and the nature of the change in the Retained Earnings balance.

Assume that Paquette Corporation recorded the closing inventory balance for 2003 as $30,000. The correct amount was $40,000. This error resulted in overstating 2003 expenses by $10,000 and understating net income by $10,000. A review of the inventory working papers after the financial statements were issued alerted the Paquette Corporation management to the mistake. The entry to record this prior-period adjustment in 2004* is

2004			
June 19	Inventory..	10,000	
	Retained Earnings		10,000
	Prior-period adjustment to correct error in		
	recording closing inventory in 2003.		

The credit to Retained Earnings adjusts retained earnings to reflect the understated income in 2003. If cost of goods sold is credited in 2004 when the prior-period adjustment is recorded, income in 2004 would be overstated. The journal entry properly locates the adjustment in the period prior to 2004 (ie., to 2003, when the error occurred.)

This prior-period adjustment would appear on the statement of retained earnings, as follows:

PAQUETTE CORPORATION
Statement of Retained Earnings
For the Year Ended December 31, 2004

Retained earnings, January 1, 2004	
as originally reported..	$390,000
Adjustment to correct error	
in recording closing inventory in 2003 (see Note XX).................	10,000
Retained earnings, December 31, 2003,	
as adjusted..	400,000
Net income for 2004..	114,000
	514,000
Dividends for 2004...	(41,000)
Retained earnings balance, December 31, 2004	$473,000

Our example shows a prior-period adjustment for additional revenue. To make a prior-period adjustment for additional expense, retained earnings is debited and the misstated asset or liability is credited.

Paragraph 1506.11 of the *CICA Handbook* suggests that, where appropriate, a change in accounting policy should be applied retroactively. Paragraph 1506.15 confirms that prior periods should be restated to reflect the change and the facts of the restatement should be disclosed in the notes. An example would be a change in amortization method. The effect of the change on prior periods' results would appear as a prior-period adjustment on the Statement of Retained Earnings, the same way as an error would.

The Decision Guidelines feature covers the major aspects of a corporate income statement.

---

*We disregard the income tax effects to simplify the illustration.

Decision	Guidelines
What are the main sections of the income statement?	**Continuing operations** • Continuing operations, including unusual (but not extraordinary) gains and losses and income tax expense **Special items** • Discontinued operations—gain or loss—less the income tax effect • Extraordinary gain or loss, less the income tax effect • Net income (or net loss) **Earnings per share** • Earnings per share—applies only to net income (or net loss) and its components
What earnings per share (EPS) figures must a corporation report?	Must compute separate EPS figures for all amounts that apply, including • Income from continuing operations • Discontinued operations • Income before extraordinary item • Extraordinary gain or loss • Net income (or net loss) • Basic EPS must be presented; fully diluted EPS should be presented by corporations that have bonds or preferred shares with conversion privileges.
How to compute basic EPS for net income?	$$EPS = \frac{\text{Net income} - \text{Preferred dividends}}{\text{Weighted-average number of common shares outstanding}}$$

Summary Problem
for Your Review

The following information was taken from the ledger of Ansong Corporation:

Loss on sale of discontinued operations	$40,000	Selling expenses	$156,000
Prior-period adjustment —credit to Retained Earnings	10,000	Common stock, 40,000 shares issued	310,000
		Sales revenue	1,240,000
Gain on sale of capital assets	42,000	Interest expense	60,000
Cost of goods sold	760,000	Extraordinary gain	52,000
Income tax expense (saving)		Operating income, discontinued operations	60,000
Continuing operations	64,000	Loss due to lawsuit	22,000
Discontinued operations		General expenses	124,000
Operating income	24,000	Preferred stock, $8.00, 1,000 shares issued	40,000
Loss on sale	(16,000)		
Extraordinary gain	20,000	Retained earnings, January 1, 2002, as	
Dividends	32,000	originally reported	206,000

Required

Prepare a single-step income statement and a statement of retained earnings for Ansong Corporation for the year ended December 31, 2002. Include the earnings per share presentation and show computations. Assume no changes in the stock accounts during the year.

Solution to Review Problem

ANSONG CORPORATION
Income Statement
For the Year Ended December 31, 2002

Revenue and gains			
Sales revenue...			$1,240,000
Gain on sale of capital assets...........................			42,000
Total revenues and gains............................			1,282,000
Expenses and losses			
Cost of goods sold		$760,000	
Selling expenses...		156,000	
General expenses..		124,000	
Interest expense		60,000	
Loss due to lawsuit...		22,000	
Income tax expense		64,000	
Total expenses and losses...........................			1,186,000
Income before discontinued operations and			
extraordinary items.....................................			96,000
Discontinued operations (Note A)			
Operating income...	$60,000		
Less income tax..	24,000	36,000	
Loss on sale of discontinued operations	(40,000)		
Less income tax saving	16,000	(24,000)	12,000
Income before extraordinary items......................			108,000
Extraordinary gain (Note B)		52,000	
Less income tax..		20,000	32,000
Net income			$ 140,000

Earnings per share	
Income before discontinued operations and	
extraordinary item [($96,000 – $8,000)/40,000 shares]........................	$2.20*
Income from discontinued operations ($12,000/40,000 shares)	0.30
Income before extraordinary items [($100,000 – $8,000)/40,000 shares].....	2.50
Extraordinary gain ($32,000/40,000 shares)	0.80
Net income [($140,000 – $8,000)/40,000 shares]...	$3.30*

Computations:

$$\text{EPS} = \frac{\text{Income} - \text{Preferred dividends}}{\text{Weighted average number of common shares outstanding}}$$

Preferred dividends: $1,000 \times \$8.00 = \$8,000$

---

* These calculations are required; the other EPS calculations are included to make the statements more informative for users.

ANSONG CORPORATION
Statement of Retained Earnings
For the Year Ended December 31, 2002

Retained earnings, January 1, 2002, as originally reported....................	$206,000
Prior-period adjustment—credit (Note X).................................	10,000
Retained earnings, January 1, 2002, as adjusted	216,000
Net income for current year..	140,000
	356,000
Dividends for current year...	(32,000)
Retained earnings, December 31, 2002...................................	$324,000

Cyber Coach

Visit the Student Resources area of the *Accounting* Companion Website for extra practice with the new material in Chapter 14.

www.pearsoned.ca/horngren

Summary

1. **Account for stock dividends.** *Retained Earnings* carries the balance of the business's net income accumulated over its lifetime, less all declared dividends and net losses. *Cash dividends* are distributions of corporate assets made possible by earnings. *Stock dividends* are distributions of the corporation's own stock to its shareholders.

2. **Distinguish stock splits from stock dividends.** Stock dividends shift amounts from retained earnings to capital stock. *Stock splits* do not change any account balance. Stock splits and stock dividends increase the number of shares outstanding and lower the market price per share of stock.

3. **Account for repurchased capital stock.** *Repurchased capital stock* is the corporation's own stock that has been issued and reacquired. The corporation may issue repurchased stock in the normal way or may cancel the repurchased shares.

4. **Report restrictions on retained earnings.** Retained earnings may be *restricted* by law or contract or by the corpo-

ration itself. An *appropriation* is a restriction of retained earnings that is recorded by formal journal entries and appears on the balance sheet as a separate Retained Earnings item.

5. **Identify the elements of a corporation's income statement.** The corporate *income statement* lists separately the various sources of income—*income before discontinued operations and extraordinary items*, which includes unusual gains and losses, *discontinued operations*, and *extraordinary gains and losses*. The bottom line of the income statement reports *net income* or *net loss* for the period. *Income tax expense* and *earnings-per-share* figures also appear on the income statement, likewise divided into different categories based on the nature of income.

6. **Prepare a statement of retained earnings.** A statement of retained earnings reports the changes in the retained earnings account, including prior-period adjustments, net income or net loss, and dividends paid. This statement may be combined with the income statement.

Self-Study Questions

Test your understanding of the chapter by marking the best answer for each of the following questions:

1. A corporation has total shareholders' equity of $200,000, including retained earnings of $38,000. The cash balance is $70,000. The maximum cash dividend the company can declare and pay is (*pp. 760–761*)

   a. $38,000   c. $130,000
   b. $70,000   d. $200,000

2. A stock dividend (*p. 761*)

   a. Decreases shareholders' equity
   b. Decreases assets
   c. Leaves total shareholders' equity unchanged
   d. None of the above

3. Meyer's Thrifty Acres Ltd. has 10,000 shares of common stock outstanding; the stock was issued at $20.00 per share. The stock's market value is $40.00 per share. Meyer's board of directors declares and distributes a common stock dividend of one share for every ten held. Which of the fol-

lowing entries shows the full effect of declaring and distributing the dividend? (pp. 762–763)

a. Retained Earnings.............. 40,000
   Common Stock Dividend
      Distributable.................... 40,000
b. Retained Earnings.............. 20,000
      Common Stock................ 20,000
c. Retained Earnings.............. 20,000
      Cash................................. 20,000
d. Retained Earnings.............. 40,000
      Common Stock................ 40,000

4. Lang Real Estate Investment Corporation declared and distributed a 50 percent stock dividend. Which of the following stock splits would have the same effect on the number of Lang shares outstanding? (p. 764)

a. 2 for 1   c. 4 for 3
b. 3 for 2   d. 5 for 4

5. A company purchased 10,000 shares of its common stock that had been issued at $1.50 per share, paying $6.00 per share. This transaction (pp. 765–768)

a. Has no effect on company assets
b. Has no effect on shareholders' equity
c. Decreases shareholders' equity by $15,000
d. Decreases shareholders' equity by $60,000

6. A restriction of retained earnings (p. 770)

a. Has no effect on total retained earnings
b. Reduces retained earnings available for the declaration of dividends
c. Is usually reported by a note
d. All of the above

7. Which of the following items is not reported on the income statement? (p. 774)

a. Issue price of stock
b. Extraordinary gains and losses
c. Income tax expense
d. Earnings per share

8. The income statement item that is likely to be most useful for predicting income from year to year is (pp. 773–776)

a. Extraordinary items
b. Discontinued operations
c. Income from continuing operations
d. Net income

9. In computing earnings per share (EPS), dividends on preferred stock are (pp. 776–778)

a. Added because they represent earnings to the preferred shareholders
b. Subtracted because they represent earnings to the preferred shareholders
c. Ignored because they do not pertain to the common stock
d. Reported separately on the income statement

10. A corporation accidentally overlooked an accrual of property tax expense at December 31, 2002. Accountants for the company detect the error early in 2003 before the expense is paid. The entry to record this prior-period adjustment for a prior year's error is (pp. 779–780)

a. Retained Earnings XXX
      Property tax expense...... XXX
b. Property tax expense.......... XXX
      Property tax payable...... XXX
c. Retained Earnings XXX
      Property tax payable...... XXX
d. Property tax payable.......... XXX
      Property tax expense...... XXX

Answers to the Self-Study Questions follow the Similar Accounting Terms.

Accounting Vocabulary

Appropriation of retained earnings (p. 770)
Earnings per share (EPS) (p. 776)
Extraordinary gain or loss (p. 775)
Extraordinary item (p. 775)
Prior-period adjustment (p. 780)

Repurchase of own stock (p. 765)
Segment of a business (p. 775)
Stock dividend (p. 761)
Stock split (p. 763)

Similar Accounting Terms

Contributed capital   Capital stock; Share capital
Extraordinary gains and losses Extraordinary items
Income Statement   Statement of Earnings
Price-to-earnings ratio   Price-earnings ratio; P/E ratio
Repurchased stock   Treasury stock
Shareholders' equity   Stockholders' equity

Assignment Material

Questions

1. Identify the two main parts of shareholders' equity.

2. Identify the account debited and the account credited from the last closing entry a corporation makes each year. What is the purpose of this entry?

3. Ametek Inc. reported a cash balance of $73 million and a retained earnings balance of $162.5 million. Explain how Ametek Inc. can have so much more retained earnings than cash. In your answer, identify the nature of retained earnings and state how it ties to cash.

4. A friend of yours receives a stock dividend on an investment. He believes stock dividends are the same as cash dividends. Explain why the two are not the same.

5. Give two reasons for a corporation to distribute a stock dividend.

6. A corporation declares a stock dividend on December 21 and reports Stock Dividend Payable as a liability on the December 31 balance sheet. Is this correct? Give your reason.

7. What value is normally assigned to shares issued as a stock dividend?

8. Explain the similarity and difference between a 100 percent stock dividend and a 2-for-1 stock split to the corporation issuing the stock dividend and the stock split.

9. Give three reasons why a corporation may repurchase its own shares.

10. What effect does the repurchase of capital stock have on the (a) assets and (b) issued and outstanding stock of the corporation?

11. What effect does the repurchase and cancellation of common stock have on the (a) assets, (b) authorized stock, and (c) issued and outstanding stock of the corporation?

12. What does the *Canada Business Corporations Act* (CBCA) require a company to do when it repurchases its own stock?

13. Are there any exceptions to the requirement of the CBCA mentioned in question 12? If so, what are they?

14. Incorporating legislation frequently has a prohibition on a corporation purchasing its own stock in certain circumstances. What are those circumstances? Why does the prohibition exist?

15. Why do creditors wish to restrict a corporation's payment of cash dividends and repurchases of the corporation's stock?

16. What are two ways to report a retained earnings restriction? Which way is more common?

17. Identify three items on the income statement that generate income tax expense. What is an income tax saving, and how does it arise?

18. Why is it important for a corporation to report income from continuing operations separately from discontinued operations and extraordinary items?

19. Give two examples of extraordinary gains and losses and four examples of gains and losses that are *not* extraordinary.

20. What is the most widely used of all accounting statistics? What is the price-earnings ratio? Compute the price-earnings ratio for a company with EPS of $2 and a market price of $12 per share of common stock.

21. What is the earnings per share of a company with net income of $5,500 and a weighted average number of common shares of 12,000?

22. What account do all prior-period adjustments affect? On what financial statement are prior-period adjustments reported?

Exercises

Exercise 14-1 *Journalizing dividends and reporting shareholders' equity* **(Obj. 1)**

TVX Wireless Inc. is authorized to issue 400,000 shares of common stock. The company issued 100,000 shares at $4.00 per share, and all 100,000 shares are outstanding. When the retained earnings balance was $300,000, TVX Wireless Inc. declared and distributed a 50 percent stock dividend, using the market value of $1.00 per share. Later, TVX declared and paid a $0.20 per share cash dividend.

Required

1. Journalize the declaration and distribution of the stock dividend.
2. Journalize the declaration and payment of the cash dividend.
3. Prepare the shareholders' equity section of the balance sheet after both dividends.

Exercise 14-2 *Journalizing a stock dividend and reporting shareholders' equity* **(Obj. 1)**

The shareholders' equity for Penwest Systems Inc. on September 30, 2002 (end of the company's fiscal year), follows:

Shareholders' Equity	
Common stock, 200,000 shares authorized,	
100,000 shares issued...	$600,000
Retained earnings..	200,000
Total shareholders' equity..	$800,000

On October 16, the market price of Penwest Systems Inc.'s common stock was $10.00 per share and the company declared a 10 percent stock dividend. Penwest Systems Inc. issued the dividend shares on October 30.

Required

1. Journalize the declaration and distribution of the stock dividend.
2. Prepare the shareholders' equity section of the balance sheet after the stock dividend distribution.

Exercise 14-3 *Reporting shareholders' equity after a stock split* **(Obj. 2)**

UTS Energy Inc. had the following shareholders' equity at May 31, 2003:

Common stock, unlimited shares authorized, 75,000 shares issued	$240,000
Retained earnings	315,000
Total shareholders' equity	$555,000

On June 7, 2003, UTS Energy Inc. split its common stock 4 for 1. Make the memorandum entry to record the stock split, and prepare the shareholders' equity section of the balance sheet immediately after the split.

Exercise 14-4 *Accounting for a reverse stock split* **(Obj. 2)**

Examine UTS Energy Inc.'s shareholders' equity section for May 31 in Exercise 14-3. Suppose UTS Energy Inc. split its common stock 1 for 2 (a reverse stock split) in order to increase the market price of its stock. The company's stock was trading at $15 immediately before the split. Make the memorandum entry to record the stock split, and prepare the shareholders' equity section of UTS Energy Inc.'s balance sheet after the stock split.

Exercise 14-5 *Using a stock split or a stock dividend to decrease the market price of a stock* **(Obj. 2)**

Fairstar Services Ltd. has prospered during the past ten years, and recently, the company's stock price has shot up to $105. Fairstar management wishes to decrease its stock price to the range of $50 to $55, which will be attractive to more investors. Should the company issue a 100% stock dividend or split the stock? Why? If you propose a stock split, state the split ratio that will accomplish the company's objective. Show your computations.

Exercise 14-6 *Effects of stock issuance, dividends, and stock repurchase transactions* **(Obj. 1, 2, 3)**

Identify the effects of these transactions on shareholders' equity. Has shareholders' equity increased, decreased, or remained the same? Each transaction is independent.

a. A 10 percent stock dividend. Before the dividend, 1,000,000 shares of common stock were outstanding; market value was $7.60 at the time of the dividend.

b. Sale of 600 shares of repurchased common stock for $10.00 per share. Cost of the stock was $7.00 per share.

c. A three-for-one stock split. Prior to the split, 100,000 shares of common stock were outstanding.

d. Purchase of 2,000 shares of common stock at $4.00 per share.

e. A 50 percent stock dividend. Before the dividend, 1,000,000 shares of common stock were outstanding; market value was $14.00 at the time of the dividend.

f. Issuance of 50,000 shares of common stock at $20.00.

Exercise 14-7 *Journalizing repurchase of stock transactions* **(Obj. 3)**

Journalize the following transactions of Arbor Transmissions Inc., a national chain of car repair shops:

Jan. 19	Issued 10,000 shares of common stock at $20 per share.
Apr. 22	Purchased 1,000 shares of stock at $19 per share.
Oct. 11	Sold 200 shares of repurchased stock at $21 per share.
Nov. 28	Sold 200 shares of repurchased stock at $15 per share.

Exercise 14-8 *Journalizing repurchase of company stock and reporting shareholders' equity* **(Obj. 3)**

Armada Inc. had the following shareholders' equity on November 30, 2002:

Shareholders' Equity	
Common stock, 1,000,000 shares authorized, 100,000 shares issued...	$ 800,000
Retained earnings...	1,040,000
Total shareholders' equity...	$1,840,000

On December 19, the company repurchased and retired 10,000 shares of common stock at $7.00 per share. Journalize this transaction and prepare the shareholders' equity section of the balance sheet at December 31, 2002.

Exercise 14-9 *Accounting for the retirement of preferred stock* **(Obj. 3)**

Study Exhibit 14-4 on page 771. Suppose the corporation retired its preferred stock. What would be the amount of the company's total shareholders' equity if the cost to retire the preferred stock was (a) $1,600 million, (b) $1,775 million, (c) $1,800 million?

Exercise 14-10 *Reporting a retained earnings restriction* *(Obj. 4)*

The agreement under which Valunet Corp. issued its long-term debt requires the restriction of $200,000 of the company's retained earnings balance. Total retained earnings is $400,000, and total capital stock is $300,000.

Required

Show how to report shareholders' equity (including retained earnings) on Valunet Corp.'s balance sheet, assuming:

a. Valunet Corp. discloses the restriction in a note. Write the note.

b. Valunet Corp. appropriates retained earnings in the amount of the restriction and includes no note in its statements.

c. Valunet Corp.'s cash balance is $220,000. What is the maximum amount of cash dividends Valunet Corp. can declare?

Exercise 14-11 *Preparing a multiple-step income statement* *(Obj. 5)*

The ledger of Blackwell Corporation contains the following information for 2003 operations:

Sales revenue	$500,000		Income tax expense—	
Operating expenses			extraordinary gain	$10,000
(not including income tax)	110,000		Income tax saving—loss on	
Cost of goods sold	325,000		discontinued operations	24,000
Loss on discontinued			Extraordinary gain	25,000
operations	60,000		Income tax expense	26,000

Required

Prepare a multiple-step income statement for 2003. Omit earnings per share. Was 2003 a good year or a bad year for Blackwell Corporation? Explain your answer in terms of the outlook for 2004.

Exercise 14-12 *Computing earnings per share* *(Obj. 5)*

Skeena Technology Corp. earned net income of $125,000 in 2002. The ledger reveals the following figures:

Preferred stock, $2.50, 2,000 shares issued and outstanding	$ 62,500
Common stock, unlimited shares authorized, 50,000 shares issued	500,000

Required

Compute Skeena Technology Corp.'s EPS for 2002, assuming no changes in the stock accounts during the year.

Exercise 14-13 *Computing earnings per share* *(Obj. 5)*

Astaware Technologies Inc. had 40,000 shares of common stock and 10,000 shares of $0.75 preferred stock outstanding on December 31, 2002. On April 30, 2003, the company issued 9,000 additional common shares and ended 2003 with 49,000 shares of common stock outstanding. Income from continuing operations of 2003 was $108,700, and loss on discontinued operations (net of income tax) was $10,120. The company had an extraordinary gain (net of tax) of $50,600.

Required

Compute Astaware Technologies Inc.'s EPS amounts for 2003, starting with income before discontinued operations and extraordinary items.

Exercise 14-14 *Preparing a statement of retained earnings* *(Obj. 5, 6)*

Best Pacific Hotels Inc., a large hotel chain, had retained earnings of $425 million at the beginning of 2002. The company showed these figures at December 31, 2002:

	($ millions)
Net income	$138
Cash dividends—preferred	3
common	89
Debit to retained earnings due to repurchase of preferred stock	8

Required

Prepare the statement of retained earnings for Best Pacific Hotels Inc. for the year ended December 31, 2002.

Exercise 14-15 *Preparing a statement of retained earnings with a prior-period adjustment (Obj. 6)*

Peyto Inc., a soft-drink company, reported a prior-period adjustment in 2002. An inventory error caused net income of prior years to be overstated by $4.8 million. Retained earnings at January 1, 2002, as previously reported, stood at $403.3 million. Net income for 2002 was $149.1 million, and dividends were $44.8 million.

Required

Prepare the company's statement of retained earnings for the year ended December 31, 2002.

Exercise 14-16 *Preparing a statement of retained earnings* *(Obj. 6)*

At December 31, 2002, Winstar Corp. reported the following shareholders' equity:

Common stock, 2,000,000 shares authorized, 180,000 shares issued	$2,550,000
Retained earnings	2,700,000
	$5,250,000

During 2003, Winstar Corp. completed these transactions and events (listed in chronological order):

a. Declared and issued a 50% stock dividend. At the time, Winstar Corp.'s stock was quoted at a market price of $18 per share.
b. Sold 1,000 shares of stock for $22 per share.
c. Sold 500 shares of common stock to employees at $15 per share.
d. Net income for the year was $510,000.
e. Declared and paid cash dividends of $270,000.

Required

Prepare Winstar Corp.'s statement of retained earnings for 2003.

Challenge Exercise

Exercise 14-17 *Recording a stock dividend and preparing a statement of retained earnings (Obj. 1, 6)*

Bluestar Systems Inc. began 2002 with 3.9 million shares of common stock issued and outstanding for $11.7 million. Beginning retained earnings was $9 million. In March 2002, Bluestar Systems Inc. issued 100,000 shares of stock at $10 per share. In December, when the stock's market price was $12 per share, the board of directors declared and distributed a 10 percent stock dividend. Net income for the year was $2.2 million.

Required

1. Make the journal entries for the issuance of stock for cash and for the 10 percent stock dividend.
2. Prepare the company's statement of retained earnings for the year ended December 31, 2002.

Beyond the Numbers

Beyond the Numbers 14-1 *Reporting special items* *(Obj. 3, 5)*

The following accounting issues have arisen at Suncrest Sportswear Inc.:

1. An investor noted that the market price of stocks seemed to decline after the date of record for a cash dividend. Why do you think that would be the case?
2. The treasurer of the company wants to disclose a large loss as an extraordinary item because Suncrest Sportswear Inc. produced too much inventory just before a very cool summer. Why do you think the treasurer wants to use that particular disclosure? Would such disclosure be acceptable?
3. Corporations sometimes repurchase their own stock. When asked why they do so, Suncrest Sportswear Inc. management responds that the stock is undervalued. What advantage would Suncrest Sportswear Inc. gain by buying and selling its own stock under these circumstances?
4. Suncrest Sportswear Inc. earned a significant profit in the year ended November 30, 2002, because land that it held was expropriated for a new highway. The company proposes to treat the sale of land to the government as operating revenue. Why do you think Suncrest Sportswear Inc. is proposing such treatment? Is this treatment appropriate?

Ethical Issue

Link Back to Chapter 1 (Accounting Principles)

GMO Resources Corporation is an independent oil producer in Alberta. In February, company geologists discovered a pool of oil that tripled the company's proven reserves. Prior to disclosing the new oil to the public, top managers of the company quietly bought most of GMO Resources Corporation stock for themselves personally. After the discovery announcement, GMO Resources Corporation's stock price increased from $13 to $40.

Required

1. Did GMO Resources Corporation managers behave ethically? Explain your answer.
2. Identify the accounting principle relevant to this situation. Review Chapter 1 if necessary.
3. Who was helped and who was harmed by management's action?

Problems (Group A)

Problem 14-1A *Journalizing shareholders' equity transactions* *(Obj. 1, 3)*

Assume Evans Software Inc. completed the following selected transactions during the current year:

April 18   Declared a cash dividend on the $4.00 preferred stock (1,000 shares outstanding). Declared a $0.40 per share dividend on the 100,000 shares of common stock outstanding. The date of record was May 2, and the payment date was May 23.

May	23	Paid the cash dividends.
June	10	Split the company's 100,000 shares of common stock 2 for 1; one new common share was issued for each old share held.
July	30	Declared a 10 percent stock dividend on the common stock to holders of record August 21, with distribution set for September 11. The market value of the common stock was $14 per share.
Sept.	11	Issued the stock dividend shares.
Oct.	26	Repurchased 3,000 shares of the company's own common stock at $12 per share. The stock had an average issue price of $6 per share. The shares were cancelled.
Nov.	8	Sold 1,000 shares of common stock for $17 per share.
Dec.	13	Sold 500 shares of common stock for $13 per share.

Required

Record the transactions in the general journal.

Problem 14-2A *Journalizing dividend and repurchase of stock transactions and reporting shareholders' equity* **(Obj. 1, 2, 3)**

The balance sheet of Alantra Inc. at December 31, 2002, reported 200,000 shares of common stock authorized, with 50,000 shares issued and a Common Stock balance of $300,000. Retained Earnings had a credit balance of $222,500. During 2003, the company completed the following selected transactions:

Mar.	15	Repurchased 7,000 shares of the company's own common stock at $5 per share. These shares will *not* be cancelled.
Apr.	30	Declared a 20 percent stock dividend on the 43,000 shares of outstanding common stock to holders of record May 1, with distribution set for May 15. The market value of Alantra Inc. common stock was $10 per share.
May	15	Issued the stock dividend shares.
Oct.	8	Sold 2,400 repurchased shares of common stock for $12 per share.
Dec.	19	Split the common stock 2 for 1 by issuing one new share for each old share held. Prior to the split, the corporation had issued 54,000 shares.
	31	Earned net income of $195,000 during the year.

Required

1. Record the transactions in the general journal. Explanations are not required.
2. Prepare the shareholders' equity section of the balance sheet at December 31, 2003.
3. Calculate the average issue price per common share on December 31, 2003.

Problem 14-3A *Increasing dividends to fight off a takeover of the corporation* **(Obj. 1)**

Current Fashions Inc. is positioned ideally in the clothing business. Located in Vancouver, Current Fashions Inc. is the only company with a highly developed import, design, and distribution network. The company does a brisk business with high-fashion stores such as Holt Renfrew. Current Fashions Inc.'s success has made the company a prime target for a takeover. Against the wishes of Current Fashions Inc.'s board of directors, an investment group from Victoria is attempting to buy 51 percent of Current Fashions Inc.'s outstanding stock. Board members are convinced that the Victoria investors would sell off the most desirable pieces of the business and leave little of value.

At the most recent board meeting, several suggestions were advanced to fight off the hostile takeover bid. One suggestion is to increase the stock outstanding by distributing a 100 percent stock dividend.

Required

As a significant shareholder of Current Fashions Inc., write a short memo to explain to the board whether distributing the stock dividend would make it more difficult for the investor group to take over Current Fashions Inc. Include in your memo a discussion of the effect that the stock dividend would have on assets, liabilities, and total shareholders' equity, that is, the dividend's effect on the size of the corporation.

Problem 14-4A *Journalizing dividend and repurchase of stock transactions; reporting retained earnings and shareholders' equity* **(Obj. 1, 3, 6)**

The balance sheet of EKZ Logistics Ltd. at December 31, 2001, reported the following shareholders' equity:

Common stock, 100,000 shares authorized, 30,000 shares issued............	$ 750,000
Retained earnings..	285,000
Total shareholders' equity	$1,035,000

During 2002, EKZ Logistics Ltd. completed the following selected transactions:

Apr.	30	Declared a 10 percent stock dividend on the common stock. The market value of EKZ Logistics Ltd. common stock was $24 per share. The record date was May 21, with distribution set for June 5.
June	5	Issued the stock dividend shares.
July	29	Repurchased 3,000 shares of the company's own common stock at $21 per share; average issue price was $24.91.
Nov.	13	Sold 600 repurchased shares of common stock for $22 per share.
	27	Declared a $0.30 per share dividend on the common stock outstanding. The date of record was December 17, and the payment date was January 7, 2003.
Dec.	31	Closed the $93,000 credit balance of Income Summary to Retained Earnings.

Required

1. Record the transactions in the general journal.
2. Prepare a statement of retained earnings at December 31, 2002.
3. Prepare the shareholders' equity section of the balance sheet at December 31, 2002.

Problem 14-5A *Preparing a single-step income statement* **(Obj. 5)**

The following information was taken from the ledger and other records of Radar Technologies Corp. at September 30, 2002:

Cost of goods sold	$212,000	Preferred stock, $1,	
Loss on sale of capital		10,000 shares authorized	
assets.......................................	10,000	5,000 shares issued............	$100,000
Sales returns...............................	4,500	Retained earnings,	
Income tax expense (saving):		October 1, 2001	44,000
Continuing operations.........	36,000	Selling expenses.....................	68,000
Discontinued segment:		Common stock,	
Operating loss..................	(3,000)	25,000 shares	
Gain on sale.....................	1,000	authorized and issued......	125,000
Extraordinary loss	(6,000)	Sales revenue	421,000
Gain on sale of discontinued		Dividends..............................	17,500
segment.................................	2,500	Operating loss,	
Interest expense.........................	5,500	discontinued segment......	7,500
General expenses	56,500	Loss on insurance	
Interest revenue.........................	2,000	settlement...........................	6,000
Extraordinary loss......................	15,000		

Required

Prepare a single-step income statement, including earnings per share, for Radar Technologies Corp. for the fiscal year ended September 30, 2002. Evaluate income for the year ended September 30, 2002, in terms of the outlook for 2003. Assume 2002 was a typical year and that Radar Technologies Corp. managers hoped to earn income from continuing operations equal to 10 percent of net sales.

Problem 14-6A *Preparing a corrected combined statement of income and retained earnings* **(Obj. 5, 6)**

Andrea McNeill, accountant for Music Classics Ltd., was injured in a skiing accident. Another employee prepared the income statement shown below for the fiscal year ended December 31, 2002.

The individual amounts listed on the income statement are correct. However, some accounts are reported incorrectly, and others do not belong on the income statement at all. Also, income tax (40 percent) has not been applied to all appropriate figures. Music Classics Ltd. issued 52,000 shares of common stock in 2000 and has not issued or repurchased stock since that time. The retained earnings balance, as originally reported at December 31, 2001, was $541,500.

Required

Prepare a corrected combined statement of income and retained earnings for 2002; include earnings per share. Prepare the income statement portion in single-step format.

MUSIC CLASSICS LTD.
Income Statement
2002

Revenue and gains		
Sales		$543,000
Proceeds from sale of repurchased stock		120,000
Gain on retirement of preferred stock		
(issued for $81,000; repurchased for $66,000)		15,000
Total revenues and gains		678,000
Expenses and losses		
Cost of goods sold	$157,500	
Selling expenses	84,000	
General expenses	91,500	
Sales returns	16,500	
Dividends	10,500	
Sales discounts	9,000	
Income tax expense	30,000	
Total expenses and losses		399,000
Income from operations		279,000
Other gains and losses		
Loss on sale of discontinued operations	$ (4,500)	
Extraordinary flood loss	(30,000)	
Operating loss on discontinued segment	(13,500)	
Prior-period adjustment—understated income		
tax for 2001 due to an error	(7,500)	
Total other losses		(55,500)
Net income		$223,500
Earnings per share		$ 4.47

Problem 14-7A *Computing earnings per share and reporting a retained earnings restriction* **(Obj. 4, 5)**

The capital structure of NewWeb Design Inc. at December 31, 2002, included 30,000 shares of $1.25 preferred stock and 66,000 shares of common stock. The 30,000 preferred shares were issued in 1997. Common shares outstanding during 2003 were 66,000 January through May; 75,000 June through August; and 90,750 September through December. Income from continuing operations during 2003 was $121,650. The company discontinued a segment of the business at a gain (net of tax) of $9,945, and an extraordinary item generated a gain (net of tax) of $50,490. The NewWeb Design Inc. board of directors restricts $150,000 of retained earnings for contingencies.

Required

1. Compute NewWeb Design Inc.'s earnings per share. Start with income from continuing operations. Income of $121,650 is net of income tax.

2. Show two ways of reporting NewWeb Design Inc.'s retained earnings restriction. Retained earnings at December 31, 2002, was $160,500, and total capital stock at December 31, 2003, is $471,000. The company declared dividends of $43,500 in 2003.

Problem 14-8A *Accounting for stock dividends, stock splits, the repurchase of capital stock, and the sale of repurchased capital stock* **(Obj. 1, 2, 3)**

Alberta Wireless Inc. had the following shareholders' equity on January 1, 2003:

Shareholders' Equity	
Preferred Stock, $1, cumulative (1 year in arrears), liquidation price of $12, 200,000 shares authorized, 10,000 shares issued and outstanding	$100,000
Common stock, unlimited number of shares authorized, 20,000 shares issued and outstanding	100,000
Total contributed capital	200,000
Retained earnings	180,000
Total shareholders' equity	$380,000

The following transactions took place during 2003:

Jan.	15	Declared a $45,000 cash dividend, payable on March 1 to the shareholders of record on February 1. Indicate the amount payable to each class of shareholder.
Feb.	28	Issued 5,000 shares of common stock for $5 per share.
Mar.	1	Paid the cash dividend declared on January 15.
Apr.	3	Declared a 20 percent stock dividend on the common stock, distributable on May 1 to the shareholders of record on April 15. The market value of the stock was $5.20 per share.
May	1	Distributed the stock dividend declared on April 3.
July	2	Repurchased 2,500 shares of the company's own common stock at $4.00 per share.
Sept.	3	Issued 2,000 shares of repurchased common stock for $5.00 per share.
Nov.	2	Split the common stock 2 for 1.
Dec.	31	Reported net income of $88,000. Closed the income summary account.

Required

1. Record the transactions in the general journal. Explanations are not required.

2. Prepare the shareholders' equity section of the balance sheet at December 31, 2003.

Problem 14-9A *Accounting for stock dividends, stock splits, and prior-period adjustments; preparing a combined statement of income and retained earnings; calculating earnings per share* **(Obj. 1, 2, 5, 6)**

Beaupre Hothouse Ltd. operates a hydroponic cucumber farm and had the following shareholders' equity on January 1, 2002:

Shareholders' Equity

Preferred Stock, $1, convertible to common on a 2 for 1 basis, 80,000 shares authorized, 40,000 shares issued and outstanding.....................	$300,000
Common stock, unlimited number of shares authorized, 80,000 shares issued	300,000
Total contributed capital...	600,000
Retained earnings	275,000
Total shareholders' equity	$875,000

The following information is available for the year ending December 31, 2002:

Feb. 1   Declared a cash dividend of $112,500, payable on March 1 to the shareholders of record on February 15. Indicate the amount payable to each class of shareholder.

Mar. 1   Paid the cash dividend declared on February 1.

May 2   Declared a 10 percent stock dividend on the common stock, distributable on July 2 to the shareholders of record on June 15. The market value of the stock was $4.50 per share.

July 2   Distributed the common stock dividend declared on May 2.

Aug. 8   Received notification from Canada Customs and Revenue Agency that Beaupre Hothouse Ltd. had made a mistake filing 2000 taxes. The reassessment showed that the company had reported and underpaid $37,500 in taxes. The amount of taxes unpaid was due on receipt of the reassessment.

Dec. 31 Beaupre Hothouse Ltd.'s records show the following:

Sales for the year..	$ 450,000
Cost of goods sold	200,000
Operating expenses	112,500
Income from discontinued operations........................	12,500
Loss on sale of discontinued operations	7,500
Extraordinary loss...	10,000

Close the income summary account, assuming the income taxes on operating income are 40 percent and on discontinued operations and extraordinary items are 20 percent.

Required

1. Record the transactions in the general journal. Explanations are not required.

2. Prepare a combined statement of income and retained earnings for the year ended December 31, 2002. Include earnings-per-share information. For purposes of the earnings-per-share calculation, the weighted average number of common shares is 88,000.

Problems (Group B)

Problem 14-1B   *Journalizing shareholders' equity transactions*   **(Obj. 1, 3)**

Epic Data Inc. completed the following selected transactions during 2003:

Feb. 6   Declared a cash dividend on the 20,000 shares of $2.00 preferred stock. Declared a $0.20 per share cash dividend on the 20,000 shares of common stock outstanding. The date of record was February 17, and the payment date was February 20.

Feb. 20 Paid the cash dividends.

Apr. 18 Declared a 50 percent stock dividend on the common stock to holders of record April 30, with distribution set for May 30. The market value of the common stock was $17 per share.

May 30 Issued the stock dividend shares.

June 18 Repurchased 2,400 shares of the company's own common stock at $11 per share; average issue price was $9 per share. The shares will be reissued in the future.

Nov. 14 Issued 800 shares of repurchased common stock for $10 per share.
Dec. 22 Issued 700 shares of repurchased common stock for $16 per share.

Required

Record the transactions in the general journal.

Problem 14-2B *Journalizing dividend and repurchase of stock transactions and reporting shareholders' equity* **(Obj. 1, 2, 3)**

The balance sheet of InternetCap Inc. at December 31, 2002, reported 1,000,000 shares of common stock authorized with 100,000 shares issued at an average price of $6.00 each. Retained Earnings had a balance of $103,000. During 2003, the company completed the following selected transactions:

Feb. 15 Repurchased 5,000 shares of the company's own common stock at $6 per share.
Mar. 8 Sold 2,000 shares of repurchased common stock for $7 per share.
Sept. 28 Declared a 10 percent stock dividend on the 97,000 shares of outstanding common stock to holders of record October 15, with distribution set for October 31. The market value of InternetCap Inc. common stock was $7 per share.
Oct. 31 Issued the stock dividend shares.
Nov. 5 Split the common stock 2 for 1; one new common share was issued for every existing share held. Prior to the split, the corporation had 106,700 shares issued and outstanding.
Dec. 31 Earned net income of $110,000 during the year.

Required

1. Record the transactions in the general journal. Explanations are not required.
2. Prepare the shareholders' equity section of the balance sheet at December 31, 2003.
3. Calculate the average issue price per common share on December 31, 2003.

Problem 14-3B *Repurchasing stock to fight off a takeover of the corporation* **(Obj. 3)**

Whitepass Corporation is positioned ideally in its industry. Located in the Yukon, Whitepass Corporation is the only company with reliable sources for its locally produced gifts. The company does a brisk business with specialty stores. Whitepass Corporation's recent success has made the company a prime target for a takeover. An investment group from Yellowknife is attempting to buy 51 percent of the company's outstanding stock against the wishes of Whitepass Corporation's board of directors. Board members are convinced that the Yellowknife investors would sell off the most desirable pieces of the business and leave little of value.

At the most recent board meeting, several suggestions were advanced to fight off the hostile takeover bid. The suggestion with the most promise is to purchase and retire a huge quantity of stock. Whitepass Corporation has the cash to carry out this plan.

Required

1. As a significant shareholder of Whitepass Corporation, write a memorandum to explain for the board how the repurchase and retirement of stock would make it more difficult for the Yellowknife group to take over Whitepass Corporation. Include in your memo a discussion of the effect that repurchasing stock would have on stock outstanding and on the size of the corporation.

2. Suppose Whitepass Corporation management is successful in fighting off the takeover bid and later issues shares at prices greater than the purchase price.

Explain what effect the sale of these shares will have on assets, shareholders' equity, and net income.

Problem 14-4B *Journalizing dividends and repurchase of stock transactions; reporting retained earnings and shareholders' equity* *(Obj. 1, 3, 6)*

The balance sheet of CHK International Inc. at December 31, 2001, presented the following shareholders' equity:

Conributed capital

Common stock, 1,000,000 shares authorized, 200,000 shares issued............	$1,600,000
Retained earnings...	440,000
Total shareholders' equity	$2,040,000

During 2002, CHK International Inc. completed the following selected transactions:

Mar. 29 Declared a 50 percent stock dividend on the common stock. The market value of CHK International Inc. common stock was $5 per share. The record date was April 19, with distribution set for May 19.

May 19 Issued the stock dividend shares.

July 13 Repurchased 8,000 shares of the company's own common stock at $6 per share.

Oct. 4 Sold 6,400 shares of common stock for $8 per share.

Dec. 27 Declared a $0.20 per share dividend on the common stock outstanding. The date of record was January 17, 2003, and the payment date was January 31, 2003.

31 Closed the $304,000 net income to Retained Earnings.

Required

1. Record the transactions in the general journal.

2. Prepare the statement of retained earnings at December 31, 2002.

3. Prepare the shareholders' equity section of the balance sheet at December 31, 2002.

Problem 14-5B *Preparing a single-step income statement* *(Obj. 5)*

The following information was taken from the ledger and other records of DataWest Inc. at June 30, 2002:

General expenses	$142,000	Extraordinary gain...................	$ 54,000
Loss on sale of		Operating gain, discontinued	
discontinued segment..........	20,000	segment	16,000
Cost of goods sold	638,000	Loss on sale of capital	
Income tax expense (saving)		assets....................................	20,000
Continuing operations.........	56,000	Dividends on preferred	
Discontinued segment:		stock......................................	12,000
Operating income............	6,400	Preferred stock, $1.00,	
Loss on sale	(8,000)	20,000 shares authorized,	
Extraordinary gain...............	21,600	8,000 shares issued..............	200,000
Interest expense	46,000	Dividends on common	
Gain on settlement of		stock......................................	24,000
lawsuit	16,000	Sales revenue	1,178,000
Sales returns	30,000	Retained earnings	
Contributed surplus from		July 1, 2001...........................	126,000
retirement of preferred		Selling expenses	174,000
stock	32,000	Common stock,	
Sales discounts..........................	14,000	unlimited shares authorized,	
		20,000 shares issued............	700,000

Required

Prepare a single-step income statement, including earnings per share, for DataWest Inc. for the fiscal year ended June 30, 2002. Evaluate income for the year ended June 30, 2002, in terms of the outlook for 2003. Assume 2002 was a typical year and that DataWest Inc. managers hoped to earn income from continuing operations equal to 10 percent of net sales.

Problem 14-6B *Preparing a corrected combined statement of income and retained earnings* **(Obj. 5, 6)**

SCAN IMAGING LTD.
Income Statement
June 30, 2003

Revenues and gains		
Sales..		$1,250,000
Gain on retirement of preferred stock		
(issued for $76,000; purchased for $59,000).............		17,000
Total revenues and gains...		1,267,000
Expenses and losses		
Cost of goods sold..	$575,000	
Selling expenses	185,000	
General expenses..	81,000	
Sales returns..	18,000	
Prior-period adjustment—understated income		
tax for 2002 due to error	6,000	
Dividends..	23,000	
Sales discounts..	30,000	
Income tax expense...	48,000	
Total expenses and losses......................................		966,000
Income from operations		301,000
Other gains and losses		
Extraordinary gain...	40,000	
Operating income on discontinued segment...............	37,000	
Loss on sale of discontinued operations......................	(60,000)	
Total other gains		17,000
Net income		$ 318,000
Earnings per share..		$ 15.90

Derrick Chan, accountant for Scan Imaging Ltd., was injured in a sailing accident. Another employee prepared the income statement, shown above, for the fiscal year ended June 30, 2003.

The individual amounts listed on the income statement are correct. However, some accounts are reported incorrectly, and others do not belong on the income statement at all. Also, income tax (40 percent) has not been applied to all appropriate figures. Scan Imaging Ltd. issued 24,000 shares of common stock in 1999 and has not issued or repurchased shares of common stock since that date. The retained earnings balance, as originally reported at June 30, 2002, was $614,000. There were no preferred shares outstanding at June 30, 2003.

Required

Prepare a corrected combined statement of income and retained earnings for fiscal year 2003; include earnings per share. Prepare the income statement portion in single-step format.

Problem 14-7B *Computing earnings per share and reporting a retained earnings restriction* **(Obj. 4, 5)**

The capital structure of Web Design Ltd. at December 31, 2001, included 10,000 shares of $2.50 preferred stock and 260,000 shares of common stock. Common shares outstanding during 2002 were 260,000 January through February; 238,000 during March; 242,000 April through October; and 256,000 during November and December. Income from continuing operations during 2002 was $743,770. The company discontinued a segment of the business at a gain of $138,320 and also had an extraordinary loss of $99,020. The board of directors of Web Design Ltd. has restricted $100,000 of retained earnings for expansion of the company's office facilities.

Required

1. Compute Web Design Ltd.'s earnings per share. Start with income from continuing operations. Income and loss amounts are net of income tax.

2. Show two ways of reporting Web Design Ltd.'s retained earnings restriction. Retained earnings at December 31, 2001 was $255,600, and total capital stock at December 31, 2002, is $1,049,220. Web Design Ltd. declared cash dividends of $529,000 during 2002.

Problem 14-8B *Accounting for stock dividends, stock splits, the repurchase of capital stock, and the sale of repurchased capital stock* **(Obj. 1, 2, 3)**

Huron Enviromental Ltd. had the following shareholders' equity on January 1, 2002:

Shareholders' Equity	
Preferred stock, $1, cumulative (1 year in arrears), liquidation price of $24, 40,000 shares authorized, 10,000 shares issued and outstanding	$200,000
Common stock, unlimited number of shares authorized, 40,000 shares issued and outstanding..	200,000
Total contributed capital	400,000
Retained earnings	350,000
Total shareholders' equity	$750,000

The following transactions took place during 2002:

Jan.	27	Declared a $50,000 cash dividend, payable on March 1 to the shareholders of record on February 1. Indicate the amount payable to each class of shareholder.
Feb.	28	Issued 20,000 shares of common stock for $6 per share.
Mar.	1	Paid the cash dividend declared on January 27.
Apr.	3	Declared a 20 percent stock dividend on the common stock, distributable on May 1 to the shareholders of record on April 15. The market value of the stock was $6.50 per share.
May	1	Distributed the stock dividend declared on April 3.
July	2	Repurchased 4,000 shares of the company's own common stock at $7.50 per share.
Sept.	3	Issued 3,000 shares of common stock for $7.00 per share.
Nov.	2	Split the common stock 3 for 1.
Dec.	31	Reported net income of $145,000. Closed the income summary account.

Required

1. Record the transactions in the general journal. Explanations are not required.

2. Prepare the shareholders' equity section of the balance sheet at December 31, 2002.

Problem 14-9B *Accounting for stock dividends, stock splits, and prior-period adjustments; preparing a combined statement of income and retained earnings; calculating earnings per share* **(Obj. 1, 2, 5, 6)**

Sudbury Meats Ltd. had the following shareholders' equity on January 1, 2003:

Shareholders' Equity

Preferred stock, $2, convertible to common on a 2 for 1 basis, 60,000 shares authorized, 30,000 shares issued and outstanding	$ 360,000
Common stock, unlimited number of shares authorized, 60,000 shares issued and outstanding...	360,000
Total contributed capital..	720,000
Retained earnings	380,000
Total shareholders' equity	$1,100,000

The following information is available for the year ending December 31, 2003:

Feb. 7 Declared a cash dividend of $140,000, payable on March 1 to the shareholders of record on February 15. Indicate the amount payable to each class of shareholder.

Mar. 1 Paid the cash dividend declared on February 7.

May 2 Declared a 20 percent stock dividend on the common stock, distributable on July 2 to the shareholders of record on June 15. The market value of the stock was $7.40 per share.

July 2 Distributed the common stock dividend declared on May 2.

Aug. 8 Received notification from Canada Customs and Revenue Agency that Sudbury Meats Ltd. had made an error in filing 2001 taxes. The reassessment showed that the company had reported and overpaid $30,000 in taxes.

Dec. 31 Sudbury Meats Ltd.'s records show the following:

Sales for the year..	$ 900,000
Cost of goods sold	390,000
Operating expenses	220,000
Income from discontinued operations........................	30,000
Loss on sale of discontinued operations	16,000
Extraordinary loss..	36,000

Close the income summary account assuming the income taxes on operating income are 40 percent and on discontinued operations and extraordinary items are 20 percent.

Required

1. Record the transactions in the general journal. Explanations are not required.

2. Prepare a combined statement of income and retained earnings for the year ended December 31, 2003. Include earnings-per-share information.

Challenge Problems

Problem 14-1C *Explaining the effects of a stock repurchase* **(Obj. 3)**

Advantedge Corp., a public company listed on the Canadian Venture Exchange, had issued 10,000 shares of common stock at incorporation at a price of $8.00. The book value per share was $15.00 at the most recent year end. The company has been paying an annual dividend of $0.64 per share.

Recently, when the market price of the stock was $10.00, the company decided to repurchase 1,000 shares at that price.

You and a friend bought 100 shares each when the stock was issued. Your friend wonders whether he should sell his shares back to Advantedge Corp. since the company was offering 25 percent more than he had paid.

Required

Analyze the information provided to help your friend decide whether or not he should sell his shares back to the company.

Problem 14-2C   *Income from continuing operations, discontinued operations, and extraordinary items   (Obj. 5)*

In the late 1980s, the CICA's Accounting Standards Board set out fairly restrictive rules for disclosure of discontinued operations and extraordinary items. The rules limited management's ability to classify a transaction as relating to discontinued operations or as being an extraordinary item.

Required

Explain why management, in the absence of the rules in the *CICA Handbook* described above, might classify a financial event or transaction as extraordinary versus classifying it as part of continuing operations.

Extending Your Knowledge

Decision Problem

1. Analyzing cash dividends and stock dividends   (Obj. 1)

Naftex Energy Inc. had the following shareholders' equity on June 30, 2003:

Common stock, 100,000 shares issued and outstanding............................	$1,500,000
Retained earnings	1,660,000
Total shareholders' equity	$3,160,000

In the past, Naftex Energy Inc. has paid an annual cash dividend of $3.00 per share. In 2002, despite a large retained earnings balance, the board of directors wished to conserve cash for expansion and did not pay a cash dividend but did distribute a 10 percent stock dividend. During 2003, the company's cash position improved. The board declared and paid a cash dividend of $2.50 per share.

Suppose you own 4,000 shares of Naftex Energy Inc. common stock, acquired January 2, 2001. The market price of the stock was $60 per share before any of the above dividends.

Required

1. How did the stock dividend affect your proportionate ownership in the company? Explain.
2. What amount of cash dividends did you receive in 2001? What amount of cash dividends did you receive in 2003? Would you expect the dividend per share to remain unchanged?
3. Immediately after the stock dividend was distributed, the market value of Naftex Energy Inc. stock decreased from $60 per share to $54.54 per share. Does this represent a loss to you? Explain.
4. Suppose Naftex Energy Inc. announces at the time of the stock dividend that the company will continue to pay the annual $3.00 cash dividend per share, even after the stock dividend. Would you expect the market price of the stock to decrease to $54.54 per share as in requirement 3 above? Explain.

Financial Statement Problem

Retained earnings and earnings per share **(Obj. 2, 5)**

Use the Intrawest Corporation financial statements in Appendix A to answer the following questions.

1. Intrawest Corporation reports capital stock on the balance sheet and gives details in the notes to the financial statements. How many shares of common stock had Intrawest Corporation issued during the year ended June 30, 2000? How many shares were outstanding at June 30, 1999?

2. Did the company issue or redeem any shares during fiscal 2000? What was the average price per share for stock issued?

3. Prepare a T-account for Retained Earnings to show the beginning and ending balances and all activity during the year ended June 30, 2000.

4. Show how to compute net income *per share* for the year ended June 30, 2000.

CHAPTER

15

Long-Term Liabilities

CHAPTER OBJECTIVES

After studying this chapter, you should be able to

1 Discuss bonds payable and account for basic bond transactions

2 Amortize bond discount and premium by the straight-line amortization method and the effective-interest amortization method

3 Account for retirement of bonds

4 Account for conversion of bonds

5 Show the advantages and disadvantages of borrowing

6 Report lease and employee future benefits liabilities

A1 Compute the future value of an investment

A2 Compute the present value of a single future amount and the present value of an annuity

A3 Determine the cost of an asset acquired through a capital lease

CanWest Global Communications

Israel Asper O.C., Q.C., LL.D, Ph.D.
Executive Chairman

"Raising the money to finance its $3.5 billion purchase of newspapers from Conrad Black's Hollinger Inc. is becoming more expensive than planned for CanWest Global Communications Group.

The autumn slump in financial markets has made investors jittery, forcing CanWest to entice them by offering higher interest rates on $800 million in bonds it is selling.

The new rate of 12 percent is about two percentage points higher than CanWest expected to pay on the bonds, which could make a difference of millions of dollars in interest payments.

Bond rating agency Standard and Poor's has rated the bonds at 'B' level, which is five steps below investment grade."

How do investors assess the risk of a bond? Analysts from bond-rating agencies like Moody's Canada Inc., Standard and Poor's Rating Services, and Canadian Bond Rating Service evaluate the company's management, operations, finances, and outlook for the future. In addition, these analysts consider general economic conditions. In the case of CanWest Global, analysts were concerned specifically with the debt burden the company would be under if the bonds were issued, the integration of the new business (newspapers) with CanWest's existing business (television stations), and the state of the economy—whether the buoyant conditions in effect at the time of the issue would continue. In other words, analysts evaluate the risk that investors would be taking if they invested in the bonds. A central truth of business is that the return on an investment depends on the risk of the investment. Stated differently, to earn a high rate of return, an investor must take a high degree of risk. An investor who is unwilling to take much risk cannot expect to earn a high rate of return on the investment.

The risk-return relationship applies to government bonds as well as corporate bonds. The bond rating attached to companies' bonds by analysts influences how much interest companies will have to pay to investors. An upgrade would reduce the borrowing costs, while a downgrade has the opposite effect. It appears that one reason for CanWest's 12 percent interest rate is the relatively low rating given its bonds by Standard and Poor's.

Source: Quoted from Canadian Press, "CanWest Global Hikes Interest Rates to Help Finance Hollinger Deal," *The Vancouver Sun*, November 2, 2000, p. D4.

CHAPTERS 13

and 14 covered two ways of financing operations: capital stock and profitable operations (retained earnings). This chapter discusses the third way to finance a company—borrowing money on long-term liabilities, including bonds and debentures payable (and notes payable), lease liabilities, and pension liabilities. The chapter appendix provides background on the valuation of long-term liabilities.

Before launching into accounting for bonds payable, let's compare stocks and bonds.

Stocks	Bonds
1. Stocks represent ownership (equity) of the corporation.	1. Bonds represent a debt (liability) of the corporation.
2. Each shareholder is an *owner* of the corporation.	2. Each bondholder is a creditor of the corporation.
3. Shareholder has the right to receive dividends, if declared.	3. Bondholder has the right to receive interest.
4. The corporation may or may not pay dividends.	4. The corporation must pay interest.
5. Dividends are *not* an expense and are not tax-deductible by the corporation.	5. Interest is a tax-deductible expense of the corporation.

| 6. Corporation is *not* obligated to repay amount invested by the shareholders. | 6. Corporation must repay the bonds at maturity. |

Bonds: An Introduction

OBJECTIVE 1
Discuss bonds payable and account for basic bond transactions

Large companies such as Nortel Networks Corporation and Air Canada Corporation cannot borrow billions from a single lender because no lender will risk lending that much money to a single company. Even smaller companies may find it impossible to borrow all they need from a bank. Banks and other lenders diversify their risk by loaning smaller amounts to numerous customers. That way, if a borrower cannot repay, the lender is not devastated.

Air Canada Corporation
www.aircanada.ca

How then do large corporations borrow a huge amount? They issue bonds to the public. A **bond** is a formal arrangement between the issuer of the bond and the holder of the bond. The bondholder lends a fixed amount of money to the issuer. The issuer promises to pay the fixed amount at some future time and to pay regular payments of interest to the bondholder over the life of the bond. A bond is a debt of the company that issued the bond. **Bonds payable** are groups of notes payable issued to multiple lenders, called bondholders. Manitoba Telecom Services Inc. can borrow large amounts from thousands of individual investors, each buying a modest amount of Manitoba Telecom Services Inc. bonds.

Purchasers of bonds receive a bond certificate, which carries the issuing company's name. The certificate also states the *principal*, which is the amount that the company has borrowed from the bondholder. This figure, typically stated in units of $1,000, is also called the bond's face value, maturity value, or par value. The bond obligates the issuing company to pay the holder the principal amount at a specific future date, called the maturity date, which also appears on the certificate.

Bondholders lend their money to earn interest. The bond certificate states the interest rate that the issuer will pay the bondholder and the dates that the interest payments are due (generally twice a year). Some bond certificates name the bondholder (the investor).

John Labatt Ltd.
www.labatt.com

Manitoba Telecom Services Inc.
www.mts.mb.ca

RBC Dominion Securities Inc.
www.rbcds.com

Issuing bonds usually requires the services of a securities firm, like RBC Dominion Securities Inc., to act as the *underwriter* of the bond issue. The **underwriter** purchases the bonds from the issuing company and resells them to its clients. Alternatively, the underwriter may sell the bonds for a commission from the issuer, agreeing to buy all unsold bonds. This guarantees that the issuer can borrow the amount of money needed.

Types of Bonds

All the bonds in a particular issue may mature at the same time (**term bonds**), or they may mature in installments over a period of time (**serial bonds**). Serial bonds are like installment notes payable.

Secured or *mortgage* bonds give the bondholder the right to take specified assets of the issuer (called collateral) if the company *defaults*, that is, fails to pay interest or principal. *Unsecured bonds,* called **debentures**, are backed only by the good faith of the borrower. Exhibit 15-1 shows an actual debenture certificate. The discussion in this chapter will generally refer to bonds and include secured bonds and debentures. When reference is made to a debenture, the instrument will be treated in the same way as a bond.

KEY POINT

A debenture is unsecured and, therefore, is riskier than a bond, which is secured.

Bond Prices

A bond issued at a price greater than its maturity (or par) value is said to be issued at a **premium**, and a bond issued at a price less than maturity (par) value has a **discount**. Bonds sell at a premium or a discount when the interest rate that will be

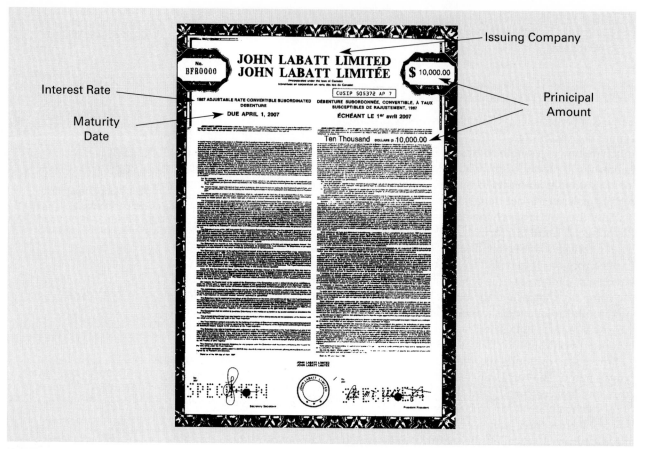

Issuing Company

Interest Rate

Maturity Date

Prinicipal Amount

EXHIBIT 15-1

Debenture Certificate

THINKING IT OVER

Refer to Exhibit 15-1. What is John Labatt Limited obligated to pay to the debenture holder?

A: John Labatt Limited is obligated to pay interest at a floating or variable rate (the debenture states the rate is adjustable) each year and to pay $10,000 on April 1, 2007.

paid on the bond is different from the interest rate available to investors elsewhere in the market. This will soon be explained more fully. As a bond nears maturity, its market price moves toward its maturity value. On the maturity date, the market value of a bond equals exactly its maturity value because the company that issued the bond pays that amount to retire the bond.

After a bond is issued, investors may buy and sell it through bond markets. The bond market in Canada is called the over-the-counter (OTC) market. It is a network of investment dealers who trade bonds issued by the Government of Canada and Crown corporations, the provinces, municipalities and regions, and corporations. Bond prices are quoted at a percentage of their maturity value using $100 as a base. For example, a $1,000 bond quoted at 100 is bought or sold for $1,000, which is 100 percent of its maturity value. The same bond quoted at 101½ has a market price of $1,015 (101½ percent of its maturity value, or $1,000 × 1.015).

Exhibit 15-2 contains actual price information for a Province of Alberta bond, taken from *The Financial Post* on January 26, 2001, On that date, the Province of Alberta's 6.375 percent $1,000 par value bonds maturing June 1, 2004, had a bid price of $103.21, or $1,032.10. This bid price provided a yield of 5.31 percent (the yield rate of a bond is influenced by the market interest rate and time to maturity). To contrast, on October 21, 1998, *The Financial Post* reported that the same bond was trading at $106.96, for a yield of 4.94 percent.

Present Value[1]

A dollar received today is worth more than a dollar received in the future. Why? Because you can invest today's dollar and earn income from it. Likewise, deferring any

---

[1] The chapter appendix covers present value in more detail.

Bonds	Int. Rate %	Maturity Date	Bid $	Yield %
Province of Alberta	6.375	June 1/04	103.21	5.31

EXHIBIT 15-2

Bond Price Information

payment until later gives your money a period to grow. Money earns income over time, a concept called the *time value of money*. Let's examine how the time value of money affects the pricing of bonds.

Assume a bond with a face value of $1,000 reaches maturity three years from today and carries no interest. Would you pay $1,000 to purchase the bond? No, because the payment of $1,000 today to receive the same amount in the future provides you with no income on the investment. You would not be taking advantage of the time value of money. Just how much would you pay today in order to receive $1,000 at the end of three years? The answer is some amount less than $1,000. Let's suppose that $750 is a fair price. By investing $750 now to receive $1,000 later, you earn $250 interest revenue over the three years. The issuing company sees the transaction this way: It pays you $250 interest expense for the use of your $750 for three years.

The amount that a person would invest *at the present time* to receive a greater amount at a future date is called the **present value** of a future amount. In our example, $750 is the present value of the $1,000 amount to be received three years from now.

Our $750 bond price is a reasonable estimate. The exact present value of any future amount depends on (1) the amount of the future payment (or receipt), (2) the length of time from the investment to the date when the future amount is to be received (or paid), and (3) the interest rate during the period. Present value is always less than the future amount. We discuss the method of computing present value in the appendix that follows this chapter. We need to be aware of the present-value concept, however, in the discussion of bond prices that follows. If your instructor so directs you, please study the appendix now.

Bond Interest Rates

Bonds are sold at market price, which is the amount that investors are willing to pay at any given time. Market price is the bond's present value, which equals the present value of the principal payment plus the present value of the cash interest payments (which are made quarterly, semiannually, or annually over the term of the bond).

Two interest rates work to set the price of a bond:

- The **contract interest rate**, or **stated interest rate**, is the interest rate that determines the amount of cash interest the borrower pays—and the investor receives—each year. The contract interest rate is set by the bond contract and may be fixed or adjustable. If the rate is fixed, it does not change during the life of the bond. For example, The Toronto-Dominion Bank's 8 percent bonds have a contract interest rate of 8 percent. Thus Toronto Dominion pays $8,000 of interest annually on each $100,000 bond. Each semiannual interest payment is $4,000 ($100,000 × 0.08 × ½).

- The **market interest rate**, or **effective interest rate**, is the rate that investors demand for loaning their money. The market interest rate varies, sometimes daily. A company may issue bonds with a contract interest rate that differs from the prevailing market interest rate. The Toronto-Dominion Bank may issue its 8 percent bonds when the market rate has risen to 9 percent. Will the Toronto Dominion bonds attract investors in this market? No, because investors can earn 9 percent on other bonds. Therefore, investors will purchase Toronto Dominion bonds only at a price less than the face or maturity value. The difference between the lower price and face value is a *discount*. Conversely, if the market interest rate is 7 percent, Toronto Dominion's 8 percent bonds will be so attractive that investors will pay more than face value for them. The difference between the higher price and face value is a *premium*.

THINKING IT OVER

Would it be better to receive $1,000 today or $1,000 in 10 years? Why?

A: $1,000 today because it can be invested today and begin earning interest. In 10 years, you would then have more than $1,000.

KEY POINT

Present value is always less than future value. You should be able to invest today's money (present value) so that it will increase (future value). The difference between present value and future value is interest.

$$\text{Present Value} + \text{Interest Earned} = \text{Future Value} \quad or$$

$$\text{Future Value} - \text{Interest Earned} = \text{Present Value}$$

KEY POINT

Because market interest rates fluctuate daily, the contract interest rate will seldom equal the market interest rate on the date the bonds are sold. Bonds sell at a premium if the market rate drops below the bonds' contract rate and at a discount if the market rate rises above the contract rate.

KEY POINT

When you buy a bond, you are really "buying" two future cash flows: principal and interest. The principal is a single sum received at maturity, and the interest is a series of receipts received each period until maturity.

LEARNING **TIP**

Use the movement of a see-saw to explain how changes in interest rates affect the present value. As interest rates rise, present value decreases. As interest rates fall, present value increases.

KEY POINT

Bonds sell at a *premium* if the market rate drops below the contract rate. Bonds sell at a *discount* if the market rate rises above the contract rate.

WORKING IT OUT

The following data will be used to illustrate various points covered in the next several Working It Outs. Assume that Quill Corp. issues, at par, $600,000 of 9%, 10-year bonds on May 31, 2002. The bonds pay interest each May 31 and November 30. What entries record issuance, first semiannual interest payment, and retirement at maturity?

A:

Issuance: May 31, 2002
Cash...................... 600,000
   Bonds Payable...... 600,000
First interest payment:
Nov. 30, 2002
Interest Expense..... 27,000
   Cash 27,000
Maturity: May 31, 2012
Bonds Payable........ 600,000
   Cash 600,000

Exhibit 15-3 shows how the contract interest rate and the market interest rate interact to determine the issuance, or selling price, of a bond.

Issuing Bonds to Borrow Money

Suppose that Air Canada Corporation has $100 million in 8 percent bonds that mature in 10 years. Assume that Air Canada issued these bonds at par on January 2, 2002. The issuance entry is

2002				
Jan.	2	Cash...	100,000,000	
		Bonds Payable.......................................		100,000,000
		To issue 8%, 10-year bonds at par.		

Air Canada, the borrower, makes this one-time entry to record the receipt of cash and the issuance of bonds. Afterward, investors buy and sell the bonds through the bond markets, similar to buying and selling shares through the stock market. The buy-and-sell transactions between investors do not involve the corporation that issued the bonds. It keeps no records of these transactions, except for the names and addresses of the bondholders. This information is needed for mailing the interest and principal payments.

Interest payments for these bonds occur each January 2 and July 2. Air Canada's entry to record the first semiannual interest payment is

2002				
July	2	Interest Expense	4,000,000	
		Cash.......................................		4,000,000
		To pay semiannual interest on bonds payable ($100,000,000 × 0.08 × ½).		

At maturity, Air Canada will record payment of the bonds as follows:

2012				
Jan.	2	Bonds Payable	100,000,000	
		Cash.......................................		100,000,000
		To pay bonds payable at maturity.		

EXHIBIT 15-3

How the Contract Interest Rate and the Market Interest Rate Interact to Determine the Price of a Bond

Issuance (Selling) Price of a Bond

Contract (stated) interest rate on a bond	equals	Market interest rate	→	Par (face, or maturity) value
Example: 8%	=	8%	→	Par: $1,000 bond issued for $1,000
Contract (stated) interest rate on a bond	less than	Market interest rate	→	Discount (price below par)
Example: 8%	<	9%	→	Discount: $1,000 bond issued below $1,000
Contract (stated) interest rate on a bond	greater than	Market interest rate	→	Premium (price above par)
Example: 8%	>	7%	→	Premium: $1,000 bond issued above $1,000

Issuing Bonds and Notes Between Interest Dates

The foregoing entries to record Air Canada's bond transactions are straightforward because the company issued the bonds on an interest payment date (January 2). However, corporations often issue bonds between interest dates because they may not need the funds in one lump sum.

Suppose Nova Scotia Power issues $200 million of 12 percent bonds due June 15, 2012. These bonds are dated June 15, 2002, and carry the price "100 plus accrued interest." An investor purchasing the bonds after the bond date must pay market value *plus accrued interest*. The issuing company will pay the full semiannual interest amount to the bondholder at the next interest payment date. Companies do not split semiannual interest payments among two or more investors who happen to hold the bonds during a six-month interest period.

Assume that Nova Scotia Power sells $100,000 of its bonds on July 15, 2002, one month after the bond date of June 15. Also assume that the market price of the bonds on July 15 is the face value. The company receives one month's accrued interest in addition to the bond's face value. Nova Scotia Power's entry to record issuance of the bonds payable is

2002				
July 15	Cash..	101,000	
	Bonds Payable...		100,000
	Interest Payable..		1,000
	To issue 12%, 10-year bonds at par, one month after the original issue date. Interest payable is $1,000 ($100,000 × 0.12 × $\frac{1}{12}$).		

Nova Scotia Power has collected one month's interest in advance. On December 15, 2002, Nova Scotia Power's entry to record the first semiannual interest payment is

2002				
Dec. 15	Interest Expense..	5,000	
	Interest Payable..	1,000	
	Cash		6,000
	To pay semiannual interest on bonds payable. Interest expense is $5,000 ($100,000 × 0.12 × $\frac{5}{12}$); cash paid is $6,000 ($100,000 × 0.12 × $\frac{6}{12}$).		

The debit to Interest Payable eliminates the credit balance in that account from July 15. Nova Scotia Power has now paid that liability.

Note that Nova Scotia Power pays a full six months' interest on December 15. After subtracting the one month's accrued interest received at the time of issuing the bond, Nova Scotia Power has recorded interest expense for five months ($5,000). This interest expense is the correct amount for the five months that the bonds have been outstanding.

Nova Scotia Power
www.nspower.com/

Sale of Bonds and Debentures Between Interest Dates—"Plus Accrued Interest"

Selling bonds and debentures between interest dates at market value plus accrued interest simplifies the borrower's accounting. Nova Scotia Power pays the same amount of interest on each bond regardless of the length of time the investor has held the bond. Nova Scotia Power need not compute each bondholder's interest payment on an individual basis.

When an investor sells bonds or debentures to another investor, the price is always "plus accrued interest." Suppose you hold Nova Scotia Power bonds as an investment for two months of a semiannual interest period and sell the bonds to another investor before you receive your interest. The person who buys the bonds will receive your two months of interest on the next specified interest date. Business practice dictates that you must collect your share of the interest from the buyer when you sell your investment. For this reason, all bond or debenture transactions are "plus accrued interest."

From the foregoing sequence of transactions, what interest would Nova Scotia Power report if it prepared financial statements immediately after December 15, 2002?

Answer: **Balance sheet:** Nothing to report because Interest Payable is $0.
Income statement: Interest Expense of $5,000.

Accounting and the e-World

Borrowers Online: Click Here to Lend Us $6 Billion

Original art, hockey memorabilia, and vintage Barbie dolls are all being sold online. Why not bonds? Companies in need of cash are stepping into e-commerce and borrowing money online.

Once the Y2K fears of financial-system collapse evaporated on January 1, 2000, bonds made their debut in cyberspace. The U.S. Government went online first—on January 5, 2000, its mortgage agency, Freddie Mac, offered a $6 billion bond issue. Ford Motor Company took the lead among corporate borrowers—five days later, Ford announced a three-year bond issue to borrow $1 billion.

Online bond selling offers some real advantages, such as a wider array of lenders. Bond issuers used to approach only large institutional investors. Now they can reach medium-sized institutions and individual investors instantly. Kim Rector of Ford Credit Europe claims: "Our strategy was based on accessing new investors, getting information to investors, getting feedback from investors, and then, quite frankly, using it as an opportunity to cross-sell. Our investors buy cars, and we'd love to see them buy Fords." As Rector says, giving and getting the latest marketing information about a company's products is another advantage of Internet trading. And online trading lets issuers see their orders filled in real time.

For all of these reasons, there has been a frenzy of activity in online borrowing. But borrowers and lenders beware: the ease of selling debt online could also be its undoing. Companies *might* be seduced into borrowing more money than they can pay back.

Based on: Chris Wright, "Cutting Through the Hype of Internet Bond Issuance," *Corporate Finance*, April 2000, pp. 5–6. Fiona Haddock, "The Seduction of Online Debt," *Global Finance*, April 2000, pp. 30–33. Antony Currie, "Bonding on the Internet," *Euromoney*, February 2000, pp. 43–50.

Issuing Bonds at a Discount

Unlike stocks, bonds are often issued at a discount. We know that market conditions may force the issuing corporation to accept a discount price for its bonds. Suppose Telus Corp. issues $100,000 of its 6 percent, 10-year bonds when the market interest rate is slightly above 6 percent. The market price of the bonds drops to $98.00, which means 98 percent of face or par value. Telus receives $98,000 ($100,000 × 0.98) at issuance. The entry is the following:

Telus Corp.
www.telus.com

2003				
Jan.	2	Cash	98,000	
		Discount on Bonds Payable	2,000	
		Bonds Payable		100,000
		To issue 6%, 10-year bonds at a discount.		
		Cash received was $98,000 ($100,000 × 0.98).		

After posting, the bond accounts have the following balances:

Bonds Payable	Discount on Bonds Payable
100,000	2,000

WORKING IT OUT

Assume that Quill Corp. issues its $600,000, 9% bonds on May 31, 2003, when the market rate of interest is just under 10%. The bonds are issued at $97.50. What entry records the issuance?

A:

May 31, 2003
Cash................... 585,000
Discount on
Bonds Payable   15,000
     Bonds Payable   600,000
($600,000 × 0.975
= $585,000)
The carrying amount on the balance sheet on May 31, 2003, is:
Bonds payable $600,000
Less: Discount on
bonds payable   15,000
Carrying amount $585,000

Telus Corp.'s balance sheet immediately after issuance of the bonds reports:

Long-term liabilities
  Bonds payable, 6%, due 2013................................ $100,000
  Less: Discount on bonds payable........................   2,000 $98,000

Discount on Bonds Payable is a contra account to Bonds Payable. Subtracting its balance from Bonds Payable yields the book value, or carrying value, of the bonds. The relationship between Bonds Payable and the Discount account is similar to the relationships between Equipment and Accumulated Amortization and between Accounts Receivable and Allowance for Uncollectible Accounts. Thus Telus Corp.'s liability is $98,000, which is the amount the company borrowed. If Telus were to pay off the bonds immediately (an unlikely occurrence), the company's required outlay would be $98,000 because the market price of the bonds is $98,000.

Interest Expense on Bonds Issued at a Discount   We earlier discussed the difference between the contract interest rate and the market interest rate. Suppose the market rate is 6.27 percent when Telus issues its 6 percent bonds. The 0.27 percent interest rate difference creates the $2,000 discount on the bonds. Telus borrows $98,000 cash but must pay $100,000 cash when the bonds mature 10 years later. What happens to the $2,000 balance of the discount account over the life of the bond issue? The $2,000 is in reality an additional interest expense to the issuing company. That amount is a cost—beyond the stated interest rate—that the business pays for borrowing the investors' money. The discount has the effect of raising the interest expense on the bonds to the market interest rate of 6.27 percent.

The discount amount is an interest expense not paid until the bond matures. However, the borrower—the bond issuer—benefits from the use of the investors' money each accounting period over the full term of the bond issue. The matching principle directs the business to match expense against its revenues on a period-by-period basis. The discount is allocated to interest expense through amortization for each accounting period over the life of the bonds. We will examine this in more detail shortly.

Issuing Bonds at a Premium

Why are bonds issued at a premium less common than bonds issued at a discount? Because companies prefer to issue bonds that pay a lower interest rate, so they price the bonds to sell at a discount. To illustrate issuing bonds at a premium, let's change the Telus Corp. example. Assume that the market interest rate is 5½ percent when the company issues its 6 percent, 10-year bonds. Because 6 percent bonds are attractive in this market, investors pay a premium price to acquire them. If the bonds are priced at $103.77 (103.77 percent of par value) Telus receives $103,770 cash upon issuance. The entry is

2003					
Jan.	2	Cash	103,770	
		Bonds Payable...		100,000
		Premium on Bonds Payable.........................		3,770
		To issue 6%, 10-year bonds at a premium.		
		Cash received is $103,770 ($100,000 × 1.0377).		

After posting, the bond accounts have the following balances:

Bonds Payable	Premium on Bonds Payable
100,000	3,770

Telus Corp.'s balance sheet immediately after issuance of the bonds reports:

Long-term liabilities
Bonds payable, 6%, due 2013 .... $100,000
Premium on bonds payable 3,770 $103,770

Premium on Bonds Payable is added to Bonds Payable to show the book value, or carrying value, of the bonds. Telus Corp.'s liability is $103,770, which is the amount that the company borrowed. Immediate payment of the bonds would require an outlay of $103,770 because the market price of the bonds at issuance is $103,770. The investors would be unwilling to give up bonds for less than their market value.

Interest Expense on Bonds Issued at a Premium   The ½ percent difference between the 6 percent contract rate on the bonds and the 5½ percent market interest rate creates the $3,770 premium. Telus borrows $103,770 cash but must pay only $100,000 cash at maturity. We treat the premium as a reduction of interest expense to Telus. The premium reduces Telus Corp.'s cost of borrowing the money and reduces the company's interest expense to an effective interest rate of 5½ percent, the market rate. We account for the premium much as we handled the discount. We amortize the bond premium as a *decrease* in interest expense over the life of the bonds.

OBJECTIVE 2
Amortize bond discount and premium by the straight-line amortization method and the effective-interest amortization method

Amortization of Bond Discounts and Bond Premiums

There are two methods for amortizing bond discounts and bond premiums: the Straight-line Method and the Effective Interest Method. Each of these will be discussed in turn.

Straight-line Method of Amortization of a Bond Discount and a Bond Premium

The *straight-line method of amortization* of bond discounts or bond premiums involves dividing the discount or premium into equal amounts for each interest period. This method is called **straight-line amortization.**

Straight-line Amortization of a Bond Discount   In our Telus Corp. example on page 810, the beginning discount is $2,000, and there are 20 semiannual interest periods during the bonds' 10-year life. Therefore, ¹⁄₂₀ of the $2,000 ($100) of bond discount is amortized each interest period. Telus Corp.'s semiannual interest entry on July 2, 2003, is[2]

---

[2] Some accountants record the payment of interest and the amortization of the discount in two separate entries, as follows:

2003
July 2   Interest Expense 3,000
               Cash 3,000
               Paid semiannual interest ($100,000 × 0.06 x 6/12).
July 2   Interest Expense 100
               Discount on Bonds Payable 100
               Authorized discount on bonds payable ($2,000/20).

WORKING IT OUT

For the $600,000 of 10-year bonds issued by Quill Corp. on May 31, 2002, at 97¹/₂, what entry on November 30, 2002, records the first semiannual interest payment and amortization of the discount?

A:
Nov. 30, 2002
Int. Expense 27,750
   Cash 27,000
   Discount on Bonds
   Payable 750
($600,000 × 0.09 × ⁶/₁₂ = $27,000 interest paid in cash, $15,000 ÷ 20 = $750 amortization)
Discount on Bonds Payable is reduced equally in each of the 20 periods until its balance reaches zero at maturity. The recording of discount amortization *increases* Interest Expense each period. That is, Interest Expense is greater than the cash paid for interest.

```
2003
July   2   Interest Expense.....................................................   3,100
                 Cash.......................................................................              3,000
                 Discount on Bonds Payable ..........................               100
                 To pay semiannual interest of $3,000 ($100,000 × 0.06 × 6⁄12) and amortize
                 discount on bonds payable ($2,000/20).
```

Interest expense of $3,100 is the sum of the contract interest ($3,000, which is paid in cash) plus the amount of discount amortized ($100). Discount on Bonds Payable is credited to amortize (reduce) the account's debit balance. Because Discount on Bonds Payable is a contra account, each reduction in its balance increases the book value of Bonds Payable. Twenty amortization entries will decrease the discount balance to zero, which means that Bonds Payable book value will have increased by $2,000 up to its face value of $100,000. The entry to pay the bonds at maturity is

```
2013
Jan.   2   Bonds Payable ......................................................   100,000
                 Cash .......................................................................            100,000
                 To pay bonds payable at maturity.
```

Straight-line Amortization of a Bond Premium   In our example on page 811, the beginning premium is $3,770, and there are 20 semiannual interest periods during the bonds' 10-year life. Therefore, 1⁄20 of the $3,770 ($188.50) of bond premium is amortized each interest period. Telus Corp.'s semiannual interest entry on July 2, 2003, is[3]

```
2003
July   2   Interest Expense.....................................................   2,811.50
                 Premium on Bonds Payable ................................      188.50
                 Cash .......................................................................            3,000.00
                 To pay semiannual interest ($100,000 × 0.06 × 6⁄12)
                 and amortize premium on bonds
                 payable ($3,770/20).
```

Interest expense of $2,811.50 is the remainder of the contract cash interest ($3,000) less the amount of premium amortized ($188.50). The debit to Premium on Bonds Payable reduces its credit balance.

Effective-Interest Method of Amortization of a Bond Discount and a Bond Premium

The straight-line amortization method has a theoretical weakness. Each period's amortization amount for a premium or discount is the same dollar amount over the life of the bonds. However, over that time, the bonds' carrying value continues to increase (with a discount) or decrease (with a premium). Thus the fixed dollar amount of amortization changes as a percentage of the bonds' carrying value, making it appear that the bond issuer's interest rate changes over time. This appearance is misleading because in fact the issuer locked in a fixed interest rate when the bonds were issued. The interest *rate* on the bonds does not change.

The **effective-interest amortization** method keeps each interest expense amount

---

[3] The payment of interest and the amortization of bond premium can be recorded in two separate entries as follows:

```
2003
July 2   Interest Expense...........................................................   3,000
                Cash......................................................................               3,000
                Paid semiannual interest ($100,000 × 0.06 × 6/12).
July 2   Premium on Bonds Payable.......................................   188.50
                Interest Expense.................................................               188.50
                Authorized discount on bonds payable ($3,770/20).
```

Assume that Quill Corp.'s $600,000 of 9%, 10-year bonds are issued on May 31, 2002, when the market rate of interest is just over 8%. The bonds are issued at $102.00. (1) What is the entry to record the issuance? (2) What is the entry on November 30, 2002, to record the first semiannual interest payment and to amortize the premium on a straight-line basis?

A:

(1) May 31, 2002

```
Cash ..........................   612,000
  Bonds Payable ........     600,000
  Premiums on
    Bonds Payable ......      12,000
```
($600,000 × 1.02 = $612,000)
The carrying amount on the balance sheet on May 31, 2002, is

```
Bonds payable              $600,000
Plus: Premium on
  bonds payable              12,000
Carrying amount           $612,000
```

(2) Nov. 30, 2002
```
Int. Expense...........   26,400
Premium on
  Bonds Payable.....      600
  Cash..................             27,000
```
($600,000 × 0.09 × 6/12 = $27,000 interest paid in cash; $12,000 ÷ 20 = $600 amortization.)

Premium on Bonds Payable is reduced equally in each of the 20 periods until the balance is fully amortized. The recording of the premium amortization decreases Interest Expense each period. Interest Expense is less than the cash paid for interest.

KEY POINT

The amount of cash paid each semiannual interest period is calculated with the formula:
Interest paid = Par value × (Contract rate/2)
This amount does not change over the term of the bond.

at the same percentage of the bonds' carrying value for every interest payment over the bonds' life. The total amount of bond discount or bond premium amortized over the life of the bonds is the same under both methods. Canadian GAAP does not specify which method should be used, although the effective-interest method is favoured because it does a better job of matching. However, the straight-line method is popular because of its simplicity.

Effective-Interest Method of Amortizing a Bond Discount   Assume that Rogers Communications Inc. issues $500,000 of 9 percent bonds at a time when the market rate of interest is 10 percent. Also assume that these bonds mature in five years and pay interest semiannually, so there are 10 semiannual interest payments. The issue price of the bonds is $480,745.[4] The discount on these bonds is $19,255 ($500,000 − $480,745). Exhibit 15-4 illustrates amortization of the discount by the effective-interest method.

Recall that we want to present interest expense amounts over the full life of the bonds at a fixed percentage of the bonds' carrying value. The 5 percent rate—the effective-interest rate (10% ÷ 2)—*is* that percentage. We have calculated the cost of the money borrowed by the bond issuer—the interest expense—as a constant percentage of the carrying value of the bonds. The dollar *amount* of interest expense varies from period to period but the interest percentage remains the same.

The *accounts* debited and credited under the effective-interest amortization method and the straight-line method are the same. Only the amounts differ. We may take the amortization *amounts* directly from the table in Exhibit 15-4. We assume that the first interest payment occurs on July 1 and use the appropriate amounts from Exhibit 15-4, reading across the line for the first interest payment date:

July	1	Interest Expense (column B)..................................	24,037	
		Discount on Bonds Payable (column C)..........		1,537
		Cash (column A)		22,500
		To pay semiannual interest and amortize discount on bonds payable.		

On page 816, Exhibit 15-5, Panel A diagrams the interest expense over the life of bonds payable issued at a discount. Panel B shows how the carrying amount of the bonds rises to the maturity date. All amounts are taken from Exhibit 15-4. Focus on the highlighted items to understand the main points of the exhibit.

Effective-Interest Method of Amortizing a Bond Premium   Let's modify the Rogers Communications Inc. example to illustrate the effective-interest method of amortizing a bond premium. Assume that Rogers issues $500,000 of five-year, 9 percent bonds that pay interest semiannually. If the bonds are issued when the market interest rate is 8 percent, their issue price is $520,500 (actually $520,497.50, rounded to $520,500 for ease of calculations).[5] The premium on these bonds is $20,500, and Exhibit 15-6 (on page 817) illustrates amortization of the premium by the effective-interest method.

Assuming that the first interest payment occurs on October 31, we read across the line in Exhibit 15-6 for the first interest payment date and pick up the appropriate amounts.

Oct.	31	Interest Expense (column B)..................................	20,820	
		Premium on Bonds Payable (column C)	1,680	
		Cash (column A)...		22,500
		To pay semiannual interest and amortize discount on bonds payable.		

On page 818, Exhibit 15-7, Panel A diagrams the interest expense over the life of the bonds issued at a premium. Panel B shows how the carrying amount of the bonds falls to maturity. All amounts are taken from Exhibit 15-6. Focus on the highlighted items.

[4]We compute this present value using the tables that appear in the appendix to this chapter.
[5]Again we compute the present value of the bonds using the tables in this chapter's appendix.

Rogers Communications Inc.
www.rogers.com

WORKING IT OUT

Back to Quill Corp. and the $600,000, 9%, 10-year bonds dated May 31, 2002. Assume that the bonds are sold on May 31, 2002, for $562,674 to yield an effective rate of 10%. Using the effective-interest method, what entry is required on Nov. 30, 2002, the first interest payment date?

A:
Nov. 30, 2002
Interest Expense   28,134*
  Discount on
    Bonds Payable   1,134†
  Cash..................   27,000

*$562,674 × 5% = $28,134
†$28,134 − $27,000 = $1,134

The Discount account has been reduced by $1,134 and has a new balance of $36,192 ($37,326−$1,134). The bonds' new carrying value is $563,808 ($600,000 − $36,192).

KEY POINT

The amount of semiannual interest expense is calculated with the formula:
Interest expense = Bond carrying value × (Market interest rate/2)
This amount will change each period as carrying value changes over the term of the bond.

Panel A: Bond Data

Maturity value—$500,000
Contract interest rate—9%
Interest paid—4½% semiannually—$22,500 ($500,000 × 0.045)
Market interest rate at time of issue—10% annually, 5% semiannually
Issue price—$480,745

EXHIBIT 15-4

Effective-Interest Method of Amortizing a Bond Discount

Panel B: Amortization Table

Semiannual Interest Period	A Interest Payment (4½% of Maturity Value)	B Interest Expense (5% of Preceding Bond Carrying Amount)	C Discount Amortization (B − A)	D Discount Account Balance (D − C)	E Bond Carrying Amount ($500,000 − D)
Issue Date				$19,255	$480,745*
1	$22,500	$24,037	$1,537	17,718	482,282
2	22,500	24,114	1,614	16,104	483,896
3	22,500	24,195	1,695	14,409	485,591
4	22,500	24,280	1,780	12,629	487,371
5	22,500	24,369	1,869	10,761	489,239
6	22,500	24,462	1,962	8,799	491,201
7	22,500	24,560	2,060	6,739	493,261
8	22,500	24,663	2,163	4,576	495,424
9	22,500	24,771	2,271	2,304	497,696
10	22,500	24,804	2,304	-0-	500,000

*Minor differences because of the effect of rounding.

Notes

Column A The semiannual interest payments are constant because they are fixed by the contract interest rate and the bonds' maturity value.

Column B The interest expense each period is computed by multiplying the preceding bond carrying amount by the market interest rate. The effect of this *effective interest rate* determines the interest expense each period. The amount of interest each period increases as the effective-interest rate, a constant, is applied to the increasing bond carrying amount (E).

Column C The excess of each interest expense amount (B) over each interest payment amount (A) is the discount amortization for the period.

Column D The discount balance decreases by the amount of amortization for the period (C) from $19,255 at the bonds' issue date to zero at their maturity. Balance of the discount + bonds' carrying amount equal the bonds' maturity value.

Column E The bonds' carrying amount increases from $480,745 at issuance to $500,000 at maturity.

LEARNING TIP

Compare and contrast the straight-line and effective-interest methods of amortization:
Straight-line: Interest expense, amortization of premium discount, and cash interest paid are the same each period. Interest expense is the cash paid +(−) the amortization of the premium or discount. The carrying amount will equal the maturity value at maturity.
Effective interest: The cash interest paid is the same as under the straight-line method; the interest expense is computed by multiplying the carrying amount by the effective interest rate. The interest expense will change each period. The carrying amount will equal the maturity value at maturity.

STOP & THINK

Over the life of a bond issued at a *discount*, will the periodic amount of interest expense increase or decrease under the effective-interest amortization method?

Answer: The periodic amount of interest expense *increases* because the carrying amount of the bond *increases* toward maturity value. To see this, refer to columns B and E of Exhibit 15-4.

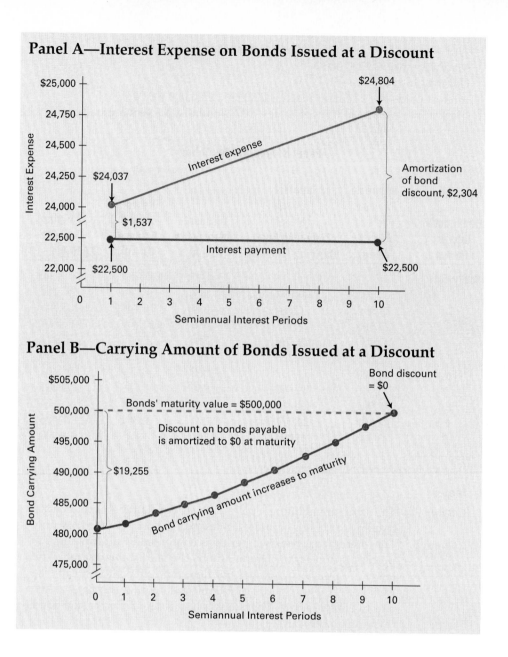

Panel A—Interest Expense on Bonds Issued at a Discount

Panel B—Carrying Amount of Bonds Issued at a Discount

STOP & THINK

How does the method of amortizing bond premium or discount affect the amount of cash
interest paid on a bond?

Answer: The amortization method for bond premium or discount has *no effect* on the
amount of cash interest paid on a bond. The amount of cash interest paid depends on the
contract interest rate stated on the bond. That interest rate, and the amount of cash interest paid, are fixed and therefore remain constant over the life of the bond. To see this,
examine column A of Exhibits 15-4 and 15-6.

EXHIBIT 15-6

Effective-Interest Method of Amortizing a Bond Premium

Panel A: Bond Data

Maturity value—$500,000
Contract interest rate—9%
Interest paid—4½% semiannually, $22,500 ($500,000 × 0.045)
Market interest rate at time of issue—8% annually, 4% semiannually
Issue price—$520,500

Panel B: Amortization Table

Semiannual Interest Period	A Interest *Payment* (4½% of Maturity Value)	B Interest *Expense* (4% of Preceding Bond Carrying Amount)	C Premium Amortization (A – B)	D Premium Account Balance (D – C)	E Bond Carrying Amount ($500,000 + D)
Issue Date				$20,500	$520,500
1	$22,500	$20,820	$1,680	18,820	518,820
2	22,500	20,753	1,747	17,073	517,073
3	22,500	20,683	1,817	15,256	515,256
4	22,500	20,610	1,890	13,366	513,366
5	22,500	20,535	1,965	11,401	511,401
6	22,500	20,456	2,044	9,357	509,357
7	22,500	20,374	2,126	7,231	507,231
8	22,500	20,289	2,211	5,020	505,020
9	22,500	20,201	2,299	2,721	502,721
10	22,500	19,779*	2,721	-0-	500,000

*Note: Numbers may not add due to rounding.

Notes:

Column A The semiannual interest payments are a constant amount fixed by the contract interest rate and the bonds' maturity value.

Column B The interest expense each period is computed by multiplying the preceding bond carrying amount by the effective-interest rate. The amount of interest decreases each period as the bond carrying amount decreases.

Column C The excess of each interest payment (A) over the period's interest expense (B) is the premium amortization for the period.

Column D The premium balance decreases by the amount of amortization for the period (C) from $20,500 at issuance to zero at maturity. The bonds' carrying amount – the premium balance = the bonds' maturity value.

Column E The bonds' carrying value decreases from $520,500 at issuance to $500,000 at maturity.

STOP & THINK

For a bond issued at a *premium*, will the periodic amount of interest expense increase or decrease? Assume the effective-interest method.

Answer: The periodic amount of interest expense *decreases* because the carrying amount of the bond *decreases* toward maturity value. To see this, study columns B and E of Exhibit 15-6. The downward-sloping line in Exhibit 15-7, Panel A, on page 818, illustrates the decreasing amount of interest expense.

EXHIBIT 15-7

Interest Expense and Bond Carrying Amount Both Decrease for Bonds Issued at a Premium

Panel A—Interest Expense on Bonds Issued at a Premium

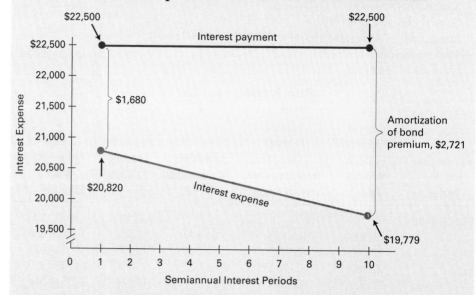

Panel B—Carrying Amount of Bonds Issued at a Premium

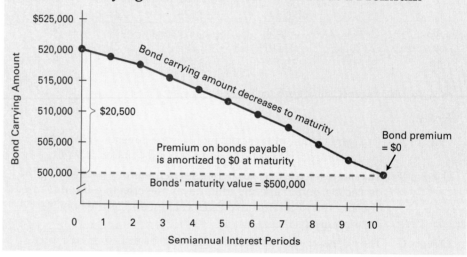

LEARNING TIP

The carrying amount in Exhibit 15-7 changes by the amortization of the premium. The new carrying amount each period can be calculated by subtracting the amortization of the premium from the previous bond carrying amount. The carrying amount at the end of the fourth period will be:

$515,256
−1,890
$513,366

Note: Just the opposite was true for bonds at a discount. The new carrying amount each period can be calculated by adding the amortization of the discount to the previous bond carrying amount.

STOP & THINK

Consider bonds issued at a discount. Which will be greater, the cash interest paid per period or the amount of interest expense? Answer the same question for bonds issued at a premium.

Answer: For bonds issued at a *discount*, interest expense will be greater than cash interest paid, by the amount of the discount amortized for the period. Remember that the company received less than face value when it issued the bonds. But at maturity, the company must pay the full value back to the bondholders. Thus, a discount increases the company's interest expense above the amount of cash interest paid each period.

For bonds issued at a *premium*, cash interest paid will be greater than interest expense, by the amount of the premium amortized for the period. This is because the premium amount received at issuance decreases the interest expense below the amount of cash interest paid each period.

Reporting Bonds Payable

Bonds payable are reported on the balance sheet at their maturity amount plus any unamortized premium or minus any unamortized discount. For example, at December 31, Telus Corp. in the example on page 813 would have amortized Premium on Bonds Payable for two semiannual periods ($188.50 × 2 = $377). The Telus Corp. balance sheet would show these bonds payable as follows:

Long-term liabilities		
Bonds Payable, 6% due 2013................................	$100,000	
Premium on bonds payable		
[$3,770 – (2 × $188.50)]..	3,393	$103,393

Over the life of the bonds, twenty amortization entries will decrease the premium balance to zero. The payment at maturity will debit Bonds Payable and credit Cash for $100,000.

Adjusting Entries for Interest Expense

Manitoba Hydro
www.hydro.mb.ca

Companies issue bonds when they need cash. The interest payments seldom occur on the end of the company's fiscal year. Nevertheless, interest expense must be accrued at the end of the period to measure net income accurately. The accrual entry may often be complicated by the need to amortize a discount or a premium for only a partial interest period.

Adjusting Entries Using the Straight-line Method

Suppose Manitoba Hydro issues $1,000,000 of 8 percent, 10-year bonds at a $20,000 discount on October 1, 2002. Assume that interest payments occur on March 31 and September 30 each year. On December 31, Manitoba Hydro records interest for the three-month period (October, November, and December) as follows:

2002				
Dec. 31	Interest Expense...	20,500		
	Interest Payable...		20,000	
	Discount on Bonds Payable		500	
	To accrue three months' interest			
	($1,000,000 × 0.08 × 3/12) and amortize discount on			
	bonds payable for three months ($20,000/10 × 3/12).			

Interest Payable is credited for the three months of cash interest that have accrued since September 30. Discount on Bonds Payable is credited for three months of amortization.

The Manitoba Hydro balance sheet at December 31, 2002, reports Interest Payable of $20,000 as a current liability. Bonds Payable appears as a long-term liability, presented as follows:

Long-term liabilities		
Bonds payable, 8%, due 2012	$1,000,000	
Less: Discount on bonds payable ($20,000 – $500)	19,500	$980,500

Observe that the balance of Discount on Bonds Payable decreases by $500. The bonds' carrying value increases by the same amount. The bonds' carrying value continues to increase over its 10-year life, reaching $1,000,000 at maturity when the discount will be fully amortized.

The next semiannual interest payment occurs on March 31, 2003, as follows:

WORKING IT OUT

For the Working It Out exercise on page 813, (1) what year-end adjusting entry is required on Dec. 31, 2002? (2) What entry will follow on May 31, 2003?

A:

(1) Dec. 31, 2002
Int. Expense 4,400
Premium on
  Bonds Payable 100
    Int. Payable 4,500
($27,000 × 1/6 = $4,500 and $600 × 1/6 = $100, both for 1 month)
The amounts recorded are 1/6 of the usual semiannual amortization and interest amounts.
(2) May 31, 2003
Int. Expense............ 22,000
Interest Payable 4,500
Premium on
  Bonds Payable 500
    Cash.................. 27,000

This entry represents 5 months of interest expense and of amortization and 6 months of interest paid in cash. Interest expense and amortization for the remaining month have been recorded in the Dec. 31, 2002, entry.

Chapter Fifteen Long-Term Liabilities   **819**

```
          2003
          Mar.  31   Interest Expense.....................................................   20,500
                     Interest Payable ...............................................   20,000
                         Cash ........................................................................            40,000
                         Discount on Bonds Payable...........................                  500
                     To pay semiannual interest
                     ($1,000,000 × 0.08 × 6/12), part of which was
                     accrued, and amortize three months' discount
                     on bonds payable ($20,000/10 × 3/12).
```

Amortization of a premium over a partial interest period is similar except that Premium on Bonds Payable is debited.

Adjusting Entries Using the Effective-Interest Method

At year end, it is necessary to make an adjusting entry for accrued interest and amortization of the bond premium for a partial period. In our example on page 814, the last interest payment occurred on October 31. The adjustment for November and December must cover two months, or one-third of a semiannual period. The entry, with amounts drawn from line 2 in Exhibit 15-6 on page 817 is

```
          Dec.  31   Interest Expense.......................................................    6,918
                     Premium on Bonds Payable ..................................      582
                         Interest Payable ..................................................             7,500
                     To accrue two months' interest
                     ($20,753 × 1/3) and amortize premium on bonds
                     payable for two months ($1,747 × 1/3).
```

The second interest payment occurs on April 30 of the following year. The payment of $22,500 includes interest expense for four months (January through April), the interest payable at December 31, and premium amortization for four months. The payment entry is the following:

```
          Apr.  30   Interest Expense .....................................................   13,835
                     Interest Payable......................................................    7,500
                     Premium on Bonds Payable..................................    1,165
                         Cash...................................................................            22,500
                     To pay semiannual interest ($13,835 = $20,753×
                     2/3), some of which was accrued ($7,500), and amor-
                     tize premium on bonds payable for four months
                     ($1,747 × 2/3).
```

If these bonds had been issued at a discount, procedures for these interest entries would be the same, except that Discount on Bonds Payable would be credited.

Take a few moments to review the first half of the chapter by studying the Decision Guidelines feature.

Decision	Guidelines
Need to pay back principal amount • All at maturity? • In installments?	Type of bonds to issue: • Term bonds • Serial bonds
Are the bonds secured? • Yes • No	Then they are • Mortgage, or secured, bonds • Debenture, or unsecured, bonds
How are bond prices • Quoted? • Determined?	 • As a percentage of maturity value (Example: A $500,000 bond priced at $510,000 would be quoted at 102 ($510,000 ÷ $500,000 = 1.02)) • Present value of the future principal amount to pay plus present value of the future periodic interest payments (see chapter appendix)
What are the two interest rates used for bonds?	• *Contract (stated) interest rate* determines the amount of cash interest the borrower pays. This interest rate is set by contract and does not change during the life of the bonds. • *Market (effective) interest rate* is the rate that investors demand for loaning their money. The market interest rate determines the borrower's true rate of interest expense. This rate varies, sometimes daily.
What causes a bond to be priced at • Par (face, or maturity) value? • A premium? • A discount?	When the bonds are issued, • Contract interest rate on the bond *equals* Market interest rate • Contract interest rate on the bond *greater than* Market interest rate • Contract interest rate on the bond *less than* Market interest rate
What is the relationship between interest expense and interest payments when bonds are issued at • Par (face, or maturity) value? • A premium? • A discount?	 • Interest expense *equals* interest payment • Interest expense *less than* interest payment • Interest expense *greater than* interest payment
How to report bonds payable on the balance sheet?	Par (face, or maturity) amount $\left\{\begin{array}{l} + \text{Premium on bonds} \\ \text{or} \\ - \text{Discount on bonds} \end{array}\right.$
What happens to the bonds' carrying amount when bonds payable are issued at • Par? • A premium? • A discount?	 • Carrying amount *stays* at par (face, or maturity) value during the life of the bonds. • Carrying amount *falls* gradually to the bonds' maturity value on their maturity date. • Carrying amount *rises* gradually to the bonds' maturity value on their maturity date.

Assume that Hydro-Québec has outstanding an issue of 9 percent bonds that mature on May 1, 2023. Further, assume that the bonds are dated May 1, 2003, and Hydro-Québec pays interest each April 30 and October 31.

Required

1. Will the bonds be issued at par, at a premium, or at a discount if the market interest rate is 8 percent at date of issuance? What if the market interest rate is 10 percent?

2. Assume Hydro-Québec issued $5,000,000 of the bonds at 104.00 on May 1, 2003.
   a. Record issuance of the bonds.
   b. Record the interest payment and straight-line amortization of the premium or discount on October 31, 2003.
   c. Accrue interest and amortize the premium or discount on December 31, 2003.
   d. Show how the company would report the bonds on the balance sheet at December 31, 2003.
   e. Record the interest payment on April 30, 2004.

Solution to Review Problem

Requirement 1

If the market interest rate is 8 percent, 9 percent bonds will be issued at a *premium*. If the market rate is 10 percent, the 9 percent bonds will be issued at a *discount*.

Requirement 2

2003

a. May 1	Cash		5,200,000	
	Bonds Payable			5,000,000
	Premium on Bonds Payable			200,000
	To issue 9%, 20-year bonds at a premium ($5,000,000 × 1.04).			
b. Oct. 31	Interest Expense		220,000	
	Premium on Bonds Payable		5,000	
	Cash			225,000
	To pay semiannual interest ($5,000,000 × 0.09 × ⁶⁄₁₂) and amortize premium on bonds payable ($200,000/40).			
c. Dec. 31	Interest Expense		73,333	
	Premium on Bonds Payable		1,667	
	Interest Payable			75,000
	To accrue interest ($5,000,000 × 0.09 × ²⁄₁₂) and amortize bond premium for two months ($200,000/40 × ²⁄₆).			

To pay semiannual interest ($5,000,000 × $0.09 \times {}^{6}\!/_{12}$) and amortize premium on bonds payable ($200,000/40).

To accrue interest ($5,000,000 × 0.09 × ${}^{2}\!/_{12}$) and amortize bond premium for two months ($200,000/40 × ${}^{2}\!/_{6}$).

d. Long-term liabilities

Bonds payable, 9%, due 2023	$5,000,000	
Premium on bonds payable		
($200,000 − $5,000 − $1,667)*	193,333	$5,193,333

---

*The calculation is for student reference only. It would not appear on the balance sheet.

2004

e. Apr. 30	Interest Expense	146,667	
	Interest Payable	75,000	
	Premium on Bonds Payable	3,333	
	Cash		225,000

To pay semiannual interest
($5,000,000 × 0.09 × %₁₂), part of which
was accrued ($75,000), and amortize
four months' premium on bonds
payable ($200,000/40 × ⅘).

Supplement to Summary Problem Solution

Bond problems include many details. You may find it helpful to check your work. We verify the answers to the Summary Problem in this supplement.

On April 30, 2004, the bonds have been outstanding for one year. After the entries have been recorded, the account balances should show the results of one year's cash interest payments and one year's bond premium amortization.

Fact 1 Cash interest payments should be $450,000 ($5,000,000 × 0.09).

Accuracy check Two credits to Cash of $225,000 each = $450,000. Cash payments are correct.

Fact 2 Premium amortization should be $10,000 ($200,000/40 semiannual periods × 2 semiannual periods in 1 year).

Accuracy check Three debits to Premium on Bonds Payable ($5,000 + $1,667 + $3,333 = $10,000). Premium amortization is correct.

Fact 3 Also we can check the accuracy of interest expense recorded during the year ended December 31, 2003.

The bonds in this problem will be outstanding for a total of 20 years, or 240 (that is, 20 × 12) months. During 2003, the bonds are outstanding for 8 months (May through December).

Interest expense for 8 months *equals* payment of cash interest for 8 months minus premium amortization for 8 months.

Interest expense should therefore be ($5,000,000 × 0.09 × ⁸⁄₁₂ = $300,000) minus [($200,000/240) × 8 = $6,667] or ($300,000 − $6,667 = $293,333).

Accuracy check: Two debits to Interest Expense ($220,000 + $73,333) = $293,333. Interest expense for 2003 is correct.

Cyber Coach

Visit the Student Resources area of the *Accounting* Companion Website for extra practice with the new material in Chapter 15.

www.pearsoned.ca/horngren

Bond Sinking Fund

Bond indentures, the contracts under which bonds are issued, often require the borrower to make regular periodic payments to a bond sinking fund. A fund is a group of assets that are segregated for a particular purpose. A *bond sinking fund* is used to retire bonds payable at maturity. A trustee manages this fund for the issuer, investing the company's payments in income-earning assets. The company's payments into the fund and the interest revenue the fund earns—which the trustee reinvests in the fund—accumulate. The target amount of the sinking fund is the face value of the bond issue at maturity. When the bonds come due, the trustee sells the sinking fund assets and uses the cash proceeds to retire the bonds. The bond sinking fund provides security of payment to investors in unsecured bonds.

Most companies report sinking funds under the heading Investments, a separate asset category between current assets and capital assets on the balance sheet. A bond sinking fund is not a current asset because it may not be used to pay current liabilities. Accounting for the interest, dividends, and other earnings on the bond sinking fund requires use of the accounts Sinking Fund and Sinking Fund Revenue.

Assume Sobeys Inc. has outstanding $18.5 million of 8 percent sinking fund debentures. The company must make annual sinking-fund payments. The entry to deposit $1,000,000 with the trustee is

Jan.	5	Sinking Fund	1,000,000	
		Cash		1,000,000
		To make annual sinking fund deposit.		

If the trustee invests the cash and reports annual sinking fund revenue of $100,000, the fund grows by this amount, and Sobeys Inc. makes the following entry at year end:

Apr.	30	Sinking Fund	100,000	
		Sinking Fund Revenue.............................		100,000
		To record sinking fund earnings.		

Assume that Sobeys Inc. has made the required sinking fund payments over a period of years and that these payments plus the fund earnings have accumulated a cash balance of $18.9 million at maturity. The trustee pays off the bonds and returns the excess cash to Sobeys Inc., which makes the following entry:

Jan.	4	Cash	400,000	
		Bonds Payable	18,500,000	
		Sinking Fund		18,900,000
		To record payment of bonds payable and receipt of excess sinking fund cash at maturity.		

If the fund balance is less than the bonds' maturity value, the entry is similar to the foregoing entry. However, the company pays the extra amount and credits Cash.

OBJECTIVE 3
Account for retirement of bonds

Retirement of Bonds

Normally companies wait until maturity to pay off, or retire, their bonds payable. All bond discount or premium has been amortized, and the retirement entry debits Bonds Payable and credits Cash for the bonds' maturity value. But companies sometimes retire their bonds payable prior to maturity. The main reason for retiring bonds early is to relieve the pressure of making interest payments. Interest rates fluctuate. The company may be able to borrow at a lower interest rate and use the proceeds from new bonds to pay off the old bonds, which bear a higher rate.

Some bonds are **callable**, which means that the bonds' issuer may *call* or pay off those bonds at a specified price whenever the issuer so chooses. The call price is usually a few percentage points above the face value or par, perhaps $104.00 or $105.00, to make the bonds attractive to lenders. Callable bonds give the issuer the benefit of being able to take advantage of low interest rates by paying off the bonds at the most favourable time. An alternative to calling the bonds is to purchase them in the open market at their current market price.

Whether the bonds are called or purchased in the open market, the journal entry is the same.

Air Products Canada Ltd. has $10,000,000 of debentures outstanding with unamortized discount of $40,000. Lower interest rates in the market may convince management to retire these bonds now. Assume that the bonds are callable at $103.00. If the market price of the bonds is $99.50 will Air Products Canada Ltd. call the bonds or purchase them in the open market? The market price is lower than the call price, so market price is the better choice. Retiring the bonds at $99.50 results in a gain of $10,000, computed as follows:

Face value of bonds being retired	$10,000,000
Unamortized discount	40,000
Book value	9,960,000
Market price ($10,000,000 × 0.9950)	9,950,000
Gain on retirement	$ 10,000

The following entry records retirement of the bonds, immediately after an interest date:

June 30	Bonds Payable	10,000,000	
	Discount on Bonds Payable......................		40,000
	Cash		9,950,000
	Gain on Retirement of		
	Bonds Payable......................................		10,000
	To retire bonds payable before maturity.		

The entry removes the bonds payable and the related discount from the accounts and records a gain on retirement. Of course, any existing premium would be removed with a debit. If Air Products Canada Ltd. had retired only half of these bonds, the accountant would remove half of the discount or premium. Likewise, if the price paid to retire the bonds exceeds their carrying value, the retirement entry would record a loss with a debit to the account Loss on Retirement of Bonds. GAAP requires that gains and losses on early retirement of debt that are both abnormal in size and unusual, be reported separately as a line item on the income statement before income tax and discontinued operations and extraordinary items.

In summary, when bonds are retired before maturity, follow these steps: (1) Record partial period amortization of premium or discount, if date is other than an interest payment date. (2) Write off the portion of Premium or Discount that relates to the portion of bonds being retired. (3) Calculate any gain or loss on retirement.

Convertible Bonds and Notes

Corporations often add *sweeteners* to their bonds—features to make the bonds more attractive to potential investors. Many corporate bonds, debentures, and notes payable have the feature of being convertible into the common stock of the issuing company at the option of the investor. These bonds and notes, called **convertible bonds** (or **convertible notes**), combine the safety of assured receipts of principal and interest on the bonds with the opportunity for large gains on the stock. The conversion feature is so attractive that investors usually accept a lower contract, or stated, interest rate than they would on nonconvertible bonds. The lower interest rate benefits the issuer. Convertible bonds are recorded like any other debt at issuance.

If the market price of the issuing company's stock gets high enough, the bondholders will convert the bonds into stock. The corporation records conversion by debiting the bond accounts and crediting the shareholders' equity accounts. Normally, the carrying value of the bonds becomes the book value of the newly issued stock, and no gain or loss is recorded.

Inco Limited reported in its 1999 annual report that it had outstanding $173 million of 5.75% Convertible U.S. Debentures due 2004 and that

> The Debentures . . . are convertible, at the option of holders, into common shares of the Company, at a conversion price of $30 (U.S.) per share.

OBJECTIVE 4
Account for conversion of bonds

Inco Limited
www.inco.com/

Assume that $3,000,000 of debentures were converted into 100,000 ($3,000,000/$30) shares of common stock on May 1, 2002. Inco Limited reports its financial statements in U.S. dollars so no conversion to Canadian dollars is necessary. The debentures were issued at par. Inco's entry to record the conversion would be:

2002				
May	1	Debentures Payable.....................................	3,000,000	
		Share Capital		3,000,000
		To record conversion of $3,000,000 debentures		
		outstanding into 100,000 common shares.		

Observe that the carrying value of the debentures ($3,000,000) becomes the amount of increase in shareholders' equity.

Current Portion of Long-Term Debt

Many companies have several issues of long-term debt outstanding where each issue has a different maturity date. For example, Inco Limited reported in its 1999 annual report that it had 10 different issues of debt outstanding aggregating $1,540 million (U.S.) and that $45 million of that total was due in one year. Inco Limited reported the debt as follows on its December 31, 1999, balance sheet:

	$ millions
Current liabilities	
Current portion of long-term debt...	$ 190
Long-term debt, excluding amounts payable within one year	1,154

The portion of long-term debt that is due within the next year is reclassified as a current liability and the long-term debt is reduced by the same amount.

Mortgage Notes Payable

You have probably heard of mortgage payments. Many notes payable are mortgage notes, which actually contain two agreements.

- The *note* is the borrower's promise to pay the lender the amount of the debt.
- The **mortgage**—a security agreement related to the note—is the borrower's promise to transfer the legal title to certain assets to the lender if the debt is not paid on schedule.

The borrower is pledging these assets as security for the note. Often the asset that is pledged was acquired with the borrowed money. For example, most homeowners sign mortgage notes to purchase their residence, pledging that property as security for the loan. Businesses sign mortgage notes to acquire buildings, equipment, and other long-term assets. Mortgage notes usually require monthly or quarterly payments.

OBJECTIVE 5
Show the advantages and disadvantages of borrowing

Advantage of Issuing Bonds versus Stock

Businesses acquire assets in different ways. Management may decide to purchase or to lease equipment. The money to pay for the asset may be financed by the business's retained earnings, a note payable, a stock issue, or a bond issue. Each financing strategy has its advantages and disadvantages as follows:

	Advantages of Financing Operations by	
	Issuing Stock	**Issuing a Note or Bonds**
	• Creates no liabilities or interest expense, which must be paid even during bad years. Less risky to the issuing corporation.	• Does not dilute stock ownership or control of the corporation. • May result in higher earnings per share because interest expense is tax-deductible and ownership is not diluted.

Exhibit 15-8 illustrates the earnings-per-share (EPS) advantage of borrowing. Recall that earnings per share (EPS) is a company's net income per share of outstanding common stock. EPS may be the most important figure on the income statement. Suppose a corporation with net income of $600,000 and with 200,000 shares of common stock outstanding needs $500,000 for expansion. Management is considering two financing plans.

- Plan 1 is to issue $1,000,000 of 10 percent bonds.
- Plan 2 is to issue 100,000 shares of common stock for $1,000,000.

Management believes the new cash can be invested in operations to earn income of $300,000 before interest and taxes.

The EPS amount is higher if the company borrows (Plan 1). The business earns more on the investment ($120,000) than the interest it pays on the bonds ($100,000). Earning more income than the cost of borrowing increases the earnings for common shareholders, and is called **trading on the equity**. It is widely used in business to increase earnings per share of common stock.

Borrowing has its disadvantages. Interest expense may be high enough to eliminate net income and lead to a cash crisis and even bankruptcy. This has happened to many Internet startups. Also, borrowing creates liabilities that accrue during bad years as well as during good years. In contrast, a company that issues stock can omit paying dividends during a bad year.

Computer spreadsheets are useful in evaluating financing alternatives issuing common stock, preferred stock, or bonds. This assessment is often called "what if" analysis—for instance, "what if we finance with common stock?" The answers to "what if" questions can be modeled on a spreadsheet to project the company's financial statements over the next few years.

	Plan 1 Borrow $1,000,000 at 10%	Plan 2 Issue $1,000,000 of Common Stock
Net income after interest and income tax, before expansion..	$600,000	$600,000
Project income before interest and income tax	$300,000	$300,000
Less: interest expense ($1,000,000 × 0.10).......	100,000	-0-
Project income before income tax	200,000	300,000
Less: income tax expense (40%)	80,000	120,000
Project net income	$120,000	$180,000
Total company net income	$720,000	$780,000
Earnings per share including expansion		
Plan 1 ($720,000/200,000 shares)	$ 3.60	
Plan 2 ($780,000/300,000 shares)		$ 2.60

EXHIBIT 15-8

Earnings-per-Share Advantage of Borrowing versus Issuing Stock

OBJECTIVE 6
Report lease and employee
future benefits liabilities

Lease Liabilities

A **lease** is an agreement in which the tenant (**lessee**) agrees to make regular, periodic payments to the property owner (**lessor**) in exchange for the exclusive use of the asset. Leasing avoids having to make the large initial cash down payment that purchase agreements require. Accountants divide leases into two types when considering the lease from the lessee's perspective: operating and capital. The lessor divides capital leases into three kinds: *operating leases*, *sales-type leases*, in which the lessor is usually a manufacturer or dealer, and *direct financing leases*, in which the lessor is usually not a manufacturer or dealer but provides financing. This text will consider the broader term, *capital lease*, and not the kinds of capital lease.

In a recent survey of 200 Canadian companies, 78 or 39 percent had operating leases only, 5 or 2.5 percent had capital leases only, and 62 or 31 percent had both operating and capital leases.[6]

Operating Leases

Operating leases are usually short-term or cancelable. Many apartment leases and most short-term car-rental agreements extend a year or less. These operating leases give the lessee the right to use the asset, but provide the lessee with no continuing rights to the asset. The lessor retains the usual risks and rewards of owning the leased asset. To account for an operating lease, the lessee debits Rent Expense (or Lease Expense) and credits Cash for the amount of the lease payment. The lessee's books report neither the leased asset nor any lease liability (except perhaps a prepaid rent amount or a rent accrual at the end of the period). However, the future lease payments for each of the next five years should be given in the notes to the financial statements. The nature of the lease commitments should also be stated in the notes.

Capital Leases

Many businesses use capital leasing to finance the acquisition of some assets. A capital lease is a long-term and noncancelable financing that is a form of debt. How do you distinguish a capital lease from an operating lease? Section 3065 of the *CICA Handbook* defines a **capital lease** as one that transfers substantially all the benefits and risks incident to ownership of property to the lessee. The section goes on to suggest that a lease is a capital lease from the perspective of the lessee if one or more of the following conditions are present at the beginning of the lease:

1. There is reasonable assurance that the lessee will obtain ownership of the leased asset at the end of the lease term.

2. The lease term is of such a length that the lessee will obtain almost all (usually 75 percent or more) of the benefits from the use of the leased asset over its life.

3. The lessor would both recover the original investment and earn a return on that investment from the lease.

KEY POINT

For an operating lease, the lessor, not the lessee, records the amortization expense on the leased asset. For a capital lease, the lessee records the amortization expense.

A lease that does not meet any of the above conditions is probably an operating lease and should be accounted for as such.

A lease is a capital lease from the perspective of the lessor if any one of the three conditions outlined above is present and *both* of the following are present:

1. The credit risk associated with the lease is normal.

2. The amounts of any unreimbursable costs to the lessor are estimable.

---

[6] Byrd, C., I. Chen and H. Chapman, *Financial Reporting in Canada 1999*, Twenty-fourth Edition. (Toronto: Canadian Institute of Chartered Accountants, 1999), p. 286.

Accounting for a Capital Lease   Accounting for a capital lease is much like accounting for a purchase. The lessor removes the asset from his or her books. The lessee enters the asset into his or her accounts and records a lease liability at the beginning of the lease term. Thus, the lessee capitalizes the asset on its own financial statements even though the lessee may never take legal title to the property.

Sierra Wireless Inc. has its head office in Vancouver. Suppose Sierra leases a building on January 2, 2002, agreeing to pay $50,000 annually for a 20-year period, with the first payment due immediately and all subsequent payments due at the beginning of the year. This meets the second condition for a capital lease given above; this arrangement is similar to purchasing the building on an installment plan. In an installment purchase, Sierra would debit Building and credit Cash and Installment Note Payable. The company would then pay interest and principal on the note payable and record amortization on the building. Accounting for a capital lease follows this pattern.

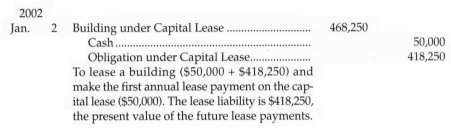

Sierra Wireless Inc.
www.sierrawireless.com

Sierra records the building at cost, which is the sum of the $50,000 initial payment plus the present value of the 19 future lease payments of $50,000 each.[7] The company credits Cash for the initial payment and credits Lease Liability for the present value of the future lease payments. Assume the interest rate on Sierra's lease is 10 percent and the present value (PV) of the future lease payments is $418,250.[8] At the beginning of the lease term, Sierra Wireless Inc. makes the following entry:

2002					
Jan.	2	Building under Capital Lease	468,250		
		Cash		50,000	
		Obligation under Capital Lease.....................		418,250	
		To lease a building ($50,000 + $418,250) and make the first annual lease payment on the capital lease ($50,000). The lease liability is $418,250, the present value of the future lease payments.			

Sierra's lease liability at January 2, 2002, is for 19 payments of $50,000 each on January 2, 2003, to January 2, 2021. However, included in those payments is interest calculated at 10 percent. The lease liability is

Cash payments January 2, 2003, to January 2, 2021	
(19 × $50,000)...	$950,000
Interest embedded in the lease payments	531,750
Present value of future lease payments	$418,250

If Sierra Wireless Inc. were to record the liability at $950,000, it would also have to record the interest included in that amount as a contra amount. Most companies net the interest against the cash payments and show the liability as the net amount (principal).

Because Sierra has capitalized the building, the company records amortization (straight-line). Assume the building has an expected life of 25 years. It is amortized over the lease term of 20 years because the lessee has the use of the building only for that period. No residual value enters into the amortization computation because the lessee will have no residual asset when the building is returned to the lessor at the expiration of the lease. Therefore, the annual amortization entry is

2002				
Dec.	31	Amortization Expense..	23,413	
		Accumulated Amortization—		
		Building under Capital Lease		23,413
		To record amortization on leased building of $23,413 ($468,250/20).		

---

[7] The chapter appendix explains present value.
[8] The formula for this computation appears in the chapter appendix.

Note that a lessee, such as Sierra, might obtain ownership of the leased asset at the end of the lease term. In such a situation, the lessee would amortize the leased asset over its useful life instead of over the term of the lease. At year end, Sierra must also accrue interest on the lease liability. Interest expense is computed by multiplying the lease liability by the interest rate on the lease. The following entry credits Lease Liability (not Interest Payable) for this interest accrual:

2002			
Dec. 31	Interest Expense	41,825	
	Obligation under Capital Lease.....................		41,825
	To accrue interest on the lease liability ($418,250 × 0.10).		

The balance sheet at December 31, 2002, reports:

Assets

Capital assets:		
Building under capital lease...	$468,250	
Less: Accumulated amortization	23,413	$444,837

Liabilities

Current liabilities:	
Lease liability (next payment due on Jan. 2, 2003)*	$50,000
Long-term liabilities:	
Lease liability..	410,075**

* The information in brackets is for student reference only. It would not appear on the balance sheet.
** $410,075 = [beginning balance ($418,250) + interest accrual ($41,825) – current portion ($50,000)]

In addition, the lessee must report the minimum capital lease payments for the next five years in the notes to the financial statements.

The lease liability is split into current and long-term portions because the next payment ($50,000) is a current liability and the remainder is long-term. The January 2, 2003, lease payment is recorded as follows:

2003			
Jan. 2	Lease Liability	50,000	
	Cash...		50,000
	To make second annual lease payment on building.		

Off-Balance-Sheet Financing

An important part of business is obtaining the funds needed to acquire assets. To finance operations, a company may issue stock, borrow money, or retain earnings in the business. All three of these financing plans affect the right-hand side of the balance sheet. Issuing stock affects preferred or common stock. Borrowing creates notes or bonds payable. Internal funds come from retained earnings.

Off-balance-sheet financing is the acquisition of assets or services whose resulting debt is not reported on the balance sheet. A prime example is an operating lease. The lessee has the use of the leased asset, but neither the asset nor any lease liability is reported on the balance sheet. In the past, most leases were accounted for by the operating method. However, the *CICA Handbook* in Section 3065 has required businesses to account for an increasing number of leases by the capital lease method. Also, Section 3065 has brought about detailed reporting of operating lease payments in the notes to the financial statements; minimum operating lease payments for the next five years must be reported. The inclusion of more lease information, be they capital or operating leases, makes the accounting information for decision making more complete. Much useful information is reported only in the notes. Experienced investors study them carefully.

Employee Future Benefits

In March 1999, the Accounting Standards Board of the CICA issued *CICA Handbook* Section 3461, "Employee Future Benefits." The new section covers both pensions and non-pension benefits. The following discussion is intended to present an overview of the topic; the subject is complex and will be covered in more advanced accounting courses.

Pensions   Most companies have a pension plan for their employees. A **pension** is employee compensation that is received during retirement. Employees earn the pensions by their service, so the company records pension expense while employees work for the company. While employees may also contribute to a company pension plan, the following discussion relates to employer contributions to a pension plan for employees.

The *CICA Handbook* in Section 3461 gives the rules for measuring pension expense. To record the company's payment into a pension plan, the company debits Pension Expense and credits Cash. Trustees such as trust companies and pension trusts manage pension plans. They receive the employer payments and any employee contributions, then invest these amounts for the future benefit of the employees. The goal is to have the funds available to meet any obligations to retirees.

While employees are perhaps those most interested in the status of their employer's pension plan, others such as creditors are also interested because pension plan assets and obligations can be large in proportion to a company's financial position. A company with a large underfunded pension liability could find itself in financial difficulties that would affect all creditors. For example, the December 31, 1999, annual report of Dofasco Inc., the Hamilton, Ontario, steelmaker, showed total assets of the company were $3,483 million while the assets of the company's pension plans totalled $1,819 million. The pension obligations were estimated at $1,543 million.

Section 3461 defines two types of pension plan: a **defined benefit pension plan**, in which the benefits to be paid to the employee upon retirement are specified and the company must ensure that adequate funds will be available to make the specified payments, and a **defined contribution plan**, in which the contribution is defined and the benefits depend on what is available when the employee retires. Each will be discussed in turn.

A *defined benefit pension plan* must have an actuarial evaluation at least every three years to ensure that there will be sufficient funds available to make the required payments to each member of the plan on his or her retirement. In conducting the valuation, the plan actuaries will determine the actuarial present value of the plan benefits, compare that to the plan assets and determine whether the plan has a surplus or deficit. Section 3461 requires that the actuarial present value of plan benefits for employee services to the reporting date and the value of pension plan assets be disclosed in the financial statements. The 2000 annual report issued by CAE Inc., the electronics and technology company, includes the following note to the financial statements:

> 14. PENSIONS
> The Corporation has defined benefit plans that provide benefits based on length of service and final average earnings. The Corporation has an obligation to ensure that there are sufficient funds in the plans to pay the benefits earned.
>
> ... The funded status of the defined benefit pension plans at March 31 was as follows [amounts in millions]:

	2000	1999
Market value of assets	$121.7	$114.8
Present value of accrued pension benefits	104.0	97.4

The accounting for defined benefits pension plans is complex and is demonstrated in subsequent accounting courses.

KEY POINT

A pension plan is a contract between a business and its employees. The contract's terms outline the retirement benefits the company will pay to retired employees.

REAL WORLD EXAMPLE

There are two types of pension plans: (1) Defined Contribution Plan: The employee, employer, or both must contribute a certain amount each period to the pension fund. The retirement benefits depend on how much is in the fund. (2) Defined Benefit Plan: The amount of the retirement benefit is defined by, say, 70% of salary in the year of retirement. The amount to be contributed to this type of pension fund requires a complex calculation and the services of an actuary.

CAE Inc.
www.cae.com

A *defined contribution plan* is an accumulation of the employer and employee contributions. The required disclosure is the present value of required future contributions by the company for employee services to the reporting date. For example, the disclosure for a typical company with a defined contribution plan might be as follows:

> NOTES TO THE FINANCIAL STATEMENTS
> 8. The Company has a defined contribution pension plan that covers all the Company's employees. The present value of required future contributions by the Company in respect of past service by employees of the Company was $759,256 at the year end.

Section 3460 of the *CICA Handbook* requires companies to disclose in a note pension assets and liabilities for defined benefit plans and unfunded obligations for past service for defined contribution plans, starting in 1990. Before that date, the pension obligation was an undisclosed liability. Companies received the benefit of their employees' service but could avoid reporting pension liabilities on the balance sheet.

Non-Pension Benefits

Section 3461 requires companies to treat non-pension future benefits in the same way as pension future benefits. Non-pension benefits include post-employment benefits such as medical insurance, extended health, and dental coverage.

The costs of the non-pension benefits should be recognized over the covered employee's service period. The annual financial statements should fully disclose costs and liabilities under the non-pension benefits plan including the accounting policies followed.

The 1999 Dofasco Inc. annual report discloses "Aggregate obligations for ... post-employment benefits, based on amounts determined by independent actuaries... are as follows:

	1999 Obligations	1998 Obligations
Other post-employment benefits (in millions)	$327	$312

The Decision Guidelines feature provides a summary of the major points of the chapter's second half.

Decision	Guidelines

How to account for the retirement of bonds?	At maturity date:
	
	Bonds Payable.. Maturity value
	    Cash... Maturity value
	
	Before maturity date (assume a discount on the bonds and a gain on retirement):
	Bonds Payable.. Maturity value
	    Discount on Bonds Payable............. Balance
	    Cash... Amount paid
	    Gain on Retirement of Bonds Payable Excess

How to account for the conversion of convertible bonds payable into common stock?	Remove all bonds payable (and related premium or discount) accounts and credit Common Stock.
What are the advantages of financing operations with • Stock? • Bonds (or notes) payable?	• Creates no liability or interest expense. Less risky to the issuing corporation. • Does not dilute stock ownership or control of the corporation. • Results in higher earnings per share—under normal conditions.

How to account for
• An operating lease?
• A capital lease?
	• Debit lease (or rent) expense when making each lease payment.
	• At the beginning of the lease period, record
	  a. Asset (as though it were purchased).
	  b. Lease liability—present value of future lease payments.
	
	Each period thereafter, record
	a. Lease payment as a debit to the Lease Liability account, a credit to Cash.
	b. Interest expense on the lease liability.
	c. Amortization expense on the asset.

Summary Problem
for Your Review

Val Morin Inc. has outstanding an issue of 8 percent convertible bonds that mature in 2022. Suppose the bonds were dated October 1, 2002, and pay interest each April 1 and October 1.

Required

1. Complete the following effective-interest amortization table through October 1, 2004.

Bond data: Maturity value—$200,000
Contract interest rate—8%
Interest paid—4% semiannually, $8,000 ($200,000 × 0.04)
Market interest rate at time of issue—9% annually, 4½% semiannually
Issue price—$90.75

Amortization table:

Semiannual Interest Period	A Interest Payment (4% of Maturity Value)	B Interest Expense (4½% of Preceding Bond Carrying Amount)	C Discount Amortization (B – A)	D Discount Account Balance (D – C)	E Bond Carrying Amount ($200,000 – D)
Oct. 1, 2002					
Apr. 1, 2003					
Oct. 1, 2003					
Apr. 1, 2004					
Oct. 1, 2004					

2. Using the amortization table, record the following transactions:
   a. Issuance of the bonds on October 1, 2002.
   b. Accrual of interest and amortization of discount on December 31, 2002.
   c. Payment of interest and amortization of discount on April 1, 2003.
   d. Conversion of one-third of the bonds payable into common stock on October 2, 2004.
   e. Retirement of two-thirds of the bonds payable on October 2, 2004. Purchase price of the bonds was $102.00.

Solution to Review Problem

Requirement 1

Amortization Table

Semiannual Interest Period	A Interest Payment (4% of Maturity Value)	B Interest Expense (4½% of Preceding Bond Carrying Amount)	C Discount Amortization (B – A)	D Discount Account Balance (D – C)	E Bond Carrying Amount ($200,000 – D)
Oct. 1, 2002				$18,500	$181,500
Apr. 1, 2003	$8,000	$8,168	$168	18,332	181,668
Oct. 1, 2003	8,000	8,175	175	18,157	181,843
Apr. 1, 2004	8,000	8,183	183	17,974	182,026
Oct. 1, 2004	8,000	8,191	191	17,783	182,217

Requirement 2

2002
a. Oct. 1 Cash ($200,000 × 0.9075) 181,500
           Discount on Bonds Payable 18,500
              Bonds Payable   200,000
           To issue 8%, 20-year bonds at a discount.

b. Dec. 31 Interest Expense ($8,168 × ⅜) 4,084
              Discount on Bonds Payable ($168 × ⅜) ..   84
              Interest Payable ($8,000 × ⅜)   4,000
           To accrue interest and amortize bond dis-
           count for three months.

2003
c. Apr. 1 Interest Expense 4,084
           Interest Payable 4,000
              Discount on Bonds Payable ($168 × ⅜) ..   84
              Cash   8,000

To pay semiannual interest, part of which
was accrued, and amortize three months'
discount on bonds payable.

2004

d.	Oct.	2	Bonds Payable ($200,000 × ⅓).......................	66,667	
			Discount on Bonds Payable		
			($17,783 × ⅓)...		5,928
			Common Stock ($182,217 × ⅓).................		60,739
			To record conversion of bonds payable.		
e.	Oct.	2	Bonds Payable ($200,000 × ⅔).......................	133,333	
			Loss on Retirement of Bonds.......................	14,522	
			Discount on Bonds Payable		
			($17,783 × ⅔)...		11,855
			Cash ($200,000 × ⅔ × 1.02).......................		136,000
			To retire bonds payable before maturity.		

Cyber Coach

Visit the Student Resources area of the *Accounting* Companion
Website for extra practice with the new material in Chapter 15.

www.pearsoned.ca/horngren

Summary

1. **Discuss bonds payable and account for basic bond transactions.** A corporation may borrow money by issuing long-term notes and *bonds.* A bond contract specifies the maturity value of the bonds, the *contract interest rate,* and the dates for paying interest and principal. Bonds may be secured (*mortgage* bonds) or unsecured (*debenture* bonds); bonds and debentures are accounted for similarly.

   Bonds are traded through organized markets, such as the over-the-counter market. Bonds are typically divided into $1,000 units. Their prices are quoted at the price per $100.00 bond. *Market interest rates* fluctuate and may differ from the contract rate on a bond. If a bond's contract rate exceeds the market rate, the bond sells at a *premium.* A bond with a contract rate below the market rate sells at a *discount.*

   Money earns income over time, a fact that gives rise to the *present-value concept.* An investor will pay a price for a bond equal to the present value of the bond principal plus the present value of the bond interest.

2. **Amortize bond discount and premium by the straight-line amortization method and the effective-interest amortization method.** *Straight-line amortization* allocates an equal dollar amount of premium or discount to each interest period. In the *effective-interest method* of amortization, the market rate at the time of issuance is multiplied by the bonds' carrying amount to determine the interest expense each period and to compute the amount of discount or premium amortization. This method allocates a constant percentage of premium or discount to each interest period.

3. **Account for retirement of bonds.** Companies may retire their bonds payable before maturity. *Callable* bonds give the borrower the right to pay off the bonds at a specified call price, or the company may purchase the bonds in the open market.

4. **Account for conversion of bonds.** *Convertible bonds* and notes give the investor the privilege of trading the bonds in for stock of the issuing corporation. The carrying amount of the bonds becomes the book value of the newly issued stock.

5. **Show the advantages and disadvantages of borrowing.** A key advantage of raising money by borrowing versus issuing stock is that interest expense on debt is tax-deductible. Thus borrowing is less costly than issuing stock. Borrowing's disadvantages result from the fact that the company *must* repay the loan and its interest.

6. **Report lease and employee future benefits liabilities.** A *lease* is an agreement between the *lessee* and the *lessor.* In an *operating lease* the lessor retains the usual risks and rights of owning the asset. The lessee debits Rent Expense and credits Cash when making lease payments. A *capital lease* is long-term, noncancelable, and similar to an installment purchase of the leased asset. In a capital lease, the lessee capitalizes the leased asset and reports a lease liability.

   In the case of *defined benefit pension plans,* companies should report *accrued pension benefits* and *pension assets* in the financial statements; in the case of *defined contribution pension plans,* companies should report *unfunded obligations* for past service. Non-pension future benefits liabilities should be reported.

Self-Study Questions

Test your understanding of the chapter by marking the best answer for each of the following questions:

1. An unsecured bond is called a (p. 805)
   a. Serial bond
   b. Registered bond
   c. Debenture bond
   d. Mortgage bond

2. How much will an investor pay for a $100,000 bond priced at $102.5 plus a brokerage commission of $1,100? (p. 806)
   a. $100,000
   b. $102,000
   c. $102,500
   d. $103,600

3. A bond with a stated interest rate of 9½ percent is issued when the market interest rate is 9¾ percent. This bond will sell at (p. 807)
   a. Par value
   b. A discount
   c. A premium
   d. A price minus accrued interest

4. Ten-year, 11 percent bonds payable of $1,000,000 were issued for $1,064,000. Assume the straightline amortization method is appropriate. The total annual interest expense on these bonds is (pp. 812–813)
   a. $103,600
   b. $110,000
   c. $116,400
   d. A different amount each year because the bonds' book value decreases as the premium is amortized

5. Repeat Question 4 but use the effective-interest method of amortization. (pp. 813–814)
   a. $103,600
   b. $110,000
   c. $116,400
   d. A decreasing amount each year because the bonds' book value decreases as the premium is amortized

6. Bonds payable with face value of $600,000 and carrying value of $576,000 are retired before their scheduled maturity with a cash outlay of $584,000. Which of the following entries correctly records this bond retirement? (pp. 824–825)
   a. Bonds Payable 600,000
      Discount on Bonds Payable.... 24,000
          Cash 584,000
          Gain on Retirement of
             Bonds Payable 40,000

   b. Bonds Payable 600,000
      Loss on Retirement of
          Bonds Payable 8,000
          Discount on Bonds Payable   24,000
          Cash 584,000
   c. Bonds Payable 600,000
          Discount on Bonds Payable   12,000
          Cash 584,000
      Gain on Retirement of
          Bonds Payable 4,000
   d. Bonds Payable 576,000
      Discount on Bonds Payable.... 24,000
      Gain on Retirement of
          Bonds Payable 16,000
          Cash 584,000

7. An advantage of financing operations with debt versus stock is (pp. 826–827)
   a. The tax deductibility of interest expense on debt
   b. The legal requirement to pay interest and principal
   c. Lower interest payments compared to dividend payments
   d. All of the above

8. In a capital lease, the lessee records (pp. 828–830)
   a. A leased asset and a lease liability
   b. Amortization on the leased asset
   c. Interest on the lease liability
   d. All of the above

9. Which of the following is an example of off-balance-sheet financing? (p. 830)
   a. Operating lease
   b. Current portion of long-term debt
   c. Debenture bonds
   d. Convertible bonds

10. A corporation's defined benefit pension plan has accumulated benefit obligations of $830,000 and assets that are worth $790,000. What will this company report for its pension plan? (pp. 831–832)
    a. Accumulated benefit obligation of $830,000
    b. Note disclosure of the $40,000 excess of accumulated benefit obligation over plan assets
    c. Long-term pension liability of $40,000
    d. The obligation of $830,000 and the assets of $790,000.

Answers to the Self-Study Questions follow the Similar Accounting Terms.

Accounting Vocabulary

Bond (p. 805)
Bond discount (p. 805)
Bond premium (p. 805)
Bonds payable (p. 805)
Callable bonds (p. 824)

Capital lease (p. 828)
Contract interest rate (p. 807)
Convertible bonds (p. 825)
Convertible notes (p. 825)
Debentures (p. 805)

Defined benefit pension plan (p. 831)
Defined contribution pension plan (p. 831)
Discount (p. 805)
Effective-interest amortization (p. 813)
Effective interest rate (p. 807)

Lease *(p. 828)*
Lessee *(p. 828)*
Lessor *(p. 828)*
Market interest rate *(p. 807)*
Mortgage *(p. 826)*
Off-balance-sheet financing *(p. 830)*

Operating lease *(p. 828)*
Pension *(p. 831)*
Premium *(p. 805)*
Present value *(p. 806)*
Serial bonds *(p. 805)*

Stated interest rate *(p. 807)*
Straight-line amortization *(p. 812)*
Term bonds *(p. 805)*
Trading on the equity *(p. 827)*
Underwriter *(p. 805)*

Similar Accounting Terms

Bond — Secured bond; Mortgage bond
Bond principal — Face value; Maturity value; Par value
Contract interest rate — Stated interest rate
Debenture — Unsecured bond
Market interest rate — Effective interest rate
Obligation under capital lease — Lease liability

Answers to Self-Study Questions

1. c
2. d [($100,000 × 1.025) + $1,100 = $103,600]
3. b
4. a [($1,000,000 × 0.11) − ($64,000/10) = $103,600]
5. d
6. b
7. a
8. d
9. a
10. d

Assignment Material

Questions

1. How do bonds payable differ from a note payable?

2. How does an underwriter assist with the issuance of bonds?

3. Compute the price to the nearest dollar for the following bonds with a face value of $10,000:
   a. $93.00   c. $101.375   e. $100.00
   b. $88.75   d. $122.50

4. In which of the following situations will bonds sell at par? At a premium? At a discount?
   a. 9% bonds sold when the market rate is 9%.
   b. 9% bonds sold when the market rate is 10%.
   c. 9% bonds sold when the market rate is 8%.

5. Identify the accounts to debit and credit for transactions (a) to issue bonds at *par*, (b) to pay interest, (c) to accrue interest at year end, and (d) to pay off bonds at maturity.

6. Identify the accounts to debit and credit for transactions (a) to issue bonds at a *discount*, (b) to pay interest, (c) to accrue interest at year end, and (d) to pay off bonds at maturity.

7. Identify the accounts to debit and credit for transactions (a) to issue bonds at a *premium*, (b) to pay

interest, (c) to accrue interest at year end, and (d) to pay off bonds at maturity.

8. Why are bonds sold for a price "plus accrued interest"? What happens to accrued interest when bonds are sold by an individual?

9. How does the straight-line method of amortizing bond discount (or premium) differ from the effective-interest method?

10. A company retires ten-year bonds payable of $100,000 after five years. The business issued the bonds at $104.00 and called them at $103.00. Compute the amount of gain or loss on retirement. How is this gain or loss reported on the income statement? The straight-line methd of amortization is used.

11. Bonds payable with a maturity value of $100,000 are callable at $102.50. Their market price is $101.25. If you are the issuer of these bonds, how much will you pay to retire them before maturity?

12. Why are convertible bonds attractive to investors? Why are they popular with borrowers?

13. McMullen Corp. has $156 million of bonds

outstanding at December 31, 2002. Of the total, $26 million are due in 2003 and the balance in 2004 and beyond. How would McMullen Corp. report its bonds payable on the balance sheet?

14. Contrast the effects on a company of issuing bonds versus issuing stock.

15. Identify the accounts a lessee debits and credits when making operating lease payments.

16. What characteristics distinguish a capital lease from an operating lease?

17. A business signs a capital lease for the use of a building. What accounts are debited and credited (a) to begin the lease term and make the first lease payment, (b) to record amortization, (c) to accrue interest on the lease liability, and (d) to make the second lease payment?

18. Show how a lessee reports on the balance sheet any leased equipment and the related lease liability under a capital lease.

19. What is off-balance-sheet financing? Give an example.

20. Distinguish a defined benefit pension plan from a defined contribution pension plan. What must be reported for each in the financial statements?

Exercises

Exercise 15-1 *Issuing bonds and paying interest* *(Obj. 1)*

Seagate Systems, Inc. issues $500,000 of 8 percent, semiannual, 20-year bonds that are dated April 30. Record (a) the issuance of bonds at par on April 30, and (b) the next semiannual interest payment on October 31.

Exercise 15-2 *Issuing bonds and paying and accruing interest* *(Obj. 1)*

On February 1, QL Technologies Inc. issues 20-year, 7 percent bonds payable with a face value of $5,000,000. The bonds sell at par and pay interest on January 31 and July 31. Record (a) issuance of the bonds on February 1, (b) the semiannual interest payment on July 31, and (c) the interest accrual on December 31.

Exercise 15-3 *Issuing bonds and paying and accruing interest* *(Obj. 1)*

McMillan Corp. issues 20-year, 8 percent bonds with a face value of $10,000,000 on March 31. The bonds sell at par and pay interest on March 31 and September 30. Record (a) issuance of the bonds on March 31, (b) payment of interest on September 30, and (c) accrual of interest on December 31.

Exercise 15-4 *Issuing bonds between interest dates* *(Obj. 1)*

Refer to the data for McMillan Corp. in Exercise 15-3. If McMillan Corp. issued the bonds on June 30, how much cash would McMillan Corp. receive upon issuance of the bonds?

Exercise 15-5 *Issuing bonds payable and paying interest* *(Obj. 1)*

Jones Corp. issues $600,000 of 7%, 20-year bonds that are dated April 30. Record (a) issuance of the bonds at par on May 31, and (b) the next semiannual interest payment on October 31.

Exercise 15-6 *Issuing bonds, paying and earning interest, and amortizing discount by the straight-line method* *(Obj. 1, 2)*

On February 1, Excel Technologies Inc. issued 20-year, 7 percent bonds with a face value of $5,000,000. The bonds sell at $98.00 and pay interest on January 31 and July 31. Excel Technologies Inc. amortizes bond discount by the straight-line method. Record (a) issuance of the bonds on February 1, (b) the semiannual interest payment on July 31, and (c) the interest accrual on December 31.

Exercise 15-7 *Issuing bonds, paying and accruing interest, and amortizing premium by the straight-line method* **(Obj. 1, 2)**

Armstrong Corp. issues 20-year, 8 percent bonds with a face value of $5,000,000 on March 31. The bonds sell at $102.00 and pay interest on March 31 and September 30. Assume Armstrong Corp. amortizes the premium by the straight-line method. Record (a) the issuance of the bonds on March 31, (b) payment of interest on September 30, and (c) accrual of interest on December 31.

Exercise 15-8 *Preparing an effective-interest amortization table; recording interest payments and the related discount amortization* **(Obj. 2)**

Top-Level Sports Ltd. is authorized to issue $1,000,000 of 7 percent, 10-year bonds. On January 2, the contract date, when the market interest rate is 8 percent, the company issues $800,000 of the bonds and receives cash of $745,320. Top-Level Sports Ltd. amortizes bond discount by the effective-interest method.

Required

1. Prepare an amortization table for the first four semiannual interest periods. Follow the format of Panel B in Exhibit 15-4 on page 815.
2. Record the first semiannual interest payment on June 30 and the second payment on December 31.

Exercise 15-9 *Preparing an effective-interest amortization table; recording interest accrual and payment, and the related premium amortization* **(Obj. 2)**

On September 30, 2003, the market interest rate is 7 percent. Biotech Ltd. issues $500,000 of 8 percent, 20-year bonds at $110.625. The bonds pay interest on March 31 and September 30. Biotech Ltd. amortizes bond premium by the effective-interest method.

Required

1. Prepare an amortization table for the first four semiannual interest periods. Follow the format of Panel B in Exhibit 15-6 on page 817.
2. Record issuance of the bonds on September 30, 2003, the accrual of interest at December 31, 2003, and the semiannual interest payment on March 31, 2004.

Exercise 15-10 *Journalizing sinking-fund transactions* **(Obj. 2)**

Kapur Inc. established a sinking fund for bonds issued on September 30, 2002. The bond issue of $1,000,000 20-year, 8 percent bonds was sold at $110.625. Record payment of $19,000 into the sinking fund on March 31, 2003. Also record sinking-fund revenue of $1,283 on December 31, 2003, and the payment of the bonds at maturity on September 30, 2022. At maturity date the sinking-fund balance was $972,000.

Exercise 15-11 *Debt payment and discount amortization schedule using a spreadsheet* **(Obj. 2)**

On January 2, 2002, Winnberg Logistics Ltd. issued $2,000,000 of 8½ percent, 5-year bonds when the market interest rate was 10 percent. Winnberg Logistics Ltd. pays interest annually at year end. The issue price of the bonds was $1,886,276.

Required

Create a spreadsheet model to prepare a schedule to amortize the discount on these bonds. Use the effective-interest method of amortization. Round to the nearest dollar, and format your answer as follows:

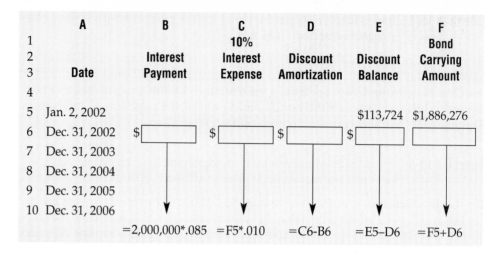

	A	B	C	D	E	F
1			10%			Bond
2		Interest	Interest	Discount	Discount	Carrying
3	Date	Payment	Expense	Amortization	Balance	Amount
4						
5	Jan. 2, 2002				$113,724	$1,886,276
6	Dec. 31, 2002	$	$	$	$	
7	Dec. 31, 2003					
8	Dec. 31, 2004					
9	Dec. 31, 2005					
10	Dec. 31, 2006					
		=2,000,000*.085	=F5*.010	=C6−B6	=E5−D6	=F5+D6

Exercise 15-12   *Recording retirement of bonds payable*   **(Obj. 3)**

Daon Management Inc. issued $1,000,000 of 8 percent bonds at $97.00 on October 1, 2002. These bonds mature on October 1, 2010, and are callable at $101.00. Daon Management Inc. pays interest each April 1 and October 1. On October 1, 2007, when the bonds' market price is $104.00, Daon Management Inc. retires the bonds in the most economical way available.

Required

Record the payment of interest and amortization of bond discount at October 1, 2007, and the retirement of the bonds on that date. Daon Management Inc. uses the straight-line method to amortize the bond discount.

Exercise 15-13   *Recording conversion of bonds payable*   **(Obj. 4)**

Nu-Mark Imaging Ltd. issued $1,000,000 of 8½ percent bonds payable on July 1, 2002, at a price of $98.50. After 5 years, the bonds may be converted into the company's common stock. Each $1,000 face amount of bonds is convertible into 40 shares of common stock. The bonds' term to maturity is 15 years. On December 31, 2007, bondholders exercised their right to convert the bonds into common stock.

Required

1. What would cause the bondholders to convert their bonds into common stock?
2. Without making journal entries, compute the carrying amount of the bonds payable at December 31, 2007. Nu-Mark Imaging Ltd. uses the straight-line method to amortize bond premium and discount.
3. All amortization has been recorded properly. Journalize the conversion transaction at December 31, 2007.

Exercise 15-14   *Accounting for the conversion of bonds*   **(Obj. 4)**

Link Back to Chapter 4 (Debt Ratio). Suppose Oracle Design Corp. has $10,000,000 of convertible bonds outstanding, with a bond premium of $800,000 also on the books. The bondholders have notified Oracle Design Corp. that they wish to convert the bonds into stock. Specifically, the bonds may be converted into 2,000,000 shares of Oracle's common stock.

Required

1. What is the carrying value of Oracle's convertible bonds payable prior to the conversion?

2. Journalize, on Oracle's books, the conversion of the bonds payable into common stock. No explanation is required.

3. How will the conversion affect Oracle's debt ratio?

Exercise 15-15 *Recording early retirement and conversion of bonds payable* **(Obj. 3, 4)**

Baca Products Ltd. reported the following at September 30, 2003:

Long-term liabilities		
Convertible bonds payable, 9%,		
due September 30, 2011	$500,000	
Discount on bonds payable	15,000	$485,000

Required

1. Record retirement of one-half of the bonds on October 1, 2003 at the call price of $101.00.

2. Record conversion of one-fourth (of the original $500,000) of the bonds into 10,000 shares of Baca Products Ltd.'s common stock on October 1, 2003.

Exercise 15-16 *Analyzing alternative plans for raising money* **(Obj. 5)**

Canadian Transport Ltd. is considering two plans for raising $2,000,000 to expand operations. Plan A is to borrow at 9 percent, and Plan B is to issue 200,000 shares of common stock. Before any new financing, Canadian Transport Ltd. has net income after interest and income tax of $1,200,000 and 200,000 shares of common stock outstanding. Management believes the company can use the new funds to earn income of $840,000 per year before interest and taxes. The income tax rate is 40 percent.

Required

Analyze Canadian Transport Ltd.'s situation to determine which plan will result in higher earnings per share. Use Exhibit 15-8 on page 827 as a guide.

Exercise 15-17 *Earnings-per-share effects of financing with bonds versus stock* **(Obj. 5)**

Foothill Financial Services Ltd. of Calgary, Alberta, needs to raise $2,000,000 to expand company operations into British Columbia. Foothill's president is considering the issuance of either

• Plan A: $2,000,000 of 8% bonds payable to borrow the money.

• Plan B: 100,000 shares of common stock at $20 per share.

Before any new financing, Foothill Financial Services Ltd. expects to earn net income of $700,000, and the company already has 200,000 shares of common stock outstanding. The president believes the expansion will increase income before interest and income tax by $400,000. The company's income tax rate is 40 percent.

Required

Prepare an analysis similar to Exhibit 15-8, page 827, to determine which plan is likely to result in the higher earnings per share. Which financing plan would you recommend for Foothill Financial Services Ltd.? Give your reasons.

Exercise 15-18 *Reporting long-term debt and pension liability on the balance sheet* **(Obj. 5)**

The chief accounting officer of Gateway Productions Ltd. is considering how to report long-term notes and pension liabilities.

a. The company's financial accountant has assembled the following for long-term notes payable.

Note 5: Long-Term Debt

Total	$800,000
Less: Current portion	50,000
Less: Unamortized discount	2,000
Long-term debt	$748,000

None of the unamortized discount relates to the current portion of long-term debt. Show how Gateway Productions Ltd.'s balance sheet would report these liabilities.

b. Gateway Productions Ltd.'s defined benefit pension plan has assets with a market value of $1,440,000. The plan's accumulated benefit obligation is $1,680,000. What should the company report in the notes to the financial statements?

Exercise 15-19 *Reporting liabilities, including capital lease obligations* *(Obj. 6)*

MNA Associates Inc. includes the following selected accounts in its general ledger at December 31, 2003:

Bonds payable...........................	$525,000	Current obligation under	
Equipment under		capital lease	$12,000
capital lease	171,000	Accounts payable	28,500
Interest payable (due		Long-term capital lease	
March 1, 2004)......................	10,500	liability	63,000
Current portion of		Discount on bonds	
bonds payable.......................	75,000	payable (all long-term)	9,000
Notes payable, long-term........	90,000		

Required

Prepare the liabilities section of MNA Associates Inc.'s balance sheet at December 31, 2003, to show how the company would report these items. Report a total for both current and long-term liabilities.

Exercise 15-20 *Journalizing capital lease and operating lease transactions* *(Obj. 6)*

A capital lease agreement for equipment requires Laporte Equipment Ltd. to make 10 annual payments of $15,000, with the first payment due on January 2, 2003, the date of the inception of the lease. The present value of the 9 future lease payments at 10 percent is $86,385.

Required

1. Calculate the present value of the lease at 10 percent if your instructor has taught present value.

2. Journalize the following lessee transactions:

2003
Jan.   2   Beginning of lease term and first annual payment.
Dec.   31   Amortization of equipment.
          31   Interest expense on lease liability.
2004
Jan.   2   Second annual lease payment.

3. Assume now that this is an operating lease. Journalize the January 2, 2003, lease payment.

Challenge Exercises

Exercise 15-21 *Analyzing bond transactions* *(Obj. 1, 2)*

This (partial) advertisement appeared in *The Financial Post*.

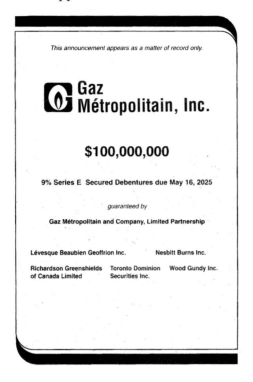

This announcement appears as a matter of record only.

Gaz Métropolitain, Inc.

$100,000,000

9% Series E Secured Debentures due May 16, 2025

guaranteed by

Gaz Métropolitain and Company, Limited Partnership

Lévesque Beaubien Geoffrion Inc.   Nesbitt Burns Inc.

Richardson Greenshields   Toronto Dominion   Wood Gundy Inc.
of Canada Limited   Securities Inc.

Interest is payable on November 16 and May 16.

Required

Answer these questions about Gaz Métropolitain, Inc.'s secured debentures (bonds):

1. Suppose investors purchased these securities at $98.50 on May 16, 2000. Describe the transaction in detail, indicating who received cash, who paid cash, and how much.
2. Compute the annual cash interest payment on the Gaz Métropolitain, Inc. bonds.
3. Compute the annual interest expense under the straight-line amortization method.
4. Prepare an effective-interest amortization table for Gaz Métropolitain, Inc.'s first two payments on November 16, 2000, and May 16, 2001. The market rate at the date of issuance was 9.2 percent.
5. Compute Gaz Métropolitain, Inc.'s interest expense for the first full year ended May 16, 2001, under the effective-interest amortization method.
6. Another company's issue of unsecured bonds for $20,000,000 was issued the same day; it bore an interest rate of 12 percent. Why was the rate so much higher for this issue than for the Gaz Métropolitain, Inc. issue?

Exercise 15-22 *Analyzing bond transactions* *(Obj. 1, 2)*

Refer to the bond situation of Gaz Métropolitain, Inc. in Exercise 15-21. Assume Gaz Métropolitain, Inc. issued the bonds at a price of $98.50 and that the company uses the effective-interest amortization method. The company's year end is December 31.

Required

1. Journalize the following bond transactions of Gaz Métropolitain, Inc.:

   2000
   May 16   Issuance of the bonds.
   Nov. 16   Payment of interest expense and amortization of discount on bonds payable. The
              market rate on the date of issuance was 9.2 percent.
   Dec. 31   Accrual of interest expense and amortization of discount on bonds payable.

2. What is Gaz Métropolitain, Inc.'s carrying amount of the bonds payable at

   a. November 16, 2000   b. December 31, 2000   c. May 16, 2001?

Beyond the Numbers

Beyond the Numbers 15-1 *Questions about long-term debt*
                             (Obj. 6 and Appendix to Chapter 15)

Link Back to Chapter 4 (Debt Ratio). The following questions are not related.

1. IMAX Corporation obtains the use of most of its theatre properties through leases. IMAX Corporation prefers operating leases over capital leases. Why is this a good idea? Consider IMAX Corporation's debt ratio.

2. IMAX Corporation likes to borrow for longer periods when interest rates are low and for shorter periods when interest rates are high. Why is this a good business strategy?

3. Suppose IMAX Corporation needs to borrow $2,000,000 to open new theatres. The company can borrow $2,000,000 by issuing 8%, 20-year bonds at a price of 96. How much will IMAX Corporation actually be borrowing under this arrangement? How much must the company repay at maturity?

Ethical Issue

Cranmore Corp., manufacturer of electronic devices, borrowed heavily during the 1990s to exploit the advantage of financing operations with debt. At first, Cranmore Corp. was able to earn operating income much higher than its interest expense and was therefore quite profitable. However, when the business cycle turned down, Cranmore Corp.'s debt burden pushed the company to the brink of bankruptcy. Operating income was less than interest expense.

Required

Is it unethical for managers to commit a company to a high level of debt? Or is it just risky? Who could be hurt by a company's taking on too much debt? Discuss.

Problems (Group A)

Problem 15-1A *Journalizing bond transactions (at par) and reporting bonds payable on
                    the balance sheet   (Obj. 1)*

The board of directors of Cook Production Co. Ltd. authorizes the issue of $10,000,000 of 7 percent, 10-year bonds. The semiannual interest dates are May 31 and November 30. The bonds are issued through an underwriter on June 30, 2003, at par plus accrued interest.

Required

1. Journalize the following transactions:
   a. Issuance of the bonds on June 30, 2003.
   b. Payment of interest on November 30, 2003.

c. Accrual of interest on December 31, 2003.

d. Payment of interest on May 31, 2004.

2. Check your recorded interest expense for 2003, using as a model the supplement to the summary problem on page 823.

3. Report interest payable and bonds payable as they would appear on the Cook Production Co. Ltd. balance sheet at December 31, 2003.

Problem 15-2A *Issuing bonds at a discount, amortizing by the straight-line method, and reporting bonds payable on the balance sheet* **(Obj. 1, 2)**

On March 1, 2002, Chung Systems Ltd. issues 8½ percent, 20-year bonds payable with a face value of $500,000. The bonds pay interest on February 28 and August 31. Chung Systems Ltd. amortizes premium and discount by the straight-line method.

Required

1. If the market interest rate is 7⅝ percent when Chung Systems Ltd. issues its bonds, will the bonds be priced at par, at a premium, or at a discount? Explain.

2. If the market interest rate is 8⅝ percent when Chung Systems Ltd. issues its bonds, will the bonds be priced at par, at a premium, or at a discount? Explain.

3. Assume the issue price of the bonds is $96.00. Journalize the following bond transactions:

   a. Issuance of the bonds on March 1, 2002.

   b. Payment of interest and amortization of discount on August 31, 2002.

   c. Accrual of interest and amortization of discount on December 31, 2002, Chung Systems Ltd.'s year end.

   d. Payment of interest and amortization of discount on February 28, 2003.

4. Check your recorded interest expense for the year ended February 28, 2003, using as a model the supplement to the summary problem on page 823.

5. Report interest payable and bonds payable as they would appear on the Chung Systems Ltd.'s balance sheet at December 31, 2003.

Problem 15-3A *Analyzing a company's long-term debt, journalizing its transactions, and reporting the long-term debt on the balance sheet* **(Obj. 2)**

The notes to SGC.com Inc.'s financial statements recently reported the following data on September 30, 2002 (amounts rounded):

NOTE 4: INDEBTEDNESS
Long-term debt at September 30, 2002 included the following:

6.00% debentures due September 30, 2021 with an effective interest rate of 7.00%, net of unamortized discount of $51,678...	$448,322
Other indebtedness with an interest rate of 8.30%, due $51,000 in 2006 and $49,000 in 2008.................................	100,000

Assume SGC.com Inc. amortizes discount by the effective-interest method.

Required

1. Answer the following questions about SGC.com Inc.'s long-term liabilities:

   a. What is the maturity value of the 6 percent debentures?

   b. What are SGC.com Inc.'s annual cash interest payments on the 6 percent debentures?

   c. What is the carrying amount of the 6 percent debentures at September 30, 2002?

2. Prepare an amortization table through September 30, 2005, for the 6 percent debentures. Round all amounts to the nearest dollar, and assume SGC.com Inc. pays interest annually on September 30.

3. Record the September 30, 2004 and 2005 interest payments on the 6 percent debentures.
4. There is no premium or discount on the other indebtedness. Assuming annual interest is paid on September 30 each year, record SGC.com Inc.'s September 30, 2003, interest payment on the other indebtedness.
5. Show how SGC.com Inc. would report the debentures payable and other indebtedness on September 30, 2005.

 Problem 15-4A *Issuing convertible bonds at a premium, amortizing by the effective-interest method, retiring bonds early, converting bonds, and reporting the bonds payable on the balance sheet* **(Obj. 2, 3, 4)**

On December 31, 2002, Douglas Holdings Ltd. issues 9 percent, 10-year convertible bonds with a maturity value of $1,500,000. The semiannual interest dates are June 30 and December 31. The market interest rate is 8 percent, and the issue price of the bonds is $106.795. Douglas Holdings Ltd. amortizes bond premium and discount by the effective-interest method.

Required

1. Prepare an effective-interest method amortization table for the first four semiannual interest periods.
2. Journalize the following transactions:
   a. Issuance of the bonds on December 31, 2002. Credit Convertible Bonds Payable.
   b. Payment of interest on June 30, 2003.
   c. Payment of interest on December 31, 2003.
   d. Retirement of bonds with face value of $500,000 on July 2, 2004. Douglas Holdings Ltd. pays the call price of $102.00.
   e. Conversion by the bondholders on July 2, 2004, of bonds with face value of $750,000 into 10,000 shares of Douglas Holdings Ltd. common stock.
3. Prepare the balance sheet presentation of the bonds payable that are outstanding at December 31, 2004.

Problem 15-5A *Journalizing bonds payable and capital lease transactions* **(Obj. 1, 6)**

Journalize the following transactions of Collier Technologies Inc.:

2003
Jan.   2   Issued $1,000,000 of 8 percent, 10-year bonds at 97.00.
       2   Signed a 5-year capital lease on equipment. The agreement requires annual lease payments of $100,000, with the first payment due immediately. The present value of the four future lease payments is $303,735.
July   2   Paid semiannual interest and amortized discount by the straight-line method on the 8 percent bonds.
Dec. 31   Accrued semiannual interest expense, and amortized discount by the straight-line method on the 8 percent bonds.
      31   Recorded amortization on leased equipment, using the straight-line method.
      31   Accrued interest expense at 12 percent on the lease liability.
2013
Jan.   2   Paid the 8 percent bonds at maturity.

Problem 15-6A *Financing operations with debt instead of with stock* **(Obj. 5)**

Two businesses must consider how to raise $10,000,000.

Cavendish Inc. is in the midst of its most successful period since it began operations 48 years ago. For each of the past 10 years, net income and earnings per share have increased by 15 percent. The outlook for the future is equally bright, with new markets opening up and competitors unable to manufacture products of Cavendish Inc.'s quality. Cavendish Inc. is planning a large-scale expansion.

Nordeg Limited has fallen on hard times. Net income has remained flat for five of the last six years, even falling by 10 percent from last year's level of profits. Top management has experienced unusual turnover, and the company lacks strong leadership. To become competitive again, Nordeg Limited desperately needs $10,000,000 for expansion.

Required

1. Propose a plan for each company to raise the needed cash. Which company should borrow? Which company should issue stock? Consider the advantages and disadvantages of raising money by borrowing and by issuing stock, and discuss them in your answer.

2. How will what you have learned help you manage a business?

Problem 15-7A *Reporting liabilities on the balance sheet* *(Obj. 6)*

The accounting records of Quadra Logistics Inc. include the following items:

Capital lease liability,		Mortgage note payable,	
long-term................................	$146,000	long-term	$134,000
Bonds payable, long-term........	320,000	Building acquired under	
Premium on bonds		capital lease	400,000
payable.................................	26,000	Interest expense	94,000
Interest payable.........................	28,400	Bonds payable,	
Interest revenue........................	10,600	current portion......................	40,000
Capital lease liability,		Accumulated amortization,	
current..................................	18,000	building...................................	216,000
		Defined benefit	
		pension plan assets................	1,560,000

Required

Show how these items would be reported on the Quadra Logistics Inc. balance sheet, including headings for capital assets, current liabilities, long-term liabilities, and so on. Note disclosures are not required.

Problem 15-8A *Amortizing bond discount and premium by the effective-interest method; retirement of bonds; conversion of bonds* *(Obj. 2, 3, 4)*

Alsask Transport Ltd. is authorized to issue $20,000,000, 10-year, 8 percent convertible bonds with interest payable on June 30 and December 31. The bonds are convertible on the basis of 50 shares of common stock for each $1,000 bond. The following bond transactions took place:

2002
Jan.   2   Sold bonds with $8,000,000 face value. Since the market rate of interest on this date was 10 percent, the bonds had a present value of $7,003,023.
June   30   Paid the interest and amortized the discount using the effective-interest amortization method.
Dec.   31   Paid the interest and amortized the discount using the effective-interest amortization method.

2003
April   1   Sold $1,600,000 (face value) of bonds at par plus accrued interest. The market rate of interest on this date was 8 percent.
June   30   Paid the interest and amortized the discount using the effective-interest amortization method.
July   2   Retired $6,000,000 (face value) of the bonds issued on January 2, 2002, at a rate of 96.
July   2   Bondholders converted $2,000,000 (face value) of bonds issued on January 2, 2002, into shares of common stock.

Required

Round all amounts to the nearest whole dollar.

1. Journalize the transactions.
2. Show the balance sheet presentation of the bonds payable on July 2, 2003.

Problem 15-9A *Amortizing bond premium by the effective-interest method; accounting for lease transactions* *(Obj. 2, 6)*

Gateway Systems Inc. had the following information available on bonds payable outstanding at December 31, 2002, its year end:

- $5,000,000—Bonds Payable, 9 percent, interest paid on April 2 and October 2. The bonds had been sold April 2, 2001, when the market rate of interest was 8 percent and were due April 2, 2005.
- $101,022—Premium on Bonds Payable

The following transactions took place after December 31, 2002:

2003

Jan.	2	Gateway Systems Inc. signed a lease to rent a building for expansion of its operations. The lease is 5 years, with an option to renew, and calls for annual payments of $50,000 per year payable on January 2. Gateway Systems Inc. gave a cheque for the first year upon signing the contract.
Jan.	2	Gateway Systems Inc. signed a lease for equipment. The lease is for 10 years with payments of $40,000 per year payable on January 2 (first year's payment was made at the signing). At the end of the lease the equipment will become the property of Gateway Systems Inc. The future payments on the lease have a present value (at 10 percent) of $230,361.
April	2	Paid the interest on the bonds payable and amortized the premium using the effective-interest method.
Oct.	2	Paid the interest on the bonds payable and amortized the premium using the effective-interest method.
Dec.	31	Recorded any adjustments required at the end of the year for the bonds payable and the lease(s).

2004

Jan.	2	Made the annual payments on the leases.
April	2	Paid the interest on the bonds payable and amortized the premium using the effective-interest method.
Oct.	2	Paid the interest on the bonds payable and amortized the premium using the effective-interest method.
Dec.	31	Recorded any adjustments required at the end of the year for the bonds payable and the lease(s).

Required

Round all amounts to the nearest whole dollar.

1. Prepare the general journal entries required to record the transactions of 2003 and 2004.
2. Show the liability section of the balance sheet on December 31, 2004.

Problems (Group B)

Problem 15-1B *Journalizing bond transactions (at par) and reporting bonds payable on the balance sheet* *(Obj. 1)*

The board of directors of Webbase Communications Ltd. authorizes the issue of $5,000,000 of 8 percent, 20-year bonds payable. The semiannual interest dates are March 31 and September 30. The bonds are issued through an underwriter on April 30, 2003, at par plus accrued interest. Webbase's year end is December 31.

Required

1. Journalize the following transactions:
   a. Issuance of the bonds on April 30, 2003.
   b. Payment of interest on September 30, 2003.
   c. Accrual of interest on December 31, 2003.
   d. Payment of interest on March 31, 2004.

2. Check your recorded interest expense for 2003, using as a model the supplement to the summary problem on page 823.

3. Report interest payable and bonds payable as they would appear on the Webbase Communications Ltd. balance sheet at December 31, 2003.

Problem 15-2B *Issuing notes at a premium, amortizing by the straight-line method, and reporting notes payable on the balance sheet (Obj. 1, 2)*

On April 1, 2002, Mason Corp. issues 7¾ percent, 10-year bonds payable with a face value of $1,000,000. The bonds pay interest on March 31 and September 30, and Mason Corp. amortizes premium and discount by the straight-line method.

Required

1. If the market interest rate is 8½ percent when Mason Corp. issues its bonds, will the bonds be priced at par, at a premium, or at a discount? Explain.

2. If the market interest rate is 7 percent when Mason Corp. issues its bonds, will the bonds be priced at par, at a premium, or at a discount? Explain.

3. Assume the issue price of the bonds is $102.00. Journalize the following bond payable transactions:
   a. Issuance of the bonds on April 1, 2002.
   b. Payment of interest and amortization of premium on September 30, 2002.
   c. Accrual of interest and amortization of premium on December 31, 2002, the year end.
   d. Payment of interest and amortization of premium on March 31, 2003.

4. Check your recorded interest expense for the year ended March 31, 2003, using as a model the supplement to the summary problem on page 823.

5. Report interest payable and bonds payable as they would appear on the Mason Corp. balance sheet at December 31, 2002.

Problem 15-3B *Analyzing a company's long-term debt, journalizing its transactions, and reporting the long-term debt on the balance sheet (Obj. 2)*

Assume that the notes to Unicore Systems Ltd.'s financial statements reported the following data on September 30, 2003 (amounts rounded):

NOTE E: LONG-TERM DEBT
5% debentures due 2022, net of unamortized discount
    of $223,162 (effective-interest rate of 6.0%) $1,776,838

Unicore Systems Ltd. amortizes discount by the effective-interest method.

Required

1. Answer the following questions about Unicore Systems Ltd.'s long-term liabilities:
   a. What is the maturity value of the 5 percent debentures?
   b. What is the carrying amount of the 5 percent debentures at September 30, 2003?
   c. What are Unicore Systems Ltd.'s annual cash interest payments on the 5 percent debentures?

2. Prepare an amortization table through September 30, 2005 for the 5 percent debentures. Unicore Systems Ltd. pays interest annually on September 30.

3. Record the September 30, 2005, interest payments on the 5 percent debentures.

4. What is Unicore Systems Ltd.'s carrying amount of the 5 percent debentures at September 30, 2005, immediately after the interest payment?

Problem 15-4B *Issuing convertible bonds at a discount, amortizing by the effective-interest method, retiring bonds early, converting bonds, and reporting the bonds payable on the balance sheet* **(Obj. 2, 3, 4)**

On December 31, 2002, Goodwin Corp. issues 8 percent, 10-year convertible bonds with a maturity value of $5,000,000. The semiannual interest dates are June 30 and December 31. The market interest rate is 9 percent, and the issue price of the bonds is $93.496. Goodwin Corp. amortizes bond premium and discount by the effective-interest method.

Required

1. Prepare an effective-interest method amortization table for the first four semi-annual interest periods.

2. Journalize the following transactions:
   a. Issuance of the bonds on December 31, 2002. Credit Convertible Bonds Payable.
   b. Payment of interest on June 30, 2003.
   c. Payment of interest on December 31, 2003.
   d. Retirement of bonds with face value of $1,000,000 on July 2, 2004. Goodwin Corp. purchases the bonds at $96.00 in the open market.
   e. Conversion by the bondholders on July 2, 2004, of bonds with face value of $2,000,000 into 50,000 shares of Goodwin Corp. common stock.

3. Prepare the balance sheet presentation of the bonds payable that are outstanding at December 31, 2004.

Problem 15-5B *Journalizing bonds payable and capital lease transactions* **(Obj. 1, 6)**

Journalize the following transactions of Khalil Communications Inc.:

2002
Jan. 2 Issued $2,000,000 of 8 percent, 10-year bonds payable at 97.00.
      2 Signed a 5-year capital lease on machinery. The agreement requires annual lease payments of $20,000, with the first payment due immediately. The present value of the four future lease payments is $63,397.
July 2 Paid semiannual interest and amortized discount by the straight-line method on the 8 percent bonds payable.
Dec. 31 Accrued semiannual interest expense and amortized discount by the straight-line method on the 8 percent bonds.
     31 Recorded amortization on leased machinery, using the straight-line method.
     31 Accrued interest expense at 10 percent on the lease liability.
2012
Jan. 2 Paid the 8 percent bonds at maturity.

Problem 15-6B *Financing operations with debt or with stock* **(Obj. 5)**

Marketing studies have shown that consumers prefer upscale restaurants, and recent trends in industry sales have supported the research. To capitalize on this trend, Branigan's Ltd. is embarking on a massive expansion. Plans call for opening 5 new restaurants within the next 18 months. Each restaurant is scheduled to be

30 percent larger than the company's existing restaurants, furnished more elaborately, with more extensive menus. Management estimates that company operations will provide $6 million of the cash needed for expansion. Branigan's must raise the remaining $4 million from outsiders. The board of directors is considering obtaining the $4 million either through borrowing or by issuing common stock.

Required

1. Write a memo to company management. Discuss the advantages and disadvantages of borrowing and of issuing common stock to raise the needed cash. Use the following format for your memo:

Date:
To: Management of Branigan's Ltd.
From: Student Name
Subject: Advantages and disadvantages of borrowing and issuing stock to raise $4 million for expansion
Advantages and disadvantages of borrowing:
Advantages and disadvantages of issuing stock:

2. How will what you have learned in this problem help you manage a business?

Problem 15-7B   *Reporting liabilities on the balance sheet*   *(Obj. 6)*

The accounting records of Potter Technologies Inc. include the following items:

Equipment acquired under capital lease	$374,000	Mortgage note payable—long-term	$164,000
Bonds payable—current portion	$150,000	Accumulated amortization, equipment	92,000
Capital lease liability—long-term	108,000	Capital lease liability—current	36,000
Discount on bonds payable—long term	14,000	Mortgage note payable—current	46,000
Interest revenue	10,000		
Interest payable	26,000	Bonds payable—long-term	600,000
Interest expense	114,000	Defined benefit pension plan—obligations	1,428,000
Defined benefit pension plan—assets at market	1,592,000		

Required

Show how these items would be reported on the Potter Technologies Inc. balance sheet, including headings for capital assets, current liabilities, long-term liabilities, and so on. Note disclosures are not required.

Problem 15-8B   *Amortizing bond discount and premium by the effective-interest method; retirement of bonds; conversion of bonds*   *(Obj. 2, 3, 4)*

Ace Systems Inc. is authorized to issue $15,000,000, 10-year, 10 percent convertible bonds with interest payable on June 30 and December 31. The bonds are convertible on the basis of 40 shares of common stock for each $1,000 bond. The following bond transactions took place:

2003
Jan.   2   Sold bonds with $9,000,000 face value. Since the market rate of interest on this date was 8 percent, the bonds had a present value of $10,223,129.
June 30   Paid the interest and amortized the premium using the effective-interest method.

Dec.	31	Paid the interest and amortized the premium using the effective-interest method.
2004		
April	1	Sold $4,000,000 of bonds at par plus accrued interest. The market rate of interest on this date was 10 percent.
June	30	Paid the interest and amortized the premium using the effective-interest method.
July	2	Retired $3,000,000 (face value) of the bonds issued on January 2, 2003, at a rate of 101.
July	2	Bondholders converted $3,000,000 (face value) of bonds issued on January 2, 2003, for common stock.

Required

Round all amounts to the nearest whole dollar.

1. Journalize the transactions.
2. Show the balance sheet presentation of the bonds payable on July 2, 2004.

Problem 15-9B *Amortizing bond discount by the effective-interest method; accounting for lease transactions* **(Obj. 2, 6)**

FirstFreight Trucking Ltd. had the following information available on bonds payable outstanding at December 31, 2002, its year end:

- $10,000,000—Bonds Payable, 9 percent, interest paid on April 2 and October 2. The bonds had been sold April 2, 2000, when the market rate of interest was 10 percent. The bonds mature on January 2, 2005.
- $177,300—Discount on Bonds Payable.

The following transactions took place after December 31, 2002:

2003		
Jan.	2	FirstFreight Trucking Ltd. signed a lease to rent a building for expansion of its operations. The lease is for 6 years, with an option to renew, and calls for annual payments of $50,000 per year payable on January 2. FirstFreight Trucking Ltd. gave a cheque for the first year upon signing the lease.
Jan.	2	FirstFreight Trucking Ltd. signed a lease for equipment. The lease is for 10 years with payments of $30,000 per year payable on January 2 (first year's payment was made at the signing). At the end of the lease the equipment will become the property of FirstFreight Trucking Ltd. The future payments on the lease have a present value (at 10 percent) of $172,770.
April	2	Paid the interest on the bonds payable and amortized the discount using the effective-interest method.
Oct.	2	Paid the interest on the bonds payable and amortized the discount using the effective-interest method.
Dec.	31	Recorded any adjustments required at the end of the year for the bonds payable and the lease(s).
2004		
Jan.	2	Made the annual payments on the leases.
April	2	Paid the interest on the bonds payable and amortized the discount using the effective-interest method.
Oct.	2	Paid the interest on the bonds payable and amortized the discount using the effective-interest method.
Dec.	31	Recorded any adjustments required at the end of the year for the bonds payable and the lease(s).

Required

Round all amounts to the nearest whole dollar.

1. Prepare the general journal entries required to record the transactions of 2003 and 2004.

2. Show the liability section of the balance sheet on December 31, 2004.

Challenge Problems

Problem 15-1C   *Understanding present value*   *(Obj. A2)*

A friend tells you that she always buys bonds that are at a discount because "You always get more than you paid when the bond matures."

Required

Discuss your friend's understanding of present value.

Problem 15-2C   *Evaluating alternative methods of financing growth*   *(Obj. 5)*

You have just inherited $1,000 and have decided to buy stock. You have narrowed your choice down to QT Logistics Inc. and Compulogic Systems Ltd. You carefully read each company's annual report to determine which company's stock you should buy. Your research indicates that the two companies are very similar. QT Logistics Inc.'s annual report states "The Company has financed its growth through long- and short-term borrowing," while the Compulogic report contains the statement "Your Company has financed its growth out of earnings retained in the business."

QT's shares are trading at $25.00 while Compulogic 's shares are trading at $13.00. You wonder if that is because QT has been paying an annual dividend of $2.00 per share while Compulogic has been paying a dividend of $1.10.

You recall that the morning newspaper had an article about the economy that predicted that interest rates were expected to rise and stay at a much higher rate than at present for the next two to three years.

Required

Explain which stock you would buy and indicate why you have selected it.

Extending Your Knowledge

Decision Problems

1. Analyzing alternative ways of raising $10,000,000 (Obj. 6)

Business is going well for Peace River Forest Products Inc. The board of directors of this family-owned company believes that the company could earn an additional $3,000,000 in income after interest and taxes by expanding into new markets. However, the $10,000,000 that the business needs for growth cannot be raised within the family. The directors, who strongly wish to retain family control of Peace River Forest Products Inc., must consider issuing securities to outsiders. They are considering three financing plans.

Plan A is to borrow at 8 percent. Plan B is to issue 100,000 shares of common stock. Plan C is to issue 100,000 shares of nonvoting, $7.50 cumulative preferred stock. The company presently has net income before tax of $6,000,000 and has 500,000 shares of common stock outstanding. The income tax rate is 40 percent.

Required

1. Prepare an analysis similar to Exhibit 15-8 to determine which plan will result in the highest earnings per share of common stock.

2. Recommend one plan to the board of directors. Give your reasons.

2. Questions about long-term debt (Obj. 6 and Appendix)

The following questions are not related.

a. Why do you think corporations prefer operating leases over capital leases? How do you think a shareholder would view an operating lease?

b. If you were to win $2,000,000 from Lotto 649, you would receive the $2,000,000 today, whereas if you were to win $2,000,000 in one of the U.S. lotteries, you would receive 20 annual payments of $100,000. Are the prizes equivalent? If not, why not?

Financial Statement Problem

Long-term debt (Obj. 1, 3)

The Intrawest Corporation income statement and balance sheet in Appendix A provide details about the company's long-term debt. Use the data to answer the following questions.

1. How much cash did Intrawest Corporation borrow on bank and other long-term debt during the year ended June 30, 2000? How much long-term debt did Intrawest repay during the year?
2. Journalize in a single entry Intrawest's interest expense on long-term debt for the year ended June 30, 2000. Assume that Intrawest paid 90 percent of the interest expense and accrued the remainder at year end.
3. What is the total amount owing to banks and others at June 30, 2000? How much is due in the year ended June 30, 2001?
4. Does the company have any convertible debt outstanding? If so, how many shares will the company have to issue if the debt is converted?
5. Does Intrawest Corporation have any operating leases? If so, what payments are due in the year ended June 30, 2001? How much is due in the years beyond 2001?

Appendix

Time Value of Money:
Future Value and Present Value

The following discussion of future value lays the foundation for present value but is not essential. For the valuation of long-term liabilities, some instructors may wish to begin on page 858.

The phrase *time value of money* refers to the fact that money earns interest over time. Interest is the cost of using money. To borrowers, interest is the expense of renting money. To lenders, interest is the revenue earned from lending. When funds are used for a period of time, we must recognize the interest. Otherwise we overlook an important part of the transaction. Suppose you invest $4,545 in corporate bonds that pay 10-percent interest each year. After one year, the value of your investment has grown to $5,000. The difference between your original investment ($4,545) and the future value of the investment ($5,000) is the amount of interest revenue you will earn during the year ($455). If you ignored the interest, you would fail to account for the interest revenue you have earned. Interest becomes more important as the time period lengthens because the amount of interest depends on the span of time the money is invested.

Let's consider a second example, but from the borrower's perspective. Suppose you purchase a machine for your business. The cash price of the machine is $8,000, but you cannot pay cash now. To finance the purchase, you sign an $8,000 note payable. The note requires you to pay the $8,000 plus 10-percent interest one year from date of purchase. Is your cost of the machine $8,000, or is it $8,800 [$8,000 plus interest of $800 ($8,000 × 0.10)]? The cost is $8,000. The additional $800 is interest expense and not part of the cost of the machine. If you ignored the interest, you would overstate the cost of the machine and understate the amount of interest expense.

Future Value

OBJECTIVE A1
Compute the future value of an investment

The main application of future value is to calculate the accumulated balance of an investment at a future date. In our first example above, the investment earned 10 percent per year. After one year, $4,545 grew to $5,000, as shown in Exhibit 15A-1. If the money were invested for five years, you would have to perform five such calculations. You would also have to consider the compound interest that your investment is earning. Compound interest is the interest you earn not only on your principal amount but also the interest you receive on the interest you have already earned. Most business applications include compound interest. The table below shows the interest revenue earned each year at 10 percent:

End of Year	Interest	Future Value
0	—	$4,545
1	$4,545 × 0.10 = $455	5,000
2	5,000 × 0.10 = 500	5,500
3	5,500 × 0.10 = 550	6,050
4	6,050 × 0.10 = 605	6,655
5	6,655 × 0.10 = 666	7,321

Earning 10 percent, a $4,545 investment grows to $5,000 at the end of one year, to $5,500 at the end of two years, and so on. Throughout this discussion we round off to the nearest dollar.

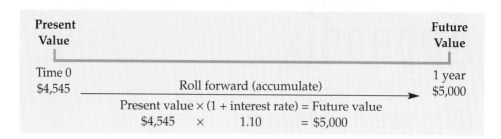

Future Value Tables

The process of computing a future value is called *accumulating* because the future value is *more* than the present value. Mathematical tables ease the computational burden. You can also use financial calculators and functions in spreadsheet programs to calculate future value. Exhibit 15A-2, Future Value of $1, gives the future value for a single sum (a present value), $1, invested to earn a particular interest rate for a specific number of periods. Future value depends on three factors: (1) the amount of the investment, (2) the length of time between investment and future accumulation, and (3) the interest rate.

The heading in Exhibit 15A-2 states $1. Future value tables and present value tables are based on $1 because unity (the value 1) is so easy to work with. Observe the Periods column and the interest rate columns 4% through 16%. In business applications interest rates are always stated for the annual period of one year unless specified otherwise. In fact, an interest rate can be stated for any period, such as 3 percent per quarter or 5 percent for a six-month period. The length of the period is arbitrary. For example, an investment may promise a return (income) of 3 percent per quarter for six months (two quarters). In that case you would be working with 3-percent interest for two periods. It would be incorrect to use 6 percent for one period because the interest is 3 percent compounded quarterly, and that amount differs somewhat from 6 percent compounded semiannually. Take care in studying future value and present value problems to align the interest rate with the appropriate number of periods.

Periods	4%	5%	6%	7%	8%	9%	10%	12%	14%	16%
1	1.040	1.050	1.060	1.070	1.080	1.090	1.100	1.120	1.140	1.160
2	1.082	1.103	1.124	1.145	1.166	1.188	1.210	1.254	1.300	1.346
3	1.125	1.158	1.191	1.225	1.260	1.295	1.331	1.405	1.482	1.561
4	1.170	1.216	1.262	1.311	1.360	1.412	1.464	1.574	1.689	1.811
5	1.217	1.276	1.338	1.403	1.469	1.539	1.611	1.762	1.925	2.100
6	1.265	1.340	1.419	1.501	1.587	1.677	1.772	1.974	2.195	2.436
7	1.316	1.407	1.504	1.606	1.714	1.828	1.949	2.211	2.502	2.826
8	1.369	1.477	1.594	1.718	1.851	1.993	2.144	2.476	2.853	3.278
9	1.423	1.551	1.689	1.838	1.999	2.172	2.358	2.773	3.252	3.803
10	1.480	1.629	1.791	1.967	2.159	2.367	2.594	3.106	3.707	4.411
11	1.539	1.710	1.898	2.105	2.332	2.580	2.853	3.479	4.226	5.117
12	1.601	1.796	2.012	2.252	2.518	2.813	3.138	3.896	4.818	5.939
13	1.665	1.886	2.133	2.410	2.720	3.066	3.452	4.363	5.492	6.886
14	1.732	1.980	2.261	2.579	2.937	3.342	3.797	4.887	6.261	7.988
15	1.801	2.079	2.397	2.759	3.172	3.642	4.177	5.474	7.138	9.266
16	1.873	2.183	2.540	2.952	3.426	3.970	4.595	6.130	8.137	10.748
17	1.948	2.292	2.693	3.159	3.700	4.328	5.054	6.866	9.276	12.468
18	2.026	2.407	2.854	3.380	3.996	4.717	5.560	7.690	10.575	14.463
19	2.107	2.527	3.026	3.617	4.316	5.142	6.116	8.613	12.056	16.777
20	2.191	2.653	3.207	3.870	4.661	5.604	6.727	9.646	13.743	19.461

Future Value of $1

Let's use Exhibit 15A-2. The future value of $1.00 invested at 4 percent for one year is $1.04 ($1.00 × 1.040, which appears at the junction under the 4% column and across from 1 in the Periods column). The figure 1.040 includes both the principal (1.000) and the compound interest for one period (0.040).

Suppose you deposit $5,000 in a savings account that pays annual interest of 4 percent. The account balance at the end of the year will be $5,200. To compute the future value of $5,000 at 4 percent for one year, multiply $5,000 by 1.040 to get $5,200. Now suppose you invest in a 10-year, 6-percent certificate of deposit (CD). What will be the future value of the CD at maturity? To compute the future value of $5,000 at 6 percent for 10 periods, multiply $5,000 by 1.791 (from Exhibit 15A-2) to get $8,955. This future value of $8,955 indicates that $5,000 earning 6 percent interest compounded annually, grows to $8,955 at the end of 10 years. In this way you can find any present amount's future value at a particular future date. Future value is especially helpful for computing the amount of cash you will have on hand for some purpose in the future.

Future Value of an Annuity

In the preceding example, we made an investment of a single amount. Other investments, called annuities, include multiple investments of an equal periodic amount at fixed intervals over the duration of the investment. Consider a family investing for a child's education. The Dietrichs can invest $4,000 annually to accumulate a college fund for 15-year-old Helen. The investment can earn 7 percent annually until Helen turns 18—a three-year investment. How much will be available for Helen on the date of the last investment? Exhibit 15A-3 (on page 858) shows the accumulation—a total future value of $12,860.

The first $4,000 invested by the Dietrichs grows to $4,580 over the investment period. The second amount grows to $4,280, and the third amount stays at $4,000 because it has no time to earn interest. The sum of the three future values ($4,580 + $4,280 + $4,000) is the future value of the annuity ($12,860), which can be computed as follows:

End of Year	Annual Investment	Interest	Increase for the Year	Future Value of Annuity
0	—	—	—	0
1	$4,000	—	$4,000	$4,000
2	4,000 +	($4,000 × 0.07 = $280) =	4,280	8,280
3	4,000 +	($8,280 × 0.07 = $580) =	4,580	12,860

These computations are laborious. As with the Future Value of $1 (a lump sum), mathematical tables ease the strain of calculating annuities. Exhibit 15A-4, Future Value of Annuity of $1, gives the future value of a series of investments, each of equal amount, at regular intervals.

What is the future value of an annuity of three investments of $1 each that earn 7 percent? The answer 3.215 can be found in the 7% column and across from 3 in the Periods column of Exhibit 15A-4. This amount can be used to compute the future value of the investment for Helen's education, as follows:

Amount of each periodic investment	×	Future value of annuity of $1 (Exhibit 15A-4)	=	Future value of investment
$4,000	×	3.215	=	$12,860

This one-step calculation is much easier than computing the future value of each annual investment and then summing the individual future values. In this way you can compute the future value of any investment consisting of equal periodic amounts at regular intervals. Businesses make periodic investments to accumulate funds for

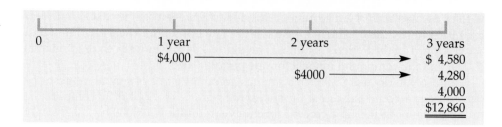

equipment replacement and other uses—an application of the future value of an annuity.

Present Value

Often a person knows a future amount and needs to know the related present value. Recall Exhibit 15A-1, in which present value and future value are on opposite ends of the same time line. Suppose an investment promises to pay you $5,000 at the *end* of one year. How much would you pay *now* to acquire this investment? You would be willing to pay the present value of the $5,000, which is a future amount.

Present value also depends on three factors: (1) the amount of payment (or receipt), (2) the length of time between investment and future receipt (or payment), and (3) the interest rate. The process of computing a present value is called *discounting* because the present value is *less* than the future value.

In our investment example, the future receipt is $5,000. The investment period is one year. Assume that you demand an annual interest rate of 10 percent on your investment. With all three factors specified, you can compute the present value of $5,000 at 10 percent for one year. The computation is

$$\frac{\text{Future value}}{(1 + \text{Interest rate})} = \frac{\$5,000}{1.10} = \$4,545$$

EXHIBIT 15A-4

Future Value of Annuity of $1

Periods	4%	5%	6%	7%	8%	9%	10%	12%	14%	16%
1	1.000	1.000	1.000	1.000	1.000	1.000	1.000	1.000	1.000	1.000
2	2.040	2.050	2.060	2.070	2.080	2.090	2.100	2.120	2.140	2.160
3	3.122	3.153	3.184	3.215	3.246	3.278	3.310	3.374	3.440	3.506
4	4.246	4.310	4.375	4.440	4.506	4.573	4.641	4.779	4.921	5.066
5	5.416	5.526	5.637	5.751	5.867	5.985	6.105	6.353	6.610	6.877
6	6.633	6.802	6.975	7.153	7.336	7.523	7.716	8.115	8.536	8.977
7	7.898	8.142	8.394	8.654	8.923	9.200	9.487	10.089	10.730	11.414
8	9.214	9.549	9.897	10.260	10.637	11.028	11.436	12.300	13.233	14.240
9	10.583	11.027	11.491	11.978	12.488	13.021	13.579	14.776	16.085	17.519
10	12.006	12.578	13.181	13.816	14.487	15.193	15.937	17.549	19.337	21.321
11	13.486	14.207	14.972	15.784	16.645	17.560	18.531	20.655	23.045	25.733
12	15.026	15.917	16.870	17.888	18.977	20.141	21.384	24.133	27.271	30.850
13	16.627	17.713	18.882	20.141	21.495	22.953	24.523	28.029	32.089	36.786
14	18.292	19.599	21.015	22.550	24.215	26.019	27.975	32.393	37.581	43.672
15	20.024	21.579	23.276	25.129	27.152	29.361	31.772	37.280	43.842	51.660
16	21.825	23.657	25.673	27.888	30.324	33.003	35.950	42.753	50.980	60.925
17	23.698	25.840	28.213	30.840	33.750	36.974	40.545	48.884	59.118	71.673
18	25.645	28.132	30.906	33.999	37.450	41.301	45.599	55.750	68.394	84.141
19	27.671	30.539	33.760	37.379	41.446	46.018	51.159	63.440	78.969	98.603
20	29.778	33.066	36.786	40.995	45.762	51.160	57.275	72.052	91.025	115.380

By turning the problem around, we verify the present value computation:

Amount invested (present value)	$4,545
Expected earnings ($4,545 × 0.10)	455
Amount to be received one year from now (future value)	$5,000

This example illustrates that present value and future value are based on the same equation:

Present value × (1 + Interest rate) = Future value

$$\frac{\text{Future value}}{(1 + \text{Interest rate})} = \text{Present value}$$

If the $5,000 is to be received two years from now, you will pay only $4,132 for the investment, as shown in Exhibit 15A-5. By turning the data around, we verify that $4,132 accumulates to $5,000 at 10 percent for two years.

Amount invested (present value)	$4,132
Expected earnings for first year ($4,132 × 0.10)......................................	413
Amount invested after one year..	4,545
Expected earnings for second year ($4,545 × 0.10)	455
Amount to be received two years from now (future value)	$5,000

You would pay $4,132—the present value of $5,000—to receive the $5,000 future amount at the end of two years at 10 percent per year. The $868 difference between the amount invested ($4,132) and the amount to be received ($5,000) is the return on the investment, the sum of the two interest receipts: $413 + $455 = $868.

Present-Value Tables

We have shown the simple formula for computing present value. However, calculating present value "by hand" for investments spanning many years presents too many opportunities for arithmetical errors. Present-value tables ease our work. Let's re-examine our examples of present value by using Exhibit 15A-6: Present Value of $1.

For the 10 percent investment for one year, we find the junction under 10% and across from 1 in the period column. The table figure of 0.909 is computed as follows: $\frac{1}{1.10}$ = 0.909. This work has been done for us, and only the present values are given in the table. The heading in Exhibit 15A-6 states present value for $1. To calculate present value for $5,000, we multiply 0.909 by $5,000. The result is $4,545, which matches the result we obtained by hand.

For the two-year investment, we read down the 10 percent column and across the Period 2 row. We multiply 0.826 (computed as $\frac{0.909}{1.10}$ = 0.826) by $5,000 and get $4,130, which confirms our earlier computation of $4,132 (the difference is due to rounding in the present-value table). Using the table we can compute the present value of any single future amount.

While we focus on tables in this text, you can also use financial calculators and functions in spreadsheet programs to calculate present value.

WORKING IT OUT

What is the present value of $1,000 to be received at the end of 5 years at 10%?

A: Look in Exhibit 15A-6 at the factor for 5 periods and 10%: 0.621. The present value is: $1,000 × 0.621 = $621. The amount of interest that could be earned over 5 years with an initial investment of $621 is $379 ($1,000 – $621).

EXHIBIT 15A-5

Two-Year Investment

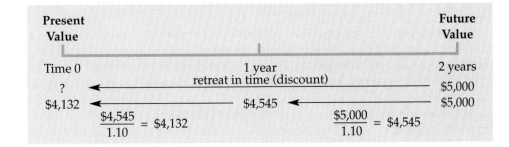

Periods	4%	5%	6%	7%	8%	10%	12%	14%	16%
1	0.962	0.952	0.943	0.935	0.926	0.909	0.893	0.877	0.862
2	0.925	0.907	0.890	0.873	0.857	0.826	0.797	0.769	0.743
3	0.889	0.864	0.840	0.816	0.794	0.751	0.712	0.675	0.641
4	0.855	0.823	0.792	0.763	0.735	0.683	0.636	0.592	0.552
5	0.822	0.784	0.747	0.713	0.681	0.621	0.567	0.519	0.476
6	0.790	0.746	0.705	0.666	0.630	0.564	0.507	0.456	0.410
7	0.760	0.711	0.665	0.623	0.583	0.513	0.452	0.400	0.354
8	0.731	0.677	0.627	0.582	0.540	0.467	0.404	0.351	0.305
9	0.703	0.645	0.592	0.544	0.500	0.424	0.361	0.308	0.263
10	0.676	0.614	0.558	0.508	0.463	0.386	0.322	0.270	0.227
11	0.650	0.585	0.527	0.475	0.429	0.350	0.287	0.237	0.195
12	0.625	0.557	0.497	0.444	0.397	0.319	0.257	0.208	0.168
13	0.601	0.530	0.469	0.415	0.368	0.290	0.229	0.182	0.145
14	0.577	0.505	0.442	0.388	0.340	0.263	0.205	0.160	0.125
15	0.555	0.481	0.417	0.362	0.315	0.239	0.183	0.140	0.108
16	0.534	0.458	0.394	0.339	0.292	0.218	0.163	0.123	0.093
17	0.513	0.436	0.371	0.317	0.270	0.198	0.146	0.108	0.080
18	0.494	0.416	0.350	0.296	0.250	0.180	0.130	0.095	0.069
19	0.475	0.396	0.331	0.277	0.232	0.164	0.116	0.083	0.060
20	0.456	0.377	0.312	0.258	0.215	0.149	0.104	0.073	0.051

Present Value of $1

EXHIBIT 15A-6

Present Value of $1

WORKING IT OUT

What is the present value of $1,000 to be received at the end of each of the next five years at 10%?

A: Look in Exhibit 15A-7 at 5 periods and 10%. The factor is 3.791. The present value of *all five* $1,000 receipts is $1,000 × 3.791 = $3,791.

Present Value of an Annuity

Return to the investment example beginning on page 859. That investment provided the investor with only a single future receipt ($5,000 at the end of two years). Annuity investments provide multiple receipts of an equal amount at fixed intervals over the investment's duration.

Consider an investment that promises *annual* cash receipts of $10,000 to be received at the end of each of three years. Assume that you demand a 12 percent return on your investment. What is the investment's present value? What would you pay today to acquire the investment? The investment spans three periods, and you would pay the sum of three present values. The computation is as follows:

Year	Annual Cash Receipt	Present Value of $1 at 12% (Exhibit 15A-6)	Present Value of Annual Cash Receipt
1	$10,000	0.893	$ 8,930
2	10,000	0.797	7,970
3	10,000	0.712	7,120
Total present value of investment			$24,020

The present value of this annuity is $24,020. By paying this amount today, you will receive $10,000 at the end of each of three years while earning 12 percent on your investment.

The example illustrates repetitive computations of the three future amounts, a time-consuming process. One way to ease the computational burden is to add the three present values of $1 (0.893 + 0.797 + 0.712) and multiply their sum (2.402) by the annual cash receipt ($10,000) to obtain the present value of the annuity ($10,000 × 2.402 = $24,020).

An easier approach is to use a present value of an annuity table. Exhibit 15A-7 shows the present value of $1 to be received periodically for a given number of periods. The present value of a three-period annuity at 12 percent is 2.402 (the junction

Present Value of Annuity of $1

Periods	4%	5%	6%	7%	8%	10%	12%	14%	16%
1	0.962	0.952	0.943	0.935	0.926	0.909	0.893	0.877	0.862
2	1.886	1.859	1.833	1.808	1.783	1.736	1.690	1.647	1.605
3	2.775	2.723	2.673	2.624	2.577	2.487	2.402	2.322	2.246
4	3.630	3.546	3.465	3.387	3.312	3.170	3.037	2.914	2.798
5	4.452	4.329	4.212	4.100	3.993	3.791	3.605	3.433	3.274
6	5.242	5.076	4.917	4.767	4.623	4.355	4.111	3.889	3.685
7	6.002	5.786	5.582	5.389	5.206	4.868	4.564	4.288	4.039
8	6.733	6.463	6.210	5.971	5.747	5.335	4.968	4.639	4.344
9	7.435	7.108	6.802	6.515	6.247	5.759	5.328	4.946	4.607
10	8.111	7.722	7.360	7.024	6.710	6.145	5.650	5.216	4.833
11	8.760	8.306	7.887	7.499	7.139	6.495	5.938	5.453	5.029
12	9.385	8.863	8.384	7.943	7.536	6.814	6.194	5.660	5.197
13	9.986	9.394	8.853	8.358	7.904	7.103	6.424	5.842	5.342
14	10.563	9.899	9.295	8.745	8.244	7.367	6.628	6.002	5.468
15	11.118	10.380	9.712	9.108	8.559	7.606	6.811	6.142	5.575
16	11.652	10.838	10.106	9.447	8.851	7.824	6.974	6.265	5.669
17	12.166	11.274	10.477	9.763	9.122	8.022	7.120	6.373	5.749
18	12.659	11.690	10.828	10.059	9.372	8.201	7.250	6.467	5.818
19	13.134	12.085	11.158	10.336	9.604	8.365	7.366	6.550	5.877
20	13.590	12.462	11.470	10.594	9.818	8.514	7.469	6.623	5.929

EXHIBIT 15A-7

Present Value of Annuity of $1

of the Period 3 row and the 12 percent column). Thus $10,000 received annually at the end of each of three years, discounted at 12 percent, is $24,020 ($10,000 × 2.402), which is the present value.

Present Value of Bonds Payable

The present value of a bond—its market price—is the present value of the future principal amount at maturity plus the present value of the future contract interest payments. The principal is a single amount to be paid at maturity. The interest is an annuity because it occurs periodically.

Let's compute the present value of 9 percent, five-year bonds of Rogers Communications Inc. The face value of the bonds is $500,000, and they pay 4½ percent contract (cash) interest semiannually. At issuance the market interest rate is 10 percent, but it is computed at 5 percent semiannually. Therefore, the effective-interest rate for each of the 10 semiannual periods is 5 percent. We use 5 percent in computing the present value of the maturity and of the interest. The market price of these bonds is $480,745, as follows:

	Effective annual interest rate ÷ 2	Number of semiannual interest payments	
PV of principal:			
$500,000 × PV of single amount at 5%	for	10 periods	
($500,000 × 0.614—Exhibit 15A-6) ...			$307,000
PV of interest:			
($500,000 × 0.045) × PV of annuity at 5%	for	10 periods	
($22,500 × 7.722—Exhibit 15A-7)			173,745
PV (market price) of bonds			$480,745

The market price of the Rogers Communications Inc. bonds shows a discount because the contract interest rate on the bonds (9 percent) is less than the market interest rate (10 percent). We discuss these bonds in more detail on page 814.

WORKING IT OUT

What is the present value of a $100,000, 12%, 10-year bond priced to yield 14% interest? Interest is paid semiannually.

A:
PV of principal:
$100,000 × 0.258 = $25,800
PV of interest:
$6,000 × 10.594 =   63,564
PV of bond $89,364

The factors are for 20 interest periods, since the 10-year bond pays interest semiannually. The interest rate used to compute the semiannual receipts of cash interest is the bond's stated rate (12%) divided by 2. The interest rate used in the present-value table is the effective rate (14%) divided by 2. How would the issue price of this bond be quoted?

A:
$89,364/$100,000 = 89.36 approximately.

Let's consider a premium price for the Rogers Communications Inc. bonds. Assume that the market interest rate is 8 percent at issuance. The effective-interest rate is 4 percent for each of the 10 semiannual periods.

	Effective annual interest rate ÷ 2	Number of semiannual interest payments	
PV of principal:			
$500,000 × PV of single amount at	4% for	10 periods	
($500,000 × 0.676—Exhibit 15A-6)			$338,000
PV of interest:			
($500,000 × 0.045) × PV of annuity at	4% for	10 periods	
($22,500 × 8.111—Exhibit 15A-7)............			$182,498
PV (market price) of bonds.................			$520,498

We discuss accounting for these bonds on page 814.

Many calculators and spreadsheet software packages can quickly and accurately perform present value calculations for bonds and leases.

Capital Leases

OBJECTIVE A3
Determine the cost of an asset acquired through a capital lease

How does a lessee compute the cost of an asset acquired through a capital lease? Consider that the lessee gets the use of the asset but does *not* pay for the leased asset in full at the beginning of the lease. A capital lease is therefore similar to borrowing money to purchase the leased asset. The lessee must record the leased asset at the present value of the lease liability. The time value of money must be weighed.

The cost of the asset to the lessee is the sum of any payment made at the beginning of the lease period plus the present value of the future lease payments. The lease payments are equal amounts occurring at regular intervals—that is, they are annuity payments.

Consider a 20-year building lease of Sierra Wireless Inc. The lease starts on January 2, 2002, and requires 20 annual payments of $50,000 each, with the first payment due immediately. The interest rate in the lease is 10 percent, and the present value of the 19 future payments is $418,250 ($50,000 × PV of annuity at 10 percent for 19 periods, or 8.365 from Exhibit 15A-7). Sierra's cost of the building is $468,250 (the sum of the initial payment, $50,000, plus the present value of the future payments, $418,250). The entries for a capital lease are illustrated on pp. 828–830.

Appendix Problems

Problem 15A-1 *Computing the future value of an investment* *(Obj. A1)*

For each situation, compute the required amount.

a. Summit Enterprises Ltd. is budgeting for the acquisition of land over the next several years. The company can invest $400,000 at 9 percent. How much cash will Summit Enterprises Ltd. have for land acquisitions at the end of five years? At the end of six years?

b. Alton Associates Inc. is planning to invest $5,000 each year for five years. The company's investment adviser believes that Alton Associates Inc. can earn 6 percent interest without taking on too much risk. What will be the value of Alton's investment on the date of the last deposit if Alton can earn 6 percent? If Alton can earn 8 percent?

Problem 15A-2 *Relating the future and present values of an investment* *(Obj. A1, A2)*

For each situation, compute the required amount.

a. Bombardier Inc.'s operations are generating excess cash that will be invested in a special fund. During 2002, Bombardier Inc. invests $11,287,000 in the fund for a planned advertising campaign for a new product to be released six years later, in 2008. If Bombardier Inc. investments can earn 10 percent each year, how much cash will the company have for the advertising campaign in 2008?

b. Bombardier Inc. will need $20 million to advertise a new type of plane in 2008. How much must Bombardier Inc. invest in 2002 to have the cash available for the advertising campaign? Bombardier Inc. investments can earn 10 percent annually.

c. Explain the relationship between your answers to (a) and (b).

Problem 15A-3 *Computing the present values of various notes and bonds* *(Obj. A2)*

Determine the present value of the following notes and bonds (notes are accounted for in the same way as bonds):

1. $50,000, five-year note payable with contract interest rate of 9 percent, paid annually. The market interest rate at issuance is 10 percent.
2. Ten-year bonds payable with maturity value of $100,000 and contract interest rate of 12 percent, paid semiannually. The market rate of interest is 10 percent at issuance.
3. Same bonds payable as in number 2, but the market interest rate is 8 percent.
4. Same bonds payable as in number 2, but the market interest rate is 12 percent.

Problem 15A-4 *Computing a bond's present value; recording its issuance at a discount and interest payments* *(Obj. A2)*

On December 31, 2003, when the market interest rate is 8 percent, Fairview Land Corporation issues $300,000 of 10-year, 7.25 percent bonds payable. The bonds pay interest semiannually.

Required

1. Determine the present value of the bonds at issuance.
2. Assume that the bonds are issued at the price computed in requirement 1. Prepare an effective-interest method amortization table for the first two semiannual interest periods.
3. Using the amortization table prepared in requirement 2, journalize issuance of the bonds and the first two interest payments.

Problem 15A-5 *Deciding between two payment plans* *(Obj. A2)*

Osaka Children's Choir needs a fleet of vans to transport the children to singing engagements throughout Japan. Nissan offers the vehicles for a single payment of 6,300,000 yen due at the end of four years. Toyota prices a similar fleet of vans for four annual payments of 1,500,000 yen each. The children's choir could borrow the funds at 6 percent, so this is the appropriate interest rate. Which company should get the business, Nissan or Toyota? Base your decision on present value, and give your reason.

Problem 15A-6 *Computing the cost of equipment acquired under a capital lease, and recording the lease transactions* *(Obj. A3)*

Rykoff Inc. acquired equipment under a capital lease that requires six annual lease payments of $10,000. The first payment is due when the lease begins, on January 2, 2002. Future payments are due on January 2 of each year of the lease term. The interest rate in the lease is 16 percent.

Required

1. Compute Rykoff Inc.'s cost of the equipment.
2. Journalize the (a) acquisition of the equipment, (b) amortization for 2002, (c) accrued interest at December 31, 2002, and (d) second lease payment on January 2, 2003.

16

Investments and International Operations

CHAPTER OBJECTIVES

After studying this chapter, you should be able to

1 Account for short-term stock investments

2 Account for long-term stock investments

3 Use the equity method to account for investments

4 Understand consolidated financial statements

5 Account for long-term investments in bonds

6 Understand how foreign-currency exchange rates are determined

"When you are in business, you either create growth or go stagnate. You can't stay still," said Frank Sobey, founder of Empire Co. Ltd. While some companies expand through internal growth, most grow through merger.

Empire Co. Ltd., owner of Sobeys Inc., one of the largest food retailers in Canada, purchased the Oshawa Group Ltd. in December, 1998. With that purchase, Sobeys, based in Nova Scotia, expanded to more than 1,200 stores across Canada.

In explaining why the Sobeys decided to move westward, Douglas Stewart, chief executive of Sobeys Inc., stated that in an industry where low profit margins are the norm, high sales volume is required to make money.

"Going national means you have more buying power and get a better bang for your buck" (*Maclean's*, p. 51).

The Sobeys 2000 Annual Report indicates that consolidated sales for the 53 weeks ended May 6, 2000, exceeded $11 billion. Empire Co. Ltd. is a major retailer in Canada with stores stretching from the Atlantic to the Pacific. Mergers like Sobeys' have costs; the 1999 Sobeys Annual Report shows restructuring and integration costs of $85 million and a loss of $8 million. But with the restructuring behind them, Sobeys had a profit of $80 million in 2000.

Sources: Adapted from John DeMont, "A Pictou Empire" and "Loblaw Fights Back," *Maclean's Magazine*, December 14, 1998, pp. 51, 53, 54; Sobeys Inc. 1999 and 2000 annual reports.

THROUGHOUT this course, you have become increasingly familiar with the financial statements of companies such as IPSCO, Intrawest, and Bombardier. This chapter continues to examine the real world of accounting by discussing long-term investments and international operations. We begin with investments. Investments extend from a few shares of stock to the acquisition of an entire company. In earlier chapters we discussed the stocks and bonds that MGI Software Corp. and CanWest Global Communications Group were hoping to issue. Here we examine stocks and bonds from the perspective of an investor who would buy them.

Why do individuals and corporations invest in stocks and bonds? You would probably make an investment in order to earn dividend revenue and to sell the stock at a higher price than you paid for it. Investment companies such as pension funds, mutual funds, insurance companies, and bank trust departments buy stocks and bonds for this same reason.

Many companies invest in stocks and bonds for a second reason: to influence or to control the other company. In the story above, in 1998 the top managers of Sobeys Inc. envisioned a need to become a national food retailer, and to remain competitive in its industry.

Different accounting methods apply to different types of investments. We begin with stock investments and then move to investments in bonds and notes.

Stock Investments: An Overview

Stock Prices

Investors buy more stock in transactions among themselves than in purchases directly from the issuing company. Each share of stock is issued only once, but it may be traded among investors many times thereafter. People and businesses buy and sell stocks from each other in markets, such as the Toronto and Montreal Stock

Sobeys Inc.
www.sobeys.ca

Toronto Stock Exchange
www.tse.com

Montreal Exchange
www.me.org

Canadian Venture Exchange (CDNX)
www.cdnx.com

 **REAL WORLD EXAMPLE**

Observe the reporting of stock prices in the financial section of a local newspaper or *The National Post*. Look for a company that has made an announcement—good (such as an earnings increase) or bad (such as a decrease in cash dividends)—to see how that news affects a stock's price.

Exchanges and the Canadian Venture Exchange (CDNX). Recall that stock ownership is transferable. Investors trade millions of shares of stock each day. Brokers like RBC Dominion Securities and Marleau, Lemire Inc. handle stock transactions for a commission.

A broker may "quote a stock price," which means state the current market price per share. The financial community quotes stock prices in dollars and cents. For example, Exhibit 16-1 shows Bombardier Class A trading at $22.20. Financial publications and many newspapers carry daily information on the stock issues of thousands of corporations. These one-line summaries carry information as of the close of trading the previous day. Many Internet sites show real-time price information.

Exhibit 16-1 presents information for the common stock of Bombardier Inc., just as it appears in *The Financial Post's* FP Investing section.[1]

During the previous 52 weeks, Bombardier Class A common stock reached a high of $26.80 and a low of $14.13. The annual cash dividend is $0.13 per share. *The National Post* comes out in the morning so the information relates to the previous day: the high and low prices were $22.45 and $21.61, while the closing price was $22.20 (if there had been no trading on the previous day, the latest, or most recent price, would be given). The closing price on the previous day was down by $0.04 from the closing price of one trading day earlier. During the previous day, 28,800 (288 × 100) shares of Bombardier A stock were traded. The yield (dividend per share divided by price per share) is 0.6 percent while the P/E ratio (ratio of earnings per share to the share price) is 35.0 for Bombardier A shares.

The newspaper also reveals that the shares split two for one during the past 52 weeks.

Investors and Investees

The person or company that owns stock in a corporation is the *investor*. The corporation that issued the stock is the *investee*. If you own shares of Bombardier common stock, you are an investor and Bombardier is the investee.

A business may purchase another corporation's stock simply to put extra cash to work in the hope of earning dividend revenue and gains on the sale of the stock. Such investments are rare, however. Most entities prefer to invest in inventory, employees, and capital assets in their own line of business. However, entities do buy the stock of other corporations to gain a degree of control over the investee's operation. An investor holding 25 percent of the outstanding stock of the investee owns one-fourth of the business. This one-quarter voice in electing the directors of the corporation is likely to give the investor influence over the conduct of the investee's business. An investor holding more than 50 percent of the outstanding shares controls the investee.

EXHIBIT 16-1

Stock Price Information for Bombardier Inc.

52 Weeks		Stock	Div Rate	High	Low	Cls or Latest	Net Chge	Vol 100s	Yield %	P/E Ratio
High	**Low**									
26.80	$14.13	Bombardier Class A	0.13	22.45	21.61	22.20	–0.04	288	0.6	35.0
26.70	13.90	Bombardier Class B	0.13	22.40	21.55	22.20	+0.26	39,368	0.6	35.0

[1] *The National Post*, March 2, 2001, p. D7.

Classifying Investments

Investments are assets to the investor. The investments may be short-term or long-term. Short-term investments are typically described on the balance sheet as **short-term investments, marketable securities**, or **temporary investments** and are current assets. To be listed on the balance sheet as current assets, investments must be liquid (readily convertible to cash). Generally, the investor intends to convert the investments to cash within one year but may continue to hold the investments for a longer period.

Investments not meeting these two requirements are classified on the balance sheet as **long-term investments**, a category of non-current assets. Long-term investments include bond sinking funds, and stocks, bonds, and other assets that the investor expects to hold longer than one year or that are not readily marketable—for instance, real estate not used in the operations of the business. Exhibit 16-2 shows the positions of short-term and long-term investments on the balance sheet.

We report assets in the order of their liquidity, starting with cash. Long-Term Investments are less liquid than current assets but more liquid than capital assets.

KEY POINT

Short-term investments include treasury bills, certificates of deposit, money market funds, and stocks and bonds of other companies.

Accounting for Short-Term Investments

Short-Term Stock Investments: The Cost Method (with LCM)

OBJECTIVE 1
Account for short-term stock investments

The **cost method** (with lower of cost or market) is used to account for short-term investments in stock. Cost is used only as the initial amount for recording investments and as the basis for measuring gains and losses on their sale. These investments are reported on the balance sheet at the *lower of their cost or market value*. When market value exceeds cost, it is customary to disclose market value in parentheses after the caption on the balance sheet or in the notes to the financial statements. Therefore, we refer to the overall method as cost (with lower of cost or market, or LCM).

All investments, including short-term investments, are recorded initially at cost. Cost is the price paid for the stock plus the brokerage commission. Accountants have no separate account for the brokerage commission paid. Suppose that Athabasca Ltd. purchases 1,000 shares of ATCO Ltd. non-voting common stock at the market price of $36.25 and pays a $500 commission. Athabasca Ltd. intends to sell this investment within one year or less and, therefore, classifies it as short-term. Athabasca Ltd.'s entry to record the investment is

Aug. 22	Marketable Securities..	36,750	
	Cash..		36,750

Purchased 1,000 shares of ATCO Ltd. non-voting common stock at $36.25 (1,000 × $36.25 = $36,250) plus commission of $500.

EXHIBIT 16-2

Reporting Investments on the Balance Sheet

Current Assets		
Cash..	$X	
Short-term investments...	X	
Accounts receivable	X	
Inventories..	X	
Prepaid expenses..	X	
Total current assets..		$X
Long-term investments (or simply **Investments**)		X
Capital assets...		X
Intangible assets		X
Other assets		X

Assume Athabasca Ltd. receives a $0.23 per share cash dividend on the ATCO Ltd. non-voting stock. Athabasca Ltd.'s entry to record receipt of the dividends is

Oct. 14	Cash	230	
	Dividend Revenue		230
	Received $0.23 per share cash dividend (1,000 × $0.23) on ATCO Ltd. non-voting common stock.		

Dividends do not accrue with the passage of time (as interest does). The investee has no liability for dividends until the dividends are declared. An investor makes no accrual entry for dividend revenue at year end in anticipation of a dividend declaration.

However, if a dividend declaration *does* occur before year end, say, on December 28, the investor *may* debit Dividend Receivable and credit Dividend Revenue on that date. The investor would then report this receivable and the revenue in the December 31 financial statements. Receipt of the cash dividend in January would be recorded by a debit to Cash and a credit to Dividend Receivable. The more common practice, however, is to record the dividend as income when it is received.

KEY POINT

Receipt of stock dividends and stock splits is recorded in a memorandum entry.

Receipt of a *stock* dividend is not income to the investor, and no formal journal entry is needed. As we have seen, a stock dividend increases the number of shares held by the investor but does not affect the total cost of the investment. The *cost per share* of the stock investment therefore decreases. The investor usually makes a memorandum entry of the number of stock dividend shares received and the new cost per share. Assume that Athabasca Ltd. receives a 10 percent stock dividend on its 1,000-share investment in ATCO Ltd. that cost $36,750. Athabasca Ltd. would make a memorandum entry like this:

Nov. 22	Received 100 shares of ATCO Ltd. common stock in a 10 percent stock dividend. New cost per share is $33.41 ($36,750/1,100 shares).

Any gain or loss on the sale of the investment is the difference between the sale proceeds and the cost of the investment. Assume that Athabasca Ltd. sells 400 shares of ATCO Ltd. stock for $35 per share, less a $280 commission. The entry to record the sale is

Dec. 18	Cash	13,720	
	Marketable Securities		13,364
	Gain on Sale of Investment		356
	Sold 400 shares of investment in ATCO Ltd. common stock. Cash received was $13,720 [(400 × $35) − $280]. Cost of common stock sold was $13,364 (400 × $33.41).		

Observe that the cost per share of the investment ($33.41) is based on the total number of shares held, including those received as a stock dividend.

Reporting Short-Term Investments at Lower of Cost or Market (LCM)

Because of accounting conservatism, short-term investments are reported at the lower of their cost or market (LCM) value. Canadian practice, in the absence of standards in the *CICA Handbook*, is to calculate market value on an investment-by-investment basis or on the portfolio as a whole. In either event, the basis of valuation for cost and market values should be disclosed. Assume a company owns three short-term investments with the following costs and market values:

Short-term Investment Portfolio

Stock	Cost	Current Market Value
Dofasco Inc.	$112,000	$92,000
Toronto-Dominion Bank	87,000	105,000
WestJet Airlines Ltd.	75,000	63,000
Total	$274,000	$260,000

The investor owning the portfolio has two choices when determining the value of the portfolio for balance sheet purposes. The first considers the portfolio on a security-by-security basis. The investor would write the book value of the two stocks (Dofasco Inc. and WestJet Airlines Ltd.) whose market price has dropped below the price paid for them, down to their market values of $92,000 and $63,000 respectively. The market price of The Toronto-Dominion Bank stock is greater than cost, so no adjustment would be made to its book value. The journal entry to record the write down would be as follows:

Loss on Marketable Securities...	32,000	
Marketable Securities..		32,000

To write down investment in Dofasco Inc. ($112,000 – $92,000 = $20,000) and WestJet Airlines Ltd. ($75,000 – $63,000 = $12,000) to market.

The investor's balance sheet would report short-term investments as follows:

Current Assets

Cash	$ XXX
Short-term investments, at lower of cost or market value (Note 4)	$242,000
Accounts receivable, net of allowance of $XXX	XXX

Note 4. Short-Term Investments
Short-term investments are reported at the lower of their cost or market value. At December 31, 2001, market value was $260,000.

Under this option, the investor would write down the book value of individual stocks to their market values, where cost was greater than market, irrespective of whether or not the total market value of the portfolio was greater than or less than cost.

The investor's other option would be to apply the LCM rule to the entire portfolio and write it down to market. The journal entry to record the write down would be

Loss on Marketable Securities...	14,000	
Marketable Securities..		14,000

To write down investment portfolio by $14,000 ($274,000 – $260,000) to market.

The investor's balance sheet would report short-term investments as follows:

Current Assets

Cash	$ XXX
Short-term investments, at market value (Note 4)	260,000
Accounts receivable, net of allowance of $XXX..	XXX

Note 4. Short-term Investments
Short-term investments are reported at the lower of their cost or market value. At December 31, 2001, cost was $274,000.

WORKING IT OUT

The short-term investment portfolio of Noxo Inc. at year end is as follows:

	Shares	Cost	Market
ClubLink	1,000	$ 5,500	$ 6,000
Western Star Trucks Holdings	300	12,300	10,200
Yogen Früz	1,000	1,500	1,700
		$19,300	$17,900

Journalize the adjusting entry needed if Noxo Inc. values the investments on (1) a portfolio basis; (2) a security-by-security basis.

A:

(1)	Loss on Marketable Securities...........1,400*	
	Marketable Securities....	1,400
(2)	Loss on Marketable Securities...........2,100†	
	Marketable Securities....	2,100

* $19,300 – $17,900 = $1,400
† $12,300 – $10,200 = $2,100

Dofasco Inc.
www.dofasco.ca

The Toronto-Dominion Bank
www.td.com

WestJet Airlines
www.westjet.ca

Under the second option, if the portfolio cost is lower than market value, the investor reports short-term investments at cost and discloses market value in the note.

Conservatism requires that an investor write the book value of stocks or portfolios down to market when cost exceeds market, but does not permit the investor to write up the book value of those same stocks or portfolios when their market value subsequently rises above the written-down book values.

Mutual funds, on the other hand, value their stock investments at market and recognize both increases and decreases in market value on the balance sheet and on the income statement. This form of accounting is appropriate for mutual funds because they invest in marketable securities and their value is determined by the market value of the mutual fund's portfolio.

Short-Term Bond Investments:The Cost Method (with LCM)

The cost method (with lower of cost or market) is used to account for investments in bonds. Like stocks, short-term bond investments are valued at the lower of cost or market on an individual investment or portfolio basis. Premiums or discounts are not amortized as the intent is to hold the bonds for only a short period.

OBJECTIVE 2
Account for long-term stock investments

Accounting for Long-Term Stock Investments

An investor may own numerous investments, some short-term and others long-term. For accounting purposes, the two investment portfolios are not mixed. They are reported separately on the balance sheet, as shown in Exhibit 16-2. *Long-term* is not often used in the account title. An investment is understood to be long-term unless specifically labelled as short-term and included with current assets.

Long-term investments may be of several different types depending on the purpose of the investment and thus the percentage of voting interest acquired. Each of the three types is introduced in the following paragraphs and discussed more fully in turn below.

An investor may make a *portfolio investment* where the purpose is similar to that of short-term investing; the investor will hold the investment to earn dividend revenue or interest but has no long-term interest in the investee. In such a situation, the investor will generally hold less than 20 percent of the voting interest of the investee and would normally play no important role in the investee's operations. Such an investor would normally account for the investment using the *cost method*.

An investor may also make an investment in the investee by purchasing from 20 percent to 50 percent of the investee's voting stock. The investor will likely be able to exert a *significant influence* over the investee and how the investee operates the business. Such an investor can likely affect the investee's decisions on dividend policy, product lines, sources of supply, and other important matters. An investor holding from 20 to 50 percent would likely account for the investment using the *equity method* (depending on the circumstances).

The investor may make an investment in the investee that exceeds 50 percent of the voting interest and thus is able to control the operations and activities of the investee. Such investees are called subsidiaries; the financial statements of subsidiaries are normally *consolidated* with those of the parent.

Long-Term Stock Investments Accounted For by the Cost Method

Accounting for portfolio investments follows the procedures outlined for short-term investments, that is, the cost method. The beginning accounting value is cost, which is debited to an Investments account at the date of purchase. Dividends are treated as income. Gains and losses are recorded on sales. Long-term investments are normally reported on the balance sheet at cost. In the *CICA Handbook*, Paragraph 3050.20 states that if the market price of one of the stocks in the portfolio drops below cost, and the decline is thought to be other than temporary, the stock's book value would be written down to market and carried at that value in the future. The determination of whether or not the decline is temporary is management's.

Long-Term Stock Investments Accounted For by the Equity Method

OBJECTIVE 3
Use the equity method to account for investments

An investee with a stock holding of from 20 percent to 50 percent of the investee's voting stock may significantly influence how the investee operates the business. Since the investor has a voice in shaping business policy and operations, accountants believe that some measure of the business's success and failure should be included in accounting for the investment. We use the *equity method* to account for investments in which the investor can significantly influence the decisions of the investee. (Note that in certain circumstances, an investor with less than a 20-percent holding may still exert significant influence if there are many other shareholders who all own few shares. In another case, a shareholder with a large holding, such as a 30 percent holding, may exert no significant influence if another shareholder owns 51% of the shares and thus has control of the corporation.)

Investments accounted for by the **equity method** are recorded initially at cost. Suppose Saltspring Corp. pays $400,000 for 30 percent of the common stock of White Rock Corporation. Saltspring Corp.'s entry to record the purchase of this investment is

2002			
Jan. 6	Investment in White Rock Corporation		
	Common Stock...	400,000	
	Cash..		400,000
	To purchase 30% investment in White Rock		
	Corporation common stock.		

KEY POINT

A simple T-account illustrates how to account for equity-method investments:

Equity Method

Original cost	Share of losses
Share of income	Share of dividends

WORKING IT OUT

Apex Ltd. purchased 40% of Base Ltd.'s stock for $750,000. Base reported $100,000 income and paid $40,000 dividends during the next year. (1) On Apex Ltd.'s books, record the purchase, the net income of Base Ltd., and dividends of Base Ltd. (2) What is the carrying amount of Apex's investment in Base Ltd.?

A:

(1) Purchase:
Investment in
   Base Ltd........ 750,000
   Cash............... 750,000
Net income of Base Ltd.:
Investment in
   Base Ltd........ 40,000
   Equity-Method
      Invest. Rev. ... 40,000
Dividends of Base Ltd.:
   Cash 16,000
   Invest. in
      Base Ltd........ 16,000

(2) $774,000 ($750,000 + $40,000 − $16,000)

Under the equity method, Saltspring Corp., as the investor, applies its percentage of ownership, 30 percent in our example, in recording its share of the investee's net income and dividends. If White Rock Corporation reports net income of $125,000 for the year, Saltspring Corp. records 30 percent of this amount as an increase in the investment account and as equity-method investment revenue, as follows:

2002			
Dec. 31	Investment in White Rock Corporation		
	Common Stock..	37,500	
	Equity-Method Investment Revenue		37,500
	To record 30% of White Rock Corporation net		
	income—$37,500 ($125,000 × 0.30).		

The Investment Revenue account carries the Equity-Method label to identify its source. This labelling is similar to distinguishing Sales Revenue from Service Revenue.

The investor increases the Investment account and records Investment Revenue when the investee reports income because of the close relationship between the two companies. As the investee's shareholders' equity increases, so does the Investment account on the books of the investor.

Saltspring Corp. records its proportionate part of cash dividends received from White Rock Corporation. Assuming White Rock Corporation declares and pays a cash dividend of $50,000, Saltspring Corp. receives 30 percent of this dividend, recording it as follows:

KEY POINT

An investor who holds 20% of a company's stock can usually influence some decisions of the board of directors and gain influence in company decisions. With more than 50% control (majority ownership), the investor can usually control the affairs of the company.

2002				
Dec. 31	Cash	....	15,000	
	Investment in White Rock Corporation			
	Common Stock	....		15,000
	To record receipt of 30% of White Rock			
	Corporation cash dividend, which is			
	$15,000 ($50,000 × 0.30).			

Observe that the Investment account is credited for the receipt of a dividend on an equity-method investment. Why? It is because the dividend decreases the investee's shareholders' equity and so it also reduces the investor's investment. In effect, the investor received cash for this portion of the investment.

After the above entries are posted, Saltspring Corp.'s Investment account reflects its equity in the net assets of White Rock Corporation (also known as its *carrying value*):

Investment in White Rock Corporation Common Stock

2002			2002		
Jan. 6	Purchase	400,000	Dec. 31	Dividends	15,000
Dec. 31	Net income	37,500			
2002					
Dec. 31	Balance	422,500			

Gain or loss on the sale of an equity-method investment is measured as the difference between the sale proceeds and the carrying value of the investment. For example, sale of one-tenth of the White Rock Corporation common stock owned by Saltspring Corp. for $41,000 would be recorded as follows:

2003				
Feb. 13	Cash	....	41,000	
	Loss on Sale of Investment	....	1,250	
	Investment in White Rock Corporation			
	Common Stock	....		42,250
	Sold one-tenth of investment in White Rock			
	Corporation common stock at a loss of $1,250			
	[$41,000 − ($422,500 × ⅒)].			

Companies with investments accounted for by the equity method often refer to the investee as an *affiliated company*. The account title Investments in Affiliated Companies refers to investments that are accounted for by the equity method.

Sometimes a company must write down an investment accounted for by the equity method. In its 1999 Annual Report, Ivaco Inc. reported in Note 12:

In December 1999, management determined that the carrying value of its investment in Laclede Steel Company has been impaired, because, among other things, Laclede continues to incur operating losses. Accordingly, the Company recognized a non-cash charge of $28.7 million to reduce the carrying amount to a nominal value.

Ivaco Inc.
www.ivaco.com

Ivaco Inc. debited an expense account "Non-recurring Losses" and credited the long-term asset "Investments" for the $28.7 million because management believes there has been a permanent decline in the value of the investment.

Joint Ventures—Accounted For by Proportionate Consolidation

A *joint venture* is a separate entity or project owned and operated by a small group of businesses. Joint ventures are common in risky endeavours such as the petroleum and construction industries. Moreover, they are widely used in regions with developing economies. Many Canadian and U.S. companies that do business abroad enter into joint ventures. For example, BCE Inc., the telephone giant, reports in its December 31, 1999, annual report that it is participating in joint ventures with companies in Latin America and the Asia Pacific Region.

Section 3055 of the *CICA Handbook* requires the use of proportionate consolidation when accounting for a joint venture. Proportionate consolidation means the venturer consolidates its proportionate interest in the assets, liabilities, revenues, and expenses of a joint venture with its own assets, liabilities, revenues, and expenses. For example, assume the venturer, V Ltd., has inventory of $50,000 and a 40 percent interest in a joint venture. The joint venture has inventory of $20,000. V Ltd. would report inventory on its consolidated statements of $58,000 ($50,000 + 40% of $20,000).

Long-Term Stock Investments Accounted For by the Consolidation Method

Most large corporations own controlling interests in other corporations. A **controlling** (or **majority**) **interest** is normally the ownership of more than 50 percent of the investee's voting stock. Such an investment enables the investor to elect a majority of the investee's board of directors and so control the investee. The investor is called the **parent** company, and the investee company, as mentioned earlier, is called the **subsidiary**. For example, Loblaw Companies Limited, the grocery store chain, is 63 percent owned by George Weston Ltd. Galen Weston and the other shareholders of George Weston Ltd. control that company and, because George Weston Ltd. owns Loblaw Companies Limited, they also control Loblaw Companies Limited, as diagrammed in Exhibit 16-3.

Why have subsidiaries? Why not have the corporation take the form of a single legal entity? Subsidiaries may limit the parent's liabilities in a risky venture, may make mergers, acquisitions, and sales easier, and may ease expansion into foreign countries. For example, Chieftain International, Inc., the natural gas and oil exploration and production company located in Edmonton, has a U.S. subsidiary, Chieftain International (U.S.) Inc., and two U.K. subsidiaries, Chieftain Exploration (U.K.) Limited and Chieftain International North Sea Limited. Those companies conduct operations for Chieftain International, Inc. in those two countries respectively. Exhibit 16-4 shows selected subsidiaries of three major Canadian companies.

Consolidation accounting is a method of combining the financial statements of two or more companies that are controlled by the same owners. This method implements the entity concept by reporting a single set of financial statements for the consolidated entity, which carries the name of the parent company. Exhibit 16-5 illustrates the accounting method used generally for stock investments according to the percentage of the investor's ownership in the investee company.

EXHIBIT 16-3

Ownership Structure of Loblaw Companies Limited

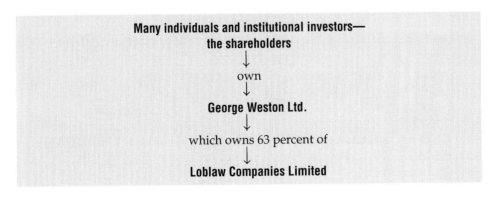

Many individuals and institutional investors—
the shareholders

↓

own

↓

George Weston Ltd.

↓

which owns 63 percent of

↓

Loblaw Companies Limited

EXHIBIT 16-4

Selected Subsidiaries of
Three Canadian Companies

Parent Company	Selected Subsidiaries
ATCO Ltd.	ATCO Structures Inc.
	ATCO Noise Management Ltd.
	Canadian Utilities Limited and its
	subsidiaries
	ATCO Electric Ltd.
	ATCO Frontenac Corp.
	ATCO Power Ltd.
Boliden Limited	Boliden Mineral AB (Sweden)
	Boliden LDM Nederland BV (Holland)
	Boliden MKM Limited (England)
	Boliden Aspirsa (Spain)
Bombardier Inc.	Bombardier Inc. (Canadair) (Canada)
	Bombardier Inc. (de Haviland) (Canada)
	Learjet Inc. (U.S.)
	Short Brothers plc (United Kingdom)
	Bombardier-Wien Schienenfahrzenge AG
	(Austria)
	Bombardier Capital Ltd. (Canada)

OBJECTIVE 4
Understand consolidated
financial statements

EXHIBIT 16-5

**Accounting Methods for
Stock Investment by
Percentage of Ownership**

Cost Method,
or Lower of Cost
and Market

20%–50%
Equity
Method

Less
than 20%

More than 50%
Consolidation
Method

Almost all published financial reports include consolidated statements. To understand the statements you are likely to encounter, you need to know the basic concepts underlying consolidation accounting. **Consolidated statements** combine the balance sheets, income statements, and other financial statements of the parent company with those of the subsidiaries into an overall set as if the parent and its subsidiaries were a single entity. The goal is to provide a better perspective on operations than could be obtained by examining the separate reports of each of the individual companies. The assets, liabilities, revenues, and expenses of each subsidiary are added to the parent's accounts. The consolidated financial statements present the combined account balances. For example, the balance in the Cash account of Loblaw Companies Limited is added to the balance in the George Weston Ltd. Cash account, and the sum of the two amounts is presented as a single amount in the consolidated balance sheet of George Weston Ltd. Each account balance of a subsidiary loses its identity in the consolidated statements. George Weston Ltd. financial statements are entitled "George Weston Ltd. and Consolidated Subsidiaries." Loblaw Companies Limited and the names of all other George Weston Ltd. subsidiaries do not appear in the statement titles. But the names of the subsidiary companies are

EXHIBIT 16-6

**Parent Company with
Consolidated Subsidiaries
and an Equity-Method
Investment**

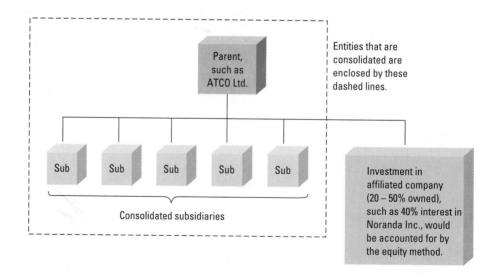

Parent,
such as
ATCO Ltd.

Entities that are
consolidated are
enclosed by these
dashed lines.

Sub   Sub   Sub   Sub   Sub

Consolidated subsidiaries

Investment in
affiliated company
(20 – 50% owned),
such as 40% interest in
Noranda Inc., would
be accounted for by
the equity method.

listed in the parent company's annual report. A reader of corporate annual reports cannot hope to understand them without knowing how consolidated statements are prepared. Exhibit 16-6 diagrams a corporate structure whose parent corporation owns controlling interests in five subsidiary companies and an equity-method investment in another investee company.

Consolidated Balance Sheet—Parent Owns All of Subsidiary's Stock Suppose that Parent Corporation purchased all the outstanding common stock of Subsidiary Corporation at its book value of $150,000. In addition, Parent Corporation loaned Subsidiary Corporation $80,000. The $150,000 is paid to the *former owners* (the shareholders) of Subsidiary Corporation as private investors. The $150,000 is *not* an addition to the existing assets and shareholders' equity of Subsidiary Corporation. *That is, the books of Subsidiary Corporation are completely unaffected by Parent Corporation's initial investment and Parent's subsequent acccounting for that investment. Subsidiary Corporation is not dissolved. It lives on as a separate legal entity but with a new owner, Parent Corporation.*

Parent Corporation Books[2]			Subsidiary Corporation Books		
Investment in Subsidiary					
Corporation..............	150,000		No entry		
Cash......................		150,000			
Note receivable from			Cash	80,000	
Subsidiary Corp.......	80,000		Note Payable		
Cash......................		80,000	to Parent Corp.		80,000

Each legal entity has its individual set of books. The consolidated entity does not keep a separate set of books. Instead a work sheet is used to prepare the consolidated statements. A major concern in consolidation accounting is this: Do not double-count—that is, do not include the same item twice.

Companies may prepare a consolidated balance sheet immediately after acquisition. The consolidated balance sheet shows all the assets and liabilities of the parent and the subsidiary. The Investment in Subsidiary account on the parent's books represents all the assets and liabilities of Subsidiary Corporation. The consolidated statements cannot show both the investment account *plus* the amounts for the subsidiary's assets and liabilities. Doing so would count the same net resources twice. To avoid this double-counting we eliminate (a) the $150,000 Investment in Subsidiary Corporation on the parent's books, and the $150,000 shareholder's equity on the subsidiary's books ($100,000 Common Stock and $50,000 Retained Earnings) and (b) the intercompany $80,000 note.

Explanation of Elimination—Entry (a) Exhibit 16-7 shows the work sheet for consolidating the balance sheet. Consider the elimination entry for the parent-subsidiary ownership accounts, which are intercompany accounts. Entry (a) credits the parent's Investment account to eliminate its debit balance. It also eliminates the subsidiary's shareholders' equity accounts by debiting Common Stock for $100,000 and Retained Earnings for $50,000. The resulting consolidated balance sheet reports no Investment in Subsidiary Corporation account, and the Common Stock and Retained Earnings are those of Parent Corporation only. The consolidated amounts are in the final column of the consolidation work sheet.

Explanation of Elimination—Entry (b) Parent Corporation loaned $80,000 to Subsidiary Corporation, and Subsidiary Corporation signed a note payable to Parent Corporation. Therefore, Parent Corporation's balance sheet includes an $80,000 note receivable and Subsidiary Corporation's balance sheet reports a note payable for this amount. This loan was entirely within the consolidated entity and so must be elimi-

---

[2]The parent company may use either the cost method of the equity method for work sheet entries to the Investment account. Regardless of the method used, the consolidated statements are the same. Advanced accounting courses deal with this topic.

	Parent Corporation	Subsidiary Corporation	Eliminations Debit	Eliminations Credit	Consolidated Amounts
Assets					
Cash.................................	12,000	18,000			30,000
Notes receivable					
from Subsidiary Corp.	80,000	—		(b) 80,000	—
Inventory	104,000	91,000			195,000
Investment in Subsidiary Corp.	150,000	—		(a) 150,000	—
Other assets	218,000	138,000			356,000
Total................................	564,000	247,000			581,000
Liabilities and Shareholders' Equity					
Accounts payable	43,000	17,000			60,000
Notes payable	190,000	80,000	(b) 80,000		190,000
Common stock	176,000	100,000	(a) 100,000		176,000
Retained earnings	155,000	50,000	(a) 50,000		155,000
Total................................	564,000	247,000	230,000	230,000	581,000

EXHIBIT 16-7

Work Sheet for Consolidated Balance Sheet—Parent Corporation Owns All of Subsidiary Corporation's Stock

> ## STOP & THINK
>
> Examine Exhibit 16-7. Why does the consolidated shareholders' equity ($176,000 + $155,000) exclude the equity of Subsidiary Corporation?
>
> **Answer:** Because the shareholders' equity of the consolidated entity is that of the parent only, and because the subsidiary's equity and the parent company's investment balance represent the same resources. Therefore, including them both would amount to double-counting.

nated. Entry (b) accomplishes this. The $80,000 credit in the elimination column of the work sheet offsets Parent Corporation's debit balance in Notes Receivable from Subsidiary Corporation. After this work sheet entry, the consolidated amount for notes receivable is zero. The $80,000 debit in the elimination column offsets the credit balance of Subsidiary Corporation's notes payable, and the resulting consolidated amount for notes payable is the amount owed to those outside the consolidated entity.

Parent Buys Subsidiary's Stock and Pays for Goodwill
A company may acquire a controlling interest in a subsidiary by paying a price above the fair value of the subsidiary's net assets (assets minus liabilities), which we assume is equal to the book value of the subsidiary's shareholders' equity. This excess is called *goodwill*.[3] Accounting for goodwill was introduced in Chapter 10 on page 529. What drives a company's market value up? The company may create goodwill through its superior products, service, or location.

The subsidiary does not record goodwill, only the purchaser does. The goodwill is identified in the process of consolidating the parent and subsidiary financial statements.

Suppose Parent Corporation paid $450,000 to acquire 100 percent of the common stock of Subsidiary Corporation, which had Common Stock of $200,000 and Retained Earnings of $180,000. Parent's payment included $70,000 for goodwill ($450,000 – $200,000 – $180,000 = $70,000).[4] The entry to eliminate Parent Corporation's Investment account against Subsidiary Corporation's equity accounts is:

LEARNING **TIP**

The accounts that would appear on consolidated financial statements:
Minority Interest—the minority shareholders' share of the company.
Goodwill—excess of the purchase price of the subsidiary over the fair value of its net assets.
The investment account, intercompany transactions, and the shareholders' equity of the subsidiary are not on the consolidated statements.

---

[3] The U.S. Financial Accounting Standards Board is considering the methods of accounting for business combinations and goodwill at the time of writing. The CICA's Accounting Standards Board is awaiting the new U.S. standard at which time revision of the Canadian standard will be considered.

[4] For simplicity, we are assuming that the fair market value of the subsidiary's net assets (assets minus liabilities) equals the book value of the company's shareholders' equity. Advanced courses consider other situations.

Common Stock, Subsidiary Corporation	200,000		
Retained Earnings, Subsidiary Corporation	180,000		
Goodwill	70,000		
Investment in Subsidiary Corporation.............................		450,000	

To eliminate cost of investment in Subsidiary Corporation against Subsidiary Corporation's equity balances and to recognize Subsidiary Corporation's unrecorded goodwill.

In *actual* practice, this entry would be made only on the consolidation work sheet. Here we show it in general journal form for instructional purposes.

The asset goodwill is reported on the consolidated balance sheet among the intangible assets, after capital assets. For example, Hollinger International Inc.'s consolidated 1999 balance sheet includes goodwill of $710.6 million with "Goodwill and Other Assets." Goodwill is amortized to expense over its useful life, not to exceed 40 years.

Consolidated Balance Sheet—Parent Owns Less Than 100 Percent of Subsidiary's Stock   When a parent company owns more than 50 percent (a majority) of the subsidiary's stock but less than 100 percent of it, a new category of balance sheet account, called *minority interest*, must appear on the consolidated balance sheet. Suppose Parent Corporation buys 75 percent of Subsidiary Corporation's common stock. The minority interest is the remaining 25 percent of Subsidiary Corporation's equity. Thus **minority interest** is the subsidiary's equity that is held by shareholders other than the parent company. While the *CICA Handbook* is silent on where minority interest should be disclosed on the balance sheet, accepted practice is to list it as a liability between liabilities and shareholders' equity.

Assume P Ltd. buys 75 percent of S Ltd.'s common stock and there is no goodwill. Also, P Ltd. owes S Ltd. $50,000 on a note payable to S Ltd. Exhibit 16-8 is the consolidation work sheet. Again, focus on the Eliminations columns and the Consolidated Amounts.

Entry (a) eliminates P Ltd.'s Investment balance of $120,000 against the $160,000 shareholders' equity of S Ltd. Observe that all of S Ltd.'s equity is eliminated even though P Ltd. holds only 75 percent of S's stock. The remaining 25 percent interest in S Ltd.'s equity is credited to Minority Interest ($160,000 × 0.25 = $40,000). Thus Entry (a) reclassifies 25 percent of S Ltd.'s equity as minority interest. Entry (b) in Exhibit 16-8 eliminates S Ltd.'s $50,000 note receivable against P Ltd.'s note payable of the same amount. The consolidated amount of notes payable ($42,000) is the amount that S Ltd. owes to outsiders.

KEY POINT

The elimination entry requires, at most, five steps: (1) Eliminate intercompany receivables and payables. (2) Eliminate the shareholders' equity accounts of the subsidiary. (3) Eliminate the Investment in Subsidiary account. (4) Record goodwill. (5) Record minority interest.

EXHIBIT 16-8

Work Sheet for Consolidated Balance Sheet: Parent (P Ltd.) Owns Less Than 100 Percent of Subsidiary's (S Ltd.) Stock

	P Ltd.	S Ltd.	Eliminations Debit	Eliminations Credit	Consolidated Amounts
Assets					
Cash..........................	33,000	18,000			51,000
Notes receivable from P Ltd................	—	50,000		(b) 50,000	—
Accounts receivable, net......................	54,000	39,000			93,000
Inventory	92,000	66,000			158,000
Investment in S Ltd.	120,000	—		(a) 120,000	—
Capital assets, net	230,000	123,000			353,000
Total..	529,000	296,000			655,000
Liabilities and Shareholders' Equity					
Accounts payable..................................	141,000	94,000			235,000
Notes payable..	50,000	42,000	(b) 50,000		42,000
Minority interest	—	—		(a) 40,000	40,000
Common stock	170,000	100,000	(a) 100,000		170,000
Retained earnings	168,000	60,000	(a) 60,000		168,000
Total...	529,000	296,000	210,000	210,000	655,000

P Ltd. purchases 80% of S Ltd. for $280,000. Their balance sheets immediately afterward are:

Assets	P Ltd.	S Ltd.
Cash	$ 200,000	$ 50,000
Accounts rec.	275,000	60,000
Inventory	300,000	80,000
Invest. in S Ltd.	280,000	
Capital assets	500,000	170,000
	$1,555,000	$360,000

Liabilities and Shareholders' Equity

Accounts pay.	$350,000	$ 60,000
Com. stock	500,000	120,000
Ret. earnings	705,000	180,000
	$1,555,000	$360,000

P Ltd. owes S Ltd. $10,000 on account. Prepare the elimination entry in general journal form.

A:

Accounts Payable...	10,000
Common Stock	120,000
Retained Earnings..	180,000
Goodwill...............	40,000*
Investment in S Ltd.	280,000
Minority Interest	60,000†
Accounts Rec.	10,000

*[$280,000 − ($300,000 × 80%)]
†($300,000 × 20%)

The consolidated balance sheet of P Ltd., shown in Exhibit 16-9, is based on the work sheet of Exhibit 16-8. The consolidated balance sheet reveals that ownership of P Ltd. and its consolidated subsidiary is divided between P Ltd.'s shareholders (common stock and retained earnings totaling $338,000) and the minority shareholders of S Ltd. ($40,000).

Income of a Consolidated Entity   The income of a consolidated entity is the net income of the parent plus the parent's proportion of the subsidiaries' net income. Suppose Parent Inc. owns all the stock of Subsidiary S-1 Inc. and 60 percent of the stock of Subsidiary S-2 Inc. During the year just ended, Parent Inc. earned net income of $330,000, S-1 Inc. earned $150,000 and S-2 Inc. had a net loss of $100,000. Parent Inc. would report net income of $420,000, computed as follows:

	Net Income (Net Loss)	Parent Inc. Shareholders' Ownership	Parent Inc. Net Income (Net Loss)
Parent Inc..........................	$330,000	100%	$330,000
Subsidiary S-1 Inc..............	150,000	100%	150,000
Subsidiary S-2 Inc..............	(100,000)	60%	(60,000)
Consolidated net income .			$420,000

The parent's net income is the same amount that would be recorded under the equity method. However, the equity method stops short of reporting the investee's assets and liabilities on the parent balance sheet because, with an investment in the range of 20–50 percent, the investor owns less than a controlling interest in the investee company.

The procedures for preparation of a consolidated income statement parallel those outlined above for the balance sheet. The consolidated income statement is discussed in an advanced accounting course.

P LTD. AND CONSOLIDATED SUBSIDIARY
Consolidated Balance Sheet
December 31, 2003

Assets

Current Assets		
Cash...	$ 51,000	
Accounts receivable, net	93,000	
Inventory...	158,000	
Total current assets		$302,000
Capital assets, net...		353,000
Total assets		$655,000

Liabilities and Shareholders' Equity

Current liabilities		
Accounts payable...		$235,000
Long-term liabilities		
Notes payable..		42,000
Total liabilities..		$277,000
Minority interest..		40,000
Shareholders' equity		
Common stock...	$170,000	
Retained earnings	168,000	
Total shareholders' equity		338,000
Total liabilities and shareholders' equity...................		$655,000

EXHIBIT 16-9

Consolidated Balance Sheet of P Ltd.

STOP & THINK

Answer these questions about consolidated financial statements:

1. Whose name appears on the consolidated statements—the parent company, the subsidiary company, or both?

2. Suppose A Ltd. owns 90% of B Ltd. What is the remaining 10% of B Ltd.'s stock called, and where does it appear, if at all, in A Ltd.'s consolidated financial statements?

3. Suppose C Ltd. paid $1 million to acquire D Ltd., whose shareholders' equity (same as net assets) totaled $700,000. What is the $300,000 excess called? Which company reports the excess? Where in the consolidated financial statements is the excess reported?

Answers:

1. A Ltd. (parent) only.

2. Minority Interest—reported on A Ltd.'s (parent) consolidated balance sheet among the liabilities.

3. Goodwill—reported on C Ltd.'s (parent) consolidated balance sheet as an intangible asset.

WORKING IT OUT

Refer to the Working It Out situation on page 878. Prepare the consolidated balance sheet.

A:

Assets	
Cash	$ 250,000
Accounts rec.	325,000
Inventory	380,000
Capital assets	670,000
Goodwill	40,000
Total	$1,665,000

Liabilities and Shareholders' Equity	
Accounts pay.	$ 400,000
Minority interest	60,000
Common stock	500,000
Ret. earnings	705,000
Total	$1,665,000

KEY POINT

Each subsidiary company keeps its own set of books and pays its own taxes, just as the parent company does; however, for reporting purposes, the parent and subsidiary companies are treated as one economic unit when they are consolidated. Intercompany receivables and payables must be eliminated.

Computers and Consolidations

Consider diversified companies such as Magna International Inc., a leading global supplier of automotive systems and parts. Magna, at December 31, 1999, had sales of $9.4 billion, and more than 58,000 employees and 146 manufacturing plants in 16 countries on four continents. Magna sells to Chrysler, Ford, General Motors, Volkswagen, BMW/Rover, and other automobile manufacturers. A company such as Magna International Inc. can prepare its consolidated financial statements automatically with a fully integrated accounting information system.

Long-Term Investments in Bonds and Notes[5]

OBJECTIVE 5
Account for long-term investments in bonds

Magna International Inc.
www.magnaint.com

Chrysler
www.chrysler.com

Ford
www.ford.ca

General Motors
www.gmcanada.com

Volkswagen
www.vw.com

BMW/Rover
www.bmw.ca

Industrial and commercial companies invest far more in stock than they do in bonds. The major investors in bonds are financial institutions, such as pension plans, trust companies, and insurance companies. The relationship between the issuer and the investor may be diagrammed as follows:

Issuing Corporation		Investor (Bondholder)
Bonds payable	⟷	Investment in bonds
Interest expense	⟷	Interest revenue

The dollar amount of a bond transaction is the same for issuer and investor, but the accounts debited and credited differ. For example, the issuer's interest expense is the investor's interest revenue.

An investment in bonds is classified either as short-term (a current asset) or as long-term. When bonds are purchased as a short-term investment, the bonds are

[5] Section 3860 of the *CICA Handbook*, Financial Instruments—Disclosure and Presentation; "... prescribes certain requirements for presentation of recognized financial instruments and identifies information that should be disclosed about ... recognized ... financial instruments." Much of the discussion in Section 3860 is beyond the scope of this text and is covered in advanced accounting courses.

recorded at cost (that is, par value plus any premium or minus any discount plus any brokerage fee). The bonds would be valued at lower of cost or market. Short-term investments in bonds are rare. Here, we focus on long-term investments in bonds and notes that the investor intends to hold until the bonds or notes mature.

Bond investments are recorded at cost, which includes the purchase price and any brokerage fees.

At maturity the investor will receive the face value of the bonds. For long-term investments, discount or premium is amortized to account more precisely for interest revenue over the period the bonds will be held. The amortization of discount or premium on a bond investment affects Interest Revenue and the carrying amount of the bonds in the same way as for the company that issued the bonds. Long-term investments in bonds are reported at their *amortized cost*, which determines the carrying amount.

The accountant records amortization on the cash interest dates and at year end, along with the accrual of interest receivable. Accountants rarely use separate discount and premium accounts for investments. Amortization of a *discount* is recorded by directly *debiting* the Long-Term Investment in Bonds account and *crediting* Interest Revenue. Amortization of a *premium* is recorded by directly *crediting* the Long-Term Investment in Bonds account. This entry *debits* Interest Revenue. These entries bring the investment balance to the bonds' face value on the maturity date and record the correct amount of interest revenue each period.

Suppose $10,000 of 6 percent Xpress Trucking Ltd. bonds were purchased on April 1, 2002, as a long-term investment. Interest dates are April 1 and October 1. These bonds mature on April 1, 2006, so they will be outstanding for 48 months. The price of $93.00 includes brokerage charges of $200; the cost of the bonds is $9,300. Assume amortization of the discount by the straight-line method. Straight-line amortization of premium or discount on a bond investment is calculated the same way as it is calculated for bonds payable (see Chapter 15, pages 812–813). The following entries illustrate accounting for a long-term bond investment:[6]

WORKING IT OUT

Assume that Quill Corp. is buying bonds to hold to maturity. Quill Corp. buys $300,000 of 9%, 10-year bonds at $104.00. The bonds pay interest on February 1 and August 1. What entries record (1) the purchase on August 1, 2002, (2) the year-end accrual, and (3) the first semiannual interest receipt and straight-line amortization of the premium?

A:

(1) Purchase on Aug. 1/02:
Invest. in
    Bonds......... 312,000
    Cash ($300,000 ×
        1.04)......... 312,000

(2) Accrual on Dec. 31/02:
Interest
    Receivable ... 11,250
    Interest
        Revenue   11,250
($300,000 × 9% × 5/12)

Interest
    Revenue..... 500
Invest. in
    Bonds....... 500
[($12,000 prem./20 semiann. int. periods) = $600 × 5/6]

(3) Interest receipt on Feb. 1, 2003:
Cash ($300,000 ×
    0.045)......... 13,500
Interest
    Receivable   11,250
Interest
    Revenue...   2,250

Interest Revenue   100
Invest. in Bonds   100
($600 × 1/6)

2002				
Apr. 1	Long-Term Investment in Bonds................................	9,300	
	Cash..		9,300
	To purchase long-term bond investment ($10,000 × 0.93).		
Oct. 1	Cash	300	
	Interest Revenue..		300
	To receive semiannual interest ($10,000 × 0.06 × $\frac{6}{12}$).		
Oct. 1	Long-Term Investment in Bonds................................	88	
	Interest Revenue..		88
	To amortize discount on bond investment for six months ([($10,000 – $9,300)/48] × 6).		

At December 31, 2002, the year-end adjustments are:

Dec. 31	Interest Receivable...	150	
	Interest Revenue..		150
	To accrue interest revenue for three months ($10,000 × 0.06 × $\frac{3}{12}$).		

---

[6] If the company were to record the investment at par value and the premium or discount in a separate contra account, the April 1 entry would be:

Long-Term Investment in Bonds	10,000	
Discount on Long-Term Bonds...		700
Cash		9,300

The entry on October 1 would be:

Discount on Long-Term Bonds	88	
Interest Revenue		88

Dec. 31	Long-term Investment in Bonds..............................	44	
	Interest Revenue...		44
	To amortize discount on bond investment for		
	three months ([($10,000 – $9,300)/48] × 3).		

The financial statements at December 31, 2002, report the following effects of this long-term investment in bonds, where $9,432 = $9,300 + $88 + $44 (assume the bonds' market price is $102.00):

Balance sheet at December 31, 2002:
Current assets:
Interest receivable... $ 150
Total current assets .... X,XXX

Long-term investments in bonds—Note 6... 9,432

_____
Note 6: Long-term investments.
Long-term bonds are reported at amortized cost. At December 31, 2002, the current market value of long-term investments in bonds was $10,200.

Income statement (multiple-step) for the year ended December 31, 2002 (where interest revenue is $582 = $300 + $88 + $150 + $44):

Other revenues:
Interest revenue $582

If the market value of a long-term stock investment declines below cost and the decline is considered to be other than temporary, the investment should be written down to market.

Summary of Accounting Methods

This chapter has illustrated how to account for various types of investments. The Decision Guidelines feature shows which accounting method to use for each type of investment.

DECISION GUIDELINES *Accounting Method to Use for Each Type of Investment*

Investment Type	Accounting Method
Short-term investment in stock or bonds	
Short-term investment	Cost (lower of cost or market)
Long-term investment in stock or bonds	
Long-term investment in stock	
Investor owns less than 20 percent of investee stock	Cost (lower of cost or market if decline in market is not temporary)
Investor owns 20–50 percent of investee stock	Equity
Investor owns greater than 50 percent of investee stock	Consolidation
Long-term investment in bonds	Amortized cost

This problem consists of four independent items.

1. Identify the appropriate accounting method for each of the following situations involving investment in common stock:

    a. Purchase of 25 percent and investor plans to hold as a long-term investment

    b. Investor intends to sell three months after year end

    c. Purchase of more than 50 percent of investee's stock

2. At what amount should the following short-term investment portfolio be reported on the December 31 balance sheet? All the investments are less than 5 percent of the investee's stock. Journalize any adjusting entry required by these data.

Stock	Investment Cost	Current Market Value
Four Seasons Hotels	$39,000	$54,000
Linamar Corp.	85,000	63,500
Loblaw Companies Ltd.	33,800	43,000

3. Investor Ltd. paid $67,900 to acquire a 40 percent equity-method investment in the common stock of Investee Ltd. At the end of the first year, Investee Ltd.'s net income was $80,000, and Investee Ltd. declared and paid cash dividends of $55,000. Journalize Investor Ltd.'s (a) purchase of the investment, (b) share of Investee Ltd.'s net income, (c) receipt of dividends from Investee Ltd., and (d) sale of Investee Ltd. stock for $80,100.

4. Parent Corp. paid $100,000 for all the common stock of Subsidiary Corp., and Parent Corp. owes Subsidiary Corp. $20,000 on a note payable. Assume the fair value of Subsidiary Corp.'s net assets is equal to book value. Complete the following consolidation work sheet:

	Parent Corp.	Subsidiary Corp.	Eliminations Debit	Eliminations Credit	Consolidated Amounts
Assets					
Cash	7,000	4,000			
Note receivable from Parent Corp.	—	20,000			
Investment in Subsidiary Corp.	100,000	—			
Goodwill	—	—			
Other assets	108,000	99,000			
Total	215,000	123,000			
Liabilities and Shareholders' Equity					
Accounts payable	15,000	8,000			
Notes payable	20,000	30,000			
Common stock	135,000	60,000			
Retained earnings	45,000	25,000			
Total	215,000	123,000			

Solution to Review Problem

1. a. Equity   b. Cost (LCM)   c. Consolidation

2. There are two possible solutions to this problem:

a. Report the investments at cost, $157,800, because total cost is less than total market ($160,500). No journal entry required.

Stock	Investment Cost	Current Market Value
Four Seasons Hotels	$ 39,000	$ 54,000
Linamar Corp.	85,000	63,500
Loblaw Companies Ltd.	33,800	43,000
Totals	$157,800	$160,500

b. Report the investments at the lower of cost or market on an investment-by-investment basis because the market value for one or more of the investments (Linamar Corp.) is less than cost.

Stock (Note)	Lower of Investment Cost and Current Market Value
Four Seasons Hotels	$39,000
Linamar Corp.	63,500
Loblaw Companies Ltd.	33,800
Total	$136,300

Note: Market value is $160,500.

Adjusting entry:

Loss on Short-Term Investments	21,500	
Short-Term Investments		21,500
To write investment down to market value		
($85,000-$63,500).		

3. a.

Investment in Investee Ltd. Common Stock	67,900	
Cash		67,900
To purchase 40 percent investment in Investee Ltd.		
common stock.		

b.

Investment in Investee Ltd. Common Stock	32,000	
Equity-Method Investment Revenue		32,000
To record 40 percent of Investee Ltd. net income		
($80,000 × 0.40).		

c.

Cash	22,000	
Investment in Investee Ltd. Common Stock		22,000
To record receipt of 40 percent of Investee Ltd. cash		
dividend ($55,000 × 0.40).		

d.

Cash	80,100	
Investment in Investee Ltd. Common Stock		77,900
Gain on Sale of Investment		2,200
Sold investment in Investee Ltd. common stock		
($67,900 + $32,000 − $22,000).		

4. Consolidation work sheet:

Assets	Parent Corp.	Subsidiary Corp.	Eliminations Debit	Eliminations Credit	Consolidated Amounts
Cash...	7,000	4,000			11,000
Note receivable from Parent Corp.	—	20,000		(a) 20,000	—
Investment in Subsidiary Corp.	100,000	—		(b) 100,000	—
Goodwill	—	—	(b) 15,000*		15,000
Other assets	108,000	99,000			207,000
Total	215,000	123,000			233,000
Liabilities and Shareholders' Equity					
Accounts payable	15,000	8,000			23,000
Notes payable.......................................	20,000	30,000	(a) 20,000		30,000
Common stock	135,000	60,000	(b) 60,000		135,000
Retained earnings.................................	45,000	25,000	(b) 25,000		45,000
Total	215,000	123,000	120,000	120,000	233,000

*$15,000 = $100,000 − ($60,000 + $25,000)

Cyber Coach

Visit the Student Resources area of the *Accounting* Companion Website for extra practice with the new material in Chapter 16.
www.pearsoned.ca/horngren

OBJECTIVE 6
Understand how foreign-currency exchange rates are determined

Alcan Aluminium
www.alcan.com

McCain Foods
www.mccain.com

Accounting for International Operations

Accounting for business activities across national boundaries makes up the field of *international accounting*. Did you know that Inco and Bombardier earn more than ninety percent of their revenues outside of Canada? It is common for Canadian companies to do a large part of their business abroad. Molson, Alcan Aluminium, McCain Foods, and others are very active in other countries, as shown in Exhibit 16-10.

The economic environment varies from country to country. Canada may be booming while countries in the Pacific Rim may be depressed economically. International accounting must deal with such differences.

Foreign Currencies and Foreign-Currency Exchange Rates

Each country uses its own national currency. Assume Research In Motion Ltd. (RIM) sells 1,000 of its Blackberry wireless email devices to a U.S. retailer. Will RIM receive

EXHIBIT 16-10

Extent of International Business

Company	Percent that is International	
	Revenue	Capital Assets
CAE	86%	57%
IPSCO Inc.	38	73
Nortel Networks	94	86

Canadian dollars or U.S. dollars? If the transaction takes place in Canadian dollars, the U.S. retailer must buy Canadian dollars in order to pay RIM in Canadian currency. If the transaction takes place in U.S. dollars, RIM will receive U.S. dollars that it exchanges for Canadian dollars. In either case, a step has been added to the transaction: one company must convert domestic currency into foreign currency, or the other company must convert foreign currency into domestic currency.

The price of one nation's currency can be stated in terms of another country's monetary unit. The price of a foreign currency is called the **foreign-currency exchange rate**. In Exhibit 16-11, the dollar value of a French franc is $0.2196. This means that one French franc could be bought for approximately twenty-two cents. Other currencies, such as the pound and the yen (also listed in Exhibit 16-11), are similarly bought and sold.

We use the exchange rate to convert the price of an item stated in one currency to its price in a second currency. We call this conversion a *translation*. Suppose an item costs two hundred French francs. To compute its cost in dollars, we multiply the amount in francs by the conversion rate: 200 French francs × $0.2196 = $43.92.

To aid the flow of international business, a market exists for foreign currencies. Traders buy and sell Canadian dollars, U.S. dollars, French francs, and other currencies in the same way that they buy and sell other commodities like beef, cotton, and automobiles. And just as supply and demand cause the prices of these other commodities to shift, so supply and demand for a particular currency cause exchange rates to fluctuate daily. When the demand for a nation's currency exceeds the supply of that currency, its exchange rate rises. When supply exceeds demand, the currency's exchange rate falls.

Two main factors determine the supply and demand for a particular currency: (1) the ratio of a country's imports to its exports, and (2) the rate of return available in the country's capital markets.

The Import/Export Ratio   Japanese exports far surpass Japan's imports. Customers of Japanese companies must buy yen (the Japanese unit of currency) in the international currency market to pay for their purchases. This strong demand drives up the price—the foreign exchange rate—of the yen. France, on the other hand, imports more goods than it exports. French businesses must sell francs in order to buy the foreign currencies needed to acquire the foreign goods. The supply of the French franc increases and so its price decreases.

The Rate of Return   The rate of return available in a country's capital markets affects the amount of investment funds flowing into the country. When rates of return are high in a politically stable country such as Canada, international investors buy stocks, bonds, and real estate in that country. This increases the demand for the nation's currency and drives up its exchange rate.

Currencies are often described in the financial press as "strong" or "weak." What do these terms mean? The exchange rate of a **strong currency** is rising relative to other nations' currencies. The exchange rate of a **weak currency** is falling relative to other currencies.

Research In Motion Ltd. (RIM)
www.rim.net

EXHIBIT 16-11

Foreign-Currency Exchange Rates

Country	Monetary Unit	Cost in Canadian Dollars	Country	Monetary Unit	Cost in Canadian Dollars
United States	Dollar	$1.5480	Britain	Pound	$2.2548
European			Italy	Lira	0.0007
Community	Euro	1.4408	Japan	Yen	0.0132
France	Franc	0.2196	Mexico	Peso	0.1599
Germany	Deutschmark	0.7365			

Source: *National Post, March 2, 2001, p.D12.*

On January 9, 1999, the exchange rate for the British pound was $2.48. On March 1, 2001, the rate had changed to $2.25. We would say that the dollar has risen against the British pound—because the pound has become cheaper, and so the dollar now buys more pounds. A stronger dollar would make travel to England more attractive to Canadians than when the pound was at $2.48.

The National Post reported a fall in the exchange rate of the euro from $1.65 to $1.44. This indicates that the euro is weaker than the dollar. European Community products are less expensive because each dollar buys more euros.

In our example situation we would describe the Canadian dollar as *stronger* than the British pound because the British pound's exchange rate fell between January 9, 1999, and March 1, 2001. For the same reason, the Canadian dollar was stronger than the euro. To determine whether the British pound is stronger than the euro, you would have to compare the euro's exchange into pounds on two different days to see whether the euro fell against the pound.

On January 1, 1999, the *euro* was introduced to harmonize financial transactions among the members of the European Community. Eleven members will use the euro: three members—Britain, Sweden and Denmark—have opted not to use the euro at the present time.

Initially all financial transactions between the eleven European Community members will be translated from the local currency into the euro and back into the local currency of the second country. For example, a transaction between a French company and a German company would be translated from francs to euros and then from euros into deutschmarks.

In 2002, the currencies of the 11 countries will disappear and all transactions among them, and between them and non-members, will be in euros.

On March 1, 2001, *The National Post* reported that the euro was trading at $1.4408 Canadian.

Foreign-Currency Transactions

When a Canadian company transacts business with a foreign company, the transaction price can be stated either in dollars or in the national currency of the other company. If the price is stated in dollars, the Canadian company has no special accounting difficulties. The transaction is recorded and reported in dollars exactly as though the other company were also Canadian.

Paying Cash in a Foreign Currency

If the transaction price is stated in units of the foreign currency, the Canadian company encounters two accounting steps. First, the transaction price must be translated into dollars for recording in the accounting records. Second, credit transactions (the most common international transaction) usually cause the Canadian company to experience a **foreign-currency transaction gain** or **loss**. This type of gain or loss occurs when the exchange rate changes between the date of the purchase on account and the date of the subsequent payment of cash.

The credit purchase creates an Account Payable that is recorded at the prevailing exchange rate. Later, when the buyer pays cash, the exchange rate has almost certainly changed. Accounts Payable is debited for the amount recorded earlier, and Cash is credited for the amount paid at the current exchange rate. A debit difference is a loss, and a credit difference is a gain.

Suppose on May 13, 2001, The Bay imports Shalimar perfume from a French supplier at a price of 200,000 francs. The exchange rate is $0.23 per French franc. The Bay records this credit purchase as follows:

May 13	Inventory	46,000	
	Accounts Payable		46,000
	To record a purchase on credit (200,000 × $0.23).		

WORKING IT OUT

(1) On December 30, the exchange rate for German marks was DM = $0.72. International Corp. (a Canadian company) purchased inventory from a German company at a cost of 50,000 DM. Record the purchase in dollars. (2) Record the payment on January 5 for a current exchange rate of DM = $0.70.

A:

(1) Inventory........ 36,000
    Accounts
      Payable......   36,000
(50,000 DM × $0.72 = 36,000)
(2) Accounts
    Payable 36,000
    Foreign-Currency
    Transaction
      Gain.......   1,000
    Cash..........   35,000
(50,000 DM × $0.70 = 35,000)

The Bay translates the French franc price of the merchandise (200,000 Fr) into dollars ($46,000) for recording the purchase and the related account payable.

If The Bay were to pay this account immediately (which is unlikely in international commerce), The Bay would debit Accounts Payable and credit Cash for $46,000. Suppose, however, that the credit terms specify payment within 60 days. On July 2, when The Bay pays this debt, the exchange rate has fallen to $0.21 per French franc. The Bay's payment entry is

July 2	Accounts Payable	46,000	
	Cash		42,000
	Foreign-Currency Transaction Gain		4,000
	To record payment of a credit purchase (200,000 × $0.21).		

The Bay
www.hbc.com

The Bay has a gain because the company has settled the debt with fewer dollars than the amount of the original account payable. If on the payment date the exchange rate of the French franc had exceeded $0.23, The Bay would have paid more dollars than the original $46,000. The company would have recorded a loss on the transaction as a debit to Foreign-Currency Transaction Loss.

Collecting Cash in a Foreign Currency

International sales on account also may be measured in foreign currency. Suppose Bombardier sells some Ski Doos to a German retailer on December 30, 2001. The price of the Ski Doos is 140,000 German marks, and the exchange rate is $0.71 per German mark. Bombardier's sale entry is

Dec. 30	Accounts Receivable	99,400	
	Sales revenue...		99,400
	To record a sale on account (140,000 × $0.71).		

Assume Bombardier collects from the German retailer on January 9, 2002, when the exchange rate has fallen to $0.69 per German mark. Bombardier receives fewer dollars than the recorded amount of the receivable and so experiences a foreign-currency transaction loss. The collection entry is

Jan. 9	Cash	96,600	
	Foreign-Currency Transaction Loss	2,800	
	Accounts Receivable..		99,400
	To record collection of a receivable (140,000 × $0.69).		

Foreign-Currency Transaction Gains and Losses are combined for each accounting period. The net amount of gain or loss can be reported as Other Revenue and Expense on the income statement.

Hedging—A Strategy to Avoid Foreign-Currency Transaction Losses

One way for Canadian companies to avoid foreign-currency transaction losses is to insist that international transactions be settled in Canadian dollars. This requirement puts the burden of currency translation on the foreign party. However, such a strategy may alienate customers and decrease sales, or it may cause customers to demand unreasonable credit terms. Another way for a company to protect itself from the effects of fluctuating foreign-currency exchange rates is by hedging.

Hedging means to protect oneself from losing money in one transaction by engaging in a counterbalancing transaction. A Canadian company selling goods to be collected in Mexican pesos expects to receive a fixed number of pesos in the future. If the peso is losing value, the Canadian company would expect the pesos to be worth fewer dollars than the amount of the receivable—an expected loss situation.

REAL WORLD EXAMPLE

If a company wants to protect the value of a receivable denominated in a foreign currency, the company will most likely purchase a *forward contract.* A forward contract is an obligation to buy or sell a specific amount of currency at a predetermined rate at a specific future date. The advantage here is that it allows the company to more accurately project cash flows.

KEY POINT

When a subsidiary prepares financial statements in a currency other than dollars, the subsidiary must translate the financial statements into dollars for the consolidated financial statements.

REAL WORLD EXAMPLE

If a company is required to make payments in a foreign currency, the most common way to exchange Canadian dollars for another currency is through a spot foreign exchange contract. A spot contract locks in an exchange rate on the date of the contract and the currency is delivered two business days later. It is the most liquid foreign exchange tool.

 **REAL WORLD EXAMPLE**

Chiquita ships more than a billion dollars of bananas annually. A small change in currency rates can mean a big change in profits. Therefore, Chiquita purchases currency options to hedge the foreign currency exchange risk. The currency options give Chiquita the right to buy foreign currencies at prescribed prices and thus enable the company to minimize losses due to any changes in the exchange rate.

REAL WORLD EXAMPLE

Several years ago Daimler Benz, the German company that builds Mercedes Benz cars, decided to list its shares on the New York Stock Exchange. Its financial statements, which showed a large net profit under German GAAP, had to be reported using U.S. GAAP. The restated statements showed a significant loss. Unfortunately, many investors are unaware of different accounting standards around the world.

The Canadian company may have accumulated payables stated in a foreign currency in the normal course of its business, such as the amount payable by The Bay to the French supplier. Losses on the receipt of pesos may be approximately offset by gains on the payment of francs to the French supplier. Most companies do not have equal amounts of receivables and payables in foreign currency, so offsetting receivables and payables is imprecise. To obtain a more precise hedge, some companies buy *futures contracts,* which are contracts for foreign currencies to be received in the future. Futures contracts can effectively create a payable to exactly offset a receivable, and vice versa. Many companies that do business internationally use hedging techniques.

Further discussion of foreign currency and international transactions is beyond the scope of this text and will be covered in more advanced accounting courses.

International Accounting Standards

For the most part, accounting principles are similar from country to country. However, some important differences exist. For example, some countries, such as Italy, require financial statements to conform closely to income tax laws. In other countries, such as Brazil and Argentina, high inflation rates dictate that companies make price-level adjustments to report amounts in units of common purchasing power. Neither practice is followed in Canada. Canada requires research costs to be expensed as incurred but, in certain circumstances, Canada permits capitalization of development costs (see Chapter 10, page 530), as does Great Britain. The United States and Germany require all research and development costs to be expensed as incurred.

Several organizations are working to achieve worldwide harmony of accounting standards. Chief among these is the *International Accounting Standards Committee (IASC)*. Headquartered in London, the IASC operates much as the CICA's Accounting Standards Board in Canada. It has the support of the accounting professions in Canada, the United States, most of the British Commonwealth countries, Japan, France, Germany, the Netherlands, Mexico, and many other countries. However, the IASC has no authority to require compliance with its accounting standards. It must rely on cooperation by the various national accounting professions. Since its creation in 1973, the IASC has succeeded in narrowing some differences in international accounting standards.

The three accounting bodies in Canada, the CICA, CGAAC, and SMAC, are members of IASC. The Appendix to Section 1501 of the *CICA Handbook* is a comparison of International Accounting Standards to the *CICA Handbook*. Paragraph 1501.02 states "The Accounting Standards Board supports the objective of harmonizing accounting standards internationally. The Board works with the IASC to minimize differences between International Accounting Standards and the corresponding Accounting Recommendations."

The Decision Guidelines feature summarizes the second half of the chapter. Study it before proceeding to the Summary Problem for Your Review.

DECISION GUIDELINES Foreign-Currency Transactions

Decision	Guidelines
When to record a • Foreign-currency transaction gain?	• When you receive foreign currency worth *more* in Canadian dollars than the amount of the receivable recorded earlier. • When you pay foreign currency that costs *less* in Canadian dollars than the amount of the payable recorded earlier.
• Foreign-currency transaction loss?	• When you receive foreign currency worth *less* in Canadian dollars than the amount of the receivable recorded earlier. • When you pay foreign currency that costs *more* in Canadian dollars than the amount of the payable recorded earlier.

Summary Problems
for Your Review

1. Journalize the following transactions of Canada Corp.:

2002

Nov. 16 Purchased equipment on account for 40,000 U.S. dollars when the exchange rate was $1.48 per U.S. dollar.

27 Sold merchandise on account to a Mexican company for 700,000 Mexican pesos. Each peso is worth $0.16.

Dec. 22 Paid the U.S. company when the dollar's exchange rate was $1.46.

31 Adjusted for the change in the exchange rate of the Mexican peso. Its current exchange rate is $0.15.

2003

Jan. 4   Collected from the Mexican company. The exchange rate is $0.165.

2. In the 2002 transactions, identify each of the following currencies as stronger or weaker.

    a. U.S. dollar   **b.** Mexican peso   **c.** Canadian dollar

Solutions to Review Problems

1. Entries for transactions stated in foreign currencies:

2002			
Nov. 16	Equipment (40,000 × $1.48)	59,200	
	Accounts Payable		59,200
27	Accounts Receivable (700,000 × $0.16)	112,000	
	Sales Revenue		112,000
Dec. 22	Accounts Payable	59,200	
	Cash (40,000 × $1.46)		58,400
	Foreign-Currency Transaction Gain		800
31	Foreign-Currency Transaction Loss		
	[700,000 × ($0.16 – $0.15)]	7,000	
	Accounts Receivable		7,000
2003			
Jan. 4	Cash (700,000 × $0.165)	115,500	
	Accounts Receivable		
	($112,000 - $7,000)		105,000
	Foreign-Currency Transaction Gain		
	[700,000 × ($0.165 - $0.15)]		10,500

2. During 2002:

    a. U.S. dollar—weaker   **b.** Mexican peso—weaker   **c.** Canadian dollar—stronger

During 2003, the Mexican peso strengthened and the Canadian dollar weakened.

Cyber Coach

Visit the Student Resources area of the *Accounting* Companion Website for extra practice with the new material in Chapter 16.

www.pearsoned.ca/horngren

Summary

1. **Account for short-term stock investments.** Investments are classified as short-term or long-term. *Short-term investments* are liquid, and, generally, the investor intends to convert them to cash within one year or less, or to use them to pay a current liability. All other investments are *long-term*.

    Different methods are used to account for stock investments, depending on the investor's degree of influence over the investee. All investments are recorded initially at *cost*. Short-term investments are accounted for by the cost method (with lower-of-cost-or-market) and are reported on the balance sheet at the lower of their cost or current market (LCM) value. Dividends received are recorded as income.

2. **Account for long-term stock investments.** Long-term investments of less than 20 percent of the investee's stock are also accounted for using the cost method. Dividends received are recorded as income. A long-term investment is written down if there is a permanent decline in the value of the investment.

3. **Use the equity method to account for investments.** The *equity* method is used to account for investments of 20 to 50 percent of the investee company's stock. Such an investment generally enables the investor to significantly influence the investee's activities. Investee income is recorded by the investor by debiting the Investment account and crediting an account entitled Equity-Method Investment Revenue. The investor records receipt of div-

idends from the investee by crediting the Investment account.

4. **Understand consolidated financial statements.** Ownership of more than 50 percent of the voting stock creates a *parent-subsidiary* relationship, and the *consolidation* method must be used. Because the parent has control over the subsidiary, the subsidiary's financial statements are included in the consolidated statements of the parent company. Two features of consolidation accounting are (1) addition of the parent and subsidiary accounts to prepare the parent's consolidated statements, and (2) elimination of intercompany items. When a parent owns less than 100 percent of the subsidiary's stock, the portion owned by outside investors is called *minority interest*. Purchase of a controlling interest at a cost greater than the fair value of the subsidiary's net assets creates an intangible asset called *goodwill*. A consolidation work sheet is used to prepare the consolidated financial statements.

5. **Account for long-term investments in bonds.** *Long-term investments* in bonds are accounted for using the *amortized-cost method*. An important part of this method is accruing interest receivable and amortizing any bond discount or premium over the life of the bond. Long-term bonds are presented on the balance sheet after current assets with long-term stock investments; interest revenue from bond investments appears on the income statement under Other revenues.

6. **Understand how foreign-currency exchange rates are determined.** *International accounting* deals with accounting for business activities across national boundaries. A key issue is the translation of foreign-currency accounts into dollars, accomplished through a *foreign-currency exchange rate*. Changes in exchange rates cause companies to experience *foreign-currency transaction gains and losses* on credit transactions.

The International Accounting Standards Committee is working to harmonize accounting principles worldwide.

Self-Study Questions

Test your understanding of the chapter by marking the best answer for each of the following questions:

1. Short-term investments are reported on the balance sheet *(p. 867)*
   a. Immediately after cash
   b. Immediately after accounts receivable
   c. Immediately after inventory
   d. Immediately after current assets

2. Byforth Inc. distributes a stock dividend. An investor who owns Byforth Inc. stock should *(p. 868)*
   a. Debit Investment and credit Dividend Revenue for the book value of the stock received in the dividend distribution
   b. Debit Investment and credit Dividend Revenue for the market value of the stock received in the dividend distribution
   c. Debit Cash and credit Investment for the market value of the stock received in the dividend distribution
   d. Make a memorandum entry to record the new cost per share of Byforth Inc. stock held

3. Short-term investments are reported at the *(pp. 868–869)*
   a. Total cost of the portfolio
   b. Total market value of the portfolio
   c. Lower of total cost or total market value of the portfolio or lower of cost or market value on an investment-by-investment basis
   d. Total equity value of the portfolio

4. Putsch Corporation owns 30 percent of the voting stock of Mazelli, Inc. Mazelli Inc. reports net income of $100,000 and declares and pays cash dividends of $40,000. Which method should Putsch Corporation use to account for this investment? *(p. 870)*

a. Cost
b. Market value
c. Equity
d. Consolidation

5. Refer to the facts of the preceding question. What effect do Mazelli Inc.'s income and dividends have on Putsch Corporation's net income? *(pp. 871–872)*
   a. Increase of $12,000
   b. Increase of $18,000
   c. Increase of $30,000
   d. Increase of $42,000

6. In applying the consolidation method, elimination entries are *(pp. 873–876)*
   a. Necessary
   b. Required only when the parent has a receivable from or a payable to the subsidiary
   c. Required only when there is a minority interest
   d. Required only for the preparation of the consolidated balance sheet

7. Parent Corp. has separate net income of $155,000. Sub A Ltd., which Parent Corp. owns 90 percent of, reports net income of $60,000, and Sub B Ltd., which Parent Corp. owns 60 percent of, reports net income of $80,000. What is Parent Corp.'s consolidated net income? *(p. 878)*
   a. $155,000
   b. $257,000
   c. $263,000
   d. $295,000

8. On May 16, the exchange rate of the German mark was $0.70. On May 20, the exchange rate is $0.71. Which of the following statements is true? *(p. 886)*
   a. The dollar has risen against the mark.
   b. The dollar has fallen against the mark.
   c. The dollar is weaker than the mark.
   d. The dollar and the mark are equally strong.

9. A strong Canadian dollar encourages *(pp. 885–886)*
   a. Travel to Canada by foreigners
   b. Purchase of Canadian goods by foreigners

c. Canadians to travel abroad

d. Canadians to save dollars

10. Canadian Tire purchased auto accessories from an English supplier at a price of 500,000 British pounds. On the date of the credit purchase, the exchange rate of the British pound was $2.25. On the payment date, the exchange rate of the pound is $2.32. If payment is in pounds, Canadian Tire experiences *(pp. 886–887)*

a. A foreign-currency transaction gain of $35,000

b. A foreign-currency transaction loss of $35,000

c. Neither a transaction gain nor loss because the debt is paid in dollars

d. None of the above

Answers to the Self-Study Questions follow the Similar Accounting Terms.

Accounting Vocabulary

Consolidated statements *(p. 874)*
Controlling interest *(p. 873)*
Cost method for investments *(p. 867)*
Equity method for investments *(p. 871)*
Foreign-currency exchange rate *(p. 885)*
Foreign-currency transaction gain *(p. 886)*
Foreign-currency transaction loss *(p. 886)*
Hedging *(p. 887)*
Long-term investment *(p. 867)*

Majority interest *(p. 873)*
Marketable security *(p. 867)*
Minority interest *(p. 877)*
Parent company *(p. 873)*
Short-term investment *(p. 867)*
Strong currency *(p. 885)*
Subsidiary company *(p. 873)*
Temporary investment *(p. 867)*
Weak currency *(p. 885)*

Similar Accounting Terms

Controlling interest   Majority interest

Short-term investments   Marketable securities; Temporary investments

---

Answers to Self-Study Questions

1. a   2. d   3. c   4. c

5. c ($100,000 × 0.30 = $30,000; dividends have no effect on investor net income under the equity method)

6. a   7. b [$155,000 + ($60,000 × 0.90) + ($80,000 × 0.60) = $257,000]

8. a   9. c   10. b [500,000 × ($2.32 – $2.25) = $35,000]

Assignment Material

Questions

1. How are stock prices quoted in the securities market? What is the investor's cost of 1,000 shares of Mitel Corp. $2.00 preferred stock at $25.25 with a brokerage commission of $290?

2. What distinguishes a short-term investment from a long-term investment?

3. Show the positions of short-term investments and long-term investments on the balance sheet.

4. Outline the accounting methods for the different types of investment.

5. How does an investor record the receipt of a cash dividend on an investment accounted for by the

cost method? How does this investor record receipt of a stock dividend?

6. An investor paid $12,000 for 1,000 shares of stock and later received a 10 percent stock dividend. Compute the gain or loss on sale of 300 shares of the stock for $2,600.

7. At what amount are short-term investments reported on the balance sheet? Are the short-term and long-term investment portfolios mixed, or are they kept separate?

8. When is an investment accounted for by the equity method? Outline how to apply the equity

method. Include in your answer how to record the purchase of the investment, the investor's proportion of the investee's net income, and receipt of a cash dividend from the investee.

9. Identify three transactions that cause debits or credits to an equity-method investment account.

10. What are two special features of the consolidation method for investments?

11. Why are intercompany items eliminated from consolidated financial statements? Name two intercompany items that are eliminated.

12. Name the account that expresses the excess of cost of an investment over the fair market value of the subsidiary's net assets. What type of account is this, and where in the financial statements is it reported?

13. When a parent company buys more than 50 percent but less than 100 percent of a subsidiary's stock, a certain type of equity is created. What is it called and how do most companies report it?

14. How would you measure the net income of a parent company with three subsidiaries? Assume that two subsidiaries are wholly (100 percent) owned and that the parent owns 60 percent of the third subsidiary.

15. Cathy Harding purchases Westcoast Energy bonds as a long-term investment. Suppose the face amount of the bonds is $100,000 and the purchase price is $101.30. The bonds pay interest at the stated annual rate of 8 percent. How much did Harding pay for the bonds? How much principal will Harding collect at maturity?

16. The purchase date of the bond investment in the preceding question was August 1, 2001. The bonds pay semiannual interest on January 31 and July 31. How much cash interest will Harding earn during the year ended December 31, 2001?

17. McKay Inc. purchased inventory from a French company, agreeing to pay 100,000 francs. On the purchase date, the franc was quoted at $0.21. When McKay Inc. paid the debt, the price of a franc was $0.22. What account does McKay Inc. debit for the $1,000 difference between the cost of the inventory and the amount of cash paid?

18. Which situation results in a foreign-currency transaction gain for a Canadian business? Which situation results in a loss?

a. Credit purchase denominated in pesos, followed by weakness in the peso
b. Credit purchase denominated in pesos, followed by weakness in the dollar
c. Credit sale denominated in pesos, followed by weakness in the peso
d. Credit sale denominated in pesos, followed by weakness in the dollar

Exercises

Exercise 16-1   *Classifying investments as short-term or long-term*   *(Obj. 1, 2)*

Prentiss Corp. reports its annual financial results on June 30 each year. Prentiss Corp. purchased 100 shares of stock in each of three companies. Classify each investment as a current asset or a long-term asset.

a. Investment to be sold within the next 9 to 12 months.
b. Investment to be sold within the next 90 days.
c. Investment to be sold within the next two years.

Exercise 16-2   *Accounting for a short-term investment*   *(Obj. 1)*

Journalize the following investment transactions of Maral Corp.:

2002
Nov. 6   Purchased 1000 shares of Titan Corporation common stock at $66.00 per share, with brokerage commission of $3,000. The shares will be sold early in 2003.
Nov. 30   Received cash dividend of $0.90 per share on the Titan Corporation investment.
Dec. 31   Market value of the Titan shares is $64,000.

2003
June 14   Sold the Titan Corporation stock for $70.00 per share, net of commissions.

Exercise 16-3 *Reporting investments at the lower of cost or market* *(Obj. 1)*

ATCO Ltd. recently reported the following information on its balance sheet:

Current Assets	(dollars in millions)
Cash and short-term investments..	$218.3

Assume that the cost of ATCO's short-term investments is $100 million and that current market value is $90 million.

Required

Apply the lower-of-cost-or-market method to ATCO's short-term investments and calculate the value of the short-term investments included in "cash and short-term investments." Write a note to identify the method used to report short-term investments, and to disclose cost and market value. Show the journal entry that would have been made by ATCO if you determine that a journal entry was needed at year end. Assume the marketable securities were purchased during the current year.

Exercise 16-4 *Journalizing transactions for a long-term investment* *(Obj. 2)*

Journalize the following investment transactions of Chateau Rose Inc.:

2002
Aug. 6   Purchased 800 shares of Madison Corporation common stock as a long-term investment, paying $44.00 per share.
Sept. 12   Received cash dividend of $1.20 per share on the Madison Corporation investment.
Nov. 23   Received 80 shares of Madison Corporation common stock in a 10% stock dividend.
Dec. 4   Unexpectedly sold the Madison Corporation stock for $29.00 per share.

Exercise 16-5 *Accounting for an investment* *(Obj. 1)*

Suppose Ruland Ltd. completed the following investment transactions in 2001.

Nov. 6   Purchased 1,000 shares of Artcor Corporation stock for $20,000. Ruland plans to sell the stock at a profit in the near future.
    30   Received a quarterly cash dividend of $0.80 per share on the Artcor Corporation stock.
Dec. 31   Current market value is $26,000.

2002
Jan. 20   Sold the Artcor Corporation stock for $27,000.

Required

1. Make the entries to record Ruland Ltd.'s investment transactions. Explanations are not required.
2. Show how Ruland Ltd. would report its investment in the Artcor Corporation stock on the balance sheet at December 31, 2001.

Exercise 16-6 *Journalizing transactions under the equity method* *(Obj. 3)*

Canadian National Railway System (CN) owns equity-method investments in several companies. Suppose CN paid $2,000,000 to acquire a 30 percent investment in Motion Engineering Ltd. Further, assume Motion Engineering Ltd. reported net income of $640,000 for the first year and declared and paid cash dividends of $400,000. Record the following entries in CN's general journal: (a) purchase of the investment, (b) CN's proportion of Motion Engineering Ltd.'s net income, and (c) receipt of the cash dividends.

Exercise 16-7 *Recording equity-method transactions in the accounts* **(Obj. 3)**

Using the information from Exercise 16-6, calculate the balance in the investment in Motion Engineering Ltd.'s Common Stock account. Assume that after all the above transactions took place, CN sold its entire investment in Motion Engineering Ltd. common stock for cash of $2,400,000. Journalize the sale of the investment.

Exercise 16-8 *Applying the appropriate accounting method for investments* **(Obj. 2. 3)**

Jacina Corporation paid $160,000 for a 30 percent investment in the common stock of Nanco Systems Inc. For the first year, Nanco Systems Inc. reported net income of $84,000 and at year end declared and paid cash dividends of $16,000. On the balance sheet date the market value of Jacina Corporation's investment in Nanco Systems Inc. stock was $134,000.

Required

1. Which method is appropriate for Jacina Corporation to use in accounting for its investment in Nanco Systems Inc.? Why?
2. Show everything that Jacina Corporation would report for the investment and any investment revenue in its year-end financial statements.
3. What role does the market value of the investment play in this situation?

Exercise 16-9 *Completing a consolidation work sheet* **(Obj. 4)**

On-Time Logistics Ltd. owns all of the common shares of Bradson Trucking Ltd. Prepare a consolidation work sheet, using the following information.

	On-Time Logistics Ltd.	Bradson Trucking Ltd.
Assets		
Cash	62,000	16,000
Accounts receivable, net	112,000	80,000
Note receivable from Bradson Trucking Ltd.	20,000	—
Parts inventory..	72,000	49,000
Investment in Bradson Trucking Ltd...	710,000	—
Capital assets, net	1,100,000	880,000
Total	2,076,000	1,025,000
Liabilities and Shareholders' Equity		
Accounts payable.....................................	108,000	53,000
Notes payable...	140,000	230,000
Other liabilities.......................................	23,000	63,000
Common stock	600,000	200,000
Retained earnings	1,205,000	479,000
Total	2,076,000	1,025,000

Exercise 16-10 *Completing a consolidation work sheet with minority interest* **(Obj. 4)**

Diamond Holdings Ltd. owns an 80 percent interest in Hearts Inc. Prepare a consolidation work sheet using the information on page 896.

	Diamond Holdings Ltd.	Hearts Inc.
Assets		
Cash	39,000	14,000
Accounts receivable, net	82,000	55,000
Note receivable from Hearts Inc.	22,000	—
Inventory	102,000	87,000
Investment in Hearts Inc.	90,000	—
Capital assets, net	286,000	129,000
Other assets	22,000	8,000
Total	643,000	293,000
Liabilities and Shareholders' Equity		
Accounts payable	44,000	26,000
Notes payable	47,000	36,000
Other liabilities	82,000	131,000
Minority interest	—	—
Common stock	310,000	80,000
Retained earnings	160,000	20,000
Total	643,000	293,000

Exercise 16-11 *Working with a bond investment* **(Obj. 5)**

Western Securities Ltd. has a large investment in corporate bonds. Suppose Western Securities Ltd. buys $1,000,000 of Government of Manitoba bonds at a price of 95. The Government of Manitoba bonds pay cash interest at the annual rate of 7.5% and mature within five years.

1. How much did Western Securities Ltd. pay to purchase the bond investment? How much will Western Securities Ltd. collect when the bond investment matures?

2. How much cash interest will Western Securities Ltd. receive each year from the Government of Manitoba?

3. Will Western Securities Ltd. annual interest revenue on the bond investment be more or less than the amount of cash interest received each year? Give your reason.

4. Compute Western Securities Ltd.'s annual interest on this bond investment. Use the straight-line method to amortize the discount on the investment.

Exercise 16-12 *Recording bond investment transactions* **(Obj. 5)**

On March 31, 2002, Crusader Corp. paid $95.25 for 8 percent bonds of Kerlawn Limited as an investment. The maturity value of the bonds is $20,000 at September 30, 2006; they pay interest on March 31 and September 30. At December 31, the bonds' market value is $96.25.

Required

1. What method should Crusader Corp. use to account for the bonds?

2. Using the straight-line method of amortizing the discount, journalize all transactions on the bonds for 2002.

3. Show how the investment would be reported by Crusader Corp. on the balance sheet at December 31, 2002.

Exercise 16-13 *Journalizing foreign-currency transactions* **(Obj. 6)**

Journalize the following foreign-currency transactions:

2002
Nov. 17 Purchased goods on account from a Japanese company. The price was 200,000 yen, and the exchange rate of the yen was $0.0132.
Dec. 16 Paid the Japanese supplier when the exchange rate was $0.0137.
      19 Sold merchandise on account to a French company at a price of 60,000 French francs. The exchange rate was $0.21.
      31 Adjusted for the decrease in the value of the franc, which had an exchange rate of $0.20.

2003
Jan. 14 Collected from the French company. The exchange rate was $0.215.

Challenge Exercise

Exercise 16-14 *Analyzing long-term investments* **(Obj. 3)**

Boliden Limited is a major integrated base metals company based in Canada with operations in North and South America, and Europe. Suppose Boliden Limited's financial statements reported the following items for affiliated companies whose stock Boliden owns in various percentages between 20 and 50 percent:

	(In millions of U.S. dollars)	
	2001	**2000**
Balance Sheet (adapted)		
Long-term investments	$98	$105
Cash Flow Statement		
Increase in equity-method investments	6	1
Income Statement		
Equity-method investment revenue (losses)	(2)	3

Assume no sales of equity-method investments during 2001 or 2000.

Required

Prepare a T-Account for Equity-Method Investments to determine the amount of dividends Boliden Limited received from investee companies during 2001. The company's year end is December 31. Show your calculations.

Beyond the Numbers

Beyond the Numbers 16-1 *Analyzing long-term investments* **(Obj. 4)**

Jing Hu inherited some investments, and she has received the annual reports of the companies in which the funds are invested. The financial statements of the companies are puzzling to Jing, and she asks you the following questions:

a. The companies label their financial statements as *consolidated* balance sheet, *consolidated* income statement, and so on. What are consolidated financial statements?

b. Notes to the statements indicate that "certain intercompany transactions, loans, and other accounts have been eliminated in preparing the consolidated financial statements." Why does a company eliminate transactions, loans, and accounts? Jing states that she thought a transaction was a transaction and that a loan obligated a company to pay real money. She wonders if the company is juggling the books to defraud Canada Customs and Revenue Agency.

c. The balance sheet lists the asset Goodwill. What is goodwill? Does this mean that the company's stock has increased in value?

Required

Respond to each of Jing Hu's questions.

Ethical Issue

Marjal Inc. owns 18 percent of the voting stock of Pyrene Corporation. The remainder of the Pyrene Corporation stock is held by numerous investors with small holdings. Chuck Ross, president of Marjal Inc. and a member of Pyrene Corporation's Board of Directors, heavily influences Pyrene Corporation's policies.

Under the cost method of accounting for investments, Marjal Inc.'s net income increases if or when it receives dividends from Pyrene Corporation. Marjal Inc. pays President Ross a bonus computed as a percentage of Marjal Inc.'s net income. Therefore, Ross can control his personal bonus to a certain extent by influencing Pyrene Corporation's dividends.

Marjal Inc. has a bad year in 2001, and corporate income is low. Ross uses his power to have Pyrene Corporation pay a large cash dividend. This action requires Pyrene Corporation to borrow a substantial sum one month later to pay operating costs.

Required

1. In getting Pyrene Corporation to pay the large cash dividend, is Ross acting within his authority as a member of the Pyrene Corporation Board of Directors? Are Ross's actions ethical? Whom can his actions harm?

2. Discuss how using the equity method of accounting for investments would decrease Ross's potential for manipulating his bonus.

Problems   (Group A)

Problem 16-1A   *Journalizing transactions under the cost and equity methods*   *(Obj. 1, 2, 3)*

KAL Corp., the conglomerate, owns numerous investments in the stock of other companies. Assume KAL Corp. completed the following investment transactions:

2002

May	1	Purchased 12,000 shares (total issued and outstanding common shares, 38,400) of the common stock of Finnegan Corp. at total cost of $810,000.
July	2	Purchased 1,600 additional shares of Finnegan Corp. common stock at a cost of $120,000.
Sept.	15	Received semiannual cash dividend of $1.40 per share on the Finnegan Corp. investment.
Oct.	12	Purchased 1,000 shares of A&L Ltd. common stock as a short-term investment, paying $22.50 per share plus brokerage commission of $500.
Dec.	14	Received semiannual cash dividend of $0.80 per share on the A&L Ltd. investment.
Dec.	31	Received annual report from Finnegan Corp. Net income for the year was $350,000. Of this amount, KAL Corp.'s proportion is 35.4 percent. The current market value for 1,000 shares of A&L Ltd. stock is $20,000.

2003

Feb.	6	Sold 1,920 shares of Finnegan Corp. stock for net cash of $169,700.

Required

Record the transactions in the general journal of KAL Corp.; the company year end is December 31.

Oct.	1	X.Teck Ltd. declared and distributed a 3-for-1 common stock split.
Nov.	1	Received the interest on the United America Ltd. bonds when the exchange rate was $1.485 Canadian per American dollar.
Dec.	20	Sold 10,000 shares of X.Teck Ltd. common stock at $6.50 and commission was $1,000.
	31	Adjusted for the accrued interest on the United America Ltd. bonds. The exchange rate was $1.46 Canadian per American dollar. The current value of the bonds is $104.50 (U.S. dollars). Scully Corp.'s year end is December 31.

2003

May	1	Received the interest on the United America Ltd. bonds when the exchange rate was $1.47 Canadian per American dollar.

Required

1. Prepare the general journal entries required to record these transactions.
2. Calculate the May 1, 2003, balance of the investment account.

Problems (Group B)

Problem 16-1B *Journalizing transactions under the cost and equity methods* **(Obj. 1, 2, 3)**

Circle 4 Investments Ltd. owns numerous investments in the stock of other companies. Assume Circle 4 Investments Ltd. completed the following investment transactions:

2002

Feb.	12	Purchased 20,000 shares (total issued and outstanding common shares, 90,000) of the common stock of Durham Mfg. Ltd. at total cost of $740,000.
July	2	Purchased 8,000 additional shares of Durham Mfg. Ltd. common stock at cost of $300,000.
Aug.	9	Received annual cash dividend of $0.90 per share on the Durham Mfg. Ltd. investment.
Oct.	16	Purchased 2,000 shares of Sydenham Ltd. common stock as a short-term investment, paying $43.00 per share plus brokerage commission of $1,200.
Nov.	30	Received semiannual cash dividend of $0.60 per share on the Sydenham Ltd. investment.
Dec.	31	Received annual report from Durham Mfg. Ltd. Net income for the year was $510,000. Of this amount, Circle 4 Investments Ltd.'s proportion is 31.11 percent.
	31	The current value of Sydenham stock is $77,000.

2003

Jan.	14	Sold 4,000 shares of Durham Mfg. Ltd. stock for net cash of $181,000.

Required

Record the transactions in the general journal of Circle 4 Investments Ltd.; the company year end is December 31.

Problem 16-2B *Applying the cost method (with LCM) and the equity method* **(Obj. 1, 2, 3)**

The December 31, 1999, balance sheet of Nortel Networks Corporation included:

Investments—Associated Companies at Equity...... $176,400,000

Suppose the company completed the following investment transactions during the year:

2000

March	2	Purchased 2,000 shares of common stock as a short-term investment, paying $12.60 per share plus brokerage commission of $800.
	5	Purchased additional shares in an associated company at cost of $600,000.
July	21	Received semiannual cash dividend of $0.50 per share on the short-term investment purchased March 2.

Aug. 17 Received cash dividend of $47,000 from an associated company.

Oct. 16 Sold 1,600 shares of the short-term investment (purchased on March 2) for $12.00 per share less brokerage commission of $200.

Nov. 8 Purchased short-term investments for $126,000, plus brokerage commission of $2,300.

17 Received cash dividend of $69,000 from an associated company.

Dec. 31 Received annual reports from associated companies. Their total net income for the year was $8,000,000. Of this amount, Nortel's proportion is 24 percent.

Required

1. Record the transactions in the general journal of Nortel Networks Corporation.

2. Post entries to the Equity Investments T-account and determine its balance at December 31, 2000.

3. Assume the beginning balance of Short-Term Investments was cost of $293,600. Post entries to the Short-Term Investments T-account and determine its balance at December 31, 2000.

4. Assuming the market value of the short-term investment portfolio is $410,000 at December 31, 2000, show how Nortel Networks would report short-term investments and investments in associated companies on the ending balance sheet. Nortel Networks compares total portfolio cost to total portfolio market value in determining the lower of cost or market. Use the following format:

Cash.. $XXX

Short-term investments, at lower of cost or market (_?_ ,___) ☐

Accounts receivable (net)... XXX

Total current assets XXX

Investments—Associated companies at equity............................. ☐

Problem 16-3B *Preparing a consolidated balance sheet; goodwill, no minority interest* **(Obj. 4)**

Dorinda Inc. paid $300,000 to acquire all the common stock of Jakester Ltd., and Jakester Ltd. owes Dorinda Inc. $81,000 on a note payable. The fair market value of Jakester's net assets equalled the book value. Immediately after the purchase on June 30, 2003, the two companies' balance sheets were as follows:

	Dorinda Inc.	Jakester Ltd.
Assets		
Cash...	$ 24,000	$ 20,000
Accounts receivable, net......................	87,000	42,000
Note receivable from Jakester Ltd.	81,000	—
Inventory	145,000	214,000
Investment in Jakester Ltd.	300,000	—
Capital assets, net................................	178,000	219,000
Total...	$815,000	$495,000
Liabilities and Shareholders' Equity		
Accounts payable	$ 57,000	$ 39,000
Notes payable	177,000	68,000
Note payable to Dorinda Inc.	—	81,000
Other liabilities	129,000	41,000
Common stock.......................................	274,000	130,000
Retained earnings................................	178,000	136,000
Total...	$815,000	$495,000

Required

Prepare a consolidation work sheet.

Problem 16-4B   *Preparing a consolidated balance sheet; with minority interest*   **(Obj. 4)**

On March 22, 2002, Pita Investments Corp. paid $245,000 to purchase 70 percent of the common stock of Lawrence Products Inc., and Pita Investments Corp. owes Lawrence Products Inc. $67,000 on a note payable. The fair market value of Lawrence Products Inc.'s net assets equalled the book value. Immediately after the purchase, the two companies' balance sheets were as follows:

	Pita Investments Corp.	Lawrence Products Inc.
Assets		
Cash	$ 41,000	$ 23,000
Accounts receivable, net	86,000	139,000
Note receivable from		
Pita Investments Corp......................	—	67,000
Inventory...	128,000	85,000
Investment in Lawrence Products Inc.	245,000	—
Capital assets, net................................	344,000	188,000
Total...	$844,000	$502,000
Liabilities and Shareholders' Equity		
Accounts payable.................................	$ 72,000	$ 65,000
Notes payable.......................................	234,000	40,000
Note payable to Lawrence		
Products Inc.	67,000	—
Other liabilities....................................	11,000	47,000
Minority interest	—	—
Common stock.......................................	141,000	100,000
Retained earnings	319,000	250,000
Total...	$844,000	$502,000

Required

Prepare a consolidation work sheet.

Problem 16-5B   *Accounting for a long-term bond investment purchased at a premium*
                       (Obj. 5)

Financial institutions such as insurance companies and pension plans hold large quantities of bond investments. Suppose Vancouver City Savings Credit Union (Van City) purchases $800,000 of 9.5 percent bonds of the Province of British Columbia for $110.00 on January 9, 2001. These bonds pay interest on July 9 and January 9 each year. They mature on January 9, 2012.

Required

1. Journalize Van City's purchase of the bonds as a long-term investment on January 9, 2001, receipt of cash interest and amortization of premium on July 9, 2001, and accrual of interest revenue and amortization of premium at November 9, 2001, the fiscal year end. Assume the straight-line method is appropriate for amortizing premium.

2. Calculate the book value of the Province of British Columbia bonds at November 9, 2001.

Problem 16-6B *Computing the cost of a bond investment and journalizing its transactions (Obj. 5)*

Link Back to Chapter 15 (Effective-interest Amortization of Discount) Suppose, on December 31, 2002, when the market interest rate is 8 percent, an investor purchases $800,000 of W & D Products Inc.'s 6-year, 7.4 percent bonds at issuance. Determine the cost (present value) of this long-term bond investment. The investor uses the effective-interest amortization method.

Required

Prepare a schedule for amortizing the discount on bond investment through December 31, 2003. Use Exhibit 15-4 on page 815 as a guide. Journalize the purchase on December 31, 2002, the first semiannual interest receipt on June 30, 2003, and the year-end interest receipt on December 31, 2003.

Problem 16-7B *Journalizing foreign-currency transactions and reporting the transaction gain or loss (Obj. 6)*

Suppose Cott Corp., the Canadian beverage company, completed the following transactions:

2001
Dec.   4   Sold soft drink syrup on account to a Mexican company for $36,000. The exchange rate of the Mexican peso is $0.155, and the customer agrees to pay in Canadian dollars.

      13   Purchased inventory on account from a U.S. company at a price of U.S. $100,000. The exchange rate of the American dollar is $1.48, and payment will be in American dollars.

      20   Sold goods on account to an English firm for 70,000 British pounds. Payment will be in pounds, and the exchange rate of the pound is $2.25.

      27   Collected from the Mexican company. The exchange rate is unchanged from December 4.

      31   Adjusted the accounts for changes in foreign-currency exchange rates. Current rates: U.S. dollar, $1.45; British pound, $2.23.

2002
Jan.   21   Paid the American company. The exchange rate of the U.S. dollar is $1.49.
Feb.   17   Collected from the English firm. The exchange rate of the British pound is $2.22.

Required

1. Record these transactions in Cott Corp.'s general journal, and show how to report the transaction gain or loss on the income statement for the year ended December 31, 2001.

2. How will what you have learned in this problem help you structure international transactions?

Problem 16-8B *Accounting for short-term stock investments using the cost method (with LCM) and long-term investments in bonds (Obj. 1, 5)*

Longhorn Holding Ltd. had the following short-term investments in marketable securities on December 31, 2001 (valued at the lower of cost or market on an investment-by-investment basis):

	LCM
Canadian Utilities Ltd.	$ 98,000
Clearnet Communications Inc.	130,000
Renaissance Energy Ltd.	48,000
Total short-term investments	$276,000

Longhorn Holding Ltd. had the following investment transactions during 2002:

Jan.	5	Purchased 5,000 shares (2 percent) of Davo Ltd. as a short-term investment. The shares were purchased at $28.00 and the commission was $1,500.
Jan.	31	Davo Ltd. reported net income of $1,900,000 and declared a cash dividend of $500,000.
Feb.	15	Received $10,000 from Davo Ltd. as a cash dividend.
April	1	Purchased $100,000 (face value) of bonds at 98 as a long-term investment. The bonds pay 10 percent interest (5 percent semiannually) on October 1 and April 1 and mature in 2 years.
Aug.	31	Received a 10 percent stock dividend from Davo Ltd.
Oct.	1	Received the interest on the bonds.
Nov.	1	Davo Ltd. declared and distributed a 2-for-1 stock split.
Dec.	15	Sold 3,000 shares of Davo Ltd. at $16.50 and the commission was $900.
	31	Recorded the adjustment for accrued interest on the bonds.
	31	The market values of the investments were:

Canadian Utilities Limited	$ 90,000
Clearnet Communications Inc.	145,000
Davo Ltd.	91,000
Renaissance Energy Ltd.	45,000
Total short-term investments	$371,000

Required

Prepare the general journal entries required to record the transactions of 2002.

Problem 16-9B *Accounting for stock investments using the equity method; accounting for investments in bonds; and accounting for transactions stated in a foreign currency* **(Obj. 3, 5, 6)**

Timbra Ltd. uses the equity method in accounting for long-term investments and had the following investment transactions:

2002

Feb.	16	Timbra Ltd. purchased 30,000 shares (40 percent) of Fidelity Sound Ltd. common stock as a long-term investment. The shares were purchased for $24.00 and the commission was $1,800.
Mar.	31	Fidelity Sound Ltd. reported net income of $200,000 and declared a dividend of $150,000.
Apr.	1	Purchased $200,000 (U.S. dollar face value) of Eagle Crest Ltd. bonds at 100 (U.S. dollars) as a short-term investment. The bonds pay annual interest of 12 percent each April 1 and October 1, and mature in 5 years. The exchange rate at the time of the transaction was $1.48 Canadian for each American dollar.
	15	Received $60,000 as a cash dividend from Fidelity Sound Ltd.
June	10	Received 3,000 shares of Fidelity Sound Ltd. common stock as a 10 percent stock dividend.
Sept.	1	Fidelity Sound Ltd. declared and distributed a 3-for-1 common stock split.
Oct.	1	Received the interest on the Eagle Crest Ltd. bonds when the exchange rate was $1.46 Canadian per American dollar.
Dec.	10	Sold 30,000 shares of Fidelity Sound Ltd. common stock at $10.50 per share and the commission was $1,000.
	31	Adjusted for the accrued interest on the Eagle Crest Ltd. bonds. The exchange rate was $1.49 Canadian per American dollar. The current value of the bonds is $97.50 (U.S. dollars).

2003

Apr.	1	Received the interest on the Eagle Crest Ltd. bonds when the exchange rate was $1.45 Canadian per American dollar.

Required

1. Prepare the general journal entries required to record these transactions. Timbra Ltd.'s year end is December 31.

2. Calculate the April 1, 2003, balance of the investment account.

Challenge Problems

Problem 16-1C   *Accounting for ownership of shares in another company*   *(Obj. 1, 2, 3, 4)*

The text lists general rules for accounting for long-term investments in the voting stock of another corporation. However, the management of the investing company may decide that, in their judgment, the rules do not apply in a particular situation.

Required

1. Identify a situation where an investing company that owns less than 20 percent might believe that the equity method was appropriate.

2. Identify a situation where an investing company that owns between 20 percent and 50 percent might believe that the cost method was appropriate.

3. Identify a situation where an investing company that owns more than 50 percent might believe that the cost method was appropriate.

Problem 16-2C   *Accounting for foreign operations*   *(Obj. 6)*

Canadian exporters are pleased when the Canadian dollar weakens against the U.S. dollar, while the federal and provincial ministers of finance are likely not happy when the dollar weakens.

Required

Explain why a weakening Canadian dollar makes the Canadian exporters happy. Why would a weaker Canadian dollar make the finance ministers unhappy?

Extending Your Knowledge

Decision Problem

Understanding the cost and equity methods of accounting for investments   *(Obj. 1, 2, 3)*

Margaret Joyce is the owner of Country Music Holdings Ltd., a newly formed company, whose year end is December 31. The company made two investments during the first week of January, 2002. Both investments are to be held for at least the next five years as investments. Information about each of the investments follows:

a. Country Music Holdings Ltd. purchased 30 percent of the common stock of Nostalgia Ltd. for its book value of $150,000. During the year ended December 31, 2002, Nostalgia Ltd. earned $85,000 and paid a total dividend of $40,000.

b. Ten percent of the common stock of Western Music Inc. was purchased for its book value of $50,000. During the year ended December 31, 2002, Western Music Inc. paid Country Music Holdings Ltd. a dividend of $5,000. Western Music Inc. earned a profit of $118,000 for that period. The market value of Country Music Holdings Ltd.'s investment in Western Music Inc. was $217,000 at December 31, 2002.

Margaret has come to you as her auditor to ask you how to account for the investments. Country Music Holdings Ltd. has never had such investments before. You attempt to explain the proper accounting to her by indicating that different accounting methods apply to different situations.

Required

Help Margaret understand by

1. Describing the methods of accounting applicable to investments such as these.

2. Identifying which method should be used to account for the investments in Nostalgia Ltd. and Western Music Inc.

Financial Statement Problem

Investments in stock   *(Obj. 1, 2, 3, 4)*

The financial statements for Intrawest Corporation are in Appendix A.

Required

1. The financial statements are labelled "consolidated." What evidence can you find in the financial statements that reveals how Intrawest Corporation accounts for its subsidiaries?
2. List six subsidiaries of Intrawest Corporation and indicate Intrawest's degree of ownership.
3. How does Intrawest Corporation account for goodwill?
4. Does Intrawest Corporation have any foreign-currency transactions? How do you know?

Comprehensive Problem
for Part Three

1. Accounting for Corporate Transactions

KA Investments Inc.'s articles of incorporation authorize the company to issue 500,000 shares of common stock and 200,000 shares of $4.00 preferred stock. During the first quarter of operations, KA Investments Inc. completed the following selected transactions:

2002
Oct. 1 Issued 50,000 shares of common stock for cash of $9.00 per share.
      4 Signed a capital lease for equipment. The lease requires a down payment of $100,000, plus 20 quarterly lease payments of $10,000. Present value of the future lease payments is $135,900 at an annual interest rate of 16 percent.
      6 Issued 2,000 shares of preferred stock, receiving cash of $100,000.
      22 Received land from the province as an incentive for locating in Manitoba. Fair market value of the land was $80,000.
      30 Purchased 5,000 shares (25 percent) of the outstanding common stock of CanTech Ltd. as a long-term investment, $80,000.
Nov. 1 Issued $400,000 of 9 percent, 10-year bonds payable at 96.
      16 Purchased short-term investments in the common stocks of Telus Corp., $24,000, and ATCO Ltd., $31,000.
      19 Experienced an extraordinary tornado loss of inventory that cost $52,000. Cash received from the insurance company was $24,000.
      20 Repurchased 2,000 shares of the company's common stock at $5.00 per share for cancellation.
Dec. 1 Received cash dividends of $560 on the Telus Corp. investment.
      16 Sold 1,000 of the company's common shares for cash of $8.00 per share.
      29 Received a report from CanTech Ltd. indicating the combined net income for November and December was $104,000.
      30 Sold merchandise on account, $716,000. Cost of the goods was $314,000. Operating expenses totaled $174,000, with $166,000 of this amount paid in cash. KA Investments Inc. uses a perpetual inventory system.
      31 Accrued interest and amortized discount (straight-line method) on the bonds payable.
      31 Accrued interest on the capital lease liability.

31   Amortized the equipment acquired by the capital lease. The company uses the double-declining-balance method.

31   Market values of short-term investments: Telus Corp. stock, $22,400, and ATCO Ltd. stock, $36,000.

31   Accrued income tax expense of $80,000.

31   Closed all revenues, expenses, and losses to Retained Earnings in a single closing entry.

31   Declared a quarterly cash dividend of $1.00 per share on the preferred stock. Record date is January 11, 2003, with payment scheduled for January 19.

Required

1. Record these transactions in the general journal. Explanations are not required.

2. Prepare a single-step income statement for the quarter ended December 31, 2002, including earnings per share. Income tax expense of $80,000 should be reported as follows: Income tax expense of $89,000 is used in arriving at income before extraordinary items. The tax effect of the extraordinary loss is an income tax saving of $9,000.

3. Report the liabilities and the shareholders' equity as they would appear on the balance sheet at December 31, 2002.

Guest-Tek Services—"With Financial Support Comes Advice"

In 1995, when Arnon Levy was 23, he and Kris Youell launched Guest-Tek Services. Guest-Tek Services designed software that allows hotel guests to plug a laptop to a socket in their hotel room to gain high-speed access to the Internet.

Guest-Tek Services has been extremely successful. Since the company's inception in 1995, the company had its product installed in 3,200 hotel rooms, with contracts for 2,500 more rooms in Canada. Clients include the Holiday Inn and Hilton chains.

The company wants to break into the U.S. and the overseas markets. In the video, we learn that the company has a problem with an installation at Swiss Hotel in Boston, and that Arnon went to Singapore to make a proposal to the up-scale Pan Pacific Hotel chain. In addition, Guest-Tek is negotiating a contract with Star Choice, the satellite TV company, to bundle TV and high-speed Internet access.

Arnon, Kris, and the other members of the team realized they needed significantly greater resources to develop their software to accommodate their rapidly expanding business. In particular, they needed more programmers and more marketing people.

In August 1999, Launchworks Inc., a Calgary venture capital fund[1], invested in the company.

Launchworks Inc. had a very "hands-on" approach and provided management support of various kinds. For example, Launchworks helped Guest-Tek hire a Chief Financial Officer. Launchworks saw its role as providing funding and mentoring for Guest-Tek. Its goal was to create "tremendous shareholder wealth" and as part of that goal, Launchworks personnel met weekly with Arnon, Kris, and their employees. Guest-Tek was growing from eight to 50 people and needed the assistance that Launchworks could provide. For example, Launchworks helped Guest-Tek develop a business plan and a marketing plan.

We see the results of Launchworks's involvement

in several ways. In one scene, the company has been selected as one of a small group to make a proposal to Disneyworld that would involve wiring 25,000 rooms, and the staff are planning their strategy. In another scene, we see that Launchworks advice creates problems in the marketing area. The video ends with the comment that Guest-Tek is well on its way to success with millions more invested by Launchworks.

CASE QUESTIONS

1. What different methods might Arnon Levy have used to gain the financial resources needed to expand? What are the advantages and disadvantages of each method?

2. What method of financing does Guest-Tek likely have with Launchworks?

3. Imagine that you are Stephen Kenny, the President of Launchworks. What kind of shares would you want Guest-Tek to issue to you in exchange for your firm's financial support?

4. Venture capital funds are willing to invest in start-up companies but there is a cost to the company receiving the investment. Was Guest-Tek better off because of Launchworks' involvement?

[1] A venture capital fund invests in start-up companies, such as Guest-Tek Services, with the goal that the start-up company will become successful and sell shares of stock to the public. The venture capital fund expects that the value of its interest in the company will be sold for some multiple of its original investment and it will earn a profit. Of course not all start-ups are successful and the typical venture capital fund will have successes and failures. The venture capital fund may also provide management assistance to the start-up. Many successful high-tech companies that are listed on the various stock exchanges received support from venture capital funds in their formative years.

Source: *Venture*, "Guest-Tek," telecast on January 25, 2000.

The Cash Flow Statement

CHAPTER OBJECTIVES

After studying this chapter, you should be able to

1 Identify the purposes of the cash flow statement

2 Report cash flows from operating, investing, and financing activities

3 Prepare a cash flow statement by the direct method

4 Compute the cash effects of a wide variety of business transactions

5 Prepare a cash flow statement by the indirect method

A1 Prepare a work sheet for the cash flow statement—indirect method

The CICA Handbook in Section 1540 states "Information about the cash flows of an enterprise enables users of financial statements to assess the capacity of the enterprise to generate cash and cash equivalents and the needs of the enterprise for cash resources."

The income statement indicates to users whether an enterprise is profitable; the cash flow statement indicates whether or not the enterprise is generating enough cash to pay the bills.

The management of Dofasco Inc., in the Management Discussion and Analysis (MD&A) section of its 1999 Annual Report, stated "Dofasco's ability to generate cash from operations is one of the Company's greatest strengths and the foundation for our focused capital investments in facilities to produce value-added products."

Although cash flow from operations decreased from $569 million in 1999 to $250 million in 2000, the cash flow was still positive. This positive cash flow allowed the company to invest $216 million in new facilities and to make a $44.8 million acquisition. The positive cash flow enabled Dofasco to repurchase common and preferred shares ($94 million) and pay dividends in 2000. Cash and cash equivalents decreased by $70 million over 1999. Users of Dofasco Inc.'s financial statements can see where Dofasco generated cash and cash equivalents and where Dofasco used cash and cash equivalents (see Exhibit 17-1).

The income statement shows net income for the period but net income is *not* the only measure of success in business. After all, a company does not pay the bills with net income—it pays the bills with cash. The cash flow statement is a basic financial statement on a par with the income statement and the balance sheet.

Source: Dofasco Inc. 1999 and 2000 Annual Reports.

THE CASH FLOW

statement, a required financial statement, reports where cash came from and how the company spent it. Like the income statement and the balance sheet, the cash flow statement provides important information about an organization. For Dofasco Inc., the results seem positive because operations are generating positive cash flow (see Exhibit 17-1). This is a positive signal about any company because operations should be the main source of cash. We begin this chapter by explaining the cash flow statement format preferred by the Accounting Standards Board as stated in Section 1540 of the *CICA Handbook*. It is very clear and is called the *direct approach*. We end the chapter with the more common format of the cash flow statement, the *indirect approach*. The method used by Dofasco Inc. in the chapter-opening vignette is the indirect approach. By the time you have worked through this chapter, you will feel more confident in your ability to analyze the cash flows of any company you might encounter.

The cash flow statement (which used to be called the statement of changes in financial position), reports where cash came from and how it was spent. We learned in Chapter 1 (Exhibit 1-8) that the cash flow statement is a required financial statement. Like the other two major financial reports—the income statement and the balance sheet—the cash flow statement enables investors and creditors to make informed decisions about a company. The income statement of a company might present one picture of the company: relatively high income; while the cash flow statement might present a different picture: not enough cash. This example underscores the challenge of financial analysis: that a company's signals may point in different directions. Astute investors and creditors know what to look for; increasingly they are focusing on cash flows.

> **THINKING IT OVER**
>
> Look at Capital Assets in Exhibit 17-8 on page 927. Notice that capital assets increase $234,000 during the year. Why?
>
> ***A***: Most likely, capital assets were purchased. Several factors could have contributed to the increase. Did the business buy $234,000 of capital assets and sell none or buy $434,000 and sell $200,000? Did Anchor Ltd. pay cash or borrow money to buy the assets? The cash flow statement answers these questions.

Dofasco Inc.
www.dofasco.ca

DOFASCO INC.
Statement of Cash Flows (Adapted)
For the Year Ended December 31, 2000

	(In millions)
Cash flows from operating activities:	
Net income and charges for the year......................................	$419.7
Less transactions not involving cash outlays (e.g., amortization)	
Changes in operating working capital............................	169.9
Other...	(1.6)
Net cash inflow from operating activities........................	251.4
Cash flows from investing activities:	
New facilities	(216.0)
Acquisition...	(44.8)
Other investments...	(0.3)
Net cash outflow from investing activities.....................	(261.1)
Cash flows from financing activities:	
Increase in bank borrowing	26.0
Increase in long-term debt	83.5
Common and preferred shares repurchased (net)	(94.4)
Dividends paid...	(80.6)
Other	5.2
Net cash outflow from financing activities.....................	(60.3)
Cash and cash equivalents:	
Decrease for the year	(70.0)
Balance at January 1, 2000...	197.1
Balance at December 31, 2000...	$127.1

The Cash Flow Statement: Basic Concepts

The balance sheet reports a company's cash balance at the end of the period. By comparing the beginning and ending balance sheets, you can tell whether cash increased or decreased during the period. However, the balance sheet does not indicate *why* the cash balance changed. The income statement reports revenues, expenses, and net income (or net loss)—clues about the sources and uses of cash but does not tell *why* cash increased or decreased.

The **cash flow statement** reports the entity's **cash flows** (cash receipts and cash payments) during the period. It shows the *causes* for the change in the cash balance. This information cannot be learned solely from the other financial statements.

The cash flow statement covers a span of time and therefore is dated "For the Year Ended XXX" or "For the Month Ended XXX." Exhibit 17-2 illustrates the timing of the financial statements.

OBJECTIVE 1
Identify the purposes of the
cash flow statement

Purpose of the Cash Flow Statement

The cash flow statement is designed to:

1. *Predict future cash flows.* It takes cash to pay the bills. In many cases, past cash receipts and cash payments are a reasonably good predictor of future cash flows.

2. *Evaluate management decisions.* Wise decisions lead to profits and strong cash flows. Unwise decisions bring bankruptcy. The cash flow statement reports on the investments a company is making.

3. *Determine the company's ability to pay dividends to shareholders and principal and interest to creditors.* Shareholders are interested in receiving dividends on their

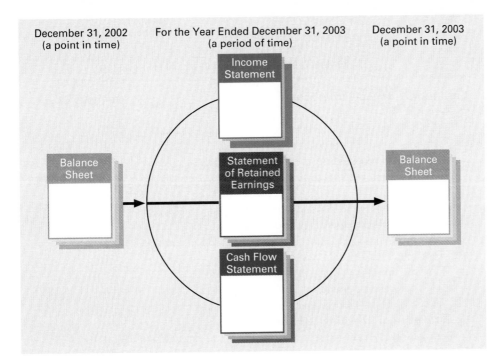

EXHIBIT 17-2

Timing of the Financial Statements

December 31, 2002 (a point in time)

For the Year Ended December 31, 2003 (a period of time)

December 31, 2003 (a point in time)

Income Statement

Balance Sheet

Statement of Retained Earnings

Balance Sheet

Cash Flow Statement

investments in the company's stock. Creditors want to receive their principal and interest amounts on time. The cash flow statement helps investors and creditors predict whether the business can make dividend and debt payments.

4. *Show the relationship of net income to cash flow.* Usually, cash and net income move together. High profits tend to lead to increases in cash, and vice versa. However, a company's cash balance can decrease when net income is high, and cash can increase when income is low. The failures of companies that were earning net income but had insufficient cash have pointed to the need for cash-flow information.

Cash and Cash Equivalents

On the financial statements, *Cash* has broader meaning than just cash on hand and cash in the bank. It includes **cash equivalents** (discussed in Chapter 7), which are highly liquid short-term investments that can be converted into cash with little delay. Because their liquidity is one reason for holding these investments, they are treated as cash. Examples of cash equivalents are investments in money-market funds and investments in Government of Canada treasury bills. Businesses invest their extra cash in these types of liquid assets rather than let cash remain idle. Throughout this chapter, the term *cash* refers to cash and cash equivalents.

Operating, Investing, and Financing Activities

A business engages in three basic categories of business activities: operating activities, investing activities, and financing activities. After the business is operational, *operations* are the most important activity, followed by *investing activities* and *financing activities*. Investing activities are generally more important than financing activities because *what* a company invests in is usually more important than *how* the company finances the acquisition.

The cash flow statement in Exhibit 17-3 on page 916 shows how cash receipts and payments are divided into operating activities, investing activities, and fi-

KEY POINT

A business operates for profit, and it must operate profitably to be a going concern. Information about net income (using the accrual basis) is found on the income statement. However, a business must have cash to pay suppliers, employees, etc. Information about cash flows is found on the cash flow statement.

OBJECTIVE 2
Report cash flows from operating, investing, and financing activities

EXHIBIT 17-3

Cash Flow Statement (Direct Method for Operating Activities)

···· **THINKING IT OVER**

How would you compare the cash flows in Exhibit 17-3 to the income statement in Exhibit 17-7 on page 926?

A: There was a net inflow of $68 from operating activities; however, Anchor Ltd.'s net income was only $41. Some of the differences are listed below:

	Cash Flow	Net Income
1. Cash rec. from customers	$271	
Sales		$284
2. Amortization	–0–	18
3. Cash pay. to suppliers	133	
COGS		150

LEARNING TIP

When preparing the cash flow statement, compare beginning cash and ending cash. Has it increased or decreased? An increase during the period means the statement will show a "net increase in cash."

KEY POINT

Cash flows from operating activities are the cash flows associated with each item on the income statement. Operating activities are all cash flows not associated with investing or financing activities.

KEY POINT

If the revenues and expenses on the income statement are converted to the cash basis, then cash flow from operations is complete. Operating activities include all cash inflows and outflows not associated with investing or financing.

ANCHOR LTD.
Cash Flow Statement
For the Year Ended December 31, 2002

		(In thousands)
Cash flows from operating activities		
Receipts:		
Collections from customers	$ 271	
Interest received on notes receivable	10	
Dividends received on investments in stock	9	
Total cash receipts		$ 290
Payments:		
To suppliers for merchandise for resale	$(113)	
To suppliers for operating expenses	(20)	
To employees	(58)	
For interest	(16)	
For income tax	(15)	
Total cash payments		(222)
Net cash inflow from operating activities		68
Cash flows from investing activities		
Acquisition of capital assets	$(306)	
Loan to another company	(11)	
Proceeds from sale of capital assets	62	
Net cash outflow from investing activities		(255)
Cash flows from financing activities		
Proceeds from issuance of common shares	$ 101	
Proceeds from issuance of long-term notes payable	94	
Payment of long-term notes payable*	(11)	
Payment of dividends	(17)	
Net cash inflow from financing activities		167
Net increase (decrease) in cash and cash equivalents		$ (20)
Cash and cash equivalents, January 1, 2002		42
Cash and cash equivalents, December 31, 2002		$ 22

*This would also include the current portion of long-term notes payable, which are NIL in this case.

---

nancing activities for Anchor Ltd., a small manufacturer of glass products. Exhibit 17-3 shows that each set of activities includes both cash inflows (receipts) and cash outflows (payments). Outflows have parentheses to indicate that payments are subtracted. Each section of the statement reports a net cash inflow (net cash receipt) or a net cash outflow (net cash payment).

Operating activities create revenues and expenses. The cash flow statement reports the cash impact of revenues and expenses. The largest cash inflow from operations is the collection of cash from customers. Smaller inflows are receipts of interest on loans and dividends on stock investments. The operating cash outflows include cash payments to suppliers and employees, and cash payments for interest and taxes. Exhibit 17-3 shows that Anchor Ltd.'s net cash inflow from operating activities is $68,000. A large positive cash inflow from operations is a good sign about a company. *In the long run, operations must be the main source of a business's cash.* Dot-com investors and lenders are well aware of this business truth.

Operating activities are related to the transactions that make up net income.[1]

---

[1]The authors thank Alfonso Oddo for suggesting this display.

Cash flows from operating activities require analysis of each revenue and expense on the income statement, along with the related current asset or current liability from the balance sheet.

Investing activities are the buying and selling of the long-term assets the business uses. A purchase or sale of a capital asset like land, a building, or equipment is an investing activity, as is the purchase or sale of a long-term investment in stock or bonds of another company. Making a current or long-term loan is an investing activity because the loan creates a receivable for the lender. Collecting on the loan is also reported as an investing activity on the cash flow statement. The acquisition of capital assets dominates Anchor Ltd.'s investing activities, which produce a net cash outflow of $255,000.

LEARNING TIP

To help organize the information for the cash flow statement, remember that
(1) most information for *operating* activities comes from the income statement, current assets, and current liabilities;
(2) most information for *investing* activities comes from the noncurrent asset section of the balance sheet;
(3) most information for *financing* activities comes from the liabilities and capital stock sections of the balance sheet.

Investing activities require analysis of the long-term asset accounts.

Investments in capital assets lay the foundation for future operations. A company that invests in plant and equipment appears stronger than one that is selling its capital assets. Why? The latter company may have to sell income-producing assets in order to pay the bills. Most companies need capital assets to operate.

Financing activities obtain the cash from investors and creditors needed to launch and sustain the business. Financing activities include issuing stock, borrowing money by issuing notes and bonds payable, and making payments to the shareholders—dividends and repurchases of the company's stock. Payments to creditors include *principal* payments only. The payment of *interest* is an operating activity. Financing activities of Anchor Ltd. brought in net cash receipts of $167,000. One thing to watch among financing activities is whether the business is borrowing heavily. Excessive borrowing has been the downfall of many companies.

Financing activities require analyis of the long-term liability accounts and the shareholders' equity accounts.

Overall, Anchor Ltd.'s cash decreased by $20,000 during 2002. The company began the year with cash of $42,000 and ended with $22,000.

Each of these categories of activities includes both cash receipts and cash payments, as shown in Exhibit 17-4. The exhibit lists the more common cash receipts and cash payments that appear on the cash flow statement.

Discontinued Operations and Extraordinary Items

Just as discontinued operations and extraordinary items are to be shown separately on the income statement, so are they to be shown separately on the cash flow statement. The cash inflow or outflow resulting from discontinued operations or from an extraordinary item should be shown as part of operating, investing, or financing activities, as is appropriate. For example, recent financial statements of Imasco Limited included a loss from discontinued operations as a reduction of cash from operating activities and proceeds from disposal as an inflow to investing activities.

Interest and Dividends as Operating Activities

You may be puzzled by the including of cash receipts of interest and dividends as operating activities. After all, these cash receipts result from investing activities. Interest comes from investment in loans, and dividends come from investments in stock. Equally puzzling is listing the payment of interest as part of operations. Interest expense results from borrowing money—a financing activity. Interest and dividends are included as operating activities because they affect the computation of net income. Interest revenue and dividend revenue increase net income, and interest expense decreases income. Therefore, cash receipts of interest and dividends

THINKING IT OVER

Is net income the amount of cash received from operations?

A: No, net income is computed by the accrual basis. Revenues are recorded when earned, and expenses when incurred. Included in accual-basis net income are some noncash expenses such as amortization. "Net cash inflow from operations" measures cash-basis net income.

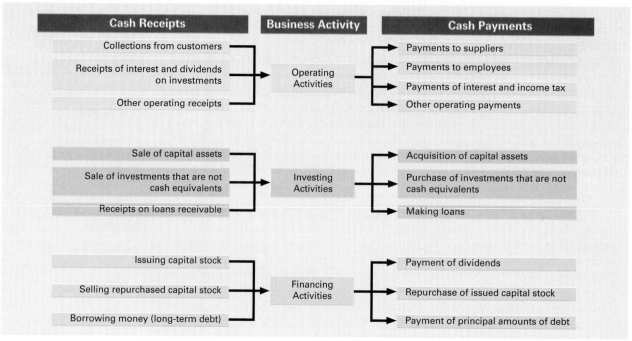

Cash Receipts	Business Activity	Cash Payments
Collections from customers	Operating Activities	Payments to suppliers
Receipts of interest and dividends on investments		Payments to employees
		Payments of interest and income tax
Other operating receipts		Other operating payments
Sale of capital assets	Investing Activities	Acquisition of capital assets
Sale of investments that are not cash equivalents		Purchase of investments that are not cash equivalents
Receipts on loans receivable		Making loans
Issuing capital stock	Financing Activities	Payment of dividends
Selling repurchased capital stock		Repurchase of issued capital stock
Borrowing money (long-term debt)		Payment of principal amounts of debt

EXHIBIT 17-4

Cash Receipts and Payments on the Cash Flow Statement

and cash payments of interest are reported as operating activities on the cash flow statement.

In contrast, note that dividend payments are reported as a financing activity. This is so because they do not enter into the computation of net income but rather are payments to the entity's shareholders, who finance the business by holding its shares.

Format of the Cash Flow Statement

KEY POINT

Under Investing Activities—Cash Payments, remember that "Making loans" means loaning money—a cash outflow.

In *CICA Handbook*, Section 1540, the Accounting Standards Board (AcSB) approved two formats for reporting cash flows from operating activities. The **direct method**, illustrated in Exhibit 17-3, lists cash receipts from specific operating activities and cash payments for each major operating activity. Section 1540 expresses a clear preference for the direct method because it reports where cash came from and how it was spent on operating activities.

In keeping with GAAP, companies' accounting systems are designed for accrual, rather than cash-basis, accounting. These systems make it easy for companies to compute cash flows from operating activities by a shortcut method. The **indirect method** starts with net income and reconciles to cash flows from operating activities. Exhibit 17-5 gives an overview of the process of converting from accrual-basis income to the cash basis for the cash flow statement.

The direct method is easier to understand, it provides better information for decision making, and the Accounting Standards Board prefers it. By learning how to compute the cash flow amounts for the direct method, you will be learning something far more important: how to determine the cash effects of business transactions. This is a critical skill for analyzing financial statements because accrual-basis accounting often hides cash effects. Then, after you have a firm foundation in cash-flow analysis, it is easier to learn the indirect method. If your instructor chooses to focus solely on the indirect method, you can study that method, which begins on page 933, with a minimum of references to earlier sections of this chapter.

The two basic ways of presenting the cash flow statement—direct and indirect—arrive at the same subtotals for operating activities, investing activities, financing activities, and the net change in cash for the period. They differ only in the manner of showing the cash flows from *operating activities*.

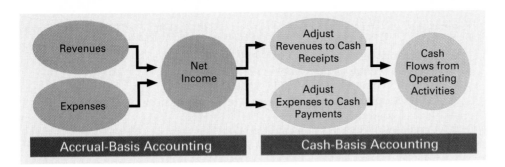

The Cash Flow Statement: The Direct Method

Let's see how to prepare the cash flow statement by the direct method illustrated in Exhibit 17-3. Suppose Anchor Ltd. has assembled the summary of 2002 transactions in Exhibit 17-6. These transactions give data for both the income statement and cash flow statement. Some transactions affect one statement, some the other. Sales, for example, are reported on the income statement, but cash collections appear on the cash flow statement. Other transactions, such as the cash receipt of dividend revenue, affect both. *The cash flow statement reports only those transactions with cash effects* (those with an asterisk in Exhibit 17-6).

To prepare the cash flow statement, follow these three steps:

1. Identify the activities that increased cash or decreased cash—those items with asterisks in Exhibit 17-6.
2. Classify each cash increase and each cash decrease as an operating activity, an investing activity, or a financing activity.
3. Identify the cash effect of each transaction.

Cash Flows from Operating Activities

Operating cash flows are listed first because they are the most important source of cash for most businesses. The failure of operations to generate the bulk of cash inflows for an extended period may signal trouble for a company. Exhibit 17-3 shows that Anchor Ltd. is sound; its operating activities were the largest source of cash, $290,000.

Cash Collections from Customers Cash sales bring in cash immediately. Credit sales bring in cash later, when cash is collected. "Collections from customers" in Exhibit 17-3 include both cash sales and collections of accounts receivable from credit sales—$271,000.

Cash Receipts of Interest Interest revenue is earned on notes receivable. The income statement reports interest revenue. As time passes, interest revenue accrues, but *cash* interest is received only on specific dates. Only the cash receipts of interest appear on the cash flow statement—$10,000 in Exhibit 17-3.

Cash Receipts of Dividends Dividends are earned on stock investments. Dividend revenue is ordinarily recorded on the income statement when cash is received. This cash receipt is reported on the cash flow statement—$9,000 in Exhibit 17-3. (Dividends *received* are part of operating activities, but dividends *paid* are a financing activity.)

EXHIBIT 17-6

Summary of Anchor Ltd.'s
2002 Transactions

Operating Activities:
1. Sales on credit, $284,000
*2. Collections of accounts receivable, $271,000
3. Interest revenue on notes receivable, $12,000
*4. Collection of interest receivable, $10,000
*5. Cash receipt of dividend revenue on investments in stock, $9,000
6. Cost of goods sold, $150,000
7. Purchases of inventory on credit, $147,000
*8. Payments to suppliers for merchandise, $113,000, and operating expenses, $20,000.
9. Salary expense, $56,000
*10. Payments of salaries, $58,000
11. Amortization expense, $18,000
12. Other operating expense, $17,000
*13. Interest expense and payments, $16,000
*14. Income tax expense and payments, $15,000

Investing Activities:
*15. Cash payments to acquire capital assets, $306,000
*16. Loan to another company, $11,000
*17. Proceeds from sale of capital assets, $62,000, including $8,000 gain.

Financing Activities:
*18. Proceeds from issuance of common shares, $101,000
*19. Proceeds from issuance of long-term note payable, $94,000
*20. Payment of long-term note payable, $11,000
*21. Declaration and payment of cash dividends, $17,000

*Indicates a cash-flow transaction to be reported on the cash flow statement.

KEY POINT

Proceeds from the issuance of stock are a *financing activity*. Payment of dividends is also considered a *financing activity*. Proceeds from and payments of short- or long-term borrowing are *financing activities*. But interest expense on these borrowings is considered an *operating activity*.

LEARNING TIP

Refer to Exhibit 17-3. Start with collections from customers, and identify the (1) *income statement account* and (2) *balance sheet account(s)* used to compute each item on the cash flow statement. Example: For collections from customers, use (1) Sales (income statement) and (2) Accounts Receivable (balance sheet). All of the other asset accounts signal *investing activities*; all of the other liability and shareholders' equity accounts signal *financing activities*.

Levi Strauss & Co.
www.levistrauss.com

McCain Foods
www.mccain.com

E.D. Smith
www.edsmith.com

Payments to Suppliers   Payments to suppliers include all cash payments for inventory and most operating expenses, but not for interest, income taxes and employee compensation expenses. *Suppliers* are entities that provide the business with its inventory and essential services. For example, a clothing store's payments to Levi Strauss & Co., Nygard International, and Stanfield are payments to suppliers. A grocery store's suppliers include McCain Foods, E.D. Smith, and Weston. Other suppliers provide advertising, utility, and other services. Payment to suppliers *excludes* payments to employees, payments for interest, and payments for income taxes because these are separate categories of operating cash payments. In Exhibit 17-3, Anchor Ltd.'s payments to suppliers are $133,000 ($113,000 + $20,000).

Payments to Employees   Salaries, wages, commissions, and other forms of employee compensation require payments to employees. Accrued amounts are excluded because they have not yet been paid. The income statement reports the expense, including accrued amounts. The cash flow statement in Exhibit 17-3 reports only the cash payments ($58,000).

Payments for Interest Expense and Income Tax Expense   These cash payments are reported separately from the other expenses. In the Anchor Ltd. example, interest and income tax expenses equal the cash payments. Therefore, the same amount appears on the income statement and the cash flow statement. In practice, this is rarely the case. Year-end accruals and other transactions usually cause the expense and cash payment amounts to differ. The cash flow statement reports the cash payments for interest ($16,000) and income tax ($15,000).

Amortization Expense   This expense is not listed on the cash flow statement in Exhibit 17-3 because it does not affect cash. Amortization is recorded by debiting the expense and crediting Accumulated Amortization. There is no debit or credit to the Cash account.

Cash Flows from Investing Activities

Investing activities are important because a company's investments determine its future. Purchases of capital assets signal expansion, which is usually a good sign about the company. Low levels of investing activities over a lengthy period mean the business is not replenishing its capital assets. Knowing these cash flows helps investors and creditors evaluate the direction that managers are charting for the business.

Cash Payments for Capital Assets, Investments, and Loans to Other Companies

All of these cash payments acquire a long-term asset. The first investing activity reported by Anchor Ltd. on its cash flow statement is the purchase of capital assets, such as land, buildings, and equipment ($306,000), shown in Exhibit 17-3. The second transaction is an $11,000 loan; Anchor Ltd. obtains a note receivable. These are investing activities because the company is investing in assets for business use rather than for resale. These transactions have no direct effect on revenues or expenses and thus are not reported on the income statement. Another transaction in this category—not shown in Exhibit 17-3—is a purchase of a stock or bond investment.

Proceeds from the Sale of Capital Assets, Investments, and the Collections of Loans

These transactions are the opposite of acquisitions of capital assets and investments, and making loans. They are cash receipts from investment transactions.

The sale of the capital assets needs explanation. The cash flow statement reports that Anchor Ltd. received $62,000 cash on the sale of capital assets. The income statement shows an $8,000 gain on this transaction. What is the appropriate amount to show on the cash flow statement? It is $62,000, the cash proceeds from the sale. If we assume Anchor Ltd. sold equipment that cost $64,000 and had accumulated amortization of $10,000, the following journal entry would record the sale:

Cash...	62,000	
Accumulated Amortization	10,000	
Equipment		64,000
Gain on Sale of Capital Assets		
(from income statement)...		8,000

The analysis indicates that the book value of the equipment was $54,000 ($64,000 – $10,000). However, the book value of the asset sold is not reported on the cash flow statement. Only the cash proceeds of $62,000 are reported on the cash flow statement. For the income statement, only the gain is reported.

Because a gain occurred, you may wonder why this cash receipt is not reported as part of operations. Operations consist of buying and selling merchandise or rendering services to earn revenue. Investing activities are the acquisition and disposition of assets used in operations. Therefore, the sale of capital assets and the sale of investments should be viewed as cash inflows from investing activities.

Investors and creditors are often critical of a company that sells large amounts of its capital assets. Such sales may signal an emergency need for cash and negative news. In other situations, selling capital assets may be positive news if the company is selling an unprofitable division or a useless capital asset. Whether sales of capital assets are positive news or negative news should be evaluated in light of a company's net income (or net loss), financial position, and other cash flows.

STOP & THINK

Suppose Canfor Corp. sold resort land at a $35 million gain. The land cost Canfor Corp. $9 million when it was purchased in 1980. What amount will Canfor Corp. report as an investing activity on the cash flow statement?

Answer: Cash receipt of $44 million (cost of $9 million plus the gain of $35 million).

Try this example to clarify which amount appears on the cash flow statement when an asset is sold—the book value, the gain or loss, or the proceeds from the sale: Suppose you sold equipment for $20,000 that originally cost $45,000 and had a book value of $25,000.

(1) What entry records the sale?
(2) What amount should appear on the cash flow statement?

A:

(1)

Cash	20,000	
Accum. Amort..	20,000	
Loss on sale	5,000	
Equipment		45,000

(2) The $20,000 should appear as an *investing activity*. The loss reduced net income but did not reduce cash; in fact, cash actually *increased* because of the sale.

Notice the entry to record the sale of equipment. Any time Cash is debited in a journal entry, it must appear on the cash flow statement as a cash inflow. Likewise, a credit signals an outflow. To think it through, make journal entries, but note that the entries are *not* to be posted and are merely a way to help you understand the cash effect of the transaction.

The *payment* of dividends, not the *declaration*, appears on the cash flow statement.

Cash Flows from Financing Activities

Cash flows from financing activities include several specific items. All are related to obtaining money from investors and lenders, and paying them back. Readers of the financial statements want to know how the entity obtains its financing.

Proceeds from Issuance of Stock and Debt   Issuing shares (preferred and common) and debt are two common ways to finance operations. In Exhibit 17-3, Anchor Ltd. issued common shares for cash of $101,000 and long-term notes payable for cash of $94,000.

Payment of Debt and Repurchases of the Company's Own Stock   The payment of debt decreases Cash, which is the opposite of borrowing money. Anchor Ltd. reports debt payments of $11,000. Other transactions in this category are repurchases of the company's stock.

Payment of Cash Dividends   The payment of cash dividends decreases Cash and is therefore reported as a cash payment. Anchor Ltd.'s $17,000 payment in Exhibit 17-3 is an example. A dividend in another form—such as a stock dividend—has no effect on Cash and is *not* reported on the cash flow statement.

Computerized Cash Flow Statements

Computerized accounting systems are programmed to generate the cash flow statement as easily as they do the balance sheet and the income statement. Consider the direct method for preparing the cash flow statement. The amounts for the operating

Accounting and the *e*-World

Cash Crunch May Turn CDNOW into "CDTHEN"

CDNOW, the online music retailer, is one of the top five U.S. websites, with 800,000 visitors a day and 3.7 million customers. Yet, like its e-retailer cousins, CDNOW cannot seem to convert customers into cash. Quarterly losses, due mainly to heavy spending on advertising and marketing, steadily outpaced revenue and reduced cash. According to an April 2000 study on e-retailers by *Market Guide* and *USA Today*, CDNOW had only enough cash to last until July 2001. CDNOW's auditing firm, Arthur Andersen, had just expressed "substantial doubt" about the company's survival due to the cash crunch at the company. In the spring of 2000, investors fled the cash-poor dot.com, slashing CDNOW's stock price by 80% to a mere $4 a share.

What can an ailing e-retailer do? Unlike traditional companies, the dot.coms do not issue bonds or try to get a loan from the bank since they would likely have to pay relatively high interest rates and they do not want to be forced to make cash payments for interest when cash flow is low. Instead, dot.coms issue shares to raise cash. The best hope for a dot.com like CDNOW is to merge with or be purchased by another company. After a proposed merger with Columbia House fell through, CDNOW's stockholders sold a 9.2% stake in the company to a Mexican billionaire. To keep the music going, CDNOW will need more investors like this one with a great deal of cash available for investment.

Based on: Charles Piller, "CDNOW Shares Plummet on Survival 'Doubt'; E-commerce: Accountants Cite Cash Crunch at One of Web's Most Visited Sites. Observers See Signal of Impending Shakeout," *The Los Angeles Times*, March 30, 2000, p. C1. Anonymous, "Mexican Billionaire Buys Stake in Online Music Retailer," *New York Times*, May 6, 2000, p. C3. Matt Krantz, "E-retailers Run Low on Fuel. Exclusive Analysis: Turn Profit Soon or Else," *USA Today*, April 26, 2000, p. 01B. Kara Scannell, "Deals & Deal Makers: When Your Start-Up Ends Way Down, Take Heart Online—Failed Entrepreneur Launches Web Site Aimed at Flops, Since No One Bats 1.000," *Wall Street Journal*, May 15, 2000, p. C22.

section can be obtained by drawing cash inflows and outflows from the posted accounts. For example, the cash receipts posted to Accounts Receivable provide the information for Cash Collections from Customers. All other cash flows for operating activities, financing activities, and investing activities are handled similarly.

Mid-Chapter Summary Problem
for Your Review

Acadia Corporation accounting records include the following information for the year ended June 30, 2003:

a. Salary expense, $104,000.
b. Amortization expense, $37,000.
c. Proceeds from issuance of common shares, $31,000.
d. Declaration and payment of cash dividends, $22,000.
e. Collection of interest on notes receivable, $7,000.
f. Payments of salaries, $110,000.
g. Collections from credit customers, $369,000.
h. Loan to another company, $42,000.
i. Proceeds from sale of capital assets, $18,000, including $1,000 loss.
j. Payments to suppliers, $319,000.
k. Income tax expense and payments, $16,000.
l. Credit sales, $358,000.
m. Cash sales, $92,000.
n. Interest revenue, $8,000.
o. Proceeds from issuance of short-term debt, $38,000.
p. Payments of long-term debt, $57,000.
q. Interest expense and payments, $11,000.
r. Loan collections, $51,000.
s. Proceeds from sale of investments, $22,000, including $13,000 gain.
t. Purchase of inventory on credit, $297,000.
u. Dividends received in cash, on stock investments, $3,000.
v. Cash payments to acquire capital assets, $83,000.
w. Cost of goods sold, $284,000.
x. Cash balance: July 1, 2002—$83,000
       June 30, 2003—$54,000

Note that, for simplicity, uncollectible accounts have been ignored.

Required

Prepare Acadia Corporation's income statement and cash flow statement for the year ended June 30, 2003. Follow the cash flow statement format of Exhibit 17-3 and the single-step format for the income statement (grouping all revenues together and all expenses together, as shown in Exhibit 17-7 on page 926).

Cyber Coach
Visit the Student Resources area of the *Accounting* Companion Website for extra practice with the new material in Chapter 17.
www.pearsoned.ca/horngren

Solution to Review Problem

ACADIA CORPORATION
Income Statement
For the Year Ended June 30, 2003

Item (Reference Letter)		(amounts in thousands)
	Revenues and gains:	
l., m.	Sales revenue	$450
s.	Gain on sale of investments	13
n.	Interest revenue	8
u.	Dividend revenue	3
	Total revenues and gains	$474
	Expenses and losses:	
w.	Cost of goods sold	284
a.	Salary expense	104
b.	Amortization expense	37
k.	Income tax expense	16
q.	Interest expense	11
i.	Loss on sale of capital assets	1
	Total expenses	453
	Net income	$ 21

ACADIA CORPORATION
Cash Flow Statement
For the Year Ended June 30, 2003

Item (Reference Letter)		(amounts in thousands)
	Cash flows from operating activities	
	Receipts:	
g., m.	Collections from customers	$461
e.	Interest received on notes receivable	7
u.	Dividends received on investments in stock	3
	Total cash receipts	$471
	Payments:	
j.	To suppliers	(319)
f.	To employees	(110)
q.	For interest	(11)
k.	For income tax	(16)
	Total cash payments	(456)
	Net cash inflow from operating activities	15
	Cash flows from investing activities	
v.	Acquisition of capital assets	(83)
h.	Loan to another company	(42)
s.	Proceeds from sale of investments	22
i.	Proceeds from sale of capital assets	18
r.	Collection of loans	51
	Net cash outflow from investing activities	(34)
	Cash flows from financing activities	
o.	Proceeds from issuance of short-term debt	38
c.	Proceeds from issuance of common shares	31
p.	Payments of long-term debt	(57)
d.	Dividends declared and paid	(22)
	Net cash outflow from financing activities	(10)
	Net decrease in cash	(29)
x.	Cash balance, July 1, 2002	83
x.	Cash balance, June 30, 2003	$ 54

Computing Individual Amounts for the Cash Flow Statement

OBJECTIVE 4
Compute the cash effects of a wide variety of business transactions

How do we compute the amounts for the cash flow statement? We use the income statement and *changes* in the related balance sheet accounts. For the *operating* cash-flow amounts, the adjustment process follows this basic approach:

Revenue or expense from the income statement	±	Adjustment for the change in the related balance sheet account(s)	=	Amount for the cash flow statement

This is called the T-account approach. Learning to analyze T-accounts is one of the most useful accounting skills you will acquire. It will enable you to measure the cash effects of a wide variety of transactions.

The following discussions use Anchor Ltd.'s income statement in Exhibit 17-7, comparative balance sheet in Exhibit 17-8, and cash flow statement in Exhibit 17-3. First, trace the $22,000 and $42,000 cash amounts on the balance sheet in Exhibit 17-8 to the bottom part of the cash flow statement in Exhibit 17-3. You see that the beginning and ending cash amounts come from the balance sheets. Now let's compute the cash flows from operating activities.

Computing the Cash Amounts of Operating Activities

Cash Collections from Customers   Collections can be computed by converting sales revenue (an accrual-basis amount) to the cash basis. Anchor Ltd.'s income statement (Exhibit 17-7) reports sales of $284,000. Exhibit 17-8 shows that Accounts Receivable increased from $80,000 at the beginning of the year to $93,000 at year end, a $13,000 increase. Based on those amounts, Cash Collections equals $271,000, as shown in the Accounts Receivable T-account:

Accounts Receivable

Beginning balance	80,000		
Sales	284,000	Collections	271,000
Ending balance	93,000		

Another explanation: Accounts Receivable increased by $13,000, so Anchor Ltd. must have received $13,000 less cash than sales revenue for the period.

The following equation shows another way to compute cash collections from customers:

Accounts Receivable

Beginning balance	+	Sales	−	Collections	=	Ending balance
$80,000	+	$284,000	−	X	=	$93,000
				$-X$	=	$93,000 - $80,000 - $284,000
				X	=	$271,000

A decrease in Accounts Receivable would mean that the company received more cash than the amount of sales revenue. This computation is summarized as the first item in Exhibit 17-9.

All collections of receivables are computed in the same way. In our example, Anchor Ltd.'s income statement, Exhibit 17-7, reports interest revenue of $12,000. Interest Receivable's balance in Exhibit 17-8 increased $2,000. Cash receipts of interest must be $10,000 (Interest Revenue of $12,000 minus the $2,000 increase in Interest Receivable). Exhibit 17-9 summarizes this computation.

LEARNING TIP
A *decrease* in Accounts Receivable indicates that cash collections were greater than sales. The decrease is *added* to Sales. An *increase* in Accounts Receivable indicates that cash collections were less than sales. The increase is *deducted* from Sales.

LEARNING TIP
Remember that each account contains four basic elements:
   Beginning Balance
   + Increases
   – Decreases
   = Ending Balance
Apply this relationship to Accounts Receivable for Anchor Ltd. Compute collections.

Beg. A/R	$ 80,000
+ Sales	284,000
– Collections*	?
= Ending Balance	$ 93,000

*Collections = $271,000

EXHIBIT 17-7

Income Statement

ANCHOR LTD.
Income Statement
For the Year Ended December 31, 2002
(amounts in thousands)

Revenues and gains:		
Sales revenue..	$284	
Interest revenue...	12	
Dividend revenue	9	
Gain on sale of capital assets................................	8	
Total revenues and gains		$313
Expenses:		
Cost of goods sold	$150	
Salary expense..	56	
Amortization expense	18	
Other operating expense..	17	
Interest expense..	16	
Income tax expense..	15	
Total expenses		272
Net income...		$ 41

Payments to Suppliers This computation includes two parts, payments for inventory related to Cost of Goods Sold and payments for operating expenses.

Payments for inventory are computed by converting cost of goods sold to the cash basis. We must analyze the Inventory and Accounts Payable accounts. To "analyze" an account means to explain each amount in the account. For companies that purchase inventory on short-term notes payable, we must also analyze Short-Term Notes Payable in the same manner as Accounts Payable. The computation of Anchor Ltd.'s cash payments for inventory is given by this analysis of the T-accounts (again, we are using Exhibits 17-7 and 17-8 for our numbers):

LEARNING TIP

An *increase* in Inventory indicates more inventory has been purchased than sold. An *increase* in inventory is *added* to COGS. A *decrease* in Inventory indicates that purchases are less than COGS. A *decrease* in inventory is deducted from COGS. A *decrease* in Accounts Payable indicates that payments for inventory were greater than purchases. The decrease is *added* to COGS. An *increase* in Accounts Payable indicates that payments for inventory were less than purchases. The increase is *deducted* from COGS.

Inventory

Beg. inventory	138,000	Cost of goods sold	150,000
Purchases	147,000		
End. inventory	135,000		

Accounts Payable

Payments for inventory	113,000	Beg. bal.	57,000
		Purchases	147,000
		End. bal.	91,000

The first equation details the activity in the Inventory account to compute Purchases, as follows:

Inventory

Beginning inventory	+	Purchases	−	Cost of goods sold	=	Ending inventory
$138,000	+	X	−	$150,000	=	$135,000
		X			=	$135,000 − $138,000 + $150,000
		X			=	$147,000

Now we can insert the purchases figure into Accounts Payable to compute the amount of cash paid for inventory, as follows:

Accounts Payable

Beginning balance	+	Purchases	−	Payments for inventory	=	Ending balance
$57,000	+	$147,000	−	X	=	$91,000
				−X	=	$91,000 − $57,000 − $147,000
				X	=	$113,000

ANCHOR LTD.
Comparative Balance Sheet
December 31, 2002 and 2001
(amounts in thousands)

Assets	2002	2001	Increase (Decrease)	
Current				
Cash	$ 22	$ 42	$(20)	
Accounts receivable	93	80	13	⎫
Interest receivable	3	1	2	⎬ Changes in current
Inventory	135	138	(3)	⎭ assets—**Operating**
Prepaid expenses	8	7	1	
Long-term receivable from another company	11	—	11	⎫ Changes in non-current
Capital assets, net of amortization	453	219	234	⎬ assets—**Investing**
Total	$725	$487	$238	
Liabilities				Changes in current
Current				liabilities—**Operating**
Accounts payable	$ 91	$ 57	$ 34	⎫ and change in current
Salary payable	4	6	(2)	⎬ portion of long-term
Accrued liabilities	1	3	(2)	⎭ debt—**Financing**
Long-term debt	160	77	83	⎫ Changes in most long-
				⎬ term liabilities and
Shareholders' Equity				⎭ capital stock—**Financing**
Common stock	359	258	101	
Retained earnings	110	86	24	⎫ Change due to net
Total	$725	$487	$238	income—**Operating** and change due to dividends—**Financing**

EXHIBIT 17-8

Comparative Balance Sheet

Beginning and ending inventory amounts come from the balance sheet, and Cost of Goods Sold from the income statement. Exhibit 17–9 shows the general approach to compute Payments to suppliers of inventory (fourth item).

By another explanation, payments for inventory appear in the Accounts Payable account. But we must first work through the Inventory account, as summarized in Exhibit 17-9 under Payments to suppliers of inventory.

LEARNING TIP

The COGS calculation requires two adjustments. The adjustments for inventory gives the amount of purchases; the adjustment for accounts payable gives the payments for inventory.

Payments for Operating Expenses Payments for operating expenses other than interest and income tax can be computed as "plug figures," or differences, by analyzing Prepaid Expenses and Accrued Liabilities, as follows for Anchor Ltd. (again, all numbers are taken from Exhibits 17-7 and 17-8):

Prepaid Expenses		Accrued Liabilities		Operating Expenses (other than Salaries, Wages, and Amortization)
Beg. bal. 7,000	Expiration of prepaid expense 7,000	Payments 3,000	Beg. bal. 3,000	Accrual of expense at year end 1,000
Payments 8,000			Accrual of expense at year end 1,000	Expiration of prepaid expense 7,000
End. bal. 8,000			End. bal. 1,000	Payments 9,000
				End. bal. 17,000

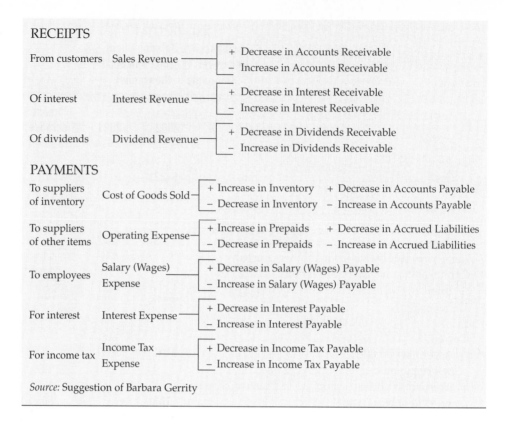

RECEIPTS

From customers   Sales Revenue   + Decrease in Accounts Receivable
                                 − Increase in Accounts Receivable

Of interest   Interest Revenue   + Decrease in Interest Receivable
                                 − Increase in Interest Receivable

Of dividends   Dividend Revenue   + Decrease in Dividends Receivable
                                  − Increase in Dividends Receivable

PAYMENTS

To suppliers of inventory   Cost of Goods Sold   + Increase in Inventory   + Decrease in Accounts Payable
                                                 − Decrease in Inventory   − Increase in Accounts Payable

To suppliers of other items   Operating Expense   + Increase in Prepaids   + Decrease in Accrued Liabilities
                                                  − Decrease in Prepaids   − Increase in Accrued Liabilities

To employees   Salary (Wages) Expense   + Decrease in Salary (Wages) Payable
                                        − Increase in Salary (Wages) Payable

For interest   Interest Expense   + Decrease in Interest Payable
                                  − Increase in Interest Payable

For income tax   Income Tax Expense   + Decrease in Income Tax Payable
                                      − Increase in Income Tax Payable

Source: Suggestion of Barbara Gerrity

WORKING IT OUT

The information listed below is taken from the financial statements of Vista Corp. for the current year:

Sales		$720
COGS	380	
Salary exp.	100	
Interest exp.	25	
Income tax exp.	15	520
Net income		$200

	Dec. 31	Jan. 1
Cash	$60	$20
Acc. rec.	16	24
Inventory	88	64
Acc. pay.	27	12
Wages pay.	32	52

Q: Compute cash flow from operating activities using the direct method.

A:

Collections from customers ($720 + $8)	$728
Payments for inventory ($380 + $24 − $15)	389
Payments to employees ($100 + $20)	120
Payments for interest	25
Payments for taxes	15	549
Cash inflow from operating activities	$179

LEARNING **TIP**

The three formulas in Exhibit 17-9 for converting accrual revenue to cash receipts are similar—*add a decrease* in the receivable; *deduct an increase* in the receivable. In computing cash payments, increases and decreases to the *payables* are treated the same as the increases and decreases in the *receivables*—*add a decrease* in the payable; *deduct an increase* in the payable. However, increases and decreases in prepaids and inventory are treated differently— *add an increase* in a prepaid or inventory; *deduct a decrease* in a prepaid or inventory.

Prepaid Expenses

Beginning balance	+	Payments	−	Expiration of prepaid expense	=	Ending balance
$7,000	+	X	−	$7,000	=	$8,000
		X			=	$8,000 − $7,000 + $7,000
		X			=	$8,000

Accrued Liabilities

Beginning balance	+	Accrual of expense at year end	−	Payments	=	Ending balance
$3,000	+	$1,000	−	X	=	$1,000
				−X	=	$1,000 − $3,000 − $1,000
				X	=	$3,000

Operating Expenses

Accrual of expense at year end	+	Expiration of prepaid expense	+	Payments	=	Ending balance
$1,000	+	7,000	+	X	=	$17,000
				X	=	$17,000 − $1,000 − $7,000
				X	=	$9,000

Total payments for operating expenses = $20,000
$8,000 + $3,000 + $9,000   = $20,000

Another explanation: Increases in prepaid expenses require cash payments, and decreases indicate that payments were less than expenses. For example, the only way for Prepaid Rent to increase is by paying the rent. Decreases in accrued liabilities can occur only from cash payments, and increases mean that cash was *not* paid. Exhibit 17-9 shows a streamlined version of this computation.

Payments to Employees   Companies keep separate accounts for salaries, wages, and other forms of employee compensation. It is convenient to combine all compensation amounts into one account. Anchor Ltd.'s calculation adjusts Salary Expense for the change in Salary Payable, as shown in the following T-account:

Salary and Wages Payable

		Beginning balance	6,000
Payments to employees	58,000	Salary expense	56,000
		Ending balance	4,000

Salary Payable

Beginning balance	+	Salary expense	−	Payments	=	Ending balance
$6,000	+	$56,000	−	X	=	$4,000
				−X	=	$4,000 − $6,000 − $56,000
				X	=	$58,000

Exhibit 17-9 summarizes this computation under Payments to Employees.

Payments of Interest and Income Tax   In our example, the expense and payment amount is the same for interest and income tax. Therefore, no analysis is required to determine the payment amount. However, if the expense and the payment differ, the payment can be computed by analyzing the related liability or prepayment account. The payment computation follows the pattern illustrated for payments to employees; Exhibit 17-9 summarizes the procedure for interest and income tax.

Computing the Cash Amounts of Investing Activities

Investing activities affect asset accounts, such as Capital Assets, Investments, and Notes Receivable. Cash flows from investing activities can be computed by analyzing these accounts. The income statement and beginning and ending balance sheets provide the data.

Acquisitions and Sales of Capital Assets   Companies keep separate accounts for Land, Buildings, Equipment, and other capital assets. It is helpful to combine these accounts into a single summary for computing the cash flows from acquisitions and sales of these assets. Also, we subtract accumulated amortization from the assets' cost and work with a net figure for capital assets. This approach allows us to work with a single total for capital assets.

To illustrate, observe that Anchor Ltd.'s balance sheet (Exhibit 17-8) reports beginning capital assets, net of amortization, of $219,000 and an ending net amount of $453,000. The income statement Exhibit 17-7 shows amortization of $18,000 and an $8,000 gain on sale of capital assets. Further, the acquisitions total is $306,000 (see Exhibit 17-3). How much are the proceeds from the sale of capital assets? First, we must compute the book value of capital assets sold as follows:

Capital Assets (net)

Beginning balance (net)	219,000	Amortization	18,000
Acquisitions	306,000	Book value of assets sold	54,000
Ending balance (net)	453,000		

LEARNING TIP

Increases and decreases in other payables (Salary Payable, Interest Payable, and Income Tax Payable) are treated in the same way as increases and decreases in Accounts Payable and Accrued Liabilities. A *decrease* in the payable indicates that payments for salaries/interest/income taxes were greater than the expense. The decrease is *added* to the expense. An *increase* in the payable indicates that payments for salaries/interest/income taxes were less than the expense. The increase is *deducted* from the expense.

KEY POINT

Changes in asset accounts, other than those used to compute cash flow from operating activities, are investing activities. An increase in an asset represents a cash outflow; a decrease in an asset represents a cash inflow.

KEY POINT

Proceeds from the sale of an asset need not equal the asset's book value. Remember:
Book value + Gain = Proceeds
Book value − Loss = Proceeds
The book value information comes from the balance sheet, the gain or loss from the income statement.

Capital Assets, Net

Beginning balance	+ Acquisitions	− Amortization	− Book value of assets sold	= Ending balance
$219,000	+ $306,000	− $18,000	− X	= $453,000
			− X	= $453,000 − $219,000 − $306,000 + $18,000
			X	= $54,000

Now we can compute the proceeds from the sale of capital assets as follows:

$$\begin{aligned} \text{Sale proceeds} &= \text{Book value of assets sold} + \text{Gain} - \text{Loss} \\ &= \$54,000 \qquad\qquad\qquad\quad + \$8,000 \;-\; \$0 \\ &= \$62,000 \end{aligned}$$

Trace the sale proceeds of $62,000 to the cash flow statement in Exhibit 17-3. If the sale had resulted in a loss of $3,000, the sale proceeds would be $51,000 ($54,000 − $3,000), and the cash flow statement would report $51,000 as a cash receipt from this investing activity.

Acquisitions and Sales of Investments, and Loans and Loan Collections   The cash amounts of investment and loan transactions can be computed in the manner illustrated for capital assets. Investments are easier to analyze, because there is no amortization to account for, as shown by the following T-account:

Investments

Beginning balance*	XXX		
Purchases**	XXX	Cost of investments sold	XXX
Ending balance*	XXX		

*From the balance sheet.
**From the accounting records, used to create the cash flow statement.

Investments (amounts assumed for illustration only)

Beginning balance	+ Purchases	− Cost of investments sold	= Ending balance
$100,000	+ $50,000	− X	= $140,000
		− X	= $140,000 − $100,000 − $50,000
		X	= $10,000

Loan transactions follow the pattern described on page 925 for collections from customers. New loans increase the receivable and decrease cash. Collections decrease the receivable and increase cash, as follows:

Loans and Notes Receivable

Beginning balance*	XXX		
New loans made**	XXX	Collections	XXX
Ending balance*	XXX		

*From the balance sheet.
**From the accounting records, used to create the cash flow statement.

Loans and Notes Receivable (amounts assumed for illustration only)

Beginning balance	+ New loans made	− Collections	= Ending balance
$90,000	+ $10,000	− X	= $30,000
		− X	= $30,000 − $90,000 − $10,000
		X	= $70,000

WORKING IT OUT

Greene Corp. reported the following:

Retirement of preferred stock	$45
Sale of bonds issued by Blue Ltd.	112
Payment of interest on mortgage note	11
Purchase of land	158
Payment of income taxes	38
Sale of common stock	105
Collection of note receivable	63
Payment of dividends	150

What is Greene Corp.'s net change in cash from investing activities?

A:
$112 − $158 + $63 = $17, a net increase. Categorize the other items.
Operating: Payment of interest, payment of taxes.
Financing: Retirement of preferred stock, sale of stock, payment of dividends.

KEY POINT

When an asset is sold, the asset account is decreased by the asset's original cost, not its selling price.

Computing the Cash Amounts of Financing Activities

Financing activities affect the liability and shareholders' equity accounts, such as Notes Payable, Bonds Payable, Long-Term Debt, Common Stock, and Retained Earnings. To compute the cash flow amounts, analyze these accounts.

Issuances and Payments of Long-Term Debt Notes Payable, Bonds Payable and Long-Term Debt accounts are related to borrowing, a financing activity. Their balances come from the balance sheet. If either the amount of new issuances or the amount of the payments is known, the other amount can be computed. New debt issuances total $94,000 (see Exhibit 17-3). Debt payments are computed from the Long-Term Debt T-account, using amounts from Anchor Ltd.'s balance sheet, Exhibit 17-8:

Long-Term Debt

		Beginning balance	77,000
Payments	11,000	Issuance of new debt	94,000
		Ending balance	160,000

Long-Term Notes Payable

Beginning balance	+	Issuance of new debt	−	Payments of debt	=	Ending balance
$77,000	+	$94,000	−	X	=	$160,000
				$-X$	=	$160,000 - $77,000 - $94,000
				X	=	$11,000

Issuances and Repurchases of Stock These financing activities are computed from the various stock accounts. It is convenient to work with a single summary account for stock. Using data from Exhibits 17-3 and 17-8, we have:

Common Stock

		Beginning balance	258,000
Retirements of shares	0	Issuance of new shares	101,000
		Ending balance	359,000

Common Stock

Beginning balance	+	Issuance of new shares	−	Retirements of shares	=	Ending balance
$258,000	+	$101,000	−	X	=	$359,000
				$-X$	=	$359,000 - $258,000 - $101,000
				X	=	0

Dividend Payments If the amount of the dividends is not given elsewhere (for example, in a statement of retained earnings), it can be computed as follows:

Retained Earnings

		Beginning balance	86,000
Dividend declaration	17,000	Net income	41,000
		Ending balance	110,000

Dividends Payable

		Beginning balance (assumed)	0
Dividend payments	17,000	Dividend declarations	17,000
		Ending balance (assumed)	0

KEY POINT

Changes in liability and shareholders' equity accounts, other than those used to compute cash flow from operating activities, are financing activities.

THINKING IT OVER

How are you able to tell, by referring to the balance sheet, if the amount of dividends paid is different from the dividends declared?

A: If there is not a Dividend Payable account (or no change in the Dividend Payable account), then the dividends declared are equal to the dividends paid.

First, we must compute dividend declarations by analyzing Retained Earnings. Then we can solve for dividend payments with the Dividends Payable account. Anchor Ltd. has no Dividends Payable account, so dividend payments are the same as declarations. The following computations show how to compute Anchor Ltd.'s dividend payments.

Retained Earnings

Beginning balance	+	Net income	–	Dividend declarations	=	Ending balance
$86,000	+	$41,000	–	X	=	$110,000
				$-X$	=	$110,000 – $86,000 – $41,000
				X	=	$17,000

Dividends Payable

Beginning balance	+	Dividend declarations	–	Dividend payments	=	Ending balance
$0	+	$17,000	–	X	=	$0
				$-X$	=	$0 – $17,000 – $0
				X	=	$17,000

Noncash Investing and Financing Activities

Companies make investments that do not require cash. For example, they may issue a note payable to buy land, or they may pay off a loan by issuing shares. Our examples thus far included none of these transactions.

Suppose Anchor Ltd. issued common shares with a stated value of $320,000 to acquire a warehouse. Anchor Ltd. would make this journal entry:

Warehouse	320,000	
Common Stock		320,000

Since this transaction has no net effect on the cash flow statement, Paragraph 1540.46 of the *CICA Handbook* requires that noncash investing and financing activities be disclosed elsewhere in the financial statements in a way that provides all the relevant information about these investing and financing activities. This can be done in a note to the financial statements or, as illustrated in Exhibit 17-10, in a schedule that accompanies the cash flow statement.

When there is a cash component to a transaction, it is appropriate to show only the net effect of the transaction on the cash flow statement. For example, if the purchase of the building had been for common stock of $300,000 and for cash of $20,000, it would be appropriate to show only the net effect on cash of $20,000 and the other components of the transaction in the notes or in an accompanying schedule.

EXHIBIT 17-10

Noncash Investing and Financing Activities (All Amounts Assumed for Illustration Only)

Noncash investing and financing activities	Thousands
Acquisition of building by issuing common shares	$320
Acquisition of land by issuing note payable	72
Payment of long-term debt by transferring investments to the creditor	104
Acquisition of equipment by issuing short-term note payable	37
Total noncash investing and financing activities	$533

Reconciling Net Income to Net Cash Flow from Operating Activities

LEARNING TIP

The cash flow statement reports the changes in all noncash accounts. To make sure that all changes have been accounted for, place a check mark by each account on the balance sheet after you have used it in preparing the statement. If a check mark is missing, further investigation may be required.

A company that formats operating activities by the direct method may wish to report a reconciliation from net income to net cash inflow (or outflow) from operating activities. The reconciliation shows how the company's net income is related to net cash flow from operating activities. Exhibit 17-11 shows the reconciliation for Anchor Ltd.

The end result—net cash inflow from operating activities of $68,000—is the same as the result we derived earlier under the *direct* method (see Exhibit 17-3). The reconciliation is also the same as the *indirect* method of computing operating cash flows. We now turn to the indirect method.

The Cash Flow Statement: The Indirect Method

OBJECTIVE 5
Prepare a cash flow statement by the indirect method

An alternative to the direct method of computing cash flows from *operating* activities is the *indirect method*, or the **reconciliation method**, as we just saw in Exhibit 17-11. This method starts with net income from the income statement and reconciles to operating cash flows. For example, the operating activities section from a recent consolidated statement of cash flows of CCL Industries Inc., one of Canada's leading packagers of consumer goods, follows:

	(in thousands)
Net earnings	$ 53,630
Items not requiring cash:	
Depreciation and amortization	84,210
Deferred income taxes	10,064
Net change in non-cash working capital	(23,199)
Cash provided by operating activities	$124,705

CCL Industries Inc.
www.cclind.com

ANCHOR LTD.
Reconciliation of Net Income to Net Cash Inflow from
Operating Activities
For the Year Ended December 31, 2002
(In thousands)

Net income		$41
Add (subtract) items that affect net income and cash flow differently:		
Amortization	$ 18	
Gain on sale of capital assets	(8)	
Increase in accounts receivable	(13)	
Increase in interest receivable	(2)	
Decrease in inventory	3	
Increase in prepaid expenses	(1)	
Increase in accounts payable	34	
Decrease in salary payable	(2)	
Decrease in accrued liabilities	(2)	27
Net cash inflow from operating activities		$68

EXHIBIT 17-11

Reconciliation of Net Income to Net Cash Inflow from Operating Activities

The indirect method shows the link between net income and cash flow from operations better than the direct method. Many companies use the indirect method for that reason. The main drawback of the indirect method is that it does not report the detailed operating cash flows—collections from customers and other cash receipts, payments to suppliers, payments to employees, and payments for interest and taxes.

These two methods (direct and indirect) of preparing the cash flow statement affect only the operating activities section of the statement. No difference exists for investing activities or financing activities.

Exhibit 17-12 is Anchor Ltd.'s cash flow statement prepared by the indirect method. Only the operating section of the statement differs from the direct-method format in Exhibit 17-3. The new items Ⓐ, Ⓑ, and Ⓒ are keyed to their explanations, which are discussed on pages 936–937. For ease of reference, we repeat Anchor Ltd.'s income statement and balance sheet here as Exhibits 17-13 and 17-14.

Logic Behind the Indirect Method

The indirect-method cash flow statement begins with net income, from the income statement. Additions and subtractions follow. These are labelled "Add (subtract) items that affect net income and cash flow differently." We discuss these items in the following sections. Refer to Exhibit 17-12.

EXHIBIT 17-12

Cash Flow Statement (Indirect Method for Operating Activities)

ANCHOR LTD.
Cash Flow Statement
For the Year Ended December 31, 2002

	(In thousands)	
Cash flows from operating activities		
Net income...		$ 41
Add (subtract) items that affect		
net income and cash flow differently:		
Ⓐ Amortization	$ 18	
Ⓑ Gain on sale of capital assets...........................	(8)	
Increase in accounts receivable.......................	(13)	
Increase in interest receivable	(2)	
Ⓒ Decrease in inventory......................................	3	
Increase in prepaid expenses	(1)	
Increase in accounts payable............................	34	
Decrease in salary payable	(2)	
Decrease in accrued liabilities.........................	(2)	27
Net cash inflow from operating activities...............		68
Cash flows from investing activities		
Acquisition of capital assets..............................	$(306)	
Loan to another company.................................	(11)	
Proceeds from sale of capital assets	62	
Net cash outflow from investing activities		(255)
Cash flows from financing activities		
Proceeds from issuance of common shares......................	$ 101	
Proceeds from issuance of long-term debt........................	94	
Payment of long-term debt................................	(11)	
Payment of dividends	(17)	
Net cash inflow from financing activities		167
Net increase (decrease) in cash and cash equivalents.......		$ (20)
Cash and cash equivalents, January 1, 2002...........................		42
Cash and cash equivalents, December 31, 2002		$ 22

From Exhibit 17-3

EXHIBIT 17-13

Income Statement

ANCHOR LTD.
Income Statement
For the Year Ended December 31, 2002
(amounts in thousands)

Revenues and gains:		
Sales revenue	$284	
Interest revenue	12	
Dividend revenue	9	
Gain on sale of capital assets	8	
Total revenues and gains		$313
Expenses:		
Cost of goods sold	$150	
Salary expense	56	
Amortization expense	18	
Other operating expense	17	
Interest expense	16	
Income tax expense	15	
Total expenses		272
Net income		$ 41

EXHIBIT 17-14

Comparative Balance Sheet

ANCHOR LTD.
Comparative Balance Sheet
December 31, 2002 and 2001
(amounts in thousands)

Assets	2002	2001	Increase (Decrease)	
Current				
Cash	$ 22	$ 42	$(20)	
Accounts receivable	93	80	13	
Interest receivable	3	1	2	Changes in current
Inventory	135	138	(3)	assets—**Operating**
Prepaid expenses	8	7	1	
Long-term receivable from another company	11	—	11	Changes in non-current
Capital assets, net of amortization	453	219	234	assets—**Investing**
Total	$725	$487	$238	
Liabilities				
				Changes in current
Current				liabilities—**Operating**
Accounts payable	$ 91	$ 57	$ 34	and change in current
Salary payable	4	6	(2)	portion of long-term
Accrued liabilities	1	3	(2)	debt—**Financing**
Long-term debt	160	77	83	Changes in most long-term liabilities and capital stock—**Financing**
Shareholders' Equity				
Common stock	359	258	101	
Retained earnings	110	86	24	Change due to net income—**Operating**
Total	$725	$487	$238	and change due to dividends—**Financing**

Amortization Expenses[Ⓐ] These expenses are added back to net income to compute cash flow from operations. Let's see why.

Amortization is recorded as follows:

Amortization Expense..	18,000	
Accumulated Amortization		18,000

This entry neither debits nor credits Cash because amortization has no cash effect. However, amortization expense is deducted from revenues to compute income. Therefore, in going from net income to cash flows from operations, we add amortization back to net income. The addback cancels the earlier deduction.

The following example should help clarify this practice: Suppose a company had only two transactions during the period, a $1,000 cash sale and amortization expense of $300. Net income is $700 ($1,000 − $300). But cash flow from operations is $1,000. To go from net income ($700) to cash flow ($1,000), we must add back the amortization amount of $300.

> **All expenses with no cash effects are added back to net income on the cash flow statement.**
>
> **Likewise, revenues that do not provide cash are subtracted from net income.**

An example of a revenue that does not provide cash is equity-method investment revenue. We learned about equity-method investment revenue in Chapter 16, pages 871–872.

Gains and Losses on the Sale of Assets[Ⓑ] Sales of capital assets are investing activities on the cash flow statement. Recall that Anchor Ltd. sold equipment with a book value of $54,000 for $62,000, producing a gain of $8,000. The $8,000 gain is reported on the income statement and is therefore included in net income. The cash receipt from the sale is $62,000, and that is what we report on the cash flow statement. The $62,000 of cash received also includes the $8,000 gain on the sale. To avoid counting the gain twice, we need to remove the gain from income and report the cash receipt of $62,000 in the investing activities section of the cash flow statement. Starting with net income, we subtract the gain. This deduction removes the gain's earlier effect on income. The sale of capital assets is reported as a $62,000 cash receipt from an investing activity, as shown in Exhibit 17-12.

A loss on the sale of capital assets is also an adjustment to net income on the cash flow statement. A loss is *added back* to income to compute cash flow from operations. The proceeds from selling the capital assets are reported under investing activities.

Changes in the Current Asset and Current Liability Accounts[Ⓒ] Most current assets and current liabilities result from operating activities. Changes in the current accounts are reported as adjustments to net income on the cash flow statement. The following rules apply:

1. **An *increase* in a current asset other than cash is subtracted from net income to compute cash flow from operations.** Suppose a company makes a sale. Income is increased by the sale amount. However, collection of less than the full amount increases Accounts Receivable. For example, Exhibit 17-14 reports that Anchor Ltd.'s Accounts Receivable increased by $13,000 during 2002. To compute the impact of revenue on Anchor Ltd.'s cash flows, we must subtract the $13,000 increase in Accounts Receivable from net income in Exhibit 17-12. The reason is this: We have *not* collected this $13,000 in cash. The same logic applies to the other current assets. If they increase during the period, subtract the increase from net income.

WORKING IT OUT

The information listed below is taken from the financial statements of Vista Corp. for the current year when net income is $200:

	Dec. 31	Jan. 1
Cash	$60	$20
Acc. Rec.	16	24
Inventory	88	64
Acc. Pay.	27	12
Wages Pay.	32	52

Q: Compute cash flow from operating activities using the indirect method.

A:

Net income	$200
Add (subtract):	
Dec. in Acc. Rec.	8
Inc. in Inventory	(24)
Inc. in Acc. Pay.	15
Dec. in Wages Pay.	(20)
Cash flow from	
operating activities	$179

Remember this:[2]

Current asset other than Cash   Cash ↓
   (Receivables, Inventory, Supplies, etc.) ↑

2. A *decrease* in a current asset other than cash is added to net income. Suppose Anchor Ltd.'s Accounts Receivable balance decreased by $4,000 during the period. Cash receipts cause Accounts Receivable to decrease and cash to increase, so decreases in Accounts Receivable and the other current assets are *added* to net income.

Symbolically,

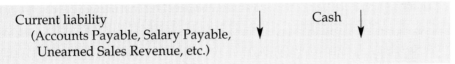

Current asset other than Cash   Cash ↑
   (Receivables, Inventory, Supplies, etc.) ↓

3. A *decrease* in a current liability is subtracted from net income. The payment of a current liability decreases both cash and the current liability, so decreases in current liabilities are subtracted from net income. For example, in Exhibit 17-12, the $2,000 decrease in Accrued Liabilities is *subtracted* from net income to compute net cash inflow from operating activities.

Current liability   Cash ↓
   (Accounts Payable, Salary Payable, ↓
    Unearned Sales Revenue, etc.)

LEARNING TIP

People often confuse the formulas for the direct and indirect method. Compare these formulas to those in Exhibit 17-9 (direct method). A change in receivables is treated the same way under both methods. But a change in payables is treated differently under the two methods.

4. An *increase* in a current liability is added to net income. Anchor Ltd.'s Accounts Payable increased during the year. This increase can occur only if cash is not spent to pay this liability, which means that cash payments are less than the related expense. As a result, we have more cash on hand. Thus, increases in current liabilities are *added* to net income.

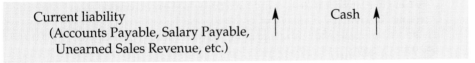

Current liability   Cash ↑
   (Accounts Payable, Salary Payable, ↑
    Unearned Sales Revenue, etc.)

KEY POINT

After you have listed all the accounts used to convert income statement items to the cash basis, notice that changes in the remaining asset accounts signal an *investing* activity. Changes in the remaining liability and shareholders' equity accounts signal *financing* activities.

    Computing net cash inflow or net cash outflow from *operating* activities by the indirect method takes a path that is very different from the direct-method computation. However, both methods arrive at the same amount of net cash flow from operating activities, as shown in Exhibits 17-3 and 17-12, both of which report a net cash inflow of $68,000.

    Exhibit 17-15 summarizes the adjustments needed to convert net income to net cash inflow (or net cash outflow) from operating activities by the indirect method.

    If you are studying *only* the indirect method for operating cash flows, please turn to pages 921–922 for coverage of investing and financing activities.

Computers and the Indirect Method of Generating the Cash Flow Statement

The computer can generate the cash flow statement by the indirect method. After the income statement is prepared, the computer picks up net income, amortization, and the other noncash expenses. Changes in the current assets and the current liabilities and the data for the investing and financing activities are obtained from the specific account balances in the general ledger.

---

[2]The authors thank Mari S. duToit for suggesting these displays.

Add (subtract)
items that affect
net income and
cash flow
differently

Net Income
+ Amortization
+ Loss on disposal or exchange of long-term asset or
  early extinguishment of debt
− Gain on disposal of long-term asset or early extinguishment
  of debt
+ Decrease in current asset other than cash
− Increase in current asset other than cash
+ Increase in current liability*
− Decrease in current liability*

Net cash inflow (or outflow) from operating activities

* Short-term notes payable for general borrowing, and current portion
of long-term debt, are related to *financing* activities, not to
operating activities.

Source: We thank Barbara Gerrity and Jean Marie Hudson for suggesting this exhibit.

STOP & THINK

Examine Anchor Ltd.'s cash flow statement, Exhibit 17-12, and answer these questions:
a. Does Anchor Ltd. appear to be growing or shrinking? How can you tell?
b. Where did most of Anchor Ltd.'s cash for expansion come from?
c. Suppose Accounts Receivable decreased by $40,000 (instead of increasing by $13,000)
   during the current year. What would Anchor Ltd.'s cash flow from operating activities be?

Answers:
a. Anchor Ltd. appears to be growing. The company acquired more capital assets
   ($306,000) than it sold during the year, and current assets changed very little.
b. Most of the cash for expansion came from issuing common stock ($101,000) and
   from borrowing ($94,000). However, cash from the balance on January 1, 2002, and
   cash from operating activities could have been used for expansion too.
c. Accounts Receivable ↓, Cash ↑
   Therefore, net cash inflow from operating activities would be $121,000 ($68,000 +
   $40,000 + $13,000).

The cash flow statement created from a computer's general ledger files is not
automatically correct from a GAAP point of view. For example, noncash investing
and financing activities of a large organization might be incorrectly combined with
the company's cash flows. The computerized system must be sophisticated enough
to distinguish among various categories of cash activities. Most important, accountants must analyze the information fed into the computer, and check that its out-
put adheres to generally accepted accounting principles.

Using Cash-Flow Information in
Investment and Credit Analysis

It is clear that cash flows are important to a company's survival. A cash shortage is
usually the most pressing problem of a struggling organization. Abundant cash allows a company to expand, invest in research and development, and hire the best
employees. How, then, do investors (and their representatives, financial analysts) and
creditors use cash-flow information for decision making?

Neither cash-flow data, net-income information, balance-sheet figures, nor the financial-statement notes tell investors all they need to know about a company. Decision making is much more complex than inserting a few numbers into a simple formula. Investors analyze a company's financial statements, articles in the financial press, data about the company's industry, and predictions about the world economy to decide whether to invest in a company's stock. To evaluate a loan request, a bank loan officer may interview a company's top managers to decide whether they are trustworthy and whether their projections for the future of the company are reasonable. Both investors and creditors are interested mainly in a company's future. They want to make predictions about a company's future net income and future cash flows.

It has been said that cash-flow data help to spot losers better than they help to spot winners. This is often true. When a company's business is booming, profits are high, and cash flows are usually improving. In almost all cases, a negative cash flow from operations warrants investigation. A cash downturn in a *single* year is not necessarily a danger signal. But negative cash flows for two *consecutive* years may lead to bankruptcy. Without cash flow from operations, a business simply cannot survive.

You may ask, "Can't the business raise money by issuing stock or by borrowing?" The answer is no, because if operations cannot generate enough cash, then shareholders will not buy the company's stock. Bankers will not lend it money. *Over the long run, if a company cannot generate cash from operations, it is doomed.*

The Decision Guidelines feature provides investors and creditors with a few suggestions on how to use cash-flow information for decision making.

DECISION GUIDELINES — Investors' and Creditors' Use of Cash-Flow and Related Information

INVESTORS

Question	Financial Statement	What to Look For
Where is most of the company's cash coming from?	Cash flow statement	Operating activities → Good sign Investing activities → Bad sign Financing activities → Neutral sign
Do high sales and profits mean the company is generating more cash?	Cash flow statement	Usually, but cash flows from *operating* activities must be the main source of cash for long-term success.
If sales and profits are low, how is the company generating cash?	Cash flow statement	If *investing* activities are generating the cash, the business may be in trouble because it is selling its long-term assets. If *financing* activities are generating the cash, that cannot go on forever. Sooner or later, creditors will demand cash flow from operating activities.
Is the cash balance large enough to provide for expansion?	Balance sheet	The cash balance should be steady (if cash is reinvested regularly) or growing over time. If not, the company may be stagnant or in trouble.

CREDITORS

Question	Financial Statement	What to Look For
Can the business pay its debts?	Income statement	Increasing net income over time.
	Cash flow statement	Cash flows from operating activities should be the main source of cash.
	Balance sheet	Current ratio, debt ratio

Summary Problem
for Your Review

Prepare the 2003 cash flow statement for Robins Corporation, using the indirect method to report cash flows from operating activities.

	December 31, 2003	December 31, 2002
Current assets		
Cash and cash equivalents	$19,000	$ 3,000
Accounts receivable	22,000	23,000
Inventories	34,000	31,000
Prepaid expenses	1,000	3,000
Current liabilities		
Notes payable (for inventory purchases)	$11,000	$ 7,000
Accounts payable	24,000	19,000
Accrued liabilities	7,000	9,000
Income and other taxes payable	10,000	10,000

Transaction data for 2003

Amortization expense	$10,000	Payment of cash dividends	$18,000
Issuance of long-term note payable to borrow cash	7,000	Net income	26,000
Issuance of common shares for cash	19,000	Purchase of long-term investment	8,000
Proceeds from sale of building	74,000	Issuance of long-term note payable to purchase patent	37,000
Repurchase of own shares	5,000		
Loss on sale of building	2,000	Issuance of common shares to retire $13,000 of bonds	13,000
Purchase of equipment	98,000		

Solution to Review Problem

ROBINS CORPORATION
Cash Flow Statement
For the Year Ended December 31, 2003

Cash flows from operating activities		
Net income		$26,000
Add (subtract) items that affect net income and cash flow differently:		
Amortization	$ 10,000	
Loss on sale of building	2,000	
Decrease in accounts receivable	1,000	
Increase in inventories	(3,000)	
Decrease in prepaid expenses	2,000	
Increase in notes payable, short-term	4,000	
Increase in accounts payable	5,000	
Decrease in accrued liabilities	(2,000)	19,000
Net cash inflow from operating activities		45,000

(Cash Flow Statement for Robins Corporation, continued)

Cash flows from investing activities

Purchase of equipment..	$(98,000)	
Sale of building..	74,000	
Purchase of long-term investment	(8,000)	
Net cash outflow from investing activities................		(32,000)

Cash flows from financing activities

Issuance of long-term note payable	$ 7,000		
Issuance of common shares..	19,000		
Payment of cash dividends	(18,000)		
Repurchase of Robins Corporation common shares	(5,000)		
Net cash inflow from financing activities.................		3,000	
Net increase in cash and cash equivalents..........................		$16,000	
Cash and cash equivalents, January 1, 2003		3,000	
Cash and cash equivalents, December 31, 2003		19,000	

Notes: 1. During the year, the company issued a long-term note payable in the amount of $37,000 in payment for a patent.
2. During the year, the company issued common shares in the amount of $13,000 to retire bonds payable in the same amount.

Summary

1. **Identify the purposes of the cash flow statement.** The *cash flow statement* reports a business's cash receipts, cash payments, and change in cash for the accounting period. It shows *why* cash increased or decreased during the period. A required financial statement, it gives a different view of the business from that given by accrual-basis statements. The cash flow statement aids prediction of future cash flows and evaluation of management decisions. Cash includes cash on hand, cash in bank, and *cash equivalents* such as liquid, short-term investments.

2. **Report cash flows from operating, investing, and financing activities.** The cash flow statement reports *operating activities, investing activities,* and *financing activities.* Operating activities create revenues and expenses in the entity's major line of business. Investing activities affect the long-term assets. Financing activities obtain from investors and creditors the cash needed to launch and sustain the business. Each section of the cash flow statement includes cash receipts and cash payments. The statement must agree with the change in cash reported on the comparative balance sheet. In addition, *noncash investing and financing activities* are reported in an accompanying schedule or in the notes to the financial statements.

3. **Prepare a cash flow statement by the direct method.** Two formats can be used to report *operating* activities— the direct method and the indirect method. The *direct method* reports collections from customers and receipts of interest and dividends minus cash payments to suppliers, payments to employees, and payments for interest and income taxes. Investing cash flows and financing cash flows are unaffected by the method used to report operating activities.

4. **Compute the cash effects of a wide variety of business transactions.** The analysis of T-accounts aids the computation of the cash effects of business transactions. The information needed comes from the balance sheet, the income statement, the statement of earnings, and the related accounts.

5. **Prepare a cash flow statement by the indirect method.** The *indirect method* starts with net income and reconciles net income to cash flow from operations. Although the Accounting Standards Board permits both the direct and the indirect method, it prefers the direct method. However, the indirect method is still more widely used.

Self-Study Questions

Test your understanding of the chapter by marking the best answer for each of the following questions:

1. The income statement and the balance sheet (p. 914)
   a. Report the cash effects of transactions
   b. Fail to report why cash changed during the period
   c. Report the sources and uses of cash during the period
   d. Are divided into operating, investing, and financing activities

2. The purpose of the cash flow statement is to (pp. 914–915)
   a. Predict future cash flows
   b. Evaluate management decisions
   c. Determine the ability to pay dividends and interest
   d. All of the above

3. A successful company's major source of cash should be (p. 916)
   a. Operating activities
   b. Investing activities
   c. Financing activities
   d. A combination of the above

4. Dividends paid to shareholders are usually reported on the cash flow statement as a (an) (p. 917)
   a. Operating activity
   b. Investing activity
   c. Financing activity
   d. Combination of the above

5. Which of the following items appears on a cash flow statement prepared by the direct method? (pp. 919–920)
   a. Amortization expense
   b. Decrease in accounts receivable
   c. Loss on sale of capital assets
   d. Cash payments to suppliers

6. In preparing a cash flow statement by the indirect method, the accountant will treat an increase in inventory as (pp. 936–937)
   a. An increase in investment cash flows
   b. A decrease in investment cash flows
   c. A decrease in operating cash flows
   d. An increase in operating cash flows

7. Net income is $17,000, and amortization is $12,000. In addition, the sale of a capital asset generated a $4,000 gain. Current assets other than cash increased by $6,000, and current liabilities increased by $8,000. What was the amount of cash flow from operations using the indirect method? (pp. 933–936)
   a. $23,000
   b. $27,000
   c. $31,000
   d. $35,000

8. Fortier Ltd. sold a long-term investment for $182,000; the selling price included a loss of $4,000. The cash flow from investing activities will show (pp. 929–930)
   a. An increase of $182,000
   b. An increase of $186,000
   c. A decrease of $182,000
   d. None of the above

9. Noncash investing and financing activities (p. 932)
   a. Are reported in the main body of the cash flow statement
   b. Are reported in a separate schedule that accompanies the cash flow statement, or in the notes
   c. Are reported on the income statement
   d. Are not reported in the financial statements

10. The work sheet approach to the preparation of the cash flow statement (Appendix, p. 972)
    a. Begins with the change in cash
    b. Ends with the change in cash
    c. Does not work as well as the T-account approach for complex situations
    d. Can only be used with the direct method of preparing the cash flow statement

Answers to the Self-Study Questions follow the Similar Accounting Terms.

Accounting Vocabulary

Cash equivalents (p. 915)
Cash flow statement (p. 914)
Cash flows (p. 914)
Direct method (p. 918)
Financing activity (p. 917)

Indirect method (p. 918)
Investing activity (p. 917)
Operating activity (p. 916)
Reconciliation method (p. 933)

Similar Accounting Terms

Cash flows	Cash receipts and cash payments
Cash flow statement	Statement of cash flows; Statement of changes in financial position

Assignment Material

Questions

1. What information does the cash flow statement report that is not shown on the balance sheet, the income statement, or the statement of retained earnings?

2. Identify four purposes of the cash flow statement.

3. Identify and briefly describe the three types of activities that are reported on the cash flow statement.

4. How is the cash flow statement dated and why?

5. What is the check figure for the cash flow statement? In other words, which figure do you check to make sure you've done your work correctly? Where is it obtained, and how is it used?

6. What is the most important source of cash for most successful companies?

7. How can cash decrease during a year when income is high? How can cash increase during a year when income is low? How can investors and creditors learn these facts about the company?

8. DeBerg Inc. prepares its cash flow statement using the *indirect* method for operating activities. Identify the section of DeBerg Inc.'s cash flow statement where each of the following transactions will appear. If the transaction does not appear on the cash flow statement, give the reason.

a. Cash	14,000	
Note Payable, Long-Term ..		14,000
b. Salary Expense	7,300	
Cash......................................		7,300
c. Cash	28,400	
Sales Revenue		28,400
d. Amortization Expense.............	6,500	
Goodwill...............................		6,500
e. Accounts Payable....................	1,400	
Cash......................................		1,400

9. Why is amortization expense *not* reported on a cash flow statement that reports operating activities by the direct method? Why and how are these expenses reported on a statement prepared by the indirect method?

10. Mainline Distributing Corp. collected cash of $92,000 from customers and $6,000 interest on notes receivable. Cash payments included $24,000 to employees, $13,000 to suppliers, $6,000 as dividends to shareholders, and $5,000 as a loan to another company. How much was Mainline Distributing Corp.'s net cash inflow from operating activities?

11. Summarize the major cash receipts and cash payments in the three categories of activities that appear on the cash flow statement prepared by the direct method.

12. Kirchner Inc. recorded salary expense of $51,000 during a year when the balance of Salary Payable decreased from $10,000 to $2,000. How much cash did Kirchner Inc. pay to employees during the year? Where on the cash flow statement should Kirchner Inc. report this item?

13. Marshall Corporation's beginning capital asset balance, net of accumulated amortization, was $193,000, and the ending amount was $176,000. Marshall Corporation recorded amortization of $37,000 and sold capital assets with a book value of $9,000. How much cash did Marshall Corporation pay to purchase capital assets during the period? Where on the cash flow statement should Marshall Corporation report this item?

14. How should issuance of a note payable to purchase land be reported in the financial statements? Identify three other transactions that fall in this same category.

15. Which format of the cash flow statement gives a clearer description of the individual cash flows

from operating activities? Which format better shows the relationship between net income and operating cash flow?

16. An investment that cost $65,000 was sold for $80,000, resulting in a $15,000 gain. Show how to report this transaction on a cash flow statement prepared by the indirect method.

17. Identify the cash effects of increases and decreases in current assets other than cash. What are the cash effects of increases and decreases in current liabilities?

18. Milano Corporation earned net income of $38,000 and had amortization expense of $22,000. Also, noncash current assets decreased by $13,000, and current liabilities decreased by $9,000. What was Milano Corporation's net cash flow from operating activities?

19. What is the difference between the direct method and the indirect method of reporting investing activities and financing activities?

20. Milgrom Corp. reports operating activities by the direct method. Does this method show the relationship between net income and cash flow from operations? If so, state how. If not, how can Milgrom Corp. satisfy this purpose of the cash flow statement?

Exercises

Exercise 17-1 *Identifying the purposes of the cash flow statement* **(Obj. 1)**

MAB Properties Ltd., a real estate developer, has experienced an unbroken string of ten years of growth in net income. Nevertheless, the business is facing bankruptcy. Creditors are calling all of MAB Properties Ltd.'s outstanding loans for immediate payment, and the cash is simply not available. In trying to explain where MAB Properties Ltd. went wrong, it becomes clear that managers placed undue emphasis on net income and gave too little attention to cash flows.

Required

Write a brief memo, in your own words, to explain for MAB Properties Ltd. managers the purposes of the cash flow statement.

Exercise 17-2 *Using a cash flow statement* **(Obj. 1)**

Suppose W.T. Grant Inc.'s cash flow statement showed a cash outflow from operations of $114,000,000.

Required

1. Suggest possible reasons for the cash outflow from operations.
2. What is the main danger signal this situation reveals?
3. Suppose W.T. Grant Inc. has two more years with the cash flows mentioned above. What is likely to happen to the company?

Exercise 17-3 *Distinguishing among operating, investing, and financing activities* **(Obj. 2)**

Describe operating activities, investing activities, and financing activities. For each category, give an example of (a) a cash receipt and (b) a cash payment.

Exercise 17-4 *Identifying activities for the cash flow statement* **(Obj. 2)**

Identify each of the following transactions as an operating activity (O), an investing activity (I), a financing activity (F), a noncash financing and investing activity (NFI), or a transaction that is not reported on the cash flow statement (N). Assume the direct method is used to report cash flows from operating activities.

_____ a. Acquisition of a building by issuance of common shares
_____ b. Accrual of salary expense
_____ c. Issuance of common shares for cash
_____ d. Payment of accounts payable
_____ e. Issuance of preferred shares for cash
_____ f. Acquisition of equipment by issuance of note payable
_____ g. Payment of long-term debt
_____ h. Purchase of long-term investment
_____ i. Payment of wages to employees
_____ j. Collection of cash interest
_____ k. Cash sale of land
_____ l. Distribution of stock dividend
_____ m. Payment of cash dividend
_____ n. Sale of long-term investment
_____ o. Amortization of equipment
_____ p. Repurchase of common stock
_____ q. Issuance of long-term note payable to borrow cash
_____ r. Amortization of bond discount
_____ s. Collection of accounts receivable

Exercise 17-5   *Classifying transactions for the cash flow statement*   *(Obj. 2)*

Indicate in which category (operating, investing, or financing), if at all, each of the following transactions would be reported on a cash flow statement prepared by the *direct* method.

a. Land...	87,700	
Cash		87,700
b. Dividends Payable	16,500	
Cash		16,500
c. Furniture and Fixtures..	22,100	
Note Payable, Short-Term		22,100
d. Salary Expense..	4,300	
Cash		4,300
e. Equipment..	18,000	
Cash		18,000
f. Cash...	7,200	
Long-Term Investment		7,200
g. Bonds Payable..	45,000	
Cash		45,000
h. Building	164,000	
Note Payable, Long-Term..		164,000
i. Cash...	1,400	
Accounts Receivable		1,400
j. Accounts Payable	8,300	
Cash		8,300
k. Cash...	81,000	
Common Stock...		81,000
l. Common Stock...	13,000	
Cash		13,000
m. Retained Earnings	36,000	
Common Stock...		36,000
n. Cash...	2,000	
Interest Revenue		2,000

Exercise 17-6   Computing cash flows from operating activities—direct method   (Obj. 3)

Analysis of the accounting records of Farmco Ltd. reveals the following:

Acquisition of land	$37,000	Net income	$21,000
Amortization	16,000	Payment of accounts	
Cash sales	29,000	payable	50,000
Collection of accounts		Payment of dividends	7,000
receivable	93,000	Payment of income tax	7,000
Collection of dividend		Payment of interest	8,000
revenue	1,000	Payment of salaries and	
Decrease in current		wages	34,000
liabilities	23,000		
Increase in current assets			
other than cash	19,000		
Loss on sale of land	8,000		

Required

Compute cash flows from operating activities by the direct method. Use the format of the operating section of Exhibit 17-3. Evaluate the operating cash flow of Farmco Ltd. Give the reason for your evaluation.

Exercise 17-7   Identifying items for the cash flow statement—direct method   (Obj. 3)

Accounts Receivable

Beginning balance	9,000	Cash receipts from customers	118,000
Sales revenue	120,000		
Ending balance	11,000		

Investments

Beginning balance	190,000	Cost of investments sold	109,000
Acquisitions	27,000		
Ending balance	108,000		

Long-Term Debt

Payments	69,000	Beginning balance	273,000
		Issuance of debt for cash	83,000
		Ending balance	287,000

Required

For each account, identify the item or items that should appear on a cash flow statement prepared by the direct method. State where to report the item.

Exercise 17-8   Preparing a cash flow statement—direct method   (Obj. 3)

Computer Animation Labs Ltd. began 2002 with cash of $28,000. During the year, the company earned service revenue of $600,000 and collected $590,000 from clients. Expenses for the year totaled $440,000, of which the company paid $410,000 in cash to employees and $15,000 in cash for supplies. Computer Animation Labs Ltd. also paid $120,000 to purchase computer equipment and a cash dividend of $30,000 to its shareholders during 2002.

Required

1. Compute net income for the year.
2. Determine the cash balance at the end of the year.

3. Prepare the company's cash flow statement for the year. Format operating activities by the direct method.

Exercise 17-9 *Preparing the cash flow statement—direct method* **(Obj. 3)**

The income statement and additional data of SR Consulting Ltd. follow:

SR CONSULTING LTD.
Income Statement
For the Year Ended September 30, 2003

Revenues		
Consulting revenue		$274,000
Expenses		
Salary expense	148,000	
Amortization expense	29,000	
Rent expense	12,000	
Insurance expense	2,000	
Interest expense	2,000	
Office supplies expense	3,000	
Income tax expense	18,000	214,000
Net income		$ 60,000

Additional data:

a. Collections from clients were $7,000 more than revenues.

b. Increase in cash balance, $10,000.

c. Payments to employees are $4,000 less than salary expense.

d. Interest expense and income tax expense equal their cash amounts.

e. Acquisition of capital assets is $116,000. Of this amount, $101,000 was paid in cash, $15,000 by signing a long-term note payable.

f. Proceeds from sale of land, $14,000.

g. Proceeds from issuance of common shares, $38,000.

h. Payment of long-term note payable, $20,000.

i. Payment of cash dividends, $15,000.

j. Payments for rent and insurance were equal to expense.

k. Payment for office supplies was $6,000 more than expense.

Prepare SR Consulting Ltd.'s cash flow statement by the direct method and accompanying schedule of noncash investing and financing activities. Evaluate SR Consulting Ltd.'s cash flow for the year. Mention all three categories of cash flows and the reason for your evaluation.

Exercise 17-10 *Computing amounts for the cash flow statement* **(Obj. 3, 4)**

Compute the following items for the cash flow statement:

a. Beginning and ending Accounts Receivable are $20,000 and $26,000, respectively. Credit sales for the period total $83,000. How much are cash collections?

b. Cost of goods sold is $82,000. Beginning Inventory balance is $28,000, and ending Inventory balance is $21,000. Beginning and ending Accounts Payable are $11,000 and $7,000, respectively. How much are cash payments for inventory?

Exercise 17-11 *Computing investing and financing amounts for the cash flow statement (Obj. 4)*

Compute the following items for the cash flow statement:

a. Beginning and ending Retained Earnings are $45,000 and $70,000 respectively. Net income for the period is $62,000, and stock dividends are $24,000. How much are cash dividend payments?

b. Beginning and ending Capital Assets, net, are $103,000 and $107,000 respectively. Amortization for the period is $18,000, and acquisitions of new capital assets are $27,000. Capital assets were sold at a $2,000 gain. What were the cash proceeds of the sale?

Exercise 17-12 *Computing cash flows from operating activities—indirect method (Obj. 5)*

The accounting records of Steitz Corporation reveal the following:

Acquisition of land	$37,000	Loss on sale of land	$ 5,000
Amortization	13,000	Net income	23,000
Cash sales	9,000	Payment of accounts	
Collection of accounts		payable	48,000
receivable	93,000	Payment of dividends	7,000
Collection of dividend		Payment of income tax	8,000
revenue	9,000	Payment of interest	16,000
Decrease in current		Payment of salaries and	
liabilities	23,000	wages	36,000
Increase in current assets			
other than cash	21,000		

Compute cash flows from operating activities by the indirect method. Use the format of the operating section of Exhibit 17-12. Then evaluate Steitz Corporation's operating cash flows as strong or weak.

Exercise 17-13 *Classifying transactions for the cash flow statement (Obj. 3, 5)*

Two transactions of Ajax Solutions Inc. are recorded as follows:

a. Cash	8,000	
Accumulated Amortization—Computer Equipment	83,000	
Computer Equipment		87,000
Gain on Sale of Computer Equipment		4,000
b. Land	290,000	
Cash		130,000
Note Payable		160,000

Required

1. Indicate where, how, and in what amount to report these transactions on the cash flow statement and accompanying schedule of noncash investing and financing activities. Are they cash inflows or outflows? Ajax Solutions Inc. reports cash flows from operating activities by the *direct* method.

2. Repeat requirement 1, assuming that Ajax Solutions Inc. reports cash flows from operating activities by the *indirect* method.

Exercise 17-14 *Preparing the cash flow statement by the indirect method (Obj. 5)*

Use the income statement of SR Consulting Ltd. in Exercise 17-9, plus these additional data during fiscal year 2003:

a. Acquisition of computer equipment was $116,000. Of this amount, $101,000 was paid in cash, $15,000 by signing a long-term note payable. SR Consulting Ltd. sold no computer equipment during fiscal year 2003.
b. Proceeds from sale of land, $14,000.
c. Proceeds from issuance of common shares, $38,000
d. Payment of long-term note payable, $20,000.
e. Payment of dividends, $15,000
f. Change in cash balance, $?
g. The comparative balance sheet:

SR CONSULTING LTD.
Comparative Balance Sheet
September 30, 2003 and 2002

	2003		2002	
Current assets				
Cash		$ 28,000		$ 18,000
Accounts receivable........................		65,000		72,000
Office supplies................................		9,000		3,000
Prepaid expenses		5,000		5,000
Total current assets		107,000		98,000
Capital assets:				
Land..		—0—		14,000
Computer Equipment	$257,000		$141,000	
Less Accumulated amortization..	(70,000)	187,000	(41,000)	100,000
Total assets		$294,000		$212,000
Current liabilities				
Accounts payable............................		$ 34,000		$ 28,000
Accrued liabilities		19,000		21,000
Total current liabilities...............		53,000		49,000
Long-term notes payable		85,000		90,000
Shareholders' equity:				
Common stock		74,000		36,000
Retained earnings		82,000		37,000
Total liabilities and shareholders' equity		$294,000		$212,000

Required

1. Prepare SR Consulting Ltd.'s cash flow statement for the year ended September 30, 2003, using the indirect method.
2. Evaluate SR Consulting Ltd.'s cash flows for the year. In your evaluation, mention all three categories of cash flows, and give the reason for your evaluation.

Exercise 17-15   *Computing cash flows from operating activities—indirect method*
                    (Obj. 5)

Sunbury Printing Ltd.'s year end is February 28. The accounting records of Sunbury Printing Ltd. at March 31, 2002, include the selected accounts shown on the next page.

Required

Compute Sunbury Printing Ltd.'s net cash inflow or outflow from operating activities during March. Use the *indirect* method. Does Sunbury Printing Ltd. have trouble collecting receivables or selling inventory? How can you tell?

Cash

Mar. 1	25,000	Dividend	8,000
Collections	42,000	Payments	46,000
Mar. 31	13,000		

Accounts Receivable

Mar. 1	18,000		
Sales	76,000	Collections	42,000
Mar. 31	52,000		

Inventory

Mar. 1	19,000		
Purchases	37,000	Cost of sales	36,000
Mar. 31	20,000		

Equipment

Mar. 1	93,000		
Mar. 31	93,000		

Accumulated Amortization—Equipment

		Mar. 1	52,000
		Amortization	6,000
		Mar. 31	58,000

Accounts Payable

		Mar. 1	14,000
Payments	32,000	Purchases	37,000
		Mar. 31	19,000

Accrued Liabilities

		Mar. 1	9,000
Payments	14,000	Expenses	11,000
		Mar. 31	6,000

Retained Earnings

Quarterly		Mar. 1	64,000
dividend	8,000	Net Income	23,000
		Mar. 31	79,000

Exercise 17-16 *Interpreting a cash flow statement—indirect method* **(Obj. 5)**

Consider three independent cases for the cash flow data of Garner Golf Products Inc.:

	Case A	Case B	Case C
Cash flows from operating activities:			
Net income	$ 30,000	$ 30,000	$ 30,000
Amortization	11,000	11,000	11,000
Increase in current assets	(1,000)	(7,000)	(19,000)
Decrease in current liabilities	–0–	(8,000)	(6,000)
	$ 40,000	$ 26,000	$ 16,000
Cash flows from investing activities:			
Acquisition of capital assets	$ (91,000)	$ (91,000)	$ (91,000)
Sales of capital assets	4,000	4,000	97,000
	$ (87,000)	$ (87,000)	$ 6,000
Cash flows from financing activities:			
New borrowing	$ 50,000	$ 104,000	$ 16,000
Payment of debt	(9,000)	(29,000)	(21,000)
	$ 41,000	$ 75,000	$ (5,000)
Net increase (decrease) in cash	$ (6,000)	$ 14,000	$ 17,000

For each case, identify from the cash flow statement how Garner Golf Products Inc. generated the cash to acquire new capital assets.

Challenge Exercise

Exercise 17-17 *Analyzing an actual company's cash flow statement* **(Obj. 1, 2, 3, 5)**

Canadian Tire Corporation, Limited's cash flow statement for the years ended January 1, 2000, and January 2, 1999, is reproduced on the next page:

CANADIAN TIRE CORPORATION, LIMITED
Consolidated Cash Flow Statement (adapted)

For the Years Ended (Dollars in thousands)	January 1 2000	January 2 1999
Cash generated from (used for):		
Operating activities		
Net earnings	**$145,929**	$ 166,980
Items not affecting cash		
Amortization of property and equipment	**106,257**	79,910
Net provision for credit charge receivables	**53,946**	56,332
Amortization of other assets	**22,085**	6,810
Loss on disposals of property and equipment	**6,068**	158
Future income tax asset (liability)	**(8,144)**	5,980
Cash generated from operations	**326,141**	316,170
Changes in other working capital components	**(2,674)**	53,278
Cash generated from operating activities	**323,467**	369,448
Investing activities		
Additions to property and equipment	**(377,349)**	(303,058)
Investment in credit charge receivables	**(206,954)**	(56,006)
Long-term receivables and other assets	**(90,927)**	(14,547)
Disposals of property and equipment	**19,457**	7,882
	(655,773)	(365,729)
Financing activities		
Issuance of long-term debt	**435,634**	435,550
Borrowing using credit charge receivables as security	**136,268**	31,858
Sale of commercial paper	**52,257**	(181,137)
Dividends	**(30,845)**	(31,299)
Class A Non-Voting Share transactions	**(29,429)**	(173,721)
Repayment of long-term debt	**(951)**	(40,000)
	562,934	41,251
Cash generated in the year	**230,628**	44,970
Cash position, beginning of year	**308,392**	263,422
Cash position, end of year	**$539,020**	$ 308,392

Required

1. Which format did Canadian Tire Corporation, Limited use for reporting cash flows from operating activities?

2. What was Canadian Tire's largest source of cash during the year ended January 1, 2000? During the year ended January 2, 1999?

3. What was Canadian Tire's largest use of cash during the year ended January 1, 2000? During the year ended January 2, 1999?

4. The operating activities section of the statement lists (in thousands of dollars) "Changes in other working capital components ($2,674). This amount includes in part:

> Accounts receivable .... ($75,908)
> Accounts payable $124,639

Did these accounts' balances increase or decrease during the year ended January 1, 2000? How can you tell?

5. During the year ended January 1, 2000, Canadian Tire sold property, plant, and equipment. Assume that the cost was $85,334,000. Journalize the sale of the property, plant, and equipment, and calculate the accumulated amortization for the assets disposed of.

6. Why are Canadian Tire's year ends shown as January 1, 2000, and January 2, 1999?

Beyond the Numbers

Beyond the Numbers 17-1 *Using cash-flow data to evaluate an investment* **(Obj. 1, 2)**

Warhale Ltd. and Altex Inc. are asking you to recommend their stock to your clients. Warhale Ltd. and Altex Inc. earn about the same net income and have similar financial positions, so your decision depends on their cash flow statements, summarized as follows:

	Warhale Ltd.		Altex Inc.	
Net cash inflows from operating activities		$90,000		$ 50,000
Net cash inflows (outflows) from investing activities:				
Purchase of capital assets	$(100,000)		$(20,000)	
Sale of capital assets	10,000	(90,000)	40,000	20,000
Net cash inflows (outflows) from financing activities:				
Issuance of common shares........		30,000		—
Issuance of long-term debt.........		—		80,000
Repayment of long-term debt....		—		(120,000)
Net increase in cash..............................		$30,000		$ 30,000

Based on their cash flows, which company looks better? Give your reasons.

Ethical Issue

Lindor Travel Ltd. is experiencing a bad year. Net income is only $40,000. Also, two important clients are falling behind in their payments to Lindor Travel Ltd., and the agency's accounts receivable are increasing dramatically. The company desperately needs a loan. The company's board of directors is considering ways to put the best face on the company's financial statements. The company's bank closely examines cash flow from operations. Gavin Shuh, a director, suggests reclassifying as long-term the receivables from the slow-paying clients. He explains to the other members of the board that removing the $30,000 rise in accounts receivable will increase net cash inflow from operations. This approach will increase the company's cash balance and may help Lindor Travel Ltd. get the loan.

Required

1. Using only the amounts given, compute net cash inflow from operations both without and with the reclassification of the receivables. Which reporting makes Lindor Travel Ltd. look better?

2. Where else in Lindor's cash flow statement will the reclassification of the receivable be reported? What cash-flow effect will this item report? What effect would the reclassification have on *overall* cash flow from all activities?

3. Under what condition would the reclassification of the receivables be ethical? Unethical?

Problems (Group A)

Problem 17-1A *Using cash-flow information to evaluate performance* *(Obj. 1)*

Top managers of Fleming Communications Corp. are reviewing company performance for 2002. The income statement reports an 18 percent increase in net income, the fifth consecutive year with an income increase above 12 percent. The income statement includes a nonrecurring loss without which net income would have increased by 20 percent. The balance sheet shows modest increases in assets, liabilities, and shareholders' equity. The assets posting the largest increases are capital assets because the company is halfway through a five-year expansion program. No other assets and no liabilities are increasing dramatically. A summarized version of the cash flow statement reports the following:

Net cash inflow from operating activities..............	$310,000
Net cash outflow from investing activities............	(285,000)
Net cash inflow from financing activities	95,000
Increase in cash during 2002.................................	$120,000

Required

Write a memo to give top managers of Fleming Communications Corp. your assessment of 2002 and your outlook for the future. Focus on the information content of the cash-flow data.

Problem 17-2A *Preparing the cash flow statement—direct method* *(Obj. 2, 3)*

Sports Products Ltd. accountants have developed the following data from the company's accounting records for the year ended July 31, 2003:

a. Salary expense, $105,300.

b. Cash payments to purchase capital assets, $172,500

c. Proceeds from issuance of short-term debt, $44,100.

d. Payments of long-term debt, $18,800.

e. Proceeds from sale of capital assets, $59,700, including $10,600 gain.

f. Interest revenue, $12,100.

g. Cash receipt of dividend revenue on stock investments, $2,700.

h. Payments to suppliers, $688,300.

i. Interest expense and payments, $37,800.

j. Cost of goods sold, $481,100.

k. Collection of interest revenue, $11,700.

l. Acquisition of equipment by issuing short-term note payable, $35,500.

m. Payment of salaries, $134,000.

n. Credit sales, $608,100.

o. Issue of long-term notes receivable, $55,000.

p. Income tax expense and payments, $56,400.

q. Amortization expense, $51,600.

r. Collections on accounts receivable, $673,100.

s. Collection of notes receivable, $74,400.

t. Proceeds from sale of investments, $34,700, including $3,800 loss.

u. Payment of long-term debt by issuing preferred shares, $150,000.

v. Cash sales, $189,000.

w. Proceeds from issuance of common shares, $114,900.

x. Payment of cash dividends, $40,000.

y. Cash balance: July 31, 2002—$75,800
   July 31, 2003—$?

Required

1. Prepare Sports Products Ltd.'s cash flow statement for the year ended July 31, 2003. Follow the format of Exhibit 17-3, but do *not* show amounts in thousands. Include a schedule of noncash investing and financing activities.

2. Evaluate 2003 in terms of cash flow. Give your reasons.

Problem 17-3A *Preparing the cash flow statement—direct method* *(Obj. 2, 3, 4)*

The 2002 comparative balance sheet and income statement of Alden Group Inc.
follow:

ALDEN GROUP INC.
Comparative Balance Sheet
December 31, 2002 and 2001

	2002	2001	Increase (Decrease)
Current assets			
Cash and cash equivalents..........................	$ 4,700	$ 15,600	$ (10,900)
Accounts receivable	41,500	43,100	(1,600)
Interest receivable	600	900	(300)
Inventories..	99,300	89,900	9,400
Prepaid expenses...	1,700	2,200	(500)
Capital assets			
Plant and equipment, net..........................	100,900	93,700	7,200
Land	40,100	10,000	30,100
Total assets..	$288,800	$255,400	$ 33,400
Current liabilities			
Accounts payable..	$ 11,400	$ 17,900	$ (6,500)
Interest payable	6,300	6,700	(400)
Salary payable...	7,100	1,400	5,700
Other accrued liabilities	18,100	18,700	(600)
Income tax payable	7,300	3,800	3,500
Long-term liabilities			
Notes payable...	45,000	65,000	(20,000)
Shareholders' equity			
Common stock..	141,100	122,300	18,800
Retained earnings...	52,500	19,600	32,900
Total liabilities and shareholders' equity	$288,800	$255,400	$ 33,400

ALDEN GROUP INC.
Income Statement
For the Year Ended December 31, 2002

Revenues:		
Sales revenue...		$438,000
Interest revenue		1,700
Total revenues		439,700
Expenses:		
Cost of goods sold	$195,200	
Salary expense	81,400	
Amortization expense...............................	15,300	
Other operating expenses	49,700	
Interest expense	24,600	
Income tax expense	16,900	
Total expenses.......................................		383,100
Net income		$ 56,600

Alden Group had no noncash investing and financing transactions during 2002.
During the year, there were no sales of land or plant and equipment, no issuances
of notes payable, and no repurchase of common shares.

Required

1. Prepare the 2002 cash flow statement, formatting operating activities by the direct method.
2. How will what you have learned in this problem help you evaluate an investment?

Problem 17-4A   *Preparing the cash flow statement—indirect method*   *(Obj. 2, 3, 5)*

Use the Alden Group Inc. data from Problem 17-3A.

Required

1. Prepare the 2002 cash flow statement by the *indirect* method. If your instructor also assigned Problem 17-3A, prepare only the operating activities section.
2. How will what you have learned in this problem help you evaluate an investment?

Problem 17-5A   *Preparing the cash flow statement—indirect method*   *(Obj. 2, 5)*

Accountants for Sweet Tooth Candy Ltd. have assembled the following data for the year ended December 31, 2003:

	December 31,	
	2003	2002
Current accounts (all result from operations)		
Current assets		
Cash and cash equivalents	$36,200	$34,800
Accounts receivable............................	68,100	73,700
Inventories	98,500	96,500
Prepaid expenses	3,200	2,100
Current liabilities		
Notes payable (for inventory purchases)	$30,300	$36,800
Accounts payable................................	72,100	67,500
Income tax payable.............................	5,900	7,800
Accrued liabilities	28,300	23,200

Transaction data for 2003:

Acquisition of building by issuing long-term note payable.........................	$132,000	Issuance of preferred shares for cash	$36,200
		Net income.............................	50,500
Acquisition of equipment......	74,000	Payment of cash dividends ...	42,800
Acquisition of long-term investment..........................	44,800	Payment of long-term debt....	47,800
		Payment of long-term debt by issuing common	
Amortization expense	20,300		
Collection of loan...................	10,300	shares	89,400
Gain on sale of investment....	3,500	Sale of long-term	
Issuance of long-term debt to borrow cash.....................	71,000	investment...........................	22,200
		Stock dividends......................	12,600

Required

Prepare Sweet Tooth Candy Ltd.'s cash flow statement, using the *indirect* method to report operating activities. Include a schedule of noncash investing and financing activities.

Problem 17-6A *Preparing the cash flow statement—indirect method* **(Obj. 2, 5)**

The comparative balance sheet of e-Tech Corp. at December 31, 2003, reported the following:

	December 31, 2003	December 31, 2002
Current assets		
Cash and cash equivalents.........................	$ 1,100	$12,500
Accounts receivable	37,100	29,300
Inventories	51,600	53,000
Prepaid expenses..	4,200	3,700
Current liabilities		
Notes payable (for inventory purchases)..	$ 9,200	$ -0-
Accounts payable	33,400	28,000
Accrued liabilities	14,300	16,800
Income tax payable	11,000	14,300

e-Tech Corp.'s transactions during 2003 included the following:

Amortization expense	$ 16,000	Net income..............................	$40,100
Cash acquisition of		Payment of cash dividends ...	17,000
building	116,000	Retirement of bonds	
Cash acquisition of		payable by issuing	
equipment	90,000	common shares....................	40,000
Issuance of common shares		Sale of long-term	
for cash	85,600	investment...........................	36,000
Issuance of long-term note		Stock dividend........................	13,000
payable to borrow cash	32,000		

Required

1. Prepare e-Tech Corp.'s cash flow statement for the year ended December 31, 2003. Use the *indirect* method to report cash flows from operating activities. Report noncash financing activities in an accompanying schedule.

2. Evaluate e-Tech Corp.'s cash flows for the year. Mention all three categories of cash flows, and give the reason for your evaluation.

Problem 17-7A *Preparing the cash flow statement—direct and indirect methods* **(Obj. 3, 5)**

To prepare the cash flow statement, accountants for Burnaby Sales Ltd. have summarized 2003 activity in two accounts as follows:

Cash

Beginning balance	87,100	Payments of operating	
Sale of common shares	60,800	expenses	46,100
Receipts of dividends	7,900	Payment of long-term debt	78,900
Sale of investments	28,400	Repurchase of common shares	10,400
Receipts of interest	2,200	Payment of income tax	6,000
Collections from customers	307,000	Payments on accounts	
		payable	101,600
		Payments of dividends	6,000
		Payments of salaries	
		and wages	67,500
		Payments of interest	21,800
		Purchase of equipment	79,900
Ending balance	75,200		

Common Stock

Repurchase of common shares	10,400	Beginning balance	103,500
		Issuance for cash	60,800
		Issuance to acquire land	75,000
		Issuance to retire long-term debt	21,100
		Ending balance	250,000

Burnaby Sales Ltd.'s 2003 income statement and selected balance sheet data follow:

BURNABY SALES LTD.
Income Statement
For the Year Ended December 31, 2003

Revenues and gains:		
Sales revenue		$317,000
Interest revenue		2,200
Dividend revenue		7,900
Gain on sale of investments		700
Total revenues and gains		327,800
Expenses:		
Cost of goods sold	$103,600	
Salary and wage expense	66,800	
Amortization expense	10,900	
Other operating expenses	44,700	
Interest expense	24,100	
Income tax expense	9,200	
Total expenses		259,300
Net income		$ 68,500

BURNABY SALES LTD.
Balance Sheet Data

	Increase (Decrease)
Current assets	
Cash and cash equivalents	$?
Accounts receivable	10,000
Inventories	5,700
Prepaid expenses	(1,900)
Loan receivable	(18,500)
Investments	(9,200)
Plant and equipment, net	69,000
Land	75,200
Current liabilities	
Accounts payable	$ 7,700
Interest payable	2,300
Salary payable	(700)
Other accrued liabilities	(3,300)
Income tax payable	3,200
Long-term debt	(100,000)
Common stock	133,600
Retained earnings	62,500

Required

1. Prepare Burnaby Sales Ltd.'s cash flow statement for the year ended December 31, 2003, using the *direct* method to report operating activities. Also prepare the accompanying statement of noncash investing and financing activities.

2. Use these data to prepare a supplementary schedule showing cash flows from operating activities by the *indirect* method. All activity in the current accounts results from operations.

Problem 17-8A *Preparing the cash flow statement—direct and indirect methods*
(Obj. 3, 4, 5)

Guildwood Inc.'s comparative balance sheet at September 30, 2002, included the following balances:

GUILDWOOD INC.
Balance Sheet
September 30, 2002 and 2001

	2002	2001	Increase (Decrease)
Current assets			
Cash	$ 48,700	$ 24,100	$24,600
Accounts receivable	41,900	41,000	900
Interest receivable	4,100	2,800	1,300
Inventories	121,700	116,900	4,800
Prepaid expenses	8,600	9,300	(700)
Long-term investments	51,100	13,800	37,300
Plant and equipment, net	131,900	104,100	27,800
Land	47,100	74,300	(27,200)
	$455,100	$386,300	$68,800
Current liabilities			
Notes payable, short-term	$ 10,000	$ -0-	$10,000
Accounts payable	61,800	70,300	(8,500)
Income tax payable	11,800	11,600	200
Accrued liabilities	17,900	29,100	(11,200)
Interest payable	4,500	3,200	1,300
Salary payable	1,500	1,100	400
Long-term note payable	123,000	131,400	(8,400)
Common stock	135,900	84,000	51,900
Retained earnings	88,700	55,600	33,100
	$455,100	$386,300	$68,800

Transaction data for the year ended September 30, 2002:

a. Net income, $87,400.

b. Amortization expense on equipment, $8,500.

c. Acquired long-term investments, $37,300.

d. Sold land for $38,100, including $10,900 gain.

e. Acquired equipment by issuing long-term note payable, $22,300 and paid $4,000 cash.

f. Paid long-term note payable, $30,700.

g. Received cash of $51,900 for issuance of common shares.

h. Paid cash dividends, $54,300.

i. Acquired equipment by issuing short-term note payable, $10,000.

Required

1. Prepare Guildwood Inc.'s cash flow statement for the year ended September 30, 2002, using the *indirect* method to report operating activities. Also prepare the accompanying schedule of noncash investing and financing activities. All current accounts, except short-term notes payable, result from operating transactions.

2. Prepare a supplementary schedule showing cash flows from operations by the *direct* method. The income statement reports the following: sales, $367,100; gain on sale of land, $10,900; interest revenue, $7,300; cost of goods sold, $161,500; salary expense, $63,400; other operating expenses, $29,600; income tax expense, $21,400; interest expense, $13,500; amortization expense, $8,500.

Problem 17-9A *Distinguishing among operating, investing, and financing activities; computing the cash effects of a wide variety of business transactions*
(Obj. 2, 5)

Indicate whether or not each of the items below would be shown on a cash flow statement (indirect method). Indicate whether the adjustment is added to, deducted from, or has no effect on the cash flow statement. If the transaction affects the cash flow statement, state whether it relates to operating activities, investing activities, or financing activities.

  a. The payment of interest on long-term debt

  b. The declaration and distribution of a common stock dividend

  c. A decrease in accounts payable

  d. The sale of office equipment for its book value

  e. The borrowing of funds for future expansion through the sale of bonds

  f. A gain on the sale of capital assets

  g. The purchase of equipment in exchange for common shares

  h. Amortization Expense—buildings

  i. A decrease in merchandise inventory

  j. An increase in prepaid expenses

  k. Amortization of the premium on bonds payable

  l. An increase in marketable securities

  m. Amortization of goodwill

Problem 17-10A *Distinguishing among operating, investing, and financing activities; using the financial statements to compute the cash effects of a wide variety of business transactions; preparing a cash flow statement by the indirect method* **(Obj. 2, 4, 5)**

The financial statements for Zoran Corp. for the year ended December 31, 2003, appear on the next page.

Additional information:

a. The Operating expenses included:
    Amortization expense on plant and equipment   = $12,000
    Amortization of goodwill   = $1,000

b. Sold equipment for its book value. The equipment cost $43,000 and had been amortized for $6,000.

c. Purchased additional equipment in December for $57,400.

d. Exchanged common shares for land valued at $40,000.

e. Declared and paid cash dividends: Preferred, $23,000; Common, $25,000.

f. Sold 5,000 common shares for $2.00 per share.

g. Paid $9,000 (of which $4,000 was interest) on the loans.

ZORAN CORP.
Balance Sheet
December 31, 2003 and 2002

	2003	2002
Assets		
Cash..	$ 1,000	$ 1,800
Marketable securities...	—0—	4,000
Accounts receivable..	18,900	17,500
Merchandise inventory	28,000	61,000
Prepaid expenses...	3,000	2,300
Plant and equipment	179,800	165,400
Less accumulated amortization	(18,000)	(12,000)
Land	40,000	—0—
Goodwill...	9,000	10,000
Total assets	$261,700	$250,000
Liabilities		
Accounts payable..	$ 17,600	$ 12,000
Salaries payable..	11,000	10,000
Loan payable...	35,000	40,000
Total liabilities..	63,600	62,000
Shareholders' equity		
Preferred shares..	50,000	50,000
Common shares...	100,000	50,000
Retained earnings...	48,100	88,000
Total shareholders' equity...................................	198,100	188,000
Total liabilities and shareholders' equity........................	$261,700	$250,000

ZORAN CORP.
Income Statement
For the Year Ended December 31, 2003

Net sales...	$160,000
Cost of goods sold	84,000
Gross margin...	76,000
Operating expenses:	
Selling expenses...	35,000
Administrative expenses..	25,000
Interest expense	4,000
Total operating expenses..	64,000
Operating income...	12,000
Income taxes...	3,900
Net income	$ 8,100

Required

1. Prepare a cash flow statement for Zoran Corp. for the year ended December 31, 2003, using the *indirect* method. Consider the marketable securities to be a cash equivalent.

2. Did the company improve its cash position in 2003? Give your reasons.

Problems (Group B)

Problem 17-1B *Using cash-flow information to evaluate performance* *(Obj. 1)*

Top managers of OnTime Delivery Ltd. are reviewing company performance for 2002. The income statement reports a 20 percent increase in net income over 2001. However, most of the increase resulted from an extraordinary gain of $20,000 on insurance proceeds covering flood damage to a warehouse. The cash proceeds were $60,000. The balance sheet shows large increases in receivables. The cash flow statement, in summarized form, reports the following:

Net cash outflow from operating activities	$(110,000)
Net cash inflow from investing activities	100,000
Net cash inflow from financing activities	50,000
Increase in cash during 2002	$ 40,000

Required

Write a memo to give OnTime Delivery Ltd. managers your assessment of 2002 operations and your outlook for the future. Focus on the information content of the cash flow data.

Problem 17-2B *Preparing the cash flow statement—direct method* *(Obj. 2, 3)*

Accounts for John's Builders' Supply Ltd. have developed the following data from the company's accounting records for the year ended April 30, 2003:

a. Credit sales, $583,900.

b. Income tax expense and payments, $37,900.

c. Cash payments to acquire capital assets, $59,400

d. Cost of goods sold, $382,600.

e. Proceeds from issuance of long-term debt, $68,000.

f. Payment of cash dividends, $48,400.

g. Collection of interest, $7,400.

h. Acquisition of equipment by issuing short-term note payable, $16,400.

i. Payment of salaries, $107,600.

j. Proceeds from sale of capital assets, $22,400, including $6,800 loss.

k. Collections on accounts receivable, $462,600.

l. Interest revenue, $3,800.

m. Cash receipt of dividend revenue on stock investments, $4,100.

n. Payments to suppliers, $368,500.

o. Cash sales, $171,900.

p. Amortization expense, $62,800.

q. Proceeds from issuance of short-term debt, $19,600.

r. Payments of long-term debt, $50,000.

s. Interest expense and payments, $13,300.

t. Salary expense, $95,300.

u. Collections of notes receivable, $2,800.

v. Proceeds from sale of investments, $9,100, including $2,000 gain.

w. Payment of short-term note payable by issuing long-term note payable, $63,000.

x. Cash balance: May 1, 2002—$79,300
April 30, 2003—$?

Required

1. Prepare John's Builders' Supply Ltd.'s cash flow statement for the year ended April 30, 2003. Follow the format of Exhibit 17-3, but do *not* show amounts in thousands. Include a schedule of noncash investing and financing activities.

2. Evaluate 2003 from a cash-flow standpoint. Give your reasons.

Problem 17-3B *Preparing the cash flow statement—direct method* *(Obj. 2, 3, 4)*

The 2003 comparative balance sheet and income statement of Armitage and Atkinson Ltd. follow:

ARMITAGE AND ATKINSON LTD.
Comparative Balance Sheet
December 31, 2003 and 2002

	2003	2002	Increase (Decrease)
Current assets			
Cash and cash equivalents............................	$ 7,200	$ 6,300	$ 900
Accounts receivable	31,600	26,900	4,700
Interest receivable...	1,900	700	1,200
Inventories...	53,600	57,200	(3,600)
Prepaid expenses...	2,500	1,900	600
Capital assets			
Plant and equipment, net.............................	56,500	49,400	7,100
Land	83,000	54,000	29,000
Total assets...	$236,300	$196,400	$39,900
Current liabilities			
Accounts payable..	$ 31,400	$ 28,800	$ 2,600
Interest payable	4,400	4,900	(500)
Salary payable...	3,100	6,600	(3,500)
Other accrued liabilities	13,700	16,000	(2,300)
Income tax payable	8,900	7,700	1,200
Long-term liabilities			
Notes payable	75,000	95,000	(20,000)
Shareholders' equity			
Common stock	58,300	34,700	23,600
Retained earnings...	41,500	2,700	38,800
Total liabilities and shareholders' equity	$236,300	$196,400	$39,900

ARMITAGE AND ATKINSON LTD.
Income Statement
For the Year Ended December 31, 2003

Revenues:		
Sales revenue..		$257,000
Interest revenue		8,600
Total revenues...		265,600
Expenses:		
Cost of goods sold	$76,600	
Salary expense...	27,800	
Amortization expense..................................	4,000	
Other operating expenses............................	10,500	
Interest expense	11,600	
Income tax expense	27,800	
Total expenses...		158,300
Net income..		$107,300

Armitage and Atkinson Ltd. had no noncash financing and investing transactions during 2003. During the year, there were no sales of land or plant and equipment, and no issuances of notes payable.

Required

1. Prepare the 2003 cash flow statement, formatting operating activities by the direct method.
2. How will what you have learned in this problem help you evaluate an investment?

Problem 17-4B *Preparing the cash flow statement—indirect method* **(Obj. 2, 3, 5)**

Use the Armitage and Atkinson Ltd. data from Problem 17-3B.

Required

1. Prepare the 2003 cash flow statement by the indirect method. If your instructor also assigned Problem 17-3B, prepare only the operating activities section of the statement.
2. How will what you learned in this problem help you evaluate an investment?

Problem 17-5B *Preparing the cash flow statement—indirect method* **(Obj. 2, 5)**

Ardnas Ltd.'s accountants have assembled the following data for the year ended December 31, 2002:

	December 31,	
	2002	**2001**
Current accounts (all result from operations)		
Current assets		
Cash and cash equivalents	$30,200	$22,700
Accounts receivable......................................	69,700	62,200
Inventories	88,600	85,000
Prepaid expenses	5,300	4,100
Current liabilities		
Notes payable (for inventory purchases) ...	$22,600	$18,300
Accounts payable..	52,900	55,800
Income tax payable.......................................	18,600	16,700
Accrued liabilities	15,500	27,200

Transaction data for 2002:

Acquisition of building	$130,300	Issuance of long-term note	
Acquisition of land by		payable to borrow cash	$ 34,400
issuing long-term note		Loss on sale of equipment	6,700
payable	107,000	Net income...............................	79,600
Acquisition of long-term		Payment of cash dividends ...	36,300
investment............................	31,600	Repurchase and retirement	
Amortization expense	24,100	of common shares...............	26,300
Collection of loan	8,700	Retirement of bonds payable	
Issuance of common shares		by issuing common shares	35,000
for cash	41,200	Sale of equipment for cash	58,000
		Stock dividends.......................	31,800

Required

Prepare Ardnas Ltd.'s cash flow statement, using the *indirect* method to report operating activities. Note any additional disclosures that are required.

Problem 17-6B *Preparing the cash flow statement—indirect method* **(Obj. 2, 5)**

The comparative balance sheet of Temagami Outfitters Ltd. at March 31, 2003, is shown on the next page.

Required

1. Prepare Temagami Outfitters Ltd.'s cash flow statement for the year ended March 31, 2003, using the *indirect* method to report cash flows from operating activities. Report noncash investing and financing activities in an accompanying schedule.
2. Evaluate Temagami Outfitters Ltd.'s cash flows for the year. Mention all three categories of cash flows, and give the reason for your evaluation.

| | March 31, | |
	2003	2002
Current assets		
Cash and cash equivalents.........................	$ 1,100	$ 6,000
Accounts receivable	34,900	21,700
Inventories...	63,200	60,600
Prepaid expenses...	1,900	1,700
Current liabilities		
Notes payable (for inventory purchases)..	$ 4,000	$ 4,000
Accounts payable	30,300	25,100
Accrued liabilities..	10,700	11,100
Income tax payable	8,000	4,700

Temagami Outfitters Ltd. transactions during the year ended March 31, 2003, included the following:

Acquisition of land by issuing note payable...............	$ 76,000	Repurchase of common shares for cash.........................	$ 13,000
Amortization expense................	11,000	Issuance of long-term note payable to borrow cash..........	50,000
Cash acquisition of building....................................	54,000	Net income	104,000
Cash acquisition of equipment..............................	78,700	Payment of cash dividend.........	30,000
		Sale of long-term investment..............................	13,700

Problem 17-7B Preparing the cash flow statement—direct and indirect methods (Obj. 3, 5)

To prepare the cash flow statement, accountants for Lake Russell Inc. have summarized activity for the year 2002 in two accounts as follows:

Cash

Beginning balance	53,600	Payments on accounts payable	373,100
Collection of loan	13,000	Payments of dividends	27,200
Sale of investment	6,200	Payments of salaries	
Receipts of interest	12,600	and wages	143,800
Collections from customers	678,700	Payments of interest	26,900
Issuance of common shares	27,800	Purchase of equipment	31,400
Receipts of dividends	4,500	Payments of operating	
		expenses	34,300
		Payment of long-term debt	41,300
		Repurchase of common shares	16,900
		Payment of income tax	18,900
Ending balance	82,600		

Common Stock

Repurchase of shares	16,900	Beginning balance	84,400
		Issuance for cash	27,800
		Issuance to acquire land	61,100
		Issuance to retire long-term debt	19,000
		Ending balance	175,400

Lake Russell Inc.'s income statement and selected balance sheet data follow:

LAKE RUSSELL INC.
Income Statement
For the Year Ended December 31, 2002

Revenues:		
Sales revenue		$706,300
Interest revenue		12,600
Dividend revenue		4,500
Total revenues		$723,400
Expenses and losses:		
Cost of goods sold	$350,600	
Salary and wage expense	150,800	
Amortization expense	24,300	
Other operating expenses	44,100	
Interest expense	28,800	
Income tax expense	16,200	
Loss on sale of investments	3,100	
Total expenses		617,900
Net income		$105,500

LAKE RUSSELL INC. Balance Sheet Data	Increase (Decrease)
Current assets	
Cash and cash equivalents	$?
Accounts receivable	27,600
Inventories	(11,800)
Prepaid expenses	600
Loan receivable	(13,000)
Long-term investments	(9,300)
Plant and equipment, net	7,100
Land	60,100
Current liabilities	
Accounts payable	$(34,300)
Interest payable	1,900
Salary payable	7,000
Other accrued liabilities	10,400
Income tax payable	(2,700)
Long-term debt	(60,300)
Common stock	91,000
Retained earnings	28,300

Required

1. Prepare the cash flow statement of Lake Russell Inc. for the year ended December 31, 2002, using the *direct* method to report operating activities. Also prepare a schedule of noncash investing and financing activities.

2. Use the data from Lake Russell Inc.'s 2002 income statement and the selected balance sheet data to prepare a supplementary schedule showing cash flows from operating activities by the *indirect* method. All activity in the current accounts results from operations.

Problem 17-8B *Preparing the cash flow statement—direct and indirect method* **(Obj. 3, 4, 5)**

Sproule Antiques Ltd.'s comparative balance sheet at June 30, 2003, included the following balances:

SPROULE ANTIQUES LTD.
Balance Sheet
June 30, 2003 and 2002

	2003	2002	Increase (Decrease)
Current assets			
Cash	$ 37,600	$ 8,600	$ 29,000
Accounts receivable.......................................	74,000	48,300	25,700
Interest receivable	2,900	3,600	(700)
Inventories	68,600	60,200	8,400
Prepaid expenses..	3,700	2,800	900
Long-term investment.....................................	10,100	5,200	4,900
Plant and equipment, net...............................	84,500	73,600	10,900
Land	42,400	96,000	(53,600)
	$323,800	$298,300	$ 25,500
Current liabilities			
Notes payable, short-term			
(for general borrowing).............................	$ 13,400	$ 18,100	$ (4,700)
Accounts payable..	46,900	40,300	6,600
Income tax payable.......................................	13,800	14,500	(700)
Accrued liabilities	8,200	9,700	(1,500)
Interest payable..	3,700	2,900	800
Salary payable..	900	2,600	(1,700)
Long-term note payable..................................	47,400	94,100	(46,700)
Common stock...	63,900	51,200	12,700
Retained earnings	125,600	64,900	60,700
	$323,800	$298,300	$ 25,500

Transaction data for the year ended June 30, 2003:

a. Net income, $86,700.

b. Amortization expense on equipment, $5,400.

c. Purchased long-term investment, $4,900.

d. Sold land for $46,900, including $6,700 loss.

e. Acquired equipment by issuing long-term note payable, $11,300, and paying $5,000 cash.

f. Paid long-term note payable, $58,000.

g. Received cash for issuance of common shares, $8,000.

h. Paid cash dividends, $26,000.

i. Paid short-term note payable by issuing common shares, $4,700.

Required

1. Prepare the cash flow statement of Sproule Antiques Ltd. for the year ended June 30, 2003, using the *indirect* method to report operating activities. Also prepare a schedule of noncash investing and financing activities. All current accounts, except short-term notes payable, result from operating transactions.

2. Prepare a supplementary schedule showing cash flows from operations by the *direct* method. The income statement reports the following: sales, $265,400; interest revenue, $10,600; cost of goods sold, $80,400; salary expense, $38,800; other operating expenses, $42,000; amortization expense, $5,400; income tax expense, $9,900; loss on sale of land, $6,700; interest expense, $6,100.

Problem 17-9B *Distinguishing among operating, investing, and financing activities; computing the cash effects of a wide variety of business transactions*
(Obj. 2, 5)

Indicate whether or not each of items below would be shown on a cash flow statement (indirect method).

Indicate whether the adjustment is added to, deducted from, or has no effect on the cash flow statement. If the transaction affects the cash flow statement, state whether it relates to operating activities, investing activities, or financing activities.

a. A loss on the sale of capital assets

b. Amortization expense—equipment

c. An increase in merchandise inventory

d. A decrease in prepaid expenses

e. Amortization of the discount on bonds payable

f. The receipt of interest on long-term investments

g. The declaration and distribution of a common stock dividend

h. An increase in trade accounts payable

i. The purchase of office equipment

j. The borrowing of funds for future expansion through the sale of bonds

k. A decrease in marketable securities

l. Amortization of goodwill

m. The purchase of land in exchange for common shares

Problem 17-10B *Distinguishing among operating, investing, and financing activities; using the financial statements to compute the cash effects of a wide variety of business transactions; preparing a cash flow statement by the indirect method*   *(Obj. 2, 4, 5)*

Bangor Sales Corp had the following financial statements for the year ended December 31:

BANGOR SALES CORP.
Income Statement
For the Year Ended December 31, 2003

Net sales	$178,000
Cost of goods sold	80,000
Gross margin	98,000
Operating expenses	
Selling expenses	49,200
Administrative expenses	29,000
Interest expense	5,800
Total operating expenses	84,000
Operating income	14,000
Income taxes	5,600
Net income	$ 8,400

BANGOR SALES CORP.
Balance Sheet
December 31, 2003 and 2002

	2003	2002
Assets		
Cash.........	$ 4,000	$ 18,400
Marketable securities.....	1,000	3,000
Accounts receivable.....	1,800	22,800
Merchandise inventory.....	30,600	72,000
Prepaid expenses.....	2,400	1,900
Plant and equipment.....	190,400	156,900
Less accumulated amortization.....	(16,000)	(10,000)
Land.....	60,000	—0—
Goodwill.....	12,000	15,000
Total assets.....	$286,200	$280,000
Liabilities		
Accounts payable.....	$ 14,200	$ 15,000
Salaries payable.....	16,000	14,000
Loans payable.....	56,000	66,000
Total liabilities.....	86,200	95,000
Shareholders' equity		
Common shares.....	110,000	100,000
Retained earnings.....	90,000	85,000
Total shareholders' equity.....	200,000	185,000
Total liabilities and shareholders' equity.....	$286,200	$280,000

Additional information:

a. The Operating expenses included:

Amortization expense on plant and equipment	=	$16,000
Amortization of goodwill	=	$3,000

b. Sold equipment for its book value. The equipment cost $23,000 and had been amortized for $10,000.

c. Purchased additional equipment for $56,500.

d. Exchanged common shares for land valued at $60,000.

e. Declared and paid cash dividends on common shares, $3,400.

f. Repurchased common shares for $50,000.

g. Paid $15,800 (of which $5,800 was interest) on the loans.

Required

1. Prepare a cash flow statement for Bangor Sales Corp. for the year ended December 31, 2003, using the *indirect* method. Consider the marketable securities to be a cash equivalent.

2. Comment on the results indicated by the cash flow statement.

Challenge Problems

Problem 17-1C *Distinguishing between the direct method and indirect method* **(Obj. 3, 5)**

Both the CICA's Accounting Standards Board (AcSB) and the Financial Accounting Standards Board (FASB) in the U.S. recommend the direct method of preparing the operating activities portion of the cash flow statement. Yet most companies use the indirect method when preparing their cash flow statement.

Required

Discuss why you think companies use the indirect method when the direct method is the method recommended by the standard-setting bodies.

Problem 17-2C   *Accounting for non-cash financing and investing activities*   *(Obj. 4)*

Initially, the *CICA Handbook* did not require financial statements to include information about noncash investing and financing activities. The financial statements reported only changes in working capital (defined as current assets less current liabilities) and so transactions such as the use of long-term debt to purchase capital assets or conversion of debt into equity were excluded.

Required

Discuss the present *CICA Handbook*'s requirements with respect to disclosure of noncash financing and investing decisions and explain why you think the required disclosure does or does not benefit users.

Extending Your Knowledge

Decision Problems

1. Preparing and using the cash flow statement to evaluate operations   *(Obj. 4, 5)*

The 2003 comparative income statement and the 2003 comparative balance sheet of Med Advances Inc. have just been distributed at a meeting of the company's board of directors.

In discussing the company's results of operations and year-end financial position, the members of the board of directors raise a fundamental question: Why is the cash balance so low? This question is especially troublesome to the board members because 2003 showed record profits. As the controller of the company, you must answer the question.

MED ADVANCES INC.
Comparative Income Statement
For the Years Ended December 31, 2003 and 2002
(amounts in thousands)

	2003	2002
Revenues and gains:		
Sales revenue	$444	$310
Gain on sale of equipment (sale price, $33)	—	18
Total revenues and gains	$444	$328
Expenses and losses:		
Cost of goods sold	$221	$162
Salary expense	48	28
Amortization expense	57	33
Interest expense	13	20
Loss on sale of land (sale price, $61)	—	35
Total expenses and losses	339	278
Net income	$105	$ 50

MED ADVANCES INC.
Comparative Balance Sheet
December 31, 2003 and 2002
(amounts in thousands)

Assets	2003	2002
Cash	$ 13	$ 63
Accounts receivable, net....................................	92	61
Inventories..	194	181
Capital assets	392	259
Accumulated amortization	(244)	(198)
Patents, net	177	188
Total assets..	$624	$554
Liabilities and Shareholders' Equity		
Notes payable, short-term		
(for general borrowing)	$ 32	$101
Accounts payable	63	56
Accrued liabilities..	12	17
Notes payable, long-term..................................	147	163
Common stock..	149	61
Retained earnings...	221	156
Total liabilities and shareholders' equity...	$624	$554

Required

1. Prepare a cash flow statement for 2003 in the format that best shows the relationship between net income and operating cash flow. The company sold no capital assets or long-term investments and issued no notes payable during 2003. The changes in all current accounts except short-term notes payable arose from operations. There were no noncash financing and investing transactions during the year. Show all amounts in thousands. Amortization expense on the patent was $11,000.

2. Answer the board members' question: Why is the cash balance so low? In explaining the business's cash flows, identify two significant cash receipts that occurred during 2002 but not in 2003. Also point out the two largest cash payments during 2003.

3. Considering net income and the company's cash flows during 2003, was it a good year or a bad year for Med Advances Inc.? Give your reasons.

2. Using the cash flow statement to evaluate a company's operations (Obj. 1)

The cash flow statement, in the not-too-distant past, included information in only two categories: sources of funds and uses of funds. Funds were usually defined as working capital (current assets minus current liabilities). The present-day statement provides information about cash flows from operating activities, investing activities, and financing activities. The earlier statement permitted the information to be about changes in working capital or in cash, while today's cash flow statement deals specifically with information about flows in cash and cash equivalents.

Required

1. Explain why you think the present-day cash flow statement, with its disclosure of the three different kinds of activities, is or is not an improvement over the earlier model that showed only sources and uses of funds.

2. Is information about cash flows more informative to users than information about working capital flows?

3. Briefly explain why comparative balance sheets and a cash flow statement are more informative than just comparative balance sheets.

Financial Statement Problem

Using the cash flow statement *(Obj. 2, 4)*

Intrawest Corporation's Consolidated Statements of Changes in Financial Position (cash flow statement) appears in Appendix A. Use this statement along with the other material in Appendix A to answer the following questions.

1. By which method of reporting does Intrawest Corporation report net cash flows from operations? How can you tell?

2. Did Intrawest Corporation improve its cash position in 2000? If so, by how much?

3. Intrawest Corporation reports cash flow differently than the method described in the chapter. What does Intrawest do differently?

4. Was Intrawest Corporation expanding or contracting in 2000? Support your answer with specific references to the financial statements.

Appendix

The Work Sheet Approach to Preparing the Cash Flow Statement

The body of this chapter discusses the uses of the cash flow statement in decision making and shows how to prepare the statement by using T-accounts. The T-account approach works well as a learning device, especially for simple situations. In practice, however, most companies face complex situations. In these cases, a work sheet can help accountants prepare the cash flow statement. This Appendix shows how to prepare that statement using a specially designed work sheet.

The basic task in preparing the cash flow statement is to account for all cash effects of transactions that took the business from its beginning financial position to its ending financial position. Like the T-account approach, the work sheet approach helps accountants identify the cash effects of all the period's transactions. The work sheet starts with the beginning balance sheet and concludes with the ending balance sheet. Two middle columns—one for debit amounts and the other for credit amounts—complete the work sheet. These columns, labelled Transaction Analysis, contain the data for the cash flow statement. Exhibit 17A-1 presents the basic framework of the work sheet. Accountants can prepare the statement directly from the lower part of the work sheet (Panel B in Exhibit 17A-1). The advantage of the work sheet is that it organizes all relevant data for the statement's preparation in one place. All the exhibits in this Appendix are based on the Anchor Ltd. data presented earlier in the chapter in Exhibit 17-6 on page 920 and repeated in this Appendix on page 973.

The work sheet can be used with either the direct method or the indirect method for operating activities. This Appendix will demonstrate the work sheet using the indirect method. As with the T-account approach, cash flows from investing activities and cash flows from financing activities are unaffected by the method used for operating activities.

EXHIBIT 17A-1

Work Sheet for Preparing the Cash Flow Statement

ANCHOR LTD.
Work Sheet for the Cash Flow Statement
For the Year Ended December 31, 2002

	Balances	Transaction Analysis		Balances
	Jan. 1, 2002	Debit	Credit	Dec. 31, 2002
PANEL A—Account Titles				
Cash				
Accounts receivable, etc.				
PANEL B—Cash Flow Statement				
Cash flows from operating activities:				
Cash flows from investing activities:				
Cash flows from financing activities:				
Net increase (decrease) in cash				

Preparing the Work Sheet—
Indirect Method for Operating Activities

The indirect method shows the reconciliation from net income to net cash inflow (or net cash outflow) from operating activities. Exhibit 17A-2 on page 974 is the work sheet for preparing the cash flow statement by the indirect method.

The Anchor Ltd. data for analyzing operating activities come from the income statement (Exhibit 17-7 on page 926) and the comparative balance sheet (Exhibit 17-8 on page 927). They are reproduced below. The analysis of investing activities and financing activities uses the information presented in Exhibit 17-6 and below.

Transaction Analysis on the Work Sheet

For your convenience, set out below are the net income amount from Exhibit 17-7 and the changes in current assets and current liabilities from Exhibit 17-8.

Operating Activities:
(a) Net income, $41,000
(b) Amortization, $18,000
(c) Proceeds from sale of capital assets, $62,000, inlcuding $8,000 gain.
(d) Increase in accounts receivable, $13,000.
(e) Increase in interest receivable, $2,000
(f) Decrease in inventory, $3,000
(g) Increase in prepaid expenses, $1,000
(h) Increase in accounts payable, $34,000
(i) Decrease in salary and wage payable, $2,000

(j) Decrease in accrued liabilities, $2,000

Investing Activities:
(k) Cash payments to acquire capital assets, $306,000
(l) Loan to another company, $11,000

Financing Activities:
(m) Proceeds from issuance of common shares, $101,000
(n) Proceeds from issuance of long-term note payable, $94,000
(o) Payment of long-term note payable, $11,000
(p) Declaration and payment of cash dividends, $17,000

Transaction Analysis under the Indirect Method

The transaction analysis on the work sheet appears in the form of journal entries. Only balance sheet accounts appear on the work sheet. There are no income statement accounts.

Refer to Exhibit 17A-2 on page 974. Net income, transaction (a), is the first operating cash inflow. Net income is entered on the work sheet as a debit to Net Income under cash flows from operating activities and a credit to Retained Earnings. Next come the additions to, and subtractions from, net income, starting with amortization transaction (b), which is debited to Amortization on the work sheet and credited to Capital Assets, Net. Transaction (c) is the sale of capital assets. The $8,000 gain on the sale is entered as a credit to Gain on Sale of Capital Assets under operating cash flows—a subtraction from net income. This credit removes the $8,000 amount of the gain from cash flow from operations because the cash proceeds from the sale were not $8,000. The cash proceeds were $62,000, so this amount is entered on the work sheet as a debit under investing activities. Entry (c) is completed by crediting the capital assets' book value of $54,000 ($62,000 – $8,000) to the Capital Assets, Net account.

Entries (d) through (j) reconcile net income to cash flows from operations for increases and decreases in the current assets other than Cash and for increases and decreases in the current liabilities. Entry (d) debits Accounts Receivable for its $13,000 increase during the year. This decrease in cash flows is credited to Increase in

Work Sheet for Cash Flow Statement—Indirect Method

ANCHOR LTD.
Work Sheet for Cash Flow Statement (Indirect Method)
For the Year Ended December 31, 2002
(Amounts in thousands)

Panel A: Account Titles	Balances Jan. 1, 2002	Transaction Analysis Debit		Transaction Analysis Credit		Balances Dec. 31, 2002
Cash	42			(q)	20	22
Accounts receivable	80	(d)	13			93
Interest receivable	1	(e)	2			3
Inventory	138			(f)	3	135
Prepaid expenses	7	(g)	1			8
Long-term receivable from another company	—	(l)	11			11
Capital assets, net	219	(k)	306	(b)	18	
				(c)	54	453
Totals	487					725
Accounts payable	57			(h)	34	91
Salary and wage payable	6	(j)	2			4
Accrued liabilities	3	(j)	2			1
Long-term debt	77	(o)	11	(n)	94	160
Common stock	258			(m)	101	359
Retained earnings	86	(p)	17	(a)	41	110
Totals	487		365		365	725

Panel B: Cash Flow Statement

		Debit		Credit	
Cash flows from operating activities					
Net income		(a)	41		
Add (subtract) items that affect net income and cash flow differently:					
Amortization		(b)	18		
Gain on sale of capital assets				(c)	8
Increase in accounts receivable				(d)	13
Increase in interest receivable				(e)	2
Decrease in inventory		(f)	3		
Increase in prepaid expenses				(g)	1
Increase in accounts payable		(h)	34		
Decrease in salary and wage payable				(i)	2
Decrease in accrued liabilities				(j)	2
Cash flows from investing activities					
Acquisition of capital assets				(k)	306
Proceeds from sale of capital assets		(c)	62		
Loan to another company				(l)	11
Cash flows from financing activities					
Proceeds from issuance of common shares		(m)	101		
Proceeds from issuance of long-term debt		(n)	94		
Payment of long-term debt				(o)	11
Payment of dividends				(p)	17
			353		373
Net decrease in cash		(q)	20		
Totals			373		373

Accounts Receivable under operating cash flows. Entries (e) and (g) are similar for Interest Receivable and Prepaid Expenses.

Entry (k) records the purchase of capital assets while entry (l) records the loan of funds to another company; both of these are investing activities. Entry (m) is the issuance of common shares for cash while entry (n) records the issuance of long-term debt for cash. Entry (o) records the repayment of long-term debt while entry (p) is for the payment of dividends. Entries (m) to (p) are financing activities.

The final item in Exhibit 17A-2 is the Net Decrease in Cash—transaction (q) on the work sheet—a credit to Cash and a debit to Net Decrease in Cash. To prepare the cash flow statement from the work sheet, the accountant merely writes Panel B of the statement, adding subtotals for the three categories of activities.

Noncash Investing and Financing Activities on the Work Sheet   Noncash investing and financing activities can also be analyzed on the work sheet. Because these types of transactions include both a financing activity and an investing activity, they require two work sheet entries. For example, suppose Anchor Ltd. purchased a building by issuing common shares of $320,000. Exhibit 17A-3 illustrates the transaction analysis of this noncash investing and financing activity. Observe that Cash is unaffected.

Work sheet entry (t1) records the purchase of the building, and entry (t2) records the issuance of the shares. The order of the entries is unimportant.

EXHIBIT 17A-3

Noncash Investing and Financing Activities on the Work Sheet

ANCHOR LTD.
Work Sheet for the Cash Flow Statement
For the Year Ended December 31, 2002
(Amounts in Thousands)

	Balances	Transaction Analysis		Balances
Panel A: Account Titles	Jan. 1, 2002	Debit	Credit	Dec. 31, 2002
Cash				
Accounts receivable..				
Building..	650,000	(t1) 320,000		970,000
Common stock	890,000		(t2) 320,000	1,210,000
Panel B: Cash Flow Statement				
Noncash investing and financing transactions:				
Purchase of building by issuance of common shares.............................		(t2) 320,000	(t1)320,000	

Appendix Problems

Problem 17A-1 *Preparing the work sheet for the cash flow statement—indirect method (Obj. A1)*

The 2002 comparative balance sheet and income statement of Baxter Tools Ltd. follow. Baxter had no noncash investing and financing transactions during 2002.

BAXTER TOOLS LTD.
Comparative Balance Sheet
December 31, 2002 and 2001

	December 31, 2002	December 31, 2001	Increase (Decrease)
Current assets:			
Cash and cash equivalents......................	$ 28,800	$ 15,600	$13,200
Accounts receivable	44,500	43,100	1,400
Interest receivable	600	900	(300)
Inventories	97,300	89,900	7,400
Prepaid expenses...................................	1,700	2,200	(500)
Capital assets:			
Plant and equipment, net.......................	100,900	93,700	7,200
Land	35,100	10,000	25,100
Total assets	$308,900	$255,400	$53,500
Current liabilities:			
Accounts payable....................................	$ 16,400	$ 17,900	$ (1,500)
Interest payable	6,300	6,700	(400)
Salary payable..	3,200	1,400	1,800
Other accrued liabilities	18,100	18,700	(600)
Income tax payable	6,300	3,800	2,500
Long-term liabilities:			
Notes payable	55,000	65,000	(10,000)
Shareholders' equity:			
Common stock...	131,100	122,300	8,800
Retained earnings...................................	72,500	19,600	52,900
Total liabilities and shareholders' equity....	$308,900	$255,400	$53,500

BAXTER TOOLS LTD.
Income Statement
For the Year Ended December 31, 2002

Revenues:		
Sales revenue.................................		$458,000
Interest revenue.............................		11,700
Total revenues..........................		469,700
Expenses:		
Cost of goods sold	$205,200	
Salary expense...............................	76,400	
Amortization expense....................	15,300	
Other operating expenses.............	49,700	
Interest expense............................	24,600	
Income tax expense	16,900	
Total expenses..........................		388,100
Net income		$ 81,600

Transaction data for the year ended December 31, 2002, are as follows:

a. Bought land for cash, $25,100.

b. Bought equipment for cash, $22,500.

c. Paid $10,000 on notes payable.

d. Paid dividends in cash, $28,700.

e. Issued common shares for cash, $8,800.

Required

Prepare the work sheet for the 2002 cash flow statement. Format cash flows from operating activities by the *indirect* method.

Problem 17A-2 *Preparing the work sheet for the cash flow statement—indirect method*
    (Obj. A1)

Saugeen Manufacturing Corp.'s comparative balance sheet at September 30, 2003, follows.

SAUGEEN MANUFACTURING CORP.
Comparative Balance Sheet
September 30, 2003 and 2002

	December 31, 2003	December 31, 2002	Increase (Decrease)
Current assets:			
Cash	$ 57,885	$ 17,600	$ 40,285
Accounts receivable	45,900	44,000	1,900
Interest receivable	4,100	2,800	1,300
Inventories	121,700	116,900	4,800
Prepaid expenses	8,600	9,300	(700)
Long-term investments	105,400	18,100	87,300
Capital assets:			
Plant and equipment, net	95,500	49,700	45,800
Land	65,800	93,000	(27,200)
Total assets	$504,885	$351,400	$153,485
Current liabilities:			
Notes payable, short-term	$ 22,000	$ —0—	$ 22,000
Accounts payable	71,800	70,300	1,500
Income tax payable	21,800	24,600	(2,800)
Accrued liabilities	23,100	29,100	(6,000)
Interest payable	4,500	3,200	1,300
Salary payable	1,500	1,100	400
Notes payable, long-term	68,900	61,300	7,600
Shareholders' equity:			
Common stock	142,100	90,200	51,900
Retained earnings	149,185	71,600	77,585
Total liability and shareholders' equity	$504,885	$351,400	$153,485

SAUGEEN MANUFACTURING CORP.
Income Statement
For the Year Ended September 30, 2003

Revenues:

Sales...		$375,600
Gain on sale of land		10,900
Interest revenue..		7,300
Total revenues......................................		$393,800

Expenses:

Cost of goods sold.....................................	$161,500	
Salary expense	63,400	
Other operating expenses	29,600	
Income tax expense....................................	18,400	
Interest expense...	13,500	
Amortization expense	8,500	
Total expenses.......................................		$294,900
Net income..		$ 98,900

Transaction data for the year ended September 30, 2003, are as follows:

a. Acquired long-term investments for cash, $87,300.

b. Sold land for cash, $38,100, including $10,900 gain.

c. Acquired equipment by issuing long-term note payable, $32,300.

d. Paid long-term note payable, $24,700.

e. Received cash of $51,900 for issuance of common shares.

f. Paid cash dividends, $21,315.

g. Acquired equipment by issuing short-term note payable, $22,000.

Required

Prepare Saugeen Manufacturing Corp.'s work sheet for the cash flow statement for the year ended September 30, 2003, using the *indirect* method to report operating activities. Include on the work sheet the noncash investing and financing activities.

Financial Statement Analysis

CHAPTER OBJECTIVES

After studying this chapter, you should be able to

1 Perform a horizontal analysis of financial statements

2 Perform a vertical analysis of financial statements

3 Prepare common-size financial statements for benchmarking against the industry average and key competitors

4 Compute the standard financial ratios used for decision making

5 Use ratios in decision making

6 Measure economic value added by a company's operations

uncor Energy Inc., whose head office is in Calgary, has three operating businesses: oil sands, oil and gas, and refining and marketing. Suncor Energy Inc. managers stated in their 1997 annual report,

"Suncor is actively pursuing new opportunities that have high growth and profit potential while remaining committed to continuously improving the profitability and sustainability of its existing businesses." The Suncor annual reports show that Suncor has been vigorously expanding its operations.

The 2000 annual report for Suncor continues the story of its success. In his message to shareholders, the President and CEO Rick George states that the record net income of $377 million and record cash flow from operations of $958 million in 2000 was based on increased oil production from the oil sands project, increased retail sales of gasoline and increased sales of natural gas. However, he points out, the Stuart Oil Shale Project in Australia is facing "environmental and technical challenges."

Many of the measures you will learn about in this chapter can be used to assess how well Suncor is performing. Suncor also uses many of the measures in assessing potential acquisitions and measuring performance of companies and divisions in the Suncor group.

Sources: Suncor Energy Inc.'s 1997, 1999, and 2000 Annual Reports.

Suncor Energy Inc.
www.suncor.com

AS THE OPENING vignette illustrates, managers rely on accounting information to make business decisions. Investors and creditors also rely on accounting information. Often they want to compare two or more similar companies. The way to compare companies of different size is to use *standard* measures. Throughout this book, we have discussed financial ratios, such as the current ratio, inventory turnover, and return on shareholders' equity. These ratios are standard measures that enable investors to compare companies of different size or companies that operate in different industries. Managers use the ratios to monitor operations and to help make business decisions. In this chapter, we discuss most of the basic ratios and related measures that managers use to run a company. Investors and lenders use the same tools to search for good investments and loan prospects. The informational value of these ratios is one reason accounting is called the "language of business."

The Objectives of Financial Statement Analysis

Financial statement analysis focuses on techniques used by internal managers and by analysts external to the organization. A major source of their information is the annual report. Annual reports usually contain:

1. The basic financial statements: balance sheet, income statement, statement of retained earnings, and cash flow statement, and the notes to the financial statements, including a statement of significant accounting policies;

2. Comparative financial information for at least the prior year;

3. The auditor's report;

4. Management's discussion and analysis (MD&A) of the past financial results and expectations for the future;

5. A management report;

6. Other financial and non-financial information about the company, such as information relating to environmental affairs.

More and more companies have web pages on the Internet where they place information about the company ranging from the annual report through information about the company and its products to news releases. Many investors and creditors gain information about companies they are interested in from these web pages.

Management's discussion and analysis is a relatively new development in financial reporting. While some companies have been providing a commentary on their past operations and expectations, it is only recently that such disclosure has become required and then only by larger companies registered with the various securities regulators in Canada, such as the Ontario Securities Commission (OSC). The description of MD&A in the OSC's Statement 5.10 is helpful in providing an understanding of the concept:

> MD&A is supplemental analysis and explanation which accompanies but does not form part of the financial statements. MD&A provides management with the opportunity to explain in narrative form its current financial situation and future prospects. MD&A is intended to give the investor the ability to look at the [company issuing the financial statements] through the eyes of management by providing a historical and prospective analysis of the business of the [issuer]. MD&A requirements ask management to discuss the dynamics of the business and to analyze the financial statements. Coupled with the financial statements this information should allow investors to assess [the issuing company's] performance and future prospects.[1]

Ontario Securities Commission
www.osc.gov.on.ca

An example of MD&A is that provided in the 2000 annual report of Intrawest Corporation, found in Appendix A. The report begins with a list of key financial objectives, the change in reporting currency from Canadian dollars to U.S. dollars, and a discussion of financial highlights. It then provides a review of ski and resort operations. Next is a review of Intrawest's other major activity, resort real estate operations. This section is followed by a review of corporate operations, discontinued operations, liquidity and capital resources, a discussion of risk and risk management, and management's outlook for the future.

Intrawest Corp.
www.intrawest.ca

Inco Limited
www.inco.com

Exhibit 18-1 shows graphical data taken from the 2000 annual report of Inco Limited. Management uses the graphical data to show how the company performed over the five years ended December 31, 2000.

The MD&A from any company, together with the accounting information in the financial statements of that company, helps investors and creditors interpret the financial statements. The balance sheet, income statement, and cash flow statement are based on historical data; they state *what* has happened but rarely provide insights into *why* it has happened. MD&A offers management's reasons for the past and glimpses into the future. Investors and creditors are also interested in where the company is headed.

Investors who purchase a company's stock expect to receive dividends and hope the stock's value will increase. Creditors make loans with the expectation of receiving cash for the interest and principal. Both groups bear the risk they will not receive their expected returns. They use financial statement analysis to (1) predict the amount of expected returns and (2) assess the risks associated with those returns.

Creditors generally expect to receive specific fixed amounts and have the first claim on a company's assets, so they are most concerned with assessing short-term liquidity and long-term solvency. **Short-term liquidity** is an organization's ability to meet current payments as they become due. **Long-term solvency** is the ability to generate enough cash to pay long-term debts as they mature.

In contrast, *investors* are more concerned with profitability, dividends, and future share prices. Why? Because dividends and future share prices depend on profitable operations. Creditors also assess profitability because profitable operations are the company's prime source of cash to repay loans.

---

[1]The authors wish to thank Brenda Eprile, FCA, former Executive Director of the Ontario Securities Commission, for her assistance in providing the authors with a copy of OSC Statement 5.10.

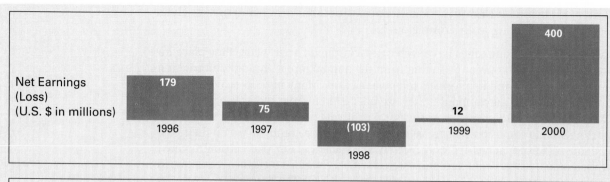

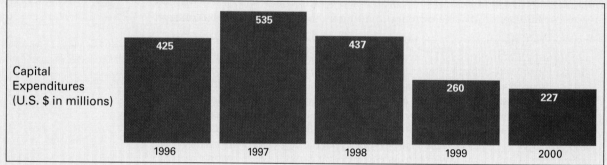

The tools and techniques that the business community uses in evaluating financial statement information can be divided into three broad categories: horizontal analysis, vertical analysis, and ratio analysis.

Horizontal Analysis

Many managerial decisions hinge on whether the dollar amounts—of revenues, income, expenses, and so on—are increasing or decreasing over time. Have revenues risen from last year? From two years ago? By how much? Revenues may have risen by $20,000. This may be interesting, but considered alone it is not very useful for decision making. The *percentage change* in the net revenues over time improves our ability to use the dollar amounts. It is better to know that revenues have increased by 20 percent than to know that revenues rose by $20,000.

The study of percentage changes in comparative statements is called **horizontal analysis**. Computing a percentage change in comparative statements requires two steps:

1. Compute the dollar amount of the change from the earlier (base) period to the later period.
2. Divide the dollar amount of change by the base-period amount.

Horizontal analysis is illustrated for Canadian National Railway Company (CN), the largest rail carrier in North America:

	(Dollar amounts in millions)		Increase (Decrease)	
	2000	**1999**	**Amount**	**Percent**
Revenues	$5,446	$5,261	$185	3.5
Net income	772	602	170	28.2

The percentage change in CN's revenues during 2000 is computed as follows:

Step 1. Compute the dollar amount of change in revenues during 2000:

	2000		1999		Increase
	$5,446	–	$5,261	=	$185

Step 2. Divide the dollar amount of change by the base-period amount to compute the percentage change during the later period:

$$\text{Percentage change} = \frac{\text{Dollar amount of change}}{\text{Base-year amount}} = \frac{\$185}{\$5,261} = 3.5 \text{ percent}$$

During 2000, CN's revenues increased by 3.5 percent.

Detailed horizontal analyses of a comparative income statement and a comparative balance sheet are shown in the two right-hand columns of Exhibits 18-2 and 18-3 from the financial statements of CN. The comparative income statement shows that net revenues increased by 3.5 percent during 2000. Expenses increased by a lesser amount ($33 million or 0.8 percent) so that income from operations increased by $152 million, or 12.3 percent.

The comparative balance sheet shows that there was little change between 1999 and 2000. Total assets increased by $439 million, or 3.0 percent, while total liabilities increased $247 million, or 2.7 percent. The increase in retained earnings of $321 million, or 19.0 percent, was partially offset by reductions in common shares and contributed surplus.

Trend Percentages

Trend percentages are a form of horizontal analysis. Trends are important indicators of the direction a business is taking. How have sales changed over a five-year period? What trend does gross profit show? These questions can be answered by analyzing trend percentages over a recent period, such as the most recent five years or ten years. To gain a realistic view of the company, it is often necessary to examine more than just a two-year or three-year period.

EXHIBIT 18-2

Comparative Income Statement—Horizontal Analysis

CANADIAN NATIONAL RAILWAY COMPANY (CN)
Consolidated Statements of Income (adapted)
For the Years Ended December 31, 2000 and December 31, 1999
(Dollar amounts in millions except per-share amounts)

	2000	1999	Increase (Decrease) Amount	Percent
Revenues	$5,446	$5,261	$185	3.5%
Expenses:				
Labour and fringe benefits	1,684	1,711	(27)	(1.6)
Purchased services	595	591	4	0.7
Other	1,370	1,326	44	3.3
Amortization	412	400	12	3.0
	4,061	4,028	33	0.8
Operating income	1,385	1,233	152	12.3
Interest expense	295	308	(13)	(4.2)
Other income	(124)	(46)	(78)	(169.6)
	171	262	(91)	(34.7)
Income before income taxes	1,214	971	243	25.0
Income taxes	442	369	73	19.8
Net income	$772	$602	$170	28.2
Earnings per share	$3.90	$3.02	$0.88	29.1
Fully diluted earnings per share	$3.81	$2.97	$0.84	28.3

Note: A decrease from any number to zero is a decrease of 100 percent. An increase from zero to any positive number is treated as an increase of 100 percent.

THINKING IT OVER

Refer to Exhibit 18-2. Identify the two items on CN's 2000 income statement that experienced the largest increases from 1999. Considering all other changes in the 2000 income statement, is this a good sign or a bad sign about the company?

A: Operating income increased by 12.3 percent and net income increased by 28.2 percent. These are good signs about the company.

EXHIBIT 18-3

Comparative Balance
Sheet—Horizontal Analysis

CANADIAN NATIONAL RAILWAY COMPANY (CN)
Consolidated Balance Sheet (adapted)
December 31, 2000 and December 31, 1999
(Dollar amounts in millions)

	2000	1999	Increase (Decrease) Amount	(Decrease) Percent
Assets				
Current assets:				
Cash and cash equivalents...........	$ 19	$ 307	$(288)	(93.8)%
Accounts receivable......................	737	803	(66)	(8.2)
Material and supplies...................	110	116	(6)	(5.2)
Future income tax asset..............	116	148	(32)	(21.6)
Other...	143	153	(10)	(6.5)
	1,125	1,527	(402)	26.3
Properties......................................	13,583	12,863	720	5.6
Other assets and deferred charges..	488	367	121	33.0
Total assets	$15,196	$14,757	$439	3.0
Liabilities and Shareholders' Equity				
Current liabilities:				
Accounts payable and				
accrued charges.......................	$ 1,393	$ 1,390	$ 3	0.2%
Current portion of				
long-term debt.........................	434	272	162	59.6
Other...	76	115	(39)	(33.9)
	1,903	1,777	126	7.1
Future income tax liability..............	2,516	2,253	263	11.7
Other liabilities and				
deferred credits............................	1,193	1,260	(67)	(5.3)
Long-term debt................................	3,886	3,961	(75)	(1.9)
Total liabilities...............................	9,498	9,251	247	2.7
Shareholders' equity:				
Common shares............................	3,124	3,311	(187)	(5.6)
Convertible preferred shares......	327	327	0	0
Contributed surplus	178	190	(12)	(6.3)
Currency translation....................	61	(9)	70	—*
Retained earnings	2,008	1,687	321	19.0
Total shareholders' equity	5,698	5,506	192	3.5
Total liabilities and				
shareholders' equity	$15,196	$14,757	$439	3.0

*Percentage changes are typically not computed for shifts from a negative amount to a positive amount, and vice versa.

Trend percentages are computed by selecting a base year, with each amount during that year set equal to 100 percent. The amounts of each following year are expressed as a percent of the base amount. To compute trend percentages, divide each item for years after the base year by the corresponding amount during the base year.

$$\text{Trend \%} = \frac{\text{Any year \$}}{\text{Base year \$}}$$

CN showed revenues and net income for the past five years as follows:

	(Amounts in millions)				
	2000	**1999**	**1998**	**1997**	**1996**
Revenues	$5,446	$5,261	$4,101	$4,313	$3,995
Income before income taxes	1,214	971	115	746	142

We want trend percentages for a four-year period starting with 1997. We use 1996 as the base year. Trend percentages for revenues are computed by dividing each revenue amount by the 1996 amount of $3,995 million. Likewise, dividing each year's income before income taxes amount by the base-year amount ($142 million) yields the trend percentages for income before income taxes. The resulting trend percentages follow (1996, the base year = 100%):

	2000	**1999**	**1998**	**1997**	**1996**
Revenues	136%	132%	103%	108%	100%
Income before income taxes	855%	684%	(81)%	525%	100%

CN's revenues have trended upwards from 1996; 2000 revenues are 136 percent of 1996 revenues. CN had a significant income tax recovery in 1996 ($694 million), which increased net income to $850 million. The illustration, therefore, shows the trend of income before income taxes to provide a more meaningful comparison. CN's income before income taxes increased sharply in 1997, declined significantly in 1998, and then increased sharply in both 1999 and 2000. This information suggests that operations may become more successful in the future. To verify this prediction, you must calculate the trend percentages for future years when information becomes available and determine whether the revenues and income before income taxes continue to trend upward.

Vertical Analysis

Horizontal analysis highlights changes in an item over time. However, no single technique provides a complete picture of a business. Another way to analyze a company is called vertical analysis.

Vertical analysis of a financial statement reveals the relationship of each statement item to the total, which is the 100 percent figure. For example, when an income statement for a merchandising company is subjected to vertical analysis, net sales is usually the base. Suppose under normal conditions a company's gross profit is 70 percent of net sales. A drop in gross profit to 60 percent of net sales may cause the company to report a net loss on the income statement. Management, investors, and creditors view a large decline in gross profit with alarm. Exhibit 18-4 shows the vertical analysis of CN's income statement as a percentage of revenues. In this case,

$$\text{Vertical analysis \%} = \frac{\text{Each income statement item}}{\text{Revenues}}$$

The 2000 comparative income statement (Exhibit 18-4) reports that labour and fringe benefts decreased from 32.5 percent of revenues in 1999 to 30.9 percent of revenues in 2000.

The gross profit is one of the most important pieces of financial information in financial analysis because it shows the relationship between sales and cost of goods sold. (For a service company like CN, operating income is one of the most important pieces of financial analysis because it shows the relationship between revenues and expenses.) Note that CN's operating income increased from 23.4 percent in 1999 (100.0% − 76.6%) to 25.4 percent in 2000 (100.0% − 74.6%). The net income percentage moved from 11.4 percent of revenues to a more positive 14.2 percent of revenues.

KEY POINT

Trend percentages indicate the change between a base year and any later year:

$$\text{Trend \%} = \frac{\text{Any year \$}}{\text{Base year \$}}$$

To calculate the % change from the base year, subtract 100% from the trend %.
For example, revenues increased 36% from 1996 to 2000 (136% − 100%).

OBJECTIVE 2
Perform a vertical analysis of financial statements

KEY POINT

While horizontal analysis shows the relationship between several years, vertical analysis shows the relationship between numbers on the financial statements for the same year.

KEY POINT

To show the relative importance of each item on the income statement, vertical analysis presents everything on that statement as a percentage of net sales.

EXHIBIT 18-4

Comparative Income
Statement—Vertical
Analysis

CANADIAN NATIONAL RAILWAY COMPANY (CN)
Consolidated Statement of Income (adapted)
For the Years Ended December 31, 2000 and December 31, 1999
(Dollar amounts in millions)

	2000 Amount	2000 Percent	1999 Amount	1999 Percent
Revenues	$5,446	100.0%	$5,261	100.0%
Expenses:				
Labour and fringe benefits..................	1,684	30.9	1,711	32.5
Purchased services	595	10.9	591	11.3
Other	1,370	25.2	1,326	25.2
Amortization.....................................	412	7.6	400	7.6
	4,061	74.6	4,028	76.6
Operating income..............................	1,385	25.4	1,233	23.4
Interest expense	295	5.4	308	5.9
Other income	(124)	(2.3)	(46)	(0.9)
	171	3.1	262	5.0
Income before income taxes.................	1,214	22.3	971	18.5
Income taxes....................................	442	8.1	369	7.0
Net income	$ 772	14.2	$ 602	11.4
Earnings per share	$ 3.90		$ 3.02	
Fully diluted earnings per share............	$ 3.81		$ 2.97	

LEARNING TIP

Refer to Exhibit 18-4. Think of
vertical analysis this way:
Consider the percentages to be
$ amounts. In other words,
Revenues for 2000, which is
100%, would be expressed as
$1.00. Labour and fringe benefits
would represent $0.309 out of
every revenue dollar, and Net
Income would be $0.142 out of
each revenue dollar.

LEARNING TIP

Often, an analysis is more helpful
if both percentage changes and
dollar changes are seen together.

The vertical analysis of CN's balance sheet (Exhibit 18-5) yields few surprises. Current assets' percentage of total assets (total assets = 100 percent) decreased in 2000, and current liabilities' percentage (total liabilities + equity = 100 percent) increased slightly. Long-term debt decreased from 26.9 percent in 1999 to 25.6 percent in 2000. Total shareholders' equity increased from 37.3 percent to 37.5 percent.

The company's financial position remains strong. The current ratio is 0.59 ($1,125 million/$1,903 million), which is appropriate for a capital-intensive company. Recall from Chapter 4 (page 179) that the current ratio is equal to total current assets divided by total current liabilities.

OBJECTIVE 3
Prepare common-size financial
statements for benchmarking
against the industry average
and key competitors

Common-Size Statements

The percentages in Exhibits 18-4 and 18-5 can be presented as a separate statement that reports only percentages (no dollar amounts). Such a statement is called a **common-size statement**.

On a common-size income statement, each item is expressed as a percentage of the net sales amount (or the revenues amount for a service company). Net sales (or revenues) is the *common size* to which we relate the statement's other amounts. In the balance sheet, the *common size* is total assets *or* the sum of total liabilities and shareholders' equity. A common-size statement eases the comparison of different companies because their amounts are stated in percentages.

Common-size statements may identify the need for corrective action. Exhibit 18-6 (p. 988) is the common-size analysis of current assets taken from Exhibit 18-5. Exhibit 18-6 shows that accounts receivable have decreased from 5.4 percent of total assets in 1999 to 4.9% of total assets in 2000. CN has no significant inventory but analysis such as this would show whether inventory had increased or decreased as a percentage of total assets. Exhibit 18-5 shows that current liabilities have increased from 12.0 percent of total assets in 1999 to 12.5 percent in 2000. Exhibit 18-6 shows that current assets have declined from 10.3 percent of total assets in 1999 to 7.4 percent of total assets in 2000. Common-size statements provide information useful for monitoring cash position and current assets, as we just saw.

EXHIBIT 18-5

Comparative Balance
Sheet—Vertical Analysis

CANADIAN NATIONAL RAILWAY COMPANY (CN)
Consolidated Balance Sheet (adapted)
December 31, 2000 and December 31, 1999
(Dollar amounts in millions)

	2000 Amount	2000 Percent	1999 Amount	1999 Percent
Assets				
Current assets:				
Cash and cash equivalents..................	$ 19	0.1%	$ 307	2.1%
Accounts receivable	737	4.9	803	5.4
Material and supplies..........................	110	0.7	116	0.8
Future income tax asset.......................	116	0.8	148	1.0
Other	143	0.9	153	1.0
	1,125	7.4	1,527	10.3
Properties	13,583	89.4	12,863	87.2
Other assets and deferred charges..........	488	3.2	367	2.5
Total assets..	$15,196	100.0%	$14,757	100.0%
Liabilities and Shareholders' Equity				
Current liabilities:				
Accounts payable and				
accrued charges	$ 1,393	9.2%	$ 1,390	9.4%
Current portion of long-term debt.....	434	2.8	272	1.8
Other	76	0.5	115	0.8
	1,903	12.5	1,777	12.0
Future income tax liability	2,516	16.6	2,253	15.3
Other liabilities and				
deferred credits.................................	1,193	7.8	1,260	8.5
Long-term debt..	3,886	25.6	3,961	26.9
Total liabilities.......................................	9,498	62.5	9,251	62.7
Shareholders' equity:				
Common shares.....................................	3,124	20.6	3,311	22.5
Convertible preferred shares	327	2.1	327	2.2
Contributed surplus	178	1.2	190	1.3
Currency translation...........................	61	0.4	(9)	(0.1)
Retained earnings................................	2,008	13.2	1,687	11.4
Total shareholders' equity..................	5,698	37.5	5,506	37.3
Total liabilities and				
shareholders' equity	$15,196	100.0%	$14,757	100.0%

WORKING IT OUT

Calculate the common-size
percentages for the following
merchandising company's income
statement:

Net sales	$150,000
COGS	60,000
Gross margin	90,000
Operating exp......	40,000
Operating income	50,000
Income tax exp. ...	15,000
Net income..........	$ 35,000

A:

Net sales	100%A
COGS	40 B
Gross margin	60 C
Operating exp......	27 D
Operating income	33 E
Income tax exp. ...	10 F
Net income..........	23%G

A $150,000 ÷ $150,000
B $60,000 ÷ $150,000
C $90,000 ÷ $150,000
D $40,000 ÷ $150,000
E $50,000 ÷ $150,000
F $15,000 ÷ $150,000
G $35,000 ÷ $150,000

Benchmarking

Benchmarking is the practice of comparing a company to a standard set by other companies, with a view toward improvement.

Benchmarking Against the Industry Average

A company's financial statements show past results and help investors predict future performance. Still, that knowledge is limited to that one company. We may learn that research and development spending decreased and net income increased last year. This information is helpful, but it does not consider how businesses in the same industry have fared over the same time period. Have other companies in the same line of business decreased research and development spending? Is there

EXHIBIT 18-6

Common-Size Analysis of
Current Assets

CANADIAN NATIONAL RAILWAY COMPANY (CN)
Common-Size Analysis of Current Assets
December 31, 2000 and December 31, 1999

	Percent of Total Assets	
	2000	1999
Current assets		
Cash and cash equivalents...	0.1%	2.1%
Accounts receivable	4.9	5.4
Material and supplies...	0.7	0.8
Other (includes future income tax asset).................	1.7	2.0
Total current assets...	7.4%	10.3%

Percent of Total Assets

Total Current Assets 7.4%
Accounts receivable 4.9%
Other current assets 2.5%
Other long-term assets and deferred charges 3.2%
Properties 89.4%

2000

Total Current Assets 10.3%
Accounts receivable 5.4%
Other current assets 4.9%
Other long-term assets and deferred charges 2.5%
Properties 87.2%

1999

an industrywide increase in net income? Managers, investors, creditors, and other interested parties need to know how one company compares to other companies in the same line of business. For example, the July 2000 issue of *The Globe and Mail's Report on Business* analyzes research and development spending as a percent of revenue for the top 50 research and development companies in Canada.[2] The rankings show that Nortel Networks spent almost $3 billion or 12.8 percent of revenue on research and development while Magna International spent $113 million or 1.2 percent of revenue and Bombardier spent $127 million or 1.1 percent of revenue.

Exhibit 18-7 gives the common-size income statement of Lucent Technologies Inc., the telecommunications networking company, compared with the average for the communications industry. This analysis compares Lucent with all other companies in its line of business. The industry averages were adapted from Robert Morris Associates' *Annual Statement Studies.* Analysts at ScotiaMcLeod and other companies specialize in a particular industry and make such comparisons in deciding which companies' stocks to buy or sell. For example, financial-service companies like ScotiaMcLeod have health-care industry specialists, paper and forest products industry specialists, merchandising industry specialists, and so on. Boards of directors evaluate top managers based on how well the company compares with other companies in the industry.

---

[2]*The Globe and Mail Report on Business*, July 2000, p. 148.

LUCENT TECHNOLOGIES INC.
Common-Size Income Statement for Comparison with Industry Average
For the Year Ended September 30, 2000

	Lucent Technologies Inc.	Industry Average
Revenues..	100.0%	100.0%
Cost of goods sold.......................................	57.8	63.9
Gross margin...	42.2	36.1
Operating expenses, other income or expenses....	34.7	32.8
Operating income		
before income taxes	7.5	3.3
Income tax expense......................................	3.9	3.5
Net income (net loss)................................	**3.6%**	**(0.2)%**

Percent of Revenues

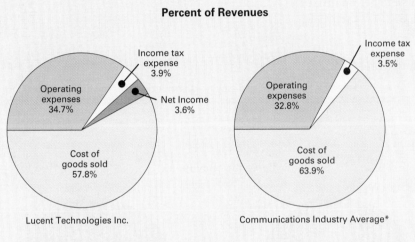

Lucent Technologies Inc.   Communications Industry Average*

*Industry Average percents total to greater than 100% because of the net loss of 0.2%.

Exhibit 18-7 shows that Lucent Technologies Inc. is more profitable than competing companies in its industry. Its gross margin percentage is much higher than the industry average. While the company's operating expenses are slightly higher as a percentage of revenues compared to the industry average, Lucent's net income as a percentage of revenues is higher than the industry average.

Benchmarking Against Another Company

Common-size statements are also used to compare individual companies. Suppose you are an industry investment specialist at ScotiaMcLeod. You are considering an investment in the stock of a manufacturing commpany and you are choosing between Magna International Inc. and Bombardier Inc. The companies are both very large but not the same size, and do not report in the same currency, so that a direct comparison of their financial statements in dollar amounts is not meaningful. However, you can convert the two companies' income statements to common size.

Exhibit 18-8 presents the common-size income statements of Magna International Inc. and Bombardier Inc. Both companies are market leaders with extensive Canadian and international operations. Although the companies differ in size and in product lines, they are very similar in their operating results.

Magna International Inc.
www.magna.ca

Bombardier Inc.
www.bombardier.ca

MAGNA INTERNATIONAL INC. AND BOMBARDIER INC.
Comparison of Common-Size Income Statements (Adapted)

	Magna International Inc.* (Year ended Dec. 31, 2000) (millions of U.S. $)	Bombardier Inc.** (Year ended Jan. 31, 2001) (millions of Cdn. $)
Revenues	100.0%	100.0%
Cost of goods sold and operating expenses	88.3	89.0
Gross margin	11.7	11.0
Amortization	3.7	1.4
Interest expense (net)	0.1	0.2
Other	(1.7)	—***
	2.1	1.6
Income before taxes	9.6	9.4
Taxes	3.4	3.0
Mino\nterest	0.3	—****
	3.7	3.0
Net income	5.9	6.4%

*Amounts shown for Magna International Inc. do not include Magna Entertainment Corp.
**Amounts shown for Bombardier Inc. do not include the financial services and real estate
  operations of the company.
***Less than 0.1 percent.
****Not applicable.

Percent of Revenues

Magna International Inc.*
- Cost of goods sold and operating expenses 88.3%
- Net Income 5.9%
- Amortization 3.7%
- Taxes on income 3.4%
- Minority interest 0.3%

Bombardier Inc.
- Cost of goods sold and operating expenses 89.0%
- Net Income 6.4%
- Amortization 1.4%
- Taxes on income 3.0%
- Other 2.2%

*Magna International Inc. percents total to greater than 100% because other and interest expense
total –1.6%.

Information Sources

Financial analysts draw their information from various sources. Annual and
quarterly reports offer readers a good look at an individual business's operations.
Publicly held companies must, in addition, submit annual reports that are more
detailed to the provincial securities commission in each province where they are
listed on a stock exchange (for example, the Ontario Securities Commission for the
Toronto Stock Exchange). Business publications such as the daily and weekend
editions of *The National Post* and the daily *Globe and Mail Report on Business* carry in-

Peer Performance: Benchmarking on the Internet

The Internet can make many accounting functions that were once time-consuming and tedious incredibly quick and easy. One of these functions is benchmarking, the practice of systematically comparing your company with a leader in your industry. In April 2000, Fourth Shift Corp. and Grant Thornton LLP announced the creation of a free financial benchmarking service on the Internet. The site lets manufacturers and service providers evaluate a number of measures and ratios, including days' sales in receivables and inventory turns. The site provides explanations of the ratios and what a company could do to improve its ratios.

At BenchmarkReport.com, you go through a four-step process to benchmark. You register your company so that the software can identify your company's relevant peer group. You then enter twelve specific data items, including cash and equivalents, trade receivables, inventory, total current assets and liabilities, total assets and liabilities, net sales, and cost of goods sold, among others. (Since this is a U.S.-based site, Canadian companies should convert all data into U.S. dollars.) When you submit your company's data, you get a benchmark report complete with charts and graphs showing how your company compares to those companies in the upper and lower quartile of your peer group. Another useful feature is that your report is archived online, so you can track your company's improvement against both its own performance and that of its peer group.

BenchmarkReport.com lists three reasons to use benchmark ratios: (1) to set goals and action programs, (2) to monitor performance, and (3) to share the results with others. Current and future stakeholders of the company can compare objectively a company's condition against other companies in the same field.

Based on: Anonymous, "Online Benchmarking Service Launched," *Electronic Buyers' News*, April 17, 2000, p. 70. Christine A. Gattenio, "Beyond Lean and Mean," *Electric Perspectives*, May/June 2000, pp. 40–52. And information from www.BenchmarkReport.com.

formation about individual companies and Canadian industries. The Globe Information Services, with its online services like globeinvestor.com, and the Financial Post DataGroup provide to subscribers data on public companies and industries in Canada. Credit agencies like Dun & Bradstreet Canada, for example, offer industry averages as part of their financial service.

globeinvestor.com
www.globeinvestor.com

Financial Post DataGroup
www.fpdata.finpost.com

Dun & Bradstreet Canada
www.dnb.ca

Mid-Chapter Summary Problem
for Your Review

Perform a horizontal analysis and a vertical analysis of the comparative income statement of TRE Corporation. State whether 2003 was a good year or a bad year and give your reasons.

TRE CORPORATION
Comparative Income Statement
For the Years Ended December 31, 2003 and 2002

	2003	2002
Total revenues	$275,000	$225,000
Expenses:		
Cost of products sold	$194,000	$165,000
Engineering, selling, and administrative expenses	54,000	48,000
Interest expense	5,000	5,000
Income tax expense	9,000	3,000
Other expense (income)	1,000	(1,000)
Total expenses	263,000	220,000
Net earnings	$ 12,000	$ 5,000

Solution to Review Problem

TRE CORPORATION
Horizontal Analysis of Comparative Income Statement
For the Years Ended December 31, 2003 and 2002

			Increase (Decrease)	
	2003	2002	Amount	Percent
Total revenues	$275,000	$225,000	$50,000	22.2%
Expenses:				
Cost of products sold	$194,000	$165,000	$29,000	17.6
Engineering, selling, and administrative expenses	54,000	48,000	6,000	12.5
Interest expense	5,000	5,000	—	—
Income tax expense	9,000	3,000	6,000	200.0
Other expense (income)	1,000	(1,000)	2,000	—*
Total expenses	263,000	220,000	43,000	19.5
Net earnings	$ 12,000	$ 5,000	$ 7,000	140.0%

*Percentage changes are typically not computed for shifts from a negative amount to a positive amount, and vice versa.

TRE CORPORATION
Vertical Analysis of Comparative Income Statement
For the Years Ended December 31, 2003 and 2002

	2003		2002	
	Amount	Percent	Amount	Percent
Total revenue	$275,000	100.0%	$225,000	100.0%
Expenses:				
Cost of products sold	$194,000	70.5	$165,000	73.3
Engineering, selling, and administrative expenses	54,000	19.6	48,000	21.3
Interest expense	5,000	1.8	5,000	2.2
Income tax expense	9,000	3.3	3,000	1.4*
Other expense (income)	1,000	0.4	(1,000)	(0.4)
Total expenses	263,000	95.6	220,000	97.8
Net earnings	$ 12,000	4.4%	$ 5,000	2.2%

*Number rounded up.

The horizontal analysis shows that total revenues increased 22.2 percent. This percentage increase was greater than the 19.5 percent increase in total expenses, resulting in a 140 percent increase in net earnings.

The vertical analysis shows decreases in the percentages of total revenues consumed by the cost of products sold (from 73.3 percent in 2002 to 70.5 percent in 2003) and the engineering, selling, and administrative expenses (from 21.3 percent in 2002 to 19.6 percent in 2003). These two items are TRE Corporation's largest dollar expenses, so their percentage decreases are quite important. The relative reduction in expenses raised 2003 net earnings to 4.4 percent of sales, compared to 2.2 percent the preceding year. The overall analysis indicates that 2003 was significantly better than 2002.

Cyber Coach

Visit the Student Resources area of the *Accounting* Companion Website for extra practice with the new material in Chapter 18.

www.pearsoned.ca/horngren

Using Ratios to Make Business Decisions

OBJECTIVE 4
Compute the standard financial ratios used for decision making

An important part of financial analysis is the calculation and interpretation of ratios. A ratio is a useful way to show the relationship of one number to another number. For example, if the balance sheet shows current assets of $100,000 and current liabilities of $25,000, the ratio of current assets to current liabilities is $100,000 to $25,000. We simplify this numerical expression to the ratio of 4 to 1, which may also be written 4:1 and 4/1. Other acceptable ways of expressing this ratio include (1) "current assets are 400 percent of current liabilities," (2) "the business has four dollars in current assets for every one dollar in current liabilities," or simply, (3) "the current ratio is 4.0."

We often reduce the ratio fraction by writing the ratio as one figure over the other, for example, 4/1, and then dividing the numerator by the denominator. In this way, the ratio 4/1 may be expressed simply as 4. The 1 that represents the denominator of the fraction is understood, not written. Consider the ratio $175,000 : $165,000. After dividing the first figure by the second, we come to 1.06 : 1, which we state as 1.06. The second part of the ratio, the 1, is understood.

A manager, lender, or financial analyst may use any ratio that is relevant to a particular decision. Many companies include ratios in a special section of their annual reports. Potash Corporation of Saskatchewan Inc. displays ratio data in the consolidated summary section of its annual report. Exhibit 18-9 shows a sampling of that summary section. Investment services—Moody's, Standard & Poor's Canada, Robert Morris Associates, and others—report these ratios for companies and industries.

The Decision Guidelines feature on page 1007 summarizes the widely used ratios that we will discuss in this chapter. The ratios may be classified as follows:

1. Ratios that measure the company's ability to pay current liabilities
2. Ratios that measure the company's ability to sell inventory and collect receivables
3. Ratios that measure the company's ability to pay short-term and long-term debt

KEY POINT

We must learn how to understand relationships among the numbers on a financial statement to help us make business decisions. Horizontal and vertical analyses were our first attempt at studying such relationships. We now learn to use ratios, which help even more in analyzing the financial statements. We compare financial statement amounts to other items to assess what the ratio indicates about the company. How do we assess a ratio? We must consider prior years, industry averages, budgeted ratios, and so on—only then does a ratio have meaning.

Moody's Investors Service
www.moodys.com

Potash Corporation
www.potashcorp.com

EXHIBIT 18-9

Consolidated Financial Summary of Potash Corporation of Saskatchewan Inc. (Dollars in millions of U.S. dollars except per-share amounts)

Years ended December 31,	2000	1999	1998	1997	1996
Operating Results					
Net income (loss)	$ 198	$ (412)	$ 261	$ 297	$ 209
Per common share	$3.78	$(7.60)	$4.82	$5.68	$4.59
Operating income (loss)	$ 327	$ (353)	$ 442	$ 442	$ 297
Financial Position					
Common share equity	$2,012	$1,962	$2,454	$2,228	$1,406
Long-term debt	$ 414	$ 437	$ 933	$1,130	$ 620
Working capital	$(149)	$(105)	$ 329	$ 282	$ 279

4. Ratios that measure the company's profitability
5. Ratios used to analyze the company's stock as an investment

How much can a computer help in analyzing financial statements for investment purposes? Time yourself as you perform one of the financial-ratio problems in this chapter. Multiply your efforts by, say, 100 companies that you are comparing by means of this ratio. Now consider ranking these 100 companies on the basis of four or five additional ratios.

On-line financial databases, such as Lexis/Nexis, Financial Post DataGroup, and Globe Information Services, offer quarterly financial figures for hundreds of public corporations going back as much as 10 years. Assume that you wanted to compare companies' recent earnings histories. You might have the computer compare hundreds of companies on the basis of price/earnings ratio and rate of return on shareholders' equity. The computer could then give you the names of the 20 (or however many) companies that appear most favourable in terms of these ratios.

Accountants use computerized financial analysis a great deal. Public accountants focus on the individual client. They want to know how the client is doing compared with the previous year and compared with other firms in the industry. Auditors want to detect any emerging trends in the company's ratios and compare the results of actual operations with expected results. To do so, an auditor can download monthly financial statistics on a spreadsheet and compute the financial ratios to gain insight into the client's situation.

Measuring the Ability to Pay Current Liabilities

Working capital is defined by the following equation:

Working capital = Current assets – Current liabilities

Working capital is widely used to measure ability to pay current liabilities with current assets. In general, the larger the working capital, the better able the business is to pay its debts. Recall that capital or shareholders' equity is total assets minus total liabilities. Working capital is like a "current" version of total capital. The working capital amount considered alone, however, does not give a complete picture of the entity's working capital position. Consider two companies with equal working capital.

········· **THINKING IT OVER**

What are the current assets in order of liquidity?

A: Cash, short-term investments, receivables, inventory, and prepaid expenses. (If you have trouble identifying current assets, refer to Chapter 4, page 174.)

	Company A	Company B
Current assets	$100,000	$200,000
Current liabilities	(50,000)	(150,000)
Working capital	$ 50,000	$ 50,000

Both companies have working capital of $50,000, but Company A's working capital is as large as its current liabilities. Company B's working capital, on the other hand, is only one-third as large as its current liabilities. Which business has the better working-capital position? Company A, because its working capital is a higher percentage of current assets and current liabilities. To use working capital data in decision making, it is helpful to develop ratios. Two decision tools based on working capital data are the *current ratio* and the *acid-test ratio*.

Current Ratio The most common ratio using current asset and current liability data is the **current ratio**, which is total current assets divided by total current liabilities. We introduced the current ratio in Chapter 4 (page 179). Recall the makeup of current assets and current liabilities. Current assets consist of cash, short-term investments, net receivables, inventory, and prepaid expenses. Current liabilities include accounts payable, short-term notes payable, unearned revenues, and all types of accrued liabilities. The current ratio measures the company's ability to pay current liabilities with current assets.

Exhibits 18-10 and 18-11 give the comparative income statement and balance sheet of Palisades Furniture, Inc. respectively. The current ratios of Palisades Furniture, Inc., at December 31, 2002, and 2001, follow, along with the average for the retail furniture industry, a benchmark for evaluating Palisades Furniture, Inc.'s ratios:

Formula	Current Ratio of Palisades Furniture, Inc.		Retail Furniture Industry Average
	2002	2001	
Current ratio = $\dfrac{\text{Current assets}}{\text{Current liabilities}}$	$\dfrac{\$262,000}{\$142,000} = 1.85$	$\dfrac{\$236,000}{\$126,000} = 1.87$	1.80

The current ratio decreased slightly during 2002. A higher current ratio suggests that the business has sufficient liquid assets to maintain normal business operations. Compare Palisades Furniture, Inc.'s current ratio of 1.85 with the 1.80 average for the retail furniture industry and with current ratios of some actual companies.

Company	Current Ratio
Boliden Limited (Mining)	1.17
Canadian Tire Corporation, Limited (Merchandising)	1.31
Clearnet Communications Inc. (Wireless provider)	1.86
IPSCO Inc. (Steel producer)	2.43
Suncor Energy Inc. (Oil and gas)	0.64

What is an acceptable current ratio? The answer to this question depends on the nature of the business. The current ratio will generally exceed 1.0, while the norm for most companies is 1.60 to 1.90. Palisades Furniture, Inc.'s current ratio of 1.85 is within the range of those values. In most industries, a current ratio of 2.0 is considered good. The companies listed above are typical of their industries; note that they range from 0.64 (Suncor's industry is a capital-intensive one with relatively low cash flows) to 2.43.

Acid-Test Ratio

The **acid-test** (or **quick**) **ratio** tells us whether the entity could pay all its current liabilities if they came due immediately. We saw in Chapter 8 (page 425) that the higher the acid-test ratio, the better able the business is to pay its current liabilities. That is, could the company pass this *acid test*? To do so, the company would have to convert its most liquid assets to cash.

To compute the acid-test ratio, we add cash, short-term investments and net current receivables (accounts and notes receivable, net of allowances) and divide by total

EXHIBIT 18-10

Comparative Financial
Statements

PALISADES FURNITURE, INC.
Comparative Income Statement
For the Years Ended December 31, 2002 and 2001

	2002	2001
Net sales	$858,000	$803,000
Cost of goods sold	513,000	509,000
Gross margin	345,000	294,000
Operating expenses:		
Selling expenses	126,000	114,000
General expenses	118,000	123,000
Total operating expenses	244,000	237,000
Income from operations	101,000	57,000
Interest revenue	4,000	—
Interest expense	(24,000)	(14,000)
Income before income taxes	81,000	43,000
Income tax expense	33,000	17,000
Net income	$ 48,000	$ 26,000

current liabilities. Inventory and prepaid expenses are *not* included in the acid-test computations because a business may not be able to convert them to cash immediately to pay current liabilities. The acid-test ratio measures liquidity using a narrower asset base than the current ratio does.

EXHIBIT 18-11

Comparative Financial
Statements

THINKING IT OVER

A Ltd. and B Ltd. of the Working It Out on page 995 have equal amounts of working capital, but their current and acid-test (quick) ratios differ. Explain.

A: A Ltd. has a higher ratio of current assets to current liabilities than B Ltd., as shown by A Ltd.'s higher current ratio. A Ltd. should be able to meet current obligations more easily as they come due. A Ltd. has a higher ratio of quick (liquid) assets to current liabilities than B Ltd., as indicated by the quick ratio—A Ltd. is more "liquid" than B Ltd. Inventory and prepaid expenses are not "quick" assets. B Ltd. has more current liabilities than quick assets. B Ltd. may have trouble paying off current debts because it must convert inventory to receivables or to cash to pay these debts. A Ltd. appears to have adequate quick assets to meet its debts. A Ltd. seems to be in a stronger current financial position than B Ltd.

PALISADES FURNITURE, INC.
Comparative Balance Sheet
December 31, 2002 and 2001

Assets	2002	2001
Current assets:		
Cash	$ 29,000	$ 32,000
Accounts receivable, net	114,000	85,000
Inventories	113,000	111,000
Prepaid expenses	6,000	8,000
Total current assets	262,000	236,000
Long-term investments	18,000	9,000
Capital assets, net	507,000	399,000
Total assets	$787,000	$644,000
Liabilities		
Current liabilities:		
Notes payable	$ 42,000	$ 27,000
Accounts payable	73,000	68,000
Accrued liabilities	27,000	31,000
Total current liabilities	142,000	126,000
Long-term debt	289,000	198,000
Total liabilities	431,000	324,000
Shareholders' Equity		
Common stock	186,000	186,000
Retained earnings	170,000	134,000
Total shareholders' equity	356,000	320,000
Total liabilities and shareholders' equity	$787,000	$644,000

Palisades Furniture, Inc.'s acid-test ratios for 2002 and 2001 are as follows:

	Formula	Acid-Test Ratio of Palisades Furniture, Inc.		Retail Furniture Industry Average
		2002	2001	
Acid-test ratio =	Cash + Short-term investments + Net current receivables / Current liabilities	$\dfrac{\$29{,}000 + \$0 + \$114{,}000}{\$142{,}000} = 1.01$	$\dfrac{\$32{,}000 + \$0 + \$85{,}000}{\$126{,}000} = 0.93$	0.60

The company's acid-test ratio improved considerably during 2002 and is significantly better than the industry average. Compare Palisades Furniture, Inc.'s 1.01 acid-test ratio with the acid-test values of some well-known companies:

Company	Acid-Test Ratio
Cominco Ltd. (Mining)..	0.75
Dofasco Inc. (Steel producer)	0.99
Magna International Inc.	0.98
Molson Inc. (Brewer and Hockey)...............................	0.41
TransAlta Corporation (Energy)	0.58

Cominco Ltd.
www.cominco.com

TransAlta Corporation
www.transalta.com

The norm ranges from 0.20 to 1.00 as reported by Robert Morris Associates. An acid-test ratio of 0.90 to 1.00 is acceptable in most industries. How can a company like TransAlta Corporation operate with such a low acid-test ratio? TransAlta Corporation has total assets of almost $6 billion; its current assets represent slightly more than 10 percent of total assets. The energy industry is a capital-intensive one with relatively low cash flows.

Measuring the Ability to Sell Inventory and Collect Receivables

The ability to sell inventory and collect receivables is fundamental to business success. Recall the operating cycle of a merchandiser: cash to inventory to receivables and back to cash. If you need to, refer to the discussion of the operating cycle in Chapter 5, page 219. This section discusses three ratios that measure the ability to sell inventory and collect receivables.

Inventory Turnover Companies generally seek to achieve the quickest possible return on their investments. A return on an investment in inventory—usually a substantial amount—is no exception. The faster inventory sells, the sooner the business creates accounts receivable, and the sooner it collects cash.

Inventory turnover is a measure of the number of times a company sells its average level of inventory during a year. We introduced inventory turnover in Chapter 5, pages 239–241. Average inventory is computed as follows: (Beginning inventory + Ending inventory)/2. In general, companies prefer a high inventory turnover. An inventory turnover of 6 means that the company sells its average level of inventory six times during the year. This is generally better than a turnover of 3 or 4. However, a high value can mean that the business is not keeping enough inventory on hand, and that can result in lost sales if the company cannot meet a customer's need. Therefore, a business strives for the *most profitable* rate of inventory turnover, not necessarily the *highest* rate.

To compute the inventory turnover ratio, we divide cost of goods sold by the average inventory for the period. We use the cost of goods sold—not sales—in the computation because both cost of goods sold and inventory are stated *at cost*. Sales are stated at the sales value of inventory and therefore are not comparable to inventory cost.

WORKING IT OUT

Refer to the Working It Out on page 995. Suppose the beginning inventories for A Ltd. and B Ltd. are $19 and $98, respectively. Compute each company's rate of inventory turnover.

A:

A Ltd.: $\dfrac{\$100}{(\$21 + \$19)/2} = 5.0$ times

B Ltd.: $\dfrac{\$135}{(\$102 + \$98)/2} = 1.35$ times

THINKING IT OVER

Evaluate the inventory turnovers of the previous Working It Out.

A: A Ltd. turns its inventory more quickly than B Ltd., which sells its inventory less than twice a year. The ratio varies widely from industry to industry, but it appears that B Ltd. is carrying goods that are hard to sell. Or B Ltd. may be carrying too much inventory for its level of sales.

Another helpful way to analyze inventory is to compare the inventory turnover days:

$$\frac{365}{\text{Inventory turnover}}$$

The calculation for Palisades Furniture, Inc. for 2002 would be

$$\frac{365}{4.58} = 80 \text{ days}$$

It took the company approximately 80 days to sell an item in inventory.

Palisades Furniture, Inc.'s inventory turnover for 2002 is

Formula	Inventory Turnover of Palisades Furniture, Inc.	Retail Furniture Industry Average
Inventory turnover $= \dfrac{\text{Cost of goods sold}}{\text{Average inventory}}$	$\dfrac{\$513,000}{\$112,000} = 4.58$ times	2.70 times

Cost of goods sold appears in the income statement (Exhibit 18-10). Average inventory is calculated by averaging the beginning inventory ($111,000) and ending inventory ($113,000). (See the balance sheet, Exhibit 18-11.) If inventory levels vary greatly from month to month, compute the average by adding the 12 monthly balances and dividing this sum by 12.

Inventory turnover varies widely with the nature of the business. Companies that remove natural gas from the ground hold their inventory for a very short period of time and have an average turnover of 30. Palisades Furniture, Inc.'s turnover of 4.58 times a year is high for its industry, which has an average turnover of 2.70. Palisades Furniture, Inc.'s high inventory turnover results from its policy of keeping little inventory on hand. The company takes customer orders and has its suppliers ship directly to customers. Leon's Furniture Ltd., with stores from St. John's, Newfoundland, to Edmonton, Alberta, turns its inventory 4.54 times, on a par with Palisades Furniture, Inc.

Inventory turnover rates can vary greatly within a company. At Toys "Я" Us, an international retailer of toys and childcare products, diapers and formula turn over more than 12 times a year, whereas seasonal toys turn over less than three times a year. The entire Toys "Я" Us inventory turns over an average of three times a year. That inventory is at its lowest point on January 31 and at its highest point around October 31, to supply Christmas and holiday shoppers.

To evaluate fully a company's inventory turnover, compare the ratio over time. A sudden sharp decline or a steady decline over a long period suggests the need for corrective action.

Accounts Receivable Turnover Accounts receivable turnover measures a company's ability to collect cash from credit customers. In general, the higher the ratio, the more successfully the business collects cash, and the better off its operations are. However, a receivable turnover that is too high may indicate that credit is too tight, causing the loss of sales to good customers. To compute the accounts receivable turnover, we divide net credit sales by average net accounts receivable. The resulting ratio indicates how many times during the year the average level of receivables was turned into cash.

KEY POINT

The accounts receivable turnover helps measure the effectiveness of credit collections.

THINKING IT OVER

Evaluate the receivable ratios of the previous Working It Out.

A: Both companies' receivables turn over between three and four times a year—it takes about 1/3 to 1/4 of the year to collect the receivables. Compare the 77 and 98 days' sales in receivables with the company's credit terms. If A Ltd.'s credit terms are 2/10 n/30, then its collection department is doing a poor job of collecting. Or credit is being extended to uncreditworthy customers. A Ltd. should sell to those customers only on the cash basis.

Palisades Furniture, Inc.'s accounts receivable turnover ratio for 2002 is computed as follows:

Formula	Accounts Receivable Turnover of Palisades Furniture, Inc.	Retail Furniture Industry Average
Accounts receivable turnover $= \dfrac{\text{Net credit sales}}{\text{Average net accounts receivable}}$	$\dfrac{\$858,000}{\$99,500} = 8.62$ times	22.2 times

The net credit sales figure comes from the income statement. Palisades Furniture, Inc. makes all sales on credit. (If a company makes both cash and credit sales, this ratio is best computed using only net *credit* sales. Average net accounts receivable is calculated using the beginning accounts receivable balance ($85,000) and the ending balance ($114,000). If accounts receivable balances exhibit a seasonal pattern, compute the average using the 12 monthly balances.

Palisades Furniture, Inc.'s receivable turnover of 8.62 times is much lower than the industry average. This is because the company is a home-town store that sells to local people who tend to pay their bills over a period of time. Leon's Furniture Ltd. does not report credit sales. Accounts receivable turnover was 37.0 times, suggesting that a large proportion of sales were cash or credit card sales. Many larger furniture stores sell their receivables to other companies called *factors*. This practice keeps receivables low and receivable turnover high. But companies that factor (sell) their receivables receive less than face value on their sale. Palisades Furniture, Inc. follows a different strategy.

Days' Sales in Receivables   Businesses must convert accounts receivable to cash. All else being equal, the lower the Accounts Receivable balance, the more successful the business has been in converting receivables into cash, and the better off the business.

The **days'-sales-in-receivables** ratio tells us how many days' credit sales remain in Accounts Receivable. Recall from Chapter 8 (page 426) that days' sales in receivables indicates how many days it takes to collect the average level of receivables. To compute the ratio, we follow a two-step process. First, divide net sales by 365 days to calculate the average sales amount for one day. Second, divide this average day's sales amount into the average net accounts receivable.

The data to compute this ratio for Palisades Furniture, Inc. for 2002 are taken from the income statement and the balance sheet (Exhibit 18-10 and 18-11).

....
THINKING IT OVER

What does the 42 days' sales in receivables indicate?
A: It takes about 42 days to collect a receivable.

Q: Is this good or bad?
A: It depends on the credit period. If the credit period is 60 days, then this ratio is good. If the credit period is 30 days, then Palisades Furniture, Inc. must alter its credit/collection policies. To a creditor of Palisades Furniture, Inc., the important point is that it takes 42 days for the cash from Palisades Furniture, Inc.'s receivables to become available to pay off a debt.

Q: How would Palisades Furniture, Inc. improve this ratio?
A: Offer discounts for early payments; tighten credit policies; use more aggressive collection procedures. For example, Canadian Tires gives Canadian Tire money for cash payments.

Formula	Days' Sales in Accounts Receivable of Palisades Furniture, Inc.	Retail Furniture Industry Average
Days' Sales in Average Accounts Receivable:		
1. One day's sales $= \dfrac{\text{Net sales}}{365 \text{ days}}$	$\dfrac{\$858,000}{365 \text{ days}} = \$2,351$	
2. Days' sales in average accounts $= \dfrac{\text{Average net accounts receivable}}{\text{One day's sales}}$ receivable	$\dfrac{\$99,500}{\$2,351} = 42 \text{ days}$	16 days

Days' sales in average receivables can also be computed in a single step: $\$99,500/(\$858,000/365 \text{ days}) = 42$ days, or 365/receivables turnover of 8.62.

Palisades Furniture, Inc.'s ratio tells us that 42 days' sales remained in average accounts receivable during the year. The company will increase its cash inflow if it can decrease this ratio. The days' sales in receivables is higher (worse) than the industry average because the company collects its own receivables. Many other furniture stores sell their receivables and carry fewer days' sales in receivables. Palisades Furniture, Inc. remains competitive because of the personal relationship with customers. Without their good paying habits, the company's cash flow would suffer.

Measuring the Ability to Pay Short-Term and Long-Term Debt

The ratios discussed so far give us insight into current assets and current liabilities. Most businesses also have long-term liabilities. Two key indicators of a business's ability to pay both short-term and long-term liabilities are the *debt ratio* and *times-in-terest-earned ratio*.

Debt Ratio   The ratio of total liabilities to total assets—called the **debt ratio**—tells us the proportion of the company's assets that it has financed with debt. We introduced the debt ratio in Chapter 4, page 179. If the debt ratio is 1, then debt has been used to finance all the assets. A debt ratio of 0.50 means that the company has used debt to finance half its assets and that shareholders' equity has financed the other half. The higher the debt ratio, the higher the strain of paying interest each year and the principal amount at maturity. The lower the ratio, the lower the business's future obligations.

WORKING IT OUT

In Working It Out on page 995, assume the beginning account receivable balances are $40 and $70, respectively. Compute (1) accounts receivable turnover; (2) days' sales in receivables.

A:
(1) A Ltd.:
$\dfrac{\$200}{(\$45 + \$40)/2} = 4.71$
B Ltd.:
$\dfrac{\$270}{(\$75 + \$70)/2} = 3.72$

(2) A: $200/365 = \$0.55$;
$\$42.5/\$0.55 = 77$ days
B: $270/365 = \$0.74$;
$\$72.5/0.74 = 98$ days

Creditors view a high debt ratio with caution. If a business seeking financing already has large liabilities, then additional debt payments may be too much for the business to handle. To help protect themselves, creditors generally charge higher interest rates on new borrowing to companies with an already-high debt ratio. Palisades Furniture, Inc.'s debt ratios at the end of 2002 and 2001 are as follows:

.... **THINKING IT OVER**

The formula for the debt ratio is

Total liabilities/Total assets

Where have we seen this ratio before?

A: It is a common-size percentage on the balance sheet, which is expressed as a percentage of total assets.

	Formula	Debt Ratio of Palisades Furniture, Inc.		Retail Furniture Industry Average
		2002	**2001**	
Debt ratio =	$\dfrac{\text{Total liabilities}}{\text{Total assets}}$	$\dfrac{\$431,000}{\$787,000} = 0.55$	$\dfrac{\$324,000}{\$644,000} = 0.50$	0.61

Palisades Furniture, Inc. expanded operations by financing the purchase of property, plant, and equipment through borrowing, which is common. This expansion explains the company's increased debt ratio. Even after the increase in 2002, the company's debt is not very high. The average debt ratio for most companies ranges around 0.57 to 0.67, with relatively little variation from company to company. Palisades Furniture, Inc.'s 0.55 debt ratio indicates a fairly low-risk debt position in comparison with the retail furniture industry average of 0.61. Leon's Furniture Ltd.'s debt ratio is 0.34, much lower than Palisades Furniture, Inc. or the industry. While Leon's shares are listed on the Toronto Stock Exchange, a majority of the shares are held by the Leon family.

KEY POINT

Palisades Furniture, Inc. has a debt ratio of 55% in 2002, which means that the company has a 45% equity ratio (the amount of assets financed by equity). The debt and equity ratios must total 100%. All assets are financed either by debt or by equity.

Times-Interest-Earned Ratio   The debt ratio measures the effect of debt on the company's *financial position* (balance sheet) but indicates nothing about its ability to pay interest expense. Analysts use a second ratio—the **times-interest-earned ratio**—to relate income to interest expense. To compute this ratio, we divide income from operations (which is *net* income + interest expense + income tax expense) by interest expense. This ratio measures the number of times that operating income can *cover* interest expense. For this reason, the ratio is also called the **interest-coverage ratio**. A high times-interest-earned ratio indicates ease in paying interest expense; a low value suggests difficulty.

Palisades Furniture, Inc's times-interest-earned ratios follow:

	Formula	Times-Interest-Earned Ratio of Palisades Furniture, Inc.		Retail Furniture Industry Average
		2002	**2001**	
Times-interest-earned ratio =	$\dfrac{\text{Income from operations}}{\text{Interest expense}}$	$\dfrac{\$101,000}{\$24,000} = 4.21$ times	$\dfrac{\$57,000}{\$14,000} = 4.07$ times	2.00 times

.... **THINKING IT OVER**

What makes a corporation with a lot of debt a more risky loan prospect than one with a lot of equity?

A: Interest on debt is contractual and not discretionary. Dividends are discretionary and do not have to be declared.

Q: What happens if interest on debt is not paid?

A: Creditors can force the company into bankruptcy.

The company's times-interest-earned ratio increased in 2002. This is a favourable sign about the company, especially since the company's liabilities rose substantially during the year. Palisades Furniture, Inc.'s new capital assets, we conclude, have earned more in operating income than they have cost the businesses in interest expense. The company's times-interest-earned ratio of around 4.00 is much better than the 2.00 average for furniture retailers. The norm for businesses, as reported by Robert Morris Associates, falls in the range of 2.00 to 3.00 for most companies. Leon's Furniture Ltd. has no long-term debt.

Based on its debt ratio and times-interest-earned ratio, Palisades Furniture, Inc. appears to have little difficulty *servicing its debt*, that is, paying its liabilities.

Measuring a Company's Profitability

The fundamental goal of business is to earn a profit. Ratios that measure profitability play a large role in decision making. These ratios are reported in the business press, by investment services, and in companies' annual financial reports.

Rate of Return on Net Sales   In business, the term *return* is used broadly and loosely as an evaluation of profitability. Consider a percentage called the **rate of return on net sales** or, simply **return on sales**. (The word *net* is usually omitted for convenience, even though the net sales figure is used to compute the ratio.) It is also called the **profit margin.** This ratio shows the percentage of each sales dollar earned as net income. The rate-of-return-on-sales ratios for Palisades Furniture, Inc. are calculated as follows:

Formula		Rate of Return on Sales of Palisades Furniture, Inc.		Retail Furniture Industry Average
		2002	2001	
Rate of return on sales	= Net income / Net sales	$48,000 / $858,000 = 0.056, or 5.6%	$26,000 / $803,000 = 0.032, or 3.2%	0.8%

The increase in Palisades Furniture, Inc.'s return on sales is significant and identifies the company as more successful than the average furniture store. Companies strive for a high rate of return. The higher the rate of return, the more net sales dollars are providing income to the business and the fewer net sales dollars are absorbed by expenses. Compare Palisades Furniture, Inc.'s rate of return on sales to the rates of some other companies:

Company	Rate of Return on Sales
ATCO Ltd. (Utilities)	4.2%
Bombardier Inc. (Diversified)	5.3
Cominco Ltd. (Mining)	9.7
BCT. TELUS Communications Inc. (Telecommunications)	6.0
Sleeman Breweries Ltd.	7.7

As these numbers indicate, the rate of return on sales varies widely from industry to industry.

One strategy for increasing the rate of return on sales is to develop a product that commands a premium price such as Bombardier's Ski-doo, Purdy's chocolates, and certain brands of clothing, such as Roots. Another strategy is to control costs. If successful, either strategy converts a higher proportion of sales into net income and increases the rate of return on net sales.

A return measure can be computed on any revenue and sales amount. Return on net sales, as we have seen, is net income divided by net sales. *Return on total revenues* is net income divided by total revenues. A company can compute a return on other specific portions of revenue as its information needs dictate.

Rate of Return on Total Assets   The **rate of return on total assets** or, simply, **return on assets** measures a company's success in using its assets to earn a profit. We first discussed rate of return on total assets in Chapter 13, page 730. Creditors have loaned money to the company, and the interest they receive is the return on their investment. Shareholders have invested in the company's shares, and net income is their return. The sum of interest expense and net income is the return to the two groups that have financed the company's operations, and this amount is the numerator of the return-on-assets ratio. Average total assets is the denominator. Palisades Furniture, Inc.'s return on total assets is computed as follows:

Formula		Rate of Return on Total Assets of Palisades Furniture, Inc.	Retail Furniture Industry Average
Rate of return on total assets	= (Net Income + Interest expense) / Average total assets	($48,000 + $24,000) / $715,500 = 0.101, or 10.1%	4.9%

Refer to the Working It Out on page 995. Compute (1) the debt ratio and (2) the times-interest-earned ratio.

WORKING IT OUT

A:
(1) A Ltd.: 50% ($150/$300)
    B Ltd.: 71% ($390/$550)
(2) A Ltd.: 13.0 times
    ($200 − $100 − $22)/$6
    B Ltd.: 3.5 times
    ($270 − $135 − $30)/$30

KEY POINT

Note the numerator in the times-interest-earned ratio: *operating income* (not net income). Some investors and creditors calculate operating income, if not given, by the formula:
Operating income = Net income + Interest expense + Income tax expense

THINKING IT OVER

Evaluate the ratios of the previous Working It Out in relation to the ability to repay long-term debt.
A: A Ltd. has a smaller percentage of total assets tied up in debt; 0.50% is a low debt ratio. B Ltd. may have more trouble paying its debts because a larger percentage of its assets are financed by liabilities as compared to equity. B Ltd. is earning only enough operating income to cover its interest 3.5 times. The lower this ratio, the more difficult it will be for B Ltd. to pay its interest. A Ltd. has a much stronger financial position than B Ltd.

KEY POINT

The denominator for rate of return on total assets is average total assets. Income is earned throughout the year. For the denominator to be stated for the same time period as the numerator, an average of assets for the year is used.

KEY POINT

The rate of return on total assets tells those who finance the assets, both creditors and owners, the level of return the company earned for each dollar invested in the assets. A return of 0.101, or 10.1%, indicates that the company earned $0.101 for each dollar invested in assets.

Net income and interest expense are taken from the income statement (Exhibit 18-10). To compute average total assets, we use beginning and ending total assets from the comparative balance sheet (Exhibit 18-11). Compare Palisades Furniture, Inc.'s rate of return on assets to the rates of some other companies:

Company	Rate of Return on Assets
Inco Limited (Mining)...	1.2%
IPSCO Inc. (Steel producer)	10.1%
Leon's Furniture Limited (Furniture retailing)	14.1%
Magna International Inc. (Automotive systems)	6.6%
TransAlta Corporation (Energy)..	5.0%

Rate of Return on Common Shareholders' Equity   Perhaps the most widely used measure of profitability is **rate of return on common shareholders' equity**, which is often shortened to **return on shareholders' equity**, or simply, **return on equity**. We examined this ratio in detail in Chapter 13, page 730.

This ratio shows the relationship between net income and common shareholders' investment in the company—how much income is earned for every dollar invested by the common shareholders. To compute this ratio, we first subtract preferred dividends from net income. The remainder is net income available to the common shareholders. We then divide net income available to common shareholders by the average common shareholders' equity during the year. The 2002 rate of return on common shareholders' equity for Palisades Furniture, Inc. is calculated as follows:

Formula		Rate of Return on Common Shareholders' Equity of Palisades Furniture, Inc.	Retail Furniture Industry Average
Rate of return on common shareholders' equity	$=$ $\dfrac{\text{Net income} - \text{Preferred dividends}}{\text{Average common shareholders' equity}}$	$\dfrac{\$48,000 - \$0}{\$338,000}$ $=$ 0.142, or 14.2%	9.3%

We compute average equity using the beginning and ending balances [($356,000 + $320,000)/2 = $338,000]. Common shareholders' equity is equal to total equity minus preferred equity.

Observe that Palisades Furniture, Inc.'s return on equity (0.142, or 14.2 percent) is higher than return on assets (0.101, or 10.1 percent). This difference results from borrowing at one rate—say, 8 percent—and investing the funds to earn a higher rate, such as the firm's 14.2 percent return on shareholders' equity. This practice is called **trading on the equity,** or the use of **leverage**. It is directly related to the debt ratio. The higher the debt ratio, the higher the leverage. Companies that finance operations with debt are said to *lever* their positions.

For Palisades Furniture, Inc. and many other companies, leverage increases profitability. That is not always the case, however. Leverage can also have a negative impact on profitability. If revenues drop, debt and interest expense still must be paid. Therefore, leverage is a double-edged sword, increasing profits during good times but compounding losses during bad times.

Compare Palisades Furniture, Inc.'s rate of return on common shareholder's equity with rates of other companies. We have used the same companies as for the previous illustration:

Company	Rate of Return on Common Shareholders' Equity
Inco Limited (Mining)	-0.28%*
IPSCO Inc. (Steel Producer)......................................	9.16%
Leon's Furniture Limited (Furniture retailing)........	21.14%
Magna International Inc. (Automotive systems).....	12.12%
TransAlta Corporation (Energy)	10.10%

*Inco paid preferred dividends of $26 million (US), which resulted in a negative rate of return.

THINKING IT OVER

Refer to the Working It Out on page 995. Assume the companies' beginning total assets are $280 and $510 and their beginning common shareholders' equity to be $130 and $140, respectively. Compute (1) the rate of return on total assets and (2) the rate of return on common shareholders' equity.

A:

(1) A Ltd.:

$$\frac{\$60 + \$6}{(\$280 + \$300)/2} = 22.8\%$$

B Ltd.:

$$\frac{\$50 + \$30}{(\$510 + \$550)/2} = 15.1\%$$

(2) A Ltd.:

$$\frac{\$60 - \$0}{(\$130 + \$150)/2} = 42.9\%$$

B Ltd.:

$$\frac{\$50 - \$1}{(\$140 + \$150)/2} = 33.8\%$$

Earnings per Share of Common Stock *Earnings per share of common stock* or, simply, **earnings per share (EPS)** is perhaps the most widely quoted of all financial statistics. Recall from Chapter 14, page 776, that GAAP requires corporations to disclose EPS figures on the income statement. EPS is the only ratio that must appear on the face of the income statement. EPS is the amount of net income per share of the company's *common* stock. Earnings per share is computed by dividing net income available to common shareholders by the weighted average number of common shares outstanding during the year. Preferred dividends are subtracted from net income because the preferred shareholders have a prior claim to their dividends. If the company has bonds or preferred shares that are convertible into common shares, the company must also disclose fully diluted earnings per share. Palisades Furniture, Inc. has no preferred stock outstanding and so has no preferred dividends. Computations of the firm's EPS for 2002 and 2001 follow (the company had 10,000 shares of common stock outstanding throughout 2001 and 2002):

Formula	Earnings per Share of Palisades Furniture, Inc.	
	2002	2001
Earnings per share of common stock (EPS) = $\dfrac{\text{Net income} - \text{Preferred dividends}}{\text{Weighted average number of shares of common stock outstanding}}$	$\dfrac{\$48,000 - \$0}{10,000} = \$4.80$	$\dfrac{\$26,000 - \$0}{10,000} = \$2.60$

Palisades Furniture, Inc.'s EPS increased 85 percent. Its shareholders should not expect such a large boost in EPS every year. Most companies strive to increase EPS by 10 to 15 percent annually, and strong companies do so. However, even the most dramatic upward trends include an occasional bad year.

Analyzing Stock as an Investment

Investors purchase stock to earn a return on their investment. This return consists of two parts: (1) gains (or losses) from selling the stock at a price that is different from the investors' purchase price, and (2) dividends, the periodic distributions to shareholders. The ratios we examine in this section help analysts evaluate stock in terms of market price or dividend payments.

Price/Earnings Ratio The **price/earnings ratio** is the ratio of the market price of a share of common stock to the company's earnings per share. This ratio, abbreviated P/E, appears in *The National Post* stock listings and other newspapers and on Internet sites giving stock information. P/E plays an important part in evaluating decisions to buy, hold, and sell stocks. It indicates the market price of $1 of earnings. If earnings are negative, the P/E is not applicable.

The calculations for the P/E ratios of Palisades Furniture, Inc. follow. The market price of its common shares was $50 at the end of 2002 and $35 at the end of 2001. These prices can be obtained from such sources as financial publications, a stockbroker, the Internet, or some other source outside the accounting records of the company.

	Formula		Price/Earnings Ratio of Palisades Furniture, Inc.	
			2002	2001
Price/ earnings ratio	$=$	Market price per share of common stock / Earnings per share	$\dfrac{\$50.00}{\$4.80} = 10.4$	$\dfrac{\$35.00}{\$2.60} = 13.5$

Given Palisades Furniture, Inc.'s 2002 price/earnings ratio of 10.4, we would say that the company's shares are selling at 10.4 times earnings. The decline from the 2001 P/E ratio of 13.5 is not a cause for alarm because the market price of the stock is not under Palisades Furniture, Inc.'s control. Net income is more controllable, and it increased during 2002. Like most other ratios, P/E ratios vary from industry to industry. P/E ratios may range from 11.9 for utilities like Gaz Métropolitain and 10.8 for BC Gas to more than 40 for stocks such as Bombardier and JDS Uniphase.

The higher a stock's P/E ratio, the higher its *downside risk*—the risk that the stock's market price will fall. Some investors interpret a sharp increase in a stock's P/E ratio as a signal to sell the stock.

.... **THINKING IT OVER**

In the Working It Out on page 995 use the following information:

	A Ltd.	B Ltd.
Market price per share	$20	$30
Shares of common stock outstanding	25	10
Dividend per share	0.75	1.50

Compute the (1) EPS, (2) P/E, and (3) dividend yield.

A:

(1) A Ltd.: $\dfrac{\$60 - \$0}{25 \text{ shares}} = \$2.40$

B Ltd.: $\dfrac{\$50 - \$1}{10 \text{ shares}} = \$4.90$

(2) A Ltd.: 8.3 ($20/$2.40)
B Ltd.: 6.1 ($30/$4.90)

(3) A Ltd.: 3.75% ($0.75/$20)
B Ltd.: 5% ($1.50/$30)

Dividend Yield **Dividend yield** is the ratio of dividends per share to the stock's market price per share. This ratio measures the percentage of a stock's market value that is returned annually as dividends, an important concern of shareholders. *Preferred shareholders*, who invest primarily to receive dividends, pay special attention to this ratio.[3]

Palisades Furniture, Inc. paid annual cash dividends of $1.20 per share in 2002 and $1.00 in 2001 and market prices of the company's common shares were $50.00 in 2002 and $35.00 in 2001. Calculation of the company's dividend yields on common shares are as follows:

	Formula		Dividend Yield on Common Stock of Palisades Furniture, Inc.	
			2002	2001
Dividend yield on common stock[3]	$=$	Dividend per share of common stock / Market price per share of common stock	$\dfrac{\$1.20}{\$50.00} = 0.024,$ or 2.4%	$\dfrac{\$1.00}{\$35.00} = 0.029,$ or 2.9%

Investors who buy Palisades Furniture, Inc.'s common shares for $50 can expect to receive almost 2½ percent of their investment annually in the form of cash dividends. Dividend yields vary widely, from more than 2.5 percent for older established firms like Manitoba Telecom Services (2.7 percent) and BCE Inc. (3.5 percent) down to a range of 0 to 2.5 percent for growth-oriented companies like Magna International (2.4 percent) and Four Seasons Hotels (0.1 percent). Palisades Furniture, Inc.'s dividend yield places the company just below the first group.

Book Value per Share of Common Stock **Book value per share of common stock** is simply common shareholders' equity divided by the number of shares of common stock outstanding. Common shareholders' equity equals total shareholders' equity less preferred equity including cumulative preferred dividends. Palisades Furniture, Inc. has no preferred stock outstanding. Calculations of its book value per share of common stock ratios are on the next page. Recall that 10,000 shares of common stock were outstanding at the end of years 2002 and 2001.

Book value indicates the recorded accounting amount for each share of common stock outstanding. Many experts argue that book value is not useful for investment analysis. Recall from Chapter 13, page 729, that book value depends on historical

---

[3]Dividend yields may also be calculated for preferred stock.

Formula	Book Value per Share of the Common Stock of Palisades Furniture, Inc.	
	2002	2001
Book value per share of common stock $=$ $\dfrac{\text{Total shareholder's equity} - \text{Preferred equity}}{\text{Number of shares of common stock outstanding}}$	$\dfrac{\$356{,}000 - \$0}{10{,}000} = \$35.60$	$\dfrac{\$320{,}000 - \$0}{10{,}000} = \$32.00$

costs, while market value depends on investors' outlook for dividends and an increase in the stock's market price. Book value bears no relationship to market value and provides little information beyond shareholders' equity reported on the balance sheet. But other investors base their investment decisions on book value. For example, some investors rank stocks on the basis of the ratio of market price to book value. To these investors, the lower the ratio, the lower the risk, and the more attractive the stock. These investors who focus on the balance sheet are called "value" investors, as contrasted with "growth" investors, who focus more on trends in a company's net income.

Limitations of Financial Analysis

OBJECTIVE 5
Use ratios in decision making

Business decisions are made in a world of uncertainty. As useful as ratios may be, they do have limitations. We may liken their use in decision making to a physician's use of a thermometer. A reading of 39°C indicates that something is wrong with the patient, but the temperature alone does not indicate what the problem is or how to cure it.

In financial analysis, a sudden drop in a company's current ratio signals that *something* is wrong, but this change does not identify the problem or show how to correct it. The business manager must analyze the figures that go into the ratio to determine whether current assets have decreased, current liabilities have increased, or both. If current assets have dropped, is the problem a cash shortage? Are accounts receivable down? Are inventories too low? Is the condition temporary? Only by analyzing the individual items that make up the ratio can the manager determine how to solve the problem. The manager must evaluate data on all ratios in the light of other information about the company and about its particular line of business, such as increased competition or a slowdown in the economy.

Legislation, international affairs, competition, scandals, and many other factors can turn profits into losses, and vice versa. To be most useful, ratios should be analyzed over a period of years to take into account a representative group of these factors. Any one year, or even any two years, may not be representative of the company's performance over the long term.

Economic Value Added (EVA®)— A New Measure of Performance

OBJECTIVE 6
Measure economic value added by a company's operations

The top managers of Imasco, Domtar, Husky Injection Moulding, Coca-Cola, Quaker Oats, and other leading companies use **economic value added (EVA®)**[4] to evaluate their company's operating performance. EVA® combines the concepts of accounting income and corporate finance to measure whether the company's operations have increased shareholder wealth. EVA® can be computed as follows:

---

[4]**EVA®** was popularized and trademarked by Stern, Steven & Co. in the United States. For more information, see Armitage, Howard M. and Vijay Jog, "Economic Value Creation," *CMA Magazine*, October 1996, pp. 21–24.

$$\text{EVA}^® = \text{Net income} + \text{Interest expense} - \text{Capital charge}$$

where

$$\text{Capital charge} = \left(\begin{array}{c} \text{Short-term} \\ \text{debt} \end{array} + \begin{array}{c} \text{Long-term} \\ \text{debt} \end{array} + \begin{array}{c} \text{Shareholders'} \\ \text{equity} \end{array} \right) \times \begin{array}{c} \text{Cost of} \\ \text{capital} \end{array}$$

Coca-Cola
www.coke.com

Quaker Oats
www.quakeroats.ca

BCE Inc.
www.bce.ca

All amounts for the EVA® computation, except the cost of capital, are taken from the financial statements. The **cost of capital** is a weighted average of the returns demanded by the company's shareholders and lenders. The cost of capital varies with the company's level of risk. For example, shareholders would demand a higher return from a start-up computer software company than from BCE Inc. because the new company is untested and therefore more risky. Lenders would also charge the new company a higher interest rate because of this greater risk. Thus the new company has a higher cost of capital than BCE Inc. The cost of capital is a major topic in finance courses. In the following discussions, we merely assume a value for the cost of capital (such as 10%, 12%, or 15%) to illustrate the computation of EVA® and its use in decision making.

The idea behind EVA® is that the returns to the company's shareholders (net income) and to its creditors (interest expense) should exceed the company's capital charge. The **capital charge** is the amount that shareholders and lenders *charge* a company for the use of their money. A positive EVA® amount indicates an increase in shareholder wealth, and the company's stock price should rise. If the EVA® measure is negative, the shareholders will probably be unhappy with the company's progress and sell its stock, resulting in a decrease in the stock's price. Different companies tailor the EVA® computation to meet their own needs.

Let's apply EVA® to Lucent Technologies Inc. Lucent's EVA® for 1999 can be computed as follows, assuming a 12% cost of capital for the company (dollar amounts in millions):

Lucent's EVA® =

$$= \begin{array}{c} \text{Net} \\ \text{income} \end{array} + \begin{array}{c} \text{Interest} \\ \text{expense} \end{array} - \left[\left(\begin{array}{c} \text{Short-term} \\ \text{debt} \end{array} + \begin{array}{c} \text{Long-term} \\ \text{debt} \end{array} + \begin{array}{c} \text{Shareholders'} \\ \text{equity} \end{array} \right) \times \begin{array}{c} \text{Cost of} \\ \text{capital} \end{array} \right]$$

$$= \$4,766 + \$406 - [(\$2,864 + \$4,162 + \$13,584) \times 0.12]$$

$$= \$5,172 - \$20,610 \times 0.12$$

$$= \$5,172 - \$2,473$$

$$= \$2,699$$

By this measure, Lucent Technologies Inc.'s operations during 1999 added $2.7 billion ($2,699 million) of value to its shareholders' wealth after meeting the company's capital charge. This performance is outstanding. Lucent's positive EVA® explains why the company's stock is popular with investors.

Efficient Markets, Management Action, and Investor Decisions

An **efficient capital market** is one in which the market prices reflect the impact of all information available to the public. Market efficiency means that managers cannot fool the market with accounting gimmicks. If the information is available, the market as a whole can translate accounting data into a "fair" price for the company's stock.

Suppose you are the president of CompSys Ltd. Reported earnings per share are $4 and the share price is $40—so the P/E ratio is 10. You believe the corporation's shares are underpriced in comparison with other companies in your industry. To correct this situation you are considering changing from accelerated to straight-line amortization. The accounting change will increase earnings per share to $5. Will the shares then rise to $50? Probably not. The stock price will likely remain at $40 because the market can understand that the change in amortization method, not improved operations, caused earnings to increase.

In an efficient market, the search for "underpriced" shares is fruitless unless the investor has relevant private information. Moreover, it is unlawful to invest based on *inside* information—information that is available only to corporate management. For outside investors in an efficient market, an appropriate investment strategy seeks to manage risk, to diversify investments so that you do not lose everything if one stock loses value, and to minimize transaction costs. The role of financial statement analysis is mainly to help measure the risks of various stocks. The goal is to manage the risk of the overall investment portfolio.

Managers, owners, investors, and creditors all use financial ratios to measure an entity's progress. The Decision Guidelines feature summarizes the ratios covered in this chapter. Memorize each ratio's computation and the information it provides because you will be using these ratios for the rest of your life.

DECISION GUIDELINES — Ratios Used in Financial Statement Analysis

Ratio	Computation	Information Provided
Measuring the company's ability to pay current liabilities:		
1. Current ratio	$\dfrac{\text{Total current assets}}{\text{Total current liabilities}}$	Measures ability to pay liabilities with current assets.
2. Acid-test (quick) ratio	$\dfrac{\text{Cash} + \text{Short-term investments} + \text{Net current receivables}}{\text{Current liabilities}}$	Shows ability to pay all current liabilities if they come due immediately.
Measuring the company's ability to sell inventory and collect receivables:		
3. Inventory turnover	$\dfrac{\text{Cost of goods sold}}{\text{Average inventory}}$	Indicates saleability of inventory—the number of times a company sells its average inventory level during a year.
4. Accounts receivable turnover	$\dfrac{\text{Net credit sales}}{\text{Average net accounts receivable}}$	Measures ability to collect cash from credit customers.
5. Days' sales in receivables	$\dfrac{\text{Average net accounts receivable}}{\text{One day's sales}}$	Shows how many days' sales remain in Accounts Receivable—how many days it takes to collect the average level of receivables.
Measuring the company's ability to pay short-term and long-term debt:		
6. Debt ratio	$\dfrac{\text{Total liabilities}}{\text{Total assets}}$	Indicates percentage of assets financed with debt.
7. Times-interest-earned ratio	$\dfrac{\text{Income from operations}}{\text{Interest expense}}$	Measures the number of times operating income can cover interest expense.
Measuring the company's profitability:		
8. Rate of return on net sales (profit margin)	$\dfrac{\text{Net income}}{\text{Net sales}}$	Shows the percentage of each sales dollar earned as net income.
9. Rate of return on total assets	$\dfrac{\text{Net income} + \text{Interest expense}}{\text{Average total assets}}$	Measures how profitably a company uses its assets.
10. Rate of return on common shareholders' equity	$\dfrac{\text{Net income} - \text{Preferred dividends}}{\text{Average common shareholders' equity}}$	Gauges how much income is earned with the money invested by common shareholders.

continued

| 11. | Earnings per share of common stock | $\dfrac{\text{Net income} - \text{Preferred dividends}}{\text{Weighted average number of shares of common stock outstanding}}$ | Gives the amount of earnings per one share of the company's common stock. |

Analyzing the company's stock as an investment:

12.	Price/earnings ratio	$\dfrac{\text{Market price per share of common stock}}{\text{Earnings per share}}$	Indicates the market price of $1 of earnings.
13.	Dividend yield	$\dfrac{\text{Dividends per share of common (or preferred) stock}}{\text{Market price per share of common (or preferred) stock}}$	Shows the percentage of the market price of each share returned as dividends to shareholders each period.
14.	Book value per share of common stock	$\dfrac{\text{Total shareholders' equity} - \text{Preferred equity}}{\text{Number of shares of common stock outstanding}}$	Indicates the recorded accounting amount for each share of common stock outstanding.

Summary Problem
for Your Review

The following financial data are adapted from the annual report of Trends Ltd., which operates a chain of clothing stores.

TRENDS LTD. Five-Year Selected Financial Data					
Operating Results	**2003**	**2002**	**2001**	**2000**	**1999**
(Dollar amounts in thousands)					
Net sales	$2,960	$2,519	$1,934	$1,587	$1,252
Cost of goods sold and occupancy expenses, excluding amortization	1,856	1,496	1,188	1,007	814
Interest expense (net)	4	4	1	3	3
Income from operations	340	371	237	163	126
Income taxes	129	141	92	65	52
Net earnings	211	230	145	98	74
Cash dividends	44	41	30	23	18
Financial Position					
Merchandise inventory	366	314	247	243	193
Total assets	1,379	1,147	777	579	481
Working capital	355	236	579	129	434
Current ratio	2.06:1	1.71:1	1.39:1	1.69:1	1.70:1
Shareholders' equity	888	678	466	338	276
Average number of shares of common stock outstanding (in thousands)	144	142	142	141	145

Required

Compute the following ratios for 2000 through 2003, and evaluate Trends Ltd.'s operating results. Are operating results strong or weak? Did they improve or deteriorate during the four-year period?

1. Gross profit percentage
2. Net income as percent of sales
3. Earnings per share
4. Inventory turnover
5. Times-interest-earned ratio
6. Rate of return on shareholders' equity

Solution to Review Problem

	2003	2002	2001	2000
1. Gross profit percentage	$\dfrac{\$2,960 - \$1,856}{\$2,960}$ $= 37.3\%$	$\dfrac{\$2,519 - \$1,496}{\$2,519}$ $= 40.6\%$	$\dfrac{\$1,934 - \$1,188}{\$1,934}$ $= 38.6\%$	$\dfrac{\$1,587 - \$1,007}{\$1,587}$ $= 36.5\%$
2. Net income as a percent of sales	$\dfrac{\$211}{\$2,960} = 7.1\%$	$\dfrac{\$230}{\$2,519} = 9.1\%$	$\dfrac{\$145}{\$1,934} = 7.5\%$	$\dfrac{\$98}{\$1,587} = 6.2\%$
3. Earnings per share	$\dfrac{\$211}{144} = \$1.47$	$\dfrac{\$230}{142} = \$1.62$	$\dfrac{\$145}{142} = \$1.02$	$\dfrac{\$98}{141} = \$0.70$
4. Inventory turnover	$\dfrac{\$1,856}{(\$366 + \$314)/2}$ $= 5.5$ times	$\dfrac{\$1,496}{(\$314 + \$247)/2}$ $= 5.3$ times	$\dfrac{\$1,188}{(\$247 + \$243)/2}$ $= 4.8$ times	$\dfrac{\$1,007}{(\$243 + \$193)/2}$ $= 4.6$ times
5. Times-interest-earned ratio	$\dfrac{\$340}{\$4} = 85$ times	$\dfrac{\$371}{\$4} = 93$ times	$\dfrac{\$237}{\$1} = 237$ times	$\dfrac{\$163}{\$3} = 54$ times
6. Rate of return on shareholders' equity	$\dfrac{\$211}{(\$888 + \$678)/2}$ $= 26.9\%$	$\dfrac{\$230}{(\$678 + \$466)/2}$ $= 40.2\%$	$\dfrac{\$145}{(\$466 + \$338)/2}$ $= 36.1\%$	$\dfrac{\$98}{(\$338 + \$276)/2}$ $= 31.9\%$

Evaluation: During this four-year period, Trends Ltd.'s operating results were outstanding. Operating results improved, with all ratio values but return on shareholders' equity higher in 2003 than in 2000. Moreover, all the performance measures indicate high levels of income and return to investors.

Summary

1. **Perform a horizontal analysis of financial statements.** Banks loan money, investors buy shares, and managers run businesses on the basis of the analysis of accounting information. *Horizontal analysis* is the study of percentage changes in financial statement items from one period to the next. To compute these percentage changes, (1) calculate the dollar amount of the change from the base (earlier) period to the later period, and (2) divide the dollar amount of change by the base-period amount. *Trend percentages* are a form of horizontal analysis.

2. **Perform a vertical analysis of financial statements.** *Vertical analysis* of a financial statement reveals the relationship of each statement item to a specified base, which is the 100% figure. On an income statement, net sales (or revenues) is usually the base. On a balance sheet, total assets is usually the base.

3. **Prepare common-size financial statements for benchmarking against the industry average and key competitors.** A form of vertical analysis, *common-size statements* report only percentages, no dollar amounts. Common-size statements ease the comparison of different companies and may signal the need for corrective action. *Benchmarking* is the practice of comparing a company to a standard set by other companies, with a view toward improvement.

4. **Compute the standard financial ratios used for decision making.** An important part of financial analysis is the calculation and interpretation of financial ratios.

A ratio expresses the relationship of one item to another. The most important financial ratios measure a company's ability to pay current liabilities (current ratio, acid-test ratio); its ability to sell inventory and collect receivables (inventory turnover, accounts receivable turnover, days' sales in receivables); its ability to pay long-term debt (debt ratio, times-interest-earned ratio); its profitability (rate of return on net sales, rate of return on total assets, rate of return on common shareholders' equity, earnings per share of common stock); and its value as an investment (price/earnings ratio, dividend yield, book value per share of common stock).

5. **Use ratios in decision making.** Analysis of financial ratios over time is an important way to track a company's progress. A change in one of the ratios over time may signal the existence of a problem. It is up to the company's managers to find the source of this problem and take actions to correct it.

6. **Measure economic value added by a company's operations.** *Economic value added (EVA®)* measures whether a company's operations have increased its shareholders' wealth. EVA® can be defined as the excess of net income and interest expense over the company's capital charge, which is the amount that the company's shareholders and lenders charge for the use of their money. A positive amount of EVA® indicates an increase in shareholder wealth; a negative amount indicates a decrease.

Self-Study Questions

Test your understanding of the chapter by marking the best answer for each of the following questions:

1. Net income was $240,000 in 2000, $210,000 in 2001, and $252,000 in 2002. The change from 2001 to 2002 is a (an) (*p. 982*)
   a. Increase of 5 percent
   b. Increase of 20 percent
   c. Decrease of 10 percent
   d. Decrease of 12.5 percent

2. Vertical analysis of a financial statement shows (*p. 985*)
   a. Trend percentages
   b. The percentage change in an item from period to period
   c. The relationship of an item to the total on the statement
   d. Net income expressed as a percentage of shareholders' equity

3. Common-size statements are useful for comparing (*p. 986*)
   a. Changes in the makeup of assets from period to period
   b. Different companies

   c. A company to its industry
   d. All of the above

4. Benchmarking allows a user of financial statements of a company to (*pp. 987–989*)
   a. Compare the performance of the company against key competitors
   b. Compare the performance of the company against best practices
   c. Compare the performance of the company against average performance
   d. All of the above

5. Cash is $10,000, net accounts receivable amount to $22,000, inventory is $55,000, prepaid expenses total $3,000, and current liabilities are $40,000. What is the acid-test ratio? (*p. 995*)
   a. 0.25   c. 2.18
   b. 0.80   d. 2.25

6. Inventory turnover is computed by dividing (*p. 997*)
   a. Sales revenue by average inventory
   b. Cost of goods sold by average inventory
   c. Credit sales by average inventory
   d. Average inventory by cost of goods sold

7. Capp Corporation is experiencing a severe cash shortage due to inability to collect accounts receivable. The decision tool most likely to help identify the appropriate corrective action is the (p. 999)
   a. Acid-test ratio
   b. Inventory turnover
   c. Times-interest-earned ratio
   d. Day's sales in receivables

8. Analysis of Mendoza Ltd. financial statements over five years reveals that sales are growing steadily, the debt ratio is higher than the industry average and is increasing, interest coverage is decreasing, return on total assets is declining, and earnings per share of common stock is decreasing. Considered together, these ratios suggest that (pp. 999–1003)
   a. Mendoza Ltd. should pursue collections of receivables more vigourously
   b. Competition is taking sales away from Mendoza Ltd.
   c. Mendoza Ltd. is in a declining industry
   d. The company's debt burden is hurting profitability

9. Which of the following is most likely to be true? (pp. 1001–1002)
   a. Return on common equity exceeds return on total assets.
   b. Return on total assets exceeds return on common equity.
   c. Return on total assets equals return on common equity.
   d. None of the above

10. How are financial ratios used in decision making? (p. 1005)
   a. They remove the uncertainty of the business environment.
   b. They give clear signals about the appropriate action to take.
   c. They can help identify the reasons for success and failure in business, but decision making requires information beyond the ratios.
   d. They are not useful because decision making is too complex.

Answers to the Self-Study Questions follow the Similar Accounting Terms.

Accounting Vocabulary

Accounts receivable turnover *(p. 998)*
Acid-test ratio *(p. 995)*
Benchmarking *(p. 987)*
Book value per share of common stock *(p. 1004)*
Capital charge *(p. 1006)*
Common-size statement *(p. 986)*
Cost of capital *(p. 1006)*
Current ratio *(p. 995)*
Days' sales in receivables *(p. 999)*
Debt ratio *(p. 999)*
Dividend yield *(p. 1004)*
Earnings per share (EPS) *(p. 1003)*
Economic value added (EVA®) *(p. 1005)*
Efficient capital market *(p. 1006)*
Horizontal analysis *(p. 982)*
Interest-coverage ratio *(p. 1000)*
Inventory turnover *(p. 997)*
Leverage *(p. 1002)*

Long-term solvency *(p. 981)*
Price/earnings ratio *(p. 1003)*
Profit margin *(p. 1001)*
Quick ratio *(p. 995)*
Rate of return on common shareholders' equity *(p. 1002)*
Rate of return on net sales *(p. 1001)*
Rate of return on total assets *(p. 1001)*
Return on assets *(p. 1001)*
Return on equity *(p. 1002)*
Return on sales *(p. 1001)*
Return on shareholders' equity *(p. 1002)*
Short-term liquidity *(p. 981)*
Times-interest-earned ratio *(p. 1000)*
Trading on the equity *(p. 1002)*
Vertical analysis *(p. 985)*
Working capital *(p. 994)*

Similar Accounting Terms

Acid-test ratio	Quick ratio
Current ratio	Working capital ratio
Leverage	Trading on the equity
Earnings per share	Earnings per share of common stock
Rate of return on common shareholders' equity	Return on shareholders' equity; Return on equity
Rate of return on net sales	Return on sales; Profit margin

Assignment Material

Questions

1. Identify two groups of users of accounting information and the decisions they base on accounting data.

2. Name the three broad categories of analytical tools that are based on accounting information.

3. Briefly describe horizontal analysis. How do decision makers use this analytical tool?

4. What is vertical analysis, and what is its purpose?

5. What is the purpose of common-size statements?

6. Why are ratios an important tool of financial analysis? Give an example of an important financial ratio.

7. Identify two ratios used to measure a company's ability to pay current liabilities. Show how they are computed.

8. Why is the acid-test ratio given that name?

9. What does the inventory-turnover ratio measure?

10. Suppose the days'-sales-in-receivables ratio of Payette, Inc. increased from 36 at January 1 to 43 at December 31. Is this a good sign or a bad sign about the company? What might Payette, Inc. management do in response to this change?

11. Kumar Inc.'s debt ratio has increased from 0.50 to 0.70. Identify a decision maker to whom this increase is important, and state how the increase affects this party's decisions about the company.

12. Which ratio measures the *effect of debt* on (a) financial position (the balance sheet) and (b) the company's ability to pay interest expense (the income statement)?

13. Sherwood Stores Ltd. is a chain of grocery stores, and Peach Inc. is a computer manufacturer. Which company is likely to have the higher (a) current ratio, (b) inventory turnover, and (c) rate of return on sales? Give your reasons.

14. Identify four ratios used to measure a company's profitability. Show how to compute these ratios and state what information each ratio provides.

15. The price/earnings ratio of WestJet Airlines was 47.8, and the price/earnings ratio of Bank of Nova Scotia was 12.0. Which company did the stock market favour? Explain.

16. Irwin Toy paid cash dividends of $0.22 (22 cents) per share when the market price of the company's stock was $7.00 per share. What was the dividend yield on Irwin Toy's stock? What does dividend yield measure?

17. Hold all other factors constant and indicate whether each of the following situations generally signals good or bad news about a company:
    a. Increase in return on sales
    b. Decrease in earnings per share
    c. Increase in price/earnings ratio
    d. Increase in book value per share
    e. Increase in current ratio
    f. Decrease in inventory turnover
    g. Increase in debt ratio
    h. Decrease in interest-coverage ratio

18. Explain how an investor might use book value per share in making an investment decision.

19. Describe how decision makers use ratio data. What are the limitations of ratios?

20. What is EVA® and how is it used in financial analysis?

Exercises

Exercise 18-1 *Computing year-to-year changes in working capital* *(Obj. 1)*

What was the amount of change, and the percentage change, in Bayshore Ltd.'s working capital during 2002 and 2001? Is this trend favourable or unfavourable?

	2002	2001	2000
Total current assets	$312,000	$290,000	$280,000
Total current liabilities..................................	130,000	117,000	150,000

Exercise 18-2 *Horizontal analysis of an income statement* *(Obj. 1)*

Prepare a horizontal analysis of the following comparative income statement of The Board Store Inc. Round percentage changes to the nearest one-tenth percent (three decimal places):

THE BOARD STORE INC.
Comparative Income Statement
For the Years Ended December 31, 2003 and 2002

	2003	2002
Total Revenue	$410,000	$375,000
Expenses		
Cost of goods sold	$202,000	$188,000
Selling and general expenses	118,000	111,000
Interest expense...	7,000	4,000
Income tax expense....................................	17,000	13,000
Total expenses...	344,000	316,000
Net Income...	$ 66,000	$ 59,000

Why was the percentage increase in net income higher than that of total revenue during 2003?

Exercise 18-3 *Computing trend percentages* *(Obj. 1)*

Compute trend percentages for Melton Ltd.'s net sales and net income for the following five-year period, using 1998 as the base year:

	2002	2001	2000	1999	1998
		(Amounts in thousands)			
Net sales	$1,410	$1,187	$1,086	$1,009	$1,043
Net income............................	119	112	83	71	85

Which grew more during the period, net sales or net income?

Exercise 18-4 *Vertical analysis of a balance sheet* *(Obj. 2)*

Saman Corp. has requested that you perform a vertical analysis of its balance sheet. Determine the component percentages of its assets, liabilities, and shareholders' equity.

SAMAN CORP.
Balance Sheet
December 31, 2003

Assets

Total current assets...	$ 81,000
Long-term investments..	35,000
Capital assets, net...	224,000
Total assets..	$340,000

Liabilities

Total current liabilities	$ 57,000
Long-term debt	123,000
Total liabilities...	180,000

Shareholders' Equity

Total shareholders' equity	160,000
Total liabilities and shareholders' equity	$340,000

Exercise 18-5 *Vertical analysis of the income statement* **(Obj. 2)**

T-Shaft Ltd. recently introduced a new titanium-strengthened shaft for its golf clubs. Demand for the product has been high, and T-Shaft Ltd. is shipping goods to many pro shops and golf stores. T-Shaft Ltd.'s comparative income statement reports these figures for 2003 and 2002:

	2003	2002
Net sales...	$193,000	$151,000
Cost of goods sold	64,000	50,000
Selling expenses...	44,000	37,000
General expenses...	18,000	17,000
Net income	$ 67,000	$ 47,000

Perform a vertical analysis of T-Shaft Ltd.'s income statements for 2003 and 2002. Does the analysis reflect favourably or poorly on the company? Give specifics in your answer.

Exercise 18-6 *Vertical analysis to correct a shortage* **(Obj. 2)**

T-Shaft Ltd. reported the following amounts on its balance sheets at December 31, 2003, 2002, and 2001.

	2003	2002	2001
Cash...	$ 6,000	$ 6,000	$ 5,000
Receivables, net	50,000	34,000	19,000
Inventory	38,000	30,000	24,000
Prepaid expenses.......................................	2,000	2,000	1,000
Capital assets, net.....................................	96,000	88,000	87,000
Total assets	$192,000	$160,000	$136,000

1. Sales and profits are high. Nevertheless, the company is experiencing a cash shortage. Perform a vertical analysis of T-Shaft Ltd.'s assets at the end of each year, 2003, 2002, and 2001. Use the analysis to explain the reason for the cash shortage.
2. Suggest a way for T-Shaft Ltd. to generate more cash.

Exercise 18-7 *Preparing a common-size income statement* **(Obj. 3)**

Prepare a comparative common-size income statement for The Board Store Inc. using the 2003 and 2002 data of Exercise 18-2 and rounding percentages to one-tenth percent (three decimal places).

Exercise 18-8 *Common-size analysis of assets* **(Obj. 3)**

Prepare a common-size analysis to compare the asset composition of Truro Inc. and Fundy Ltd. (amounts in millions).

Assets	Truro Inc.	Fundy Ltd.
Current assets:		
Cash and equivalents..	$ 262	$ 146
Short-term investments	—	363
Accounts receivable, net..	1,346	438
Inventories..	931	2,700
Other current assets	188	62
Total current assets...	2,727	3,709
Capital assets, net..	1,967	5,437
Goodwill and other intangibles	75	87
Other assets	106	109
Total assets...	$4,875	$9,342

To which company are *current assets* more important? Which company places more emphasis on its *capital assets?*

Exercise 18-9 *Computing five ratios* **(Obj. 4)**

The financial statements of Val Morin Inc. include the following items:

	2002	2001
Balance sheet		
Cash..	$ 17,000	$ 22,000
Short-term investments......................	11,000	26,000
Net receivables	74,000	73,000
Inventory..	87,000	71,000
Prepaid expenses...............................	6,000	8,000
Total current assets............................	195,000	200,000
Total current liabilities......................	121,000	86,000
Income statement		
Net credit sales	$482,000	
Cost of goods sold.............................	271,000	

Required

Compute the following ratios for 2002: (a) current ratio, (b) acid-test ratio, (c) inventory turnover, (d) accounts receivable turnover, and (e) days' sales in average receivables.

Exercise 18-10 *Using ratio data to reconstruct a balance sheet* **(Obj. 4)**

A skeleton of Darlin Ltd.'s balance sheet at June 30, 2003 (as adapted) appears as follows (amounts in millions):

Balance Sheet

Cash............................	$53	Total current liabilities........	$2,414
Receivables........................	(a)		
Inventories	755	Long-term debt..................	(e)
Prepaid expenses................	(b)	Other long-term liabilities..	876
Total current assets.........	(c)		
Capital assets, net..............	(d)	Common stock....................	285
Other assets.........................	2,150	Retained earnings...............	2,456
Total assets	$7,015	Total liabilities and equity..	$(f)

Use the following ratio data to complete Darlin Ltd.'s balance sheet:

a. Debt ratio is 0.6092.

b. Current ratio is 0.7306.

c. Acid-test ratio is 0.3161.

Exercise 18-11 *Analyzing the ability to pay current liabilities* *(Obj. 4, 5)*

Chiliwack Plastic Products Ltd. has requested that you determine whether the company's ability to pay its current liabilities and long-term debts has improved or deteriorated during 2002. To answer this question, compute the following ratios for 2002 and 2001: (a) current ratio, (b) acid-test ratio, (c) debt ratio, and (d) times-interest-earned ratio. Summarize the results of your analysis in a written report.

	2002	2001
Cash...	$ 24,000	$ 47,000
Short-term investments..........................	28,000	—
Net receivables	106,000	112,000
Inventory...	226,000	263,000
Prepaid expenses.....................................	12,000	9,000
Total assets..	503,000	489,000
Total current liabilities...........................	207,000	245,000
Total liabilities..	261,000	273,000
Income from operations	172,000	158,000
Interest expense	36,000	39,000

Exercise 18-12 *Analyzing profitability* *(Obj. 4, 5)*

Compute four ratios that measure ability to earn profits for Keswick Farm Supplies Ltd., whose comparative income statement appears below. Additional data follow.

KESWICK FARM SUPPLIES LTD.
Comparative Income Statement
For the Years Ended December 31, 2003 and 2002

	2003	2002
Net sales..	$174,000	$158,000
Cost of goods sold	93,000	84,000
Gross profit...	81,000	74,000
Selling and general expenses.....................................	48,000	42,000
Income from operations...	33,000	32,000
Interest expense	21,000	10,000
Income before income tax..	12,000	22,000
Income tax expense	3,000	5,000
Net income..	$ 9,000	$ 17,000

Additional data	2003	2002
a. Average total assets..	$204,000	$191,000
b. Average common shareholders' equity	99,000	92,000
c. Preferred dividends	3,000	3,000
d. Shares of common stock outstanding............................	20,000	20,000

Did the company's operating performance improve or deteriorate during 2003?

Exercise 18-13 *Evaluating a stock as an investment* **(Obj. 4, 5)**

Evaluate the common shares of Veinot Solutions Inc. as an investment. Specifically, use the three stock ratios to determine whether the shares have increased or decreased in attractiveness during the past year.

	2002	2001
Net income	$ 62,000	$ 55,000
Dividends (half on preferred stock)	36,000	28,000
Common shareholders' equity at year end		
(80,000 shares)...	530,000	500,000
Preferred shareholders' equity at year end	200,000	200,000
Market price per share of common stock at year end.......	$9.47	$7.75

Exercise 18-14 *Using economic value added to measure corporate performance* **(Obj. 6)**

Two companies with very different economic-value-added (EVA®) profiles are IHOP, the restaurant chain, and Texaco, the giant oil company. Adapted versions of the two companies' recent financial statements are presented here (in millions):

	IHOP	Texaco
Balance sheet data		
Total assets..	$252	$24,937
Interest-bearing debt.......................................	$ 35	$ 4,240
All other liabilities..	109	11,178
Shareholders' equity..	108	9,519
Total liabilities and shareholders' equity	$252	$24,937
Income statement data		
Total revenue..	$164	$36,787
Interest expense	(9)	(483)
All other expenses	(139)	(35,697)
Net income	$ 16	$ 607

Required

1. Before performing any calculations, which company do you think would represent the better investment? Give your reason.

2. Compute the EVA® for each company, and then decide which company's stock you would rather hold as an investment. Assume each company's cost of capital is 14 percent.

Challenge Exercises

Exercise 18-15 *Using ratio data to reconstruct a real company's income statement*
  (Obj. 2, 3, 4)

The following data (dollar amounts in millions) are from the financial statements of McDonald's Corporation, operator of more than 14,000 restaurants in 65 countries.

	Dollars in Millions
Average shareholders' equity	$3,815
Interest expense	$ 413
Preferred stock	–0–
Operating income as a percent of sales	25.54%
Rate of return on sales	11.13%
Rate of return on shareholders' equity	20.50%
Income tax rate	37.53%

Required

Complete the following condensed income statement. Report amounts to the nearest million dollars:

Sales	$?
Operating expense	?
Operating income	?
Interest expense	?
Pretax income	?
Income tax expense	?
Net income	$?

Exercise 18-16   *Using ratio data to reconstruct a company's balance sheet*   **(Obj. 2, 3, 4)**

The following data (dollar amounts in thousands) are from the financial statements of Household Plumbing Supplies Ltd.

Total liabilities	$11,806
Preferred stock	–0–
Total current assets	$10,196
Accumulated amortization	$ 2,692
Debt ratio	57.408%
Current ratio	1.80%

Required

Complete the following condensed balance sheet. Report amounts to the nearest thousand dollars:

Current assets		$?
Capital assets	$?	
Less accumulated amortization	?	?
Total assets		$?
Current liabilities		$?
Long-term liabilities		?
Shareholders' equity		?
Total liabilities and shareholders' equity		$?

Beyond the Numbers

Beyond the Numbers 18-1   *Understanding the components of accounting ratios*
(Obj. 4, 5)

Consider the following business situations.

1. Susan Willis has asked you about the stock of a particular company. She finds it attractive because it has high dividend yield relative to another stock she is also considering. Explain to her the meaning of the ratio and the danger of making a decision based on it alone.

2. Laurent Textiles Ltd.'s owners are concerned because the number of days' sales in receivables has increased over the previous two years. Explain why the ratio might have increased.

Beyond the Numbers 18-2   *Taking unethical action to improve the ratios*   **(Obj. 4)**

Marie Hurd is the controller of Rapid Sales Inc., whose year end is June 30. Hurd prepares cheques for suppliers in June and posts them to the appropriate accounts in that month. However, she holds on to the cheques and mails them to the suppliers in July. What financial ratio(s) are most affected by the action? What is Hurd's purpose in undertaking the activity?

Ethical Issue

W and D Products Ltd.'s long-term debt agreements make certain demands on the business. For example, W and D may not repurchase company shares in excess of the balance of Retained Earnings. Long-term Debt may not exceed Shareholders' Equity, and the current ratio may not fall below 1.50. If W and D fails to meet these requirements, the company's lenders have the authority to take over management of the corporation.

Changes in consumer demand have made it hard for W and D Products Ltd. to sell its products. Current liabilities have mounted faster than current assets, causing the current ratio to fall to 1.40. Prior to releasing financial statements, W and D management is scrambling to improve the current ratio. The controller points out that an investment can be classified as either long-term or short-term, depending on management's intention. By deciding to convert an investment to cash within one year, W and D can classify the investment as short-term (a current asset). On the controller's recommendation, W and D Products Ltd.'s board of directors votes to reclassify long-term investments as short-term.

Required

1. What effect will reclassifying the investment have on the current ratio? Is W and D Products Ltd.'s financial position stronger as a result of reclassifying the investment?

2. Shortly after releasing the financial statements, sales improve and so, then, does the current ratio. As a result, W and D Products Ltd. management decides not to sell the investments it had reclassified as short-term. Accordingly, the company reclassifies the investments as long-term. Has management behaved unethically? Give your reason.

Problems (Group A)

Problem 18-1A   *Trend percentages, return on common equity and comparison with the industry*   **(Obj. 1, 4, 5)**

Net sales, net income, and common shareholders' equity for Kubitz Products Ltd. for a six-year period follow:

	2002	2001	2000	1999	1998	1997
			(Amounts in thousands)			
Net sales...	$761	$697	$637	$662	$642	$634
Net income...	61	47	35	48	41	40
Ending common shareholders'						
equity..	386	354	333	304	272	252

Required

1. Compute trend percentages for 1998 through 2002, using 1997 as the base year.
2. Compute the rate of return on average common shareholders' equity for 1998 through 2002, rounding to three decimal places. In this industry, rates of 13 percent are average, rates above 16 percent are considered good, and rates above 20 percent are viewed as outstanding.
3. How does Kubitz Products Ltd.'s return on common shareholders' equity compare with the industry?

Problem 18-2A *Common-size statements, analysis of profitability, and comparison with the industry* *(Obj. 2, 3, 4, 5)*

Calgary Central Vac Ltd. has asked your help in comparing the company's profit performance and financial position with the average for the central vacuum cleaner industry. The proprietor has given you the company's income statement and balance sheet, and also the following industry average data for central vacuum cleaner companies:

CALGARY CENTRAL VAC LTD.
Income Statement
Compared with Industry Average
For the Year Ended December 31, 2002

	Calgary Central Vac Ltd.	Industry Average
Net sales	$781,000	100.0%
Cost of goods sold	497,000	65.8
Gross profit	284,000	34.2
Operating expenses	163,000	19.7
Operating income	121,000	14.5
Other expenses	7,000	0.4
Net income	$114,000	14.1%

CALGARY CENTRAL VAC LTD.
Balance Sheet
Compared with Industry Average
December 31, 2002

	Calgary Central Vac Ltd.	Industry Average
Current assets	$355,000	70.9%
Capital assets, net...............	69,000	23.6
Intangible assets, net...........	4,000	0.8
Other assets.........................	22,000	4.7
Total assets	$450,000	100.0%
Current liabilities.................	$202,000	48.1%
Long-term liabilities............	67,000	16.6
Shareholders' equity	181,000	35.3
Total liabilities and shareholders' equity	$450,000	100.0%

Required

1. Prepare a two-column common-size income statement and a two-column common-size balance sheet for Calgary Central Vac Ltd. The first column of each statement should present Calgary Central Vac Ltd.'s common-size statement, and the second column should show the industry averages.
2. For the profitability analysis, compute Calgary Central Vac Ltd.'s (a) ratio of gross profit to net sales, (b) ratio of operating income to net sales, and (c) ratio of net income to net sales. Compare these figures to the industry averages. Is Calgary Central Vac Ltd.'s profit performance better or worse than the industry average?
3. For the analysis of financial position, compute Calgary Central Vac Ltd.'s (a) ratio of current assets to total assets and (b) ratio of shareholders' equity to total assets. Compare these ratios to the industry averages. Is Calgary Central Vac Ltd.'s financial position better or worse than the industry averages?

Problem 18-3A *Effects of business transactions on selected ratios* *(Obj. 4, 5)*

Financial statement data of Souris Supplies Ltd. include the following items:

Cash	$ 25,000
Short-term investments	19,000
Accounts receivable, net	83,000
Inventories	152,000
Prepaid expenses	8,000
Total assets	663,000
Short-term notes payable	49,000
Accounts payable	103,000
Accrued liabilities	42,000
Long-term notes payable	160,000
Other long-term liabilities	31,000
Net income	71,000
Number of common shares outstanding	30,000

Required

1. Compute Souris Supplies Ltd.'s current ratio, debt ratio, and earnings per share.
2. Compute each of the three ratios after evaluating the effect of each transaction that follows. Consider each transaction *separately*.
   a. Purchased merchandise of $26,000 on account, debiting Inventory.
   b. Paid long-term liabilities, $22,000.
   c. Declared, but did not pay, a $22,000 cash dividend on common shares.
   d. Borrowed $85,000 on a long-term note payable.
   e. Sold short-term investments for $18,000 (cost, $11,000); assume no income tax on the gain.
   f. Issued 5,000 shares of common stock on January 2, 2003, receiving cash of $120,000.
   g. Received cash on account, $19,000.
   h. Paid short-term notes payable, $24,000.

Use the following format for your answer:

Requirement 1		Current Ratio	Debt Ratio	Earnings per Share

Requirement 2	Transaction (letter)	Current Ratio	Debt Ratio	Earnings per Share

Problem 18-4A *Using ratios to evaluate a stock investment* **(Obj. 4, 5)**

Comparative financial statement data of Fung Foods Ltd. appear below:

FUNG FOODS LTD.
Comparative Income Statement
For the Years Ended December 31, 2003 and 2002

	2003	2002
Net sales	$462,000	$427,000
Cost of goods sold	229,000	218,000
Gross profit	233,000	209,000
Operating expenses	136,000	134,000
Income from operations	97,000	75,000
Interest expense	11,000	12,000
Income before income tax	86,000	63,000
Income tax expense	17,000	13,000
Net income	$ 69,000	$ 50,000

FUNG FOODS LTD.
Comparative Balance Sheet
December 31, 2003 and 2002
(selected 2001 amounts given for computation of ratios)

	2003	2002	2001
Current assets:			
Cash...	$ 96,000	$ 97,000	
Current receivables, net..............................	112,000	128,000	$103,000
Inventories..	172,000	150,000	201,000
Prepaid expenses......................................	16,000	7,000	
Total current assets................................	396,000	382,000	
Capital assets, net....................................	189,000	178,000	
Total assets...	$585,000	$560,000	598,000
Total current liabilities..............................	$206,000	$215,000	
Long-term liabilities.................................	119,000	125,000	
Total liabilities.....................................	325,000	340,000	
Preferred stock, $6.00................................	70,000	70,000	
Common stock..	130,000	120,000	70,000
Retained earnings....................................	60,000	30,000	20,000
Total liabilities and shareholders' equity	$585,000	$560,000	

Other information:

a. Market price of Fung Foods Ltd. common stock: $49.00 at December 31, 2003, and $41.00 at December 31, 2002.

b. Common shares outstanding: 10,000 during 2003 and 9,000 during 2002. There are 1,000 preferred shares outstanding at December 31, 2002 and 2003.

c. All sales on credit.

Required

1. Compute the following ratios for 2003 and 2002:
   a. Current ratio
   b. Inventory turnover
   c. Accounts receivable turnover
   d. Times-interest-earned ratio
   e. Return on assets
   f. Return on common shareholders' equity
   g. Earnings per share of common stock
   h. Price/earnings ratio
   i. Book value per share of common stock

2. Decide (a) whether Fung Foods Ltd.'s financial position improved or deteriorated during 2003, and (b) whether the investment attractiveness of its common stock appears to have increased or decreased.

3. How will what you have learned in this problem help you evaluate an investment?

Problem 18-5A   *Using ratio data to complete a set of financial statements*   *(Obj. 4)*

Link Back to Chapter 17 (Cash Flow Statement). Incomplete and adapted versions of the financial statements of Whitehorse Outfitters Ltd. follow (amounts in thousands).

WHITEHORSE OUTFITTERS LTD.
Income Statement
For the Year Ended May 31, 2003

Net sales...	$28,472
Cost of goods sold	(a)
Gross margin..	(b)
Selling and general expenses...	11,094
Other expense (income)...	881
Income before income tax	(c)
Income tax expense (22%)	(d)
Net income	$ (e)

WHITEHORSE OUTFITTERS LTD.
Comparative Balance Sheet
May 31, 2003 and 2002

Assets	2003	2002
Current:		
Cash..	$ (f)	$ 227
Short-term investments	1,157	1,574
Receivables, net	2,051	1,933
Inventories...	970	875
Prepaid expenses..	(g)	500
Total current assets..	(h)	5,109
Capital assets	19,720	18,597
Total assets	$(i)	$23,706
Liabilities		
Current liabilities..	$ 5,270	$ 6,575
Long-term liabilities..	(j)	10,792
Total liabilities...	(k)	17,367
Shareholders' Equity		
Common shareholders' equity	(l)	6,339
Total liabilities and equity..	$ (m)	$23,706

WHITEHORSE OUTFITTERS LTD.
Cash Flow Statement
For the Year Ended May 31, 2003

Net cash inflow from operating activities	$ 4,116
Net cash outflow from investing activities..	(2,361)
Net cash outflow from financing activities..	(1,251)
Net increase (decrease) in cash during 2003......................................	$ (n)

Ratio data:

a. Current ratio at May 31, 2003, is 0.9874.

b. Inventory turnover for year ended May 31, 2003, was 14.485.

c. Debt ratio at May 31, 2003, is 0.72346.

Required

Complete the financial statements. Start with the income statement, then go to the cash flow statement. Complete the balance sheet last.

Problem 18-6A *Using ratios to decide between two stock investments* *(Obj. 4, 5, 6)*

Assume you are purchasing an investment and have decided to invest in a company in the air-conditioning and heating business. Suppose you have narrowed the choice to Airflow Ltd., and Alltemp Products Ltd. You have assembled the following selected data:

Selected income statement data for current year

	Airflow Ltd.	Alltemp Products Ltd.
Net sales (all on credit)	$497,000	$371,000
Cost of goods sold	258,000	209,000
Income from operations	138,000	79,000
Interest expense	19,000	—
Net income	72,000	48,000

Selected balance sheet and market price data at end of current year

	Airflow Ltd.	Alltemp Products Ltd.
Current assets:		
Cash	$19,000	$ 22,000
Short-term investments	18,000	15,000
Current receivables, net	46,000	40,000
Inventories	100,000	94,000
Prepaid expenses	3,000	2,000
Total current assets	186,000	173,000
Total assets	328,000	265,000
Total current liabilities	98,000	108,000
Total liabilities	131,000*	108,000*
Preferred stock: $5.00 (200 shares)	20,000	
Common stock (2,000 shares)		10,000
(5,000 shares)	12,500	
Total shareholders' equity	197,000	157,000
Market price per share of common stock	$98	$189

*Notes payable: Airflow Ltd., $86,000;
 Alltemp Products Ltd., $1,000.

Selected balance sheet data at beginning of current year

	Airflow Ltd.	Alltemp Products Ltd.
Current receivables, net	$ 48,000	$ 35,000
Inventories	88,000	98,000
Total assets	285,000	259,000
Preferred shareholders' equity, $5.00 (200 shares)	20,000	—
Common stock (2,000 shares)		10,000
(5,000 shares)	12,500	
Total shareholders' equity	135,000	118,000

Your investment strategy is to purchase the stocks of companies that have low price/earnings ratios but appear to be in good shape financially. Assume you have analyzed all other factors, and your decision depends on the results of the ratio analysis to be performed.

Required

1. Compute the following ratios for both companies for the current year and decide which company's stock better fits your investment strategy:

a. Current ratio
b. Acid-test ratio
c. Inventory turnover
d. Day's sales in average receivables
e. Debt ratio
f. Times-interest-earned ratio
g. Return on net sales

h. Return on total assets
i. Return on common shareholders' equity
j. Earnings per share of common stock
k. Book value per share of common stock
l. Price/earnings ratio

2. Compute each company's economic-value-added (EVA®) measure, and determine whether their EVAs confirm or alter your investment decision. Each company's cost of capital is 11 percent. Round all amounts to the nearest $1,000.

Problem 18-7A *Preparing a horizontal analysis of a financial statement, computing the standard financial ratios used for decision making, using ratios in decision making   (Obj. 1, 4, 5)*

Granby Wood Products Ltd.'s financial statements for the year ended December 31, 2002, are shown below.

Required

1. Perform a horizontal analysis of the comparative balance sheets. Comment on the analysis.
2. Calculate each of the following ratios for the year ended December 31, 2002. The industry standards are provided in parentheses for some of the ratios.
   a. Current ratio (2:1)
   b. Acid-test ratio
   c. Inventory turnover
   d. Days' sales in receivables
   e. Debt ratio (0.45)
   f. Times-interest-earned ratio
   g. Rate of return on net sales

   h. Rate of return on total assets
   i. Rate of return on common shareholders' equity
   j. Price/earnings ratio—the market price per share is $28.00 (8.0)
   k. Dividend yield (7%)

3. Comment on your calculations for Granby Wood Products Ltd. in requirement 2. Include comments for those ratios for which industry standards were provided (items a, e, j, and k).

GRANBY WOOD PRODUCTS LTD.
Income Statement
For the Year Ended December 31, 2002

Net sales..	$350,000
Cost of goods sold	192,000
Gross profit margin..	158,000
Operating expenses:	
Selling expenses...	58,000
Administrative expenses...	30,000
Interest expense	6,000
Total operating expenses..	94,000
Operating income..	64,000
Income taxes (21.875%)...	14,000
Net income	$ 50,000

GRANBY WOOD PRODUCTS LTD.
Statement of Retained Earnings
For the Year Ended December 31, 2002

Retained earnings, January 1, 2002		$62,000
Add: Net income for 2002		50,000
		112,000
Less: Dividends: Preferred	$6,000	
Common	20,000	26,000
Retained earnings, December 31, 2002		$86,000

GRANBY WOOD PRODUCTS LTD.
Balance Sheet
December 31, 2002 and 2001

	2002	2001
Assets		
Cash	$ 33,000	$ 17,000
Marketable securities	5,000	3,000
Accounts receivable	18,000	24,000
Merchandise inventory	32,000	55,000
Prepaid expenses	2,000	3,000
Capital assets	241,000	189,000
Less accumulated amortization	(35,000)	(12,000)
Goodwill	16,000	18,000
Total assets	$312,000	$297,000
Liabilities		
Accounts payable	$10,000	$21,000
Notes payable (due in 30 days)	1,000	4,000
Mortgage payable (secured—capital assets)	35,000	60,000
Total liabilities	46,000	85,000
Shareholders' equity		
Preferred shares (1,000 shares, $6)		
callable at $110 per share	100,000	100,000
Common shares		
(2002—10,000 shares), (2001—5,000 shares)	80,000	50,000
Retained earnings	86,000	62,000
Total shareholders' equity	266,000	212,000
Total liabilities and shareholders' equity	$312,000	$297,000

Problem 18-8A   *Preparing a vertical analysis of a financial statement, computing the standard financial ratios used for decision making, using ratios in decision making   (Obj. 2, 4, 5)*

Digby Office Supplies Ltd.'s financial statements for the year ended December 31, 2003, are shown on the next page; the financial statements and additional information are in thousands of dollars:

Required

1. Prepare a vertical analysis of the income statement. The industry standards are gross profit of 40 percent and net income of 15 percent. Comment on the results.

2. Calculate each of the following for December 31, 2003 (industry standards are shown in parentheses for some items):

   a. Acid-test ratio (0.55:1)
   b. Inventory turnover (3.0 times)
   c. Days' sales in receivables (45 days)
   d. Debt ratio (40 percent)

e. Rate of return on total assets
   (10 percent)
f. Rate of return on shareholders'
   equity

g. Earnings per share
h. Price/earnings ratio (market price is
   $38 per share)
i. Dividend yield

3. Comment on the ratios in requirement 2 for which an industry standard was provided (items a to e).

4. Digby Office Supplies Ltd. has a policy of increasing purchases (all on credit) in the final month of the year to achieve inventory levels that are 60 percent higher than required. Thus, the inventory balance of $32,000 at December 31, 2003, is 160 percent higher than it would be normally. This is done to give the purchasing department a break after a hectic Christmas season. Management is concerned about the effects this policy may have on the acid-test ratio and inventory turnover. Calculate what these ratios would have been without the policy and comment on the results.

DIGBY OFFICE SUPPLIES LTD.
Balance Sheet
December 31, 2003

Assets

Cash	$ 10,000
Accounts receivable	20,000
Inventory	32,000
Prepaid expenses	10,000
Long-term investments	90,000
Capital assets (net)	160,000
Total assets	$322,000

Liabilities

Accounts payable	$ 40,000
Salaries payable	10,000
Dividends payable	10,000
Bonds payable	134,000
Total liabilities	194,000

Shareholders' Equity

Common stock (5,000 shares)	80,000
Retained earnings	48,000
Total shareholders' equity	128,000
Total liabilities and shareholders' equity	$322,000

DIGBY OFFICE SUPPLIES LTD.
Income Statement
For the Year Ended December 31, 2003

Sales	$290,000
Cost of goods sold	155,000
Gross profit	135,000
Operating expenses:	
Selling expense	45,000
Administrative expenses	38,000
Interest expense	3,000
Total operating expenses	86,000
Operating income	49,000
Income taxes	12,000
Net income	$ 37,000

Account Balances, January 1, 2003:

Total assets	$295,000
Accounts receivable	30,000
Inventory	24,000
Retained earnings	21,000

Problems (Group B)

Problem 18-1B *Trend percentages, return on sales, and comparison with the industry*
(Obj. 1, 4, 5)

Net sales, net income, and total assets for Andros Corp. for a six-year period follow.

	2003	2002	2001	2000	1999	1998
			(Amounts in thousands)			
Net sales	$351	$313	$266	$281	$245	$241
Net income	29	21	12	19	14	13
Total assets	296	254	209	201	181	166

Required

1. Compute trend percentages for 1999 through 2003. Use 1998 as the base year.
2. Compute the return on net sales for 1999 through 2003, rounding to three decimal places. In this industry, rates above 5 percent are considered good, and rates above 7 percent are viewed as outstanding.
3. How does Andros Corp.'s return on net sales compare to the industry?

Problem 18-2B *Common-size statements, analysis of profitability and comparison with the industry* **(Obj. 2, 3, 4, 5)**

Top managers of Ing Steel Corp., a specialty steel company, have asked for your help in comparing the company's profit performance and financial position with the average for the specialty steel industry. The accountant has given you the company's income statement and balance sheet, and also the following actual data for the specialty steel industry:

ING STEEL CORP.
Income Statement
Compared with Industry Average
For the Year Ended December 31, 2003

	Ing Steel Corp.	Industry Average
Net sales	$957,000	100.0%
Cost of goods sold	653,000	65.9
Gross profit	304,000	34.1
Operating expenses	261,000	28.1
Operating income	43,000	6.0
Other expenses	3,000	0.4
Net income.........................	$ 40,000	5.6%

ING STEEL CORP.
Balance Sheet
Compared with Industry Average
December 31, 2003

	Ing Steel Corp.	Industry Average
Current assets	$448,000	74.4%
Capital assets, net...............	127,000	20.0
Intangible assets, net...........	37,000	0.6
Other assets	13,000	5.0
Total assets	$625,000	100.0%
Current liabilities.................	$246,000	35.6%
Long-term liabilities............	154,000	19.0
Shareholders' equity	225,000	45.4
Total liabilities and shareholders' equity	$625,000	100.0%

Required

1. Prepare a two-column common-size income statement and a two-column common-size balance sheet for Ing Steel Corp. The first column of each statement should present Ing Steel Corp.'s common-size statement, and the second column should show the industry averages.
2. For the profitability analysis, compare Ing Steel Corp.'s (a) ratio of gross profit to net sales, (b) ratio of operating income (loss) to net sales, and (c) ratio of net income (loss) to net sales. Compare these figures with the industry averages. Is Ing Steel Corp.'s profit performance better or worse than average for the industry?
3. For the analysis of financial position, compare Ing Steel Corp.'s (a) ratio of current assets to total assets and (b) ratio of shareholders' equity to total assets. Compare these ratios with the industry averages. Is Ing Steel Corp.'s financial position better or worse than the average for the industry?

Problem 18-3B *Effects of business transactions on selected ratios* **(Obj. 4, 5)**

Financial statement data of Sound Marina Ltd. include the following items:

Cash	$ 47,000
Short-term investments	21,000
Accounts receivable, net	116,000
Inventories	274,000
Prepaid expenses	15,000
Total assets	950,000
Short-term notes payable	72,000
Accounts payable	96,000
Accrued liabilities	50,000
Long-term notes payable	146,000
Other long-term liabilities	78,000
Net income	123,000
Number of common shares outstanding	22,000

Required

1. Compute Sound Marina Ltd.'s current ratio, debt ratio, and earnings per share.
2. Compute each of the three ratios after evaluating the effect of each transaction that follows. Consider each transaction *separately*.
   a. Borrowed $76,000 on a long-term note payable.
   b. Sold short-term investments for $44,000 (cost $66,000); assume no tax effect of the loss.
   c. Issued 12,000 shares of common stock on January 2, 2002, receiving cash of $168,000.
   d. Received cash on account, $6,000.
   e. Paid short-term notes payable, $45,000.
   f. Purchased merchandise of $48,000 on account, debiting Inventory.
   g. Paid long-term liabilities, $40,000.
   h. Declared, but did not pay, a $31,000 cash dividend on the common shares.

Use the following format for your answer:

Requirement 1		Current Ratio	Debt Ratio	Earnings per Share

Requirement 2	Transaction (letter)	Current Ratio	Debt Ratio	Earnings per Share

Problem 18-4B *Using ratios to evaluate a stock investment* *(Obj. 4, 5)*

Comparative financial statement data of Arnprior Outdoors Store Ltd. are as follows:

ARNPRIOR OUTDOORS STORE LTD.
Comparative Income Statement
For the Years Ended December 31, 2003 and 2002

	2003	2002
Net sales	$667,000	$599,000
Cost of goods sold	378,000	283,000
Gross profit	289,000	316,000
Operating expenses	125,000	147,000
Income from operations	164,000	169,000
Interest expense	57,000	41,000
Income before income tax	107,000	128,000
Income tax expense	30,000	42,000
Net income	$ 77,000	$ 86,000

ARNPRIOR OUTDOORS STORE LTD.
Comparative Balance Sheet
December 31, 2003 and 2002
(Selected 2001 amounts given for computation of ratios)

	2003	2002	2001
Current assets:			
Cash	$ 37,000	$ 40,000	
Current receivables, net	208,000	151,000	$130,000
Inventories	347,000	286,000	184,000
Prepaid expenses	10,000	20,000	
Total current assets	602,000	497,000	
Capital assets, net	287,000	276,000	
Total assets	$889,000	$773,000	697,000
Total current liabilities	$266,000	$267,000	
Long-term liabilities	265,000	235,000	
Total liabilities	531,000	502,000	
Preferred stock, $2.00	50,000	50,000	
Common stock	160,000	140,000	140,000
Retained earnings	148,000	81,000	8,000
Total liabilities and shareholders' equity	$889,000	$773,000	

Other information:

a. Market price of Arnprior Outdoors Store Ltd. common shares: $32.00 at December 31, 2003, and $41.00 at December 31, 2002.

b. Weighted-average number of common shares outstanding: 15,000 during 2003 and 14,000 during 2002.

c. There are 2,000 shares of preferred stock outstanding.

d. All sales on credit.

Required

1. Compute the following ratios for 2003 and 2002:
   a. Current ratio
   b. Inventory turnover
   c. Accounts receivable turnover
   d. Times-interest-earned ratio
   e. Return on assets
   f. Return on common shareholders' equity
   g. Earnings per share of common stock
   h. Price/earnings ratio
   i. Book value per share of common stock

2. Decide (a) whether Arnpior Outdoors Store Ltd.'s financial position improved or deteriorated during 2003, and (b) whether the investment attractiveness of its common stock appears to have increased or decreased.

3. How will what you have learned in this problem help you evaluate an investment?

Problem 18-5B   *Using ratio data to complete a set of financial statements*   *(Obj. 4)*

Link Back to Chapter 17 (Cash Flow Statement). Incomplete and adapted versions of the financial statements of Argosy Products Inc. follow (amounts in thousands).

Ratio data:

a. Current ratio at December 31, 2002 is 0.7771.

b. Inventory turnover for 2002 was 6.414.

c. Debt ratio at December 31, 2002 is 0.6306.

ARGOSY PRODUCTS INC.
Income Statement
For the Year Ended December 31, 2002

Net sales..	$18,018
Cost of goods sold	(a)
Gross margin..	(b)
Selling and general expenses...	6,986
Other expense (income)...	(236)
Income before income tax	(c)
Income tax expense (25%)	(d)
Net income	$ (e)

ARGOSY PRODUCTS INC.
Comparative Balance Sheet
December 31, 2002 and 2001

Assets	2002	2001
Current:		
Cash...	$ (f)	$ 1,386
Short-term investments	148	145
Receivables, net..	1,750	1,525
Inventories..	1,117	1,047
Prepaid expenses	(g)	1,102
Total current assets..	(h)	5,205
Capital assets..	9,591	8,668
Total assets...	$(i)	$13,873
Liabilities		
Current liabilities...	$7,348	$ 6,177
Long-term liabilities.......................................	(j)	2,461
Total liabilities..	(k)	8,638
Shareholders' Equity		
Common shareholders' equity	$ (l)	5,235
Total liabilities and shareholders' equity	$ (m)	$13,873

ARGOSY PRODUCTS INC.
Cash Flow Statement
For the Year Ended December 31, 2002

Net cash inflow from operating activities...	$ 3,375
Net cash outflow from investing activities..	(1,013)
Net cash outflow from financing activities..	(2,321)
Net increase (decrease) in cash during 2002...	$ (n)

Required

Complete the financial statements. Start with the income statement. Then go to the cash flow statement. Complete the balance sheet last.

Problem 18-6B *Using ratios to decide between two stock investments* **(Obj. 4, 5, 6)**

Assume you are purchasing shares of stock in a company in the restaurant supply business. Suppose you have narrowed the choice to O'Boyle Inc. and Patel Ltd. and have assembled the following data:

Selected income statement data for current year

	O'Boyle Inc.	Patel Ltd.
Net sales (all on credit)	$519,000	$603,000
Cost of goods sold	387,000	454,000
Income from operations	72,000	93,000
Interest expense	8,000	—
Net income	38,000	56,000

Selected balance sheet and market price data at end of current year

	O'Boyle Inc.	Patel Ltd.
Current assets:		
Cash	$ 39,000	$ 25,000
Short-term investments	13,000	6,000
Current receivables, net	149,000	189,000
Inventories	198,000	211,000
Prepaid expenses	15,000	19,000
Total current assets	414,000	450,000
Total assets	938,000	974,000
Total current liabilities	338,000	366,000
Total liabilities	691,000*	667,000*
Preferred stock $4.00 (250 shares)	25,000	
Common stock (75,000 shares)		150,000
(25,000 shares)	100,000	
Total shareholders' equity	247,000	307,000
Market price per share of common stock	$42	$20

*Notes and bonds payable: O'Boyle Inc., $303,000; Patel Ltd., $4,000.

Selected balance sheet data at beginning of current year

	O'Boyle Inc.	Patel Ltd.
Current receivables, net	$179,000	$142,000
Inventories	207,000	209,000
Total assets	909,000	802,000
Preferred shareholders' equity, $4.00 (250 shares)	25,000	
Common stock (75,000 shares)		150,000
(25,000 shares)	100,000	
Total shareholders' equity	215,000	241,000

Your investment strategy is to purchase the shares of companies that have low price/earnings ratios but appear to be in good shape financially. Assume you have analyzed all other factors, and your decision depends on the results of the ratio analysis to be performed.

Required

1. Compute the following ratios for both companies for the current year and decide which company's stock better fits your investment strategy:

  a. Current ratio

  b. Acid-test ratio

  c. Inventory turnover

  d. Days' sales in average receivables

  e. Debt ratio

  f. Times-interest-earned ratio

  g. Return on net sales

  h. Return on total assets

  i. Return on common shareholders' equity

  j. Earnings per share of common stock

  k. Book value per share of common stock

  l. Price/earnings ratio

2. Compute each company's economic-value-added (EVA®) measure, and determine whether their EVAs confirm or alter your investment decision. Each company's cost of capital is 10 percent.

Problem 18-7B *Preparing a horizontal analysis of a financial statement, computing the standard financial ratios used for decision making, using ratios in decision making* *(Obj. 1, 4, 5)*

Red Deer Autotronics Ltd.'s financial statements for the year ended December 31, 2003, are shown below.

Required

1. Perform a horizontal analysis of the comparative balance sheets. Comment on the analysis.

2. Calculate each of the following ratios for the year ended December 31, 2003. The industry standards are provided in parentheses for some of the ratios.

   a. Current ratio (2:1)
   b. Acid-test ratio
   c. Inventory turnover
   d. Days' sales in receivables
   e. Debt ratio (0.45)
   f. Times-interest-earned ratio
   g. Rate of return on net sales
   h. Rate of return on total assets
   i. Rate of return on common shareholders' equity
   j. Price/earnings ratio—the market price per share is $9.00 (11.0)
   k. Dividend yield (6%)

3. Comment on your calculations for Red Deer Autotronics Ltd. Include comments for those ratios for which industry standards were provided (items a, e, j, and k).

RED DEER AUTOTRONICS LTD.
Income Statement
For the Year Ended December 31, 2003

Net sales..	$230,000
Cost of goods sold..	120,000
Gross profit margin..	110,000
Operating expenses:	
Selling expenses..	40,000
Administrative expenses......................................	26,000
Interest expense	6,000
Total operating expenses..	72,000
Operating income...	38,000
Income taxes (20%)..	7,600
Net income	$ 30,400

RED DEER AUTOTRONICS LTD.
Statement of Retained Earnings
For the Year Ended December 31, 2003

Retained earnings, January 1, 2003..............................		$55,000
Add: Net income for 2003		30,400
		85,400
Less: Dividends: preferred	$16,000	
common	23,800	39,800
Retained earnings, December 31, 2003.........................		$45,600

RED DEER AUTOTRONICS LTD.
Balance Sheet
December 31, 2003 and 2002

	2003	2002
Assets		
Cash	$ 21,600	$ 3,000
Accounts receivable..	20,000	26,000
Merchandise inventory...	38,000	55,000
Prepaid expenses	1,000	4,000
Capital assets...	170,000	148,000
Less accumulated amortization............................	(34,000)	(10,000)
Goodwill	12,000	15,000
Total assets..	$228,600	$241,000
Liabilities		
Accounts payable	$15,000	$23,000
Notes payable (due in 30 days)	2,000	5,000
Mortgage payable (secured—capital assets)	40,000	50,000
Total liabilities..	57,000	78,000
Shareholders' equity		
Preferred shares (8,000 shares; $2,		
callable at $7 per share)...	48,000	48,000
Common shares		
(2003—15,000 shares, 2002—6,000 shares)	78,000	60,000
Retained earnings...	45,600	55,000
Total shareholders' equity	171,600	163,000
Total liabilities and shareholders' equity	$228,600	$241,000

Problem 18-8B *Preparing a vertical analysis of a financial statement, computing the standard financial ratios used for decision making, using ratios in decision making (Obj. 2, 4, 5)*

Cobourg Computers Ltd.'s financial statements for the year ending December 31, 2002, are shown on the next page. The financial statements and additional information are in thousands of dollars.

Required

1. Prepare a vertical analysis of the income statement. The industry standards are gross profit of 50 percent and net income of 12 percent. Comment on the results.

2. Calculate each of the following for December 31, 2002 (industry standards are shown in parentheses for some items):
   a. Acid-test ratio (1:1)
   b. Inventory turnover (2.0 times)
   c. Days' sales in receivables (80 days)
   d. Debt ratio (0.40)
   e. Rate of return on total assets (7 percent)
   f. Rate of return on shareholders' equity
   g. Earnings per share
   h. Price/earnings ratio (market price is $20 per share)
   i. Dividend yield

3. Comment on the ratios in requirement 2 for which an industry standard was provided (items a to e).

4. Cobourg Computers Ltd. has a policy of increasing purchases (all on credit) in the final month of the year to achieve inventory levels that are 100 percent higher than required. Thus, the inventory balance of $45,000 at December 31, 2002, is more than twice as high as it would be normally. This is done to give the purchasing department a break after a hectic Christmas season. Management is concerned

about the effects this policy may have on the acid-test ratio and inventory turnover. Calculate what these ratios would have been without the policy and comment on the results.

COBOURG COMPUTERS LTD. Balance Sheet December 31, 2002		COBOURG COMPUTERS LTD. Income Statement For the Year Ended December 31, 2002	
Assets		Sales	$134,000
Cash	$ 6,000	Cost of goods sold	82,000
Accounts receivable	15,000	Gross profit	52,000
Inventory	45,000		
Prepaid expenses	12,000		
Capital assets (net)	150,000	Operating expenses:	
Long-term investments	80,000	Selling expense	7,000
Total assets	$308,000	Administrative expenses	9,000
Liabilities		Interest expense	6,000
Accounts payable	$ 39,000	Total operating	
Salaries payable	7,000	expenses	22,000
Dividends payable	9,000	Operating income	30,000
Bonds payable	140,000	Income taxes	9,000
Total liabilities	195,000	Net income	$ 21,000
Shareholders' equity			
Common stock		**Account Balances, January 1, 2002:**	
(6,000 shares)	70,000	Total assets	$290,000
Retained earnings	43,000	Accounts receivable	27,000
Total shareholders'		Inventory	32,000
equity	113,000	Retained earnings	31,000
Total liabilities and			
shareholders' equity	$308,000		

Challenge Problems

Problem 18-1C   *Using horizontal analysis to analyze the financial statements of a company (Obj. 1)*

Recently newspapers carried stories about a company that fired three top executives for management fraud. The three had been using improper accounting practices to overstate profits. The improper practices included improperly recording assets on the company's balance sheet, overstating sales, and understating cost of goods sold by inflating inventory numbers. When inventory got out of line, the executives would debit capital assets and credit inventory to further hide their fraud.

   The company had been growing at a very rapid pace, outdistancing its competitors. However, there were warning signals or "red flags" that revealed that all was not well with the company and that suggested that the books might have been "cooked" in order to report the rapid growth. For example, sales, which were almost all on credit, grew much faster than did accounts receivable when that balance on the company's financial statements was compared with industry data. Inventory turnover was lower than that of competitors while sales were unusually low relative to capital assets.

Required

Which items would be misstated in a horizontal analysis of the company's income statement? Which items would be misstated in a horizontal analysis of the company's balance sheet? Indicate the direction of the misstatement.

Problem 18-2C *Understanding the impact of improper accounting practices on the financial statements of a company* **(Obj. 4)**

Refer to the information given in Problem 18-1C.

Required

1. Sales grew faster than receivables. Would this situation create an unusually high or unusually low turnover?
2. Why was the fact that sales grew faster than receivables relative to other companies in the industry a "red flag"?
3. Explain why inventory turnover was too low.
4. Why was the fact that inventory turnover was low relative to other companies a "red flag"?
5. Compare the company's receivable turnover with inventory turnover. Does the comparison suggest a "red flag"? If so, what is it?

Extending Your Knowledge

Decision Problem

Identifying action to cut losses and establish profitability (Obj. 2, 4, 5)

Suppose you manage Mrs. Johnston's Corner Store Ltd., a variety store, which lost money during the past year. Before you can set the business on a successful course, you must first analyze the company and industry data for the current year in an effort to learn what is wrong. The data appear below.

Required

On the basis of your analysis of these figures, suggest three courses of action Mrs. Johnston's Corner Store Ltd. should take to reduce its losses and establish profitable operations. Give your reasons for each suggestion.

Mrs. Johnston's Corner Store Ltd. Income Statement Data		
	Mrs. Johnston's Corner Store Ltd.	Industry Average
Net sales..	100.0%	100.0%
Cost of sales..	(68.2)	(64.8)
Gross profit..	31.8	35.2
Operating expense	(37.1)	(32.3)
Operating income (loss)	(5.3)	2.9
Interest expense	(5.8)	(1.3)
Other revenue	1.1	0.3
Income (loss) before income tax.................	(10.0)	1.9
Income tax (expense) saving........................	4.4	(0.8)
Net income (loss)...	(5.6%)	1.1%

Mrs. Johnston's Corner Store Ltd. Balance Sheet Data

	Mrs. Johnston's Corner Store Ltd.	Industry Average
Cash and short-term investments..............	0.1%	10.3%
Accounts receivable	10.0	0.0
Inventory	74.3	68.0
Prepaid expenses.......................................	1.0	0.0
Total current assets................................	85.4	78.3
Capital assets, net.......................................	10.6	15.2
Other assets	4.0	6.5
Total assets..	100.0%	100.0%
Bank loan, 18%..	10.0%	0.0%
Notes payable, short-term, 12%	18.1	14.0
Accounts payable	14.1	25.1
Accrued liabilities.......................................	7.8	7.9
Total current liabilities	50.0	47.0
Long-term debt, 11%....................................	19.7	16.4
Total liabilities...	69.7	63.4
Common shareholders' equity..................	30.3	36.6
Total liabilities and shareholders' equity..	100.0%	100.0%

Financial Statement Problem

Measuring profitability and analyzing stock as an investment (Obj. 4, 5)

The Intrawest Corporation annual report is in Appendix A. The first page of the annual report gives the Five-Year Historical Review, with data for the fiscal years ended June 30, 1996 to 2000.

Required

1. Using the Five-Year Historical Review in Appendix A, page 1041, perform a four-year trend analysis of
   a. Revenues
   b. Net income
   c. Earnings per share of common stock

   Start with 1997 and end with 2000; use 1996 as the base year.

2. Evaluate Intrawest Corporation's profitability trend during this four-year period.

Comprehensive Problem
for Part Four

Analyzing a Company for its Investment Potential

In its 2000 annual report, Loblaw Companies Limited included an eight-year operating and financial record (see below). Loblaw Companies Limited operates a range of stores in all ten provinces, the Yukon, and the Northwest Territories. One of Loblaw Companies Limited's best known products is the "President's Choice" line of products.

Analyze the company's Operating and Financial Record for the fiscal years 1993 to 2000 to decide whether to invest in the common shares of Loblaw Companies Limited. Include the following sections in your analysis and fully explain your final decision:

- Trend analysis (use 1993 as the base year)
- Profitability analysis
- Measuring ability to pay liabilities and debt

LOBLAW COMPANIES LIMITED
Eight-Year Operating and Financial Record

($ millions)	2000	1999	1998	1997	1996	1995	1994	1993
Sales	20,121	18,783	12,497	11,008	9,848	9,854	10,000	9,356
Operating income	976	811	529	428	361	322	274	203
Interest expense	143	112	68	44	46	54	63	54
Net earnings (loss)	473	376	261	213	174	147	126	90
Financial position								
Working capital	(291)	(397)	(707)	202	154	179	29	148
Fixed assets	4,174	3,549	3,194	2,093	1,738	1,491	1,603	1,414
Goodwill	1,641	1,685	1,363	38	40	42	44	49
Total assets	9,025	7,979	7,105	4,013	3,531	3,197	3,042	2,743
Total debt (1)	2,216	1,999	1,842	513	435	287	525	506
Total shareholders' equity	3,124	2,904	2,595	1,495	1,311	1,160	1,105	985
Cash flow								
Cash flows from operating before acquisition restructuring and other charges	846	791	530	426	262	270	328	279
Capital investment	943	802	599	517	389	302	339	315
Per Common Share ($)								
Earnings before goodwill charges	1.87	1.52	1.06	0.88	0.73	0.61	0.50	0.37
Net earnings	1.71	1.37	1.06	0.88	0.72	0.60	0.50	0.36
Dividend rate (period end)	0.40	0.24	0.20	0.16	0.12	0.12	0.09	0.08
Cash flows from operating before acquisition restructuring and other charges (2)	3.07	2.88	2.15	1.76	1.08	1.12	1.35	1.15
Capital Investment	3.42	2.92	2.43	2.14	1.62	1.25	1.41	1.34
Book value	11.31	10.56	9.46	6.08	5.35	4.74	4.27	3.79
Market value (period end)	50.50	35.25	37.40	26.00	14.25	10.29	7.96	7.63
Shares outstanding (millions)	276	274	246	242	242	245	252	250

(1) Total debt is defined as total debt and debt equivalents less cash and short-term investments.
(2) Cash flows from operating activities before acquisition restructuring and other charges per common share is after preferred dividends.

The company acquired Provigo Inc. and Agora Foods, two major food retailers located principally in Quebec and Atlantic Canada, respectively, in late 1998.

Aggasiz Brewing Co.: The Problem Is Cash Flow

When Gary DePape played professional hockey in Germany, he developed a taste for German beer produced by small breweries, also known as microbreweries. At the age of 31, he returned to Manitoba and decided to start his own microbrewery to produce the kind of beer that he liked, reasoning that his friends and peers would also like and buy the beer. The brewery he started was Aggasiz Brewing Company, a $1,300,000 project.

Gary sold shares in the brewery to a number of small investors. It appeared that many or all of the investors had never invested in a private operation such as Aggasiz Brewing. They were more familiar with investing in public companies, where you invest your money and the company does not ask you for more money.

Winnipeg seemed ready for a microbrewery, especially if it was local. As one of Gary's hockey-playing friends noted, Molsons and Labatts had closed down, and even the Winnipeg Jets had left town. There is one microbrewery in Winnipeg already, Fort Garry Brewing, and some ex-Molsons and Labatts people are starting Twin Rivers Brewing Company.

Aggasiz Brewing Company's construction is on schedule but the budget (cash flow) is stretched. Gary hired two brew masters and a sales manager in anticipation of the beer flowing according to his plan, but there are problems that will delay production. The used bottling line that Gary purchased is missing parts and the seller won't install it. More cash is needed to fix the line. And cash is needed to start marketing Aggasiz's three brews.

The investors are nervous. The project is behind schedule and Gary needs more money. The investors have tried his new products and liked them but wonder when the cash outflow will stop and be replaced by a cash inflow. Nonetheless, they provide Gary with more cash; they still have confidence in his dream.

The problems continue. The cooling system breaks down. But in March, finally, Aggasiz Brewing Company has a product, and the bottles and bulk beer and ale start to flow to bars and restaurants and beer stores. At last, the cash outflow will be replaced with cash inflow.

Source: *Venture*, "Baron of Beer," telecast November 16, 2000.

CASE QUESTIONS

1. How has Gary financed his company to date? What are the potential problems of such an approach?

2. There is discussion in the video about "aggressive projections." What does the term mean and what are the ramifications of aggressive projections?

3. What is driving Aggasiz Brewing Company to get its beer and ale to market?

4. Could Gary have avoided his cash-flow problems?

Appendix A

GREAT PLAYGROUNDS OF THE WESTERN WORLD

CORPORATE PROFILE

Intrawest Corporation is the leading developer and operator of village-centered destination resorts across North America. It is redefining the resort world with its ten mountain resorts, one warm-weather resort, eighteen golf courses, a premier vacation ownership business—Club Intrawest—and five world-class resort villages at other locations, including one in France. In addition, Intrawest has a significant investment in Compagnie des Alpes, the largest ski company in the world in terms of skier visits, and Alpine Helicopters, owner of the largest heli-skiing operation in the world. The company has expertise in all aspects of resort living including lodging, food and beverage, themed retail, animated operations and real estate development. Its 16,000 employees are uniquely positioned to service the company's 6.2 million skier visits and 546,000 golf rounds, providing the best possible resort experience again and again. Intrawest Corporation's shares are listed on the New York (IDR) and Toronto (ITW) stock exchanges. The company is headquartered in Vancouver, British Columbia.

FIVE-YEAR HISTORICAL REVIEW

Years ended June 30	2000	1999	1998	1997	1996
Consolidated Operations		(in millions of U.S. dollars except per share amoun			
Revenue					
Resort operations	$ **452.1**	$ 382.5	$ 259.1	$ 192.7	$ 121
Real estate (sales and rental)	**348.4**	221.2	162.8	88.8	82
Other	**14.8**	5.9	2.5	3.2	4
Total revenue	**815.3**	609.6	424.4	284.7	208
Expenses					
Resort operations	**358.5**	300.9	200.5	143.3	91
Real estate costs	**285.5**	177.4	130.9	71.7	70
Interest	**35.2**	24.8	16.1	15.3	10
Depreciation and amortization	**51.4**	40.2	26.8	19.0	12
General, administrative and other	**32.6**	27.7	19.8	14.7	9
Total expenses	**763.2**	571.0	394.1	264.0	193
Income from continuing operations	$ **52.1**	$ 38.6	$ 30.3	$ 20.7	$ 14
Income per share from continuing operations	$ **1.20**	$ 0.96	$ 0.88	$ 0.74	$ 0.
Weighted average number of shares (in thousands)	**43,362**	40,237	34,486	27,809	23,0
Total Company EBITDA*	$ **165.4**	$ 128.8	$ 91.4	$ 64.8	$ 42
Consolidated Balance Sheets					
Assets					
Resort operations	$ **784.7**	$ 699.0	$ 471.5	$ 294.6	$ 186
Properties – resort	**569.3**	460.9	296.9	233.6	151
– discontinued operations	**9.6**	20.6	27.2	55.2	75
Other	**353.8**	311.7	203.6	211.9	138
Total assets	$ **1,717.4**	$ 1,492.2	$ 999.2	$ 795.3	$ 552

Liabilities and shareholders' equity

KEY FINANCIAL OBJECTIVES

Over the past few years the Company has been acquiring and expanding its portfolio of assets and the focus has now changed from building the platform for future growth, to improving returns on the existing asset base. Fiscal 2000 was a transition year. Only one small acquisition was made – Swaneset, a golf and country club in metropolitan Vancouver. Capital expenditures were reduced by approximately 18% from last year and they will decline further in the future. On the real estate side of the business, the marketability of all of the Company's properties has now been proven with successful first-time sales launches during the year at Blue Mountain, Sandestin and Squaw Valley. The pace of investment in infrastructure is expected to decline over the next 24 months as the villages at the Company's resorts reach greater maturity.

The Company's key financial objectives over the next few years are clearly defined.

- Maintain earnings per share growth of at least 20% per annum.

- As resort villages are built out, increase operating profit margins as Intrawest's resort model takes effect.

- Focus on increasing free cash flow and maximizing returns on capital.

- Combine the capital of other parties with in-house expertise to carry out new business opportunities.

- Maintain a conservative risk profile in both the operations and real estate businesses.

- Sell non-core assets and redeploy capital in more profitable or higher-returning businesses.

CHANGE IN REPORTING CURRENCY

At the beginning of fiscal 2000, the Company changed its reporting currency from Canadian to U.S. dollars. This change was made in response to the recent growth in the Company's U.S. asset and revenue base (more than 60% of both assets and revenue was expected to be U.S.-based in fiscal 2000), the Company's increasing profile in the U.S. investment community and the Company's desire to gain closer comparability with other publicly traded leisure companies. **Unless otherwise stated, all dollar amounts in this Management's Discussion and Analysis and in the Consolidated Financial Statements that follow it are in U.S. dollars.**

OPERATING HIGHLIGHTS

The operating highlights for the year include:

- A 33.7% increase in total revenue from $609.6 million to $815.3 million, with ski and resort revenue increasing 18.2% and real estate sales revenue increasing 58.2%.

- A 34.9% increase in income from continuing operations to $52.1 million and a 25.0% increase in income per share from continuing operations to $1.20. The per share amount reflects a 7.8% increase in the weighted average number of shares outstanding in 2000.

- A 14.8% increase in operating profit from ski and resort operations and a 44.3% increase in operating profit from real estate sales.

- A 28.4% increase in Total Company EBITDA from $128.8 million to $165.4 million. Total Company EBITDA is computed as income before interest (including previously capitalized interest in real estate cost of sales), taxes, non-controlling interest, depreciation and amortization. It is not a term that has an established meaning under generally accepted accounting principles; however, management believes it is an important measure of operating performance.

REVIEW OF SKI AND RESORT OPERATIONS

The following table highlights the results of the ski and resort operations business.

	2000	1999	Change
Skier visits[1]	5,694,000	5,791,000	-1.7%
Revenue ($millions)	452.1	382.5	18.2%
EBITDA ($millions)	93.7	81.6	14.8%
Margin	20.7%	21.3%	

(1) All resorts are at 100% except Mammoth at 59% and Blue Mountain at 50%.

Revenue from ski and resort operations increased 18.2% from $382.5 million in 1999 to $452.1 million in 2000. Revenue from mountain resorts increased 16.0% from $340.2 million to $394.6 million while revenue from warm-weather resorts increased 35.9% from $42.3 million to $57.5 million.

Mountain resorts

The $54.4 million increase in mountain resort revenue was due to:

	($millions)
Timing of acquisitions in 1999	17.2
Reduction in skier visits	(7.6)
Increase in revenue per skier visit	36.5
Increase in non-skier visit revenue	8.3
	54.4

The Company acquired its 50% interest in Blue Mountain and its 45% interest in Alpine in the third quarter of 1999. Intrawest Vacations was purchased in the fourth quarter of 1999 and contributed no revenue in that year. The impact of including a full year of revenue for these businesses in 2000 versus a partial year of revenue in 1999 was $17.2 million.

Skier visits decreased 1.7% from 5,791,000 in 1999 to 5,694,000 in 2000. Skier visits declined 0.4% at the Company's Canadian resorts and 3.3% at its U.S. resorts. Weaker than expected millennium bookings and fears over possible repercussions from the Y2K problem impacted business across the entire travel sector during the important Christmas/New Year period and into January. The 1999/2000 winter season was also generally a difficult one for weather. In the northeast, the season started slowly and ended prematurely due to unusually warm weather, and the late timing of Easter impacted skier visits further in that region. Lack of snow at the start of the season in Colorado and California reduced skier visits at Copper and Mammoth. Mammoth had purchased skier visit insurance and collected $0.7 million under the policy. Skier visits at Copper were also impacted by construction of the central four buildings in the new village. Only Whistler/Blackcomb, Panorama and Snowshoe showed an increase in skier visits over 1999 with each resort registering all-time record skier visits. The impact of the reduction in skier visits in 2000 was estimated to decrease mountain resort revenue by $7.6 million.

Revenue per skier visit increased 12.1% from $51.89 in 1999 to $58.19 in 2000. Revenue per skier visit increased at every one of the Company's resorts ranging from 7% at Copper, Snowshoe and Mammoth to 32% at Mountain Creek. Revenue per skier visit is a function of ticket prices and ticket yields, and revenue from non-ticket sources includes retail

13

and rental stores, lodging, ski school and food services. Ticket yields reflect the mix of ticket types (e.g., adult, child, season pass and group), the proportion of day versus destination visitors (destination visitors tend to be less price sensitive), and the amount of discounting of full-price tickets. Revenue per visit from non-ticket sources is also influenced by the mix of day versus destination visitors, the affluence of the visitor base, and the quantity and type of amenities and services offered at the resort.

The Company's strategy at all of its resorts is to offer the highest quality product within its market area at a premium ticket price. In addition, the strong competitive position of each of the Company's resorts, created by the resort villages and the significant capital investments that have been made over the past few years, helps to attract destination visitors and reduces reliance on discounts to attract local visitors in favor of committed regional visitors. During 2000 the Company moved to a variable pricing policy at most of its resorts, adjusting ticket prices depending on peak or non-peak season and holidays. The effective ticket price (i.e., total ticket revenue divided by total skier visits) across all of the Company's resorts was 11.1% higher in 2000 than in 1999. On average, ticket prices increased by 3.3% and the balance of the increase in effective ticket price in 2000 was due to ticket mix and yield management. The impact of these factors was to increase revenue by $15.8 million.

Revenue per visit from non-ticket sources increased 13.3% in 2000. The strongest performance was in retail and rental, which increased 18.2% mainly because of new or renovated stores at Whistler/Blackcomb (including the acquisition of two Westbeach stores), Tremblant and Snowshoe. Lodging and property management revenue per visit increased 15.6% due both to growth in the inventory of managed properties and to yield improvements. The construction completion of several condo-hotel properties in advance of the ski season increased the available room inventory by 9.3% and revenue per available room (REVPAR)

increased by 7.6% across the mountain resorts. Revenue per visit from food and beverage increased 8.2% with improvements at Whistler/Blackcomb, Mountain Creek and Mammoth being partially offset by declines at Tremblant and Snowshoe. The overall impact of increases in revenue per visit from non-ticket sources was to increase revenue by $20.7 million.

For the purposes of this analysis, non-skier visit revenue comprises revenue from golf and other summer activities and revenue from businesses such as Alpine and Breeze which do not have skier visits. During 2000 the Company opened new golf courses at Mammoth and Panorama and revenue from existing mountain resort courses increased 20.4% compared with 1999. Revenue from other summer activities also increased at each of the mountain resorts as the Company's strategy to grow its revenue through all four seasons began to show positive results. Alpine experienced a strong winter season with year-over-year revenue growth of 11.1% while revenue at Breeze was approximately the same in 2000 as 1999 due primarily to weather factors in Colorado and to a significant decline in destination visitors to that state. Overall non-skier visit revenue increased by $8.3 million in 2000.

Warm-weather resorts
The $15.2 million increase in warm-weather resort revenue in 2000 was due to the acquisition of Swaneset, which added $3.9 million of revenue, and to increased revenue at both Sandestin and Raven. Revenue at Sandestin increased 32.9% with significant improvements in lodging, golf, and food and beverage revenue. A re-focused marketing program initiated last year resulted in a 16.5% increase in occupied room nights in 2000. This higher occupancy and the completion of the fourth golf course during the year generated a 58.9% increase in golf revenue. Revenue at Raven increased 6.9% in 2000. The number of rounds played was approximately the same in both years, with revenue per round higher in 2000.

The factors described above changed the composition of ski and resort operations revenue as follows:

	2000 Revenue (millions)	2000 Proportion (%)	1999 Revenue (millions)	1999 Proportion (%)	Increase in Revenue (millions)	Percentage Increase (%)
Mountain operations	$ 177.1	39.2	$ 155.6	40.7	$ 21.5	13.8
Retail and rental shops	72.8	16.1	65.0	17.0	7.8	12.0
Food and beverage	60.1	13.3	54.8	14.3	5.3	9.7
Lodging and property management	53.5	11.8	38.4	10.0	15.1	39.3
Ski school	25.8	5.7	22.2	5.8	3.6	16.2
Golf	30.9	6.8	21.3	5.6	9.6	45.1
Other	31.9	7.1	25.2	6.6	6.7	26.6
	$ 452.1	100.0	$ 382.5	100.0	$ 69.6	18.2

14

Since 1995 the proportion of revenue from mountain operations (i.e. lift tickets and heli-skiing) has fallen from 52.6% to 39.2%. This trend is likely to continue as the resort villages are built out, expanding the inventory of lodging units and changing the customer mix in favor of destination visitors who spend more on retail and rental, ski school, and food and beverage.

Ski and resort operations expenses increased from $300.9 million in 1999 to $358.5 million in 2000, in line with the increase in ski and resort operations revenue. EBITDA from ski and resort operations increased 14.8% from $81.6 million in 1999 to $93.7 million in 2000. The EBITDA margin was 20.7% in 2000 compared with 21.3% in 1999. The margin in 2000 was impacted by the weaker-than-expected millennium bookings and by the difficult weather conditions, which necessitated constant rebuilding of the snow base. Not only were visits reduced during the normally high-margin Christmas period, but the mix of visits was changed with relatively fewer destination visitors because people were not travelling. A significant decline in destination visitors to Colorado (mainly because of below-average snow conditions for the past two seasons) reduced EBITDA from Breeze. The moderate decline in EBITDA margin at the mountain resorts was partially offset by an increased margin at the warm-weather resorts from 13.2% in 1999 to 16.0% in 2000. The Company expects margins going forward to increase at both the mountain resorts and the warm-weather resorts as its villages mature, driving higher mid-week destination visits, and as it takes further advantage of economies of scale.

REVIEW OF RESORT REAL ESTATE OPERATIONS
The following table highlights the results of the real estate business.

	2000	1999	Change
Units delivered	1,317	1,126	17.0%
Revenue ($millions)	341.5	215.9	58.2%
Operating profit ($millions)	59.6	41.3	44.3%
Margin	17.5%	19.1%	

Revenue from the sale of real estate increased 58.2% from $215.9 million in 1999 to $341.5 million in 2000. The increase was due to volume and price increases in the traditional real estate business and to significantly higher revenue in the resort club (timeshare) business. Real estate revenue increased 8.0% at the Company's Canadian resorts and 84.6% at its U.S. resorts.

A total of 443 units were delivered at the Company's Canadian resorts in 2000 compared with 496 units last year. The average price per unit increased 20.9% from Cdn.$237,000 in 1999 to Cdn.$286,000 in 2000 due to the mix of resorts and product types. Comparatively more units were delivered at higher-priced Whistler/Blackcomb and comparatively less at Tremblant and Panorama in 2000 than in 1999. Furthermore the Company delivered more than twice as many townhouses and 43% fewer condo-hotel units in 2000 than in 1999. Condo-hotel units typically have a higher price per square foot than townhouses but a lower absolute price because of their smaller size.

The Company delivered 874 units at its U.S. resorts in 2000 compared with 630 units in 1999. Solitude and Three Peaks closed units for the first time in 2000 and significantly more units were closed at Copper and Mammoth than in 1999. The average price per unit was $285,000 in 2000 (after adjusting the number of units for the impact of joint ventures at Keystone and Sandestin), up from $267,000 in 1999. The mix of product types at U.S. resorts was similar in 2000 and 1999, approximately 70% condo-hotel, 10% townhouse and 20% single-family lots.

The Resort Club generated $29.2 million in sales revenue in 2000, up 87.2% from $15.6 million in 1999. The opening of the new club location at Palm Desert, California accounted for 22.6% of this increase. The balance of the increase was attributable to a 42.7% increase in the number of points sold at the Blackcomb and Tremblant club locations and two price increases during the year totaling approximately 10%. The significant improvement in sales at Blackcomb and Tremblant was due to the implementation of a variable pricing policy and changes within the sales and marketing organization. These changes included the establishment of a 100-seat call centre in Vancouver and a special team to handle referral and add-on point sales to existing members. Revenue from member referrals and add-on points increased 40% in 2000 to $2.6 million reflecting high member satisfaction and growing acceptance of the Resort Club's unique points system.

Standard real estate accounting practice requires that all costs in connection with the development of real estate be capitalized to properties under development and then expensed in the period when the properties are delivered and the revenue is recognized. Such costs include general and administrative costs of personnel directly involved in the development, construction and sale of real estate as well as interest on specific real estate debt and on the portion of general corporate debt used to fund real estate development expenditures. The amount of capitalized real estate costs has increased proportionally with the ramp-up in real estate production from approximately 500 units per year in 1996 to approximately 1,500 in 2000.

Operating profit from resort real estate sales increased 44.3% from $41.3 million in 1999 to $59.6 million in 2000. The profit margin was 17.5% in 2000 compared with 19.1% in 1999. The decline in margin in 2000 was due mainly to the mix of resorts and particularly the maturity of their villages. Normally margins are lower in the early years of development of a resort. There are a number of reasons for this.

- Land and infrastructure costs are estimated for the entire build-out of a resort and the resulting total cost is allocated to projects on the basis of buildable area. The land and infrastructure cost per buildable square foot is therefore relatively fixed for all the developable units at a resort. Since sales prices escalate over time, margins rise as villages mature.

- As the resort is built out, supply and demand factors tend to increase sales prices faster than project costs. In addition, enhancements to the resort during build-out (e.g., capital improvements on the mountain or reaching critical mass in the village) will increase demand for (and therefore the prices of) real estate.

Intrawest's historical real estate experience at Blackcomb, Tremblant and Keystone confirms this trend. At Tremblant, for example, margins realized on the first two condo-hotel projects built in the village in 1993 and 1994 were approximately half the margins on later and current condo-hotel projects.

The first condo-hotel projects in the new villages at Copper, Mammoth and Solitude completed construction during 2000. The villages at each of these resorts are in the early stage of development. Sales at these resorts accounted for 32.4% of the Company's total real estate sales in 2000 (compared with 6.6% in 1999) and the margin on these sales was 14.2%. This compares with an average margin of 22.4% in 2000 at Whistler/Blackcomb, Tremblant and Keystone.

As of August 31, 2000, the Company had pre-sold 1,158 units for approximately $390 million which it expects to close in fiscal 2001 and a further 425 units for approximately $190 million due to close in fiscal 2002. Intrawest follows a conservative accounting policy for real estate

15

sales whereby it does not recognize any revenue until title to a completed unit has been transferred to a purchaser and the Company has received the full cash proceeds. The Company's strategy of pre-selling real estate projects before the start of construction reduces market risk and helps to maintain margins since sales concessions are not required and holding costs are more readily determinable. Furthermore, pre-selling real estate increases the predictability of real estate earnings.

Rental Properties
The majority of the condo-hotel projects the Company develops contain ground-level retail space which is either leased to third-party operators or used by the Company for its own sports shops. At June 30, 2000, the Company owned 341,000 square feet of commercial space compared with 310,000 square feet at the end of the previous year. Rental revenue derived from third party operators increased from $5.4 million in 1999 to $6.9 million in 2000. The increase was due to additional leasing from recently completed condo-hotel properties at Tremblant, Keystone and Snowshoe. Operating profit from rental properties increased from $2.6 million in 1999 to $3.3 million in 2000, in line with the increase in rental revenue.

REVIEW OF CORPORATE OPERATIONS

Interest and Other Income
Interest and other income increased from $3.7 million in 1999 to $12.4 million in 2000. During 2000 the Company sold its investment in a property management business in Whistler/Blackcomb and recorded a gain of $5.2 million. The Company offers central reservations to many hotel and rental management partners at Whistler/Blackcomb through its division Resort Reservations Whistler, and ownership of a property management company was no longer considered necessary to the Company's success in the resort. The balance of the increase in interest and other income was due mainly to higher fee income and miscellaneous gains.

The Company's investment in Compagnie des Alpes generated $2.3 million of earnings in 2000 compared with $2.1 million in 1999. Compagnie des Alpes experienced record revenues and profits during 2000.

Interest Costs
The Company incurred total interest costs of $66.4 million in 2000 compared with $50.6 million in 1999. Interest on the $135 million debentures issued in January 2000 along with a full year of interest on the $200 million debentures issued in 1999 accounted for $11.2 million of the increase. Proceeds from the $135 million debentures were initially used to reduce the Company's revolving credit facility, a portion of which was subsequently redrawn and invested in the extensive real estate development program. The balance of the change in interest costs was mainly due to increased construction financing.

Interest incurred is either capitalized to real estate properties and resort assets under development or charged to income. Interest capitalized to real estate assets is subsequently expensed (as a component of real estate costs) in the period when those properties are delivered. During 2000 $46.6 million of interest incurred was charged to income—$35.2 million as interest expense, $10.9 million as a component of real estate costs, and $0.5 million in discontinued operations. By comparison, in 1999 a total of $31.7 million of interest incurred was charged to income. In addition, real estate costs for 2000 and 1999 included $5.9 million and $4.8 million, respectively, of interest that was incurred and capitalized to properties in prior years, principally 1999.

Depreciation and Amortization
Depreciation and amortization expense increased from $40.2 million in 1999 to $51.4 million in 2000. A full year of depreciation expense for the resorts and businesses acquired part way through 1999 accounted

for $1.7 million of the increase and the balance of the increase was due mainly to depreciation of capital expenditures made at the resorts during 2000. Capital expenditures are planned to decline by 20-25% in 2001 and 2002 and as a result the growth in depreciation and amortization will flatten out in the future.

General and Administrative Costs
All general and administrative costs incurred by the resorts are included in ski and resort operation expenses. Similarly, general and administrative costs incurred in the development of real estate are initially capitalized to properties, and then expensed to real estate costs in the period when the properties are delivered. Corporate general and administrative costs, which mainly comprise certain executive employee costs, public company costs, audit and legal fees, and capital taxes, increased from $7.4 million in 1999 to $8.0 million in 2000. As a percentage of revenues, corporate general and administrative costs declined from 1.2% in 1999 to 1.0% in 2000. The Company continually reviews its overhead costs and has instituted procedures to reduce or eliminate costs where appropriate.

Income Taxes
The Company provided for income taxes of $15.4 million in 2000 compared with $13.5 million in 1999. This equates to an effective tax rate of 20.1% in 2000, down from 22.9% in 1999. The lower rate was due mainly to a change in the Company's policy of accounting for income taxes.

The Canadian Institute of Chartered Accountants has changed the accounting standard related to income taxes from the deferred method to the asset and liability method. The differences between the two methods are explained in note 1(n) to the Consolidated Financial Statements. The adoption of the asset and liability method brings generally accepted accounting principles (GAAP) in Canada closer to GAAP in the United States.

The Company adopted the new standard retroactively to July 1, 1999 without restating the financial statements of any prior year. Due to the number of acquisitions that the Company has made over the past few years, the impact of the change on the Company's balance sheet was significant. The cumulative effect of differences between the accounting and tax bases of assets and liabilities, amounting to $57.5 million at July 1, 1999, was charged against retained earnings in 2000 with a corresponding increase mainly to future income taxes payable. The benefit of this charge to retained earnings will be felt in future years (as well as in 2000) through a somewhat lower income tax expense.

Non-Controlling Interest
The Company has a 23% limited partner in the two partnerships which own Whistler/Blackcomb and there is a 5% non-controlling interest in Sandestin. The results of all three entities are fully consolidated into the Company's financial statements with the outside partner's share of earnings shown as non-controlling interest. Non-controlling interest increased from $6.8 million in 1999 to $9.3 million in 2000. Approximately half of the increase was due to the gain on sale of the property management business referred to above in "Interest and Other Income" and the balance was due to increased operations and real estate earnings at both Whistler/Blackcomb and Sandestin.

DISCONTINUED OPERATIONS
The consolidated financial statements disclose the results of the Company's non-resort business as discontinued operations. The discontinued operations incurred a loss of $0.1 million in 2000 compared with a loss of $4.6 million (including $3.5 million of property write-downs) in 1999. During 2000 the Company sold $11.2 million of non-resort properties including Whitemud Crossing Shopping Centre in

16

Edmonton and the remaining units in the Coach Hill project in Calgary.

At June 30, 2000, the Company had $16.8 million of remaining non-resort assets, mainly comprising two properties—the AirCare vehicle emission testing centres and the Gateway commercial land site—and a receivable of $6.4 million related to an earlier sale of non-resort properties (see note 19 to the Consolidated Financial Statements). The liquidation of these remaining non-resort assets has no impact on the common shareholders. The net income or loss generated by the non-resort assets accrues to the holders of the non-resort preferred ("NRP") shares and the net cash flow from these assets can only be used to redeem NRP shares. During 2000 the Company used $19.5 million to redeem 9,246,000 NRP shares and a further $0.1 million to purchase 62,900 NRP shares under the Company's normal course issuer bid at an average cost of Cdn.$1.74.

Up to June 30, 1999, the results of discontinued operations were included in retained earnings. During 2000 the Company's shareholders passed a resolution to reduce the redemption price of the NRP shares from Cdn.$3.82 to Cdn.$2.65 per share. As a result, the cumulative loss from discontinued operations since the creation of the NRP shares, amounting to $7.6 million, was charged against NRP share capital and retained earnings was increased by the same amount.

LIQUIDITY AND CAPITAL RESOURCES

Analysis of Cash Flows

Intrawest generally funds its operating and capital requirements from cash flow from operations, bank and other indebtedness, and equity issues. Since 1996 the Company has been acquiring and upgrading its portfolio of resorts and ramping up its production of real estate units, and although cash flow from operations grew at an average annual rate of 47.5%, it has been insufficient to fund the Company's growth. During this period approximately one-quarter of the $1.2 billion increase in total assets has been funded by cash flow from operations and the balance from debt, equity and other sources. This trend is now changing and in 2000 only $70.9 million of net new financing was required to fund the Company's growth compared with $341.4 million in 1999.

The major sources and uses of cash in 2000 and 1999 were as follows.

($millions)	2000	1999	Change
Cash flow from continuing operations	122.5	90.6	31.9
Net new investment in real estate properties developed for sale	(83.4)	(86.9)	3.5
Expenditures on acquisitions	(19.3)	(181.8)	162.5
Expenditures on resort operations improvements	(118.6)	(144.2)	25.6
Other net receipts (expenditures)	24.4	(16.4)	40.8
Net cash outflows before financing inflows	(74.4)	(338.7)	264.3
Net proceeds from financing	70.9	341.4	(270.5)
Increase (decrease) in cash	(3.5)	2.7	(6.2)

In 2000 $122.5 million of cash flow was provided by continuing operations compared with $90.6 million in 1999. Cash flow from continuing operations comprises income from continuing operations adjusted for non-cash items, such as depreciation and amortization, and future income taxes. The components of, and year-over-year changes in, cash flow from continuing operations have been discussed earlier in the review of operations.

In the past few fiscal years the real estate business has been a net user of cash. In 2000 the Company spent $365.2 million on developing real estate properties and recovered $281.8 million of development costs from sales of properties, resulting in a net new investment in real estate properties of $83.4 million. This compares with a net new investment of $86.9 million in 1999. There are two main reasons why the real estate business has required net new investment. First, significant amounts have been expended on up-front infrastructure costs and second, the production of units has increased every year as development activity has taken place at recently acquired resorts.

Since 1996 the number of real estate units under construction each year has increased at an average annual rate of approximately 30%. During this period the first projects were built and sold at Stratton, Snowshoe, Copper, Mammoth, Sandestin and Solitude. The ramp-up in the production of real estate units is expected to continue in 2001, 2002 and 2003 as more units are built at these resorts and units are built for the first time at Blue Mountain, Squaw Valley, Mountain Creek and the recently announced Les Arcs and Lake Las Vegas properties. Between 2000 and 2003 it is expected that the annual production of units will increase by approximately 15% each year and then level off at about 2,100 units per year.

During the ramp-up stage, as production increases from 1,500 units per year to 2,100 units, it is likely that the Company's net new investment in real estate properties will increase. To some extent this will be offset by a decline in annual expenditures on infrastructure costs starting in 2002. When the increase in production levels off, the real estate business will become a significant generator of cash.

In 1999 the Company announced that it planned to spend less on acquisitions and capital improvements and focus on increasing returns from existing assets. The acquisition of Swaneset and buying out the Company's partner in the Lodestar lands at Mammoth used $19.3 million of cash in 2000. By comparison, in 1999 the Company invested a total of $181.8 million in new resorts and businesses, including Sandestin, Raven, Breeze, Alpine and Blue Mountain. Capital expenditures on ski and resort assets used $118.6 million of cash flow in 2000, down 17.8% from 1999. The Company estimates that it will make capital expenditures at its mountain and warm-weather resorts totaling approximately $90 million in fiscal 2001, comprising approximately $23 million of maintenance capital and $67 million of expansion capital. The expansion capital requirements are being driven mainly by the development of the villages at the Company's resorts. For example, planned expenditures for 2001 include $15 million to build out the retail store space in the base of new condo-hotels and $7 million for village infrastructure. Approximately $15 million of capital has been allocated to upgrading and enhancing information technology systems, including building e-commerce distribution and marketing capability and standardizing both customer interactive and back-of-the-house systems across resorts.

The Company expects to fund its real estate development and expenditures on resort operations improvements from cash flow from operations, construction financing and available lines of credit. It does not foresee a requirement to raise additional equity capital. Cash is also expected to be provided by the sale of certain non-core assets.

17

Analysis of Debt

At June 30, 2000, total debt amounted to $833.2 million, an increase of $106.1 million from June 30, 1999. During the year the Company issued $135 million of 10.5% senior unsecured debentures due 2010. The proceeds were principally used to repay the Company's revolving credit facility. Since December 1997 the Company has issued $419.5 million of unsecured debentures in the public market. At year-end, this type of financing constituted 52.2% of total debt compared with 41.6% at the end of the previous year. The Company expects to continue to raise debt at the corporate level and to reduce its secured debt at the subsidiary level.

At June 30, 2000, 35.5% of total debt bore interest at floating rates, down from 43.3% at June 30, 1999. Intrawest has developed a hedging policy to manage its interest rate risk. Interim financing for real estate construction is normally arranged on a floating rate basis. Since the Company pre-sells its projects and mainly develops wood-frame buildings with a construction period of 9 to 18 months, exposure to higher interest rates on construction financing is not significant. Debt on defined-income stream properties (for example, commercial rental properties) is normally arranged on a longer-term, fixed-rate basis with the objective of matching the financing with the duration characteristics of the property. It is also the Company's policy to fix the interest on at least 50% of its general corporate and ski and resort operations debt, although a lower proportion may be hedged temporarily in anticipation of a refinancing. At year-end, 29.8% of such debt bore interest at floating rates. A 1% change in the rate of interest on this debt would impact annual earnings by approximately $2.1 million before income taxes.

The Company has various operating lines of credit totaling approximately $230 million, of which $61.4 million was drawn at June 30, 2000. These lines of credit are available to fund seasonal cash requirements and capital expenditures at the resorts, real estate development activity, and for general corporate purposes. In addition, the Company has three revolving credit facilities totaling approximately $185 million available for real estate construction, of which $87.6 million was drawn at June 30, 2000. Real estate projects must meet certain conditions (including pre-sales thresholds) in order to qualify for funding under these facilities. Once the conditions are satisfied, up to 85% of costs will be funded.

BUSINESS RISKS

Intrawest is subject to various risks and uncertainties that can cause volatility in its earnings. The Company's resort operations and resort real estate businesses are managed to deal with risks that are common to most companies, i.e., the risks of severe economic downturn, competition and currency fluctuations, and the more industry-specific risks of unfavorable weather conditions, seasonality of operations and construction overruns.

Economic Downturn

A severe economic downturn could reduce spending on resort vacations and weaken sales of recreational real estate. Although leisure and travel are discretionary activities that one might expect to be impacted by a significant economic slowdown, Intrawest's operating results have not historically shown this to be the case. Since the Company acquired Blackcomb in 1986, cash flow has increased every year at that resort despite widely varying economic conditions. Blackcomb, as well as Intrawest's other resorts, attracts customers who have incomes well above the national average and are therefore less likely to have their vacation plans impacted by an economic recession. In addition, Intrawest's resorts draw their visitors from a wide variety of locations and this diversity shelters these resorts somewhat from regional economic conditions.

Real estate developers face two major risks from an economic downturn: land risk and completed inventory risk. Land risk arises when land is purchased with debt and economic conditions deteriorate resulting in higher holding costs and reduced profitability, or worse, loan defaults and foreclosure. Intrawest has reduced its land risk by acquiring land at low cost with the purchase of a resort or by securing land through options and joint ventures. The extensive land holdings at Tremblant, Stratton, Snowshoe, Mountain Creek and Panorama were all low-cost acquisitions with the resort. At Blackcomb and Squaw Valley and the recently announced developments at Lake Las Vegas and Les Arcs, the Company secured its land holdings through a series of rolling options rather than outright purchases. Options are exercised for specific project sites only when permits are in place and construction is set to start. Similarly, at Whistler the land acquisition financing is repaid when building permits are issued, subject to minimum annual repayments. Intrawest secured its land holdings at Keystone by forming a joint venture with the land owner under which land is only paid for as completed units are sold and construction financing is repaid.

Completed inventory risk arises when completed units cannot be sold and construction financing cannot be repaid. Intrawest has mitigated this risk by pre-selling a significant portion of its units prior to commencement of, and during, construction. At June 30, 2000, the Company had 141 unsold units in its resort real estate inventory (representing 10.7% of the units delivered in 2000) and 80% of the approximately 1,500 resort units under construction on that date were pre-sold. Purchasers are required to make a significant non-refundable deposit (generally in the range of $50,000 – $60,000) prior to construction completion which has historically ensured that rescissions have been kept to an extremely low level. Furthermore, the Company generally has sufficient pre-sales in place to cover its construction and other real estate debt by 1.5 to 2 times. In the event of a severe economic downturn in the real estate business, the Company could complete construction of its pre-sold units, transfer title to purchasers and repay all of its real estate financing.

Competition

The mountain resort industry has significant barriers to entry (e.g., very high start-up costs and significant environmental hurdles) that prevent new resorts from being created. Competition therefore is essentially confined to existing resorts. Intrawest's resorts compete for destination visitors with other mountain resorts in Canada, the United States, Europe and Japan, and with other leisure industry companies, such as cruise lines. They also compete for day skiers with other ski areas within each resort's local market area. Skier visits in North America have been relatively flat over the past ten years, which has increased competition between resort owners. The Company's strategy is to acquire resorts that have natural competitive advantages (e.g., in terms of location, vertical drop and quality of terrain) and to enhance those advantages by investing in capital improvements on the mountain. Since 1997 the Company has invested a total of $390.8 million in such capital improvements. The Company's principal strength compared with its industry competitors is its ability to combine expertise in resort operations and real estate development, particularly in building master-planned resort villages. Increasingly the village has become the dominant attraction in generating visits to a resort.

The Company owns substantially all of the supply of developable land at the base of its resorts and hence competition in real estate is somewhat restricted. Expertise in all aspects of the development process, including resort master-planning, project design, construction, sales and marketing, and property management also gives the Company a distinct competitive advantage. In the resort club business, the Company

18

has established a competitive position through its ownership of the mountain facilities, and by offering a high standard of accommodation and a flexible points-based system.

Currency Fluctuations
Over the past several years the Company's Canadian resort operations have benefited from the lower Canadian dollar relative to the U.S. dollar, the Japanese yen and European currencies. This has made the price of a ski lift ticket at Intrawest's Canadian resorts 70% or less of the price at comparable U.S. resorts when denominated in the same currency. Along with accommodation and food and beverage costs, this has made vacationing in Canada more affordable for foreign visitors and it has encouraged Canadians to vacation at home. A significant shift in the value of the Canadian dollar, particularly against its U.S. counterpart, could impact earnings at Canadian resorts.

Intrawest finances its U.S. assets with U.S. dollar debt and its Canadian assets with Canadian dollar debt. Generally the Company services its debt with revenue denominated in the same currency. In addition, cash flow generated by Canadian operations is generally retained in Canada and invested in expansion of Canadian assets. Similarly cash flow generated at the U.S. resorts is generally reinvested in the United States. Cross-border cash transactions and currency exchanges are kept to a minimum.

Since Intrawest reports its earnings in U.S. dollars but its income is derived from both Canadian and U.S. sources, the Company is exposed to foreign currency exchange risk in its reported earnings. Revenues and expenses of the Company's Canadian operations will be impacted by changes in exchange rates when such operations are reported in U.S. dollars. The impact of Canadian/U.S. dollar exchange rate changes on the balance sheet are reflected in the foreign currency translation amount included in shareholders' equity and does not affect reported earnings.

Unfavorable Weather Conditions
The Company's ability to attract visitors to its resorts is influenced by weather conditions and the amount of snowfall during the ski season. Intrawest manages its exposure to unfavorable weather in three ways: by being geographically diversified, by seeking to build its visits as evenly as possible through the seasons and by investing in snowmaking.

Geographically diversified companies like Intrawest can reduce the risk associated with a particular region's weather patterns. Every ski season since 1995, favorable and unfavorable weather conditions at different times across North America have offset one another, allowing the Company to come within 2% of its budgeted winter season ski and resort operations revenue on a same-resort basis. The more a resort can attract its visitors evenly through the season the less vulnerable it is to unfavorable weather at a particular time. In order to spread its visits, Intrawest attempts to increase traffic mid-week and at non-peak times by marketing to destination visitors who book in advance, stay several days and are less likely than day visitors to change their vacation plans. Investing in snowmaking can also mitigate the impact of poor natural snow conditions. Snowmaking is particularly important in eastern North America due to the number of competing resorts and less reliable snowfall. Intrawest has invested heavily in snowmaking at all of its resorts over the past few years.

Seasonality of Operations
Ski and resort operations are highly seasonal. In fiscal 2000 approximately 70% of the Company's ski and resort operations revenue was generated during the period from December to March. Furthermore, during this period a significant portion of ski and resort operations revenue is generated on certain holidays, particularly Christmas/New

Year, Presidents' Day and school spring breaks, and on weekends. Conversely, Sandestin's peak operating season occurs during the summer months, partially offsetting the seasonality of the mountain resorts. The Company's real estate operations tend to be somewhat seasonal as well, with construction primarily taking place during the summer and the majority of sales closing in the December to June period. This seasonality of operations impacts reported quarterly earnings. The operating results for any particular quarter are not necessarily indicative of the operating results for a subsequent quarter or for the full fiscal year. The Company has taken steps to smooth its revenue and earnings throughout the year by investing in four-season amenities (e.g., golf) and growing its summer and shoulder-season businesses. As a result of these initiatives, the proportion of ski and resort operations revenue earned outside the historically strong third fiscal quarter has increased to 46.9% in 2000 from 32.7% three years ago.

Construction Overruns
Intrawest is not in the construction business but rather engages general contractors to construct its real estate projects. The Company's practice is to structure its construction contracts on a fixed-price basis so that cost overruns are at the contractor's risk. In addition construction contracts are priced only after the Company has completed full working drawings. The Company employs construction experts who oversee the general contractors and ensure that problems are properly and quickly resolved. The Company has also developed a comprehensive and sophisticated project reporting system, which helps to identify potential cost overruns early enough to permit corrective action.

OUTLOOK
The Company will continue to execute the same strategic plan in 2001 that guided its operations in 2000. The focus will be on increasing returns from the existing asset base by reducing capital spending, improving margins, and leveraging expertise to grow the business.

On the resort operations side of the business, the Company has a number of initiatives to increase revenue and limit cost growth at its resorts. These initiatives include the establishment of a national destination sales team to generate increased lodging bookings and higher occupancy, the roll-out of e-commerce sales and customer relationship systems, and plans to control labor costs (which account for more than 40% of total ski and resort operation costs). At the same time the Company expects to benefit from approximately 1,300 new units of accommodation across its resorts, access to the new village at Copper, and a return to more normal travel patterns during the important Christmas holiday period after the travel slowdown experienced in 2000 because of Y2K/millennium issues.

On the real estate side of the business, the Company has accelerated its development program. Incremental returns on these new projects are very high because of the speed that equity is rolled over, due to the Company's success in pre-selling. The accelerated expansion of the villages will also result in benefits to the operations by increasing the accommodation base for destination visitors and adding to the attractions at the resort. The Company has a record backlog of sales – approximately $580 million for delivery in 2001 and 2002 compared with $330 million this time last year.

Sales at the Resort Club continue to improve and margins are strengthening in this business. The Company expects to expand the Resort Club to new locations in 2001, including Sandestin, Blue Mountain and Vancouver.

19

Management's Responsibility

The consolidated financial statements of Intrawest Corporation have been prepared by management and approved by the Board of Directors of the Company. Management is responsible for the preparation and presentation of the information contained in the consolidated financial statements. The Company maintains appropriate systems of internal control, policies and procedures which provide management with reasonable assurance that assets are safeguarded and that financial records are reliable and form a proper basis for preparation of financial statements.

The Company's independent auditors, KPMG LLP, have been appointed by the shareholders to express their professional opinion on the fairness of the consolidated financial statements. Their report is included below.

The Board of Directors ensures that management fulfills its responsibilities for financial reporting and internal control through

an Audit Committee which is composed entirely of outside directors. This committee reviews the consolidated financial statements and reports to the Board of Directors. The auditors have full and direct access to the Audit Committee.

Joe S. Houssian
Chairman, President and Chief Executive Officer

Daniel O. Jarvis
Executive Vice President and Chief Financial Officer
September 5, 2000

Auditors' Report to the Shareholders

We have audited the consolidated balance sheets of Intrawest Corporation as at June 30, 2000 and 1999 and the consolidated statements of operations, retained earnings, and cash flows for the years then ended. These financial statements are the responsibility of the Company's management. Our responsibility is to express an opinion on these financial statements based on our audits.

We conducted our audits in accordance with Canadian generally accepted auditing standards. Those standards require that we plan and perform an audit to obtain reasonable assurance whether the financial statements are free of material misstatement. An audit includes examining, on a test basis, evidence supporting the amounts and disclosures in the financial statements. An audit also includes assessing the accounting principles used and significant estimates made by management, as well as evaluating the overall financial statement presentation.

In our opinion, these consolidated financial statements present fairly, in all material respects, the financial position of the Company as at June 30, 2000 and 1999 and the results of its operations and

its cash flows for the years then ended in accordance with Canadian generally accepted accounting principles. As required by the Company Act (British Columbia), we report that, in our opinion, these principles have been applied on a consistent basis except for the change in the method of accounting for income taxes and employee future benefits as explained in notes 1(n) and 1(t) to the consolidated financial statements.

Significant differences between Canadian and United States accounting principles as they affect these consolidated financial statements are explained and quantified in note 21.

KPMG LLP
Chartered Accountants
Vancouver, British Columbia
September 5, 2000

20

Consolidated Statements of Operations

(expressed in U.S. dollars)

For the years ended June 30, 2000 and 1999
(in thousands of dollars except per share amounts)

	2000	1999
Revenue:		
Ski and resort operations	$ 452,141	$ 382,525
Real estate sales	341,455	215,867
Rental properties	6,905	5,368
Interest and other income	12,449	3,720
Income from equity accounted investment	2,333	2,145
	815,283	609,625
Expenses:		
Ski and resort operations	358,453	300,942
Real estate costs	281,845	174,598
Rental properties	3,641	2,771
Interest (note 15)	35,217	24,813
Depreciation and amortization	51,399	40,199
General and administrative	7,985	7,384
	738,540	550,707
Income before undernoted	76,743	58,918
Provision for income taxes (note 12)	15,394	13,473
Income before non-controlling interest and discontinued operations	61,349	45,445
Non-controlling interest	9,258	6,817
Income from continuing operations	52,091	38,628
Results of discontinued operations (note 3)	(99)	(4,565)
Net income	$ 51,992	$ 34,063
Income per common share:		
Income from continuing operations	$ 1.20	$ 0.96
Net income	1.20	0.96
Weighted average number of common shares outstanding (in thousands)	43,362	40,237

See accompanying notes to consolidated financial statements.

21

Consolidated Balance Sheets

(expressed in U.S. dollars)

June 30, 2000 and 1999
(in thousands of dollars)

	2000	1999
Assets		
Current assets:		
Cash and cash equivalents	$ 78,985	$ 82,457
Amounts receivable (note 6)	72,233	79,453
Other assets (note 7(a))	78,966	46,059
Properties (note 5):		
Resort	254,801	175,710
Discontinued operations	103	10,129
Future income taxes (note 12)	4,445	–
	489,533	393,808
Ski and resort operations (note 4)	784,725	698,958
Properties (note 5):		
Resort	314,481	285,193
Discontinued operations	9,521	10,504
	324,002	295,697
Amounts receivable (note 6)	35,262	28,009
Other assets (note 7(b))	67,999	56,565
Goodwill	15,834	19,147
	$ 1,717,355	$ 1,492,184

22

June 30, 2000 and 1999
(in thousands of dollars)

	2000	1999
Liabilities and Shareholders' Equity		
Current liabilities:		
Amounts payable	$ **146,648**	$ 119,069
Deferred revenue (note 9)	**70,832**	38,314
Bank and other indebtedness, current portion (note 8):		
Resort	**158,144**	148,758
Discontinued operations	**84**	5,526
	375,708	311,667
Bank and other indebtedness (note 8):		
Resort	**670,539**	568,651
Discontinued operations	**4,394**	4,137
	674,933	572,788
Due to joint venture partners (note 13)	**16,963**	11,411
Deferred revenue (note 9)	**26,974**	20,398
Future income taxes (note 12)	**82,522**	–
Deferred income taxes	**–**	14,493
Non-controlling interest in subsidiaries	**28,983**	22,959
	1,206,083	953,716
Shareholders' equity:		
Capital stock (note 11)	**413,719**	437,938
Retained earnings	**131,953**	136,288
Foreign currency translation adjustment	**(34,400)**	(35,758)
	511,272	538,468
Contingencies and commitments (note 14)		
	$ **1,717,355**	$ 1,492,184

Approved on behalf of the Board:

Joe S. Houssian
Director

R. Thomas M. Allan
Director

See accompanying notes to consolidated financial statements.

23

Consolidated Statements of Retained Earnings

(expressed in U.S. dollars)

For the years ended June 30, 2000 and 1999
(in thousands of dollars)

	2000	1999
Opening retained earnings:		
As previously reported	$ 136,288	$ 106,607
Adjustment to reflect change in accounting for income taxes (note 1(n))	(57,457)	—
Adjustment to reflect change in accounting for employee future benefits (note 1(t))	(1,743)	—
As restated	77,088	106,607
Net income	51,992	34,063
Reduction in redemption price of non-resort preferred shares (note 11(a))	7,588	—
Dividends	(4,715)	(4,382)
Retained earnings, end of year	$ 131,953	$ 136,288

See accompanying notes to consolidated financial statements.

24

Consolidated Statements of Cash Flows (expressed in U.S. dollars)

For the years ended June 30, 2000 and 1999
(in thousands of dollars)

	2000	1999
Cash provided by (used in):		
Operations:		
Income from continuing operations	$ 52,091	$ 38,628
Items not affecting cash:		
Depreciation and amortization	51,399	40,199
Future income taxes	12,109	7,075
Income from equity accounted investment	(2,333)	(2,145)
Non-controlling interest	9,258	6,817
Cash flow from continuing operations	122,524	90,574
Recovery of costs through real estate sales	281,845	174,598
Increase in amounts receivable, net	(8,890)	(1,993)
Acquisition and development of properties for sale	(365,249)	(261,530)
Changes in non-cash operating working capital (note 20)	32,332	12,373
Cash provided by continuing operating activities	62,562	14,022
Cash provided by discontinued operations (note 3)	10,699	5,845
	73,261	19,867
Financing:		
Proceeds from bank and other borrowings	341,373	466,559
Repayments on bank and other borrowings	(244,285)	(193,292)
Issue of capital stock for cash, net of issuance costs	1,254	79,209
Redemption of non-resort preferred shares	(19,520)	(13,621)
Proceeds on dilution of partnership interest	—	9,714
Dividends paid	(4,715)	(4,382)
Distributions to non-controlling interests	(3,234)	(2,805)
	70,873	341,382
Investments:		
Expenditures on:		
Revenue-producing properties	1,315	(3,868)
Ski and resort operation assets	(118,614)	(144,195)
Other assets	(11,026)	(28,639)
Business acquisitions, net of cash acquired of		
$207 (1999 – $8,597)	(19,281)	(181,826)
	(147,606)	(358,528)
Increase (decrease) in cash and cash equivalents	(3,472)	2,721
Cash and cash equivalents, beginning of year	82,457	79,736
Cash and cash equivalents, end of year	$ 78,985	$ 82,457

Supplementary information (note 20)

See accompanying notes to consolidated financial statements.

25

Intrawest Corporation is incorporated under the Company Act (British Columbia) and, through its subsidiaries, is engaged in the development and operation of mountain and golf resorts principally throughout North America.

1. SIGNIFICANT ACCOUNTING POLICIES:

(a) Basis of presentation:
The consolidated financial statements are prepared in accordance with generally accepted accounting principles in Canada as prescribed by The Canadian Institute of Chartered Accountants ("CICA"). Information regarding United States generally accepted accounting principles as it affects the Company's consolidated financial statements is presented in note 21.

(b) Principles of consolidation:
The consolidated financial statements include:

(i) the accounts of the Company and its subsidiaries;

(ii) the accounts of all incorporated and unincorporated joint ventures to the extent of the Company's interest in their respective assets, liabilities, revenues and expenses.

The Company's principal subsidiaries and joint ventures are as follows:

	Percentage interest held by the Company
Blackcomb Skiing Enterprises Limited Partnership	77%
Whistler Mountain Resort Limited Partnership	77%
Blue Mountain Resorts Limited (note 2)	50%
Alpine Helicopters Ltd. (note 2)	45%
Mont Tremblant Resorts and Company, Limited Partnership	100%
IW Resorts Limited Partnership	100%
Swaneset Bay Golf Course Ltd. (note 2)	100%
Intrawest Resort Ownership Corporation	100%
The Stratton Corporation	100%
Snowshoe Resort, Inc.	100%
Copper Mountain, Inc.	100%
Mountain Creek Resort, Inc.	100%
Mammoth Mountain Ski Area	59.5%
Keystone/Intrawest L.L.C.	50%
Intrawest Retail Group, Inc. (note 2)	100%
Intrawest Sandestin Company, L.L.C. (note 2)	100%
Intrawest Golf Holdings, Inc. (note 2)	100%
Intrawest/Lodestar Limited Partnership (note 2)	100%
Mt. Tremblant Reservations Inc. (note 2)	100%
Whistler Blackcomb Resorts Inc. (note 2)	100%

All significant intercompany balances and transactions have been eliminated.

(c) Accounting for investments:
The Company accounts for investments in which it is able to exercise significant influence in accordance with the equity method. Under the equity method, the original cost of the shares is adjusted for the Company's share of post-acquisition earnings or losses, less dividends.

(d) Measurement uncertainty:
The preparation of financial statements in conformity with generally accepted accounting principles requires management to make estimates and assumptions that affect the reported amounts of assets and liabilities and disclosure of contingent assets and liabilities at the date of the financial statements and the reported amounts of revenues and expenses during the reporting period. Actual results could differ from those estimates.

The significant areas requiring management estimates include useful lives for depreciation, the impairment of ski and resort operations and properties, and the recoverability of amounts receivable.

(e) Cash equivalents:
The Company considers all highly liquid investments with terms to maturity of three months or less when acquired to be cash equivalents.

(f) Properties:
(i) Properties under development and held for sale:
Properties under development and held for sale are recorded at the lower of cost and net realizable value. Cost includes all expenditures incurred in connection with the acquisition, development and construction of these properties. These expenditures consist of all direct costs, interest on general and specific debt, and general and administrative expenses. Incidental operations related specifically to such properties are treated as an increase in or a reduction of costs.

Costs associated with the development of sales locations of the vacation ownership business, including operating and general and administrative costs incurred until a location is fully operational, are capitalized. Incidental operations related specifically to a location are treated as an increase in or a reduction of costs during the start-up period. These net costs are amortized on a straight-line basis over seven years.

The Company provides for write-downs where the carrying value of a particular property exceeds its net realizable value.

(ii) Revenue-producing properties:
Revenue-producing properties are stated at the lower of cost, net of accumulated depreciation, and net recoverable amount. Buildings are depreciated using the declining balance method at annual rates of 3.3% to 5%. Leasehold improvements and other tenant inducements are amortized using the straight-line method over the lease term. Furniture and equipment are depreciated on a declining balance basis at 20% per annum.

(iii) Classification:
Properties that are currently under development for sale and properties available for sale are classified as current assets. Related bank and other indebtedness is classified as a current liability.

(g) Ski and resort operations:
The assets of the ski and resort operations are stated at cost less accumulated depreciation. Costs of ski lifts, area improvements and buildings are capitalized. Certain buildings, area improvements and equipment are located on leased or licensed land. Depreciation is provided over the estimated useful lives of each asset category using the declining balance method as follows:

Buildings	3.3% to 5.0%
Ski lifts	5.0% to 8.0%
Golf courses	2.0% to 3.3%
Area improvements	2.0% to 3.3%
Automotive, helicopters and other equipment	10.0% to 50.0%
Leased vehicles	20.0% to 25.0%

26

Inventories are recorded at the lower of cost and net realizable value, and consist primarily of retail goods, food and beverage products, and mountain operating supplies.

(h) Administrative furniture, equipment and leasehold improvements:
Administrative furniture and equipment are stated at cost less accumulated depreciation. Depreciation is provided using the declining balance method at annual rates of 20% and 30%, respectively.

Leasehold improvements are stated at cost less accumulated amortization. Amortization is provided using the straight-line method over the lease term.

(i) Deferred financing costs:
Deferred financing costs consist of legal and other fees related to the financing of the Company's ski and resort operations. These costs are amortized over the term of the related financing.

(j) Goodwill:
Goodwill is amortized on the straight-line basis over a period of 10 to 40 years based on the nature of the acquired business. In determining whether there is a permanent impairment in value, recoverability is based on undiscounted estimated future cash flows.

(k) Deferred revenue:
Deferred revenue mainly comprises real estate deposits, season pass revenue, golf club initiation deposits, government grants and the exchange gains arising on the translation of long-term monetary items that are denominated in foreign currencies (note 1(o)). Deferred revenue which relates to the sale of season passes is recognized throughout the season based on the number of skier visits. Deferred revenue which relates to golf club initiation deposits is recognized on a straight-line basis over the estimated membership terms. Deferred revenue which relates to government grants for ski and resort operation assets is recognized on the same basis as the related assets are amortized. Deferred revenue which relates to government grants for properties under development is recognized as the properties are sold.

(l) Government assistance:
The Company periodically applies for financial assistance under available government incentive programs. Non-repayable government assistance relating to capital expenditures is reflected as a reduction of the cost of such assets.

(m) Revenue recognition:
(i) Ski and resort revenue from ski and resort operations is recognized as the service is provided.

(ii) Revenue from the sale of properties is recorded when title to the completed unit is conveyed to the purchaser and the purchaser becomes entitled to occupancy.

(iii) Points revenue associated with membership in the vacation ownership business of Club Intrawest (which revenue is included in real estate sales) is recognized when the purchaser has paid the amount due on closing, all contract documentation has been executed and all other significant conditions of sale are met.

(iv) Revenue from revenue-producing properties is recognized upon the earlier of attaining break-even cash flow after debt servicing or the expiration of a reasonable period of time following substantial completion. Prior to this time, the properties are categorized as properties under development, and incidental operations related to such properties are applied to development costs.

(n) Future income taxes:
During fiscal 2000 the Company has adopted the provisions of Section 3465 of the CICA Handbook, Income Taxes ("Section 3465") which requires a change from the deferred method of accounting for income taxes to the asset and liability method of accounting for income taxes.

Under the asset and liability method of Section 3465, future tax assets and liabilities are recognized for future tax consequences attributable to differences between the financial statement carrying amounts of existing assets and liabilities and their respective tax bases.

Future tax assets and liabilities are measured using enacted or substantively enacted tax rates expected to apply to taxable income in the years in which those temporary differences are expected to be recovered or settled. Under Section 3465, the effect on future tax assets and liabilities of a change in tax rates is recognized in income in the period that includes the enactment date.

Pursuant to the deferral method, which was applied in prior years, deferred income taxes were recognized for income and expense items that were reported in different years for financial reporting purposes and income tax purposes using the tax rate applicable for the year of the calculation. Under the deferral method, deferred taxes were not adjusted for subsequent changes in tax rates.

The Company has calculated the effect of adopting the provisions of Section 3465 retroactively to July 1, 1999. The cumulative effect of this change in accounting for income taxes of $57,457,000 is reported separately in the fiscal 2000 consolidated statement of retained earnings as an adjustment to the opening balance of retained earnings for the year ended June 30, 2000. This charge represents the cumulative effect to July 1, 1999 of differences between accounting and tax bases of assets and liabilities principally due to differences arising on acquisition of ski and resort operations.

The financial statements for the year ended June 30, 1999 have not been restated to reflect the provisions of Section 3465.

(o) Foreign currency translation:
These consolidated financial statements are presented in U.S. dollars. The majority of the Company's operations are located in the United States and are conducted in U.S. dollars. The Company's Canadian operations use the Canadian dollar as their functional currency. The Canadian entities' financial statements have been translated into U.S. dollars using the exchange rate in effect at the balance sheet date for asset and liability amounts and at the average rate for the period for amounts included in the determination of income.

Cumulative unrealized gains or losses arising from the translation of the assets and liabilities of these operations are recorded as a separate component of shareholders' equity.

Exchange gains or losses arising on the translation of long-term monetary items that are denominated in foreign currencies to the applicable currency of measurement are deferred and amortized on a straight-line basis over the remaining terms of the related monetary item. Other exchange gains or losses are included in income as realized.

Prior to the year ended June 30, 2000, these consolidated financial statements were presented in Canadian dollars. Fiscal 1999's

27

comparative figures have been restated into U.S. dollars using exchange rates consistent with those in effect at the dates of the underlying transactions to the financial statements. The consolidated statement of operations for the year ended June 30, 1999 has been restated into U.S. dollars using an average exchange rate of 1.5103.

(p) Interest allocated to discontinued operations:
Interest allocated to discontinued operations is the total of interest on debt directly attributable to the discontinued operations and an allocation of interest on general corporate debt not directly attributable to continuing operations.

(q) Per share calculations:
Income per common share has been calculated using the weighted average number of common shares outstanding during the year. Fully diluted per common share amounts have not been presented as the effect of outstanding options is not materially dilutive.

(r) Cash flow from continuing operations:
Cash flow from continuing operations is computed as income from continuing operations adjusted for future income taxes, depreciation and amortization of capital items, non-controlling interest, income from equity accounted investment and other non-cash items. Cash flow from continuing operations is different from cash flow from continuing operating activities since it excludes the cash provided by or used for non-cash operating working capital accounts such as real estate inventory, amounts receivable and amounts payable.

(s) Stock options:
The Company has a stock option plan as described in note 11(c). No compensation expense is recognized when shares or stock options are issued. Any consideration paid on the exercise of options or purchase of shares is credited to capital stock.

(t) Employee future benefits:
During fiscal 2000 the Company has adopted the provisions of Section 3461 of the CICA Handbook, Employee Future Benefits ("Section 3461") which requires that the Company accrue its obligations under employee benefit plans and the related costs, net of plan assets as the underlying services are provided. The Company has adopted the following policies:

- The cost of pensions and other retirement benefits earned by employees is actuarially determined using the projected benefit method pro rated on service and management's best estimate of expected plan investment performance, salary escalation, retirement ages of employees and expected health care costs.

- For the purpose of calculating the expected return on plan assets, those assets are valued at fair value.

- Past service costs from plan amendments are amortized on a straight-line basis over the average remaining service period of employees active at the date of amendment.

- Experience gains and losses are amortized into pension expense over the plan membership's expected average remaining service lifetime using the straight-line amortization method.

The Company has calculated the effect of adopting the provisions of Section 3461 retroactively to July 1, 1999. The cumulative effect of this change in accounting for employee future benefits of $1,743,000 is reported separately in the fiscal 2000 consolidated statement of retained earnings as an adjustment to

the opening balance of retained earnings for the year ended June 30, 2000. This change represents the cumulative obligation at July 1, 1999 of employee future benefits previously calculated under different methods. The financial statements for the year ended June 30, 1999 have not been restated to reflect the provisions of Section 3461.

(u) Comparative figures:
Certain comparative figures for 1999 have been reclassified to conform with the financial presentation adopted in the current year.

2. ACQUISITIONS:
During the year ended June 30, 2000, the Company completed the following acquisitions each of which was accounted for by the purchase method with effect from the date of acquisition:

(a) On January 17, 2000, the Company acquired the assets of Swaneset Bay Resort & Country Club ("Swaneset"), including two golf courses and developable real estate in British Columbia. The purchase price of the assets acquired was as follows:

Net assets acquired at assigned values:	
Ski and resort operations	$ 9,486
Property under development	5,348
Net working capital	263
Other amounts	648
Assumption of debt	(4,253)
	11,492
Cash	207
	$ 11,699

Financed by:	
Cash	$ 5,988
Bank and other indebtedness	5,711
	$ 11,699

(b) During fiscal 2000 the Company increased its interest in Intrawest/Lodestar Limited Partnership ("Lodestar") in California from 60% to 100% through the acquisition of the other partner's interest for cash of $13,500,000. Effective from November 1, 1999, the Company has consolidated the results of Lodestar with the operations of the Company. Prior to this date the operations were proportionately consolidated as the partners shared joint control. The net assets acquired at assigned values consisted primarily of land and properties under development.

During the year ended June 30, 1999, the Company completed the following acquisitions each of which was accounted for by the purchase method with effect from the date of acquisition:

(a) Effective July 13, 1998, the Company acquired 100% of the shares of Sandestin Resort & Club, Inc. ("Sandestin"), owner of Sandestin Resort, a golf, tourist and retirement destination in northwestern Florida. The purchase price of the shares acquired was $127,455,000 for which the Company paid cash. Concurrent with the acquisition, the Company sold, at assigned cost, 50% of specific real estate assets and 5% of all other assets.

(b) Effective July 23, 1998, the Company acquired the assets of the Raven Golf Group ("Raven"), including two golf courses in Arizona, U.S.A. The purchase price of the assets acquired was $30,613,000, including costs, which was settled by the issuance of 125,000 common shares of the Company, the issuance of a promissory note payable in the amount of $4,711,000 and by the payment of cash.

28

(c) Effective September 3, 1998, the Company acquired all of the shares of Breeze, Inc. ("Breeze") and Max Snowboard, Inc. ("Max") (now named Intrawest Retail Group, Inc.). Intrawest Retail Group, Inc. rents ski and snowboard equipment and also owns sports retail stores in the western United States. The purchase price of the shares acquired was $15,160,000, including costs, which was settled through the payment of cash.

(d) Effective December 27, 1998, the Company acquired a 45% equity interest in Alpine Helicopters Ltd. ("Alpine"), parent company of Canadian Mountain Holidays Inc., which provides helicopter skiing, mountaineering and hiking services in southeastern British Columbia. The purchase price of the shares acquired was $14,729,000, including costs. The purchase price was settled by the issuance of 200,000 common shares of the Company and the balance was paid in cash.

(e) Effective January 27, 1999, the Company acquired a 50% equity interest in Blue Mountain Resorts Limited ("Blue"), owner and operator of a mountain resort in Ontario. The purchase price of the shares acquired of $10,159,000, including costs, was settled through the payment of cash.

(f) Effective March 31, 1999, the Company acquired 100% of the shares of Mt. Tremblant Reservations Inc. and 100% of the shares of Whistler Blackcomb Resorts Inc. ("MTR/WBR"). Both companies are engaged in the business of providing vacation rental, real estate and property management services at the Company's resorts in Mont Tremblant, Quebec and Whistler, British Columbia. The purchase price of the shares acquired was $4,202,000, including costs, and was settled through the payment of cash and the issuance of 74,458 common shares of the Company subsequent to year end.

The assignment of the purchase prices for the above acquisitions is as follows:

	Sandestin	Raven	Breeze/Max	Alpine	Blue	MTR/WBR	Total
Net assets acquired at assigned values:							
Ski and resort operations	$ 51,964	$ 31,102	$ 2,590	$ 24,197	$ 12,231	$ 161	$ 122,245
Properties under development	75,304	–	–	–	–	–	75,304
Goodwill	–	–	15,329	–	–	3,644	18,973
Net working capital	(14,111)	(262)	(391)	(2,461)	1,849	(404)	(15,780)
Other amounts	15,242	–	–	(1,965)	(1,069)	(11)	12,197
Assumption of debt	(6,252)	(681)	(2,667)	(6,182)	(3,421)	(15)	(19,218)
	122,147	30,159	14,861	13,589	9,590	3,375	193,721
Cash	5,308	454	299	1,140	569	827	8,597
	$ 127,455	$ 30,613	$ 15,160	$ 14,729	$ 10,159	$ 4,202	$ 202,318
Financed by:							
Cash	$ 127,455	$ 23,480	$ 15,160	$ 11,190	$ 10,159	$ 2,979	$ 190,423
Bank and other indebtedness	–	4,711	–	–	–	1,223	5,934
Issue of common shares (note 11(b))	–	2,422	–	3,539	–	–	5,961
	$ 127,455	$ 30,613	$ 15,160	$ 14,729	$ 10,159	$ 4,202	$ 202,318

29

Notes to Consolidated Financial Statements

(expressed in U.S. dollars)

For the years ended June 30, 2000 and 1999
(tabular amounts in thousands of dollars unless otherwise indicated)

3. DISCONTINUED OPERATIONS:

For reporting purposes, the results of operations and cash flow from operating activities of the non-resort real estate business have been disclosed separately from those of continuing operations for the periods presented.

The results of discontinued operations are as follows:

	2000	1999
Revenue	$ 13,148	$ 11,694
Loss before current income taxes	$ (99)	$ (4,565)
Provision for current income taxes	–	–
Loss from discontinued operations	$ (99)	$ (4,565)

Assets and liabilities presented in the consolidated balance sheets include the following assets and liabilities of discontinued operations:

	2000	1999
Current assets:		
Properties	$ 103	$ 10,129
Other current assets, excluding cash	2,845	10,038
Properties	9,521	10,504
Other non-current assets	4,331	6,753
Current liabilities	(602)	(8,003)
Non-current liabilities	(4,317)	(4,861)

The cash flows from discontinued operations are as follows:

	2000	1999
Cash provided by (used in):		
Operations	$ 10,699	$ 5,845
Financing	(24,458)	(14,348)
Investments	6,989	1,398
Decrease in cash and cash equivalents	$ (6,770)	$ (7,105)

The cash flow used for financing activities in fiscal 2000 includes a $19,520,000 (1999 – $13,621,000) redemption of non-resort preferred ("NRP") shares (note 11(a)). The Company has the right to apply the net cash flow from the discontinued operations from January 1, 1997 to the redemption of NRP shares. The shares are redeemable quarterly at Cdn.$2.65 per share, except for the final redemption which shall be subject to a premium or discount based on available cash flow relating to the non-resort assets.

4. SKI AND RESORT OPERATIONS:

		2000	
	Cost	Accumulated depreciation	Net book value
Ski operations:			
Land	$ 49,752	$ –	$ 49,752
Buildings	205,832	34,765	171,067
Ski lifts and area improvements	386,708	85,974	300,734
Automotive, helicopters and other equipment	94,411	60,538	33,873
Leased vehicles	5,681	2,388	3,293
	742,384	183,665	558,719
Resort operations:			
Land	21,579	–	21,579
Buildings	55,183	7,062	48,121
Golf courses	108,963	6,517	102,446
Area improvements	65,012	11,152	53,860
	250,737	24,731	226,006
	$ 993,121	$ 208,396	$ 784,725

		1999	
	Cost	Accumulated depreciation	Net book value
Ski operations:			
Land	$ 48,028	$ –	$ 48,028
Buildings	182,400	29,979	152,421
Ski lifts and area improvements	351,911	75,257	276,654
Automotive, helicopters and other equipment	84,005	51,303	32,702
Leased vehicles	4,783	1,700	3,083
	671,127	158,239	512,888
Resort operations:			
Land	20,275	–	20,275
Buildings	50,744	5,537	45,207
Golf courses	74,627	3,169	71,458
Area improvements	56,393	7,263	49,130
	202,039	15,969	186,070
	$ 873,166	$ 174,208	$ 698,958

The ski and resort operations have been pledged as security for certain of the Company's bank and other indebtedness (note 8).

30

1060   **Appendix A** Intrawest Corporation Financial Statements

5. PROPERTIES:

	2000	1999
Properties under development and held for sale:		
Acquisition costs	$ 167,119	$ 187,598
Interest	46,427	35,733
Development costs	298,415	176,887
Administrative	30,786	25,075
	$ 542,747	$ 425,293

2000	Cost	Accumulated depreciation	Net book value
Revenue-producing properties:			
Land	$ 6,062	$ –	$ 6,062
Buildings	33,472	5,478	27,994
Leasehold improvements and equipment	3,410	1,307	2,103
	$ 42,944	$ 6,785	$ 36,159

1999	Cost	Accumulated depreciation	Net book value
Revenue-producing properties:			
Land	$ 6,816	$ –	$ 6,816
Buildings	53,865	7,120	46,745
Leasehold improvements and equipment	5,108	2,426	2,682
	$ 65,789	$ 9,546	$ 56,243

Summary of properties:

	2000	1999
Properties under development and held for sale	$ 542,747	$ 425,293
Revenue-producing properties	36,159	56,243
	$ 578,906	$ 481,536

Properties are classified for balance sheet purposes as follows:

	2000	1999
Current assets:		
Resort	$ 254,801	$ 175,710
Discontinued operations	103	10,129
Long-term assets:		
Resort	314,481	285,193
Discontinued operations	9,521	10,504
	$ 578,906	$ 481,536

During the year ended June 30, 2000, the Company capitalized interest of $30,004,000 (1999 – $22,979,000) (note 15), and administrative expenses of $20,418,000 (1999 – $18,939,000) to properties.

Properties have been pledged as security for certain of the Company's bank and other indebtedness (note 8).

6. AMOUNTS RECEIVABLE:

	2000	1999
Receivable from sales of real estate	$ 19,672	$ 26,881
Ski and resort operation receivables	29,485	25,630
Loans, mortgages and notes receivable (note 19)	37,020	39,897
Funded senior employee share purchase plan (note 11(e))	560	677
Other accounts receivable	20,758	14,377
	107,495	107,462
Less: current portion	72,233	79,453
	$ 35,262	$ 28,009

Receivables are due approximately as follows:

Year ending June 30, 2001	$ 72,233
2002	6,543
2003	3,094
2004	3,394
2005	2,777
Subsequent to 2005	19,454
	$ 107,495

The loans, mortgages and notes receivable bear interest at both fixed and floating rates which averaged 11.69% per annum as at June 30, 2000 (1999 – 11.15%). These amounts have been pledged as security for certain of the Company's bank and other indebtedness (note 8).

7. OTHER ASSETS:

(a) **Current:**

	2000	1999
Ski and resort operation inventories	$ 23,828	$ 18,207
Restricted cash deposits	41,952	17,064
Prepaid expenses and other	13,186	10,788
	$ 78,966	$ 46,059

(b) **Long-term:**

	2000	1999
Investment in Compagnie des Alpes, at equity	$ 30,741	$ 26,422
Deferred financing costs	14,526	14,377
Administrative furniture, equipment and leasehold improvements, net of accumulated depreciation of $6,651,000 (1999 – $3,141,000)	7,598	5,085
Other	15,134	10,681
	$ 67,999	$ 56,565

31

Notes to Consolidated Financial Statements

(expressed in U.S. dollars)

For the years ended June 30, 2000 and 1999
(tabular amounts in thousands of dollars unless otherwise indicated)

8. BANK AND OTHER INDEBTEDNESS:

The Company has obtained financing for its ski and resort operations and properties from various financial institutions by pledging individual assets as security for such financing. Security for general corporate debt is provided by general security which includes a floating charge on the Company's assets and undertakings, fixed charges on real estate properties, and assignment of mortgages and notes receivable. The following table summarizes the primary security provided by the Company, where appropriate, and indicates the applicable type of financing, maturity dates and the weighted average interest rate at June 30, 2000:

	Maturity dates	Weighted average interest rate	2000	1999
Ski and resort operations:				
Mortgages and bank loans	Demand-2017	6.73%	$ 211,561	$ 229,595
Obligations under capital leases	2001-2005	8.28%	3,771	4,306
			215,332	233,901
Properties				
Interim financing on properties under development and held for resale	2001-2019	8.12%	111,609	116,545
Mortgages on revenue-producing properties	2001-2015	8.57%	12,425	15,739
			124,034	132,284
General corporate debt	2001	8.01%	59,210	58,076
Unsecured debentures	2002-2010	9.35%	434,585	302,811
			833,161	727,072
Less: current portion			158,228	154,284
			$ 674,933	$ 572,788

Principal repayments and the components related to either floating or fixed interest rates are as follows:

	Interest rates		Total
	Floating	Fixed	Repayments
Year ending June 30, 2001	$ 127,967	$ 30,261	$ 158,228
2002	5,127	117,017	122,144
2003	141,706	26,525	168,231
2004	3,794	339,374	343,168
2005	1,166	7,934	9,100
Subsequent to 2005	16,185	16,105	32,290
	$ 295,945	$ 537,216	$ 833,161

The Company has entered into a swap agreement to fix the interest rate on a portion of its floating rate debt denominated in Canadian dollars. The Company had Cdn.$30,000,000 (1999 – Cdn.$30,000,000) of bank loans swapped against debt with a fixed interest rate of 6.5% (1999 – 6.5%) per annum, excluding applicable stamping fees, under an agreement expiring in 2001 (note 16(a)).

Bank and other indebtedness includes indebtedness in the amount of $349,277,000 (1999 – $369,616,000), which is repayable in Canadian dollars of $517,140,000 (1999 – $540,748,000).

The Company is subject to certain covenants in respect of some of the bank and other indebtedness which require the Company to maintain certain financial ratios. The Company is in compliance with these covenants at June 30, 2000.

9. DEFERRED REVENUE:

	2000	1999
Deposits on real estate sales	$ 51,200	$ 21,114
Government assistance (note 10)	8,917	8,724
Exchange gains	3,309	8,025
Golf club initiation deposits	15,463	6,780
Season pass revenue	11,236	5,881
Other deferred amounts	7,681	8,188
	97,806	58,712
Less: current portion	70,832	38,314
	$ 26,974	$ 20,398

10. GOVERNMENT ASSISTANCE:

The federal government and the Province of Quebec have granted financial assistance to the Company in the form of interest-free loans and grants for the construction of specified four-season tourist facilities at Mont Tremblant. The loans, which are fully advanced, totaled $9,658,000 and are repayable over 17 years starting in 2000. The grants, which will total $37,156,000 (1999 – $39,608,000) when they are fully advanced, amounted to $18,925,000 at June 30, 2000 (1999 – $19,578,000). During the year ended June 30, 2000, grants received of $1,289,000 (1999 – $2,874,000) were credited as follows: $359,000 (1999 – $322,000) to ski and resort operation assets, $930,000 (1999 – $2,552,000) to properties.

11. CAPITAL STOCK:

(a) Share capital reorganization:

Effective March 14, 1997, the Company completed a reorganization of its share capital designed to separate the remaining non-resort real estate assets from the rest of the Company's business. Under the reorganization, each existing common share was exchanged for one new common share and one non-resort preferred ("NRP") share. The new common shares have the same attributes as the old common shares.

The NRP shares were initially recorded at a value of $64,545,000 (Cdn.$3.82 per share) before deduction of issue costs of $240,000, equal to the book value of the net equity of the non-resort assets at December 31, 1996, and the value assigned to the common shares was reduced by the same amount. The Company expects that the non-resort assets will be disposed of in an orderly manner and the net cash flow from these assets distributed to the NRP shareholders, primarily by way of redemption of their shares as described in note 3. The amount ultimately realized by the Company and distributed to the NRP shareholders will be subject to prevailing real estate market conditions. As at June 30, 2000, the book value of the net equity of the remaining non-resort assets was $14,206,000 (1999– $33,655,000).

On November 15, 1999, the shareholders of the Company passed a resolution reducing the redemption price of the NRP shares from Cdn.$3.82 to Cdn.$2.65 per share. As a result, the carrying value of the NRP shares has been reduced by $7,588,000 and retained earnings has been increased by the same amount.

32

For the years ended June 30, 2000 and 1999
(tabular amounts in thousands of dollars unless otherwise indicated)

(b) Capital stock:
The Company's capital stock comprises the following:

	2000	1999
Common shares	$ 395,795	$ 393,153
NRP shares	17,924	44,785
	$ 413,719	$ 437,938

(i) Common shares:
Authorized:
200,000,000 without par value
Issued:

	Number of common shares	2000 amount	Number of common shares	1999 amount
Balance, beginning of year	43,254,386	$ 393,153	38,359,786	$ 308,303
Issued for cash, net of issue cost	–	–	4,450,000	77,902
Issued for settlement of bank and other indebtedness	74,458	1,236	–	–
Issued on acquisitions	–	–	325,000	5,961
Stock option plan	134,450	1,007	119,600	987
Future income tax adjustment	–	399	–	–
Balance, end of year	43,463,294	$ 395,795	43,254,386	$ 393,153

(ii) NRP shares:
Authorized:
50,000,000 without par value
Issued:

	Number of NRP shares	2000 amount	Number of NRP shares	1999 amount
Balance, beginning of year	16,726,586	$ 44,785	21,811,911	$ 58,086
Stock option plan	343,275	321	374,675	320
Purchased for cancellation	(62,900)	(74)	–	–
Redemption	(9,246,000)	(19,520)	(5,460,000)	(13,621)
Reduction in redemption price	–	(7,588)	–	–
Balance, end of year	7,760,961	$ 17,924	16,726,586	$ 44,785

(iii) Preferred shares:
Authorized:
20,000,000 without par value
Issued – nil

(c) Stock options:
The Company has a stock option plan which provides for grants to officers and employees of the Company and its subsidiaries of options to purchase common shares and NRP shares of the Company. Options granted under the stock option plan may not be exercised except in accordance with such limitations as the Company's Human Resources Committee may determine.

The following table summarizes the status of options outstanding under the Plan:

	2000 share options outstanding	Weighted average price	1999 share options outstanding	Weighted average price
Outstanding, beginning of year	3,257,850	$ 14.44	2,894,650	$ 13.36
Granted	255,500	17.09	542,500	19.30
Exercised	(134,450)	9.20	(119,600)	9.55
Forfeited	(157,300)	18.38	(59,700)	16.00
Outstanding, end of year	3,221,600	$ 14.68	3,257,850	$ 14.44
Exercisable, end of year	1,758,650	$ 11.94	1,369,350	$ 9.37

The following table provides details of options outstanding at June 30, 2000:

Range of exercise prices	Number outstanding June 30, 2000	Weighted average life remaining (years)	Weighted average price	Number exercisable June 30, 2000	Weighted average price
$7.64-$11.72	1,248,100	3.1	$ 9.43	1,206,900	$ 9.40
$14.96-$19.77	1,973,500	7.7	18.00	551,750	17.50
	3,221,600	5.9	$ 14.68	1,758,650	$ 11.94

(d) Employee share purchase plan:
The employee share purchase plan permits certain full-time employees of the Company and its subsidiaries and limited partnerships to purchase common shares through payroll deductions. The Company contributes $1 for every $3 contributed by an employee. To June 30, 2000, a total of 65,809 (1999 – 65,809) common shares have been issued from treasury under this plan. A further 100,000 common shares have been authorized and reserved for issuance under this plan.

(e) Funded senior employee share purchase plan:
The Company has a funded senior employee share purchase plan which provides for loans to be made to designated eligible employees to be used to subscribe for common shares. At June 30, 2000, loans to employees under the funded senior employee share purchase plan amounted to $560,000 with respect to 131,150 common shares and 37,272 NRP shares (1999 – $677,000 with respect to 131,150 common shares and 83,160 NRP shares). The loans are interest-free, secured by a promissory note and a pledge of the shares and mature by 2005. A further 96,400 common shares have been authorized and reserved for issuance under this plan.

12. INCOME TAXES:
(a) Provision for income taxes:

	2000	1999
Current	$ 3,285	$ 6,398
Future	12,109	7,075
	$ 15,394	$ 13,473

33

The reconciliation of income taxes calculated at the statutory rate to the actual income tax provision is as follows:

	2000	1999
Statutory rate	45.58%	45.58%
Income tax charge at statutory rate	$ 34,934	$ 24,775
Non-deductible depreciation and amortization	825	3,329
Large corporations tax	373	1,616
Taxes related to non-controlling interest share of earnings	(4,220)	(3,107)
Taxes related to equity accounted investment	(1,063)	(978)
Foreign taxes different from statutory rate	(15,754)	(13,278)
Other	299	1,116
Provision for income taxes	$ 15,394	$ 13,473

(b) The tax effects of temporary differences that give rise to significant portions of the future tax assets and future tax liabilities at June 30, 2000 are presented below:

	2000
Future tax assets:	
Non-capital loss carry forwards	$ 25,573
Share issue and financing costs	708
Differences in working capital deductions for tax and accounting purposes	1,854
Other	1,321
Total gross future tax assets	29,456
Less: valuation allowance	(6,910)
Net future tax assets	22,546
Future tax liabilities:	
Differences in depreciation and undepreciated capital cost:	
Ski and resort assets	93,472
Properties	6,287
Other	864
Total gross future tax liabilities	100,623
Net future tax liabilities	$ 78,077

(c) At June 30, 2000, the Company has non-capital loss carryforwards for income tax purposes of approximately $86,049,000 that are available to offset future taxable income through 2015.

13. JOINT VENTURES:

The following amounts represent the Company's proportionate interest in joint ventures and non-controlled partnerships including Mammoth, Alpine, Blue and Keystone/Intrawest L.L.C.:

	2000	1999
Properties, current	$ 40,977	$ 46,472
Other current assets	26,638	18,609
	67,615	65,081
Current liabilities	(53,927)	(34,383)
Working capital	13,688	30,698
Ski and resort operations	132,589	104,238
Properties, non-current	78,699	90,716
Bank and other indebtedness, non-current	(41,498)	(58,042)
Other, net	(14,760)	7,826
	$ 168,718	$ 175,436

	2000	1999
Revenue	$ 136,557	$ 123,282
Expenses	127,496	110,563
Income for continuing operations before income taxes	9,061	12,719
Results of discontinued operations	97	444
	$ 9,158	$ 13,163

	2000	1999
Cash provided by (used in):		
Operations	$ 26,107	$ 23,562
Financing	483	4,009
Investments	(28,720)	(26,213)
Increase (decrease) in cash and cash equivalents	$ (2,130)	$ 1,358

Due to joint venture partners is the amount payable to the Company's joint venture partners in various properties for costs they have incurred on the Company's behalf. Payments to the joint venture partners are governed by the terms of the respective joint venture agreement.

14. CONTINGENCIES AND COMMITMENTS:

(a) The Company holds licenses and land leases with respect to certain of its ski operations. These leases expire at various times between 2032 and 2051 and provide for annual payments generally in the range of 2% of defined gross revenues.

(b) The Company has estimated costs to complete ski and resort operation assets and properties currently under construction and held for sale amounting to $327,788,000 at June 30, 2000 (1999 – $250,323,000). These costs are substantially covered by existing financing commitments.

(c) The Company has entered into various operating lease commitments, payable as follows:

Year ending June 30,		
2001	$	4,953
2002		3,863
2003		3,421
2004		2,223
2005		2,112
Subsequent to 2005		3,483
	$	20,055

(d) The Company is contingently liable for indebtedness at June 30, 2000 of $8,698,000 (1999 – $13,722,000) which relates to certain non-resort properties under development sold during the year ended September 30, 1994 (note 19). The purchasers of these properties have provided guarantees to the Company in respect of the indebtedness and have indemnified the Company for any potential losses resulting from the contingent liability.

(e) The Company is contingently liable for the obligations of certain joint ventures and limited partnerships. The assets of these joint ventures and limited partnerships, which in all cases exceed the obligations, are available to satisfy such obligations.

34

15. INTEREST EXPENSE:

	2000	1999
Total interest incurred	$ 66,426	$ 50,552
Less:		
Interest capitalized to ski and resort operation assets	721	1,883
Interest capitalized to properties, net of capitalized interest included in real estate cost of sales of $10,875,000 (1999 – $6,004,000)	19,129	16,975
	$ 46,576	$ 31,694

	2000	1999
Interest was charged to income as follows:		
Real estate costs	$ 10,875	$ 6,004
Interest expense	35,217	24,813
Discontinued operations	484	877
	$ 46,576	$ 31,694

Real estate costs and discontinued operations also include $5,892,000 (1999 – $4,746,000) and $nil (1999 – $605,000), respectively, of interest incurred in prior years.

16. FINANCIAL INSTRUMENTS:

(a) Fair value:

The Company has various financial instruments including cash and cash equivalents, amounts receivable, certain amounts payable and accrued liabilities. Due to their short-term maturity or, in the case of amounts receivable, their market comparable interest rates, the instruments' book value approximates their fair value. Debt and interest swap agreements are also financial instruments. The fair values at June 30, 2000 and 1999 were estimated by discounting future cash flows at estimated market rates and are summarized as follows:

	2000 Book value	2000 Fair value	1999 Book value	1999 Fair value
Bank and other indebtedness including the effect of interest swap agreements	$ 833,161	$ 1,022,700	$ 727,072	$ 721,612

(b) Interest rate risk:

As described in note 8, $295,945,000 of the Company's debt instruments bear interest at floating rates. Fluctuations in these rates will impact the cost of financing incurred in the future.

(c) Credit risk:

The Company's products and services are purchased by a wide range of customers in different regions of North America and elsewhere. Due to the nature of its operations, the Company has no concentrations of credit risk.

17. EMPLOYEE BENEFITS:

The Company has two defined benefit pension plans for certain of its senior executives. Information about these defined benefit plans is as follows:

	2000	1999
Accrued benefit obligation:		
Balance at beginning of year	$ 3,810	$ 3,435
Current service cost	208	203
Interest cost	231	172
Balance at end of year	4,249	3,810
Plan assets:		
Fair value at beginning of year	2,016	1,454
Contributions	231	214
Actual return on plan assets	68	92
Contribution receivable	242	256
Balance at end of year	2,557	2,016
Plan deficit	(1,692)	(1,794)
Unamortized past service costs	–	1,814
Accrued benefit asset (liability)	$ (1,692)	$ 20

The significant actuarial assumptions adopted in measuring the Company's accrued benefit obligations are as follows (weighted-average assumptions as of June 30):

	2000	1999
Discount rate	7%	3.5%
Expected long-term rate of return on plan assets	8%	3.5%
Rate of compensation increase	6%	4%

The company's net benefit plan expense is as follows:

	2000	1999
Current service costs	$ 208	$ 203
Interest cost	231	172
Expected return on plan assets	(68)	(92)
Amortized past service costs	–	159
	$ 371	$ 442

3 5

18. SEGMENTED INFORMATION:

The Company has four reportable segments: ski and resort operations, real estate operations, warm-weather operations, and corporate and all other. The ski and resort segment includes all of the Company's mountain resorts and associated activities. The real estate segment includes all of the Company's real estate activities. The warm-weather operations include all of the Company's stand-alone golf courses that are not located at mountain resorts.

The Company evaluates performance based on profit or loss from operations before interest, depreciation and amortization, and income taxes. Intersegment sales and transfers are accounted for as if the sales or transfers were to third parties.

The Company's reportable segments are strategic business units that offer distinct products and services, and that have their own identifiable marketing strategies. Each of the reportable segments has senior level executives responsible for the performance of the segment.

The following table presents the Company's results from continuing operations by reportable segment:

Revenue:	2000	1999
Ski and resort	$ 394,630	$ 340,205
Real estate	348,360	221,235
Warm-weather	57,511	42,320
Corporate and all other	14,782	5,865
	$ 815,283	$ 609,625

	2000	1999
Operating profit before interest, depreciation and amortization, and income taxes:		
Ski and resort	$ 85,136	$ 75,947
Real estate	62,874	43,865
Warm-weather	8,552	5,637
Corporate and all other	14,782	5,865
	171,344	131,314
Less:		
Interest	(35,217)	(24,813)
Depreciation and amortization	(51,399)	(40,199)
General and administrative	(7,985)	(7,384)
	(94,601)	(72,396)
	$ 76,743	$ 58,918

Segment assets:	2000	1999
Ski and resort	$ 696,406	$ 633,487
Real estate	578,915	460,903
Warm-weather	104,153	84,618
Corporate and all other	321,081	266,655
Discontinued operations	16,800	46,521
	$ 1,717,355	$ 1,492,184

Capital acquisitions:	2000	1999
Ski and resort	$ 103,303	$ 138,660
Real estate	–	3,858
Warm-weather	15,311	5,535
Corporate and all other	6,501	5,476
	$ 125,115	$ 153,529

Geographic information:

Revenue:	2000	1999
Canada	$ 336,320	$ 260,415
United States	478,963	349,210
	$ 815,283	$ 609,625

	2000	1999
Operating income before income taxes, non-controlling interest and results of discontinued operations:		
Canada	$ 52,520	$ 40,718
United States	24,223	18,200
	$ 76,743	$ 58,918

Identifiable assets:	2000	1999
Canada	$ 777,762	$ 658,714
United States	922,793	786,949
Discontinued operations	16,800	46,521
	$ 1,717,355	$ 1,492,184

36

19. RELATED PARTY TRANSACTIONS:

Effective April 1, 1994, the Company sold substantially all of its industrial and non-resort residential properties under development in British Columbia and Washington State to two partnerships formed by a group of investors. An officer and a director of the Company is the majority shareholder of corporations that invested in a 20% interest in the partnerships. Such corporations are also the managing general partners of the partnerships.

The consideration for the sale included a vendor take-back note originally for $22,926,000, of which $8,230,000 was outstanding at June 30, 1999. During the year ended June 30, 2000, the partnerships repaid $6,663,000 leaving $1,567,000 outstanding at June 30, 2000. This amount is due, with interest at 10 % per annum, in two installments: $892,000 on July 31, 2000 (paid) and $675,000 on January 31, 2001.

The Company committed to provide the partnerships various credit facilities, including a $4,728,000 revolving line of credit until January 31, 2001, reducing to $4,052,000 until July 31, 2001 and thereafter to $2,702,000 until the availability terminates on January 31, 2002. The line of credit earns interest at prime plus 2% per annum. At June 30, 2000, $4,708,000 (1999 – $4,765,000) was advanced under these facilities and accrued and unpaid interest amounted to $142,000 (1999 – $480,000). In addition, the Company agreed to provide financial assistance by way of continuing liability in respect of certain indebtedness and liabilities of the partnerships. The Company earns fees in consideration for this financial assistance. The partnerships have guaranteed repayment of these facilities and indemnified the Company for any losses under them.

20. CASH FLOW INFORMATION:

The changes in non-cash operating working capital balance consist of the following:

	2000	1999
Cash provided by (used in):		
Amounts receivable	$ 531	$ (33,683)
Other assets	(32,837)	(8,334)
Amounts payable	23,365	22,862
Due to joint venture partner	5,736	13,806
Deferred revenue	35,537	17,722
	$ 32,332	$ 12,373
Supplemental information:		
Interest paid	$ 63,789	$ 39,323
Taxes paid	2,575	1,176
Non-cash investing and financing activities		
Capital stock issued on acquisitions	$ –	$ 5,961
Capital stock issued for settlement of bank and other indebtedness	1,236	–
Bank and other indebtedness incurred on acquisitions	5,711	5,934

21. DIFFERENCES BETWEEN CANADIAN AND UNITED STATES GENERALLY ACCEPTED ACCOUNTING PRINCIPLES:

The consolidated financial statements have been prepared in accordance with generally accepted accounting principles ("GAAP") in Canada. The principles adopted in these financial statements conform in all material respects to those generally accepted in the United States and the rules and regulations promulgated by the Securities and Exchange Commission ("SEC") except as summarized below:

	2000	1999
Income from continuing operations in accordance with Canadian GAAP	$ 52,091	$ 38,628
Effects of differences in accounting for:		
Cost of sales pursuant to SFAS 109 (d)	–	(942)
Depreciation pursuant to SFAS 109 (d)	(549)	(1,776)
Provision for future taxes pursuant to SFAS 109 (d)	–	1,073
Foreign exchange pursuant to FAS 52 (g)	(4,716)	8,025
Income from continuing operations in accordance with United States GAAP	46,826	45,008
Results of discontinued operations in accordance with Canadian and United States GAAP	(99)	(4,565)
Net income in accordance with United States GAAP	46,727	40,443
Opening retained earnings in accordance with United States GAAP (b)	127,645	91,584
Reduction in redemption price of non-resort preferred shares	7,588	–
Common share dividends	(4,715)	(4,382)
Closing retained earnings in accordance with United States GAAP	$ 177,245	$ 127,645
Weighted average number of shares outstanding (in thousands)	43,362	40,237
Income per common share (basic and diluted; in dollars)		
Income from continuing operations	$ 1.08	$ 1.12
Net income	$ 1.08	$ 1.12

	2000	1999
Comprehensive income		
Net income in accordance with United States GAAP	$ 46,727	$ 40,443
Other comprehensive income (loss)	1,358	(8,010)
	$ 48,085	$ 32,433

37

	2000	1999
Total assets in accordance with Canadian GAAP	$ 1,717,355	$ 1,492,184
Effects of differences in accounting for:		
Shareholder loans (c)	(560)	(677)
Ski and resort assets (d)	4,893	4,231
Goodwill (d)	37,943	39,156
Properties (d)	710	710
Total assets in accordance with United States GAAP	$ 1,760,341	$ 1,535,604

	2000	1999
Total liabilities in accordance with Canadian GAAP	$ 1,206,083	$ 953,716
Effects of differences in accounting for:		
Future income taxes (d)	–	56,381
Employee future benefits (i)	–	1,743
Foreign exchange (g)	(3,309)	(8,025)
Total liabilities in accordance with United States GAAP	$ 1,202,774	$ 1,003,815

	2000	1999
Capital stock in accordance with Canadian GAAP	$ 413,719	$ 437,938
Effects of differences in accounting for:		
Extinguishment of options and warrants (a)	1,563	1,563
Future income taxes (d)	–	399
Shareholder loans (c)	(560)	(677)
Capital stock in accordance with United States GAAP	414,722	439,223
Closing retained earnings in accordance with United States GAAP	177,245	127,645
Accumulated other comprehensive income (h)	(34,400)	(35,758)
Shareholders' equity in accordance with United States GAAP	$ 557,567	$ 531,110

(a) Extinguishment of options and warrants:

Payments made to extinguish options and warrants can be treated as capital items under Canadian GAAP. These payments would be treated as income items under United States GAAP. As a result, payments made to extinguish options in prior years impact the current year's capital stock and retained earnings. No payments were made during the years ended June 30, 2000 and 1999.

(b) Retained earnings:

Opening retained earnings in accordance with United States GAAP for the year ended June 30, 1999 includes the effects of:

(i) adopting SFAS 109 as described in (d). The net decrease in retained earnings was $11,717,000.

(ii) treating payments made to extinguish options and warrants as income items as described in (a). The net decrease in retained earnings was $1,563,000.

(iii) recognizing post employment benefits as described in (i). The net decrease in retained earnings was $1,743,000.

(c) Shareholder loans:

The Company accounts for loans provided to senior employees for the purchase of shares as amounts receivable. Under the rules of the SEC, these loans, totaling $560,000 and $677,000 as at June 30, 2000 and 1999, respectively, would be deducted from share capital.

(d) Income taxes:

As described in note 1(n), the Company adopted Section 3465 in its year ended June 30, 2000 and has calculated the provisions of Section 3465 retroactively to July 1, 1999. Prior to this date, the Company had adopted the Statement of Financial Accounting Standards ("SFAS") 109, "Accounting for Income Taxes", for the financial statement amounts presented under United States GAAP. SFAS 109 requires that future tax liabilities or assets be recognized for the difference between assigned values and tax bases of assets and liabilities acquired pursuant to a business combination except for non tax-deductible goodwill and unallocated negative goodwill, effective from the Company's year ended September 30, 1994. The effect of adopting SFAS 109 increases the carrying values of certain balance sheet amounts at June 30, 2000 and 1999 as follows:

	2000	1999
Ski and resort assets	$ 4,893	$ 4,231
Goodwill	37,943	39,156
Properties	710	710
Capital stock	–	399
Future income tax liability	–	56,381

38

The tax effects of temporary differences that give rise to significant portions of the future tax assets and future tax liabilities at June 30, 1999 are presented below:

	1999
Future tax assets:	
Non-capital loss carry forwards	$ 24,711
Share issue and financing costs	1,861
Other	911
Total gross future tax assets	27,483
Less: valuation allowance	(11,323)
Net future tax assets	16,160
Future tax liabilities:	
Differences in depreciation and undepreciated capital cost:	
Ski and resort assets	77,704
Properties	6,417
Differences in working capital deductions for tax and accounting purposes	479
Other	2,434
Total gross future tax liabilities	87,034
Net future tax liabilities	$ 70,874

(e) Joint ventures:

In accordance with Canadian GAAP, joint ventures are required to be proportionately consolidated regardless of the legal form of the entity. Under United States GAAP, incorporated joint ventures are required to be accounted for by the equity method. However, in accordance with practices provided for by the SEC, the Company has elected for the purpose of this reconciliation to account for incorporated joint ventures by the proportionate consolidation method (note 13).

(f) Stock compensation:

Statement of Financial Accounting Standards No. 123 ("FAS 123"), Accounting for Stock-Based Compensation, requires that stock-based compensation be accounted for based on a fair value methodology, although it allows an entity to elect to continue to measure stock-based compensation costs using the intrinsic value based method of accounting proscribed by Accounting Principles Board Opinion No. 25, "Accounting for Stock Issued to Employees" ("APB 25"). The Company has elected to account for stock-based compensation in accordance with APB 25 for purposes of this United States GAAP reconciliation. Accordingly, no compensation expense has been recognized for the years presented.

Had compensation expense been determined in accordance with the provisions of FAS 123 using the Black-Scholes option pricing model at the date of the grant, the following weighted average assumptions would be used for option grants in:

	2000	1999
Dividend yield	0.6%	0.7%
Risk-free interest rate	6.25%	5.0%
Expected option life	7 years	5 years
Expected volatility	69%	39%

Using the above assumptions, the Company's net income under United States GAAP would have been reduced to the pro forma amounts indicated below:

	2000	1999
Net income in accordance with United States GAAP:		
As reported	$ 46,727	$ 40,443
Estimated fair value of option grants	(2,894)	(2,403)
Pro forma	$ 43,833	$ 38,040

Pro forma net income reflects only options granted since June 30, 1996. Therefore, the full impact of calculating compensation costs for stock options under FAS 123 is not reflected in the pro forma net income amounts presented above because compensation cost is reflected over the options' vesting period of 7 years (1999 – 5 years) and compensation cost for options granted prior to July 1, 1996 is not considered.

(g) Foreign exchange on bank and other indebtedness:

Under Canadian GAAP the Company defers and amortizes foreign exchange gains and losses on bank and other indebtedness denominated in foreign currencies over the remaining term of the debt. Under United States GAAP, foreign exchange gains and losses are included in income in the period in which the exchange rate fluctuates.

(h) Other comprehensive income:

Statement of Financial Accounting Standards No. 130, Reporting Comprehensive Income ("FAS 130") requires that a company classify items of other comprehensive income by their nature in a financial statement and display the accumulated balance of other comprehensive income separately from retained earnings and capital stock in the equity section of the balance sheet.

The foreign currency translation adjustment in the amount of $34,400,000 (1999 – $35,758,000) presented in shareholders' equity under Canadian GAAP would be considered accumulated other comprehensive income under United States GAAP. The change in the balance of $1,358,000 would be other comprehensive income for the year (1999 – loss of $8,010,000).

(i) Employee future benefits:

As discussed in note 1(t), the Company has adopted new requirements in Canada for the recognition of post employment benefits. This adoption eliminates a previously existing Canada – United States GAAP difference. The application of these principles to the fiscal 1999 income reported under United States GAAP was not material.

(j) Comparative figures:

Certain comparative figures for 1999 have been reclassified to conform with the financial presentation adopted in the current year.

39

Appendix B

Summary of Generally Accepted Accounting Principles (GAAP)

Every technical area has professional associations and regulatory bodies that govern the practice of the profession. Accounting is no exception. In Canada, the Canadian Institute of Chartered Accountants (CICA) has the responsibility for issuing accounting standards that form the basis of generally accepted accounting principles (GAAP). The authority for setting GAAP was delegated to the CICA by the federal and provincial governments and the Canadian Securities Administrators in the 1970s.

The CICA's pronouncements, called *Recommendations,* are collected in Volume I of the *CICA Handbook.* The Recommendations specify how to account for particular business transactions and must be followed, except in those rare cases where a particular Recommendation or Recommendations would not lead to fair presentation. In those cases, the accountant should, using professional judgment, select the appropriate accounting principles. An accountant who determines that the *CICA Handbook* is not appropriate and selects some other basis of accounting must be prepared to defend that decision.

Each new Recommendation issued by the CICA becomes part of GAAP, the "accounting law of the land." In the same way that our laws draw authority from their acceptance by the people, GAAP depends on general acceptance by the business community. Throughout this book, we refer to GAAP as the proper way to do financial accounting.

The Objective of Financial Reporting

The basic objective of financial reporting is to provide information that is useful in making investment and lending decisions. Accounting information can be useful in decision making only if it is *understandable, relevant, reliable, comparable,* and *consistent.*

Accounting information must be *understandable* to users if they are to be able to use it. *Relevant* information is useful in making predictions and for evaluating past performance—that is, the information has feedback value. For example, Canadian Tire Corporation, Limited's disclosure of the profitability of each of its lines of business is relevant for investor evaluations of the company. To be relevant, information must be timely. *Reliable* information is free from significant error—that is, it has validity. Also, it is free from the bias of a particular viewpoint—that is, it is verifiable and neutral. *Comparable* and *consistent* information can be compared from period to period to help investors and creditors assess the entity's progress through time. These characteristics combine to shape the concepts and principles that comprise GAAP. Exhibit B-1 on page 1071 summarizes the concepts and principles that accounting has developed to provide useful information for decision making.

Summary of Important Accounting Concepts, Principles, and Financial Statements

Concepts, Principles, and Financial Statements	Quick Summary	Text Reference
Concepts		
Entity Concept	Accounting draws a boundary around each organization to be accounted for.	Chapter 1
Going-concern concept	Accountants assume the business will continue operating for the foreseeable future.	Chapter 1
Stable-monetary-unit concept	Accounting information is expressed primarily in monetary terms.	Chapter 1
Time-period concept	Ensures that accounting information is reported at regular intervals.	Chapter 3
Conservatism concept	Accountants report items in the financial statements in a way that avoids overstating assets, shareholders' equity, and revenues and avoids understating liabilities and expenses.	Chapter 9
Materiality concept	Accountans consider the4 materiality of an amount when making disclosure dicisions.	Chapter 9
Principles		
Reliability (objectivity) principle	Accounting records and statements are based on the most reliable data available	Chapter 1
Cost principle	Assets and services, revenues and expenses are recorded at their actual historical cost.	Chapter 1
Revenue principle	Tells accountants when to record revenue (only after it has been earned) and the amount of revenue to record (the cash value of what has been received).	Chapter 3
Matching principle	Directs accountants to (1) identify all expenses incurred during the period, (2) measure the expenses, and (3) match the expenses against the revenues earned during the period. The goal is to measure net income.	Chapter 3
Consistency principle	Businesses should use the same accounting methods from period to period.	Chapter 9
Disclosure principle	A company's financial statements should report enough information for outsiders to make informed decisions about the company.	Chapter 9
Financial Statements		
Balance sheet	Assets = Liabilities + Owners' Equity at a point in time (for proprietorships and partnerships). Assets = Liabilities + Shareholders' Equity at a point in time (for corporations).	Chapters 1 and 13
Income statement	Revenues and gains −Expenses and losses =Net income or net loss for the period.	Chapters 1 and 14
Cash flow statement	Cash receipts −Cash disbursements =Increase or decrease in cash during the period, grouped under operating, investing, and financing activities.	Chapters 1 and 17
Statement of retained earnings	Beginning retained earnings +Net income (or − Net loss) −Dividends =Ending retained earnings	Chapter 1
Statement of shareholders' equity	Shows the reason for the change in each shareholders' equity account, including retained earnings.	Chapter 14

Appendix C

Present-Value Tables and Future-Value Tables

This appendix provides present-value tables (more complete than those appearing in Chapter 15) and future-value tables.

Table C-1   *Present Value of $1*

Periods	1%	2%	3%	4%	5%	6%	7%	8%	9%	10%	12%
1	0.990	0.980	0.971	0.962	0.952	0.943	0.935	0.926	0.917	0.909	0.893
2	0.980	0.961	0.943	0.925	0.907	0.890	0.873	0.857	0.842	0.826	0.797
3	0.971	0.942	0.915	0.889	0.864	0.840	0.816	0.794	0.772	0.751	0.712
4	0.961	0.924	0.888	0.855	0.823	0.792	0.763	0.735	0.708	0.683	0.636
5	0.951	0.906	0.883	0.822	0.784	0.747	0.713	0.681	0.650	0.621	0.567
6	0.942	0.888	0.837	0.790	0.746	0.705	0.666	0.630	0.596	0.564	0.507
7	0.933	0.871	0.813	0.760	0.711	0.665	0.623	0.583	0.547	0.513	0.452
8	0.923	0.853	0.789	0.731	0.677	0.627	0.582	0.540	0.502	0.467	0.404
9	0.914	0.837	0.766	0.703	0.645	0.592	0.544	0.500	0.460	0.424	0.361
10	0.905	0.820	0.744	0.676	0.614	0.558	0.508	0.463	0.422	0.386	0.322
11	0.896	0.804	0.722	0.650	0.585	0.527	0.475	0.429	0.388	0.350	0.287
12	0.887	0.788	0.701	0.625	0.557	0.497	0.444	0.397	0.356	0.319	0.257
13	0.879	0.773	0.681	0.601	0.530	0.469	0.415	0.368	0.326	0.290	0.229
14	0.870	0.758	0.661	0.577	0.505	0.442	0.388	0.340	0.299	0.263	0.205
15	0.861	0.743	0.642	0.555	0.481	0.417	0.362	0.315	0.275	0.239	0.183
16	0.853	0.728	0.623	0.534	0.458	0.394	0.339	0.292	0.252	0.218	0.163
17	0.844	0.714	0.605	0.513	0.436	0.371	0.317	0.270	0.231	0.198	0.146
18	0.836	0.700	0.587	0.494	0.416	0.350	0.296	0.250	0.212	0.180	0.130
19	0.828	0.686	0.570	0.475	0.396	0.331	0.277	0.232	0.194	0.164	0.116
20	0.820	0.673	0.554	0.456	0.377	0.312	0.258	0.215	0.178	0.149	0.104
21	0.811	0.660	0.538	0.439	0.359	0.294	0.242	0.199	0.164	0.135	0.093
22	0.803	0.647	0.522	0.422	0.342	0.278	0.226	0.184	0.150	0.123	0.083
23	0.795	0.634	0.507	0.406	0.326	0.262	0.211	0.170	0.138	0.112	0.074
24	0.788	0.622	0.492	0.390	0.310	0.247	0.197	0.158	0.126	0.102	0.066
25	0.780	0.610	0.478	0.375	0.295	0.233	0.184	0.146	0.116	0.092	0.059
26	0.772	0.598	0.464	0.361	0.281	0.220	0.172	0.135	0.106	0.084	0.053
27	0.764	0.586	0.450	0.347	0.268	0.207	0.161	0.125	0.098	0.076	0.047
28	0.757	0.574	0.437	0.333	0.255	0.196	0.150	0.116	0.090	0.069	0.042
29	0.749	0.563	0.424	0.321	0.243	0.185	0.141	0.107	0.082	0.063	0.037
30	0.742	0.552	0.412	0.308	0.231	0.174	0.131	0.099	0.075	0.057	0.033
40	0.672	0.453	0.307	0.208	0.142	0.097	0.067	0.046	0.032	0.022	0.011
50	0.608	0.372	0.228	0.141	0.087	0.054	0.034	0.021	0.013	0.009	0.003

Table C-1   *(cont'd)*

						Present Value					
14%	15%	16%	18%	20%	25%	30%	35%	40%	45%	50%	Periods
0.877	0.870	0.862	0.847	0.833	0.800	0.769	0.741	0.714	0.690	0.667	1
0.769	0.756	0.743	0.718	0.694	0.640	0.592	0.549	0.510	0.476	0.444	2
0.675	0.658	0.641	0.609	0.579	0.512	0.455	0.406	0.364	0.328	0.296	3
0.592	0.572	0.552	0.516	0.482	0.410	0.350	0.301	0.260	0.226	0.198	4
0.519	0.497	0.476	0.437	0.402	0.328	0.269	0.223	0.186	0.156	0.132	5
0.456	0.432	0.410	0.370	0.335	0.262	0.207	0.165	0.133	0.108	0.088	6
0.400	0.376	0.354	0.314	0.279	0.210	0.159	0.122	0.095	0.074	0.059	7
0.351	0.327	0.305	0.266	0.233	0.168	0.123	0.091	0.068	0.051	0.039	8
0.308	0.284	0.263	0.225	0.194	0.134	0.094	0.067	0.048	0.035	0.026	9
0.270	0.247	0.227	0.191	0.162	0.107	0.073	0.050	0.035	0.024	0.017	10
0.237	0.215	0.195	0.162	0.135	0.086	0.056	0.037	0.025	0.017	0.012	11
0.208	0.187	0.168	0.137	0.112	0.069	0.043	0.027	0.018	0.012	0.008	12
0.182	0.163	0.145	0.116	0.093	0.055	0.033	0.020	0.013	0.008	0.005	13
0.160	0.141	0.125	0.099	0.078	0.044	0.025	0.015	0.009	0.006	0.003	14
0.140	0.123	0.108	0.084	0.065	0.035	0.020	0.011	0.006	0.004	0.002	15
0.123	0.107	0.093	0.071	0.054	0.028	0.015	0.008	0.005	0.003	0.002	16
0.108	0.093	0.080	0.060	0.045	0.023	0.012	0.006	0.003	0.002	0.001	17
0.095	0.081	0.069	0.051	0.038	0.018	0.009	0.005	0.002	0.001	0.001	18
0.083	0.070	0.060	0.043	0.031	0.014	0.007	0.003	0.002	0.001		19
0.073	0.061	0.051	0.037	0.026	0.012	0.005	0.002	0.001	0.001		20
0.064	0.053	0.044	0.031	0.022	0.009	0.004	0.002	0.001			21
0.056	0.046	0.038	0.026	0.018	0.007	0.003	0.001	0.001			22
0.049	0.040	0.033	0.022	0.015	0.006	0.002	0.001				23
0.043	0.035	0.028	0.019	0.013	0.005	0.002	0.001				24
0.038	0.030	0.024	0.016	0.010	0.004	0.001	0.001				25
0.033	0.026	0.021	0.014	0.009	0.003	0.001					26
0.029	0.023	0.018	0.011	0.007	0.002	0.001					27
0.026	0.020	0.016	0.010	0.006	0.002	0.001					28
0.022	0.017	0.014	0.008	0.005	0.002						29
0.020	0.015	0.012	0.007	0.004	0.001						30
0.005	0.004	0.003	0.001	0.001							40
0.001	0.001	0.001									50

Table C-2 *Present Value of Annuity $1*

					Present Value						
Periods	**1%**	**2%**	**3%**	**4%**	**5%**	**6%**	**7%**	**8%**	**9%**	**10%**	**12%**
1	0.990	0.980	0.971	0.962	0.952	0.943	0.935	0.926	0.917	0.909	0.893
2	1.970	1.942	1.913	1.886	1.859	1.833	1.808	1.783	1.759	1.736	1.690
3	2.941	2.884	2.829	2.775	2.723	2.673	2.624	2.577	2.531	2.487	2.402
4	3.902	3.808	3.717	3.630	3.546	3.465	3.387	3.312	3.240	3.170	3.037
5	4.853	4.713	4.580	4.452	4.329	4.212	4.100	3.993	3.890	3.791	3.605
6	5.795	5.601	5.417	5.242	5.076	4.917	4.767	4.623	4.486	4.355	4.111
7	6.728	6.472	6.230	6.002	5.786	5.582	5.389	5.206	5.033	4.868	4.564
8	7.652	7.325	7.020	6.733	6.463	6.210	5.971	5.747	5.535	5.335	4.968
9	8.566	8.162	7.786	7.435	7.108	6.802	6.515	6.247	5.995	5.759	5.328
10	9.471	8.983	8.530	8.111	7.722	7.360	7.024	6.710	6.418	6.145	5.650
11	10.368	9.787	9.253	8.760	8.306	7.887	7.499	7.139	6.805	6.495	5.938
12	11.255	10.575	9.954	9.385	8.863	8.384	7.943	7.536	7.161	6.814	6.194
13	12.134	11.348	10.635	9.986	9.394	8.853	8.358	7.904	7.487	7.103	6.424
14	13.004	12.106	11.296	10.563	9.899	9.295	8.745	8.244	7.786	7.367	6.628
15	13.865	12.849	11.938	11.118	10.380	9.712	9.108	8.559	8.061	7.606	6.811
16	14.718	13.578	12.561	11.652	10.838	10.106	9.447	8.851	8.313	7.824	6.974
17	15.562	14.292	13.166	12.166	11.274	10.477	9.763	9.122	8.544	8.022	7.120
18	16.398	14.992	13.754	12.659	11.690	10.828	10.059	9.372	8.756	8.201	7.250
19	17.226	15.678	14.324	13.134	12.085	11.158	10.336	9.604	8.950	8.365	7.366
20	18.046	16.351	14.878	13.590	12.462	11.470	10.594	9.818	9.129	8.514	7.469
21	18.857	17.011	15.415	14.029	12.821	11.764	10.836	10.017	9.292	8.649	7.562
22	19.660	17.658	15.937	14.451	13.163	12.042	11.061	10.201	9.442	8.772	7.645
23	20.456	18.292	16.444	14.857	13.489	12.303	11.272	10.371	9.580	8.883	7.718
24	21.243	18.914	16.936	15.247	13.799	12.550	11.469	10.529	9.707	8.985	7.784
25	22.023	19.523	17.413	15.622	14.094	12.783	11.654	10.675	9.823	9.077	7.843
26	22.795	20.121	17.877	15.983	14.375	13.003	11.826	10.810	9.929	9.161	7.896
27	23.560	20.707	18.327	16.330	14.643	13.211	11.987	10.935	10.027	9.237	7.943
28	24.316	21.281	18.764	16.663	14.898	13.406	12.137	11.051	10.116	9.307	7.984
29	25.066	21.844	19.189	16.984	15.141	13.591	12.278	11.158	10.198	9.370	8.022
30	25.808	22.396	19.600	17.292	15.373	13.765	12.409	11.258	10.274	9.427	8.055
40	32.835	27.355	23.115	19.793	17.159	15.046	13.332	11.925	10.757	9.779	8.244
50	39.196	31.424	25.730	21.482	18.256	15.762	13.801	12.234	10.962	9.915	8.305

Table C-2 (cont'd)

					Present Value						
14%	**15%**	**16%**	**18%**	**20%**	**25%**	**30%**	**35%**	**40%**	**45%**	**50%**	**Periods**
0.877	0.870	0.862	0.847	0.833	0.800	0.769	0.741	0.714	0.690	0.667	1
1.647	1.626	1.605	1.566	1.528	1.440	1.361	1.289	1.224	1.165	1.111	2
2.322	2.283	2.246	2.174	2.106	1.952	1.816	1.696	1.589	1.493	1.407	3
2.914	2.855	2.798	2.690	2.589	2.362	2.166	1.997	1.849	1.720	1.605	4
3.433	3.352	3.274	3.127	2.991	2.689	2.436	2.220	2.035	1.876	1.737	5
3.889	3.784	3.685	3.498	3.326	2.951	2.643	2.385	2.168	1.983	1.824	6
4.288	4.160	4.039	3.812	3.605	3.161	2.802	2.508	2.263	2.057	1.883	7
4.639	4.487	4.344	4.078	3.837	3.329	2.925	2.598	2.331	2.109	1.922	8
4.946	4.772	4.607	4.303	4.031	3.463	3.019	2.665	2.379	2.144	1.948	9
5.216	5.019	4.833	4.494	4.192	3.571	3.092	2.715	2.414	2.168	1.965	10
5.453	5.234	5.029	4.656	4.327	3.656	3.147	2.752	2.438	2.185	1.977	11
5.660	5.421	5.197	4.793	4.439	3.725	3.190	2.779	2.456	2.197	1.985	12
5.842	5.583	5.342	4.910	4.533	3.780	3.223	2.799	2.469	2.204	1.990	13
6.002	5.724	5.468	5.008	4.611	3.824	3.249	2.814	2.478	2.210	1.993	14
6.142	5.847	5.575	5.092	4.675	3.859	3.268	2.825	2.484	2.214	1.995	15
6.265	5.954	5.669	5.162	4.730	3.887	3.283	2.834	2.489	2.216	1.997	16
6.373	6.047	5.749	5.222	4.775	3.910	3.295	2.840	2.492	2.218	1.998	17
6.467	6.128	5.818	5.273	4.812	3.928	3.304	2.844	2.494	2.219	1.999	18
6.550	6.198	5.877	5.316	4.844	3.942	3.311	2.848	2.496	2.220	1.999	19
6.623	6.259	5.929	5.353	4.870	3.954	3.316	2.850	2.497	2.221	1.999	20
6.687	6.312	5.973	5.384	4.891	3.963	3.320	2.852	2.498	2.221	2.000	21
6.743	6.359	6.011	5.410	4.909	3.970	3.323	2.853	2.498	2.222	2.000	22
6.792	6.399	6.044	5.432	4.925	3.976	3.325	2.854	2.499	2.222	2.000	23
6.835	6.434	6.073	5.451	4.937	3.981	3.327	2.855	2.499	2.222	2.000	24
6.873	6.464	6.097	5.467	4.948	3.985	3.329	2.856	2.499	2.222	2.000	25
6.906	6.491	6.118	5.480	4.956	3.988	3.330	2.856	2.500	2.222	2.000	26
6.935	6.514	6.136	5.492	4.964	3.990	3.331	2.856	2.500	2.222	2.000	27
6.961	6.534	6.152	5.502	4.970	3.992	3.331	2.857	2.500	2.222	2.000	28
6.983	6.551	6.166	5.510	4.975	3.994	3.332	2.857	2.500	2.222	2.000	29
7.003	6.566	6.177	5.517	4.979	3.995	3.332	2.857	2.500	2.222	2.000	30
7.105	6.642	6.234	5.548	4.997	3.999	3.333	2.857	2.500	2.222	2.000	40
7.133	6.661	6.246	5.554	4.999	4.000	3.333	2.857	2.500	2.222	2.000	50

Table C-3   *Future Value of $1*

							Future Value						
Periods	1%	2%	3%	4%	5%	6%	7%	8%	9%	10%	12%	14%	15%
1	1.010	1.020	1.030	1.040	1.050	1.060	1.070	1.080	1.090	1.100	1.120	1.140	1.150
2	1.020	1.040	1.061	1.082	1.103	1.124	1.145	1.166	1.188	1.210	1.254	1.300	1.323
3	1.030	1.061	1.093	1.125	1.158	1.191	1.225	1.260	1.295	1.331	1.405	1.482	1.521
4	1.041	1.082	1.126	1.170	1.216	1.262	1.311	1.360	1.412	1.464	1.574	1.689	1.749
5	1.051	1.104	1.159	1.217	1.276	1.338	1.403	1.469	1.539	1.611	1.762	1.925	2.011
6	1.062	1.126	1.194	1.265	1.340	1.419	1.501	1.587	1.677	1.772	1.974	2.195	2.313
7	1.072	1.149	1.230	1.316	1.407	1.504	1.606	1.714	1.828	1.949	2.211	2.502	2.660
8	1.083	1.172	1.267	1.369	1.477	1.594	1.718	1.851	1.993	2.144	2.476	2.853	3.059
9	1.094	1.195	1.305	1.423	1.551	1.689	1.838	1.999	2.172	2.358	2.773	3.252	3.518
10	1.105	1.219	1.344	1.480	1.629	1.791	1.967	2.159	2.367	2.594	3.106	3.707	4.046
11	1.116	1.243	1.384	1.539	1.710	1.898	2.105	2.332	2.580	2.853	3.479	4.226	4.652
12	1.127	1.268	1.426	1.601	1.796	2.012	2.252	2.518	2.813	3.138	3.896	4.818	5.350
13	1.138	1.294	1.469	1.665	1.886	2.133	2.410	2.720	3.066	3.452	4.363	5.492	6.153
14	1.149	1.319	1.513	1.732	1.980	2.261	2.579	2.937	3.342	3.798	4.887	6.261	7.076
15	1.161	1.346	1.558	1.801	2.079	2.397	2.759	3.172	3.642	4.177	5.474	7.138	8.137
16	1.173	1.373	1.605	1.873	2.183	2.540	2.952	3.426	3.970	4.595	6.130	8.137	9.358
17	1.184	1.400	1.653	1.948	2.292	2.693	3.159	3.700	4.328	5.054	6.866	9.276	10.76
18	1.196	1.428	1.702	2.026	2.407	2.854	3.380	3.996	4.717	5.560	7.690	10.58	12.38
19	1.208	1.457	1.754	2.107	2.527	3.026	3.617	4.316	5.142	6.116	8.613	12.06	14.23
20	1.220	1.486	1.806	2.191	2.653	3.207	3.870	4.661	5.604	6.728	9.646	13.74	16.37
21	1.232	1.516	1.860	2.279	2.786	3.400	4.141	5.034	6.109	7.400	10.80	15.67	18.82
22	1.245	1.546	1.916	2.370	2.925	3.604	4.430	5.437	6.659	8.140	12.10	17.86	21.64
23	1.257	1.577	1.974	2.465	3.072	3.820	4.741	5.871	7.258	8.954	13.55	20.36	24.89
24	1.270	1.608	2.033	2.563	3.225	4.049	5.072	6.341	7.911	9.850	15.18	23.21	28.63
25	1.282	1.641	2.094	2.666	3.386	4.292	5.427	6.848	8.623	10.83	17.00	26.46	32.92
26	1.295	1.673	2.157	2.772	3.556	4.549	5.807	7.396	9.399	11.92	19.04	30.17	37.86
27	1.308	1.707	2.221	2.883	3.733	4.822	6.214	7.988	10.25	13.11	21.32	34.39	43.54
28	1.321	1.741	2.288	2.999	3.920	5.112	6.649	8.627	11.17	14.42	23.88	39.20	50.07
29	1.335	1.776	2.357	3.119	4.116	5.418	7.114	9.317	12.17	15.86	26.75	44.69	57.58
30	1.348	1.811	2.427	3.243	4.322	5.743	7.612	10.06	13.27	17.45	29.96	50.95	66.21
40	1.489	2.208	3.262	4.801	7.040	10.29	14.97	21.72	31.41	45.26	93.05	188.9	267.9
50	1.645	2.692	4.384	7.107	11.47	18.42	29.46	46.90	74.36	117.4	289.0	700.2	1,084

Table C-4 *Future Value of Annuity of $1*

Periods	1%	2%	3%	4%	5%	6%	7%	8%	9%	10%	12%	14%	15%
						Future Value							
1	1.000	1.000	1.000	1.000	1.000	1.000	1.000	1.000	1.000	1.000	1.000	1.000	1.000
2	2.010	2.020	2.030	2.040	2.050	2.060	2.070	2.080	2.090	2.100	2.120	2.140	2.150
3	3.030	3.060	3.091	3.122	3.153	3.184	3.215	3.246	3.278	3.310	3.374	3.440	3.473
4	4.060	4.122	4.184	4.246	4.310	4.375	4.440	4.506	4.573	4.641	4.779	4.921	4.993
5	5.101	5.204	5.309	5.416	5.526	5.637	5.751	5.867	5.985	6.105	6.353	6.610	6.742
6	6.152	6.308	6.468	6.633	6.802	6.975	7.153	7.336	7.523	7.716	8.115	8.536	8.754
7	7.214	7.434	7.662	7.898	8.142	8.394	8.654	8.923	9.200	9.487	10.09	10.73	11.07
8	8.286	8.583	8.892	9.214	9.549	9.897	10.26	10.64	11.03	11.44	12.30	13.23	13.73
9	9.369	9.755	10.16	10.58	11.03	11.49	11.98	12.49	13.02	13.58	14.78	16.09	16.79
10	10.46	10.95	11.46	12.01	12.58	13.18	13.82	14.49	15.19	15.94	17.55	19.34	20.30
11	11.57	12.17	12.81	13.49	14.21	14.97	15.78	16.65	17.56	18.53	20.65	23.04	24.35
12	12.68	13.41	14.19	15.03	15.92	16.87	17.89	18.98	20.14	21.38	24.13	27.27	29.00
13	13.81	14.68	15.62	16.63	17.71	18.88	20.14	21.50	22.95	24.52	28.03	32.09	34.35
14	14.95	15.97	17.09	18.29	19.60	21.02	22.55	24.21	26.02	27.98	32.39	37.58	40.50
15	16.10	17.29	18.60	20.02	21.58	23.28	25.13	27.15	29.36	31.77	37.28	43.84	47.58
16	17.26	18.64	20.16	21.82	23.66	25.67	27.89	30.32	33.00	35.95	42.75	50.98	55.72
17	18.43	20.01	21.76	23.70	25.84	28.21	30.84	33.75	36.97	40.54	48.88	59.12	65.08
18	19.61	21.41	23.41	25.65	28.13	30.91	34.00	37.45	41.30	45.60	55.75	68.39	75.84
19	20.81	22.84	25.12	27.67	30.54	33.76	37.38	41.45	46.02	51.16	63.44	78.97	88.21
20	22.02	24.30	26.87	29.78	33.07	36.79	41.00	45.76	51.16	57.28	72.05	91.02	102.4
21	23.24	25.78	28.68	31.97	35.72	39.99	44.87	50.42	56.76	64.00	81.70	104.8	118.8
22	24.47	27.30	30.54	34.25	38.51	43.39	49.01	55.46	62.87	71.40	92.50	120.4	137.6
23	25.72	28.85	32.45	36.62	41.43	47.00	53.44	60.89	69.53	79.54	104.6	138.3	159.3
24	26.97	30.42	34.43	39.08	44.50	50.82	58.18	66.76	76.79	88.50	118.2	158.7	184.2
25	28.24	32.03	36.46	41.65	47.73	54.86	63.25	73.11	84.70	98.35	133.3	181.9	212.8
26	29.53	33.67	38.55	44.31	51.11	59.16	68.68	79.95	93.32	109.2	150.3	208.3	245.7
27	30.82	35.34	40.71	47.08	54.67	63.71	74.48	87.35	102.7	121.1	169.4	238.5	283.6
28	32.13	37.05	42.93	49.97	58.40	68.53	80.70	95.34	113.0	134.2	190.7	272.9	327.1
29	33.45	38.79	45.22	52.97	62.32	73.64	87.35	104.0	124.1	148.6	214.6	312.1	377.2
30	34.78	40.57	47.58	56.08	66.44	79.06	94.46	113.3	136.3	164.5	241.3	356.8	434.7
40	48.89	60.40	75.40	95.03	120.8	154.8	199.6	259.1	337.9	442.6	767.1	1,342	1,779
50	64.46	84.58	112.8	152.7	209.3	290.3	406.5	573.8	815.1	1,164	2,400	4,995	7,218

Appendix D

*Typical Charts of Accounts for Different Types of Businesses
(For Businesses Discussed in Chapters 1–12)*

SERVICE PROPRIETORSHIP

ASSETS	LIABILITIES	OWNER'S EQUITY
Cash	Accounts Payable	Owner, Capital
Accounts Receivable	Notes Payable, Short-Term	Owner, Withdrawals
Allowance for Uncollectible Accounts	Salary Payable	**Revenues and Gains**
Notes Receivable, Short-Term	Wages Payable	Service Revenue
GST Receivable	Goods and Services Tax Payable	Interest Revenue
Interest Receivable	Employee Income Tax Payable	Gain on Sale of Land (or Furniture, Equipment, or Building)
Supplies	Employment Insurance Payable	**Expenses and Losses**
Prepaid Rent	Canada Pension Plan Payable	Salary Expense
Prepaid Insurance	Quebec Pension Plan Payable	Wages Expense
Notes Receivable, Long-Term	Employee Benefits Payable	Payroll Benefits Expense
Land	Interest Payable	Insurance Expense for Employees
Furniture	Unearned Service Revenue	Rent Expense
Accumulated Amortization—Furniture	Notes Payable, Long-Term	Insurance Expense
Equipment		Supplies Expense
Accumulated Amortization—Equipment		Uncollectible Account Expense
Building		Amortization Expense—Furniture
Accumulated Amortization—Building		Amortization Expense—Equipment
		Amortization Expense—Building
		Property Tax Expense
		Interest Expense
		Miscellaneous Expense
		Loss on Sale (or Exchange) of Land (Furniture, Equipment, or Buildings)

SERVICE PARTNERSHIP
Same as Service Proprietorship, except for Owners' Equity:

OWNER'S EQUITY
Partner 1, Capital
Partner 2, Capital
Partner N, Capital
Partner 1, Withdrawals
Partner 2, Withdrawals
Partner N, Withdrawals

(For Businesses Discussed in Chapters 13–26)

Merchandising Corporation

ASSETS	LIABILITIES	SHAREHOLDERS' EQUITY	

ASSETS

Cash
Short-Term Investments
(Trading Securities)
Accounts Receivable
Allowance for Uncollectible
Accounts
Notes Receivable, Short-
Term
Goods and Services Tax
Receivable
Interest Receivable
Inventory
Supplies
Prepaid Rent
Prepaid Insurance
Notes Receivable, Long-
Term
Investments in Subsidiaries
Investments in Stock
Investments in Bonds
Other Receivables, Long-
Term
Land
Land Improvements
Accumulated
Amortization—Land
Improvements
Furniture and Fixtures
Accumulated
Amortization—Furniture
and Fixtures
Equipment
Accumulated
Amortization—
Equipment
Buildings
Accumulated
Amortization—Buildings
Organization Cost
Franchises
Patents
Leaseholds
Goodwill

LIABILITIES

Accounts Payable
Notes Payable, Short-Term
Current Portion of Bonds
Payable
Salary Payable
Wages Payable
Goods and Services Tax
Payable
Employee Income Tax
Payable
Employment Insurance
Payable
Canada Pension Plan
Payable
Quebec Pension Plan
Payable
Employee Benefits Payable
Interest Payable
Income Tax Payable
Unearned Service Revenue
Notes Payable, Long-Term
Bonds Payable
Lease Liability

SHAREHOLDERS' EQUITY

Common Stock
Retained Earnings
Dividends

Revenues and Gains

Sales Revenue
Interest Revenue
Dividend Revenue
Equity-Method Investment
Revenue
Gain on Sale of Investments
Gain on Sale of Land
(Furniture and Fixtures,
Equipment, or Building)
Discontinued Operations—
Gain
Extraordinary Gains

Expenses and Losses

Cost of Goods Sold
Salary Expense
Wages Expense
Commission Expense
Payroll Benefits Expense
Insurance Expense for
Employees
Rent Expense
Insurance Expense
Supplies Expense
Uncollectible Accounts
Expense
Amortization Expense—
Land Improvements
Amortization Expense—
Furniture and Fixtures
Amortization Expense—
Equipment
Amortization Expense—
Buildings
Incorporation Expense
Amortization Expense—
Franchises
Amortization Expense—
Leaseholds
Amortization Expense—
Goodwill
Income Tax Expense
Loss on Sale of Investments
Loss on Sale (or Exchange)
of Land (or Furniture
and Fixtures, Equipment,
or Buildings)
Discontinued Operations—
Loss
Extraordinary Losses

Manufacturing Corporation

Same as Merchandising Corporation, except for Assets and Certain Expenses:

ASSETS

Inventories:
  Materials Inventory
  Work in Progress Inventory
  Finished Goods Inventory
Factory Wages
Factory Overhead

EXPENSES (CONTRA EXPENSES IF CREDIT BALANCE)

Direct Materials Price Variance
Direct Materials Efficiency Variance
Direct Labour Price Variance
Direct Labour Efficiency Variance
Overhead Flexible Budget Variance
Overhead Production Volume Variance

Glossary

Accounts receivable turnover Ratio of net credit sales to waverage net accounts receivable. Measures ability to collect cash from credit customers (p. 998).

Acid-test ratio Ratio of the sum of cash plus short-term investments plus net current receivables to current liabilities. Tells whether the entity could pay all its current liabilities if they came due immediately. Also called the quick ratio (p. 995).

Appropriation of retained earnings Restriction of retained earnings that is recorded by a formal journal entry (p. 770).

Articles of incorporation The document issued by the federal or provincial government giving the incorporators permission to form a corporation (p. 709).

Authorization of stock Provision in a corporation's articles of incorporation that permits a corporation to sell a certain number of shares of stock (p. 710).

Benchmarking Comparison of current performance with some standard. The standard often is the performance level of a leading outside organization (p. 987).

Board of directors Group elected by the shareholders to set policy for a corporation and to appoint its officers (p. 710).

Bond A formal agreement in which a lender loans money to a borrower, who agrees to repay the money loaned at a future date and agrees to pay interest regularly over the life of the bond (p. 805).

Bond discount Amount of bond's issue price under its maturity (par) value (p. 805).

Bond premium Excess of bond's issue price over its maturity (par) value (p. 805).

Bonds payable Groups of notes payable (bonds) issued to multiple lenders called bondholders (p. 805).

Book value Amount of shareholders' equity on the company's books for each share of its stock (p. 728).

Book value per share of common stock Common shareholders' equity divided by the number of shares of common stock outstanding (p. 1004).

Bylaws Constitution for governing a corporation (p. 710).

Callable bonds Bonds that the issuer may call or pay off at a specified price whenever the issuer wants (p. 824).

Capital charge The amount that shareholders and lenders charge a company for the use of their money (p. 1006).

Capital lease Lease agreement that transfers substantially all of the benefits and risks of ownership from the lessor to the lessee (p. 828).

Cash equivalents Highly liquid short-term investments that can be converted into cash with little delay (p. 915).

Cash flow statement Reports cash receipts and cash payments classified according to the entity's major activities: operating, investing, and financing (p. 914).

Cash flows Cash receipts and cash payments (disbursements) (p. 914).

Chairperson (of board) Elected person on a corporation's board of directors; usually the most powerful person in the corporation (p. 710).

Common-size statement A financial statement that reports only percentages (no dollar amounts); a type of vertical analysis (p. 986).

Common stock The most basic form of capital stock. In describing a corporation, the common shareholders are the owners of the business (p. 712).

Consolidated statements Financial statements of the parent company plus those of majority-owned subsidiaries as if the combination were a single legal entity (p. 874).

Contract interest rate Interest rate that determines the amount of cash interest the borrower pays and the investor receives each year. Also called the stated interest rate (p. 807).

Contributed capital A corporation's capital from investments by the shareholders. Also called share capital or capital stock (p. 711).

Controlling interest Ownership of more than 50 percent of an investee company's voting stock (p. 873).

Convertible bonds (or notes) Bonds (or notes) that may be converted into the common stock of the issuing company at the option of the investor (p. 825).

Convertible preferred stock Preferred stock that may be exchanged by the preferred shareholders, if they choose, for another class of stock in the corporation (p. 727).

Cost method for investments The method used to account for short-term investments in stock and for long-term investments when the investor generally holds less than 20 percent of the investee's voting stock. Short-term investments should be written down to market if the market declines below cost; long-term investments carried under the cost method should be written down to market if the decline is thought to be other than temporary (p. 867).

Cost of capital A weighted average of the returns demanded by a company's shareholders and lenders (p. 1006).

Cumulative preferred stock Preferred stock whose owners must receive all dividends in arrears before the corporation pays dividends to the common shareholders (p. 726).

Current ratio Current assets divided by current liabilities. Measures the ability to pay current liabilities from current assets (p. 995).

Days' sales in receivables Ratio of average net accounts receivable to one day's sales. Tells how many days' sales remain in Accounts Receivable awaiting collection (p. 999).

Debentures Unsecured bonds, backed only by the good faith of the borrower (p. 805).

Debt ratio Ratio of total liabilities to total assets. Tells the proportion of a company's assets that it has financed with debt (p. 999).

Deficit Debit balance in the retained earnings account (p. 713).

Defined benefit pension plan Benefits to be paid to the employee upon retirement are specified (p. 831).

Defined contribution pension plan The contribution to the plan is defined and the benefits to be paid to the employee depend on funds available at retirement (p. 831).

Direct method Format of the operating activities section of the cash flow statement that shows cash receipts from and cash payments for operating activities (p. 918).

Discount Amount of bond's issue price under its maturity (par) value (p. 805).

Dissolution Ending of a partnership (p. 664).

Dividend yield Ratio of dividends per share of stock to the stock's market price per share. Tells the percentage of a stock's market value that the company pays to shareholders as dividends (p. 1004).

Dividends Distributions by a corporation to its shareholders (p. 713).

Donated capital Special category of shareholders' equity created when a corporation receives a donation (gift) from a donor who receives no ownership interest in the company (p. 709).

Double taxation Corporations pay their own income taxes on corporate income. Then, the shareholders pay personal income tax on the cash dividends that they receive from corporations (p. 709).

Earnings per share (EPS) Amount of a company's net income per share of its outstanding common stock (pp. 776, 1003).

Economic Value Added (EVA®) Combines the concepts of accounting income and corporate finance to measure whether the company's operations have increased shareholder wealth (p. 1005).

Effective-interest amortization (of a bond) Amortization method in which a different amount of amortization expense is assigned to each year (or period) of the bond's life. The amount of amortization expense is the same percentage of a bond's carrying value for every period over a bond's life (p. 813).

Effective interest rate Another name for market interest rate (p. 807).

Efficient capital market One in which the market prices fully reflect all information available to the public (p. 1006).

Equity method for investments The method used to account for investments in which the investor generally has 20 to 50 percent of the investor's voting stock and can significantly influence the decisions of the investee. The investment account is debited for ownership in the investee's net income and credited for ownership in the investee's dividends (p. 871).

Extraordinary gain or loss, or extraordinary item A gain or loss that is not typical of the business and does not depend on a management decision (p. 775).

Financing activity Activity that obtains the funds from investors and creditors needed to launch and sustain the business; a section of the cash flow statement (p. 917).

Foreign-currency exchange rate The measure of one currency against another currency (p. 885).

Foreign-currency transaction gain The gain that occurs when a cash payment is less than the related account payable or a cash receipt is greater than the related account receivable due to a change in exchange rate between the transaction date and the payment date (p. 886).

Foreign-currency transaction loss The loss that occurs when a cash payment is greater than the related account payable or a cash receipt is less than the related account receivable due to a change in exchange rate between the transaction date and the payment date (p. 886).

Future income tax asset The difference that occurs when income tax expense is greater than income tax payable for a given period. Can be classified as a current or long-term asset depending on the expected reversal date (p. 732).

Future income tax liability The difference that occurs when income tax payable is greater than income tax expense for a given period. Can be classified as a current or long-term liability depending on the expected reversal date (p. 732).

General partnership A form of partnership in which each partner is an owner of the business, with all the privileges and risks of ownership (p. 666).

Hedging A way to protect oneself from losing money in a foreign-currency transaction by engaging in a counterbalancing foreign-currency transaction (p. 887).

Horizontal analysis Study of percentage changes in comparative financial statements (p. 982).

Indirect method Format of the operating activities section of the cash flow statement that starts with net income and shows the reconciliation from net income to operating cash flows. Also called the reconciliation method (p. 918).

Interest-coverage ratio Another name for the times-interest-earned ratio (p. 1000).

Inventory turnover Ratio of cost of goods sold to average inventory. Measures the number of times a company sells its average level of inventory during a year (p. 997).

Investing activity Activity that increases and decreases the long-term assets available to the business; a section of the cash flow statement (p. 917).

Lease Agreement in which the tenant (lessee) agrees to make rent payments to the property owner (lessor) in exchange for the exclusive use of the asset (p. 828).

Lessee Tenant in a lease agreement (p. 828).

Lessor Property owner in a lease agreement (p. 828).

Leverage Another name for trading on the equity (p. 1002).

Limited liability No personal obligation of a shareholder for corporation debts. The most that a shareholder can lose on an investment in a corporation's stock is the cost of the investment (p. 709).

Limited liability partnership (LLP) A partnership in which each partner's personal liability for the business's debts is limited to a certain dollar amount (p. 666).

Limited partnership A partnership with at least two classes of partners: a general partner and limited partners (p. 665).

Liquidation The process of going out of business by selling the entity's assets and paying its liabilities. The final step in liquidation of a business is the distribution of any remaining cash to the owners (p. 680).

Long-term investment Separate asset category reported on the balance sheet between current assets and capital assets (p. 867).

Long-term solvency The ability to generate enough cash to pay long-term debts as they mature (p. 981).

Majority interest Another name for controlling interest (p. 873).

Market interest rate Interest rate that investors demand in order to loan their money. Also called the effective interest rate (p. 807).

Market value (of stock) Price for which a person could buy or sell a share of stock (p. 728).

Marketable security Another name for short-term investment (p. 867).

Minority interest A subsidiary company's equity that is held by shareholders other than the parent company (p. 877).

Mortgage Borrower's promise to transfer the legal title to certain assets to the lender if the debt is not paid on schedule (p. 826).

Mutual agency Every partner can bind the business to a contract within the scope of the partnership's regular business operations (p. 664).

No-par-value shares Shares of stock that do not have a value assigned to them by the articles of incorporation (p. 716).

Off-balance-sheet financing Acquisition of assets or services with debt that is not reported on the balance sheet (p. 830).

Operating activity Activity that creates revenue or expense in the entity's major line of business. A section of the cash flow statement. Operating activities affect the income statement (p. 916).

Operating lease Usually a short-term or cancelable rental agreement (p. 828).

Organization cost The costs of organizing a corporation, including legal fees, taxes, and charges by promoters for selling the stock. Organization cost is an intangible asset (p. 721).

Outstanding stock Stock in the hands of a shareholder (p. 711).

Parent company An investor company that generally owns more than 50 percent of the voting stock of a subsidiary company (p. 873).

Partnership An unincorporated business with two or more owners (pp. 6, 662).

Partnership agreement Agreement that is the contract between partners specifying such items as the name, location, and nature of the business; the name, capital investment, and duties of each partner; and the method of sharing profits and losses by the partners (p. 663).

Pension Employee compensation that will be received during retirement (p. 831).

Preferred shares Shares of stock that gives its owners certain advantages over common shareholders, such as the priority to receive dividends before the common shareholders and the priority to receive assets before the common shareholders if the corporation liquidates (p. 714).

Premium Excess of bond's issue price over its maturity (par) value (p. 805).

Present value Amount a person would invest now to receive a greater amount at a future date (p. 807).

President Chief operating officer in charge of managing the day-to-day operations of a corporation (p. 710).

Pretax accounting income Income before income tax from the income statement (p. 731).

Price/earnings ratio Ratio of the market price of a share of common stock to the company's earnings per share. Measures the value that the stock market places on $1 of a company's earnings (p. 1003).

Prior-period adjustment A correction to retained earnings for an error of an earlier period or to reflect retroactive application of a change in accounting policy (p. 780).

Profit margin Another name for the rate of return on net sales (p. 1001).

Quick ratio Another name for the acid-test ratio (p. 995).

Rate of return on common shareholders' equity Net income minus preferred dividends, divided by average common shareholders' equity. A measure of profitability. Also called return on common shareholders' equity (pp. 730, 1002).

Rate of return on net sales Ratio of net income to net sales. A measure of profitability. Also called return on sales (p. 1001).

Rate of return on total assets The sum of net income plus interest expense divided by average total assets. This ratio measures the success a company has in using its assets to earn income for the persons who finance the business. Also called return on assets (pp. 730, 1001).

Reconciliation method Another name for the indirect method of creating the cash flow statement (p. 933).

Repurchase of own stock A corporation may repurchase its own stock that it has issued previously (p. 765).

Retained earnings A corporation's capital that is earned through profitable operation of the business (p. 712).

Return on assets Another name for rate of return on total assets (pp. 730, 1001).

Return on equity Another name for rate of return on common shareholders' equity (pp. 730, 1002).

Return on sales Another name for the rate of return on net sales (p. 1001).

Return on shareholders' equity Another name for rate of return on common shareholders' equity (p. 1002).

Segment of a business One of various separate divisions of a company (p. 775).

Serial bonds Bonds that mature in installments over a period of time (p. 805).

Shareholder A person who owns stock in a corporation (p. 709).

Shareholders' equity Owners' equity of a corporation (p. 711).

Short-term investment Investment that is readily convertible to cash and that the investor intends either to convert to cash in one year or to use to pay a current liability; also called a marketable security, a current asset (p. 867).

Short-term liquidity Ability to meet current payments as they come due (p. 981).

Stated interest rate Another name for the contract interest rate (p. 807).

Stated value Another name for par value, an arbitrary amount assigned to a share of stock (p. 716).

Stock Shares into which the owners' equity of a corporation is divided (p. 709).

Stock dividend A proportional distribution by a corporation of its own stock to its shareholders (p. 761).

Stock split An increase in the number of outstanding shares of stock coupled with a proportionate reduction in the book value of each share (p. 763).

Straight-line (SL) amortization Amortization method in which an equal amount of amortization expense is assigned to each year (or period) of asset use (p. 812).

Strong currency A currency that is rising relative to other nations' currencies (p. 885).

Subsidiary company An investee company in which a parent company owns more than 50 percent of the voting stock (p. 873).

Taxable income Income from the income tax return filed with Canada Customs and Revenue Agency; the basis for computing the amount of tax to pay the government (p. 731).

Temporary difference The amount that arises when a revenue or expense is deductible for financial statement purposes and income tax purposes in different periods. Temporary differences reverse over time. Also called a timing difference (p. 732).

Temporary investment Another name for short-term investment (p. 867).

Term bonds Bonds that all mature at the same time for a particular issue (p. 805).

Times-interest-earned ratio Ratio of income from operations to interest expense. Measures the number of times that operating income can cover interest expense. Also called the interest-coverage ratio (p. 1000).

Timing difference Another name for a temporary difference (p. 732).

Trading on the equity Earning more income on borrowed money than the related expense, thereby increasing the earnings for the owners of the business (pp. 827, 1002).

Underwriter Organization that purchases the bonds from an issuing company and resells them to its clients, or sells the bonds for a commission, agreeing to buy all unsold bonds (p. 805).

Unlimited personal liability When a partnership (or a proprietorship) cannot pay its debts with business assets, the partners (or the proprietor) must use personal assets to meet the debt (p. 664).

Vertical analysis Analysis of a financial statement that reveals the relationship of each statement item to the total, which is 100 percent (p. 985).

Weak currency A currency that is falling relative to other nations' currencies (p. 885).

Working capital Current assets minus current liabilities; measures a business's ability to meet its short-term obligations with its current assets (p. 994).

Index

P12-1A No check figure

P12-2A Total assets, $120,000; Jay Woeller, Capital, $49,000; Claudette LeBlanc, Capital, $49,000

P12-3A Req. 3: Rivers' capital, $45,000; Req. 4, Rivers' capital, $51,750

P12-4A Req. 1d: Net income to: Kantor, $70,667; Karlin, $60,667; Schipper, $50,666

P12-5A Req. 5. Dr. Mutchler, Capital, $60,000

P12-6A Req. 1a. Cash to: Cheung, $54,600; Kosse, $158,400; Lufkin, $45,000

P12-7A Req. 3. Cash to: Ryan, $12,375; Morales, $10,125; Goldberg, $13,500

P12-8A Req. 2: Dhal, Capital: $254,358; Sung, Capital, $301,642

P12-9A Jan 3, 2004 loss on disposal: Chapin, $18,450; Dawson, $12,300; Yee, $30,750

P12-1B No check figure

P12-2B Total assets, $102,000; Chris Mak, Capital, $41,000; Sean Russell, Capital, $41,000

P12-3B Req. 3: Oldham's capital, $144,000; Req. 4, Oldham's capital, $68,000

P12-4B Req. 1d: Net income to: Aplevich, $138,667; Davis, $106,667; Diehl, $114,666

P12-5B Req. 5. Dr. Dune, Capital, $57,900

P12-6B Req. 1a. Cash to: Amping, $64,000; Blair, $84,000; Trippi, $88,000

P12-7B Req. 3. Cash to: Bell, $19,500; Pastena, $11,500; O'Donnell, $6,000

P12-8B Req. 2: Dikolli, Capital: $274,727; McCracken, Capital, $237,273

P12-9B Jan 3, 2004 loss on disposal: Press, $53,600; Ewing, $80,400; Visser, $134,000

P12-1C No check figure

P12-2C Profit distributed to: Antoine, $36,400; Chui, $18,200; May, $36,400

DP 1 No check figure

FSP 1 2. $166 per hour; 3. $117,444

P13-1A No check figure

P13-2A Req. 2. Total shareholders' equity, $377,000

P13-3A Req. 5. Total shareholders' equity, $455,000

P13-4A Total shareholders' equity: Magellan Fotographic Inc., $1,020,000; Teksystems Inc., $674,000

P13-5A Req. 5b. Dividends payable: Preferred, $51,849,936; Class VBN, $24,730,332; Common, $173,419,733

P13-6A 1. Total assets, $1,286,000; total shareholders' equity, $976,000

P13-7A Req. 1b. Year 2003: Preferred, $10,000; Common, $30,000

P13-8A Req. 5. Book value per share, Preferred, $8.50; common, $5.75

P13-9A Req. 3. Net income, $120,000

P13-10A Total shareholders' equity, $652,000

P13-11A Req. 2. Total liabilities and shareholders' equity, $4,690,000

P13-1B No check figure

P13-2B Req. 2. Total shareholders' equity, $276,000

P13-3B Req. 5. Total shareholders' equity, $442,000

P13-4B Total shareholders' equity: Atrium Inc., $1,325,000; Carnival Corp., $670,000

P13-5B Req. 3. Total preferred dividends, $156,546

P13-6B 1. Total assets, $840,000; total shareholders' equity, $624,000

P13-7B Req. 1b. Year 2003: Preferred, $40,000; Common, $185,000

P13-8B Req. 6. Book value per share, Preferred, $52.55; common, $8.43

P13-9B Req. 3. Net income, $301,000

P13-10B Total shareholders' equity, $517,500

P13-11B Req. 2. Total liabilities and shareholders' equity, $2,910,000

P13-1C No check figure

P13-2C Convertible preferred rate of return, 5.5%

DP 1 Total shareholders' equity: Plan 1, $425,900; Plan 2, $410,900

FSP 1 Req. 4. Book value of common shares, $11.44

P14-1A Oct. 26 Dr. Retained earnings, $18,000

P14-2A Req. 2. Total shareholders' equity, $711,300

P14-3A No check figure

P14-4A Req. 2. Retained earnings, Dec. 31, 2002, $296,820; Req. 3. Total shareholders' equity, $1,069,020

P14-5A Net income, $12,500; Earnings per share, $0.30

P14-6A Net income, $81,900; Retained earnings, Dec. 31, 2002, $605,400

P14-7A Req. 1. Earnings per share, $1.89; Req. 2. Total shareholders' equity, $770,085

P14-8A Req. 2. Total shareholders' equity, $448,000

P14-9A Req. 2. Net income, $78,500; Retained earnings, Dec. 31, 2002, $167,500

P14-1B June 18 Dr. Retained earnings, $4,800

P14-2B Req. 2. Total shareholders' equity, $506,800

P14-3B No check figure

P14-4B Req. 2. Retained earnings, Dec. 31, 2002, $184,320; Req. 3. Total shareholders' equity, $2,287,520

P14-5B Net income, $104,000; Earnings per share, $4.80

P14-6B Net income, $323,200; Retained earnings, June 30, 2003, $908,200

P14-7B Req. 1. Earnings per share, $3.07; Req. 2. Total shareholders' equity, $1,558,890

P14-8B Req. 2. Total shareholders' equity, $971,760

P14-9B Req. 2. Net income, $156,400; Retained earnings, Dec. 31, 2003, $337,600

P14-1C New dividend, $0.71 per share

P14-2C No check figure

DP 1 Req. 2. Cash dividends before, $12,000; after, $11,000

FSP 1 Req. 2. Average issue price per share: common shares, $10.74

P15-1A Req. 1. May 31, 2004, Interest expense, $291,667; Req. 3. Current liabilities, $58,333; Long-term liabilities, $10,000,000

P15-2A Req. 3c. Interest expense, $14,500; Req. 5. Current liabilities, $14,167; Long-term liabilities, net, $480,833

P15-3A Req. 2. Bond carrying amount, Sept. 30, 2005, $452,767; Req. 3 Sept. 30, 2005, Interest expense, $31,583

P15-4A Req. 1. Bond carrying amount, Dec. 31, 2004, $1,587,383; Req. 3 Convertible bonds payable, net, $264,564

P15-5A Dec. 31, 2003, Interest expense, $41,500; Dec. 31, 2003, Amortization expense, $80,747

P15-6A No check figure

P15-7A Total current liabilities, $86,400; Total long-term liabilities, $626,000

P15-8A Req. 2. Long-term liabilities, $1,600,000

P15-9A Req. 2. Bonds payable, $5,012,019; Long-term liabilities, $194,737

P15-1B Req. 1d. Interest expense, $100,000; Req. 3. Current liabilities, $100,000; Long-term liabilities, $5,000,000

P15-2B Req. 3c. Interest expense, $18,875; Req. 5. Current liabilities, $19,375; Long-term liabilities, net, $981,500

P15-3B Req. 2. Bond carrying amount, Sept. 30, 2005, $1,790,455; Req. 3 Interest expense, $107,007

P15-4B Req. 1. Bond carrying amount, Dec. 31, 2004, $4,719,148; Req. 3 Convertible bonds payable, net, $1,887,659

P15-5B Dec. 31, 2002, Interest expense, $83,000; Dec. 31, 2002, Amortization expense, $16,679

P15-6B No check figure

P15-7B Total current liabilities, $255,200; Total long-term liabilities, $846,800

P15-8B Req. 2. Long-term liabilities, net, $6,634,831

P15-9B Req. 2. Bonds payable, net, $9,976,191; Long-term liabilities, $146,052

P15-1C No check figure

P15-2C No check figure

DP 1 Earnings per share: Plan A, $9.84; Plan B, $9.00; Plan C, $9.30

DP 2 No check figure

FSP 1 Req. 1. Increase, $97,088,000

P15A-1 (a) 5 years: $615,600; (b) 6%: $28,185

P15A-2 (a) $20,000,564; (b) $11,280,000

P15A-3 Present value Req. 1: $48,110; Req. 2: $112,472; Req. 3: $127,140; Req. 4: $100,020

P15A-4 Req. 1. Present value of bonds $284,591; Req. 2 Bond carrying amount, Dec. 31, 2004, $285,629

P15A-5 Present value: Nissan ¥4,989,600, Toyota ¥5,197,500

P15A-6 Req. 1 $42,740; Req. 2b Amortization expense $7,123; Req. 2c Interest expense $5,238

P16-1A	Feb. 6, 2003, gain on sale of investment, $23,602
P16-2A	Req. 2. Investments in significantly influenced and other companies balance, $9,461,808,000; Req. 3. Short-term investments balance, $150,228,500
P16-3A	Consolidated total assets, $746,000
P16-4A	Consolidated total assets, $1,010,000
P16-5A	Req. 2. Book value of bonds, $682,071
P16-6A	Req. I. Investment carrying amount, Dec. 31, 2003, $194,177
P16-7A	Req. 1. Foreign currency transaction loss, $1,500
P16-8A	Dec. 31, 2002, loss on short-term securities, $30,332
P16-9A	Req. 2. Short-term investment, $147,000; Long-term investments, $253,697
P16-1B	Jan. 14, 2003, gain on sale of investment, $13,363
P16-2B	Req. 2. Equity investments balance, $178,804,000; Req. 3. Short-term investments balance, $426,500
P16-3B	Consolidated total assets, $963,000
P16-4B	Consolidated total assets, $1,034,000
P16-5B	Req. 2. Book value of bonds, $873,940
P16-6B	Req. 1. Present value of bond investment, $777,796; Req. 2. Investment carrying amount, Dec. 31, 2003, $780,880
P16-7B	Req. 1. Foreign currency transaction gain, $1,600
P16-8B	Dec. 31, 2001, loss on marketable securities, $22,920
P16-9B	Req. 2. Short-term investment in bonds, $290,000; Long-term investments, $517,100
P16-1C	No check figure
P16-2C	No check figure
DP 1	No check figure
FSP 1	No check figure
CP 1	Req. 2. Net income, $111,667; Req. 3. Total shareholders' equity, $735,667

P17-1A	No check figure
P17-2A	Req. 1. Net cash outflow from operating activities, $40,000; Net increase in cash, $1,500
P17-3A	Req. 1. Net cash inflow from operating activities, $66,600; Net decrease in cash, $10,900
P17-4A	Req. 1. Net cash inflow from operating activities, $66,600; Net decrease in cash, $10,900
P17-5A	Net cash inflow from operating activities, $71,100; Net increase in cash, $1,400
P17-6A	Req. 1. Net cash inflow from operating activities, $58,000; Net decrease in cash, $11,400
P17-7A	Req. 1. Net cash inflow from operating activities, $74,100; Net decrease in cash, $11,900
P17-8A	Req. 1. Net cash inflow from operating activities, $60,900; Net increase in cash, $24,600
P17-9A	No check figure
P17-10A	Req. 1. Net cash inflow from operating activities, $58,600; Net decrease in cash, $4,800
P17-1B	No check figure
P17-2B	Req. 1. Net cash inflow from operating activities, $118,700; Net increase in cash, $82,800
P17-3B	Req. 1. Net cash inflow from operating activities, $105,900; Net increase in cash, $900
P17-4B	Req. 1. Net cash inflow from operating activities, $105,900; Net increase in cash, $900

P17-5B	Net cash inflow from operating activities, $89,700; Net increase in cash, $7,500
P17-6B	Req. 1. Net cash inflow from operating activities, $107,100; Net decrease in cash, $4,900
P17-7B	Req. 1. Net cash inflow from operating activities, $98,800; Net increase in cash, $29,000
P17-8B	Net cash inflow from operating activities, $68,000; Net increase in cash, $29,000
P17-9B	No check figure
P17-10B	Req. 1. Net cash inflow from operating activities, $90,500; Net decrease in cash, $16,400
P17-1C	No check figure
P17-2C	No check figure
DP 1	Req. 1. Net cash inflow from operating activities, $120; Net decrease in cash, $50
DP-2	No check figure
FSP 1	Req. 2. Cash and short-term deposits decreased to $78,985,000
P17A-1	Panel B: Transaction analysis, Total Dr., $110,800
P17A-2	Panel B: Transaction analysis, Total Dr., $201,300

P18-1A	Req. 1. 2002: Net sales 120%; Req. 2. 2002: 0.165, or 16.5%
P18-2A	Req. 1. Net income 14.6%; Shareholders' equity, 40.2%
P18-3A	Req. 1. Current ratio 1.48; debt ratio 0.58; Req. 2a. Current ratio 1.42; debt ratio 0.60
P18-4A	Req. 1. 2003: b. Inventory turnover 1.42; e. Return on total assets 14.0%; h. Price/earnings ratio 7.8
P18-5A	(e) $2,445 million; (l) 6,892 million
P18-6A	Req. 1l. Price/earnings ratio: Airflow Ltd. 6.9; Altemp Products Ltd. 7.9
P18-7A	Req. 2d. Days' sales in receivables 21.9 days; Req. 2j. Price/earnings ratio 4.8
P18-8A	Req. 2c. Days' sales in receivables 31.47 days; Req. 2h. Price/earnings ratio 5.14
P18-1B	Req. 1. 2003: Net sales 146%; Req. 2. 2003: 0.082, or 8.2%
P18-2B	Req. 1. Net income 4.2%; Shareholders' equity, 36.0%
P18-3B	Req. 1. Current ratio 2.17; debt ratio 0.47; Req. 2a. Current ratio 2.52; debt ratio 0.50
P18-4B	Req. 1. 2003: b. Inventory turnover 1.19; e. Return on total assets 16.1%; h. Price/earnings ratio 6.6
P18-5B	(e) $3,246 million; (l) 5,652 million
P18-6B	Req. 1l. Price/earnings ratio: O'Boyle Inc. 28.4; Patel Ltd. 26.7
P18-7B	Req. 2d. Days' sales in receivables 36.5 days; Req. 2j. Price/earnings ratio 9.4
P18-8B	Req. 2c. Days' sales in receivables 57.2 days; Req. 2h. Price/earnings ratio 5.7
P18-1C	No check figure
P18-2C	No check figure
DP 1	No check figure
FSP 1	Req. 1. 2000: Revenues 391.8%; income from continuing operations 361.8%; earnings per share 190.5%
CP 1	2000: Sales 215.1%; net earnings 525.6%; shareholders' equity per share 317.2%